The Gay & Lesbian

Theatrical Legacy

TRIANGULATIONS
Lesbian/Gay/Queer ▲ Theater/Drama/Performance

Series Editors
Jill Dolan, University of Texas
David Román, University of Southern California

Titles in the series:

Tony Kushner in Conversation
  edited by Robert Vorlicky

*Passing Performances: Queer Readings of Leading Players
in American Theater History*
  edited by Robert A. Schanke and Kim Marra

*When Romeo Was a Woman: Charlotte Cushman
and Her Circle of Female Spectators*
  by Lisa Merrill

Camp: Queer Aesthetics and the Performing Subject
  edited by Fabio Cleto

Staging Desire: Queer Readings of American Theater History
  edited by Kim Marra and Robert A. Schanke

A Problem Like Maria: Gender and Sexuality in the American Musical
  by Stacy Wolf

A Queer Sort of Materialism: Recontextualizing American Theater
  by David Savran

Margaret Webster: A Life in the Theater
  by Milly S. Barranger

*The Gay and Lesbian Theatrical Legacy: A Biographical Dictionary of
Major Figures in American Stage History*
  edited by Billy J. Harbin, Kim Marra, and Robert A. Schanke

Cast Out: Queer Lives in Theater
  edited by Robin Bernstein

Queering Mestizaje: Transculturation and Performance
  by Alicia Arrizón

The Gay & Lesbian Theatrical Legacy

A Biographical Dictionary of Major Figures

in American Stage History in the Pre-Stonewall Era

Edited by Billy J. Harbin, Kim Marra, and Robert A. Schanke

THE UNIVERSITY OF MICHIGAN PRESS
Ann Arbor

First paperback edition 2007
Copyright © by the University of Michigan 2005
All rights reserved
Published in the United States of America by
The University of Michigan Press
Manufactured in the United States of America
⊗ Printed on acid-free paper

2010   2009   2008   2007   5   4   3   2

A CIP catalog record for this book is available from the British Library.

Library of Congress Cataloging-in-Publication Data

The gay and lesbian theatrical legacy : a biographical dictionary of major figures in American stage history in the pre-Stonewall era / edited by Billy J. Harbin, Kim Marra, and Robert A. Schanke.
      p. cm. — (Triangulations)
   Includes bibliographical references and index.
   ISBN 0-472-09858-6 (alk. paper) —
   ISBN 0-472-06858-X (pbk. : alk. paper)
      1. Gay actors—United States—Biography—Dictionaries.
2. Gay theatrical producers and directors—United States—Biography—
Dictionaries.   3. Gay dramatists—United States—Biography—
Dictionaries. 4. Actors—United States—Biography—Dictionaries.
5. Theatrical producers and directors—United States—Biography—
Dictionaries.   6. Dramatists, American—United States—Biography—
Dictionaries.   7. Theater—United States—Biography—Dictionaries.
I. Harbin, Billy J., 1930- II. Marra, Kim, 1957– III. Schanke,
Robert A., 1940– IV. Series.
PN2286.5.G38 2005
792'.092'273—dc22   2004020338

ISBN 978-0-472-09858-3 (alk. paper)
ISBN 978-0-472-06858-6 (pbk. : alk. paper)

For Billy J. Harbin (1930–2004),
beloved friend, teacher, and colleague.

Billy was in his late sixties when he first joined this
project, coming to it through his research on the
closeted gay actor Monty Woolley. At the first symposium on queer American theater history, held at
the Center for Gay and Lesbian Studies in New
York City in 1998, Billy movingly expressed what
this project meant to him, in words he had never
before uttered in so public a forum:

"Exploring the double lives of Monty Woolley led
me on a journey that helped liberate myself from
the need to be a public Dr. Harbin and a private
Billy. Not all of us who contributed to this project,
of course, are gay. However, I am. And being
involved in this worthy work helped me to bring
my own double lives into one."

Acknowledgments

As the third of three volumes we contracted with the University of Michigan Press on gays and lesbians in American theater history, this book represents a culmination of ten years of work. We must first thank our editor at the press, LeAnn Fields, without whose vision, commitment, and masterful strategizing these books would not have happened. We are also grateful to series editor Jill Dolan and David Román for their advice and support in including this book along with our two previous volumes, *Passing Performances* and *Staging Desire,* in the Triangulations series.

Among the many scholars with whom we have had the good fortune to collaborate on this project, the late Billy J. Harbin holds a very special place. He contributed an essay on actor Monty Woolley to the first volume and one on playwright George Kelly to the second, and he worked closely with us as co-editor on this volume. Whereas the two of us each served as primary contact person with the press and contributors on one of the previous volumes, Billy fulfilled that role for this one, which proved a larger task because of the many more authors involved. We shared the editorial work, but Billy was Command Central, coordinating the assignment of entries, forwarding comments to authors, obtaining and soliciting permissions for the many illustrations, merging the entries into a master manuscript, and working directly with the press. This book became his major scholarly focus for the last decade of his life. Billy's enthusiasm for discovery and his unflagging dedication, patience, kindness, and gentle wit through a long, sometimes trying editorial process inspired all whom he touched. He died suddenly while completing a long-planned European theater tour in London on 24 June 2004, just after the press had sent us the copyedited manuscript. Thanks to his careful record-keeping, and help from his dear friend Gresdna Doty who gained access to his papers at his home in Baton Rouge, we were able to shepherd the manuscript through production. Mixed with our great sadness that Billy did not live to see his years of work come to fruition are great gratitude for his enormous contribution and great pride in dedicating the book to him. Unfortunately, because of Billy's untimely death, we do not know all the people he would have acknowledged had he lived. But among those he certainly would have included are:

Cary Saurage, Wayne Womack, and Jon Emerson—for their intimate friendship of thirty years; Gresdna Doty and her husband Jim Traynham—for their enduring friendship of nearly forty years and thirty years of teamwork at Louisiana State University; Elizabeth Williams, Owen Peterson, and Mary Francis Hopkins—for their years of friendship and frequent discussions about the progress of this book; Michael Tick—Chair of the Department of Theatre at Louisiana State University during the final stages of Billy's work on this volume; Mary Julia Curtis—a friend of many years who helped gather the illustrations for this volume; Kevin Winkler—Chief Librarian, Circulating Collections at the New York Public Library for the Performing Arts; Louise Martzinek and Jeremy Megraw—from the Billy Rose Theatre Collection at The New York Public Library for the Performing Arts; Tom Lisanti—Manager, Photographic Services and Permissions, The New York Public Library; and Marcia LaBrenz—Senior Copyediting Coordinator, University of Michigan Press.

We apologize if, in Billy's absence, we have neglected to mention anyone else whom he would have listed.

Others who offered us assistance on this volume and merit our thanks include CLAGS staff member Jordan Schildcrout, for sending us a videotape of the 1998 symposium from which we were able to transcribe Billy's memorable words for the dedication, and University of Iowa colleagues Kathleen Diffley, Laura Rigal, and Leslie Schwalm, for reading and commenting on early drafts of the introduction.

On behalf of all three co-editors, we must extend a final thank you to our 56 contributors who stayed with the project all these years and gamely responded to numerous calls for revision. This book is also a testament to their dedication and good will.

We remain ever grateful to our partners, Meredith Alexander and Jack Barnhart, whose love and support make our work possible.

—Kim Marra and Robert A. Schanke

Contents

Illustrations   xi

Introduction   1

The Biographies   13

Listing by Occupation   397

Contributors   401

Index   411

Illustrations

Helen Arthur	31
Gladys Bentley	57
George Birimisa	64
Maurice Browne	74
Al Carmines	83
Lynne Carter and Stormé DeLarverié	88
Mart Crowley	115
Owen Dodson	140
Lehman Engel	153
Stephen Foster	168
Paul Guilfoyle	178
Nancy Hamilton	181
Robert Heide	188
Annie Hindle	194
Josephine Hutchinson	206
Robert Joffrey	219
Harry Koutoukas	238
Sanford Meisner	277
Kathleen Mulqueen	293
John Patrick	305
Livingston Platt	315
Hassard Short	335
Virgil Thomson	352
John Van Druten	355
Jean-Claude van Itallie	358
Ella Wesner	375

Introduction

The theater has long borne the reputation of being a "haven for homosexuality." As such, it has been both denigrated as a denizen of depravity by members of the dominant, straight culture and sought after as a refuge by queer people, those whose sexual desires deviated from prevailing norms. If the haven has allowed indulgence in transgressive behavior, it has also served as a closet, as both straights and queers have been heavily invested in obscuring the sexual identities of its specific inhabitants. Straight culture has preferred to keep the desires of its entertainers behind a veil of false presumptions, while queer culture has sought the protection of theatrical masking and relished the titillations of communicating in code. These dynamics of closeting have been particularly salient in the United States, where the nation's puritanical roots and Edenic mythology meant historically high stakes for sexual deviance, especially before the 1969 Stonewall Riots launched the lesbian and gay rights movement. Thus, for all the queers rumored to have inhabited the theatrical haven, precise knowledge of who they were and what they did has remained, until recently, very shrouded, and it is still largely diffuse, couched in a relatively few studies focused on individual figures that dare to deal openly with their sexuality. *The Gay and Lesbian Theatrical Legacy* seeks to make queer American theater history more visible and accessible by collecting in a single volume biographical entries on more than one hundred notable figures whose careers flourished in the century and a half before Stonewall.

Conceived and formatted as a biographical dictionary, *The Gay and Lesbian Theatrical Legacy* furthers the larger historical recovery project Robert A. Schanke and Kim Marra undertook with two previous volumes in this series. Each of those books offered fourteen extended essays that read in depth the workings of same-sex sexual desires in the careers of selected theater practitioners: *Passing Performances* (1998) examined actors, directors, producers, and agents; *Staging Desire* (2002) analyzed playwrights, lyricists, critics, and designers. *The Gay and Lesbian Theatrical Legacy* completes this trilogy by offering shorter entries focused on 113 theatrical personalities from across the full range of theatrical occupations. Whereas the longer essays in the previous volumes could take a broader view of the workings of same-sex desire in individuals' careers (including desires they aroused in others regardless of what their own might have been), the more concise entries in this volume deal with figures for whom there is evidence that they themselves were motivated by same-sex desire. The volume consolidates and expands the field by functioning as a resource for finding basic biographical information about a large number of queer theater practitioners' sexual identities and professional accomplishments and by provoking further research.

While it differs from the earlier volumes in format and function, *The Gay and Lesbian Theatrical Legacy* is rooted in the same convictions and methodological principles. Although we are doing what historians do, that is, uncovering information that enables new understandings of the past, we are aware that when the subject is sexuality, especially transgressive sexuality, certain ethical questions about "outing" are raised.[1] We have always agreed with the point made by Larry Kramer, a staunch defender of outing, at a symposium marking the publication of *Passing Performances,* that it is not enough simply to identify people as queer; the meaning of their sexuality and value of the knowledge must be established.[2] We argue that knowledge of the role of same-sex sexual desire in historical figures' theatrical careers is central to understanding their contributions and essential both to writing a fuller and more accurate account of history and to changing current attitudes. As Martin Duberman, Martha Vicinus, George Chauncey Jr., and other historians of sexuality have powerfully demonstrated, this facet of humanity cannot be relegated to a discreet realm of the private and ignored in assessments of people's public activities.[3] Sexuality permeates people's beliefs, actions, and social relations; it is not only a question of whom they sexually desire but how they see and function in the world. Our larger project has been to examine how societal and cultural attitudes shaped our subjects' sense of sexual difference in their respective periods and the interplay of their on- and offstage lives in this context; how their sexuality affected their choices of intimates, professional associates, the kind of work they did, and how they performed it; how shared understandings with people of like persuasion both enabled and inhibited their collaborations; and how they and their associates exploited as well as suffered from modes of discrimination and oppression. Far from irrelevant, these questions, in acknowledging sexuality as a historical force, inquire into the very fabric of the past.

Moreover, the knowledge we seek to produce doesn't just enlarge but transforms the record. If biography is "the prism of history," as Barbara Tuchman has argued,[4] then the facet of sexuality, added along side other facets of identity, such as gender, race, ethnicity, and class, changes the shape of the whole and vastly complicates what we see looking through it. Information about artists' sexualities can prompt a reexamination of their careers and the social and cultural dynamics surrounding their work. The longer case studies in *Passing Performances* and *Staging Desire* provided selected examples of how such reexamination might be undertaken; the many more and shorter entries in *The Gay and Lesbian Theatrical Legacy* offer evidentiary and analytical tools and gesture toward this type of revision and recuperation to foster further scholarship in the field. Acknowledging and analyzing the sexualities of notable historical figures not only corrects distortions of their individual lives but helps debunk negative stereotypes oppressive to all members of the gay and lesbian community. In demonstrating the specificity and diversity of sexualities through time, historical recovery work counters constructions of a monolithic, unchanging "homosexuality" which stigmatizes and denies people their individual differences and civil rights.

As many historians and theorists inside and outside the growing field of gay and lesbian theater studies have helped us understand, undertaking this recovery project raises key questions about the ways knowledge of historical figures' same-sex sexual desires is produced, what constitutes that knowledge, and what its current ramifications are.[5] A central question concerns how we as authors position ourselves in relation to our recovery projects. Here, as in Marra and Schanke's earlier volumes, we are using a rubric of "queer readings" within which we can both retain the historical specificity and political agency of our respective identities and embrace the multiplicities, fluidities, and contradictions contained in contemporary notions of queerness. One can identify as lesbian, gay, bisexual, transgender, or straight, as the contributors to this volume variously do, and perform queer interventions. As Jill Dolan stated, "To be queer is not who you are, it's what you do, it's your relation to dominant power, and your relation to marginality, as a place of empowerment."[6] When we factor same-sex eroticism into the complex network of forces determining our subjects' careers, we and our contributors are doing queer theater history, working from various identity positions and rereading the past in ways which challenge the normalizing presumptions of heterosexuality.

Doing queer theater history entails wrestling with complex problems of terminology and evidence. To determine what to call our subjects, we must ask a number of questions. What were the salient conceptual frameworks of sexual normalcy and deviance within which our subjects functioned? How and to what extent did they identify their desires and behavior as transgressive? What were the terms used to describe sexual deviance in our subjects' time and how did they relate to them? Labels such as *homosexual, heterosexual, lesbian, gay,* and *queer* all date from specific historical periods and need to be used with an awareness of those derivations.[7]

Even more vexed is the question of evidence. How do we know that our subjects desired members of the same sex? Most people's sexual desires—straight or queer—have not been conclusively documented with direct forms of proof such as eyewitness accounts, explicit photographs, or soiled bedclothes. Moreover, an individual's sexual behavior may neither coincide with her desire nor remain consistent. The standard of "hard" evidence is elusive for different-sex desire as well, but biographers have not traditionally been faced with having to prove heterosexual subjects' sexuality; it is simply presumed, automatically buttressed less by facts than by hegemonic assumptions. Historically, many subjects never stated their same-sex desires publicly; often these subjects vehemently eschewed any imputation of sexual abnormality. Revelatory letters or photographs, if they ever existed, have likely been destroyed or kept hidden from researchers to protect reputations. But the absence of such evidence neither proves nor disproves the existence of the desire. In fact, in John D'Emilio's words, "absence" of or "inaccuracies" in evidence may be registering the "ways misinformation is purposely used to deflect attention away from 'who one is' or 'who one is not.'"[8]

To recover our subjects' same-sex desires and their historical impact, we have had to build circumstantial cases in which all evidence is relative and most is ersatz. The process is one of reading multiple signs, including those of absence, relative to historically contingent sign systems. Dolan's argument that the "signs of sexuality are inherently performative" enables us to read our subjects' erotically charged behaviors both within and without the theater as modes of staging their same-sex sexual desires.[9] Most of our subjects managed to appear straight while registering signs of other passions in strategies of self-concealment and subversion of dominant role expectations. In expressing desire, the primary register of sexual identification is gender; that is, sexual deviance is often expressed through coded manipulation of gender stereotypes in practitioners' personal styles and in the representations they fashion for the stage.

In addition, there are signs of concealment and erasure deployed by family and friends, the media, public opinion, and the scholarly community. What William J. Mann has termed "gay flags" or "queer markers" include phrases in the biographical record and obituaries such as "never married," "lifelong bachelor," or "there are no immediate survivors." Census reports and wills can provide some indication of domestic partnerships and intimate relations not acknowledged by other family members.[10] Where possible, we have tried to find evidence of direct expressions of same-sex desire in subjects' private papers, if these are accessible, or in the documented printed accounts of close associates. As noted, however, this kind of evidence is very rare because of the obvious risks involved in creating such documentation. Often what has remained is an ephemeral oral history handed down through generations within subcultural theatrical circles and recoverable through interviews. This oral history can yield confirmation that a particular marriage was bearded, that certain same-sex friendships and associations were also sexual, or that her "sort of secretary" or his "loyal valet" were domestic partners.[11] Of course, neither an insider's comment nor any other single piece of evidence, such as cross-dressing or an estate left to an in-house secretary, can be conclusive on its own. A circumstantial case about the workings of same-sex desire in a particular theatrical career must be built through an accretion of signs. Each sign must be read in relation to the others and in relation to the subject's own level of consciousness about the meaning of her or his behavior. The authors of the entries included here have worked to establish how it is that each of their subjects can be responsibly incorporated into a queer American theatrical past.

Vexed and elusive as the evidence of same-sex sexual desire can be, gathering it is vital because of the manifold ways historical icons affect the self-conceptions of people across the social spectrum, both in their own time and now. The ramifications are both personal and political. While those of us who identify as gay and lesbian have always projected fantasies of desire and identification onto putatively heterosexual stars, it can be immensely validating, not to mention arousing, to know that these fantasies are not pure projection, that, in the face of our continuing degradation, widely worshiped icons were at least in some measure like us. For those who identify as straight, evidence of the role of same-sex sexual desire in star performers' careers can be profoundly disorienting. Certainly it increases awareness of the constructed and shifting nature of all sexualities, including their own. For queers and straights, it can change how we consume and understand the meaning of familiar as well as new cultural products. As the dozens of entries in this volume attest, desire for persons of the same as well as the opposite sex has been deeply implicated in the production of the icons that shape the dominant cultural expectations of us all, from Edwin Forrest's paragons of American masculinity to Elsie de Wolfe's and Julian Eltinge's American Girls, the quintessentially American music of Stephen Foster and Aaron Copland, and, indeed, that quintessentially American theatrical form, the Broadway musical.[12] Straights cannot simply say of queers: "Why don't they just keep it to themselves?" Who "we" are is part of who "they" are.

Accordingly, while *The Gay and Lesbian Theatrical Legacy* is useful as a resource for looking up individual figures, its many entries also have a cumulative impact. Reading through the book as a whole, one is reminded of numerous usual suspects while learning about less familiar ones and building a more concrete sense of the presence of queer practitioners and the breadth and depth of their influence on American theatrical—and, by reciprocal influence, social and cultural—history. As numerous as our subjects are, we cannot claim that the volume is comprehensive. On a purely practical level, an exhaustive effort would exceed the bounds of a single book. More importantly, because of the risks involved in writing about queer subjects, we decided when we began the project in 1993–94 that we would collect these entries chiefly by putting out calls and letting prospective contributors volunteer. We achieved further coverage by enlisting some of those volunteers to take on other subjects. A number of entries originally slated for the book did not materialize because of authors' difficulties with evidence or their desire to withhold some of their most recent research findings for their own books. Despite the inevitable gaps, however, significant lines and dynamics of historical influence emerge from the abundance of entries collected here.

With so many figures covered in a single volume, numerous networks of affiliation through which queer theater practitioners impacted American theater history are discernible. For example, the close working relationship among several of the most powerful and influential people in the business in the late nineteenth and early twentieth centuries—including the era's biggest star, Maude Adams, its most successful playwright, Clyde Fitch (both of whose careers were supported by the empathetic producer, Charles Frohman) and Elisabeth Marbury, the pioneering theatrical agent dubbed the "fourth estate of the dramatic world"—was instrumental in solidifying the institution of modern commercial Broadway. Their network was formed and sustained through shared queer lifestyles, understandings, and aesthetics along with shared financial interests. Similar common bonds were a factor in the formation (and ultimate dissolution through interpersonal tension, which compounded economic strain) of the American Repertory Theatre by Eva LeGallienne, Margaret Webster, and Cheryl Crawford, as well as in the genesis of the Off-Off-Broadway movement at the Caffe Cino, where founder Joe Cino gave a hearing to plays by Robert Heide, H. M. Koutoukas, Robert Patrick, Lanford Wilson, and others. Recognizing the queerness of such affiliates makes same-sex desire more tangible and visible as a historical force.

Because of the interdisciplinary nature of theater, many practitioners included in this volume crossed over into other performing arts, further extending the lines of queer cultural and historical influence. In another major network of affiliation animated in part by shared lifestyle choices, Aaron Copland, Marc Blitzstein, Lehman Engel, and Virgil Thomson, all of whom wrote music for theatrical works, joined to form Arrow Music Press, which was dedicated to publishing American composers. Numerous dancers and choreographers covered here, such as Isadora Duncan, Loie Fuller, Robert Joffrey, Ted Shawn, Merce Cunningham, and Jerome Robbins, circulated from theater to dance productions. And many actors and directors—including Tallulah Bankhead, Montgomery Clift, George Cukor, James Dean, Farley Granger, Danny Kaye, Charles Laughton, Clifton Webb, and Monty Woolley—moved from theater to film, as a result of which their images proliferated into still wider arenas of popular culture.[13]

Cutting across arts disciplines and often forming the core of culturally productive networks of affiliation are a number of significant couples. These include the bearded but devoted marriages of actors Alfred Lunt and Lynn Fontanne, actor Katharine Cornell and director Guthrie McClintic, and writers Jane and Paul Bowles. More numerous are the same-sex domestic partnerships that united such influential interdisciplinary duos as agent Elisabeth Marbury and actor/interior decorator Elsie de Wolfe; actor/director Eva LeGallienne and director Margaret Webster; the producer-manager team of Helen Arthur and Agnes Morgan, who with sisters Irene and Alice Lewisohn formed the Neighborhood Playhouse; choreographer/dancers Jerome Robbins and Gerald Arpino; choreographer Merce Cunningham and composer John Cage; playwright Jean-Claude van Itallie and director Joseph Chaikin; and playwright Megan Terry and actor Joanne Schmidmann, who met at Chaikin's Open Theatre and moved west to form the Omaha Magic Theatre. In some cases, the personal and professional lives of the individuals in these couples so intertwine that the authors have chosen to cover them together in a single entry.

Through the wide coverage this volume affords, multiple intersections of race, ethnicity, and class with sexuality and gender are discernible.

There are entries on numerous African American figures, many of whose careers were launched during the Harlem Renaissance, including Josephine Baker, Gladys Bentley, Owen Dodson, Langston Hughes, Gertrude "Ma" Rainey, and Bessie Smith. If white bourgeois status served the respectable images cultivated by such queer female performers as Maude Adams and Elsie Janis, and helped insulate them from stigma, Gladys Bentley's and Ma Rainey's blackness compounded the sexual transgressions linked to their brassy performance styles and "lower" nightclub venues. White female impersonators Julian Eltinge and Lynn Carter played on the sexualization of race and exoticized their gender acts by appearing in blackface. Queer writers on both sides of the color line— such as Langston Hughes in *Mulatto* and Arthur Laurents in *Hallelujah, Baby!*—used themes of miscegenation to code forbidden desire. A number of queer white theater artists took up the positions of those othered on the basis of race and ethnicity in gestures of empathy informed by their own experience of difference. For example, Margaret Webster fought to star Paul Robeson in *Othello* (1943), making him the first African American actor to play the role on Broadway; Virgil Thomson was the first to cast all African American singers in his chorus for *Four Saints in Three Acts* (1934); and the prizewinning playwright and historian Martin Duberman began his career as a civil rights activist. Similarly, gentile playwrights and critics, such as Mercedes de Acosta and Eric Bentley, argued vociferously against anti-Semitism as well as racism and homophobia in their work. For Jewish theater artists such as Lorenz Hart and George Cukor, the stigma of ethnicity intensified that of queer sexuality, prompting some of their ironic, witty, and often bitter, as well as adulatory, takes on iconic WASP American culture.

Another crosscurrent running through the volume is a temporal one involving figures whose careers began before and extended beyond the 1969 Stonewall Riots, linking past and present. Writers such as Larry Kramer, Lanford Wilson, Eric Bentley, Terrence McNally, and Megan Terry were able to be "out" in their personal lives and so could deal with lesbian and gay subject matter more openly in their work. For Kramer and others, their outness and activism made them the target of violent attacks, but they persisted. By contrast, poet and playwright Owen Dodson and acting teacher Sanford Meisner are notable examples of those who retreated from the greater visibility wrought by Stonewall and remained all the more closeted. For some, such as Dodson, the hiding itself brought acute personal suffering. A number of our subjects lived to partake of the new liberation and express some of its energies and tensions in their works only to die prematurely of AIDS. These included Charles Ludlam and Michael Bennett, who both died at forty-four; Robert Moore, who died at fifty-six; and Robert Joffrey, who died at sixty. The different experiences these artists had with the gay and lesbian rights movement illustrate the difficulties inherent in making generalized assumptions about queer peoples' responses to historical change.

Reckoning with the particular identities and diversity of these artists, their large numbers, and the breadth and depth of their reach fosters further recognition of how same-sex sexual desire has permeated and shaped the nation's social and cultural landscapes over centuries. Such a reckoning exposes the fallacy of still salient stereotypes that would separate the theatrical "haven" and its inhabitants from a larger—and increasingly mythical—"mainstream." This history rooted in the specificity of individual lives powerfully shows that in vilifying queer culture and denying queers equal rights, straight America denigrates itself. We offer *The Gay and Lesbian Theatrical Legacy* as a contribution to the vital cause of cultural self-recognition and extend, as we did with *Passing Performances* and *Staging Desire,* the hope that more scholars will join us in recovering queer lives and acknowledging the operations of same-sex sexual desire in American theater history.

Aids to Using *The Gay and Lesbian Theatrical Legacy*

Because the volume is a biographical compendium, entries are arranged alphabetically to enable ready referencing and browsing. A "Listing by Occupation," which follows the biographical entries, sorts the names of subjects by theatrical occupation (actors, directors, designers, playwrights, and so on). To facilitate cross-referencing, especially among partners and collaborators in wider networks of affiliation, the names of figures referred to in an entry who are subjects of another appear in bold type when first mentioned. An index of proper names enables readers to track individuals throughout the volume. Bibliographies at the end of each entry both provide documentation and indicate key sources for further research.

The volume contains twenty-six photographs chosen with an eye toward making lesser-known figures more visible. This visual text is thus intended to further the larger project of *The Gay and Lesbian Theatrical Legacy*. The photos appear with the entries on their respective subjects and can be quickly located by consulting the page references in the list of illustrations.

Notes

1. See, for example, Larry Gross, *Contested Closets: The Politics and Ethics of Outing* (Minneapolis: University of Minnesota Press, 1993). The post-Stonewall choreographer and director Tommy Tune discusses how he has been the victim of "inning"—being kept in the closet, which ultimately fosters rather than avoids the shame and risk surrounding homosexuality—in his memoir *Footnotes* (New York: Simon and Schuster, 1997).

2. Passing Performances: Queering American Theater History, a symposium sponsored by the Center for Lesbian and Gay Studies (CLAGS), Proshansky Auditorium, City University of New York, October 1998.

3. Martin Duberman, Martha Vicinus, and George Chauncey Jr., eds., *Hidden from History: Reclaiming the Gay and Lesbian Past* (New York: Penguin, 1989).

4. Barbara W. Tuchman, *Practicing History: Selected Essays* (New York: Knopf, 1981), 73–74, 80.

5. Research in the history of sexuality grounds the methodology and provides crucial material about the larger sociocultural context within which we read our respective moments of theater history. In addition to *Hidden from History*, we are especially indebted to the essays gathered in Kathy Peiss and Christina Simmons, eds., *Passion and Power: Sexuality in History* (Philadelphia: Temple University Press, 1989). The work of some historians of sexuality directly intersects the world of the theater. See, for example, Martha Vicinus, "'They Wonder to Which Sex I Belong': The Historical Roots of the Modern Lesbian Identity," in *The Lesbian and Gay Studies Reader*, edited by Henry Abelove, Michele Ana Barale, and David M. Halperin (New York: Routledge, 1993), 432–52; George Chauncey Jr., *Gay New York: Gender, Urban Culture, and the Making of the Gay Male World, 1890–1940* (New York: Basic Books, 1994); Lillian Faderman, *Surpassing the Love of Men: Romantic Friendship and Love between Women from the Renaissance to the Present* (New York: Morrow, 1981); Lillian Faderman, *Odd Girls and Twilight Lovers: A History of Lesbian Life in Twentieth-Century America* (New York: Penguin, 1991); Eric Garber, "A Spectacle in Color: The Lesbian and Gay Subculture of Jazz Age Harlem," in Duberman, Vicinus, and Chauncey, *Hidden from History*, 318–31; Esther Newton, *Cherry Grove, Fire Island: Sixty Years in America's First Gay and Lesbian Town* (Boston: Beacon, 1993); and Martin Duberman, ed., *Queer Representations: Reading Lives, Reading Cultures* (New York and London: New York University Press, 1997). Of the scholars centered in the theater who contribute to gay and lesbian studies, relatively few are theater historians and fewer still are American theater historians. Kaier Curtin's pioneering *We Can Always Call Them Bulgarians* (Boston: Alyson, 1987); Nicholas de Jongh's *Not in Front of the Audience* (New York and London: Routledge, 1992); and Alan Sinfield's *Out on Stage: Lesbian and Gay Theatre in the Twentieth Century* (New Haven: Yale University Press, 1999) usefully set the theatrical context. Further historical background is provided in Carl Miller, *Stages of Desire: Gay Theatre's Hidden History* (London: Cassell, 1996), which charts the history of lesbian and gay representation onstage from the beginnings of drama in English until the nineteenth century. Rather than focusing on the relationships between individual subjects' lives and work as our books do, however, the primary aim of these books is to analyze plays featuring representations of homosexuality and lesbianism. Laurence Senelick's studies of cross-dressing are exemplary in their examination of the interplay of gender and sexuality in those specialized theater artists' careers. See, for example, his "Lady and the Tramp: Drag Differentials in the Progressive Era," in *Gender in Performance: The Presentation of Difference in the Performing Arts*, edited by Laurence Senelick (Hanover, N.H.: University Press of New England, 1992), 260–45; "Boys and Girls Together: Subcultural Origins of Glamour Drag and Male Impersonation on the Nineteenth-Century Stage," in

Crossing the Stage: Controversies on Cross-Dressing, edited by Lesley Ferris (New York: Routledge, 1993), 80–95; and *The Changing Room: Sex, Drag, and Theatre* (London and New York: Routledge, 2000). Robert A. Schanke's *Shattered Applause: The Lives of Eva Le Gallienne* (Carbondale: Southern Illinois University Press, 1992); James V. Hatch's *Sorrow Is the Only Faithful One: The Life of Owen Dodson* (Urbana: University of Illinois Press, 1993); and Lisa Merrill's *When Romeo Was a Woman: Charlotte Cushman and Her Circle of Female Spectators* (Ann Arbor: University of Michigan Press, 1998) offer rigorous scholarly treatments of the issues of homosexuality and lesbianism in their subjects' lives and work. Our books continue these efforts by factoring same-sex sexual desire into readings of a wider variety of figures from the American theatrical past.

The majority of scholars currently working in lesbian and gay theater studies specialize more in the areas of theory and criticism than theater history. While many focus largely on contemporary theater, their perspectives have informed how we read theater history. In her engagements with postmodern theory, Sue-Ellen Case's insistence on the agency of a lesbian subject positioned both inside and outside ideology and able to change the conditions of her existence continues to be inspirational. See, for example, her "Toward a Butch-Femme Aesthetic," in Abelove, Barale, and Halperin, *Gay and Lesbian Studies Reader,* 294–306; "Performing Lesbian in the Space of Technology, Part I," *Theatre Journal* 47 (March 1995): 1–18; and "Performing Lesbian in the Space of Technology, Part II," *Theatre Journal* 47 (October 1995): 329–43. Jill Dolan's paradigmatic theorizations of feminist spectatorship and the dynamics of lesbian desire in various kinds of performances have been especially important to this project. See her *The Feminist Spectator as Critic* (1988; reprint, Ann Arbor: University of Michigan Press, 1991); and *Presence and Desire: Essays on Gender, Sexuality, and Performance* (Ann Arbor: University of Michigan Press, 1993). The ways in which Stacy Wolf has continued these and other queries in exploring the "use value" of cold war era American musicals in shaping lesbian subjectivity have also enriched our understandings of theatrical reception. See her "The Queer Pleasures of Mary Martin and Broadway: *The Sound of Music* as a Lesbian Musical," *Modern Drama* 39 (spring 1996): 51–63; "'Never Gonna Be a Man/Catch If You Can/I Won't Grow Up': A Lesbian Account of Mary Martin as Peter Pan," *Theatre Journal* 49 (1997): 493–509; and "Mary Martin: Washin' That Man Right Outta Her Hair," in Schanke and Marra, *Passing Performances,* 283–302. Leading readings of gay male sexuality in modern American drama and theater are provided in John Clum, *Acting Gay: Male Homosexuality in Modern Drama* (New York: Columbia University Press, 1992); John Clum, *Something for the Boys: Musical Theatre and Gay Culture* (New York: Palgrave, 1999); David Savran, *Communists, Cowboys, and Queers: The Politics of Masculinity in the Work of Arthur Miller and Tennessee Williams* (Minneapolis: University of Minnesota Press, 1992); and David Savran, "Ambivalence, Utopia, and a Queer Sort of Materialism: How *Angels in America* Reconstructs the Nation," *Theatre Journal* (May 1995): 207–27. Theoretical analyses of the intersections of sexuality and gender with race, ethnicity, and class have pushed us to consider these always interlocking dynamics more fully. See especially Kate Davy, "Outing Whiteness: A Feminist/Lesbian Project," *Theatre Journal* 47 (May 1995): 189–205; David Romàn, "Teatro Viva! Latino Performance and the Politics of AIDS in Los Angeles," in *Etiendes? Queer Readings, Hispanic Writings,* edited by Emile L. Bergmann and Paul Julian Smith (Durham: Duke University Press, 1995); David Romàn, *Acts of Intervention: Performance, Gay Culture, and AIDS* (Bloomington: Indiana University Press, 1998); Jennifer Brody, "Hyphen-Nations," in *Cruising the Performative: Interventions into the Representation of Ethnicity, Nationality, and Sexuality,* edited by Sue-Ellen Case, David Brett, and Susan Leigh Foster (Bloomington: Indiana University Press, 1995); and *Impossible Purities: Blackness, Femininity, and Victorian Culture* (Durham: Duke University Press, 1998).

6. Queer Theatre: A Conference with Performances, Center for Lesbian and Gay Studies (CLAGS), New York, New York, April 27–29, 1995.

7. The terms *homo-* and *hetero-sexuality* first appeared in print in the United States in the early 1890s as the theories of German sexologists, most influentially those of Richard von Krafft-Ebing, entered English-language medical discourse. See, for example, Jonathan Ned Katz, *The Invention of Heterosexuality* (New York: Penguin, 1996), 19–21. The medical profession did not "invent" homo- and heterosexuality; rather, doctors coined these terms in response to preexisting social phenomena. Well before the medical publications, people were self-identifying with terms such as *queer, fairy,* and *Sapphic* and not only refused to internalize but resisted the pathology the sexologists imposed on them. See George Chauncey Jr., "From Sexual Inversion to Homosexuality: The Changing Medical Conceptualization of Female Deviance," in *Passion and Power: Sexuality in History,* edited by Kathy Peiss and Christina Simmons (Philadelphia: Temple University Press, 1989), 109. The more popular terms *gay* and *lesbian* were in common subcultural usage in the decades prior to World War II, but, even as many in the subculture embraced these terms as more affirming alternatives to the then pathologized *homosexual,* others vehemently eschewed them because of their connection to perversion and scandal. As terms used without as well as within subcultural circles, *gay* and *lesbian* gained widespread currency only in the last third of the twentieth century. Common usage of the term *gay* to refer to both men and women who sexually desire members of their own sex is problematic because it subsumes women into a male universal. Similarly, as lesbian theorists remind us, the term *homoerotic* primarily connotes male desire. While many people of all sexes have reappropriated the term *queer* as a militant gesture of pride, its long history as an extreme pejorative makes it difficult for some people to use it to describe either themselves or their predecessors.

8. John D'Emilio, oral presentation at the Lesbian and Gay History Conference, City University of New York Graduate Center, October 6–7, 1995.

9. Jill Dolan, "Breaking the Code: Musings on Lesbian Sexuality and the Performer," in Dolan, *Presence and Desire,* 139.

10. William J. Mann, *Behind the Screen: How Gays and Lesbians Shaped Hollywood, 1910–1969* (New York: Viking, 2001), xvii.

11. In gathering this evidence and reading performances of sexuality, we cannot dismiss the value of gossip. As Edith Becker, Michelle Citron, Julia Lesage, and B. Ruby Rich have argued, gossip provides "official unrecorded history": "Long denigrated in our culture, gossip nevertheless serves a crucial purpose in the survival of subcultural identity within an oppressive society. If oral history is the history of those denied control of the printed record, gossip is the history of those who cannot even speak in their own first-person voice." See their "Lesbians and Film," in *Out in Culture: Gay, Lesbian, and Queer Essays on Popular Culture,* edited by Corey K. Creekmur and Alexander Doty (Durham: Duke University Press, 1995), 31.

12. For an engaging recent discussion of the implications of queer sexuality in the production and reception of American musical theater, see Clum, *Something for the Boys.*

13. From the relatively short, theater-centered entries included in this volume, one can pursue further analysis of the impact of many of these figures' sexualities on dance and film in such recent studies as Jane C. Desmond, ed., *Dancing Desires: Choreographing Sexualities on and off the Stage* (Madison: University of Wisconsin Press, 2001); and Mann, *Behind the Screen.*

The Biographies

ADAMS, Maude (Ewing Kiskadden) (1872–1953), actress, stage lighting innovator, and teacher, was born in Salt Lake City, Utah, to actress Annie (Ansenath Ann) Adams and banker James Henry Kiskadden. An only child, she made her acting debut as a nine-month-old infant when her mother carried her onstage in a production of *The Lost Child* with a Salt Lake City Mormon stock company. She adopted her mother's maiden name and performed as a child actor in various venues in California, Nevada, and Utah until 1882. Then, too tall for children's parts, she returned to Salt Lake City to live with her grandmother and undertake what may have been her only formal schooling: less than two years at the Collegiate Institute. Following her father's death in 1883, she resumed acting with her mother and headed east with traveling stock companies. She made her New York debut in *The Paymaster* in 1888 and played mainly secondary roles before coming under the management of Charles Frohman, an association that endured from 1890 until his death on the *Lusitania* in 1915. Beginning with **Clyde Fitch**'s *The Masked Ball* in 1892, she played female leads for five seasons opposite John Drew. In 1896, James M. Barrie saw Adams in *Rosemary* and adapted his novel *The Little Minister* into her first starring vehicle. Her enormous success in the role of Lady Babbie heralded a luminous career as Frohman's biggest star and Barrie's favored muse.

Thereafter, Adams provided the premier American incarnations of numerous Barrie roles, including Phoebe in *Quality Street* (1901), Maggie in *What Every Woman Knows* (1908), the title role in *The Legend of Leonora* (1914), and Miss Thing in *A Kiss for Cinderella* (1916). But the Barrie character she inspired that made her legendary was the eponymous hero of *Peter Pan.* In a continuous run from its opening on November 6, 1905, until June 9, 1906, the American premiere production became the longest single engagement at Frohman's Empire Theatre. With this run, tours, and revivals throughout her career, Adams played Peter an estimated fifteen hundred times. In a letter to the actress, Mark Twain expressed the widespread belief that *"Peter Pan* is a great and refining and uplifting benefaction to this sordid and money-mad age" (qtd. in Robbins, *Maude Adams: The Intimate Portrait,* 90–92). Adams won additional notoriety in breeches roles in two plays by Edmond Rostand, *L'Aiglon* (1900) and *Chantecler* (1911). Momentous, too, was her incarnation of

Joan of Arc in a spectacular adaptation of Schiller's *The Maid of Orleans,* which Frohman produced for a single performance in Harvard Stadium to benefit the German Department in 1909. Adams made pleasing but less successful attempts at Viola in *Twelfth Night* (1908) and Rosalind in *As You Like It* (1910), and her performance in *Romeo and Juliet* (1899) was regarded by the most generous critics as "charming" rather than great. Reviews overwhelmingly attest that she was at her best in roles that traded on the sentimental and uplifting appeal of winsome youthfulness and inviolate virtue and altogether avoided "the fierce elemental passions of animal sex" (Gray, 737). In this line, her stardom proved incomparably popular and profitable. She was forced to retire in 1918 after a severe bout of influenza, but she made a few subsequent stage appearances, including a tour as Portia in *Merchant of Venice* (1931–32), a summer stock turn as Maria in *Twelfth Night* (1934), and reprises of some of her most treasured roles, including Peter Pan and Lady Babbie, for radio (1934).

Adams's professional accomplishments in the theater extended beyond her acting career. While under Frohman's management, she became involved in the technical aspects of production, especially stage lighting, which she often supervised on her star tours. In addition, she designed the light bridge at New York's Empire Theatre, the center of Frohman's operations. Later she worked with the General Electric Company in Schenectady, New York, to create an incandescent bulb for use in film production (1921–23). Her technical as well as artistic skills found yet another outlet in 1937 when the president of Stephens College, a women's institution in Columbia, Missouri, hired her to establish a drama department. Adams taught and directed plays there until 1950.

The charming, youthful, and virtuous image Adams maintained throughout her long theatrical career was abetted by her notoriously reclusive lifestyle. It was a key part of Frohman's scheme that Adams be known exclusively for her stage roles and that none of her offstage activities taint the purity of her star persona. In following his dictates, Adams was able to maintain a private life filled with intimate relations with other women. While the actress apparently never involved herself romantically with a man, she engaged in two long-term same-sex domestic partnerships, which endured in each case until the beloved's death. The first, dating from the early 1890s until 1901, was with Lillie Florence, and the second, from 1905 to 1951, was with Louise Boynton. Because Adams burned all of her personal papers except her correspondence with J. M. Barrie, "hard" evidence from the principals about the nature of their relationships is elusive. However, it is clear from biographical accounts by those who knew them personally (e.g., Phyllis Robbins) that Florence and Boynton were Adams's significant others.

Like other Boston marrieds of the period, Adams's relationships with her partners transpired within a close circle of women friends who also led homosocial lives. For Adams, some of these friendships evolved out of ardent star worship. Phyllis Robbins and Laura Kennedy, for example, made their adoration of Adams into an all-consuming hobby, which involved attending multiple performances of all of her shows, following her on tour, and saving in extensive scrapbooks every ticket stub, program, photograph, and printed word about her that they could find. In Robbins's case, her constant presence—usually in the front row—moved Adams to invite her backstage and eventually into her private life. The Harvard Theatre Collection's extensive holdings on Maude Adams contain the correspondence of another female friend, Nan Hodgkins, with whom Adams was close from 1902 into the 1930s; access to this correspondence was restricted until 1993. The Hodgkins letters are significant for what they reveal about the circulation of female desire around Adams. In addition to shared feelings of adoration for the star, the letters discuss jealousies among Adams's friends, competition for her attention, and the various pleasures and strains in the correspondents' respective same-sex companionate marriages.

These aspects of Adams's private life placed her at the center of a homoerotic economy that worked subversively against the patriarchal order of both the contemporary theater industry and the larger society. The media portrayed her as the deferential creation of her manager, who owned her and controlled her every move. However, for Frohman and Adams this heterosexist Pygmalion/Galatea paradigm, together with dominant cultural assumptions about female sexuality, covered other relational dynamics. Like Adams, Frohman never married in the conventional sense and cohabited with a longtime companion of the same sex, Charles Dillingham (Kuehnl, 408; Marcosson and Frohman, 360–84). Star and manager may have had a mutual understanding about their private lives that contributed to the high degree of trust they placed in each other and allowed Adams a greater degree of power and autonomy than other female stars under autocratic male management. Adams's involvement in the technical aspects of theater, for example, was but one facet of a larger authority Frohman often granted her over the appearance and direction of her productions.

Throughout the major portion of her career, Adams was also shielded by bourgeois presuppositions about female "passionlessness" that prevailed until the popularization of sexologists' theories in the United States in the decades after World War I (Cott, 162–81). Her apparent obeisance to a successful, paternalistic, male manager and scrupulous eschewal of sexualized liaisons with men enabled her to overcome the moral stigma of her profession. Given the discreet nature of her private life and the extraordinarily high level of social respectability she achieved, her relationships with her partners could be viewed within the honorable and presumably chaste Victorian tradition of female romantic friendship. Her longtime association (dating from 1901) with nunneries, in which she often sought sanctuary and to which she made generous donations, further certified the personal chastity underpinning the virtue of her stage persona. Adams's performances—quintessentially her Peter Pan— transcended the conventional codes by which breeches roles had traditionally proffered female bodies for male pleasure (Davis). Instead, as the nature and intensity of Adams's relationships with female fans and intimate friends indicate, the "passionlessness" she purportedly embodied on- and offstage provided a differently coded cultural space within which the most respectable women could exchange the most ardent desires.

See M. Adams, "The One I Knew Least of All," *Ladies Home Journal,* (March 1926–May 1927); Maude Adams Collection, Harvard Theatre Collection, Cambridge, Mass.; Maude Adams Personality File and Broadway Show Folders on *Chantecler, The Little Minister, Peter Pan, What Every Woman Knows,* Theatre Collection, Museum of the City of New York; Maude Adams Scrapbooks and Clipping Files, Billy Rose Theatre Collection, New York Public Library, Lincoln Center; S. Archer, *American Actors and Actresses,* Detroit, 1983; N. F. Cott, "Passionlessness: An Interpretation of Victorian Sexual Ideology, 1790–1850," in *A Heritage of Her Own: Toward a New Social History of American Women,* edited by N. F. Cott and E. H. Pleck, New York; T. C. Davis, "Maude Adams," *American National Biography,* 1999, 1:115–16; D. Gray, "Maude Adams, a Public Influence," *Hampton's Magazine* (June 1911): 725–37; E. K. Kuehnl, "Maude Adams, an American Idol," Ph.D. diss., University of Wisconsin-Madison, 1984; I. F. Marcosson and D. Frohman, *Charles Frohman: Manager and Man,* New York, 1916; P. Robbins, *Maude Adams: An Intimate Portrait,* New York, 1956; and P. Robbins, *The Young Maude Adams,* New York, 1959.

Kim Marra

ALBEE, Edward (1928–), playwright, was adopted by Reed and Frances Albee of Larchmont, New York, soon after his birth to a woman named Louise Harvey on March 12, 1928, in Washington, D.C. The Albees, who named their new son Edward F. Albee III, were part of an old American family that can trace its New England roots back to the late seventeenth century. Reed Albee's wealth was inherited from his father, who owned a large chain of vaudeville theaters, allowing him to retire in his early forties, the same year he adopted Edward. The family was virtually untouched by both the Depression and World War II, as was much of the exclusive Larchmont society around them, and Edward was raised with upper middle class luxuries. Albee's gayness, while seldom overtly apparent in his work, became instrumental in shaping his artistic vision, for it animated his critical perspective on the elite bourgeois society of the Northeast, as it did those of **Tennessee Williams** on the South and **William Inge** on the Midwest. Marginal sexuality, observes John Clum, helped give these writers "the tools to theatricalize the other for whom they were The Other. No heterosexual writer has done it so well since" (153).

Albee was educated at Choate, where he wrote his first play, his first novel, and poetry that was published in the school's literary magazine. He went on to Trinity College for three semesters before being dismissed for lack of attendance in classes and mandatory chapel. He had joined the college theater group and continued writing plays and poetry but spent most of his time in Hartford drinking and engaging in sexual experimentation, dating women and visiting gay bars. Albee claims that he was "going to bed with boys from age thirteen on and enjoyed it greatly. If I went to bed with girls, I never felt the same pleasure from it" (Gussow, 70).

After leaving Trinity, he tried to live at home but moved into Greenwich Village in 1949 after relations with his parents deteriorated. "I didn't feel I was left any alternative," Albee said, "and it had nothing to do with homosexuality. That's another fiction. That was never discussed between us. . . . I was aware of my own sexual nature and that I would never be able to function according to their standards. I'm sure that in the background that helped motivate me in my decision to take off" (Gussow, 71). He would not see his mother again for seventeen years.

On a six-month trip to Europe in 1952, Albee became romantically involved with the composer William Flanagan, and on their return to New York they shared an apartment. Albee took a number of odd jobs, his favorite being a messenger for Western Union, while he continued to write. He and Flanagan socialized with aspiring composers, writers, and artists at various haunts in Greenwich Village, especially gay bars, where they drank heavily. Later Albee would say of Flanagan: "I know he started me on the road to alcoholism" (Gussow, 80). It was at one of their favorite gay bars in 1954 that Albee noticed that someone had scrawled "Who's Afraid of Virginia Woolf?" on a mirror, which amused him at the time and obviously stuck in his mind.

Albee and Flanagan also frequented the theater, especially Off-Broadway, as their limited budget would permit. Two plays by gay playwrights proved to be important influences on Albee: Jean Genet's *Deathwatch* in 1957 and Tennessee Williams's *Suddenly Last Summer* the next year. In February of 1958, on the verge of his thirtieth birthday and despairing that he'd never reach his potential as an important writer, Albee began *The Zoo Story,* with its daring depiction (for the time) of a homoerotic encounter that turns murderous. The play opened in Berlin in September 1959 on a double bill with Samuel Beckett's *Krapp's Last Tape,* where it enjoyed significant success. Before Albee left for Germany, he and Flanagan separated after seven years together. One reason for the split was Albee's rising career prospects; another was that he had met **Terrence McNally** in February 1959 at a party, beginning a romantic relationship that lasted just over five years.

Albee had written *The Death of Bessie Smith,* a one-act play concerning the fatally racist denial of medical attention to the legendary bisexual jazz singer, as a companion piece to *The Zoo Story.* Both plays received separate readings at the Actors Studio in New York, but *The Zoo Story* would eventually be produced Off-Broadway in 1960 at the Provincetown Playhouse, with *Krapp's Last Tape* as its companion piece. The production marked the beginning of the long professional relationship between Albee and Richard Barr that established both Albee's reputation as a playwright and Barr's success as a producer. In his first stint as a director, Albee staged a national touring company production of *The Zoo Story.*

The Death of Bessie Smith opened in Berlin in April 1960. Another play, *The Sandbox,* written for and about his grandmother during the same period, was given its first performance that same month in New York. That summer Albee wrote *The American Dream,* an excoriation of the Oedipal triangle that is supposed to underpin patriarchal family relations, in which a domineering mother and her henpecked husband murder their only son for failing to live up to their aspirations. He also completed a libretto for Flanagan's one-act opera, *Bartleby.* Richard Barr produced a double bill of *The American Dream* and *Bartleby,* which opened Off-Broadway in January 1961. The Albee play received mixed notices, but the Flanagan opera fared less well, and Barr removed it from the evening, eventually replacing it with *The Death of Bessie Smith.* The joint production garnered even greater critical respect for Albee and became a long-running success.

Although Albee had begun a new full-length play about two academic couples in 1960, it was not until the spring of 1962 that producer Richard Barr and director Alan Schneider got to read the completed version of *Who's Afraid of Virginia Woolf?* While both loved the play, they had Broadway aspirations, and Barr was wary of some of the harsh language. Nevertheless, the play opened at the Billy Rose Theatre on October 13, 1962, making Albee the first playwright since Eugene O'Neill to successfully move from Off-Broadway to Broadway. Its depiction of the alcoholic theatrics staged by middle-aged hosts George and Martha (played by Arthur Hill and Uta Hagen) on a private New England college campus to amuse themselves with a neophyte professor and his young wife (George Grizzard and Melinda Dillon) shocked and titillated audiences. Some leading critics, such as Howard Taubman, insinuated that the hosts were a gay couple in disguise rather than accepting the play as a portrait of a happy heterosexual marriage unblinkingly portrayed through gay eyes. Aided by critical controversy, the play became a hit, running for two years on Broadway with subsequent productions around the globe. It won the New York Drama Critics Circle Award, the Outer Circle Award, and the Foreign Press Association Award and was nominated for six Tony awards, winning five, including best play. It was the only nomination for a Pulitzer Prize, but a divided Pulitzer committee rejected the nomination and no prize in drama was awarded for 1963, causing John Mason Brown and John Gassner, who had nominated it, to resign from the committee in protest.

Albee's next work was an adaptation of **Carson McCullers**'s novella *The Ballad of the Sad Café.* Directed by Alan Schneider, and starring Colleen Dewhurst, the play opened on October 30, 1963, to mixed reviews and closed after 123 performances. Soon after the opening, Albee went to the Soviet Union with his friend John Steinbeck on a cultural exchange program. When he returned, he found that his relationship with Terrence McNally was over. McNally had become involved with the actor Robert Drivas.

Albee began a full-length play, *Tiny Alice,* on a ship returning home from a European vacation with his new lover, William Pennington, an interior decorator. Since its opening production in 1964, starring John Gielgud and Irene Worth and directed by Alan Schneider, *Tiny Alice* has bewildered critics and audiences. It is an allegorical work trading on incubus/succubus motifs that feature a cardinal, his lawyer ex-lover, his celibate lay secretary Julian, and Miss Alice, the world's richest woman, who wants to make a huge bequest to the Church. Julian is seduced by Miss Alice and dies. Philip Roth's review of *Tiny Alice* in the *New York Review of Books* decried the play for its "ghastly pansy rhetoric and repartee" (qtd. in Clum, 144).

Albee's adaptation of James Purdy's *Malcolm,* another religious allegory, depicts the corruption of a teenaged boy by an elderly astrologer, who leads him into a series of destructive worldly experiences. The play opened on Broadway in 1966 and failed quickly. It was followed by *A Delicate Balance,* which, like *The American Dream,* drew from the milieu of Albee's upbringing and offered a stinging critique of Northeastern bourgeois family life. It starred Jessica Tandy, Hume Cronyn, Marian Seldes as their daughter, Henderson Forsythe, and Carmen Matthews. The play opened at the Martin Beck Theater on September 22, 1966, received generally favorable notices, and won the Pulitzer Prize for drama.

In August of 1969, William Flanagan died, and Albee, in tribute to his former lover and mentor, opened the William Flanagan Memorial Creative Persons Center in Montauk, New York. It was, and remains today, a colony for those artists who can show both poverty and talent. The death of Flanagan came soon after the loss of John Steinbeck, and both deaths may have provoked Albee to complete a short play he had begun in 1967, then called *Death,* which opened as the full-length play *All Over* in 1971. Directed by John Gielgud, the cast included Jessica Tandy, Colleen Dewhurst, and George Voskovec. But, with the notable exception of Harold Clurman in *The Nation,* the critical reception was poor. That year Albee met Jonathan Thomas, a Canadian painter and sculptor, who became his life companion.

Albee had begun writing a companion piece to *Death,* entitled *Life,* which eventually became the full-length play *Seascape.* It opened at the Shubert Theater on Broadway, directed by Albee himself, on January 26, 1975, starring Frank Langella, Deborah Kerr, and Maureen Anderman. Langella won a Tony Award for his performance, and Albee received his second Pulitzer Prize for drama.

Albee was awarded the Gold Medal in Drama from the American Academy and Institute of Arts and Letters in 1980, but the three plays that followed were miserable failures: *The Lady from Dubuque* (1980), an adaptation of Vladimir Nabokov's *Lolita* (1981), and *The Man Who Had Three Arms* (1982–83). He blames this nadir of his career in part on his battle with alcoholism. With the help of Jonathan Thomas, he was finally able to stop drinking. Amid the struggle, he wrote the one acts *Walking* and *Finding the Sun,* the latter focusing openly on a gay couple and their relational problems. He also accepted a teaching position at the University of Houston, and Houston became a second cultural home for him.

In 1989, Albee's mother died, and a year later he began writing *Three Tall Women,* which was based on her life and reckoned with his conflicted feelings about this looming figure who never let him forget he was adopted. After premiering in Vienna and then Off-Broadway in January 1994, the play moved to The Promenade Theater, where it played 582 performances, starring Marian Seldes and Myra Carter, and became Albee's longest-running show in New York since *Virginia Woolf.* It heralded a major resurgence of Albee's career, winning him his third Pulitzer

Prize (a record topped only by O'Neill) and the New York Drama Critics Circle Award for Best Play. He also won an Obie Award for Sustained Achievement. The play went on to London's West End, where it starred Maggie Smith, who won the *Evening Standard* Award, as did the play. On Broadway in 1996, *A Delicate Balance* at the Lincoln Center Theater was awarded the Tony for best revival. Albee received the National Medal of Arts and the Kennedy Center Lifetime Achievement Award, being the fourth playwright, after Tennessee Williams, Arthur Miller, and Neil Simon, to receive the honor.

Albee directed the American premiere of *The Play about the Baby* at the Alley Theater in Houston on April 12, 2000, and it opened Off-Broadway on February 1, 2001, starring Marian Seldes and Brian Murray. During that same season, another new play, *Occupant,* about the life of his friend, the famed sculptor Louise Nevelson, was produced Off-Broadway by the Signature Theater for a limited run starring Anne Bancroft. Albee won the Lucille Lortel Award for Outstanding Achievement Off-Broadway in May 2002.

Albee returned to Broadway with *The Goat, or Who Is Sylvia?* starring Mercedes Ruehl and Bill Pullman and directed by David Esbjornson, on March 10, 2002. The play received the Outer Critics Circle Award, the New York Drama Critics Circle Award, and a Drama Desk Award (in a tie) and was nominated for two Tony Awards, winning the award for best play. Set in a well-heeled Northeastern suburb, the play depicts the nuclear family of a prizewinning architect in which the husband and wife appear to be comfortable and liberal and even supportive of their gay teenaged son. However, the marriage implodes and father-son relations grow strangely more intimate when the wife learns that her husband has been having a sexual affair with a goat and, evoking the ritual origins of tragedy, slaughters the ruminant. With perhaps his most sardonic critique yet, Albee tested the limits of putative tolerance at the turn of the millennium in order to expose the hollow conventions and ever more grotesque hypocrisies of the dominant class, especially with regard to sex and sexuality.

See J. M. Clum, *Still Acting Gay: Male Homosexuality in Modern Drama,* New York, 2000; M. Gussow, *Edward Albee: A Singular Journey,* New York, 1999; P. C. Kolin, ed., *Conversations with Edward Albee,* Jackson, Miss., 1988; C. J. Summers, ed., *The Gay and Lesbian Literary Heritage,* New York, 1995; S. Malinowski, ed., *Gay and Lesbian Literature,* Detroit, 1994; and A. Sinfield, *Out on Stage: Lesbian and Gay Theatre in the Twentieth Century,* New Haven, 1999.

Jon Fraser

ALEXANDER, Cris (Christopher) (1920–), actor and photographer, was born in Tulsa, Oklahoma, where he attended school with the actor Tony Randall. He enrolled at the University of Oklahoma and worked as a radio announcer in 1937 in Oklahoma City. In 1938, he moved to New York to attend the Feagin School of Dramatic Art. At the same time, he opened a successful portrait photography studio.

In 1944, he was chosen by George Abbott to play Chip in *On the Town,* the first Broadway musical for composer **Leonard Bernstein,** as well as for writers Betty Comden and Adolph Green. Alexander's naive, hick sailor was paired with the aggressive cabdriver, Hildy, played by Nancy Walker, and together they sang the comic duet "Come Up to My Place."

Two years later Alexander acted with **Clifton Webb** in Nöel Coward's *Present Laughter.* Brooks Atkinson singled out Alexander's performance, stating that "something should be said in praise of [his] belligerent acting" (Atkinson, 31).

Before teaming up again with the creators of *On the Town* for their next Broadway production, Alexander became personally involved with a New York City Ballet dancer, Shaun O'Brien. After four and a half decades with his partner, Alexander said in an interview, "Our life is . . . the greatest life imaginable" (Klain, 39).

When the Bernstein group returned to Broadway with Rosalind Russell in *Wonderful Town,* so did Alexander. He played drugstore manager Frank Lippencott, whose banana split story is one of the high points of comic mediocrity in the song "Conversation Piece." *Wonderful Town* was to occupy Alexander for much of the 1950s. He stayed with the show for the entire original run, playing opposite Russell and later Carol Channing (Klain, 37). In 1958, he reunited with Nancy Walker for a City Center revival of the musical. In November of the same year, he repeated his role in a television production with Russell.

Alexander's personal and professional association with Russell continued in *Auntie Mame.* In both the stage and film versions, he played Mr. Loomis, the store manager who fires Mame. Onstage he also understudied Mame's nephew Patrick. Offstage, he painted a portrait of Russell's son for her (Russell and Chase, 196).

Alexander's last acting role was as an aging homosexual in Lanford Wilson's *The Madness of Lady Bright* in 1966. Stanley Kauffmann dismissed the role of Leslie Bright as "a person who is not much more than a mechanic of the mattress, growing old and desperate." But of the actor he says, "Cris Alexander, willowy and waxen-faced in the solo role, is up to its demands" (Kauffmann, 42).

Alexander's last work on Broadway was creating visual production slides for Richard Rodgers's *Two by Two* in 1970. Walter Kerr credited Alexander with enhancing the musical's "essential charm" through "swift crackling spatters of everything from Michelangelo to Van Gogh that [he] has arranged to represent the visual thunder of God's voice" (Kerr, B1).

Alexander's photography also enlivened two books by *Auntie Mame* author Patrick Dennis, *Little Me* and *First Lady*. The former, a masterpiece of theatrical camp, is the tell-all autobiography of a fictional actress, Belle Poitrine. In it, Alexander features his lover, O'Brien, as the nearly nude Mr. Musgrove leaping out of bed in their apartment (Klain, 39).

Never a leading force in the theater, Cris Alexander nevertheless contributed steadily and devotedly for more than twenty-five years. In the early 1990s, he and O'Brien retired to upstate New York. Although he is privately open about his homosexuality, Alexander rarely made it the focus of his work. But his roles, such as the shy sailor, the actor-adoring playwright, and the officious floorwalker, share an amount of understated preliberation gay sensibility.

See B. Atkinson, "Review of *Present Laughter,*" *New York Times,* October 30, 1946; S. Kauffmann, "Lanford Wilson's Plays Open at Theater East," *New York Times,* March 23, 1966; W. Kerr, "Review of *Two by Two,*" *New York Times,* November 22, 1970; J. Klain, "Cris Alexander: In Tune, in Focus," *Show Music* 10 (winter 1994–95): 35–39; R. McGill, ed., *Notable Names in the American Theatre,* Clifton, N.J., 1976; and R. Russell and C. Chase, *Life is a Banquet,* New York, 1977.

Stephen E. Long

ALTON, Robert (Robert Alton Hart) (1897–1957), choreographer and director for stage and screen, was one of New York's busiest and most successful dance directors in the 1930s and early 1940s before he pursued a career in Hollywood. His credits include some of the liveliest Broadway musicals of the period, among them *Anything Goes, Leave It to Me, Du Barry Was a Lady, Pal Joey,* and *Panama Hattie,* and he provided the choreography for many of MGM's golden era musicals, including *The Harvey Girls, Easter Parade,* and *Annie Get Your Gun.* He was married to his former dance partner, Marjory Fielding, who was the mother of his son, Robert Alton Hart Jr. But Alton's homosexual relationships were well known among Hollywood insiders. In particular, he was linked with another musical comedy choreographer/director, Charles Walters, with whom he "enjoyed a long-standing affair" (Shipman, 132). Although Alton's choreography on stage and film did not depict homo- and bisexual relations, his work may be read as "queer," with its conscious rejection of homogenized, monolithic chorus formations and an emphasis on individuality and diversity within the corps of dancers.

The youngest of seven children, Alton was born in Bennington, Vermont, where he began dancing at the age of three. After the death of his father, he moved to Springfield, Massachusetts, in pursuit of a dance education and then to New York to study with ballet director Mikhail Mordkin. Alton danced as a soloist in Mordkin's troupe before finding work in the chorus of such shows as the *Greenwich Village Follies,* the Marx Brothers' vehicle *I'll Say She Is,* and numerous vaudeville engagements. His first job as a choreographer, however, was in a St. Louis movie theater staging an amateur vaudeville act, which attracted the attention of a Warner Brothers film executive. He remained briefly in Hollywood before returning to New York, where he eventually choreographed a J. J. Shubert show. This provided the exposure he needed, and a string of Broadway hits followed. By the end of the 1930s, his attention to detail, demand for perfection from his dancers, and intricate dance patterns had earned him the reputation as one of Broadway's strictest choreographers, a quality that won him a great deal of respect from his dancers.

Alton is not generally recognized for revolutionizing musical theater dance, but his work is of great importance. Gene Kelly, whom Alton cast in *Leave It to Me* (1938), Kelly's first Broadway show, said in a 1975 interview, "Bob never invented a new style of dance the way Jack Cole did or the way I always tried to do. What he did, the fusion of the styles that remained there, was so excellent, was so good, he should be given far more credit" (Kelly, 31). Kelly does, however, regard Alton's work for *Pal Joey* (1940), a show in which Kelly originally starred, as the genesis of the "dream ballet," which became a major component of musical theater and was later perfected by Agnes DeMille in Rodgers and Hammerstein's *Oklahoma!* and *Carousel* (Kelly, 55). Alton was particularly noted for his ability to individualize each dancer in the chorus instead of treating the group as a uniform ensemble. This quality was described in an article in the *New York Times* in 1940.

> The old chorus line with twenty girls kicking precisely together, evolving every step in unison, all cogs in a dancing machine, is gone from Broadway. . . . Instead, each dancer of Alton's is now an entity, doing different steps, the many blending into one whole pleasing unit. Many postures, many steps, many varying poses and effects— that is what an Alton dance number is made of. ("Dances by Robert Alton")

Reading Alton's work as queer, one may appreciate the way in which the chorus numbers in the musicals he choreographed created a new space for difference and individualism. Metaphorically, the dances achieved what many agree is the central project of queer theory and identity politics. His work reflected the possibility of allowing individuals access into a mainstream culture "without denying or losing their oppositional identities . . . without necessarily assimilating" (Creekmur and Doty, 2).

See "Robert Alton," Clippings File, Billy Rose Theatre Collection, New York Public Library; C. K. Creekmur and A. Doty, eds., *Out in Culture: Gay, Lesbian, and Queer Essays on Popular Culture,* Durham and London, 1995; "Dances by Robert Alton," *New York Times,* March 3, 1940; G. Kelly, Transcript of interview with Marilyn Hunt, March 10–14, 1975, Dance Collection, New York Public Library; D. Shipman, *Judy Garland: The Secret Life of an American Legend,* New York, 1992.

James F. Wilson

ANDERSON, Dame Judith (Frances Margaret Anderson-Anderson) (1898–1992), actress, was born in Australia on February 10, 1898, the fourth and youngest child of James Anderson-Anderson and Jessie Margaret Saltmarsh. She may have developed her distaste for the institution of marriage (which in a 1990 interview she likened to the unpleasant shock of jumping into an ice-cold lake) from her parents' unhappy union. "Her father, who had once been known as the 'Silver King of Australia,' lost his money through gambling and left his family when Frances was five" (Head, 20). Her strong-willed mother moved the family to Sydney, where she ran a grocery to support them. When, at the age of seven, Frances saw a concert by the Australian singer Dame Nellie Melba, she decided on a career in performance. Lacking any remarkable musical talent, she soon gave up singing and settled on an acting career. Frances Anderson made her stage debut in Sydney at the age of seventeen in the Theatre Royal's production of *A Royal Divorce* (1915).

Accompanied by her mother, she moved to the United States in 1918 and secured a position in the stock company of the Fourteenth Street Theatre, where she played bit parts for two seasons. After changing her name to Judith, she received her first critical notice as Elise Von Zile in *Cobra* (1924). In 1928, she replaced **Lynn Fontanne** as Nina Leeds in O'Neill's *Strange Interlude,* and in 1932 she returned to Broadway as Lavinia Mannon in his *Mourning Becomes Electra.* Her performance caught the attention of gay theatrical producer and director **Guthrie McClintic.** He cast Anderson first as Gertrude in *Hamlet* (1936), opposite John Gielgud, then as the Scottish Lady opposite Olivier's Macbeth at the Old Vic in 1937. Her alliance with Gielgud and McClintic provided a turning point in her career; thereafter, she became known as a classical interpreter of strong, vengeful, and complex female characters.

The hallmark of her acting career came in 1947 when she played Medea under Gielgud's direction in a new adaptation of the tragedy written for Anderson by Robinson Jeffers. Anderson gave a triumphant performance. *Medea* ran for 214 performances on Broadway, toured the United States for eight months, and earned Anderson her reputation as a menacing, larger-than-life personality. The account of her brutal, aggressive, and passionate portrayal in the *New Republic* of November 3, 1947, is representative of the press she received.

> The ovations are for the performance of Judith Anderson—a performance that is nothing so much as a full cavalry charge across an open plain, squarely at the tenuous positions held by the audience. And it is difficult to report clearly. There was a swirl of hooves and sabers, a noise as of a million guns, and the positions were taken. (Young, 1:19)

Although Anderson had an impressive film career, she never gave up the stage. When she was nearly seventy-three, she portrayed Hamlet in a production that toured the United States, including two performances at Carnegie Hall on January 14–15, 1971. The production was condemned in nearly every town in which it played. Mel Gussow wrote in the *New York Times,* "Should any 72-year old lady attempt to play Hamlet? Not this 72-year old lady" (Gussow, 18). She steadfastly refused to retire; she received a kinder reception for her portrayal of the Nurse opposite Zoe Caldwell's Medea (1982). The *New Yorker* praised Anderson, "who, at eighty-four, is as strong-voiced and commanding a stage presence as ever" (Head, 22). When asked if she had ever wished to play softer roles, she dismissed the question. **Eva LeGallienne** said of her, "She cannot by nature play wall flowers" (Madsen, 175).

Anderson's reputation for playing repressed lesbian characters was gained primarily through her legendary screen role, Mrs. Danvers, in Alfred Hitchcock's *Rebecca* (1940). While Anderson claimed that she considered Mrs. Danvers to be "sexless," the lesbian subtext of the role—a sadistic housekeeper who remains psychotically devoted to the beautiful Rebecca even after her death—is barely suggested in the film. Much later she gave a sympathetic and poignant portrayal of Big Mama in the 1957 film version of *Cat on a Hot Tin Roof.* She confessed, however, that "**Ten-**

nessee **Williams** informed me that all his gentlemen friends were convinced it was a stretch for me to play a heterosexual" (169).

In *Hollywood Lesbians,* Boze Hadleigh attempted to document Anderson's sexual and romantic past through both an interview with her and anecdotal evidence provided by those who knew her. He writes, "The gay husband of lesbian stage star **Katharine 'Kit' Cornell** told gay critic **Alec Woollcott,** 'Judith may never find someone manlier than herself to act with or engage'" (Hadleigh, 160). Anderson endured two brief, unhappy marriages, the first (1937–39) to Benjamin Harrison Lehman, a professor of English at the University of California at Berkeley, and the second (1946–50) to theatrical producer Luther Greene. She would say little about the marriages except that "neither experience was a jolly holiday" (169). "After 1950," she said, "I never looked back or gave [marriage] another thought" (160). When Hadleigh asked Anderson if it would bother her to be thought of as a lesbian, she responded, "Many people already do. . . . it doesn't bother me, it's they [the people who ask] who bother me" (176). When pressed to divulge her "romantic orientation," she replied, "I am no romantic! *That* is my orientation! . . . But I wouldn't 'come out' in a million years" (176).

Although her career was spent primarily in the United States, Anderson retained her Australian citizenship, and in 1960 she was named a Dame Commander of the Most Excellent Order of the British Empire during Queen Elizabeth II's 1960 Birthday Honors. Although she considered it "quite an honor," when asked how it had changed her life she quipped that she found herself "wearing gloves more often" (Hadleigh, 161).

Her American tribute came in 1984 when the Lion Theater on West Forty-second Street in New York was renamed the Judith Anderson Theater. In an interview conducted at the time, Anderson stated that she was grateful for the honor but complained that her celebrity would mean little if she were not employed. She played a cameo role in the film *Star Trek III* (1984) and worked on the soap opera *Santa Barbara* from 1984 to 1987. When questioned about the suitability of television drama for her prodigious talents, Anderson said that she felt certain her heroine, Sarah Bernhardt, if given the opportunity, would have done the same.

See M. Gussow, "Stage: A Lady Hamlet," *New York Times,* January 15, 1971; B. Hadleigh, *Hollywood Lesbians,* New York, 1994; F. E. Head, "Judith Anderson," in *Notable Women in the American Theatre: A Biographical Dictionary,* edited by A. M. Robinson, V. Mowry Roberts, and M. S. Barranger, New York, 1989; I. Herbert, ed., with C. Baxter and R. E. Finley, *Who's Who in the Theatre: A Biographical Record of the Contemporary Stage,* 17th ed., Detroit, 1978; E. Johns, *Dames of the Theatre,* New Rochelle, N.Y., 1975; A. Madsen, *The Sewing Circle: Hollywood's Greatest Secret: Female Stars Who Loved Other*

Women, New York, 1995; E. Pace, "Dame Judith Anderson Dies at 93: An Actress of Powerful Portrayals," *New York Times,* January 4, 1992; W. C. Young, *Famous Actors and Actresses of the American Stage: Documents of American Theater History,* New York, 1975.

Susan McCully

ARTHUR, Helen Jean (1879–1939), producer and manager, was born in Lancaster, Pennsylvania, on March 29, 1879. She grew up in an upper middle class family in Evanston, Illinois, where her father was employed in real estate and law. She graduated from Evanston Township High School, spent a year at Northwestern University in 1897–98, and attended New York University in 1900–1901, from which she graduated with a Bachelor of Laws degree. She is said to have been the first woman to try a criminal case in the state of New York. She met Lillian Wald, founder of the Henry Street Settlement on New York's Lower East Side, in her capacity as an attorney and spent the summer of 1906 as a resident at Henry Street. A letter to Wald mentions an incest case that Arthur took on as a favor to her. Arthur is one of (at least) two women with whom Wald had brief, intense, romantic relationships (Coss, 9–10).

Arthur's career path began to swerve when she started writing drama reviews in order to obtain free tickets. In the theater, she served as a press representative, company manager, and personal manager before landing a job as executive secretary for the Shubert brothers. A 1930s program mentions that she had met **Agnes Morgan** at a party around 1907, when both were trying to break into the "boys' club" of New York theater production. Wald introduced Arthur to Alice and Irene Lewisohn, and by 1909 Arthur was volunteering part time on the Henry Street festivals and plays directed by the Lewisohn sisters. Arthur introduced Morgan to Sarah Cowell Le Moyne, Alice Lewisohn's mentor, which led to Morgan's help with the play *The Shepherd* in 1912. In 1917, Arthur left the Shubert organization, tried producing independently for a short period, and returned to become business manager of the Neighborhood Playhouse, a salaried position. Arthur, Morgan, and the two Lewisohns formed the producing staff of the Neighborhood Playhouse, where they were collaboratively responsible for all artistic and managerial decisions until its dissolution in 1927. Alice Lewisohn later described Arthur and Morgan as "the lithe, shirt-waisted, and stiff-collared Helen Arthur, dapper, bright-eyed, keen; and her friend the quiet, serious, watchful Agnes Morgan" (Crowley, 31). The two women lived and worked together for the rest of Arthur's life and were referred to by company members as "the Morgan-Arthurs" (handwritten photograph dedications, *The Grand Street Follies,*

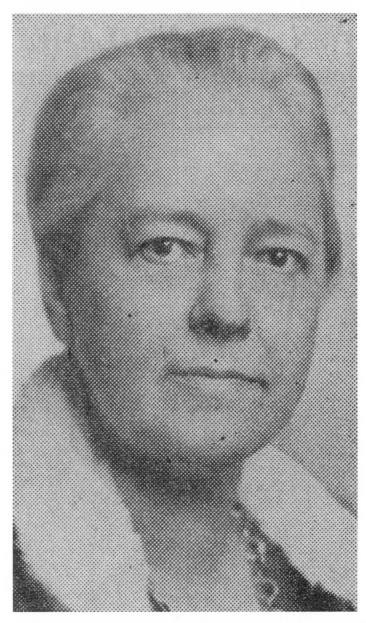

Helen Arthur in her fifties. (Photo by Brandenburg, courtesy of the Billy Rose Theatre Collection, New York Public Library for the Performing Arts, and the Astor, Lenox, and Tilden Foundations.)

Neighborhood Playhouse Gift, Billy Rose Theatre Collection, New York Public Library of the Performing Arts). Paula Trueman, a Neighborhood Playhouse performer, said in an interview years later that Arthur and Morgan "were a lesbian couple. Just everyone knew" (Coss, 10). Arthur enjoyed dressing in masculine clothing such as ties and high collars. Another Neighborhood Playhouse performer described her as "quite a pixie, bright as a whistle, and a little devilish too" (10).

Arthur had continued to work as Ruth Draper's personal manager throughout the Neighborhood Playhouse years, and after 1927 she picked up several more out of town performers as clients, including Mrs. Patrick Campbell, Angna Enters, Marion Kirby, and the Dance Repertory Company formed by Tamiris, Graham, Humphrey, and Weidman. She was the executive director and Morgan the stage director of Actor-Managers, Inc., a company developed out of the Neighborhood Playhouse team that presented *The Grand Street Follies.* Actor-Managers produced three editions of *The Grand Street Follies* and several Broadway productions, including Ring Lardner's *The Love Nest,* Lord Dunsany's *If,* Simon Gantillon's *Maya,* and Morgan's *If Love Were All.* Arthur and Morgan produced several shows at the Newport Casino Theater in Rhode Island between 1935 and 1939, including *At Marian's,* starring Laurette Taylor, and Morgan's play *Grandpa.* In 1936, they joined the Popular Price Unit of the Federal Theater Project, presenting *American Holiday, Thirteenth Chair,* and *Class of '29.* They also managed the Ann Arbor Drama Festival in 1938 and 1939. Arthur died in New York on December 9, 1939, of cerebral thrombosis, in virtual poverty due to the Depression, with Agnes Morgan by her side. Morgan died on May 25, 1976.

See D. F. Benardete, "The Neighborhood Playhouse in Grand Street," Ph.D. diss., New York University, 1949; M. N. Blood, "The Neighborhood Playhouse from 1915 to 1927: A History and Analysis," Ph.D. diss., Northwestern University, 1993; C. Coss, *Lillian D. Wald: Progressive Activist,* New York, 1989; A. L. Crowley, *The Neighborhood Playhouse: Leaves from a Theater Scrapbook,* New York, 1957; Helen Arthur folders of clippings and programs, Billy Rose Theatre Collection, New York Public Library for the Performing Arts; Helen Arthur files, Bobst Library, New York University Archives; Helen Arthur letters to Lillian Wald, Lillian Wald Collection, Special Collections, Columbia University.

Melanie Blood

ARTHUR, Jean (Gladys Georgianna Greene) (b. ca. 1900–1905, d. 1991), actress, was born in New York City, the only daughter of Herbert and Johanna Greene and the youngest of four children. She attended school in

Washington Heights, except when her father, a professional photographer, went on location for extended periods, taking his family with him. Arthur intended to become a dancer or a tightrope walker and then decided to become a foreign language teacher, but a chance encounter in high school led to a modeling job. An advertisement featuring her photograph was noticed by a Fox talent scout, who arranged a screen test (Vermilye, 330); the result was a contract and a debut in John Ford's silent film *Cameo Kirby* (1923). Although this is usually credited as her first film, Arthur had actually been cast in the starring role of *The Temple of Venus* but was replaced (with Mary Philbin) because she was deemed inadequate; she appeared as an extra. A subsequent film, *Somebody Lied,* opened a week before *Cameo Kirby* (Pierce and Swarthout, 3–5). At the studio's request, she changed her name, choosing one that reflected her romantic interests: Jean for Joan of Arc and Arthur for the legendary king of Camelot, although Pierce and Swarthout suggest other possibilities (3).

For the next few years, Arthur made nearly two dozen films, mostly westerns and slapstick comedies, the most memorable being Buster Keaton's *Seven Chances* (1925) (Bauer, 27). In 1928, she signed a contract with Paramount and the next year made her first talkie, *The Canary Murder Case,* unleashing a voice that was to become legendary. Frank Capra said it sounded "like a thousand tinkling bells" (Bauer, 28); others have called it "wistful-husky" and "a cross between sandpaper and a caress" (Drabelle, "Revisited," G10) and a sound that "brushes against the ear as tinglingly as Orson Welles's Tiffany baritone" (Drabelle, "Goop," 21). Arthur made some twenty pictures under Paramount, including *The Mysterious Dr. Fu Manchu* (1929) and *The Greene Murder Case* (1929). But when her contract expired in 1931 she headed for Broadway to learn more about acting and to further her career.

The move was bold but successful. During the next two years, she appeared in nine plays on Broadway or in summer stock, including *Foreign Affairs* (1932) and *The Man Who Reclaimed His Head* (1932), with Claude Rains (Bauer, 28). In 1932, she married Frank Ross Jr., a successful real estate businessman, who had ventured briefly into acting and later became involved in movie production.

Having gained confidence and prominence, Arthur returned to Hollywood in 1933, becoming in the next decade "a central figure in romantic comedy" (Drabelle, "Revisited," G9). After appearing in *Whirlpool* (1934), she was given a long-term contract with Columbia, during which she produced much of her best work (Bauer, 28). Although she set her image in *The Whole Town's Talking* (1935), with Edward G. Robinson ("the Depression-era working girl who shields herself by raising a hard facade in front of her soft heart" [Drabelle, "Goop," 19]), it was Frank Capra's *Mr. Deeds Goes to Town* (1936) that launched her stardom. She brought a fresh type of leading lady to the screen—liberated and independent, tough but gentle (Bauer, 29). This saucy figure strode through a string of hits, including *Easy Living* (1937), *You Can't Take It with You* (1938), *Mr. Smith Goes to Washington* (1939), *The Talk of the Town* (1942), and *The More the Merrier* (1943), for which she received her only Academy Award nomination. In 1935, she also established a radio career that would span nearly two decades and include over two dozen appearances.

When her contract ended in 1944, Arthur abandoned movies to attend college in Missouri for six weeks, studying philosophy and sociology, and then returned to Hollywood to continue her studies at UCLA. She did not appear on stage or screen again until 1948, in *A Foreign Affair,* which was so successful that Paramount signed her to a three-picture contract (Vermilye, 337). But Arthur rejected all scripts offered and during the late 1940s spent three summers studying psychology and anthropology at Bennington College in Vermont; in 1949, she took dancing lessons in New York (338).

Arthur's marriage to Ross had been deteriorating for some time, and they divorced in 1949 on grounds of incompatibility; they were, in one view, "[t]emperamentally mismatched" (Drabelle, "Goop," 23). But accounts of the relationship vary; at the time of the divorce, Ross was already involved in an affair with actress Joan Caulfield (whom he subsequently married and divorced), and Arthur accused him of cold indifference toward her (Pierce and Swarthout, 73), with her divorce action alleging "extreme cruelty." But Ross's niece and his third wife both portrayed him as quite the opposite—a gentle and caring man (Oller, 126). In the early 1980s, after years of bitterness, the two did reconcile in a tenuous friendship (280–81).

Early in 1950, Arthur starred in *Peter Pan,* a role she had long yearned for and which earned her high praise; the production had a long and successful run on Broadway. Three years later, she made her last film, the critically acclaimed *Shane* (1953), as well as her final radio appearance. In subsequent years, she made occasional television appearances, including in her own short-lived 1966 program, the *Jean Arthur Show,* which ran for only twelve episodes. She made her final return to Broadway in 1967 in an ill-fated show, *The Freaking Out of Stephanie Blake,* which closed after previews. In the following year, she began a four-year teaching career at Vassar College, followed in 1972 by a short stint at the North Carolina School of the Arts; by 1974, she had returned to her home in Carmel, California, for good. She made a brief appearance in a 1975 Cleveland production of *First Monday in October,* but she had to withdraw because of ill health. She lived the rest of her life as a recluse in Carmel. In contrast to her tough screen persona, "Arthur's personal insecurities made it impossible to sustain her career once its momentum faltered" (Harvey, 434). She died of a heart ailment in June 1991 at a Carmel nursing home.

Arthur's winsome film image as a confident and forthright woman whose feminine toughness masks vulnerability was quite different from her real life. Offscreen she was intensely private, high-strung, and insecure, beset with "a pathological shyness born of fear and self-doubt" and plagued continually "by stage and camera fright" (Oller, 3). Growing up with three older brothers, who she felt led much more adventurous lives than she, strengthened her determination "to do things that were exciting, or at least interesting" and no doubt fed the plucky image she conveyed onscreen (28). Her sense of inferiority and loneliness was probably exacerbated by the fact that her father, whom she adored, periodically abandoned his family from the time Arthur was eight.

Arthur herself had no children, and despite her marriages (the one to Ross and an earlier one-day marriage to Julian Ancker), her sexual tendencies were ambiguous. Fellow actor Patsy Kelly overtly acknowledged (in an interview) Arthur's lesbianism (Hadleigh, 62), while **Agnes Moorehead** did not contradict an interviewer who grouped Arthur with actresses who "have enjoyed lesbian or bi-relationships." Moorehead simply said that "different people thought different things about" her and that, like most women, Arthur was "emotionally intricate" (193). Arthur was rumored to have been romantically involved with Mary Martin, gossip that seemed validated by a 1966 novel, *The Princess and the Goblin,* allegedly a roman à clef about their relationship; it was several years before its author, Paul Rosner, acknowledged that the story was wholly imagined, though he did draw on his own impressions of the two women in writing it (Oller, 128–30). Speculation about Arthur's sexual orientation was revived by Donald Spoto's biography of **Marlene Dietrich,** *Blue Angel,* which cited Arthur and Martin among the "charter member[s] of America's creative lesbian community" (Spoto, 105), while Hadleigh's book assumed Arthur's lesbianism or bisexuality "as a given" (Oller, 130).

See S. Bauer, "A Star of The Golden Age: Remembering Jean Arthur," *Journal of Popular Film and Television* 17 (spring 1989): 27–36; D. Drabelle, "Jean Arthur, Revisited," *Washington Post,* October 6, 1991; D. Drabelle, "What Do You Think I Am, a Goop?" *Film Comment* 32 (March–April 1996): 18–25; B. Hadleigh, *Hollywood Lesbians,* New York, 1994; S. Harvey, "Jean Arthur: Passionate Primrose," in *Close-ups,* edited by Danny Peary, New York, 1978, 431–69; J. Oller, *Jean Arthur: The Actress Nobody Knew,* New

York, 1997; A. Pierce and D. Swarthout, *Jean Arthur: A Bio-Bibliography,* New York, 1990; M. Rosen, *Popcorn Venus,* New York, 1973; A. Rothe, ed., *Current Biography,* New York, 1945; D. Spoto, *Blue Angel,* New York, 1992; J. Vermilye, "Jean Arthur," *Films in Review* 17 (June–July 1966): 329–46; and R. Wolfe, "Jean Arthur: In Appreciation," *Journal of Popular Film and Television* 17 (spring 1989): 24–25.

Karen Blansfield

AUDEN, W. H. (Wystan Hugh) (1907–73), poet, playwright, librettist, critic, essayist, teacher, and translator, was born in York, England, on February 21, 1907, the third of three sons, to George Augustus and Constance Rosalie Bicknell Auden. Both parents were devoutly religious (High Church Anglican) and well educated: he, a doctor, in medicine and psychology, and she in music. Auden always remained close to his family, and to his mother especially; their religious, intellectual, and artistic interests were vital to his life and work.

In 1915, at the age of eight, Auden enrolled in Saint Edmund's, a preparatory school in Surrey, where he met **Christopher Isherwood,** another student, with whom he began a lifelong friendship. Intent on becoming a mining engineer from the age of six, Auden impressed his fellow students with his wide knowledge of the sciences, and in 1920 he enrolled in Gresham's School in Holt, Norfolk, which was known for excellence in scientific education. At Gresham's, Auden underwent momentous changes: he discovered his calling for poetry, he lost his religious faith, and he recognized and accepted his homosexuality. Though attracted to other boys, he remained sexually inexperienced while at Gresham's, due largely to its repressive honor code, which had been fashioned to forestall homosexual activity among the students.

On entering the college of Christ Church, Oxford, in 1925, on a scholarship in natural science, Auden found that his scientific interests had flagged, and after three years he received a third-class Honours degree (in English). For his poetry, it was a time of development: he discovered the work of T. S. Eliot, which served as a model for his own, and he edited and published poetry in numerous magazines.

Auden was promiscuous during his first year at Oxford, having sex with friends, acquaintances, and strangers (e.g., on the train to London). He recounted his encounters with relish to his friends, cultivating an image of himself as a daring sensualist, enjoying promiscuous, homosexual sex without inhibition or guilt. But to his closest friends he expressed uneasiness, writing to one in 1927: "There still lingers in my mind the idea of something indecent in a mutual homosexual relation" (Carpenter,

49). While undergoing psychoanalysis in 1928, he told his brother John of his intention "to develop heterosexual traits" (Bucknell, xl). Certainly, Auden's sexual habits, as far as they knew of them, were a cause of distress to his parents. After unpleasant scenes at home during the Christmas holidays, Auden decided to stay celibate in 1927.

In 1928, Auden and Isherwood continued their friendship in Berlin, where both were impressed by the political theater. No longer celibate, Auden engaged the services of a callboy, Manfred, who reportedly received English lessons in exchange. The next year Auden became a schoolmaster at Larchfield Academy in Scotland, where he taught French and English. Recognition as a poet came with *Paid on Both Sides,* a play (he called it a "charade") written in verse and published in *Criterion* by T. S. Eliot in 1930. The play develops the ideas of John Layard, which posit that physical and mental health are determined by one's moral state.

In 1932, Auden began to teach at the Downs School, Colwall, where he continued to write poetry and numerous plays, the latter mainly in collaboration with Isherwood, most of which were published and produced by the Group Theatre: *The Dance of Death* (1933), *The Dog beneath the Skin* (1935), and *Ascent of F6* (1936). Revealing considerable experimentation in form and tone, these plays are polemical, Marxist leaning, reflective of the didactic theater in Berlin during the 1920s (particularly Brecht's), and reflective as well of Auden's abiding interest in Freudian psychology. They were not enthusiastically received by audiences and critics. Not until the productions of the Royal Court Theatre twenty years later would anything close to Brechtian staging find a responsive audience in London.

Auden began sleeping with Isherwood in 1926, but by the 1930s his thoughts on sexuality were moving away from sensualism. He began to value lasting, emotional relationships over those centered around sexual encounters, although he had not as yet found such a relationship. In 1932, he was troubled by what he perceived as a lack of emotional commitment in both hetero- and homosexual relationships: "The mere fact that A prefers girls and B boys is unimportant. The real cause for alarm lies in the large number of nervous and unhappy people who are incapable of any intimate faithful relationship at all" (qtd. in Carpenter, 105). His marriage in 1935 to Thomas Mann's daughter Erika was a formality necessary to secure her safety from the Nazis.

Traveling to Spain in 1937 in support of the Republican cause, Auden witnessed and wrote of events in the Spanish Civil War. His poem *Spain 1937* received considerable attention, favorable and otherwise. George Orwell wrote: "Mr. Auden's brand of amoralism is only possible if you are the kind of person who is always somewhere else when the trigger is pulled" (Davenport-Hines, 167). Auden himself, while not agreeing with Orwell's critique, regretted the last lines of the poem, which refer to "necessary murder." The harsh treatment and killing of priests and the closing of churches in Republican Spain greatly dismayed Auden and aroused his sympathy for the religious faithful.

In 1939, after a trip with Isherwood to China, where they witnessed the Sino-Japanese War, both writers moved to the United States. While Isherwood left for California, Auden settled in New York City, remaining there until 1972 and taking American citizenship in 1946. Shortly after his arrival, he met **Chester Kallman,** a young man whose brilliance and Brooklynite aplomb charmed the famous poet, and he soon felt that he had found someone to whom he could remain devoted for a lifetime. With Kallman, Auden fulfilled his longing for some form of marriage, and the two remained together until death, though theirs was not a faithful nor often a joyous union. Dorothy Farnan writes of her son-in-law: "Chester . . . by nature sought variety and sexual liberty" (Farnan, 53). The relationship between the two, which Auden considered a marriage, survived sexual infidelity, though often as a source of anguish to Auden. Heavy drinkers and smokers throughout their lives, both men suffered increasingly from alcoholism and ill-health. At the time Auden met Kallman, he also returned to his Christian faith and began to attend services of the Episcopal Church.

Over the next decade, Auden taught at various American colleges and universities and continued to write and publish poetry and edit literary anthologies. In 1941, his *Paul Bunyan,* an operetta written in collaboration with Benjamin Britten, was performed at Columbia University, but it disappointed both the collaborators and the critics. In 1948, Auden spent the first of many summers in a rented house on the Italian island of Ischia.

For the stage, after his move to New York, Auden turned from writing new plays to translations, adaptations, and libretti, often in collaboration with Kallman. Most of the projects with Kallman were produced in Europe, although the New York City Ballet presented their translation of Brecht's *The Seven Deadly Sins of the Lower Middle Class,* with music by Kurt Weill.

Auden's early political writings and later religious and psychological explorations offer no direct commentary on issues of homosexuality. Regardless of the orientation, Auden preferred privacy in matters of sexuality, and in 1969 he "had little to say in favor of the new Gay Liberation movement which was bringing homosexuality out into the open"

(Carpenter, 433). In *A Certain World,* his most autobiographical work, he cautioned against interpreting poetry with attention to the poet's private life, for "his private life is, or should be, of no concern to anybody except himself, his family and his friends" (Auden, vii).

In 1972, he left New York to live at Christ Church, Oxford. Unhappy there, he planned to move back to New York the following year. He died on September 29, 1973, in Kirschstetten, Austria, where he was buried.

See W. H. Auden, *A Certain World,* New York, 1970; R. R. Bozorth, *Auden's Games of Knowledge: Poetry and the Meanings of Homosexuality,* New York, 2001; K. Bucknell, ed., *Juvenilia,* Princeton, 1994; H. Carpenter, *W. H. Auden: A Biography,* London, 1981; R. Davenport-Hines, *Auden,* New York, 1995; D. Farnan, *Auden in Love,* New York, 1984; and W. Johnson, *Auden,* New York, 1990.

Eric Wiley

BAKER, Josephine (1906–75), dancer, singer, and entertainer, was born in Saint Louis, Missouri, to Carrie McDonald. Biographers have never determined with certainty the identity of her father. When Baker was five, and her brother Richard was three, Carrie married Arthur Martin, and they subsequently had two children, Margaret and Willie Mae. At the age of eight, Baker began working as a domestic to provide the family with much needed income. Her stage aspirations and ambition for material possessions in young adulthood grew in part from her early years of deprivation. In addition to her poverty, the racial tensions that eventually erupted into the East Saint Louis race riot of 1917 impressed upon her the inequalities facing black Americans. Throughout her life, she worked to eliminate racial prejudice, often at the expense of her career.

In 1920, Baker made her theatrical debut at the Booker T. Washington Theatre, at Twenty-third and Market Street, St. Louis. There Clara Smith, billed as "the South's Favorite Coon Shouter," took a fancy to her. Smith insisted that manager Bob Russell hire her to join their vaudeville troupe, the Dixie Steppers (Baker and Chase, 38). Baker started as a dresser, but she quickly found her way onto the stage, eventually performing in the chorus. According to an associate of Russell's, she was Clara Smith's "lady lover" (38). Clara Smith also played a significant role in Baker's career by introducing her to "black glamour" (Rose, 50). Certainly, Baker's early experiences in vaudeville provided the foundation for her celebrated theatrical career, which was built in part on her ability to construct and capitalize on a glamorous persona.

Baker's initial success came from her appearance in the 1921 tour of Noble Sissle and Eubie Blake's *Shuffle Along.* Her comic antics, high energy, and spontaneity proved immensely popular with audiences, if not with other chorus members (Baker and Chase, 57). After *Shuffle Along* closed, Sissle and Blake hired Baker for their next review, *In Bamville* (1924), later titled *Chocolate Dandies*. A review in the *New York Times* noted that Baker's clowning was "quite a hit" (September 2, 1924, 22). After *Chocolate Dandies* closed in 1925, she worked at New York's Plantation Club, where Caroline Dudley Reagan recruited her to perform in a black review in France.

Baker's debut in Paris created a sensation. In the Revue Nègre, she danced with such liberated sexuality that audiences were shocked and dazzled: "Hips, stomach, and rump had never moved so violently on a Paris stage" (Rose, 21). Baker's lack of sexual inhibitions contributed to her power as a dancer; restraint was not within her nature. As Phyllis Rose described the essence of the performer's liberated attitude, "sex was a pleasurable form of exercise, like dancing, and she wasn't notably fussy about her partners" (107).

According to Jean-Claude Baker, Josephine's bisexual experiences continued throughout most of her career. Baker states that Josephine believed men were of greater importance than women because men had economic power; however, her passions were not confined to men: "Once in a while—starting with Clara Smith—there would be a lady lover in Josephine's life" (Baker and Chase, 63). Her insistence of crossing conventional sexual boundaries became an integral part of her life both onstage and off.

After her triumph in the Revue Nègre, Baker joined the Folies Bergère and became increasingly popular with Parisian audiences. At the height of her early popularity, she met Pepito Abatino, who became her lover and manager. Abatino arranged a two-year world tour (1928–29) for Baker and inventively worked to increase her fame. Under his careful tutelage, she became increasingly appealing to sophisticated audiences, and, although she still displayed an uninhibited sensuality onstage, her performances now imparted a style that had "'class,'" dignity, and artistry" (Rose, 121).

Baker was very much aware of her international star status and worked carefully to construct that image. Sociologist Bennetta Jules-Rosette notes that the artist "fashioned herself as an icon through performance" and asserts that Baker employed cross-dressing to emphasize her difference (59). While Jules-Rosette rejects any link between Baker's crossdressing and "a bisexual subculture," she does note that her "gender-doubled imagery haunted Baker's . . . stage personae throughout her life" (66). Baker's sexual fluidity and her ability to cross boundaries would become a hallmark of her career.

Despite the careful crafting of her image, not all of Baker's performances received critical acclaim. She returned to the United States in 1936 to perform in the Ziegfeld Follies, which opened in New York on January 31, 1936. Baker received harsh reviews. One critic suggested that she had "refined her art until there was nothing left in it" (*New York Times,* January 31, 1936, 17). Subsequently, Baker returned to Paris and the Folies Bergère.

World War II again altered the path of Baker's career. She became a French citizen by means of a short-lived marriage to Jean Lion in 1937, and when the Nazis invaded France she joined the Resistance. Lynn Haney notes that because she was an entertainer she had more freedom from Nazi restrictions than others did and therefore she was able to pass along valuable military information (224).

Baker's contributions to the war effort were halted in 1941 when she gave birth to a stillborn child; complications resulted in a hysterectomy, and she remained seriously ill for well over a year. Upon her recovery, she performed for the Allied troops, insisting on integrated seating for black and white soldiers. She continued touring throughout the war and returned to Paris after its liberation in August 1944. After the war, France awarded her the Medal of Resistance with rosette and subsequently the Legion of Honor for her valor and service.

In 1944, Baker married Jo Bouillon, a French orchestra leader. This fourth marriage proved to be a successful working partnership for over thirteen years. However, Jean-Claude Baker notes that both Josephine and Jo continued relationships with other partners. "Jo would come to our house with another man [and] Josephine would find happiness with a girl from the Paris ballet company" (335).

In an effort to revive Baker's career, which had floundered after the war, Jo and Josephine decided to try an American tour in 1951. In addition to promoting her own career, Baker worked to foster racial harmony by integrating black and white audiences. She also publicized any failure on the part of management to achieve this goal (Rose, 213). Ironically her fight against racism did not prevent her from becoming its victim. On a visit to New York's Stork Club, she was ignored for an hour and a half. Walter Winchell, an influential radio personality and columnist, was in the restaurant when she arrived. After the incident, Baker sent a telegram to Winchell that rebuked him for his lack of support. Winchell, who had been initially supportive of Baker's career, was surprised and offended by her insinuation. He later maligned her, calling her "Josa-phoney Baker" and claiming that she was a communist (226–29). As a result, her American tour was cut short and her career damaged.

At the age of forty-eight, Baker began adopting children of various nationalities to demonstrate that people of different races and religions could live together in peace. Between 1954 and 1965, she adopted twelve children, calling them the Rainbow Tribe. But by 1969 the financial strain of raising them and maintaining Les Milandes, the family home, bankrupted her. After a forcible eviction from Les Milandes, Baker's personal and professional situations plummeted to an all time low. She worked diligently to rebuild her career and by 1974 had reversed her fortunes by achieving success as the star of *Josephine,* a show about her life. It officially opened in Paris on April 8, 1975. Six days later, Baker died of a stroke.

Josephine Baker possessed a liberated spirit and unique talents, which enabled her to achieve success and fame despite the racial struggles of her era. The theater provided her with a haven from sexual, racial, and economic oppression, although within the United States taboos and prejudices remained virtually insurmountable during her lifetime. Like many American artists of the 1920s, her self-imposed exile to Paris freed her to move beyond these barriers both onstage and off.

See Jean-Claude Baker and C. Chase, *Josephine: The Hungry Heart,* New York, 2001; L. Haney, *Naked at the Feast: A Biography of Josephine Baker,* New York, 1981; B. Jules-Rosette, "Two Loves: Josephine Baker as Icon and Image," *Emergences,* October 1, 2000, 55–77; P. Rose, *Jazz Cleopatra: Josephine Baker in Her Time,* New York, 1989; *New York Times,* September 2, 1924, 22; *New York Times,* January 31, 1936, 17; J. C. Smith, ed., *Notable Black American Women,* Detroit, 1992, 43–47.

Amy Cuomo

BANKHEAD, Tallulah Brockman (1902–68), stage and film actress, once said, "Daddy warned me about men and alcohol, but he never said anything about women and cocaine" (Brian, 13). Bankhead, now primarily remembered for her loud, throaty laugh, devastating wit, and flamboyant personality, remains a gay icon not so much for her handful of outstanding performances as for the battles she waged against social and moral expectations with her offstage antics. She flaunted her bisexuality, for example, and took pleasure in the shock it often caused. Lee Israel writes: "Her homosexual humor, while it amused some, offended others mightily." She describes a rather typical Bankhead party gag: "In her own living room or in other people's, she would frequently pick out the stodgiest looking woman in the room, throw her arms around her, and whisper, 'Surely, you must know by now that I'm mad about you!'" (141). At once sexy and sophisticated, vulgar and base, Bankhead called attention to the performance of being a star. Through her self-conscious acting and highly publicized, uninhibited mischief, she attacked societal notions of respectability as well as the inveterate conventions of femininity.

The daughter of the Speaker of the U.S. House of Representatives and Congressman from Alabama, William Bankhead, and Adelaide Eugenia Sledge, who died a few days after her birth, the young Tallulah was destined for a life in show business. As a child, to procure her grandmother or father's attention, which was usually directed toward her older, sweeter, and more attractive sister Eugenia, she turned cartwheels or went into one of her frequent "spells," the term the family used to describe her obstreperous temper tantrums (Rice, 24). At fifteen, she entered a contest advertised in *Picture Play* magazine and was chosen as one of twelve women who would appear in a film to be shot in New York City.

Chaperoned by her aunt, Bankhead arrived in New York in 1917 and moved into the famous Algonquin Hotel, the renowned meeting place of the "Roundtable," a theatrical and literary group of luminaries that included **Alexander Woollcott,** Charles MacArthur, and Dorothy Parker. Even at fifteen, her glamorous beauty and devilish wit allowed her instant access to this distinguished group. Within a year, she had made her Broadway debut as a walk-on in a short-lived play called *The Squab Farm* (1918) and had appeared in three (rather forgettable) films. Her heart, though, was in the theater, and in 1918 she wrote to a former congressman and friend of her grandfather's, Joseph L. Rhinock, a financial backer for Lee and J. J. Shubert, powerful New York producers: "I am writing you a little note to remind you that I am still very anxious to go on the stage in preference to pictures. . . . I would be so very grateful to you if you would get me a good part in a dramatic show" (Carrier, 4). Her first break arrived, however, without the help of her Shubert connection when she became the weekend replacement for Constance Binney in **Rachel Crothers**'s *39 East* (1919). Impressed with Bankhead's work, Crothers wrote several plays expressly for her, including *Nice People* (1921) and *Everyday* (1921).

Although Bankhead performed in eight plays between 1918 and 1922, her greatest notoriety came from her active social life. She was the life of many grand Broadway parties with her outrageous behavior and imitations of famous personalities, and she was regularly spotted in the free-spirited Harlem nightclubs with celebrities such as Noël Coward and **Cole Porter.** According to Jeffrey Carrier, at this time "she was introduced to cocaine, which came in little packages the size of tea bags that sold for $50 each, [and] probably engaged in a few lesbian affairs (Estelle Winwood is rumored to have been her first lover)" (8). The young actress publicly belied the presumed proper conduct of a senator's grand-daughter and congressman's daughter: she represented the emerging independent and pleasure-seeking generation of the 1920s.

Dissatisfied with the way her career was progressing in New York, Bankhead took the advice of an astrologer, who told her she would find fame "across the water," and accepted a part in Gerald du Maurier's *The Dancers* (1923). Almost immediately, she became a phenomenon in London and remained there for eight years. The Bankhead mania that ensued is evident in Alan Dale's review in the *New York Journal-American* of Noël Coward's *Fallen Angels* (1925), her fifth play in the West End: "[*Fallen Angels*] at the Globe Theatre . . . encloses the large, tumultuous, volumi-nous and dominant American damsel, Tallulah Bankhead. Tallulah is 'it' in London. Tallulah is quite the vogue here. . . . Hail, Tallulah!"

Once again, her reputation as an actress was connected to the unbri-dled social portrait of her painted by the British gossip columnists. Inter-estingly, her huge number of admirers, as Jeffrey Carrier states, "con-sisted almost entirely of young women, an oddity which the press of the day was at a loss to explain" (11). The Bankhead persona undoubtedly represented to these young women the possibility of liberation from pre-scribed gender and social constraints. Her rejection of conventional fem-ininity and bourgeois morals, not to mention heterosexual marriage, signified the possibility of sexual and class autonomy at a time when, according to Brooks Atkinson, "young people were tired of respectability and believed in nothing except themselves" (*Broadway,* 357).

She returned to the United States in 1931 to embark on another attempt at a film career, but the media focus was on her marital status. Once again rejecting a woman's traditional role, she told interviewer George Britt in the *World Telegram:* "When I am flat and low in my mind I always think I'll just end it all by getting married. I've been back in America five months now. And I wouldn't even look at a wedding ring. That's how well I like it here." After five failed pictures and a series of Broadway shows ranging from a minor success (e.g., in **George Kelly**'s *Reflected Glory* [1936]) to an outright debacle (in *Antony and Cleopatra* [1937]), she married John Emery in 1937. They divorced four years later. Bankhead triumphed, however, in 1939 when she starred as Regina Gid-dens in Lillian Hellman's *The Little Foxes.* In his review of the play at the National Theatre on Broadway, Brooks Atkinson declared: "That sigh of relief that has been sweeping across the country is reflex action caused by the fact that Tallulah Bankhead has found a good play" (*"Little Foxes"*). Bankhead's disciplined, brilliant performance once again can be seen as an affront to presumed womanliness. In her autobiography, she referred to Regina Giddens as "a rapacious bitch, cruel, and callous. Etched in acid by Miss Hellman, who at first thought I was too young for the role, she was a frightening opportunist who stopped at nothing to further her prestige and fortune. . . . For profit she would have slit her mother's throat, but not before so staging the crime that the guilt would be pinned on another" (237).

Her next role of note, that of Sabina, the French maid in **Thornton Wilder**'s *The Skin of Our Teeth* (1942), confirmed her reputation as a formidable actress and allowed her to prove her comic abilities as well. The highlights of the performance were the occasions in which the actress stepped out of character to comment on the confusion of the play. The iconoclastic role and play were ideally suited to the image the actress had cultivated. Singling out Bankhead among her costars (Frederic March and Florence Eldridge), John Anderson of the *New York Journal-American* stated: "It is Miss Bankhead, as the eternal hussy, who gives [the play] vitality and warmth, and puts humanity into its carefully naive laughter." She received the prestigious New York Drama Critics Circle Award for her performance.

She finally achieved critical and popular approval in film for her performance in Hitchcock's *Lifeboat* (1944) and had some further success onstage in a revival of Coward's *Private Lives* (1949), but by the 1950s she had become camp. She perpetuated the outspoken, flamboyant, and sardonic image of herself on radio and television and developed a large homosexual following. In a deliberate attempt to revitalize her career and escape her public image, she undertook the complex and challenging role of Blanche in a revival of **Tennessee Williams**'s *A Streetcar Named Desire.* In its disastrous trial run at the Coconut Playhouse in Miami, Williams himself articulated the problem: audiences counted on Bankhead to be campy and excessive. He wrote: "There were all these faggots in the house. Tallulah began to play to them. . . . I got very drunk and at the conclusion I was sulking around and somebody said: 'Come over and speak to Tallulah.' And I said: 'I don't want to. She pissed on my play'" (Brian, 196). The production encountered similar difficulties when it opened at the City Center in New York on February 15, 1956. In his *New York Times* review, Brooks Atkinson notes the laughter that regretfully arose during the opening night performance. He claims the reason for this lay in the fact that Bankhead's "fabulous vitality" could not be suppressed within the "neurotic terrors of Blanche duBois" ("Miss Bankhead"). Actor James Kirkwood also recalled the reception Bankhead received: "It seemed as if the whole homosexual community was up in the balcony and they wouldn't give her a chance. Whenever she had a line that could be construed as camp, like the one that refers to a constellation of stars and she says, 'The girls are out tonight,' it got a huge laugh and a hand" (qtd. in Brian, 197).

Bankhead's outrageousness and unconcealed bisexuality account for her popularity among gay audiences, and her mordant wit and sophisticated style reflected the possibility of a noncompulsive heterosexual world. For her, restricted sexuality was something with which only common folk concerned themselves. As Lillian Faderman writes, Bankhead

> presented herself as being above the laws of mere mortals and even as phenomenally bored and blasé with the shocking privileges she took for herself. "Sex?" she shouted in one group. "I'm bored with sex. What is it, after all? If you go down on a woman, you get a crick in your neck. If you go down on a man, you get lockjaw. And fucking just gives me claustrophobia." (176)

This was the kind of outrageous image of the star that prevailed long after her reputation as an outstanding actress had begun to fade.

Other plays followed *Streetcar,* including Williams's *The Milk Train Doesn't Stop Here* (1964), her last Broadway play. There were also a few more films, such as *Die! Die! My Darling!* (1965), and television appearances, which ended with *Batman* (1967), her final acting role. On December 16, 1968, in New York she died of pneumonia complicated by emphysema. In *Broadway,* Brooks Atkinson writes: "Since Miss Bankhead lived as she wanted to, there is no point in deploring the loss of a talented actress" (358). She will certainly be remembered as a woman who did not allow societal expectations to stand in the way of living her life as she wished.

See J. Anderson, *"The Skin of Our Teeth Opens at Plymouth,"* *New York Journal-American,* November 19, 1942; B. Atkinson, *Broadway,* New York, 1970; B. Atkinson, "Miss Bankhead Heads City Center Cast," *New York Times,* February 16, 1956; B. Atkinson, *"The Little Foxes," New York Times,* February 26, 1939; T. Bankhead, *Tallulah,* New York, 1952; D. Brett, *Tallulah Bankhead: A Scandalous Life,* New York, 1997; D. Brian, *Tallulah, Darling,* New York, 1972; G. Britt, "Tallulah Bankhead Knows She's Happy When She Isn't Thinking of Marriage," *World Telegram,* June 24, 1931; J. Carrier, *Tallulah Bankhead: A Bio-Bibliography,* New York, 1991; A. Dale, "Tallulah Bankhead Success in London," *New York Journal-American,* July 13, 1925; L. Faderman, *Odd Girls and Twilight Lovers: A History of Lesbian Life in Twentieth-Century America,* New York, 1991; B. Hadleigh, *Hollywood Lesbians,* New York, 1994, 56; L. Israel, *Miss Tallulah Bankhead,* New York, 1972; A. Madsen, *The Sewing Circle,* New York, 1995; W. J. Mann, *Behind the Screen: How Gays and Lesbians Shaped Hollywood, 1910–1969,* New York, 2001; and R. Rice, "Now Meet Tallulah!" undocumented article, Tallulah Bankhead Clippings File, Billy Rose Theatre Collection, New York Public Library for the Performing Arts.

James F. Wilson

BARNES, Djuna Chappell (1892–1982), playwright, journalist, poet, novelist, and artist, was born in Cornwall-on-Hudson, New York, to Elizabeth and Wald Barnes in the two-story cabin built by her father on his brother's estate at Storm King Mountain. Sharing the small dwelling with her parents, four brothers, her paternal grandmother, her father's live-in mistress, and her three children by Wald Barnes, Djuna had an upbringing that was neither conventional nor boring. Her father never held a job, preferring to spend his days as a "gentleman" farmer, painting, composing, playing musical instruments, fixing things around the house, and occasionally tending to the farm animals and planting. The household was meagerly supported mainly through the efforts of Grandmother Zadel, a journalist, suffragette, spiritualist, and poet, who sometimes resorted to writing letters to famous personalities begging for money. Wald and Zadel, advocates of free love and opponents of the public school system, educated the Barnes children almost entirely at home, reading to them from the Bible and a wide range of authors, including Chaucer, Shakespeare, Dickens, Swinburne, Montaigne, Proust, and Donne. The children were taught music and art and encouraged in their natural curiosities.

Wald Barnes viewed sexual freedom as beneficial to society, and he practiced it frequently. There is strong evidence that Djuna's sexual initiation took place with either her father or her grandmother, and themes of sexuality and incest are frequent in Barnes's mature works. In any case, by 1912, when Elizabeth divorced her husband and took Djuna and her brothers to live in New York, the girl bore the imprint of her childhood: artistically gifted, bohemian in spirit, highly literate, and sexually experienced.

Obligated to support her mother and three younger brothers, Barnes quickly abandoned her studies at the Pratt Institute and took a job writing for the *Brooklyn Eagle,* which led to further assignments with the *New York Press, New York World Magazine, New York American, New York Tribune,* and *New York Morning Telegraph.* Over the next twenty years, she would support herself primarily as a journalist and freelance feature writer for newspapers and magazines such as *Theatre Guild, Little Review, Dial, Others, Parisienne, Charm, Smart Set, Shadowland, Vanity Fair, McCall's, Transatlantic Review,* and *transition.* More than 170 articles are focused on theater or popular entertainment, and her first plays were published in the *New York Morning Telegraph Sunday Magazine* (1916).

Settling in Greenwich Village, the strikingly attractive and bitingly witty Barnes had little trouble making the acquaintance of some of the more notable personalities of the day, including John Reed, Eugene O'Neill, Mabel Dodge, James and Susan Light, Dorothy Day, Berenice Abbott, Edna St. Vincent Millay, Kenneth Burke, and Peggy Guggenheim, who would become one of her benefactors in later years. Her common-law marriage to Courtenay Lemon, which lasted from 1917 to 1919, gained Barnes introductions to many of the individuals who formed the Provincetown Players. Despite the apparent harmony of her relationship with Lemon, her many close friendships with the ladies of Greenwich Village suggest that her primary attraction was to women. Phillip Herring credits a previous Barnes beau, Putzi Hanfstaengl, with citing Barnes's "continuing sexual interest in women" as the reason for the end of their engagement in 1916. Other compelling evidence is found in a letter to Barnes from her father, also quoted in Herring, dated December 5, 1913: "You say that you are in love. . . . Male or female this time? And who's th' lucky dorg (or dorgess)?" (Herring, 71).

Her first book, published in 1915 as part of the Bruno Chapbooks series, was *The Book of Repulsive Women*. It created a negative stir among both heterosexuals and lesbians, causing Barnes later to express the desire that this collection of unflattering homoerotic poems and drawings had never been published. Between 1916 and 1923, Barnes published eighteen plays in various newspapers, periodicals, and magazines. Her official debut with the Provincetown Players came in 1919, when *Three from the Earth* was performed, followed by *An Irish Triangle* and *Kurzy of the Sea* in 1920. From the beginning of her playwriting career, Barnes was dogged by criticism similar to **Alexander Woollcott**'s review of the play he renamed *"Three from the Birth,"* writing that "the greatest indoor sport this week is guessing what it means." Labeled "obscure," "bewildering," and likened to "reading **Gertrude Stein** by candlelight on a merry-go-round," Barnes's plays remained in the category of "art" rather than commercially viable theater (Woollcott).

Most of the plays deal with the impossibility of meaningful and harmonious relationships between men and women. With the exception of *The Dove* (1923), few have blatantly lesbian themes, though most have heavy sexual subtexts. In that she was forced to rely on innuendo and coded action to express the meanings in her plays, it is hardly surprising that Barnes's chief literary successes took the form of novels.

Barnes is perhaps best known for her controversial book *Nightwood* (1936), a literary purging of her passionate and doomed relationship with Thelma Wood in Paris between 1921 and 1928. In later years, this would be the single lesbian relationship that she freely and publicly acknowledged. Although she had a series of affairs with both men and women, she was referring to her relationship with Thelma when she wrote in a letter to Emily Coleman that she had already had the "great love" of her life and "there will never be another" (qtd. in Herring, 166).

During her years with Thelma, Barnes published prolifically, including *A Book* (1923), a collection of short stories and plays; *Ryder* (1928), a short satire of her father's sexual antics; and *Ladies Almanac* (1928). *Ladies Almanac,* a "slight wigging" of Natalie Barney's lesbian circle of friends, gained for Barnes the lifelong patronage of the expatriate heiress. Following her breakup with Wood, up to the beginning of World War II Barnes divided her time between the United States and Europe, working on *Nightwood* and completing assignments for various magazines, including *Theatre Guild.* Her "Playgoer's Almanac" (which later evolved into "The Wanton Playgoer") was a regular feature, in addition to her interviews with some of the most prominent theater people of the time: the **Lunts, Alla Nazimova, Rachel Crothers,** and Jo Mielziner.

By 1940, Barnes had moved into the residence at 5 Patchin Place that would be her home for the rest of her life. Consumed by problems of alcoholism, ill health, and her work on *The Antiphon,* a full-length autobiographical play, she became a recluse, treating the rare visitor to her vitriolic tongue and bitter memories. She relied on the benefices of her old friends to scrape out an existence. Championed by Edwin Muir and T. S. Eliot, *The Antiphon* was eventually brought to the attention of Dag Hammarskjold, who helped to translate the play into Swedish and made possible its premiere in 1961 at the Royal Dramatic Theatre in Stockholm. Turning down at least two lucrative offers for the film rights to *The Antiphon* and *Nightwood,* Barnes kept body, if not soul, together by selling her papers and manuscripts to the University of Maryland in 1972. She spent the last years of her life in failing health, working on a bestiary, called "Creatures in an Alphabet," and writing poetry. Bitter over her failure to achieve recognition in the literary world, she referred to herself as "the most famous unknown author in the world."

See the Barnes Collection, University of Maryland; and *Kurzy of the Sea,* an unpublished manuscript at the Library of Congress. *Three from the Earth* originally appeared in the *Little Review* (November 1919): 3–15, and was republished, along with *The Dove,* in *A Book,* New York, 1923. See also Barnes's The *Antiphon,* London, 1959; *The Book of Repulsive Women,* New York, 1915; *Ryder,* New York, 1928; *Nightwood,* London, 1936; and *Creatures in an Alphabet,* New York, 1982. Secondary sources include M. L. Broe, ed., *Silence and Power: A Revaluation of Djuna Barnes,* Carbondale, Ill., 1989; S. F. Clark, "Misalliance: Djuna Barnes and the American Theatre," Ph.D. diss., Tufts University, 1989; A. Field, *Djuna: The Formidable Miss Barnes,* Austin, Tex., 1985; P. Herring, *Djuna: The Life and Work of Djuna Barnes,* New York, 1995; and D. Messerli, *Djuna Barnes: A Bibliography,* New York, 1975; A. Woollcott, "Second Thoughts on First Nights: The Provincetown Plays," *New York Times,* November 9, 1919, Sec. 8, p. 2.

Susan F. Clark

BENNETT, Michael (1943–87), dancer, choreographer, and director, was born in Buffalo, New York, to working-class parents (his father was a machinist, his mother a secretary). Bennett's interest in dance became apparent quite early. At the age of two, he danced to music on the radio; by three, he was taking dance lessons. While still in high school, he worked in summer stock and obtained his first professional role in the 1960 tour of *West Side Story,* dropping out of high school to participate in the European tour of the show. He was often self-conscious about his lack of formal education, never having returned to school. During the tour, he met Bob Avian, who became his most important assistant during the next twenty-five years. Avian was the associate choreographer or assistant director of Bennett's most successful shows, including *Promises, Promises; Coco; Company; Follies; Twigs; Seesaw;* and *A Chorus Line.*

Since his particular interest was choreography, Bennett danced in only three shows on Broadway: *Subways Are for Sleeping* (1961), *Here's Love* (1963), and *Bajour* (1964). He supplemented his income in the early 1960s by teaching dance, choreographing sequences for several television variety shows (including the *Ed Sullivan Show* and *Dean Martin Show*), and appearing on television as a dancer on the NBC rock-and-roll series *Hullabaloo.* His first opportunity to assist with choreography came in 1962 when he worked with Donald Driver in developing the movement for the Washington Shakespeare Festival production of *A Midsummer Night's Dream.*

The 1966 production of *A Joyful Noise* was Bennett's first major work as a choreographer. Marred by book and casting problems, the show was a failure in all respects except one: Bennett's unique contribution as choreographer. Although the show quickly closed, Bennett received his first nomination for a Tony Award; he lost to **Ronald Field,** who won for *Cabaret.* Bennett's first notable success, *Promises, Promises,* came only two years later. With 1,281 performances, it would be his longest run prior to *A Chorus Line.*

During the next few years, Bennett worked on a variety of shows. *Coco* (1969), a musical based on the life of Coco Chanel, attracted sizable audiences (despite relatively bad reviews) because it starred Katherine Hepburn in her only musical role. In 1970, Bennett choreographed **Stephen Sondheim**'s innovative musical *Company,* and in 1971 his choreography and codirection of *Follies* brought him Tonys in both categories. Also in 1971 he directed *Twigs,* the first of the two nonmusical shows of his career; the second, *God's Favorite,* followed two years later. When Bennett was asked to salvage *Seesaw* in 1973, his success with that production confirmed his growing reputation as one of the country's most promising choreographer/directors; it was also the first show over which he had total control.

Bennett's greatest success came with the 1975 production of *A Chorus Line.* Opening to rave reviews, the production broke the record for Broadway's longest-running show with its 3,389th performance on September 29, 1983; it continued to run for seven more years, closing in 1990 after 6,137 performances. With *A Chorus Line,* Bennett began the practice (which became standard) of sharing a portion of his royalties with the dancers who had assisted in the development of the show. *A Chorus Line* emerged from a series of workshops that began on January 18, 1974, with the book largely based on events in the lives of the workshop participants, many of whom also appeared in the production. Although the collaborative/workshop method had been used previously in plays, *A Chorus Line* marked its first use in the development of a musical.

None of his subsequent work attained the success of *A Chorus Line,* but Bennett remained a vital force in musical theater until illness due to AIDS forced his retirement. His production of *Stardust Ballroom* (1978) failed, but his last produced show, *Dreamgirls* (1981), gained considerable public attention and acceptance. He began working on *Scandal* in 1984, but during the preparatory stages he was diagnosed as HIV positive and he abandoned the project. Late in 1985, he began work on *Chess,* but three months prior to opening night he withdrew from the production because of declining health. He told only a few of his closest friends the truth about his departure from the show, announcing to the press that he was forced to leave because of a heart condition. On July 2, 1987, at the age of forty-four, he died.

Though primarily attracted to men, Bennett had several important relationships with women, including a marriage to dancer Donna McKechnie. He never publicly acknowledged being bisexual or homosexual, but when asked about the gay characters in *A Chorus Line* he told *Newsweek:* "I would be lying . . . if I did not deal with homosexuality in this show" (qtd. in Kroll and Guthrie, 68). Bennett's work frequently focused on African Americans, older dancers, and others who (like gay men and lesbians) have been marginalized and disenfranchised. *A Chorus Line* is very much concerned with being different, being on the outside, and wanting to gain acceptance. *Dreamgirls* deals with the experience of African American performers, *Stardust Ballroom* with older dancers and illicit love, and *Scandal* with a woman's growing sexual freedom.

Both brilliant and manipulative, Bennett used any method, including deceit, to get the best from his dancers. He had no interest in developing a "Bennett style," in the sense that Bob Fosse and others had identifiable styles. Rather, he sought to adapt his approach to meet the unique demands and potential of each production. He was inducted into the Theatre Hall of Fame in April 1986.

See "It Started with Watergate," *Time,* July 28, 1975; J. Kroll and C. Guthrie, "Broadway's New Kick," *Newsweek,* December 1, 1975; K. Mandelbaum, *A Chorus Line and the Musicals of Michael Bennett,* New York, 1989; and the Internet sites <www.isd.net/stage/shows/chorus.line.html> and <www.artsnet.heinz.cmu.edu/OnBroadway>, accessed on October 15, 1996.

Wendell Stone

BENTLEY, Eric Russell (1916–), playwright and critic, was born in Bolton, Lancashire, England, on September 16, 1916. He began his education at the Bolton School, continued at Oxford University, and came to Yale University for the Ph.D. in drama. He has lived in the United States ever since and became an American citizen in 1948. He has taught at many colleges and universities, spending the greatest amount of time at Columbia University in New York, where he held the distinguished position of Brander Matthews Professor (1952–69). He also taught at Harvard University, the State University of New York at Buffalo, the University of Minnesota, and the University of Maryland. Bentley established himself as a respected critic, theorist, and historian during the 1940s. During this decade and later, he wrote a number of critical volumes on various topics, including *A Century of Hero Worship: A Study of the Idea of Heroism in Carlyle and Nietzsche* (1944); *The Playwright as Thinker: A Study of Drama in Modern Times* (1946); *Bernard Shaw: A Reconsideration* (1947); *In Search of Theatre* (1953); *What Is Theatre?* (1956); *The Life of the Drama* (1964); *The Theatre of Commitment and Other Essays on Drama in Our Society* (1967); and *Theatre of War: Comments on 32 Occasions* (1974). In Bentley's opinion, the most profound of these works is *The Playwright as Thinker,* wherein he divided theater into two models: a "popular" theater in the Brechtian sense and an "art" theater for the more intellectually elite "avant-garde." In each model, he called for a "political theatre" that would also be considered entertaining, mildly anti-Broadway, and anti-capitalist. Most important to theater history, however, *The Playwright as Thinker* introduced Brecht and Sartre to American readers and theater audiences.

In the 1950s, Bentley began writing dramatic reviews and criticism for various periodicals, especially the *New Republic,* where he was drama critic from 1952 to 1956. He also continued to publish books. One such critical study, *The Dramatic Event,* included a lengthy discussion of homosexuality, which arose in response to Ruth and Augustus Goetz's dramatic adaptation of André Gide's novel *The Immoralist*. Written in 1954, his critique rather daringly champions the homosexual cause, while coming far short of serving as a vehicle for his personal coming out. In describing the nature of homosexuality in drama, he states: "Up to now, as Gide told them [the Goetzes] in an interview, homosexuality in the theatre has been an accusation. Its standard form at present is, in fact, the unjust accusation; for our public has reached the point where it will allow the subject of homosexuality to come up, provided that the stigma is removed before the end of the evening" (207). In addition, he has translated several modern European playwrights, including Brecht, Pirandello, Sternheim, Wedekind, and Gogol. He has also directed plays, in various languages, in a number of cities around the world, including Salzberg, Padua, Dublin, and New York. Notable among these was his codirection of O'Neill's *The Iceman Cometh* in its German-language premiere (1950) and his own translation of Brecht's *The Good Person of Setzuan* in New York (1956).

Bentley's work as a playwright began with his adaptations of others' works. His earliest play, *Orpheus in the Underworld,* was published in 1956. From the plays of Euripides and Sophocles, he created *A Time to Live,* which was published with a second play, *A Time to Die,* in 1967. Other plays include *The Red White and Black* (1970), an examination of American sociopolitical problems of the time; *Expletive Deleted* (1974), a drama about Nixon's White House tapes; *Are You Now or Have You Ever Been: The Investigation of Show-Business by the Un-American Activities Committee, 1947–1956; The Recantation of Galileo Galilei;* and *From the Memoirs of Pontius Pilate.* The latter three plays were published in *Rallying Cries* in 1977. According to Bentley, critics have offered a "gay" reading of the play on Galileo, asserting that the relationship between Galileo and the young priest was more romantic than professional. In retrospect, Bentley sees how this reading could emerge, but he denies an intention to create a sexual relationship (interview with the author, April 15, 1997).

Bentley's trilogy, *The Kleist Variations* (1978), adapts three plays by Heinrich von Kleist (*The Broken Jug, Penthesilea,* and *Cathy of Heilbronn,* which he entitles *Concord, The Fall of the Amazons,* and *Wannsee).* Although Kleist's writings (especially his letters) reveal his homoerotic desires and relationships, in his own version Bentley makes no direct reference to the homosexuality of Kleist (or, indeed, of his own). In fact, the 1982 published version of *The Kleist Variations* contains an interview by the Voice of America radio network wherein Bentley defends himself against the question of his "championing" gay liberation. Although he does not completely deny being gay, he leads the interviewer, and thus the reader, to believe that he is indeed denying it. However, when *The Kleist Variations* appeared in a new edition in 1990, Bentley added a preface to *The Fall of the Amazons,* entitled "On Hating the Other Sex," in which he relates his experience with homoerotic desires at Yale in 1940 as a natural sexual inclination. Societal condemnation of homosexuality in that repressive era forced him into denial for many years (66–69).

Kleist himself is quoted in Bentley's next play, *Lord Alfred's Lover* (1981). Kleist declared in a letter to his friend Ernst von Pfuel in 1805: "All the law giving of Lycurgus—also his conception of the love of young men—became quite clear to me through the feelings you had awakened. Come to me! [and] be my wife, children, and grandchildren!" *Lord Alfred's Lover* analyzes the complex relationship between Oscar Wilde and Lord Alfred Douglas. While playwrights have seen this as a story about Wilde's imprisonment, Bentley sees it as a coming out story; the title, he claims, is a joke, an irony. Bentley's Oscar Wilde was not Lord Alfred's lover. He did not understand himself as a "sodomite" until the very end of his life. For Bentley, the most important line of the play is when Wilde says, "'Posing as a sodomite'—the fateful phrase *is* libel now. I do not *pose* as a sodomite. I *am* a sodomite." In his dying words, he comes out. In this play, his first to deal with homosexuality as a central theme, Bentley, through the historical characters, describes the nature of his own double life, his own closeted existence. *Lord Alfred's Lover,* he claims, is more autobiographical than anything else he has written (interview with author, April 15, 1997).

Bentley, who has two sons, came out when he was in his fifties, after two unsuccessful marriages. By 1968, the pressures of leading a double life had brought him to accept and eventually declare his homosexuality. In an interview in *The Advocate* in 1991, he defended his earlier decisions to marry.

> You went into a marriage, typically, not being certain and thinking that because you like or love a woman, you will very likely end up totally straight. And you had every reason to be straight in those days. No wonder that people misunderstood you. You hadn't understood yourself, and you gave out mixed signals. (Raymond, 75)

Bentley found the writing of *Lord Alfred's Lover* to be self-liberating and hence a relatively easy and rewarding creative process. But his next gay-themed play, *Round 2* (1986–91), was more difficult because it was drawn solely from his imagination and experience rather than historical records. The play, a gay version of Schnitzler's *La Ronde*, depicts a round-robin of ten male sexual liaisons wherein one partner of one affair meets a new person for the next encounter. *Round 2* marked Bentley's public declaration of his homosexual identity. Many critics considered the play inappropriate for the post-AIDS era. In fact, the Glines, a gay producing organization, rejected the work when it was first submitted in 1986. In 1991, Bentley spoke publicly with *The Advocate,* answering critics who claimed that *Round 2* promoted a negative gay image.

> I wanted to write about the give-and-take of fairly typical, ordinary gay people in how they conduct their love life and to be perfectly natural and simple about it. I did not have any ax to grind or try to set up any positive images. I don't want [the situation to be one in which] when you say "gay" everybody shouts "hurrah." (Raymond, 75)

To answer the critics, however, Bentley later added a subtitle, *New York in the '70s,* thereby distancing his play from AIDS in the gay community of the 1980s. The point often missed in production, according to Bentley, is that the character of the soldier is the only one that seeks purely physical sex. The others are searching, unsuccessfully, for love through the sexual act. In production, the play is often mistaken for a titillating comedy rather than a dark discussion of unfulfilled longing.

In his openly gay life, Bentley first attempted to duplicate the model of heterosexual marriage. "It seemed like it worked for a year or two, and then it didn't. My little philosophy is that people that really wish to stay together beyond six years have to put it on a nonsexual basis, a friendship, a partnership" (75). In the fall of 1991, Bentley followed up his *Advocate* interview with one in the *Drama Review.* Here, he discusses the need to portray nonflamboyant, nonglamorous gay characters: "What the public won't take is that someone on 92nd street, not particularly good looking and not all that youthful, is not straight and not dying. They don't want to hear about that. What the straight public doesn't seem to be ready for yet is ordinary gay people" (DiGaetani, 90). He claims that this is what keeps *Round 2* from being successful: "I have ten characters in the play, and only one is a transvestite. The other nine are ordinary people, not in the sense of being contemptible or mediocre, but in the sense that they would not be immediately recognizable as gay or straight. They are people who happen to be gay" (90). "What is striking about this succession of sexual encounters," notes one critic, "is how very interesting even dull people become in such situations. Sex overturns, even if for a short time, the economic order" (Wilcox, n.p.).

Bentley dismisses the idea of serving as a gay role model, claiming: "It's an overdone idea—we don't have to be surrounded by them." Further, he condemns the idea of outing as a means of proliferating gay role models: "Is Malcolm Forbes a role model simply because he is famous and rich? If a person hasn't come out on his own, he is *ipso facto* not a role model" (Raymond, 75). Most recently, Bentley has angered gay activists and theater practitioners by siding with Catholic University administrators who chose to reject a production of Tony Kushner's *Angels in America.* He respects their right to do this: "To not choose a play is not to censor it. A Catholic College is not an ACLU office" (*American Theatre,* 2).

Eric Bentley received a Special Citation at the 1977–78 Obie Awards for lifetime service in the theater. He lives in New York.

See *American Theatre,* February 1997; E. Bentley, *The Dramatic Event,* London, 1954; E. Bentley, *The Kleist Variations,* Carbondale, Ill., 1990; E. Bentley, *Lord Alfred's Lover,* in *Monstrous Martyrdoms: 3 Plays,* Buffalo, 1985; E. Bentley, *Round 2,* in *Gay Plays Four,* London, 1990; J. L. DiGaetani, "The Thinker as Playwright: An Interview with Eric Bentley," *Drama Review* 35 (fall 1991): 85–92; D. Nadon, "The Gay Man as Thinker: Eric Bentley's Many Closets," in *Staging Desire: Queer Readings of American Theater History,* edited by K. Marra and R. Schanke, Ann Arbor, 2002, 288–307; G. Raymond, "A Sage's Advice: Eric Bentley Muses on the Real-Life Drama of Love and Sex," *The Advocate,* April 9, 1991; and M. Wilcox, ed., Introduction to *Gay Plays,* vol. 4, London, 1990, n.p.

Daniel-Raymond Nadon

BENTLEY, Gladys (1907–60), male impersonator and headline attraction in ribald nightclub revues, represents the sexually free spirit of 1920s and 1930s Harlem. Performing in her characteristic white tuxedo and weighing 250 pounds, Bentley was noted for replacing popular song lyrics with licentious verses. As Wilbur Young points out, "So adept was she at this art that she could take the most tender ballad and convert it into a new low with her filthy lyrics" (Young, 1). She prompted the audience to sing along with her, and "it was just a matter of time before the house got raided" (Young, 1). Onstage and off, scandalous Gladys Bentley also proudly proclaimed her lesbian identity by wearing men's clothing and publicly marrying a woman.

Born in Philadelphia to a mother who prayed for a son and refused to nurse the infant for the first six months, Bentley was the oldest of four children and the "problem child" of the family (Bentley, 96). Even as a youngster, she preferred boy's clothing to dresses, which made her the object of ridicule among her peers. She later recalled her first attraction to

Gladys Bentley, probably in *Brevities in Bronze* (1937), in which she appeared in white tails and sang "Gladys Isn't Gratis Any More." (Courtesy of Jim Wilson and the Moorland-Spingarn Research Center, Howard University.)

a woman, a beautiful schoolteacher with long hair, although she did not comprehend these feelings at the time. When her parents discovered their child was "different," they took her to a number of doctors in an attempt to "supplant the malignant growth festering inside of [her]" (Bentley, 96).

At sixteen, Bentley ran away to New York, where after establishing a recording career she quickly found work as a piano player, first as a substitute and then as a featured act, in many of the most popular nightclubs of the day, including the Mad House, Connie's Inn, and the Cotton Club. She attracted the attention of New York's elite, white and black, including **Langston Hughes,** who wrote: "Miss Bentley was an amazing exhibition of musical energy—a large, dark, masculine lady, whose feet pounded the floor while her fingers pounded the keyboard" (qtd. in Garber, 56). By the early 1930s, she was headlining a string of revues at the Ubangi Club on Seventh Avenue and 131st Street, where she performed for several years. Her lyrics were noticeably less lewd, but the shows were known for their risqué specialty numbers. The *New York World Telegram,* on April 17, 1937, for example, described one of the shows, *Brevities in Bronze,* as "the kind of show one expects from the bronze belt; fast, robust, dancing across—and through—the thin ice of good taste with a laugh and a leer." The author of the review wrote of the show's star: "Portly Gladys Bentley, in white tails, gives her number 'Gladys Isn't Gratis Any More' all she has (about 300 pounds) and there are other attractions, some more shocking than their fellows."

At the end of the 1930s and with the demise of the Harlem Renaissance, Bentley moved to California, where she continued to record and perform (sometimes under the name Bobbie Minton) throughout the 1940s and into the 1950s. In 1952, most likely in an effort to salvage her musical career in the midst of the homophobic McCarthy era, as Eric Garber maintains, she published an autobiographical article in *Ebony* entitled "I Am a Woman Again." In it, she denounces "the sex underworld in which [she] once lived" and hopes "to help others who are trapped in its dark recesses by telling [her] story" (Bentley, 94). Her "miraculous" cure, she contends, was brought about by the love of a man, as well as monthly female hormonal injections, which stimulated her to let "the world . . . know that those of us who have taken the unusual paths to love are not hopeless; that we can find someone in the opposite sex who can teach us love as love really ought to exist" (98). She died at fifty-two on January 18, 1960, of influenza.

See Gladys Bentley Clippings File, Billy Rose Theatre Collection, New York Public Library; G. Bentley, "I Am a Woman Again," *Ebony,* August 1952, 92–98; L. Faderman,

Odd Girls and Twilight Lovers: A History of Lesbian Life in Twentieth-Century America, New York, 1991; E. Garber, "Gladys Bentley: The Bulldagger Who Sang the Blues," *Out/Look,* spring 1988, 52–61; Ubangi Club Clippings File, Billy Rose Theatre Collection, New York Public Library; c. Mitchell, "Creations of Fantasies/Constructions of Identities: The Oppositional Lives of Gladys Bentley," in *The Greatest Taboo: Homosexuality in Black Communities,* edited by D. C. Simms, Los Angeles, 2000; and W. Young, "Gladys Bentley," in *Biographical Sketches: Negroes of New York,* New York City, 1939, copy in the Schomburg Collection, New York Public Library.

James F. Wilson

BERNSTEIN, Leonard (Louis) (1918–90), composer and conductor, was born in Lawrence, Massachusetts, the eldest of three children of Russian-Jewish immigrants. He demonstrated his musical talent and theatrical impulses early in life; as a teenager, he staged operas and musicals in Sharon, Massachusetts, where his family had a summer home. He attended the Boston Latin School, graduated from Harvard in 1939, and completed advanced musical studies at the Curtis Institute in 1941. In 1943, he achieved instant fame as a conductor when he substituted for the ailing Bruno Walter in a broadcast concert with the New York Philharmonic. At this time, he also began composing symphonies and other "serious music," as well as works for the stage. In the 1940s and 1950s, he juggled his growing international conducting career with work as a composer for ballet and Broadway. His reputation in the theater grew steadily with the musicals *On the Town* (1944), *Peter Pan* (1950), *Wonderful Town* (1953), *Candide* (1956), and *West Side Story* (1957); the ballets *Fancy Free* (1944) and *Facsimile* (1946); and the opera *Trouble in Tahiti* (1952). In 1958, he was named musical director of the New York Philharmonic, a post he held until 1969; in these years, he sharply curtailed his composing while boosting his fame as conductor and host of the Young People's Concerts on television. After 1969, he continued to conduct orchestras around the world and returned to composing, though with much less success than in his earlier years. His theater works from this period include *Mass* (1971), which was written for the opening of the Kennedy Center in Washington, D.C.; the ballet *The Dybbuk* (1974); the failed Broadway musical *1600 Pennsylvania Avenue* (1976); *A Quiet Place* (1983), his only full-length opera; and a number of unfinished projects. He died at his home in New York in 1990. After his death, unfounded rumors arose that he had died of AIDS. The actual cause was emphysema and heart failure, brought on from a lifetime of heavy smoking and drinking.

Bernstein's frenetic sexual life was widely rumored but little discussed in the press or the many biographies written about him until near the end of his life. While still at Harvard, Bernstein had sexual encounters with other men and less frequently with women. There is evidence that he had a brief affair with the conductor Dimitri Mitropoulos, who would become an important mentor in his early career (Secrest, 51). Another important mentor was Serge Koussevitzky, conductor of the Boston Symphony, with whom he studied at Tanglewood. Koussevitzky disapproved of Bernstein's homosexuality and made it clear that he would not get a major conducting position unless he married. In 1946, he became engaged to the Chilean actress Felicia Montealegre. The engagement was broken off in 1947, then resumed, and the two were finally married in 1951. Bernstein's later biographers report that he and his wife had a strong sexual relationship (they had three children), but that Montealegre was also aware of Bernstein's homosexuality. She demanded discretion as a condition of their marriage; Bernstein was generally able to comply until he met Tom Cothran in 1971. His relationship with Cothran caused a rift in an already stormy marriage, and in 1976 Bernstein moved out of his New York apartment to live with Cothran. Montealegre died of cancer in 1978; Bernstein blamed himself for her death for the rest of his life. In the 1980s, he became increasingly less interested in hiding his homosexuality, and he had a series of brief relationships with younger men (H. Burton, 473). He toyed with the idea of coming out in public, but until his death his sexuality remained in effect an open secret.

Bernstein's life, both professional and personal, was dominated by two characteristics: unbounded energy and deep internal conflict. From his earliest days, no one ever doubted that he would be a star because he attacked his work with such fervor. His hyperactive power generated much criticism but was also at the heart of his success. As a conductor, his personal intensity generated equivalent levels of excitement in the musicians who played for him; he was famous for the "Bernstein leap," a conducting move in which he literally jumped off the podium into the air. His theatricality transformed the Broadway stage; no musical before *West Side Story* had laid bare such raw emotion. He also threw his energy into a range of political causes throughout his life. When the new state of Israel was formed in the 1940s, he risked his life to conduct the Israel Philharmonic; he organized fund-raisers for the Black Panthers and Amnesty International in the 1970s; and, after Cothran died of AIDS in 1986, he conducted concerts to benefit the American Foundation for AIDS Research. His manic intensity also characterized his sexual life. He greeted everyone he knew with kisses and bear hugs. Bernstein's most thoughtful biographer, Humphrey Burton, documents the extent and variety of his voracious sexual appetites with a series of letters in which the young Bernstein describes his erotic exploits over a few months in 1943 (H. Burton, 108–9). When Mark Taylor, his last lover, asked Bernstein if he had loved his wife passionately, he replied, "Everyone I love, I love passionately" (507).

But Bernstein's unbounded energy was marred by internal conflicts. Professionally, he was continually torn between conducting and composing. He thought of himself primarily as a composer, but he craved the fame and notoriety that came from conducting, even though it kept him from composing. He wanted to be remembered as a serious composer of symphonies and operas, but his most successful works were written for Broadway. He agonized over these divisions, which prevented him from being able to compose as he wished. His professional ambivalence also found a parallel in his sexual life. At Harvard, as Burton reports, he felt that he was swinging like a pendulum between homosexuality and heterosexuality (H. Burton, 49). He expressed hostility toward effeminate gay men while pursuing them as lovers (Secrest, 148). According to several biographers, his close friend **Aaron Copland,** who was gay, called Bernstein "PH" (Phony Homosexual) or "BH" (Bluff Homosexual) and told him "you are not one of us" (Peyser, 54; Secrest, 180). Bernstein had a hard time maintaining long-term relationships and could never completely reconcile himself to his sexual desires (he spent many years in analysis). As his friend, composer David Diamond, observed, both Bernstein's work and his personal life were hampered by his self-destructive tendencies (W. Burton, 23).

While Bernstein's works for the theater rarely evoke gay issues, it is possible to locate a certain gay sensibility in them. There is some campy comedy in *On the Town* and *Candide* (the revised versions of *Candide* in the 1970s highlight gay issues more directly than the original Lillian Hellman version). A similar sensibility can be located in the overt emotionality of *West Side Story.* Notably, all the major figures involved in creating this piece—Bernstein, **Stephen Sondheim,** Jerome Robbins, **Arthur Laurents,** and **Jean Rosenthal**—were gay. Bernstein, however, reserved his most direct evocations of gay sexuality for his nontheatrical works: his Symphony no. 2, based on **W. H. Auden**'s poem "The Age of Anxiety"; the Serenade for violin and orchestra, after Plato's *Symposium;* and the settings of poems by Walt Whitman, **Gertrude Stein,** and **Langston Hughes** in *Songfest.* Bernstein created only one openly gay character in his works for the stage, Junior, in his opera *A Quiet Place.* Junior is a deeply troubled character, who has conflicted feelings about his homosexuality. This unhappy character is arguably an autobiographical reflection;

Junior's father in the opera is named Sam, as was Bernstein's own father. If so, this character suggests that he remained unresolved about his sexuality even toward the end of his life.

Several years before Bernstein's death, Joan Peyser published a tell-all biography of sometimes questionable accuracy, which characterized Bernstein as a "homosexual" except during the years when he was married. Peyser theorizes that, like Thomas Mann and Oscar Wilde, marriage inhibited Bernstein's promiscuous homosexuality and allowed him to write his important symphonic and theatrical works (378). Burton, in his more thoroughly researched and reasonably argued biography, points out Peyser's sensationalistic aims and the homophobia implicit in her attitude toward Bernstein's sexuality (H. Burton, 490). Burton identifies Bernstein as bisexual (211), but even this label may be too limiting to describe his intense sexuality and the impact it had on his art. While he was certainly more attracted to men than women, Bernstein was a sexual omnivore; he consumed lovers as he consumed cigarettes and scotch, constantly and voraciously but with a lingering sense of guilt. Other than his own driven personality, there was little to prevent him from fulfilling his personal and professional desires. In his friends and acquaintances Aaron Copland, David Diamond, Ned Rorem, Giancarlo Menotti, Samuel Barber, and Benjamin Britten he had clear role models, serious composers who lived relatively open and happy lives as gay men. But such openness was more problematic in the public spheres where Bernstein found his greatest success, conducting and the Broadway theater. Bernstein gave his last concert as musical director of the New York Philharmonic a month before the Stonewall Riots took place. In subsequent years, he tried to change with the times, but he could never erase the conflicts of his past. In spite of Peyser's arguments, Bernstein was not destroyed by his homosexuality. He was, however, a victim of the divisiveness of gay life in mid-twentieth-century America. The internal conflicts generated by the public stigma attached to gay sexuality can be seen in Bernstein's life and career, amplified—as with everything else in his life—to vast proportions.

See B. Bernstein, *Family Matters,* New York, 1982; L. Bernstein, *The Joy of Music,* New York, 1959; L. Bernstein, *The Infinite Variety of Music,* New York, 1966; L. Bernstein, *Findings,* New York, 1982; S. Bernstein, *Making Music: Leonard Bernstein,* Chicago, 1963; J. Briggs, *Leonard Bernstein,* New York, 1961; H. Burton, *Leonard Bernstein,* New York, 1994; W. Burton, *Conversations about Bernstein,* New York, 1995; S. Chapin, *Leonard Bernstein: Notes from a Friend,* New York, 1992; D. Ewen, *Leonard Bernstein,* London, 1967; J. Fluegel, *Bernstein Remembered,* New York, 1991; M. Freedland, *Leonard Bernstein,* London, 1987; J. Gottlieb, ed., *Bernstein on Broadway,* New York, 1981; P. Gradenwitz, *Leonard Bernstein,* London, 1987; J. Gruen, *The Private World of Leonard Bernstein,* New York,

1968; Leonard Bernstein Archive, Library of Congress, Washington, D.C.; J. Peyser, *Bernstein: A Biography,* New York, 1987; N. Rorem, *Knowing When to Stop,* New York, 1994; M. Secrest, *Leonard Bernstein: A Life,* New York, 1994.

Sam Abel-Palmer

BIRIMISA, George (1924–), playwright, actor, and director, was born in Santa Cruz, California, one of five children of Yugoslavian immigrants. He spent most of his childhood in foster homes and orphanages and received a ninth-grade education. After serving in the U.S. Naval Reserve during World War II, he supported himself as (among other things) a factory worker, bartender, disc jockey, health studio manager, television network page, prostitute, and Howard Johnson's counterman. At the age of forty-one, he studied acting with Uta Hagen at the Herbert Berghof Studio in New York and became determined to become a playwright. His first play, *Degrees* (1966), produced at Theater Genesis in the East Village, was an autobiographical portrait of a gay relationship. At the time, gay plays were usually denied serious artistic attention: "For years, even gay people would ask me, 'When are you going to write your first real play?'"

Birimisa became an Off-Off-Broadway celebrity with *Daddy Violet* (1967), an antiwar fantasia structured around improvisations. He directed and appeared in the play, which subsequently toured colleges in the United States and Canada and appeared at the 1968 International Theater Festival in Vancouver. In 1973, he said that *Daddy Violet* was about "how the individual's fantasy can lead to the burning of women and children in Vietnam" (Kirkpatrick, 54). Today he acknowledges that he wrote it as a parody of the abstract, improvisational plays then in vogue on Off-Off-Broadway. *Mr. Jello* (1968), Birimisa's first two-act play, features diverse characters, including a female impersonator, a gay married man, and a hustler, in realistic vignettes that intersect to become a surreal social statement. In 1969, Birimisa became the first openly gay playwright to receive a Rockefeller Foundation grant, which enabled him to attend rehearsals for the London production of *Mr. Jello.*

Georgie Porgie (1968), another play of vignettes, illustrates the destructive force of self-hatred in gay men. The original Off-Off-Broadway production won Birimisa some of the best reviews of his career.

> Birimisa's dialogue is graceful and pointed, his characterization swift and penetrating, and astonishingly, his most agonizing scenes are often his most hilarious, as if he's able to reach greater heights

George Birimisa, New York, 2002. (Photo by James Eilers.)

of pain and laughter by having the two lean on each other. . . . Birimisa's considerable talent [is] as fluid as it is raw, as passionate as it is brutal. (Wetzsteon, 46)

Georgie Porgie was listed as a highlight of the Off-Off-Broadway season in *The Best Plays of 1968–1969* (Schroeder, 41). The play was optioned for Off-Broadway, but investors were scared away by its unvarnished language, male nudity, and simulated sex. In 1971, the play finally opened Off-Broadway.

Georgie Porgie at Greenwich Village's Fortune Theatre is a play written by a homosexual, about a homosexual, with a special interest for homosexuals. This is not to say that it isn't a serious effort. Indeed, it's a well performed attempt to accurately portray the totality of the homosexual experience. . . . [C]hildhood ridicule, repulsion by parental heterosexual relations, brutality and beatings directed against homosexuals, falsified testimony by police vice squads, male prostitution, black and white homosexual attraction, bicep worship, marriage between homosexuals and women are all touched upon. . . . *Georgie Porgie,* then, is a limited appeal show since so many find the entire subject unpopular and distasteful. (Scholem, n.p.)

Birimisa moved to Los Angeles in 1976. He believes that his next three plays, *A Dress Made of Diamonds* (1976), *Pogey Bait* (1976), and *A Rainbow in the Night* (1978), do not live up to his earlier work (although *A Rainbow in the Night,* an autobiographical play about two gay men living in the Bowery in 1953, won a *Drama-Logue* award). He moved to San Francisco in 1980 and did not write another play for almost ten years. In 1994, *The Man with Straight Hair,* a revised version of *A Rainbow in the Night,* was produced in the Studio at Theatre Rhinoceros. A one-man show, *Looking for Mr. America* (1995), appeared at Josie's Cabaret and Juice Joint and subsequently in New York at the La Mama Experimental Theater Club. Birimisa himself performed the piece at the age of seventy-one, in the role of a man recounting a lifelong sexual addiction, offering "an eloquent and touching portrait of a particular gay man's journey through the last half of the 20th Century" (Goodman, 24).

George Birimisa's career as a playwright is especially notable for his participation in the explosion of gay-themed plays Off-Off-Broadway in the mid-1960s. His work is characterized by emotionally raw, sexually explicit depictions of pre-Stonewall, often closeted, working-class homosexual men. According to Michael Smith, Birimisa "links the pain of human isolation to economic and social roots" (Kirkpatrick, 54).

See G. Birimisa, *Looking for Mr. America,* Dallas, 1995; G. Birimisa, *The Man with Straight Hair,* Dallas, 1995; G. Birimisa, "*Pogey Bait,*" *Drummer* 12 (1977): 19, and 13 (1977): 19; G. Birimisa, *Georgie Porgie,* in *More Plays from Off Off Broadway,* edited by M. Smith, New York, 1971, 34–126; G. Birimisa, "*Daddy Violet,*" *Prism International* (Vancouver) 7, no. 3 (spring 1968): 83–102; D. Goodman, "San Francisco Scene," *Drama-Logue,* September 28, 1995; D. L. Kirkpatrick, ed., *Contemporary Dramatists,* 4th ed., Chicago, 1988; F. C. Locher, ed., *Contemporary Authors,* vols. 89–92, Detroit, 1980; R. J. Scholem, "Greater New York Radio Theatre Review," WGSM radio, August 11, 1971; R. J. Schroeder, "The 1968–69 Off-Off Broadway Season," in *The Best Plays of 1968–1969,* edited by O. L. Guernsey Jr., New York, 1969, 39–41; and R. Wetzsteon, "Theatre Journal," *Village Voice,* November 28, 1968. See also unpublished manuscripts in the Joe Cino Memorial Library, Lincoln Center Library of the Performing Arts, New York.

Paul Sagan

BLITZSTEIN, Marc (Marcus Samuel) (1905–64), composer, librettist, and translator, was born in Philadelphia to a family of socialist Russian-Jewish bankers. From an early age, he showed prodigious talent at the piano. He is the only American to have studied with both Nadia Boulanger (in Paris) and Arnold Schoenberg (in Berlin). At first, he was drawn to the beaux arts tradition, composing in an avant-garde, even dadaistic vein. In the late 1920s, he set to music homoerotic poems in Walt Whitman's "Calamus" series, shocking critics with both his jazz rhythms and the black singer he engaged. His audacity set the tone for a lifetime of subverting the existing musical, theatrical, and political order.

Not an innovator in strictly musical ways, Blitzstein is remembered more as an amalgamator of the arts in a series of works that brought new subject matter and character types to the American stage. Such theater pieces as *The Cradle Will Rock, No for an Answer, Regina, Reuben Reuben,* and *Juno,* as well as song and choral works (*Airborne Symphony* and *This Is the Garden*) reveal numerous coded, Whitman-like messages to the future. Long before Stonewall, he perceived and alluded to the position of the homosexual in society, though often subsuming his observations in a general critique of capitalism.

The Cradle Will Rock (1936–37), a labor musical, has a quasi-vaudevillian scene featuring a feuding painter and a violinist, both of whom are played with obvious homosexual overtones. In *No for an Answer* (1937–41), an opera concerning immigrant Greek laborers, Blitzstein struggled to develop a homosexual character, but in the final version, unable to supersede prevailing homophobic conditions, he abandoned the issue of homosexuality.

The major work resulting from Blitzstein's World War II service with the Eighth Army Air Force was the *Airborne Symphony,* an hour-long cantata for men's voices that has been performed by many gay men's choruses. Blitzstein wrote homoerotic passages about men in bombardier uniform, reflecting his all-male military environment. After the war, the composer took Lillian Hellman's popular play *The Little Foxes* as the basis for his Broadway opera *Regina* (1946–49). In this gothic tale of southern treachery, Blitzstein followed the original play, dropping the standard love story that Hellman had scripted into the film version. Instead, he had a pair of young black males peeking through a window at a fancy ball and imitating the flirting they see inside. The enormous risks he assumed in avoiding commercial convention, in part reflecting personal anxiety over his own sexuality, invited critical censure.

After the success of his translation of Kurt Weill and Bertolt Brecht's *Three Penny Opera* in the early 1950s, Blitzstein wrote the libretto and music for another Broadway opera, *Reuben Reuben* (1950–55), a resetting of the Faust story in contemporary New York City. His lead character, Reuben, will commit suicide unless he finds true love. He is affected by aphonia, the inability to speak, suggesting "the love that dares not speak its name." Although love appears in the background of other works, for the first time in his career Blitzstein built a full-length theatrical work around this theme. Revealingly, the relationship he constructs between Reuben and his female counterpart fails to convince. The show closed out of town.

In his 1957 cantata, *This Is the Garden,* Blitzstein wrote achingly of lovers who wander the streets of New York "in twos" with no place to be alone together. Tellingly, the genders of the couple are not specified. In *Juno* (1957–59), which is based on Sean O'Casey's play *Juno and the Paycock,* men and women lead lives largely in isolation from each other. The male principal even sings an ode to life on the sea, where no unwelcome female curves can be seen. In one of his last uncompleted projects, an opera about the anarchists Sacco and Vanzetti, who were executed in 1927 on trumped-up murder charges, Blitzstein may well have been aware of Vanzetti's questionable sexuality.

Known in theatrical and musical circles to be homosexual, Blitzstein for a time in the late 1940s openly introduced his lover, William Hewitt, an American he had met in London during the war. After that relationship ended, he never again had a steady lover. He died in Fort-de-France,

Martinique, where he was wintering, on January 22, 1964, a few hours after being robbed and beaten by three sailors.

In subject matter and treatment, Blitzstein was a pathbreaker who, owing to his left-wing politics and his status as a homosexual outsider, was ultimately unable in his own era to reach the wider audience he sought. Subsequent generations have gradually come to recognize his contributions: *The Cradle Will Rock* is often staged, and *Regina* has become recognized as one of the foremost American operas. Because of his countercultural reputation and the manner of his death, he is regarded, perhaps more than any other composer, as a gay role model, a status he likely would not have appreciated.

See E. A. Gordon, *Mark the Music: The Life and Work of Marc Blitzstein,* New York, 1989; and D. Metzer, "Reclaiming Walt: Marc Blitzstein's Whitman Settings," *Journal of the American Musicological Society* 48, no. 2 (summer 1995): 240–71.

Eric A. Gordon

BOURBON, Rae/Ray (Ramon Icarez) (ca. 1893–1971), actor and female impersonator, was born in Texas somewhere along the U.S.-Mexican border. Ray Bourbon's act, onstage and in recordings, was not impersonating famous female performers but telling "risqué" stories and singing "racy" songs. Bourbon sang only specialty songs written for him, such as "Mr. Wong Has Got the Biggest Tong in China." His stage persona, Rae Bourbon, was a professional vulgarian, not to be confused with glamour drag.

The mainstay of Bourbon's act was storytelling, often prefaced by, "Oh, it was such a camp, I'll never forget it, even if I live to be normal." One of his trademarks was an infectious laugh, which started as a high-pitched "hee-hee-hee" and often morphed into a hacking giggle. His monologues were peppered with "Mary," "sister," "honey," and "miss," delivered with attitude, affectation, and southern charm. On his *A Trick Ain't Always a Treat* album, he relates an anecdote from a previous night-club engagement: "I stooped over to sneeze and my Tampax shot the cat. I have never been so embarrassed in my life, standing in an elegant lounge with a dead pussy."

More popular in nightclubs than in vaudeville, Bourbon branched out into silent films during the 1920s, including four with Rudolph Valentino. He claimed that he not only "discovered" Valentino but was his lover. "Ray told so many lies about so many things that no one could say anything certain about him unless it happened while you were present," reported Robert Wright (qtd. in Gavin, 54).

Bart Howard, Bourbon's accompanist in 1935, recalled: "Ray was very kind to me, and I even lived with him for a while because we were working together so closely. But he didn't want me to have any other friends. Whenever anyone came over he put sugar in their gas tanks or punctured their tires. He tried to treat me like his possession" (qtd. in Gavin, 54). Bourbon developed infatuations with many of the young men with whom he worked—which led to romantic overtures that were rarely reciprocated.

During the height of his popularity in the 1930s and 1940s, Bourbon presented his drag act in such respectable nightclubs as Finocchio's (San Francisco), Rue Angel (Hollywood), the Jewel Box (Kansas City), the Bishop's Club (Cairo), the Frolics (Paris), the Coon Chicken Inn (Salt Lake City), and the Blue Angel and Jimmy's Back Yard (New York City). In 1944, Mae West cast him (along with Gene Barry and Robert Morse) in the Broadway premiere of her play *Catherine Was Great*. Lavishly produced by Michael Todd, the production ran for 191 performances with Bourbon playing a French hairdresser. West hired him again for the 1949 Broadway revival of *Diamond Lil*.

While performing at the 544 Club in New Orleans in 1956, Bourbon was arrested for "wearing the clothes of the opposite sex." His attempt to revive his nightclub career was not successful. Sending out press releases that he had undergone a sex change operation, "Miss Rae Bourbon's" new act was called, "She Lost It in Juarez (?)" (Bourbon's punctuation). Later in 1956, Beverly Hills sheriff's deputies arrested him at the Melody Room for impersonating a woman. With his act declared "obscene and profane," he was prohibited from completing his engagement (*Daily Variety*, n.p.). Three years later he was arrested in New Orleans for "doing an alleged lewd dance" at a club located at 800 Bourbon Street. Disaster struck while he was driving through Texas in 1965 when his old car caught fire. Leaving his fifteen dogs in a local pet shop, he hit the road again, sending money for their care whenever he could. But while performing in Kansas City he was arrested for the murder of the pet shop owner. He pleaded innocent but was convicted and sentenced to ninety-nine years in prison. In 1970, he wrote to *Variety*, "I seem to have been forgotten by everyone, especially ones I have done favors for. . . . I am now on an appeal. But I need help" (Bourbon, 51). He died of a heart attack on July 19, 1971, at the age of seventy-eight.

See R. Bourbon, letter to *Variety*, June 3, 1970; *Daily Variety*, August 16, 1956; J. Gavin, *Intimate Nights*, New York, 1991; J. Newlin, "Rae Bourbon . . . Tells All!" *Wavelength*, July 1988; "Rae Bourbon, a Protégé of Mae West, Dead at 78," *New York Times*, July 22, 1971; A. Slide, *Encyclopedia of Vaudeville*, Westport, Conn., 1994; R. Smith, *Comedy on Record*, New York, 1988; *Variety*, July 28, 1971.

Bud Coleman

BOWLES, Jane (Sydney Auer) (1917–73), and **Paul BOWLES** (1910–1999), writers and, in his case, a composer and translator, are well known as a couple whose home in Tangier served for decades as a hub for visiting counterculture literati. Both had limited involvement with the theater. Jane's play, *In the Summer House* (1953), was produced in New York to mixed reviews, and Paul composed ballets and incidental theater music for over thirty plays, including **Tennessee Williams**'s *The Glass Menagerie* (1945), *Summer and Smoke* (1948), and *Sweet Bird of Youth* (1959).

Jane was born Jane Sydney Auer on February 22, 1917, in New York City, the only child of Sydney and Claire Auer. After her father's death in 1930, she began a lifelong pattern of moving and traveling, frequently abroad. In 1943, she published *Two Serious Ladies,* a novel, and ten years later her play, *In the Summer House,* was produced on Broadway. Many of her short stories and a puppet play, *The Quarreling Pair* (1945), were also published. A stroke in 1957 ended her writing career, and the remaining years of her life were marked by a steady decline in her physical and mental condition.

Paul was born Paul Frederick Bowles on December 30, 1910, in New York City, the only child of Claude Dietz and Rena Winewisser Bowles. He began his career as a composer under the guidance of **Aaron Copland** and **Virgil Thomson,** but devoted himself to writing and translating from the mid-1940s until his death. His first novel, *The Sheltering Sky* (1948), was published two years after his translation of Jean-Paul Sartre's *Huis Clos* (*No Exit*) was produced in New York. His prolific and varied writing includes novels, short stories, poetry, essays, screenplays, diaries, letters, and translations from French, Spanish, Italian, Arabic, and Moghrebi.

Jane's homosexuality is well established, Paul's less so. In a letter written in 1935, when she was eighteen, Jane relates an argument at home in which her mother maintained "that this Lesbian business was just an adolescent phase" (qtd. in Dillon, *Out in the World,* 14). In Millicent Dillon's biography of Jane, the sexual experiences of Paul and Jane prior to their meeting in 1937 are encapsulated: "He had had affairs with men and women, she only with women" (Dillon, *A Little Original Sin,* 43). Shortly after their marriage in 1938, on Jane's insistence, sex ceased to be part of the relationship, which nonetheless proved a lasting and close union.

Apart from numerous, minor affairs, Jane established strong and lasting attachments to two women, Helvetia Perkins and Cherifa, a Moroccan peasant. Jane's involvement with Helvetia, who was twenty-two years her senior, began in 1940 and lasted seven years. A fiercely independent woman, Helvetia had lived for many years in Europe after divorcing her husband in 1921, and she prided herself on her informed, leftist politics. Eventually, as Jane refused to leave Paul, the relationship between the women deteriorated. In 1942, Jane slit her wrists in a suicide attempt, though the reasons for it are unclear. Paul was unsettled by the amount of alcohol Jane was drinking at the time, though she also drank heavily before and after her years with Helvetia. Millicent Dillon sees in *The Quarreling Pair* a dramatization of Jane's relationship with Helvetia. In the play, two puppets, sisters, exchange severe accusations, as well as words of endearment, as they reveal their suffocating bond to each other. The publication in 1943 of Jane's novel, *Two Serious Ladies,* was not met with the critical approval nor with the popularity she had desired, though a number of important writers hailed its achievement; her play, *In the Summer House,* evoked a similar divided response.

The 1953 production of *In the Summer House* at the Playhouse Theatre in New York represents Jane's greatest foray into the American theater. Opening on December 29, it featured **Judith Anderson** in the leading role of Gertrude Eastman Cuevas; José Quintero directed, with music by Paul Bowles. Confronted with a complex and mystifying plot, critics have concentrated on the characters and their relationships as the most laudable feature of the play. And, though all of the main characters in the play (and in her novel) are women, critics have not found them to represent a specifically lesbian outlook. Three pairs of mother-daughter relationships figure in the play, with Gertrude Eastman Cuevas and her daughter Molly providing the central conflict, which Edith Oliver characterizes as a mother's efforts "to dominate her daughter and the consequences of that attempt" (Oliver, 83). The play was revived on Broadway in 1993 under the direction of Joanne Akalaitis. Forty years after the original production, the critics remained unreceptive.

In 1948, after ending her relationship with Helvetia, Jane left the United States to join Paul in Morocco. She met Cherifa that same year and fell in love with the young, black-haired Moroccan, an illiterate social maverick and a lesbian. Cherifa expected and received money from Jane in return for intimacy, and in 1956 Jane gave her a house. Later Cherifa moved in with Jane, as her servant. Jane's health steadily deteriorated after her stroke in 1957, and she began slipping into severe depressions and experiencing obsessive fears, usually about money. Twice in the next decade she underwent electric shock treatments. Cherifa continued to obtain money from Jane, who often expressed fear of her, but Paul was unable to keep Cherifa away, despite an attempt to fire her.

Jane spent the last five years of her life as a patient at the Clinica de Los

Angeles in Malaga, Spain, where she died on May 4, 1973. After her death, Paul came to realize how much their lives had been interwoven. To Millicent Dillon, he wrote of his sense of loss following Jane's death: "I think I lived vicariously largely and didn't know it. And when I had no one to live through or for, I was disconnected from life" (Dillon, *A Little Original Sin*, 421).

The couple had a profound marital bond that withstood challenges from intimates of both spouses. The marriage also weathered the strains of professional rivalry, periods of separation, mental and physical debilitation, and drug and alcohol addiction. Theirs was not a sham marriage, and Paul's sexual modesty no doubt played a role in its success.

The circumstances of Paul's marriage to a lesbian, his residence in a country renowned for its hospitality to Western homosexuals, and his close relations and occasional cohabitation with gay men throughout his life all suggest that his sexual orientation was homosexual or perhaps bisexual. His confirmation of affairs with both men and women permit one to draw such a conclusion.

But even those who knew Bowles well find his sexual preference difficult to locate, and most claim that he seemed to have an aversion to physical intimacy. Apart from a few passing references to affairs, he kept his sexual life a secret. Virgil Thomson indicated that he may have feigned homosexuality, stating: "He made out in his life as if he were queer" (Caponi, *Paul Bowles,* 58).

In her biography, *Paul Bowles: Romantic Savage,* Gena Dagel Caponi notes that there were advantages "to being homosexual in the 1920s and 1930s; overt homosexuals dominated French high culture . . . and homosexuals were prominent in the New York world of music and theater" (58). Christopher Sawyer-Laucanno's *An Invisible Spectator: A Biography of Paul Bowles* argues the same point. Certainly, Paul enjoyed the countercultural associations of his youthful image as a homosexual, and he speaks of his vocal opposition to heterosexuality during his twenties as a "gesture of social defiance" (Caponi, 58).

In later years, Paul entered into a long relationship with a Moroccan painter, Ahmed Yacoubi, the strength of which threatened the Bowles's marriage; Jane began to feel estranged when the three were together. Paul met Ahmed in 1947 and four years later began to live and travel with him. The relationship ended in 1957, when Ahmed was jailed on charges of sexual involvement with a German youth; later he emigrated to the United States, married, and lost contact with Paul.

Paul protected his privacy throughout his life and to a far greater degree than most of his homosexual friends. His wife and closest friends knew him to be quiet and remarkably reserved, one who cultivated the role of observer and saw himself as living vicariously through others. This reserve bears on his sexuality, as well as his disinclination to discuss it, and helps to explain the general view of his friends that he had a tendency to remain sexually inactive. He did not embrace homosexuality as a social movement, contending that it "would necessitate that each individual conceive of himself as a member of a segregated community, that he see himself not as a free spirit, but as one of many. A definite diminution" (Caponi, *Paul Bowles,* 164). This protection of his privacy probably stemmed in part from his determination not to be categorized. In this, both he and Jane succeeded, and their lives and works continue to defy easy analysis. Paul died in Tangier on November 18, 1999.

See P. Bowles, *Without Stopping: An Autobiography,* New York, 1991; G. D. Caponi, ed., *Conversations with Paul Bowles,* Jackson, Miss., 1993; G. D. Caponi, *Paul Bowles: Romantic Savage,* Carbondale, Ill., 1994; M. Dillon, *A Little Original Sin: The Life and Work of Jane Bowles,* New York, 1981; M. Dillon, ed., *Out in the World: Selected Letters of Jane Bowles, 1935–1970,* Santa Barbara, 1985; M. Dillon, *You Are Not I: A Portrait of Paul Bowles,* Berkeley, 1998; M. Green, *The Dream at the End of the World,* New York, 1991; E. Oliver, "Twenty-four Years Later," *New Yorker,* May 23, 1977; and C. Sawyer-Laucanno, *An Invisible Spectator: A Biography of Paul Bowles,* New York, 1989.

Eric Wiley

BROWNE, Maurice (1881–1955), writer, actor, director, and producer, was born in Reading, England, on February 12, 1881, the first of four children, to Marsie and Frederick Herbert Browne. The latter served as headmaster and pastor at a preparatory school in Ipswich until his death by suicide when Maurice was fourteen years old. Thereafter, the mother supported the family by opening and operating a number of private schools in succession. At boarding schools from the age of eleven, Browne distinguished himself as a student of classical languages, and, after serving briefly in the Boer War, he entered Cambridge University in 1900.

At college, Browne developed a passion for poetry that stayed with him for the rest of his life. Although he stopped writing verse shortly after his graduation, with honors, in 1903, his poetic values greatly informed his career in the theater. After eight years of teaching, tutoring, traveling, lecturing, and for a short time publishing his own and others' poetry at Samurai Press, which he cofounded with Harold Monro, Browne met Ellen Van Volkenburg, a gifted American actress, at a restaurant in Florence. Almost immediately he embarked with her on a life in the theater.

Engaged to Nellie Van, as she was called, within days of their meeting,

Maurice Browne in his thirties at about the time the Chicago Little Theatre was founded in 1912. (Photo by Vandamm Studio, courtesy of the Billy Rose Theatre Collection, New York Public Library for the Performing Arts.)

Browne joined his fiancée in her native Chicago, where after their marriage they founded the Chicago Little Theatre in 1912. His leadership of this innovative amateur company during its five years of operation earned Browne his reputation as father of the American Little Theater movement, as hundreds of little theaters appeared across the country between 1912 and 1920. Browne protested this popular designation, for it overlooked the important contributions of others, such as Laura Dainty Pelham's work with the Hull House Players, which dated back to 1907.

But the influence of the Chicago Little Theatre was particularly widespread due to its practice of touring productions to other cities and to the publication of articles by Browne on the company's work. In characterizing Browne's influence on other theaters, Bernard Dukore states that he "advanced the ideas of a non-commercial dramatic literature, a non-professional theatre, unity of production under the guidance of a single directing mind, and the new stagecraft" (125). In *The New Movement in the Theatre* (1914), Sheldon Cheney asserts that Browne "has whipped into shape an organization which stands to-day as one of the most vital expressions of the new dramatic spirit in America" (179).

Following the disbanding of the Chicago Little Theatre in 1917, Browne spent a decade restlessly moving around the United States, teaching sporadically, directing, and, increasingly, producing theater. Browne and Nellie Van divorced, after years of his infidelity with other women, though they continued to work together professionally for many years. A second marriage, to Ellen Janson, proved short-lived after the birth of a son, whom Ellen raised in California after Browne returned to England in 1927. Two years later, Browne produced R. C. Sheriff's *Journey's End,* and with that play's extraordinary success, which was followed by others in the West End, he became one of London's preeminent theatrical producers. He continued to produce until 1942, when poverty and ill health required him to withdraw from the theater. Over the course of his career, several of his own plays were produced, including *The King of the Jews* (1916), at the Chicago Little Theatre, but none significantly enhanced his reputation. In the last years of his life, he became a devout Christian and wrote an autobiography, posthumously published as *Too Late to Lament,* in which he frankly relates his sexual history, including a homosexual past.

Browne maintained that sexual desire had played a dominant role in his life, describing it as "that evil-good which from puberty to impotence had been my curse and my ecstasy" (15). Throughout most of his adult life, he was both heterosexual and promiscuous; the two periods of homosexuality discussed in his autobiography occurred in his youth and early manhood. The nature of the link between his youthful homosexual experiences and his later work in the theater, while certainly present, remains difficult to determine without additional factual information.

Writing of his years at Winchester (1894–97), a preparatory school for boys, Browne describes the practice of being "tarted" by an older student, explaining that "tarting did not necessarily imply sexual activity; it meant merely an elder's favorable regard" (42). But sexuality was often part of the boys' relationships, and Browne mentions having desired some of his fellow students. He also relates the occasional outrage he and others suffered through homosexual rape by an older student and his "cronies." Following one assault when he was fourteen, Browne recalls his anguish in the third person, writing that "in a paroxysm of rage and pain he shakes his fists at a hypothetical heaven and curses aloud the parents who gave him life and the hour in which he was born" (42).

Browne's experience of rape did not lead then, nor later, to an ill-disposition toward homosexuality. At college, he sometimes had sex with other boys, referring to it as a release of sexual desire "in the public-school manner" (69). Not until his second year at Cambridge did he have his first heterosexual encounter, which he describes as "a furtive business in a back street" (69). A misdiagnosis caused him to believe for several years that he had contracted gonorrhea from the woman and led to a "flight toward homosexuality for two or three years, through fear of further infection or of infecting others" (70).

In his autobiography, Browne treats his homosexual past as an early phase in the development of his adult heterosexuality. Perhaps the distinction between his homosexual and heterosexual experiences, which he rather neatly categorizes as youthful experimentation versus mature behavior, reflects his later thinking, when as a Christian near the end of his life he wrote of his years at Cambridge. His homosexuality as a young man does not seem to be adequately described by the word *flight,* and his failure to provide further information on this period effectively excludes it from the otherwise detailed narrative of his early years. Nevertheless, Browne's insistence on including not only an admission of his homosexual past but the narration of scenes of it, at a time when such confessions in memoirs were virtually taboo, demonstrates his validation of that past as a significant facet in the revelation of his identity. He died on January 21, 1955.

See M. Browne, *Too Late to Lament,* London, 1955; S. Cheney, *The New Movement in the Theatre,* New York, 1914; and B. F. Dukore, "Maurice Browne and the Chicago Little Theatre," Ph.D. diss., University of Illinois, 1957.

Eric Wiley

CAGE, John (1912–92), composer, musician, mixed-media performer, writer, and philosopher, was born in Los Angeles. He graduated from Los Angeles High School in 1928 and then attended Pomona College in Claremont for two years. He traveled throughout France, Spain, and Germany and returned to California in 1931, where he studied counterpoint and analysis with Arnold Schoenberg (Snyder, 36). In June 1935, he married Xenia Andreyevna Kashevaroff, a young art student (Gill, 29).

In 1938, Cage formed a percussion orchestra and began composing music for objects such as automobile brake drums, Chinese rice bowls, tin cans, audio frequency oscillators, and buzzers (Cage, n.p.). This was also the year he met **Merce Cunningham,** the dancer and choreographer who would later become his lifelong partner, at the Cornish School (now Cornish College of the Arts) in Seattle, Washington, where Cage was a composer and accompanist for dance classes under the direction of Bonnie Bird (Snyder, 37). In 1939, Cage began composing pieces for the prepared piano, which he developed by placing objects such as screws, bolts, and pie pans between and on top of the piano strings (Charles, 51).

In 1945, Cage and Kashevaroff were divorced, and Cage moved to New York's Lower East Side (Snyder, 37). He resumed working with Cunningham, touring with the Merce Cunningham Dance Company and later becoming its musical director (38). In a 1966 interview, he described his collaborations with Cunningham: "We started at a time when dancers were very proud. They made the dance first, and then a musician came in like a tailor. From about 1952 on, our music was no longer fitted to the dance. The music could go on for any length of time; so there no longer needed to be rehearsals of the dance and music together" (Kostelanetz, "Conversation," 21). Cage continued working with the Merce Cunningham Dance Company in a variety of capacities— as "program designer, agent, pianist, composer, chauffeur, food gatherer, impresario, apologist, fund raiser, chef de cuisine, comedian, and spiritual mentor" (Klosty, 11)—until his death in 1992.

Shortly after his divorce, Cage began seriously studying Indian philosophy and music with Gita Sarabhai, an Indian musician, who gave him a copy of *The Gospel of Sri Ramakrishna;* Cage enthusiastically embraced Ramakrishna's message "of living unattached in the world" (Pritchett, 36). Aldous Huxley's *The Perennial Philosophy* piqued Cage's interest in Zen Buddhism and led him to the works of Meister Eckhart, Chuang Tze, Huang Po, and Lao Tze. He studied Zen Buddhism with D. T. Suzuki at Columbia University (74). However, it was Ananda K. Coomaraswamy's *The Transformation of Nature in Art* and *The Dance of Shiva* that most influenced Cage's musical thinking (36–37).

One of the most obvious ways in which Cage's interest in Eastern philosophy manifested itself in his work was in the composition process. In 1950, he began composing using "chance operations," a process that involved consulting methods set forth in the *I Ching* and tossing coins to determine the arrangements of sounds in his compositions (Johnston, 147). Cage accepted the Zen "view of a totally interpenetrating and non-dualistic reality" and soon applied it to music (Pritchett, 75). He argued that musical knowledge limited the composer to a fixed scope of sounds and composition methods. Chance operations, on the other hand, allowed the composer "to explore freely the infinite space of musical possibilities," leading to the Zen state of "no-mindedness," which "meant that the mind should be alert to sounds, but empty of musical ideas" (76–77).

In 1951, Cage began to experiment with silence after spending time in an anechoic chamber at Harvard University. In this supposedly "silent" room, Cage heard two sounds—the sounds of his nervous system and his circulatory system—thus proving that the total absence of sound did not exist (De Visscher, 125). He composed *4'3"*, which was performed for the first time in 1952 (125). In *4'3"*, the pianist sits at the piano, and for three movements no sounds are intentionally produced. The audience, with their coughs and creaking chairs, becomes part of the piece; consequently, the "silent piece" is different each time it is performed (Johnston, 148).

In 1952, Cage put together what Richard Kostelanetz has described as "the first truly mixed-means performance in America," an untitled piece performed at Black Mountain College (Kostelanetz, *Theatre of Mixed-Means,* 50). In the untitled piece, which scholars consider to be a precursor to the "happenings" of the 1960s and 1970s, various performances took place in and around the audience: Cage read a lecture on Meister Eckhart, M. C. Richards recited from a ladder, Charles Olsen and other performers in the audience stood when their time came and said a few words, David Tudor played the piano; movies were projected on the ceiling, Robert Rauschenberg played records on an old phonograph, and Merce Cunningham improvised a dance around the audience (Kirby, 19).

Between 1967 and 1969, Cage collaborated with Lejaren Hiller, who was composing computer music. The result was *HPSCHD*—named after the computer program developed by Hiller—a piece composed with a computer for up to seven harpsichords and fifty-one tapes. The performance included several thousand slides, several films, black lights, spotlights, and a mirrored ball (Pritchett, 159–60). Cage continued to experiment with various media, and his early multimedia performances paved the way for the work of various performance artists of the 1970s and 1980s.

Throughout the 1960s, 1970s, and 1980s, Cage published several collections of his writings. He was committed to anarchy, and statements about the evils of government often appeared in his writings and music (Pritchett, 192). His political and artistic philosophies were in sync; he believed that sounds, as well as people, should be "unimpeded and inter-penetrating." He also believed that technology would eventually be able to meet everyone's material needs, and the need for government would diminish, allowing individuals to live freely and independently (192). During the last years of his life, he composed primarily instrumental music, which resulted in forty-three pieces for various ensembles (199).

Some argue that Cage's refusal to speak publicly about his sexual orientation was politically problematic, especially given his outspokenness about other political issues throughout his career (Gill, 26–27). However, for over forty years he and Cunningham collaborated on numerous works, and Cage dedicated many of his compositions and writings to the dancer. The two lived together openly as a gay couple. In 1988, *Architectural Digest* visited their New York loft, noting that the two had begun "sharing their lives" after Cage and his wife separated in the early 1940s (Gruen, 272). Throughout his life, Cage tried to separate himself (and his personal life) from his work, insisting that his work should stand on its own (Pritchett, xii). He died on August 12, 1992, having suffered a stroke while preparing evening tea for himself and Cunningham (Kostelanetz, *John Cage, Writer,* xvii).

See: J.-Y. Bosseur and D. Caux, *John Cage,* Paris, 2000; J. Cage, "A Program of Percussion Music," in *John Cage,* edited by R. Kostelanetz, New York, 1970, n.p.; D. Charles, "About John Cage's 'Prepared Piano,'" in *Writings about John Cage,* edited by R. Kostelanetz, Ann Arbor, 1993, 46–54; E. De Visscher, "'There's no such a thing as silence . . .': John Cage's Poetics of Silence," in *Writings about John Cage,* edited by R. Kostelanetz, Ann Arbor, 1993, 117–33; W. Duckworth, *Talking Music: Conversations with John Cage, Philip Glass, Laurie Anderson, and Five Generations of American Experimental Composers,* New York, 1999; W. Fetterman, "Merce Cunningham and John Cage: Choreographic Cross-Currents," *Choreography and Dance* 4, no. 3 (1997): 59–78; J. Gill, *Queer Noises: Male and Female Homosexuality in Twentieth-Century Music,* Minneapolis, 1995; J. Gruen, "*Architectural Digest* Visits John Cage and Merce Cunningham," *Architectural Digest,* November 1988; J. Johnston, "There Is No Silence Now," in *John Cage,* edited by R. Kostelanetz, New York, 1970, 145–49; M. Kirby, "Happenings: An Introduction," in *Happenings and Other Acts,* edited by M. E. Sanford, London, 1995, 1–28; J. Klosty, introduction to *Merce Cunningham,* edited by J. Klosty, New York, 1975, 11–17; H. Koegler, "Lifelong Companions," *Neue Zeitschrift für Musik* 155, no. 5 (September 1994): 29–31; R. Kostelanetz, ed., *John Cage, Writer: Selected Texts,* New York, 2000; R. Kostelanetz, *John Cage (Ex)plain(ed),* New York, 1996; R. Kostelanetz, "Second Preface," in *John Cage, Writer: Previously Uncollected Pieces,* edited by R. Kostelanetz, New York, 1993, xvii–xviii; R. Kostelanetz, *The Theatre of Mixed-Means: An Introduction to Happenings, Kinetic Environments, and Other Mixed-Means Presentations,* New York, 1980; R. Kostelanetz, "Conversation with John Cage," in *John Cage,* edited by R. Kostelanetz, New York, 1970, 6–35; L. Kuhn, "Cunningham + Cage," *Ballet Review* 26, no. 3 (fall 1998): 80–98; D. Nicholls, *The Cambridge Companion to John Cage,* Cambridge, 2002; D. W. Patterson, *John Cage: Music, Philosophy, and Intention, 1933–1950,* New York, 2002; M. Perloff and C. Junkerman, eds., *John Cage: Composed in America,* Chicago, 1994; J. Pritchett, *The Music of John Cage,* Cambridge, 1993; J. Retallack, ed., *Musicage: Cage Muses on Words, Art, Music,*

Hanover, N.H., 1995; D. Revill, *The Roaring Silence: John Cage, a Life,* New York, 1992; S. Richards, *John Cage as - /,* Oxford, 1996; C. Shultis, *Silencing the Sounded Self: John Cage and the American Experimental Tradition,* Boston, 1998; and E. J. Snyder, "Chronological Table of John Cage's Life," in *John Cage,* edited by R. Kostelanetz, New York, 1970, 36–41.

Krista L. May

CAPOTE, Truman (Truman Streckfus Persons) (1924–84), writer of plays, novels, short stories, and screenplays, was born in New Orleans but spent much of his childhood in Monroeville, Alabama, under the care of his maternal family. His mother, Nina (née Lillie Mae Faulk), was motivated in part to marry Arch Persons in order to escape her meddlesome family, but the union lasted only until Truman's fourth birthday. While Nina struggled to escape the limited vistas of a rural existence and Arch followed various get rich quick schemes, Truman was left with his elderly cousins. He developed a unique attachment to Sook Faulk and would later recall their gentle bond in short stories such as "A Christmas Memory." Nina married Joe Capote in 1932 and brought Truman to live with them in New York later that year. Joe proved to be an indulgent stepfather and Truman was officially adopted in 1935, but the future writer's relationship with his mother proved uneasy. Nina's principal anger toward her son had always stemmed from "his inability to look, act, or be like other boys" (Clarke, 62). Perhaps in an effort to toughen her son, Nina enrolled him at St. John's Military Academy in Ossining New York, and it was there that he experienced his first sexual contacts with other boys. Capote likened his matriculation at the academy to prison. Eventually, he was enrolled at Greenwich High School in Millbrook, Connecticut, later making conflicting claims as to whether or not he ever earned a diploma.

From 1943 to 1945, Capote worked as a copyboy at the *New Yorker,* and the experience familiarized him with the world of publishing and writers. During this period, some of his short stories were published in various magazines, but the appearance of his novella *Other Voices, Other Rooms* in 1948 "made him famous" (Inge, 314). The provocative photograph of the author on the dust jacket created additional publicity for Capote's literary debut and indicates his first striving for celebrity. Also in 1948, Capote met Jack Dunphy, a former Broadway dancer and future writer who would become his lifelong companion. Their relationship proved to be a wary alliance. Dunphy recalled: "Though close and loving, ever so comfortable in one another's company, we were both at the same time propelled by the compulsion to wander apart. . . . We did not have the same tastes. . . . We had a taste for one another's company above all others, but that's about all, but not always, nor for all the time" (162).

Between 1948 and 1951, Capote produced a new work annually. He adapted his novel *The Grass Harp* for the stage in 1952, but the production, despite praise from Brooks Atkinson, enjoyed only 36 performances. Later that year, Capote went on location in Italy for the filming of his screenplay *Beat the Devil,* directed by John Huston. He returned to Broadway in 1954 as playwright and lyricist for *House of Flowers,* with music by Harold Arlen, starring Pearl Bailey, and directed by Peter Brook (later replaced by Herbert Ross, but Brook retained credit in the program). The production had 165 performances but lost money on its original investment. The critic from the *Daily News* believed that the first scene was conceived "out of a dirty little mind" (Suskin, 321). Perhaps homophobia contributed to the lack of enthusiasm: "*House of Flowers'* book was slight but charming, [but] its humor and outlook possess[ed] a decidedly gay sensibility that may not have pleased straight audiences in the fifties" (Mandelbaum, 257).

Capote ceased writing plays and returned to prose. He traveled with the American Company of *Porgy and Bess* to the Soviet Union in 1955 and reported his experiences in *The Muses are Heard* (1956). He followed this work with the two creations for which he is probably best remembered today—the novella *Breakfast at Tiffany's* (1958) and the nonfiction novel *In Cold Blood* (1965). He worked for six years on the latter, often spending months in isolation while he wrote, and his efforts gained enthusiastic praise from most critics. In need of recreation and perhaps wishing to add to the publicity his book was generating, Capote hosted the now famous black and white masked ball at the Plaza Hotel in 1966. Costumes from the event were eventually collected by the Museum of the City of New York; the guest list included rich and famous personages from all over the globe. The black and white party may indicate the moment when Capote solidified his image as a celebrity/artist. As the years passed, his celebrity status began to overshadow his artistic output.

While Capote ceased direct involvement with the stage, his works continued to reach Broadway. In 1966, he declined the opportunity to adapt a musical version of *Breakfast at Tiffany's,* and the task fell to **Edward Albee.** Despite advance ticket sales exceeding other musicals of the season such as *Cabaret, Breakfast at Tiffany's* (called *Holly Golightly* in the Philadelphia and Boston tryouts) received only four preview performances. Producer David Merrick closed the show "rather than subject the drama critics and the theatergoing public—who invested one million dollars in advance sales—to an excruciatingly boring evening" (Mandelbaum, 17). The musical version of *The Grass Harp* (1971) lasted only one week at the Martin Beck Theater.

Meanwhile, Capote's artistic output declined. In 1969, he adapted (with Frank and Eleanor Perry) three of his stories for television under the title *Trilogy*. A collection of essays, *The Dogs Bark: Public People and Private Places,* appeared in 1973. Four excerpts from his frequently self-promoted novel *Answered Prayers* were printed in *Esquire* in the mid-1970s and alienated Capote from the privileged circles of glitterati he had come to know. *Answered Prayers* "was to be Capote's masterwork—a nonfiction novel culled from his diaries, letters, and journals written between 1943 and 1965" (Grobel, 199), but no additional chapters appeared, nor were any discovered after his death. Capote often claimed that this unfinished work would be his *Remembrance of Things Past.* Abandoned by most of his friends, his health declined, and he was hospitalized for treatment of drug and alcohol addictions. He published two more works, *Music for Chameleons* (1980) and *One Christmas* (1983) before his death in 1984, a month prior to his sixtieth birthday.

Capote wrote, "I'm an alcoholic. I'm a drug addict. I'm homosexual. I'm a genius" (261). We have his life as proof of these first three statements, but only his works and posterity may establish the last. Capote's contributions to the theater are relatively minor, yet his high profile as a celebrity and his frank acknowledgment of his homosexuality made him an early role model in the television age. Furthermore, this self-assessment implies that he valued his sexual identity as much as his artistry, which attests to his courage in an era that was marked by homophobia. While Capote's works remain widely available and few twentieth-century writers attempted as many genres, his celebrity ultimately eclipsed his artistic achievements.

See T. Capote, *Music for Chameleons,* New York, 1980; G. Clarke, *Capote: A Biography,* New York, 1988; J. Dunphy, *"Dear Genius: A Memoir of My Life with Truman Capote,* New York, 1987; L. Grobel, *Conversations with Capote,* New York, 1985; M. Inge, ed., *Truman Capote: Conversations,* Jackson, Miss., 1987; K. Mandelbaum, *Not since "Carrie,"* New York, 1991; G. Plimpton, *Truman Capote: In Which Various Friends, Enemies, Acquaintances, and Detractors Recall His Turbulent Career,* New York, 1997; and S. Suskin, *Opening Night on Broadway,* New York, 1990.

Mark Zelinsky

CARMINES, Al (Alvin) (1936–), minister, composer, lyricist, and performer, was born in Hampton, Virginia. He graduated from Swarthmore College and has a B.D. and S.T.M. from Union Theological Seminary. First

Al Carmines at about the time of his first Obie Award in 1966 for the musical *Home Movies*. (Photo by Conrad Ward, courtesy of the Billy Rose Theatre Collection, New York Public Library for the Performing Arts.)

ordained at Central Methodist Church in Richmond, Virginia, he is Pastor of the Rauschenbusch Memorial United Church of Christ and Trinity Presbyterian in New York City, which have played a leading role in Presbyterian Welcome, an organization that accepts all people as ministers or elders regardless of their sexual orientation. He is Adjunct Professor of Musical Theater at Columbia University. From 1960 to 1981, he was Associate Minister of the Judson Memorial Church in Greenwich Village, where he founded the Judson Poets' Theater and administered the Judson Dance Theater (birthplace of the postmodern movement in American dance) and the Judson Art Gallery.

While running the Judson Poets' Theater, he improvised some music for George Dennison's *Vaudeville Skit* (1962) and discovered that he had a talent for composing tuneful theater music. He soon began writing shows of his own, which were performed by an informal stock company that included members of the Judson congregation as well as professionals. The shows, many of them directed by Lawrence Kornfeld, were among the most important manifestations of the growing Off-Off-Broadway theater movement of the 1960s. The originality of Carmines's compositions lay in his setting of texts by such writers as **Gertrude Stein,** Aristophanes, Maria Irene Fornes, A. A. Milne, Ruth Krauss, and Mao Zedong to an eclectic mix of popular musical forms. His first setting of a Stein text was the exquisite *What Happened,* which was performed by members of the Judson Dance Theater in 1963.

He collaborated with George Dennison again on *Patter for a Soft Shoe Dance,* which was performed at the Off-Broadway Pocket Theater in 1964. It was followed the same year by *Sing Ho for a Bear,* a musical adapted from the Winnie-the-Pooh books of A. A. Milne by Kornfeld and Robert Sargent. *The Promenade,* with text by Maria Irene Fornes, was presented at Judson in 1965 and 1966, as was Remy Charlip's production of Ruth Krauss's *A Beautiful Day. Pomegranada,* by **Harry M. Koutoukas,** followed in 1966. Carmines's first Obie Award was for the musical *Home Movies* (Rosalyn Drexler), also in 1966. *San Francisco's Burning* (Helen Adams) opened in January 1967.

In due course, he composed a cantata based on the biblical stories entitled *Song of Songs* (1967) and another called *The Sayings of Mao Tse-Tung* (1968). Also in 1968, Judson presented *Peace,* which was adapted from Aristophanes by Carmines and Tim Reynolds, and James Waring's production of *The Poor Little Match Girl* (Arthur Williams). A secular oratorio, *The Urban Crisis,* with text by Carmines himself (1969), was followed in December of the same year by *Christmas Rappings,* an oratorio based on texts from the Old and New Testaments. This became a Judson tradition for the next eleven years, and it has continued to be performed in other venues since then. Another oratorio, *About Time* (Theo Barnes), followed in 1970. The next year saw the production of *The Journey of Snow White* (text by Carmines himself), *Wanted* (David Epstein), and *Joan,* his own version of the legend of Joan of Arc set in the East Village. *A Look at the Fifties,* which takes place on a basketball court, and *The Making of Americans,* another Stein adaptation (by Leon Katz), were both presented in 1972.

Homosexuality had been a primary and explicit element in *Joan;* not only did the character share an apartment with a gay couple, but she fell in love with a vision of the Virgin Mary. The revue *The Faggot* (1973) included numbers sung by Oscar Wilde (played by Carmines himself) and his lover Lord Alfred Douglas and by Gertrude Stein and Alice B. Toklas, as well as commentaries on contemporary gay life. Carmines found his subject matter in American history in two shows presented in 1976: *The Bonus Army* and *Camp Meeting* (at the Greenwich Mews Theater).

Ten of his shows have been produced Off-Broadway, some of them as transfers from Judson, notably *Promenade,* which inaugurated the theater of that name in a new production in 1969; *In Circles; Peace; Wanted; Joan;* and *The Faggot. A Look at the Fifties,* was presented at the Arena Stage in Washington, D.C., in 1974 and at the Second Stage of the Seattle Repertory Theater, in a production by Arne Zaslove, in 1975. Both *The Journey of Snow White* and *Christmas Rappings* were revived with some original cast members during the Judson Centennial celebrations of 1990. *The Making of Americans* was presented at Center Stage in Baltimore in 1994, *Wanted* was presented at the Wooly Mammoth Theater in Washington, D.C., in 1995; and new productions of *In Circles* played at the John Houseman Theater in New York in 1996 and at the Salon in 1997.

Carmines has received five Obie awards, including one for Sustained Achievement, as well as four Drama Desk Awards, the Vernon Rice Award (for his performance in *In Circles*), the New York State Award, and the New York City Medal for his pioneering work in the arts as well as for his own works.

Gertrude Stein's posthumous collaboration with Carmines has also included adaptations of *Listen to Me* (1974), *A Manoir* (1977), and *Dr. Faustus Lights the Lights* (1979). In 1969, he composed the songs for Peter Gill's production of *Much Ado about Nothing* at Stratford, Connecticut. In 1972, he was commissioned by the Metropolitan Opera Guild to write an opera for young people, *The Duel,* based on the lives of Alexander Hamilton and Aaron Burr, which played in New York City schools. He has also been commissioned by the United Methodist Church, the United Presbyterian Church, and the United Church of Christ to write hymns; his hymn "Many Gifts One Spirit" is contained in the new *Methodist Hymnal* and the new *UCC Century Hymnal.*

As a singer and pianist, Carmines has appeared in concert and cabaret in New York, London, Paris, and Canada, alone and with David Vaughan, singing his own songs and those of such composers as Irving Berlin, George Gershwin, and Jerome Kern. He began acting as a student at Union Theological Seminary, playing the lead in T. S. Eliot's *The Family Reunion,* under the direction of E. Martin Browne. Professionally, he has appeared in Peter Parnell's *Romance Language* (as Walt Whitman) at Playwrights Horizons (1984), in William Gaskill's production of *The Comedy of Errors* for Theater for a New Audience (1990), on the television series *The Equalizer* and *Kojak,* on the *Tonight Show* and the *Today Show,* and in the film *Lorenzo's Oil.* With Margaret Wright (a frequent Judson performer) and Vaughan, he appeared in a CBS *Camera Three* show about Irving Berlin.

In addition to Columbia, he has taught at New York University, the New York Seminar of Earlham College, and Union Theological Seminary, frequently collaborating with his students on the creation of an original musical, for example, *Maslova,* adapted by David Boles from Tolstoy's novel *Resurrection,* with music and lyrics by Carmines (Columbia University, 1992) and *Martyrs and Lullabies* (Union Theological Seminary, 1996). He has served on the board of Christians and Jews and Arts, Religion, and Culture and as vice moderator of the Metropolitan United Church of Christ. In 1995, he was awarded the Union Theological Seminary's Distinguished Alumnus Medal. Since 1996, with Howard Stein, the former chair of the Columbia University Theater Department, he has taught yearly courses at Fifth Avenue Presbyterian Church on the problems of various religions and philosophies throughout the world. In these courses, he has been assisted by the choreographers Gladys Roman and, more recently, Elaine Shipman. In 2003 he received the Robert Chesley Award for lesbian and gay playwriting.

Concerning his sexual orientation, Reverend Carmines has said that he regards being bisexual as a fact of which he is neither particularly proud nor ashamed. He regards being a Christian and an artist as facts of his life for which he is grateful. Being bisexual is simply what he is—a creation of God, who seeks to create in words and music his view of the universe.

See the Al Carmines file, Billy Rose Theatre Collection, New York Public Library of the Performing Arts. This essay is based on interviews and materials furnished by Carmines and the archives of the Judson Memorial Church.

David Vaughan

CARTER, Lynne (c. 1924–1985), actor and female impersonator, was born in Cleveland, Ohio. He served in the navy during World War II and returned to Cleveland to work as a florist. He began his show business career in Cleveland when he entered a Halloween contest, imitating Hildegarde, in 1947. This exposure landed him a twenty-eight-week engagement as a female impersonator at a small Chicago nightclub.

Although he was Caucasian, one of Carter's most famous impersonations was that of Pearl Bailey. Since he had not seen her perform live, he based his enactment on her recordings and photographs. When Bailey saw Carter's act in Chicago, she was so impressed that she gave him the charts of two of her top songs and one of her gowns. This generosity was later surpassed by **Josephine Baker,** who gave Carter some of her musical arrangements and three taxicabs full of her 1950s Paris fashions. Kay Thompson, on the other hand, threatened to sue Carter in 1953 if he did not remove spoofs of her from his act. The publicity surrounding this threat helped establish his career in Los Angeles.

Carter did not lip-sync to recordings, nor did he appear in blackface when he impersonated performers such as Pearl Bailey, Eartha Kitt, and Josephine Baker. With his "regular" makeup and a blonde wig for Pearl, Carter created the illusion of his target through voice mimicry and body language. Even though Carter was famous for his personification of female stars of the stage and screen, he preferred to be called an illusionist, not a female impersonator or drag queen. For Carter, the cultural construct of woman made his job easier: "I have found that women always wear a mask. It's made of cosmetics and fashion. . . . But they end up being caricatures of themselves, which makes them easy to mimic" (qtd. in Christy, n.p.).

Esther Newton places the performance style of Carter in the category of camp, since he did not aim for pure glamour drag: "Carter does not make a good-looking woman. His features are sharp—comic, rather than beautiful" (91). Often Carter would establish a character, break the illusion to speak to the audience in his "male" voice, and then resume the characterization. For years, he would begin his act with the song "There Is Nothing Like a Dame." When he got to the line, "What ain't I got?" Carter would look down at his chest and tell the audience, "You know damn well." His Hildegarde set included a bit in which he would look at himself in a mirror and exclaim: "Oh, I scared myself! I thought it was an old man with a bloody mouth." After a double take, he would conclude: "It *is* an old man with a bloody mouth" (qtd. in Newton, 92).

Comedy in Carter's act came about through a variety of means. He

Lynne Carter and Stormé DeLarverié. (Photo courtesy of Bud Coleman.)

would perform original material, such as a song in which Mae West has a fantasy about being the Statue of Liberty ("Miss Liberty's Gonna Be Liberal from Now On"); a number mocking the evils of illegal narcotics ("Please, Stay off the Grass"); and "The Boy from Fire Island," which was sung to the tune of "The Girl from Ipanema." Other numbers derived their humor from a change in context, for example, a rendition of "Bill Bailey, Won't You Please Come Home" as it would be performed by Bette Davis.

In addition to his club work, Carter appeared as the star of the Jewel Box Revue during the late 1950s and the 1960s. In 1968, he starred in an Off-Broadway revue, *Fun City.* He appeared in several films, including *The Man From O.R.G.Y.* (1970), a spoof of "dirty" movies. Listed in the credits as Lynn Carter, he performed in drag, playing the madam of a brothel. With little reason or justification, he also performed his impersonations of Hermione Gingold, **Marlene Dietrich,** Bette Davis, and **Tallulah Bankhead.**

On January 20, 1971, Carter became the first female impersonator to star in a concert at Carnegie Hall. He performed his impressions of famous women, as well as original characters, such as an old woman who never intended her daughter to be a Playboy bunny. A sold-out house gave him a standing ovation, and *Variety* announced: "Carter is one of the top female impressionists working today" (Sege., 50).

Carter told a reporter in 1971 that one of his biggest problems after being in show business for twenty-five years was trying to find new women to impersonate. With the exception of Barbra Streisand, he thought the new generation of actresses had few distinctive mannerisms that could be copied: "People have said, 'Why don't you do Jane Fonda?' But what would I do—run around and protest?" (qtd. in Klemesrud, 14).

Frequent illnesses in the mid-1970s greatly impeded Carter's career, and by the 1980s he had stopped performing and was working as a secretary. In 1983, he auditioned for the "femme part of the team" in the Broadway musical version of *La Cage aux Folles.* When George Hearn saw him dressed as Marlene Dietrich, he reportedly shrieked, "I've lost the part!" (qtd. in Bell, 36). Weakened by AIDS, Carter died of pneumonia at the age of sixty.

See A. Bell, "Bell Tells," *Village Voice,* January 4, 1983; M. Christy, *Boston Globe,* March 12, 1971; J. Klemesrud, "Lynne Carter, Female Impersonator, Will Perform at Carnegie Hall," *New York Times,* January 16, 1971; "Lynne Carter, Impersonator," *New York Times,* January 14, 1985; E. Newton, *Mother Camp,* Chicago, 1972; Sege., *Variety,* January 27, 1971; *Variety,* January 23, 1985; and "Wrong Lynne," *New York Post,* September 26, 1977.

Bud Coleman

CHRISTIANS, Mady (1900–51), German American stage and film actress, was born Marguerita Maria Christians in Vienna, Austria, on January 19, 1900, into a theatrical family. Her father, Rudolph Christians, was a well-known actor-manager, and her mother, Bertha Klein Christians, was an opera and concert singer. Because her parents were often on tour, Mady

Christians (her parents called her Madi) was educated in the Ursulerin-nen, a convent in Berlin. The family came to New York City in 1912 and lived on East Fifteenth Street while her father acted with the German-language repertory company at the Irving Place Theater nearby. At age sixteen, Christians made her stage debut as the heroine of the operetta *Brüderlein fein,* produced at the Irving Place Theater, where her father had become director-manager. She also appeared in the silent film *Audrey.* Encouraged by her success, she determined to study and become a professional actress. Accompanied by her mother, she returned to Berlin in 1917 (German-language theater had proved unpopular in the United States following World War I) and enrolled in Max Reinhardt's acting school. Two years later her father left New York and went to Hollywood as an actor under contract to Universal Pictures. He died of pneumonia in Pasadena in 1921.

Christians made her professional debut as "Mady Christians" in Molière's *L'Avare* at the Deutsches Theater in Berlin. Under Reinhardt's management, she rose to stardom in Europe and was celebrated in musical comedy and plays by Shakespeare, Lessing, Goethe, Rostand, and Pirandello. She married and later divorced Dr. Sven von Mueller, a writer and government official. She also established herself as a film star and appeared in over sixty European and American films between 1922 and 1948.

In 1931, Christians toured the United States in *Marching By* and returned to Berlin with a contract to appear on Broadway in *The Divine Drudge* by Vicki Baum and John Golden, authors of *Grand Hotel.* Upon her return to the United States in 1933, she began a full-blown American stage career, first in *The Divine Drudge* (1933), and then in *Races* (1934), *Alice Takat* (1936), *Save Me the Waltz* (1938), and George Bernard Shaw's *Heartbreak House* (1938) at the Mercury Theater. While Christians was playing Hesione Hushabye in *Heartbreak House,* **Margaret Webster,** the Anglo-American director who had teamed up with actor Maurice Evans to bring Shakespeare to Broadway, was searching for an actress to play the Queen in *Hamlet* opposite Evans in the title role. Webster found Queen Gertrude in the regal, five-foot-seven Christians. Webster later described her as "distinguished, opulent . . . [with] a slight German accent" (*Don't Put Your Daughter on the Stage,* 26). Webster had also found a friend and companion in the actress, who was by then a refugee from Hitler's Germany.

Cast as the queen in the Evans-Webster *Hamlet* (1938), Christians was taken into Margaret Webster's circle of friends, which included the actresses **Eva Le Gallienne** and Marion Evensen. During rehearsals for

Hamlet, their professional relationship evolved into a deeper friendship and most probably a love affair. Although the two women did not share an apartment (in the early 1940s, Christians lived at 42 West Fifty-eighth Street in New York), they vacationed together on Martha's Vineyard and shared their passion for working in the theater. *Hamlet* was followed in 1939 with another Evans-Webster production and national tour of *Henry IV, Part I,* with Christians playing Lady Percy. Then Christians accepted a part in *The Lady Who Came to Stay,* directed by **Guthrie McClintic,** and carried the play with her forceful acting. She next soared to acclaim in Lillian Hellman's *Watch on the Rhine,* playing the American-born wife of a German anti-Fascist. Critic Brooks Atkinson wrote that her performance was "full of womanly affection and a crusader's resignation to realities" (Atkinson, 1941). In 1941, she was also elected to the Equity Council, the governing board of the Actors' Equity Association, but already the rumors that she was "foreign born" and therefore a communist were circulating in the entertainment industry. It was true that during World War II Christians, like so many citizens, supported charitable causes to assist refugees, exiles, and writers in war-torn Europe. Her support of Russian and Spanish aid committees later brought her to grief during the years of the House Un-American Activities Committee investigations.

Their separate careers were not keeping Christians and Margaret Webster apart as much as was the purposeful intervention of Eva Le Gallienne, who asserted her influence on Webster's life and career in the early 1940s. Christians's film career likewise proved disruptive of the relationship between the two women. Beginning with *A Wicked Woman* in 1934, Christians appeared in supporting roles in eleven Hollywood films. During two intervals in 1943–44 when Christians was in Hollywood, Webster remained in New York City, where she directed nine Broadway plays in five years and began planning with Le Gallienne and **Cheryl Crawford** their grand enterprise, the American Repertory Theatre.

Christians seemingly expressed an ambiguous sexuality in her lifestyle. She never remarried, she continued her friendship with Webster long after they were no longer romantically involved, and she maintained a devoted circle of male acquaintances, including the actor Walter Slezak and playwrights Elmer Rice and **John Van Druten.**

Following the national tour of *Watch on the Rhine,* Christians departed for Hollywood, where she appeared in *Tender Comrade* with Ginger Rogers and *Address Unknown* with Paul Lukas. After returning to New York, she read a collection of Kathryn Forbes's stories entitled *Mama's Bank Account.* She proceeded to write to Richard Rodgers, who had optioned the material for a Broadway play, and asked to be considered for the lead. Shortly thereafter, John Van Druten adapted the stories as the play *I Remember Mama* and suggested Christians for the role of Mama along with Marlon Brando, who would play her fifteen-year-old son. (Druten dedicated the published edition to the actress.) For her distinction as the gentle, wise matriarch of the Norwegian American family, Christians won unanimous critical praise and the Delia Austrian Medal awarded by the Drama League of New York for the most distinguished performance of the 1944–45 season. She played 720 performances for two Broadway seasons, toured with the play across America, and performed the role in London in 1948. She also made two films in 1948, including *All My Sons,* with Edward G. Robinson and Burt Lancaster, and *A Letter from an Unknown Woman,* with Joan Fontaine and Louis Jourdan.

Unknown to Christians, her life was drawing to a close. She taught a master class in acting at Columbia University for a summer term and directed Arthur Schnitzler's *The Affairs of Anatole* for the Equity Library Theatre. Her final Broadway appearances were as Margaret Hayden in James Parish's *Message to Margaret* (1947), with Miriam Hopkins and Roger Pryor, and as Laura in August Strindberg's *The Father* (1949), with Raymond Massey and Grace Kelly. She received glowing reviews as the wife in Strindberg's play: "Miss Christians plays her part in that almost inhuman key. She is defiant and powerful—a terrible force let loose on the stage" (*New York Times,* November 17, 1949). Earlier she had become the first theatrical star to record for the Talking Books program of the Library of Congress, which distributed recordings for use by the seeing impaired. She also was heard on four radio broadcasts in the early 1940s, including performances of Maxwell Anderson's *Elizabeth the Queen* and a reprise of her role in *I Remember Mama* for the *U.S. Steel Hour.*

Mady Christians, émigrée from Nazi Germany and an outspoken anti-Fascist, had become an American citizen in 1939, but, like many of her friends and coworkers, including Lillian Hellman and Margaret Webster, she awoke one morning in June 1950 to discover her name published in *Red Channels: The Report of Communist Influence in Radio and Television* compiled by former FBI agents and listing so-called communists and sympathizers in the entertainment industry. What followed were false accusations, FBI investigations, and blacklisting by film studios and radio and television networks. Subsequently, she grew ill and began to suffer from high blood pressure, but doctors dismissed her symptoms as a psychosomatic illness. Her health improved when the CBS program *Maugham Television Theater* offered her a role (she had been featured in an earlier broadcast), but the offer was quickly withdrawn when her blacklisting was brought to the producer's attention. In an effort to continue working, she took a role in a revival of George Bernard Shaw's *Getting Married,* directed by Cedric Hardwick, and toured for a month. Then she joined the touring company of Lesley Storm's *Black Chiffon,* which opened in Ohio in early October. While on tour with *Black Chiffon,* she became ill and returned to her country home in New Canaan, Connecticut. She died at the age of fifty-one of a cerebral hemorrhage in the Northwalk General Hospital on October 28, 1951, and was buried in Ferncliff Cemetery in Ardsley, New York.

Christians's friends believed that her vivid memories of the persecutions of artists in Nazi Germany and her ubiquitous blacklisting brought on her medical condition and her death. Elmer Rice, John Van Druten, and Margaret Webster were the most outspoken on this matter. Rice described her as: "A great actress bred in a great tradition, a fine, vital, warm-hearted human being, her career brought to an untimely end by the relentless, sadistic persecution to which she was subjected" (Rice, n.p.). Druten wrote of her persecution, "which greatly speeded her death" (Druten). And Margaret Webster attested to her late friend's patriotism, compassion, and exceptional talent (*One More Word,* n.p.).

Christians's death was attributed to memories of earlier persecutions of artists in Germany, to the humiliations of blacklisting, and to her fears of unemployment and financial ruin. As a German immigrant who became a U.S. citizen and a successful artist, her persecutors made her, according to Stefan Kanfer, into "the classic figure" of the twentieth century: the exile. She was the patriotic émigrée victimized by her former homeland and her adopted country. She did not live to confront her accusers; it was left to her friends to declare her innocence.

Several years before her death, Mady Christians stated in an interview that "life wasn't meant to be easy. And I think it is better that way—you don't have to be at the top so long—when you get there late" (Funke).

See B. Atkinson, "Watch on the Rhine," *New York Times,* April 2, 1941, n.p.; J. Van Druten, "To the Drama Editor," *New York Times,* November 11, 1951, n.p.; M. Barranger, *Margaret Webster: A Life in the Theater,* Ann Arbor, 2004; *Current Biography 1945,* New York, 1945; *Current Biography 1951,* New York, 1951; L. B. Funke, "Mama Mady Remembers," *New York Times,* November 19, 1944, n.p. S. Kanfer, *A Journal of the Plague Years,* New York, 1973; Mady Christians Collection, New York Public Library for the Performing Arts, New York; Obituaries, *New York Times,* October 29, 1951, November 1, 1951; H. Ormsbee, "Mady Christians Recalls How Nazis 'Cleansed' the Theatres," *New York Herald Tribune,* July 13, 1941; E. Rice, "A Note on the Death of an Actress," *New York Times,* November 4, 1951; H. Sheehy, *Eva Le Gallienne: A Biography,* New York, 1996; M. Webster, *Don't Put Your Daughter on the Stage,* New York, 1972; M. Webster, "One More Word," *New York Times,* November 25, 1951.

Milly S. Barranger

CINO, Joseph (1931–67), producer and director, was born on November 20, 1931. While the Caffe Cino, the seminal Off-Off-Broadway theater he founded, has passed into legend, very little has been written about this intriguing personality. One problem in obtaining reliable information is that, like many gay men and other theatrical characters, Cino created several alternative personas, embellishing the truth when it suited his fancy to do so. He sometimes professed to have been born in New York's Little Italy, but it is more likely that his birthplace was Buffalo, where he spent the majority of his youth. His mother, Mary, was kept busy rearing her four sons, while Joe led people to believe that his Sicilian father had some connection to the Mafia. There can be no doubt, however, that Joe Cino was not only an early instigator behind what would eventually become known as Off-Off-Broadway but was also the first, and for many years the only, entrepreneur to openly encourage the depiction of homosexuality on the New York stage at a time when it was still illegal to do so.

Photos of the young Cino reveal a round face with an olive complexion, bulbous nose, wide-set dark eyes, thick-lipped mouth, and high forehead with curly dark hair; later photos show him with straggly hair and a full beard. Although he felt that he was overweight and too short, he harbored dreams of becoming a professional dancer. He studied dance in Buffalo and made his first theatrical appearance at the age of twelve on *Uncle Ben's Liberty Shoe Hour.*

After dropping out of high school, Cino arrived in Manhattan by bus during a blizzard on February 7, 1948, barely sixteen years old, to pursue his career. Recalling those days for an interview in 1965, Cino said, "I didn't have a dime . . . and I don't have one now. . . . I enrolled in the Henry Street Playhouse and took courses in everything—acting, dancing, speech, makeup, things like that. I was there for two years" (Smith, 1, 14). In the summer of 1953, he was given a dance scholarship to Jacob's Pillow. He also danced with Mary Anthony's company, and in March 1957 he toured with Alfred Brooks and Maxine Munt.

The liberating atmosphere of the big city seemed to agree with Cino, and he felt free to express his homosexual orientation—an unusually brave move for anyone in the repressive Eisenhower years. The playwright **Robert Heide** recalls that the first time he met Joe, in 1963, he was warned that he ran with a rather wild bunch and that his idea of fun was to dress in drag and walk the streets in an effort to pick fights with punks and beat them up. The playwright **Robert Patrick** says that he and Cino sometimes visited gay bathhouses together for furtive, anonymous sex and that there were even occasional sex parties after closing time at the theater itself. By the time the Caffe Cino was in full operation, however,

Joe had become involved in a long-term, tempestuous relationship with a man named Johnny Torry, who worked as a theatrical electrician.

When Joe realized that his physical size, or perhaps lack of talent, precluded any chance for real success in the dance field, he opened a small coffeehouse in 1958 at 31 Cornelia Street in Greenwich Village. Although the rent was modest, until 1960 Joe continued to hold a day job as a typist to supplement the meager income he derived from the sale of comestibles. He envisioned his coffeehouse as a place where his friends could relax, sip coffee, display their art and photography, read Beat poetry, and discuss philosophy; he never envisioned it as a theater. Eventually, however, he began to allow folk singers to try out their material; impromptu poetry readings soon followed. The first theatrical offerings were initiated by an acting student named Phoebe Mooney; aspiring thespians would try out monologues and short scenes prior to performing them for their classes, occasionally passing the hat for recompense. The first recorded "production," appropriately enough, was a cutting from Oscar Wilde's *The Importance of Being Earnest* performed on February 7, 1959. The initial offerings tended to be from classics in the public domain or pirated one-acts and adapted short stories. The first original script at the Cino was an otherwise forgotten entity by James Howard entitled *Flyspray* that was produced sometime during the summer of 1960. However, by 1963 virtually all the shows at the Caffe Cino were from new, original scripts. Approximately 250 productions were mounted there during the Caffe's nine-year existence.

The importance and lasting significance of the Caffe Cino can be more fully appreciated when one realizes that during that era no other places existed where unknown playwrights could try out experimental work on a shoestring budget or where material could be presented that would have been shocking to the vast majority of the downtown audience. The need for such a testing ground was evident, and perhaps inevitable, but it was part of the genius of Joe Cino that he provided it in a tawdry little coffeehouse in the Village. In providing such a venue, Cino was meeting not only his personal needs for artistic expression but the communal needs of a fledgling homosexual community that was taking its own first steps toward recognition and validation. It is certainly not coincidental that most of the people that Cino allowed to work at his theater were overtly homosexual men. These included the actors Charles Stanley and George Harris (the latter of whom, under his drag name "Hibiscus," would go on to found the radical drag troupe Les Cockettes), actor-directors Neil Flanagan and Andy Milligan, directors Tom O'Horgan, Marshall Mason, Ron Link, Michael Smith, and Robert Dahdah, and a plethora of now established playwrights: Tom Eyen, Paul Foster, **William M. Hoffman,** Robert Patrick, **Jean-Claude van Itallie,** Doric Wilson, and **Lanford Wilson.** Less recognizable names equally vital to this initial flurry of gay-themed drama include Soren Agenoux, **George Birimisa,** Haal Borske, Alan Causey, Robert Heide, Allan James, **H. M. Koutoukas,** David Starkweather, Ronald Tavel, and Jeff Weiss. When the content itself was not blatantly homosexual, the plays were often presented in what could best be described as a gay, often campy style.

Several pivotal Cino plays were notable for their groundbreaking gay content. Lanford Wilson's elegy for a lonely middle-aged drag queen, *The Madness of Lady Bright* debuted at the Cino in May 1964 and would play over two hundred performances in its frequent revivals. In Robert Patrick's first play, *The Haunted Host* (1964), a gay playwright exorcises the ghost of his dead lover when a straight boy, the lover's spitting image, invades his apartment. William M. Hoffman's *Thank You, Miss Victoria* (1965) dealt with phone sex decades before it became a 1990s safe sex staple, while his *Goodnight, I Love You* (1965) portrayed a gay man's fantasies of being impregnated by his lover. George Haimsohn's campy *Dames at Sea, or Golddiggers Afloat* was notable both for ushering in a craze for 1930s-style nostalgia musicals and for introducing a chubby, unknown seventeen year old named Bernadette Peters in her first semiprofessional engagement.

Payola to the authorities to guarantee nonintervention in these illegal products was commonplace. Patrick remembers: "I used to see Joe slip bills to some of the neighborhood cops. Others he'd take in the back and they'd come out red-eyed or zipping their flies. The cops never bothered us while Joe was alive" ("Other Brick Road," 3). The sexual favors to the cops became a bone of contention between Cino and Torry, occasioning more than one breakup during their on-again, off-again relationship.

Tragedy struck the Caffe Cino in the form of a fire, which gutted the interior on March 5, 1965—appropriately enough, on Ash Wednesday. Though officially blamed on a gas leak, Heide (interview with the author) said the fire was set, accidentally or on purpose, during one of Torry's periodic drunken rages. The productions scheduled for the following month were allowed to perform on the off nights at other Off-Off-Broadway theaters, while several benefit performances were organized to help pay for the reconstruction.

The influx of the trendy Andy Warhol crowd at the renovated theater inadvertently spelled the beginning of the end for the Caffe Cino. Although casual drug use had been a part of the Cino scene almost from the beginning, Warhol's minions brought a hard drug experience to the fore. Pot and pills gave way to heroin, speed, and acid. Heide recalls:

> Joe went to a doctor during this agitated period of his life and was advised to stop taking all drugs, that his heart could not stand the strain. He then flew home to Buffalo, to his mother, where he planned to stay two weeks and go cold turkey. He returned to Manhattan after three days, following a convulsion. Joe seemed to need drugs to assuage his intense emotional pain. (Heide and Gilman, 31)

This "intense emotional pain" came from a combination of factors, not least of which was the sudden death of Torry, who, toward the end of 1966 went to New Hampshire to work on the lights for a stock production. Torry, who surely knew better, was not wearing gloves as he hung the lights. Whether he intentionally touched a live wire, as some believe, or a wrench he wore on his belt accidentally brushed against one, he was electrocuted and died instantly. The death of his lover, combined with his drug problems and his despondency over growing older and fatter, proved to be too much for Cino.

Four months after Torry's death, on the night of March 31, 1967, Cino began hallucinating from LSD someone had slipped him earlier in the evening. The landlady overheard an argument in the Caffe: someone was screaming at Joe, daring him to kill himself and end it all. Cino took a kitchen knife and cut his wrists and arms and opened his flabby stomach. He maintained consciousness long enough to phone for help to a friend, the director Michael Smith. Joe was rushed by ambulance to St. Vincent's Hospital, where he lingered. News that Cino was out of danger and would recover came almost simultaneously with the announcement of his death. He died April 2, 1967, at the age of thirty five—ironically, on Johnny Torry's birthday.

The Cino regulars tried to make a go of running the Caffe without Joe, but the life, literally, had gone out of the place. Without the protection that Joe's payola and supposed or real Mafia connections afforded, the authorities swooped down on the still illegal operation. Over twelve hundred violations quickly accumulated, and the attempt to save the Cino ultimately failed. The last production was performed in March 1968, after which the legendary Caffe Cino closed its doors for good.

The impact that this tiny theater/coffeehouse and its proprietor had, and continue to have, on the American dramatic landscape is immeasurable. Without the Caffe Cino's seminal and courageous example, would there have ever been an Off-Off-Broadway? The extraordinary number of theater artists who honed their skills at the tacky storefront is legion. But perhaps Joe Cino's most honorable accomplishment is that, as an openly and unapologetically gay man in an incredibly repressive age and society, he put himself and his establishment on the line to foster the first honest, literate, and compassionate portrayals of homosexuality to appear on the New York stage.

See R. Buck and M. Dominic, "Caffe Cino and Its Legacy" (exhibition catalog), New York, 1985; J. Cino, "Notes on the Caffe Cino," in *Eight Plays from Off-Off Broadway,* New York, 1966, 53–54; D. Crespy, *Off-Off-Broadway Explosion,* New York, 2003; M. Dominic, "Caffe Cino Part VIII," *Other Stages,* July 12, 1979; M. Feingold, "Caffe Cino 20 Years after Magic Time," *Village Voice,* May 14, 1985; R. Heide, "Magic Time at the Caffe Cino," *New York Native,* May 6–19, 1985; R. Heide and J. Gilman, *Greenwich Village,* New York, 1995; "Joe Cino's World Goes up in Flames," *Village Voice,* March 11, 1965; R. Patrick, "Caffe Cino: Memories by Those Who Worked There," *Los Angeles Theatres,* November 1994; R. Patrick, "The Other Brick Road," *Other Stages,* February 8, 1979; A. Poland and B. Mailman, eds., *The Off Off Broadway Book,* New York, 1972; M. Smith, "The Caffe Cino: Homage to a Patron of the Arts," *The Day,* March 24, 1985; W. Stone, *Caffe Cino: The Birthplace of Off-Off-Broadway,* Carbondale, 2005; and "Theatre Journal," *Village Voice,* April 6, 1967.

Douglas W. Gordy

CLIFT, Montgomery (Edward Montgomery) (1920–66), actor, was born in Omaha, Nebraska, several hours after a twin sister, Roberta. His father, Bill Clift, was first vice president of the Omaha National Bank, which provided the family with sufficient wealth to afford both a nurse and a maid. His mother, Sunny, who had been adopted at birth by a lower-class family, vowed to raise her twins and their older brother, Brooks, in the princely environment that she had been denied. "Monty" therefore grew up in a world of private tutors and extended trips to Europe; Brooks Clift later noted that his brother's contact with the sexually liberal European culture helped him to accept his own bisexuality at an early age (Bosworth, 74). In later years, however, Clift would agonize over his inability to choose one sex over the other. "I don't understand it. I love men in bed but I really love women," he once said to a friend, Bill Le Massena (McCann, 61).

By the age of fourteen, Monty had convinced his parents that he wanted a career in the theater. This inspired them to get him a job in the summer stock production of Dorothy Bennett and Irving White's *Fly Away Home* in Stockbridge, Massachusetts. The production transferred to Broadway on January 15, 1935, ran for seven months, and received favorable reviews. "I had found my calling," Clift later remarked (McCann, 37). After a series of further Broadway appearances, which included **Cole Porter** and Moss Hart's *Jubilee* (1935), and a successful stint at modeling (which he hated), he obtained a substantial role in the Theatre Guild's production of Andre Birabeau's *Dame Nature* in 1938. Although the production failed on Broadway, his performance drew positive critical attention (Bosworth, 67).

In January of 1939, Clift, then nineteen, began a short-lived relationship with the conductor **Lehman Engel,** who was ten years his elder. In the late spring of that year, the two traveled to Mexico, where Clift contracted amoebic dysentery. The disease would plague him with stomach pains for the rest of his life and motivated him to become an expert on prescription drugs. Later in life, he turned to mood elevators, such as Ritalin, and eventually to hard drugs; he also became known for his binges of drinking and party going, which perhaps were attempts to sedate his sexual guilt, as well as reactions against his mother's oppressive control of his childhood (McCann, 40).

In late 1939, Clift first encountered the successful husband and wife team, **Alfred Lunt** and **Lynn Fontanne,** when he was cast in their production of *There Shall Be No Night,* which earned Robert Sherwood his third Pulitzer Prize. The Lunts quickly became a surrogate family for Clift, as he deliberately removed himself from the controlling influence of his mother; one of his most prized possessions, in fact, was a photograph of the Lunts, inscribed with the words "from your *real* mother and father" (Bosworth, 79). Alfred Lunt served as a powerful influence on Clift's acting style during the formative years of his career, as he frequently mimicked Lunt's voice and movements (McCann, 40–41).

In the 1940s, Clift acted in several additional Broadway plays and established himself as one of America's brightest young talents. During this time, his self-confidence increased and he explored his own sexual orientation, having affairs with both men and women. One such affair, with an aspiring actor whom Clift biographer Patricia Bosworth names only as "Josh," lasted two years. According to Josh, "One of the things that was starting to torture Clift back in 1940 was the fact that he had to hide his sexual feelings. He despised deception, pretense, and he felt the intolerable strains of living a lie." The affair ended when Josh joined the Navy in 1942, "but we saw each other frequently as friends after that, even after Monty became a big star" (Bosworth, 82).

In 1942, Clift appeared with **Tallulah Bankhead** and Fredric March in **Thornton Wilder**'s Pulitzer Prize play, *The Skin of Our Teeth,* under the direction of Elia Kazan. He later played George Gibbs in a 1944

revival of *Our Town.* Although he had met Wilder during the former production, they did not develop a close friendship until 1945, apparently
when they discovered they were both twins. Wilder rapidly became an
intellectual guru for Clift, and they spent a great deal of time together
that year. Over the following years, they kept in contact and continued to
meet occasionally.

In 1946, Clift accepted his first film role in Howard Hawks's *Red River,*
which starred John Wayne. Although Wilder had entreated him to avoid
Hollywood, Clift took the role because he was thirteen hundred dollars in
debt at the time. *Red River* was not released until 1948, after his second
film, *The Search* (1948), had brought him considerable public attention
and earned him his first Academy Award nomination. Each of these films
gained critical success, and Clift became one of the most sought after
male leads in Hollywood.

Although he was billed as "Hollywood's latest sex symbol," Clift abandoned the traditional tough guy image of a Gable, Tracy, or Wayne.
Instead, his acting style presented a sensitive personality that seemed
anguished and quietly distanced. His appeal was subtle, radiating from
his mystery and vulnerability; Jane Fonda recalled her first impression of
Clift on the screen: "No one had ever seen an attractive man who was so
. . . vulnerable. He was like a wound" (McCann, 47).

The Actors' Studio began holding classes in 1947, and Clift attended
its first sessions. Also attending was Marlon Brando, whom Clift
described as "erratic and impetuous, lacking the necessary patience to
think things through." Likewise, Brando commented that Clift acted
"like he's got a Mixmaster up his ass and doesn't want anyone to know it"
(McCann, 42). In spite of their obvious rivalry, the two men maintained
a mutual respect and offered one another advice throughout Clift's lifetime. Clift, however, was relatively unimpressed with the Actors' Studio
and privately referred to Lee Strasberg as "a charlatan" (Miller, 359).

In 1951, Clift was catapulted into superstardom with the release of *A
Place in the Sun,* which earned him his second Academy Award nomination. During the filming, Clift developed a close relationship with eigh-
teen-year-old Elizabeth Taylor (they even briefly spoke of marriage), and
she remained a close companion throughout his life. Clift had several lifelong friendships with women that were consistently described as "maternal" in nature (even when sexual) by Clift's friends. According to Elia
Kazan, "Monty's sexuality was that of a child waiting for his mother to
put her arms around him" (597). Besides Taylor, other notable female
figures in Clift's life included Libby Holman, Mira Rostova (who served
as his acting coach), Myrna Loy, and Marilyn Monroe.

In 1953, Clift starred with Burt Lancaster, Deborah Kerr, and Frank Sinatra in the film *From Here to Eternity,* which earned him a third Academy Award nomination. In 1954, he returned to the stage (for the last time) as Treplev in *The Seagull,* with Mira Rostova (who received scathing reviews) as Nina. Although the production received mixed reviews, Clift's acting was consistently praised and the performances sold out for the entire two-month run. During this time, however, his behavior became increasingly self-destructive, particularly with regard to drug and alcohol abuse. By the fall of 1954, he "was being compared to Jekyll and Hyde by many of the people who saw him regularly" (Bosworth, 276).

Although he was offered several film roles, Clift did not work again until 1956, when he accepted the lead in *Raintree County* as a favor to costar Elizabeth Taylor. Halfway through the shooting, he crashed his car into a telephone pole on the twisting road to Taylor's house after leaving a dinner party there. His face, the most valuable of his physical attributes, was almost entirely destroyed structurally. After reconstruction and limited plastic surgery, he was eventually able to complete *Raintree County,* but the accident left his left cheek paralyzed, and he numbed the frequent headaches with an increased use of painkillers and alcohol. Elia Kazan later stated: "He was no longer handsome, and there was strain everywhere in him—even, it seemed, in his effort to stand erect" (597).

Clift continued to work, but his subsequent films were all critical failures until he took a small part in Stanley Kramer's *Judgment at Nuremberg* for no salary in 1961. Although his scene was only seven minutes long, Clift, as the feeble-minded Jew testifying against the Nazis, received an Academy Award nomination for best supporting actor. He died suddenly, of occlusive coronary artery disease, at the age of forty-five, on July 23, 1966.

From a historical perspective, Montgomery Clift's acting style is remembered primarily for its distinctiveness; surely, no male actor preceding or succeeding him has fully matched his subtlety and sensitivity, which emanated in part from his gay sensibility. The singularity of his style inspired and paved the way for many actors who followed, most notably, **James Dean** and Warren Beatty. Even Marlon Brando admitted: "In some ways Monty's success made possible my success" (McCann, 77). Clift's greatest contribution to acting was to introduce and win acceptance for traits such as vulnerability and introspection in Hollywood's (and the public's) perception of the leading male persona.

See P. Bosworth, *Montgomery Clift,* New York, 1978; J. Huston, *An Open Book,* New York, 1980, 288–305; E. Kazan, *A Life,* New York, 1988; J. Kotsilibas-Davis and M. Loy, *Myrna Loy,* New York, 1987; R. La Guardia, *Monty,* New York, 1977; M. Leonard,

Montgomery Clift, London, 1997; G. McCann, *Rebel Males,* London, 1991; and A. Miller, *Timebends,* London, 1987.
Robert Brooks

COPLAND, Aaron (1900–1990), composer, was born in Brooklyn to Jewish immigrant parents. He studied piano and composition in New York; in 1921, he went to France to study composition with Nadia Boulanger. He returned to the United States in 1924, where he rapidly gained public notoriety with the premieres of several jazz-based compositions that many audiences found shockingly avant-garde. In the 1920s, he composed a series of pieces that in his autobiographies he calls "music for musicians," experimental works that increased his reputation among critics but found only a small popular audience. In the 1930s, he began to write works in a different style, which he calls "music for the people," highly popular compositions on American national themes, using traditional and folk melodies. These works, many of them written for stage or film, established Copland's reputation as the "dean of American composers": the ballets *Billy the Kid* (1938), *Rodeo* (1942), and *Appalachian Spring* (1944); the film scores for *Of Mice and Men* (1939) and *Our Town* (1940); and the opera *The Tender Land* (1954). In his later works, he returned to his experimental style; he stopped composing actively in the early 1970s.

When Copland died in 1990, after a long battle with Alzheimer's disease, many Americans were shocked by the revelation that he was gay and had been in a long-term relationship with the violinist and photographer Victor Kraft from the time they met in the early 1930s until Kraft's death in 1976. While Copland's homosexuality was widely known in musical circles, it was virtually unknown to the general public. He kept a strict separation between his public and private lives, in keeping with the social norms for a gay public figure in the early twentieth century. He also showed no desire to discuss his sexuality outside his close group of friends; when, toward the end of his life, **Leonard Bernstein** urged him to come out, Copland said: "I think I'll leave that to you, boy" (Burton, 473). On the other hand, he never actively denied his sexuality, nor did he, like many other prominent gay figures, make a public display of pretended heterosexuality by getting married. In his two autobiographies, he regularly mentions Kraft, though he does not specify the nature of their relationship, describing him as "a pupil, companion, secretary, and friend" (Copland and Perlis, *Copland: 1900 through 1942,* 213). Throughout the two books, Kraft's presence is simply assumed, as Copland's traveling partner and housemate. Copland leaves hints for the astute reader; he includes several quotations from friends clearly referring to the two as a couple. He quotes Kraft complaining about their New York studio and the fire hazard caused by the "Femininos," presumably flamboyant Latino youth, so flamingly gay that they posed a fire hazard (19). He does not deny his relationship, but he remains sufficiently vague that any reader wishing to ignore the gay implications has a convenient means of denial.

Copland lived two lives, a private life spent almost exclusively in gay male circles, and a public life as one of the country's most prominent symbols of mainstream Americana. In his private life, Copland stood at the center of a large group of gay composers and musicians who virtually defined American serious music in the twentieth century: **Virgil Thomson,** Henry Cowell (who was jailed for four years in the 1930s for having sex with a minor), David Diamond, Giancarlo Menotti, Samuel Barber, **Marc Blitzstein,** Leonard Bernstein, Ned Rorem, and the British composer Benjamin Britten and his lover, the tenor Peter Pears. In his public life, primarily through the popularity of his works for the stage, Copland came to represent the "real" America. His firm hold on this public perception is remarkable because he was in almost every way the least likely representative of mainstream America: a New York Jew, a sometime expatriate with left-leaning politics, and a homosexual. Copland was aware of his divided personality and tells this story:

> I met Groucho Marx at a modern music concert one evening. Groucho heard my *Piano Sonata* played at the concert, and at intermission, he expressed surprise at the advanced idiom of the piece. "Well," I said, "you see, I have a split personality." And Groucho shot back, "It's okay, Copland—as long as you split it with Sam Goldwyn." (Copland and Perlis, *Copland: 1900 through 1942,* 18)

The split in Copland's music parallels the division in his personal life. Notably, he began to write works in a popular idiom in the mid-1930s, at a time when antigay crackdowns began to intensify in the United States and in the years when his friend Henry Cowell was in jail for homosexual acts. The "American" idiom that made him so popular was an adopted style; his musical roots were in Eastern European Jewish music and the French avant-garde, not Protestant hymns and Appalachian folk tunes. Copland's early works were based in his own traditions; his shift away from the avant-garde, and his creation of an American musical voice based on folk melodies, represented a conscious move away from his earlier identity, an act of artistic closeting. Notably, not only did Copland consciously change his style, but he chose the most public venues, music for stage and film, for his most American works while continuing to write his more experimental music for less popular audiences. The theater was his central means of erecting his highly effective musical closet.

Copland's life, then, stands as a notable example of the disjunction between the public image of mainstream America and the private lives of those who generate that image. The public was surprised at the revelation of Copland's homosexuality because it did not want to see the obvious. Copland, whose own life bore little relationship to mythical middle America, used music and the theater to turn this myth into a powerful semblance of reality. He wrote the music that signifies America to many people in the United States and the rest of the world; that image is not reality but only the door to a carefully constructed closet.

See H. Burton, *Leonard Bernstein,* New York, 1994; A. Copland and V. Perlis, *Copland: 1900 through 1942,* New York, 1984; A. Copland and V. Perlis, *Copland: Since 1943,* New York, 1989; Aaron Copland Papers, Performing Arts Research Center, New York Public Library; A. Dobrin, *Aaron Copland: His Life and Times,* New York, 1967; R. Kostelanetz, *Aaron Copland: A Reader: Selected Writings, 1926–1972,* New York, 2003; N. Rorem, *Knowing When to Stop: A Memoir,* New York, 1994.

Sam Abel-Palmer

CORNELL, Katharine (1893–1974), actress, and **Guthrie McClintic** (1893–1961), director, were married in 1921, just as her Broadway career began to take off. From that point on, "The First Lady of the Theater" (as **Alexander Woollcott** dubbed her) developed into a popular and commanding presence on Broadway. By 1931, Cornell and McClintic were a formidable producing team that had garnered a series of hits and long-running successes.

Katharine Cornell made her New York debut with the Washington Square Players in 1916 and continued to work with them as a company member for two years. In the summer of 1918, she joined Jessie Bonstelle's Stock Company in Buffalo, New York. In her second summer with the company (1919), she began to play second leads, and in November of the same year she debuted as Jo in *Little Women* in London, receiving enthusiastic reviews. In the spring of 1920, she returned to the Jessie Bonstelle Company to play alternate leads and met the new assistant stage director, Guthrie McClintic. In March 1921, she opened in her first Broadway show, *Nice People,* with **Tallulah Bankhead,** which had an impressive thirty-one-week run. In September 1921, she married Guthrie

McClintic, and in the following month she received splendid reviews for her first Broadway hit, *A Bill of Divorcement,* which closed after 173 performances. She appeared in various roles after this success, including the lead in *The Way Things Happen,* her first play under her husband's direction since their marriage. In 1924, she received critical acclaim for *Candida,* and in the following year her role in *The Green Hat* with Leslie Howard made her an official Broadway star. In 1931, Cornell and McClintic founded the Cornell-McClintic Corporation, and she served as producer-manager while Guthrie was the director. Their first project together under this new arrangement was the highly successful *The Barretts of Wimpole Street,* in which she played Elizabeth Barrett. This is usually considered the greatest success of her long, prolific career.

Guthrie McClintic studied acting at the American Academy of Dramatic Arts and began appearing on the stage in supporting roles in 1913. His first New York appearance was in 1914. He had a ten-year association with Winthrop Ames, a producer/director who was a leader in the art theater movement in the early twentieth century. During his career, he was one of the most celebrated directors in American theater. He directed more than ninety plays in his lifetime, and two of the scripts he premiered won Pulitzer Prizes (*The Old Maid* and *Winterset,* both staged in 1935).

The actors he worked with are a roll call of top American performers: Gregory Peck, Kirk Douglas, Orson Welles, Ethel Waters, Maureen Stapleton, and Tyrone Power. In 1937, he directed Marlon Brando in the second revival of the ever popular *Candida* with Cornell. He directed his wife in twenty-five plays, and the greatest success of his career, like hers, was *The Barretts of Wimpole Street,* which he revived four times.

In 1933, "Kit" and "Guth," as they were known to their friends, launched a transcontinental repertory tour with *The Barretts of Wimpole Street, Candida,* and *Romeo and Juliet.* They were taking great financial risks. Many people, including members of the theatrical press, thought the road was dead. Only a few actors were still touring, and they usually took a single show. The Cornell-McClintic company toured 17,000 miles in seven months, their 225 performances played to 500,000 people, and they set box office records in every town they visited. By putting their faith in the road, they are often credited with reviving the viability of a repertory tour.

In 1934, they brought *Romeo and Juliet* to New York to outstanding reviews. Cornell received the New York Drama League Award for her performance, which was considered by many to be the foremost American

Juliet of her generation. In 1937, she was the first actress to receive a Gold Medal of National Achievement Award, presented to her at the White House by First Lady Eleanor Roosevelt.

When in 1961 McClintic died of cancer, Katharine Cornell retired from the stage, prompting the closing narrative of her professional life: without her life partner, who had helped promote and shape her career, she could not continue working. While the public at large was unaware of the private lives of the couple, their marriage and professional partnership helped to create a seamless portrayal of marital bliss. But those close to the couple in the show business world knew otherwise. It was a well-known fact among theater people that Kit and Guth had a lavender marriage: a marriage of convenience and companionship while each maintained homosexual relationships. (Lavender marriages were common in Hollywood as a ploy to cover up homosexual relationships and divert attention from same-sex partners. Studio press agents used the lavender marriage to spin good romantic press material steeped in heterosexual "normality.")

Cornell's career falls into two periods: her early hits, in which she specialized in a series of dangerous, wanton women; and her self-produced work, which featured wholesome female characters. In her first hit, *A Bill of Divorcement,* she played a brash, self-assured, excitable girl of seventeen. The production of *The Green Hat* in 1925, which made her a household name, cast her in the controversial role of Iris March, a passionate, independent young woman driven to promiscuity. Cornell's performance made her wildly popular with the female public, and Iris March became a model for aspiring young sophisticates. In her 1930 performance as the murderous but seductive Madeleine Cary in *Dishonored Lady,* theater critics compared her sultry stage decadence to that of Greta Garbo. Beginning in 1931, with *The Barretts of Wimpole Street,* Cornell's acting roles changed significantly to parts that were considered safely "artistic": Elizabeth Barrett, Juliet, and Joan of Arc. This shift in her professional persona was accompanied by her employment of Ray Henderson, a press agent, who promoted her as a thoughtful, calm, dignified lady of the theater known to the press as "Miss Cornell."

There is little published material that discusses openly the homosexual relationships of either Cornell or McClintic. One significant source is the biography by Tad Mosel and Gertrude Macy entitled *Leading Lady: The World and Theater of Katharine Cornell.* Macy worked for Cornell beginning in 1928 as a secretary and was the stage manger for *The Barretts of Wimpole Street.* Her discretion and efficiency eventually landed her the position of general manager for Cornell, with responsibility for all of her box office and financial dealings and personal correspondence. In the 1930s, Macy introduced Cornell to **Nancy Hamilton,** a comic review writer and actress who was to become Kit's lifetime companion and lover. The Mosel and Macy biography avoids giving specific details about their relationship, only referring to the "passionate friendships" with women enjoyed by Cornell. Mosel and Macy are more forthcoming about McClintic's promiscuity and his short-lived but numerous relationships.

Two other documents that attest to their sexual preferences are fictional works that present troubling caricatures while referencing reality. Moss Hart's *Light Up the Sky* (1948) has an effeminate director, Carleton Fitzgerald, who is considered a parody of McClintic. While McClintic had a reputation as one of the best directors of his generation, he was also known for his volatile, flashy behavior, which is clearly made fun of in Hart's comedy of backstage life. The second document is the theatrical novel *Quicksilver* (1942). The novel offers a fresh, perceptive, and detailed account of life in a large theater company from the point of view of the bit players while they tour a Broadway success—*Romeo and Juliet*—on the road. Fitzroy Davis, the author, began his professional theater career in a small role in Katharine Cornell's 1935 tour of *Romeo and Juliet*. The novel, which received acclaim for its authentic depiction of backstage life, simultaneously caused a scandal because the leading actress was clearly an unflattering portrayal of Katharine Cornell. Not only is the fictional star of *Romeo and Juliet* in Davis's novel a grasping diva, but she is also a lesbian.

During the later years of Cornell's career, she was feted and honored with numerous awards and honorary degrees. Her last production before McClintic's death was a twenty-seven-week tour of *Dear Liar* in 1960, which ended with a respectable run at the Billy Rose Theatre in New York. She retired to her home on Martha's Vineyard with her partner Nancy Hamilton, where they lived until her death from pneumonia on June 12, 1974 (Hamilton died in 1985). In January of that year, she was awarded the American National Theater and Academy's National Artist Award for her "incomparable acting ability." In April 1974, the New York Public Library's Theater Collection at Lincoln Center dedicated the Katharine Cornell–Guthrie McClintic Room, and the couple's personal papers were made available to theater scholars.

See K. Cornell, *I Wanted to Be an Actress: The Autobiography of Katharine Cornell,* New York, 1938; F. Davis, *Quicksilver,* New York, 1942; L. Ferris, "Kit and Guth: A Lavender Marriage on Broadway," in *Passing Performances: Queer Readings of Leading Players in American Theater History,* edited by R. A. Schanke and K. Marra, Ann Arbor, 1998, 197–220; A. Madsen, *The Sewing Circle: Hollywood's Greatest Secret—Female Stars Who Loved Other Women,* New York, 1995; G. Malvern, *Curtain Going Up! The Story of Katharine Cornell,*

New York, 1943; G. McClintic, *Me and Kit,* Boston: Little, Brown, 1955; T. Mosel and G. Macy, *Leading Lady: The World and Theater of Katharine Cornell,* Boston, 1978; L. M. Pederson, *Katharine Cornell: A Bio-Bibliography,* Westport, Conn., 1994; C. Shattuck, "Quicksilver Revisited: A Portrait of the Stage in the 1930's," in *The American Stage: Social and Economic Issues from the Colonial Period to the Present,* edited by R.Engle and T. L. Miller, Cambridge, 1993, 190–99; and J. K. Tillinghast, "Guthrie McClintic, Director," Ph.D. diss., Indiana University, 1964.

Lesley Ferris

CRAWFORD, Cheryl (1902–86), producer and director, was born in Akron, Ohio, the only daughter of realtor Robert Kingsley and Luella Elizabeth (Parker) Crawford. Cheryl had a "healthy, happy childhood" (Crawford, 13), despite the fact that her unconventional behavior, which ranged from smoking and drinking to refusing to eat the crusts of her bread, did not conform to the expectations of her mother and father (the latter of whom also served as superintendent of the Congregational Church).

Crawford performed in amateur theatrical productions as early as the third grade, but it was not until she enrolled at Smith College in 1921 that she realized her passion for the stage. Her low voice and ability to imitate men won her breeches roles as a freshman and sophomore. "Adorned in white satin britches, an embroidered coat and a white wig, [she] became a campus star" following her performance in *A Marriage of Conscience* (Crawford, 16). Eventually, her popularity won her the presidency of Smith's Dramatic Association. A faculty committee, however, was appointed by the outgoing officers to supervise Crawford. It was feared that she "might choose something outlandish and dangerous to young ladies' morals" (17). Rumors circulated around Smith that Crawford not only smoked and drank but lectured on Nietzsche and sex to innocent young women. As a senior, she was denied Phi Beta Kappa honors because she lacked "moral excellence" (25).

Crawford interned with the Provincetown Players during the summer of her junior year, which strengthened her resolve to pursue a professional career in the theater. Following her graduation from Smith in 1925, she moved to New York and enrolled in the Theatre Guild School. She later recalled: "Of course after Provincetown [I] wanted to live in Greenwich Village among the Bohemians" (Crawford, 30). Early in her "long love affair" with the guild, she supported herself through poker, bootlegging, and a "sugar daddy" who asked "nothing more than to enjoy our high spirits" (39). She regularly visited the jazz clubs and speakeasies in Harlem. She also became attracted to someone who shared her romantic interests; unfortunately, "physical attraction was deplorable to the sages I was reading" (Crawford, 38).

In 1931, Crawford abandoned the comfort and security of her position as a casting director and general assistant at the guild to direct the Group Theatre with Harold Clurman and Lee Strasberg. Seduced by Clurman's "jeremiads" and "Whitmanesque moods," she thought her cofounders would be sympathetic to the problems confronting women directors (Crawford, 52). She assisted Strasberg on the theater's first production, Paul Green's *The House of Connelly* (1931), and went on to direct Dawn Powell's *Big Night* (1933), Clifford Odets's *Till the Day I Die* (1935), and Nelisse Childs's *Weep for the Virgins* (1935). Her primary duties, however, were to conduct the company's financial and business affairs, arrange for summer retreats, read scripts, and shepherd productions such as Paul Green and Kurt Weill's *Johnny Johnson* (1936). She also kept the peace between Clurman and Strasberg. In a satirical sketch staged for members of the group, Margaret Barker characterized Crawford "as a kind of female cowboy, addressing herself with laconic shrewdness to her quixotic partners" (Clurman, 97).

As was the case throughout her career, Crawford publicly claimed that her life was absorbed by work. An affair with Dorothy Patten (who was well known with the group) suggests otherwise. Crawford rented her apartment to **Aaron Copland** so that she could move in with Patten. Their vacations together included visits to their family homes in Akron and Chattanooga.

Following a period of struggle between the directors and the acting ensemble, Crawford resigned from the Group Theatre in 1937 to pursue a career as an independent producer. Among her early productions were *Family Portrait* (1939), starring **Judith Anderson** and directed by **Margaret Webster**, and *Another Sun* (1940), written by Dorothy Thompson. Crawford also found success with a stock company in Maplewood, New Jersey, where her weekly productions featured the talents of **Tallulah Bankhead**, Ethel Barrymore, Edna Ferber, José Ferrer, Helen Hayes, Canada Lee, Paul Robeson, and Gloria Swanson, among others. The transfer of a revival of *Porgy and Bess* from Maplewood to Broadway in 1942 became the first of several musicals produced by Crawford. Other notable productions included *One Touch of Venus* (1943), starring Mary Martin, *Brigadoon* (1947), *Regina* (1949), and *Paint Your Wagon* (1951).

By 1941, Crawford was regarded as one of the most successful women producers in the American theater. She was known both as the "Lady from Akron" and "The Great Poker Face." She "rarely display[ed] feelings in a world of temperaments and hysterics" (Michaelson, 25). "Along with a masculine mind," added Florence Ramon, she had "close-cropped light brown hair, a soap and water face, small thrifty looking hands and a very firm handclasp" (Ramon, n.p.). Crawford was also believed to have a "special feminine formula" for producing musicals, which included the "elimination of a lot of customary, costly, masculine waste" (Flanner, 34).

Crawford's success and visibility as a Broadway producer made her part of an elite group of lesbians and gay men in the theater who spent their summers in Cherry Grove, New York, during the 1940s and 1950s. Many of her closest associates (both personal and professional) vacationed on Fire Island, including **Carson McCullers, Jane Bowles, Tennessee Williams,** Oliver White, and Janet Flanner, among others. "Several old timers said they heard of the Grove through [Crawford] or wanted to come because they knew through theatrical grapevines that she was there" (Newton, 209). Crawford frequently rented Pride House with cookbook author Ruth Norman and served on the advisory board for the Cherry Grove Follies during its first season. As it became more diversified in terms of class, Crawford and Norman joined the migration of "ladies" from Cherry Grove to the Connecticut countryside. Their weekend guests at their Eastham estate included, among many others, neighbors Mary Martin and Richard Halliday, as well as Tennessee Williams and Frank Merlo.

Although Crawford enjoyed the sense of freedom associated with her position as an independent producer, she longed to belong to a company. In 1945, she cofounded, with **Margaret Webster** and **Eva Le Gallienne,** the American Repertory Theatre. It was hoped that the company could be established as a classical repertory theater along the lines of the Old Vic. Crawford was excited to work with two pillars of strength such as Le Gallienne and Webster, who were lovers at the time. Her enthusiasm faded, however, when the company encountered unprecedented demands from theater unions, as well as a lukewarm reception from reviewers. Crawford resigned from the company in 1947, feeling unfulfilled after a season plagued with artistic and managerial compromises.

Later that year Crawford reunited with Elia Kazan and Robert Lewis to found the Actors Studio as a training school for young artists. She produced *Strange Interlude* (1963), *Marathon 33* (1963), *Blues for Mr. Charlie* (1964), and *Three Sisters* (1964) for the Studio Theatre. She also produced plays for the American National Theatre and Academy, notably, *Galileo* (1947), starring **Charles Laughton,** and *Peer Gynt* (1951).

Crawford's "proudest experience" as a producer was her work on four plays by Tennessee Williams (Crawford, 183). She won an Antoinette Perry (Tony) Award for *The Rose Tattoo* (1951), and productions followed of *Camino Real* (1953), *Sweet Bird of Youth* (1959), and *Period of Adjustment* (1960).

In 1957, Crawford received a Creative Arts Award from Brandeis University, as well as a subpoena to appear before the House Un-American Activities Committee. The summons disturbed Crawford, who claimed that politics had always been an "incidental" matter for her: "Would McCarthy and his cohorts believe that I kept my nose to the theatrical grindstone to the exclusion of everything else—love, for instance, which certainly would have come before politics if there had been world enough and time?" (Crawford, 256). Her appearance before the committee was indefinitely postponed.

Although her career declined in the last two decades of her life, Crawford remained active as a producer until her death (of complications from a fall) in 1986.

See C. Adams, "Our Greatest Stars Came from Her 'Womb,'" *New York Post,* October 9, 1986; H. Clurman, *The Fervent Years: The Group Theatre and the Thirties,* New York, 1975; C. Crawford, *One Naked Individual: My Fifty Years in the Theatre,* Indianapolis, 1977; J. Flanner, "A Woman in the House," *New Yorker,* May 8, 1948; A. Klein, "Innovation: The Producer and the Poet," *New York Times,* August 29, 1982; J. Michaelson, "Our Town's Leading Business Women," *New York Post Magazine,* September 1, 1964; A. Murphy, "At Home with . . . Cheryl Crawford," *New York Post,* October 9, 1960, 15; E. Newton, *Cherry Grove, Fire Island: Sixty Years in America's First Gay and Lesbian Town,* Boston, 1993; F. Ramon, "Cheryl's Chock Full of Stage Ideas," *Morning Telegraph,* May 30, 1941; W. Smith, *Real Life Drama: The Group Theatre and America, 1931–1940,* New York, 1990; G. Turner, "She Knows What We Like," *New York Herald Tribune,* May 24, 1942; J. Wilson, *From Chattanooga to Broadway: The Dorothy Patten Story,* Chattanooga, 1986; "Woman Producer: Miss Crawford a Success in Tough Career," *Philadelphia Inquirer,* March 2, 1947; and "Women Who Produce Plays," *Independent Woman,* February 1946.

Jay Plum

CROTHERS, Rachel (1878–1958), playwright and director, was born in Bloomington, Illinois, to a family of physicians (both father and mother), who held the theater to be an abomination. Nevertheless, the child developed a passion for the theater by giving her dolls dialogue and costumes. Her first written and produced play, at the age of twelve, was an outgrowth of her loneliness, and together with a school friend she delivered "the complete thing" to an astounded audience of her parents' friends (Crothers, n.p.).

After attending Illinois State Normal School and teaching briefly, Crothers went to Boston in 1892 to study acting and later to New York, where she enrolled in the well-known Stanhope-Wheatcroft School of

Acting. Her acting debut, with the eminent E. H. Sothern Company in New York, was reported in the Chicago papers as "Beginning a Histrionic Career under Flattering Auspices" (*Chicago Tribune*). Crothers built her craft at the Wheatcroft School by working as a coach after her graduation and by staging her own one-act plays. Through these experiences, she learned all phases of the theater, took advantage of the many opportunities for theatergoing, and absorbed the cultural atmosphere of New York in the early twentieth century.

Crothers's first Broadway success, *The Three of Us* (1906), launched a thirty-year Broadway career of writing and directing over twenty-five plays. Her central theme, with variations, that of women in conflict, and the timeliness of her plots dealing with the New Woman in American society, brought her considerable attention, and she became a significant literary influence.

Considered a feminist in her own day (which she always denied, although she clearly wrote with a feminine and feminist bias), Crothers herself was influenced by the radical humanism of Henrik Ibsen and by the liberating ideas of male-female equality of such nineteenth-century thinkers as John Stuart Mill. In her view, the ideal male-female relationship can be realized, as she attempted to demonstrate in her plays, if both husband and wife share as equals in a marriage.

The principal subjects and themes of her plays were with the problems women encountered in their marriages, including economic dependence and career frustrations. Her plays, in other words, considered the new, independent woman in society, revealing her growing need for individual identity and equality to match that of the male in the household and the workplace.

Crothers never married, and no evidence has emerged to suggest that she had a romantic heterosexual relationship anytime in her life. Those in the theater who knew and worked with her in the 1920s and 1930s said that it was known among their ranks that she lived with a woman companion in an elegant house in Redding, Connecticut. J. K. Curry notes that Crothers in a newspaper article, "'What Do Women Think of Other Women?' Men Are More Tolerant and Good Natured," answered several questions about a relationship with another woman: "Modern women are capable of splendid friendships for each other. That is a matter on which I feel very strongly. I myself have lived for ten years with a woman friend and the relation has been ideal. I have my work and she has hers. I write plays and she keeps my apartment" (Curry, 56–57; *Pantagraph*, n.p.). Curry identifies Crothers's companion as Eula Seeley Garrison, "who shared Crothers's home in Connecticut for decades" (57). Garrison died around 1951, and at Crothers's death in 1958 her entire estate was left to her lifetime partner's niece, Mrs. Anthony Hoagland, who donated Crothers's materials to the Museum of the City of New York.

Among her dramas and social comedies dealing with issues generated by "women's nature," ten furnish telling examples of twentieth-century, feminine, middle-class life and its hardships. Written with insight, humor, and irony, they fall into groupings that can be briefly identified. *Three of Us* (1906) and *A Man's World* (1910) are early dramas of women's emancipation from double standards. *Old Lady 31* (1916) and *He and She* (1920), plays of the World War I era, deal with conventional marital loyalty and with marriage-career conflicts, respectively. *Nice People* (1921) treats the flapper era, *Mary the Third* (1923) the generation gap, and *Let Us be Gay* (1929) postwar divorce. *As Husbands Go* (1931), Crothers's example of sophisticated comedy, demonstrates that marriages can be kept together through mutual work and understanding. In *When Ladies Meet* (1932), she explored the ironies that result when a wife and a mistress leave a man simultaneously and in collusion. *Susan and God* (1937) depicts those women who pursue their own interests and causes at the expense of their families.

Crothers thought that women were especially important in the arts. In an early interview, she stated:

> Women are by far the stronger element in the development of drama because they are the prevailing part of the audience and therefore really largely decide what plays should be seen . . . [I]n general, women's taste in theatre is much wider than men's . . . [T]he majority of plays have for their central figure a woman—a study of her character, place, and influence in society. . . . [M]ost of the great modern plays are studies of women. I suppose it is because women in themselves are more dramatic than men, more changing, and a more significant note of the hour in which they live because of their own evolution. If you want to see the signs of the times, watch women. Their evolution is the most important thing in modern life. (*Boston Evening Transcript,* n.p.)

Crothers pioneered the pathway for the women playwrights who followed her, including Lillian Hellman, Corinne Jacker, Maureen Duffy, and especially Wendy Wasserstein.

See *Boston Evening Transcript,* February 14, 1912; *Chicago Tribune,* September 25, 1897; R. Crothers, "The Box in the Attic," unfinished typescript of autobiographical notes, 1953, Museum of the City of New York; J. K. Curry, "Rachel Crothers: An Exceptional

Woman in a Man's World," in *Staging Desire: Queer Readings of American Theater History,* edited by K. Marra and R. A. Schanke, Ann Arbor, 2002, 55–80; E. Flexner, *American Playwrights, 1918–1938,* New York, 1938; Z. C. Kaplan, "Woman in Focus in Major Plays and Productions of Rachel Crothers," Ph.D. diss., City University of New York, 1979; M. Lawrence, *The School of Femininity,* New York, 1936; J. Mersand, *When Ladies Write Plays,* New York, 1937; M. Moses, *The American Dramatist,* Boston, 1925; *Pantagraph* (Bloomington, Ill.), October 6, 1909; and P. M. Spacks, *The Female Imagination,* New York, 1975.

Zoe Coralnik Kaplan

CROWLEY, Mart (Edward Martino) (1935–), playwright, screenwriter, and producer, was not trying to break new ground when his groundbreaking play, *The Boys in the Band,* opened in 1968. "I was just getting a lot of resentment off my chest," he says (interview with the author, June 16, 1996), but before the play closed two years later the Stonewall Riots (1969) would mark the beginning of an era in which many gay people shed resentment and accepted their homosexuality.

Born in Vicksburg, Mississippi, on August 21, 1935, Crowley was the only child of Edward Joseph and Pauline Crowley. "Eddie" was the proprietor of Crowley's Smoke House, a billiard parlor and sports center for men, whose motto was "Where All Good Fellows Meet." An avid sports enthusiast, a staunch Irish Catholic, and an alcoholic, Eddie took Mart to the Sugar Bowl football game every year ("which I loathed," said Crowley) (Tallmer, n.p.). His mother, Pauline, was "not the normal housewife," being plagued by years of drug addiction and illness. "My mother and I were close when I was a child," Crowley has said. "The older I got, the closer I got to my father. I was spoiled rotten, but I had to take care of them until the end of their lives. I didn't have any childhood. I was the grown-up, they were the children" (interview with author).

Crowley escaped from an unhappy family life into the movies. The summer after his graduation from St. Aloysius High School in Vicksburg at the age of seventeen, he went to Los Angeles with a friend, whose aunt lived in Glendale. But instead of staying in Glendale he got a job washing dishes at the University of Southern California, rented his own apartment, and snuck onto film lots in his free time. He wanted to go to UCLA to study film, but when his father discovered that he was not living in Glendale and wanted to stay in Los Angeles he had his son meet him in Chicago and tried to convince him to attend Notre Dame. As a compromise, they agreed on the Catholic University of America in Washington, D.C., which had a notable drama department. Crowley was not the best student, and he spent his summers making up courses at Georgetown

Mart Crowley in about 1968, the year of the release of *The Boys in the Band.* (Courtesy of the Billy Rose Theatre Collection, New York Pubic Library for the Performing Arts.)

University and UCLA. At Catholic University, he decided to become a set designer and spent his weekends in New York City seeing plays. He graduated from Catholic University with a Bachelor of Arts in drama in 1957.

During a Christmas break from college in 1955, Crowley went home to Vicksburg. Nearby, in the Mississippi Delta, Elia Kazan was shooting *Baby Doll.* He had seen Kazan's production of *Cat on a Hot Tin Roof,* as well as other Broadway plays directed by Kazan, and hung around the set until he finally met the director, whom he called "my idol" (interview with the author). Kazan told Crowley to look him up in New York when he finished college, but it was the script supervisor from *Baby Doll,* Roberta Hodes, who got him his first job when he arrived in New York.

She was working on a remake of *The Last Mile,* and Crowley became a production assistant on the three-week project.

He then got production assistant jobs on *The Fugitive Kind* and *Butterfield 8* but left the latter midproduction to join Kazan, who was then preparing *Splendor in the Grass.* It was on the set of this film that he met Natalie Wood and eventually her husband, Robert Wagner. Crowley became friends with the couple (later he was the godfather of their two children), and when the film was completed Wood suggested that he join her in Los Angeles, where she could introduce him to agents while he worked as her personal assistant. Part of his job was to read the scripts and books sent to Wood for her consideration. When television's *Playhouse 90* producer Martin Manulis sent her a novel by Dorothy Baker called *Cassandra at the Wedding,* Crowley read the book and returned to Vicksburg to write the screenplay, which he sent to Manulis. Manulis, who loved the screenplay by this apparently unknown writer, sent it to Wood, who was equally enthusiastic. Twentieth Century Fox purchased *Cassandra* for Manulis in 1962. Crowley went to Rome that summer to visit Robert Wagner and stayed eight months before returning to Hollywood to work on *Cassandra.* The French director Serge Bourguignon had been hired to make the film, but at the last minute the project fell through (interview with author).

This disappointment was followed by a six-month stint with Four Star Television, where Crowley wrote scripts for Bette Davis, none of which were produced. When another movie fell through at Paramount Pictures, a dejected Crowley left for Mexico, where he "stayed drunk for awhile" (interview with the author, June 16, 1996). When he returned, Natalie Wood offered to pay for six months of psychoanalysis. "She thought I was in need of it, and I was. I was just very neurotic." Without a job, money, or prospects, Crowley sublet his apartment and accepted a housesitting offer from actress Diana Lynn in the summer of 1967, feeling "hysterical, washed up, and, in my mind, finished" (Raymond, 45–46). There, in a period of five weeks, he wrote *The Boys in the Band.*

After an initial rejection of the script by a New York agent, Richard Barr and **Edward Albee** presented a workshop production of *The Boys in the Band* in New York City, and its success encouraged Barr and Charles

Woodward to produce it Off-Broadway for a regular run. Directed by Robert Moore, it opened on April 14, 1968, at Theatre Four, received an enthusiastic critical and public response, and played for 1,001 performances. Clive Barnes, writing the opening night review for the *New York Times,* called it

> by far the frankest treatment of homosexuality I have ever seen on the stage. . . . [T]his is not a play about a homosexual, but a play that takes the homosexual milieu, and the homosexual way of life, totally for granted and uses this as a valid basis of human experience. . . . The power of the play . . . is the way in which it remorselessly peels away the pretensions of its characters and reveals a pessimism so uncompromising in its honesty that it becomes in itself an affirmation of life. (Barnes, 48)

Considered a breakthrough in American theater, the play presented for the first time gay characters who took their sexuality as a given rather than a secret to be revealed in the last act or a condition in need of a cure (Reed, B2).

The landmark play opened in London at the Wyndham Theatre on February 11, 1969, and was made into a film in 1970 with William Friedkin directing the original cast. A twenty-fifth anniversary production at the Fountain Theatre in Los Angeles sold out in 1993. By that time, five of the nine original "boys," as well as the director and both producers, had died of complications of HIV infection. Proceeds from the limited engagement in Los Angeles went to Equity Fights AIDS, with the cast, crew, and Crowley donating their talents ("A Tranquil Place"). In the same year, Crowley began planning a sequel to *The Boys in the Band,* entitled *The Men from the Boys* (Kramer, B9). "It wasn't until AIDS that I've begun to feel that maybe I have something else to say," he stated (Raymond, n.p.). In 1996, Crowley went to New York City to help prepare another major revival of the play, which opened at the WPA Theater on June 20 and once again sold out. In a retrospective interview, he said, "Among other things, I think this play is about the difficulty of coming out. And perhaps that was what I was doing, you see. It later occurred to me that I was not only announcing things to my family; I was announcing it to the world" (Dunlap, 28). In 1999, the American Theater Critics Association identified *The Boys in the Band* as one of the twenty-five most significant plays of the twentieth century.

Crowley's plays after *The Boys in the Band* were less successful. *Remote*

Asylum, starring William Shatner, was produced at the Ahamson Theatre in Los Angeles in 1970. *A Breeze from the Gulf,* starring Ruth Ford, was produced at the Eastside Playhouse in New York City in 1973 and ran for only six weeks despite favorable reviews.

Disappointment from the failure of these two plays sent a depressed Crowley to the South of France. "For almost two years I didn't do much except drink white wine and stare out to sea . . . ." But at a meeting with Robert Wagner and Natalie Wood in Paris he was persuaded to return to Hollywood to help Wagner with his new television series, *Hart to Hart.* He began rewriting scripts for Wagner and became the producer of the series for ABC in 1979 (Franklin, 29).

In 1984, he wrote *The Spirit of It All,* which was presented at the Williamstown Theatre Festival and starred Marsha Mason. It was subsequently substantially rewritten and retitled *Avec Schmalz.* He adapted James Kirkwood's *There Must Be a Pony,* which was produced by ABC in 1986, starring Elizabeth Taylor, Robert Wagner, and James Coco. Other adaptations for television include Dominick Dunne's *People Like Us* as an NBC miniseries, and Barbara Taylor Bradford's *Remember,* a CBS miniseries.

In 1993, he wrote the play *For Reasons That Remain Unclear,* which was produced by the Olney Theater in Olney, Maryland (Crowley had spent some of his summers during college as an intern at this theater, which is located just outside Washington, D.C.). It is included in *Three Plays by Mart Crowley,* where, in an introduction, Crowley writes, "To more than a considerable extent, with the works and with the laughs, has come a release from the unhappiness and the resentment" (Crowley, x). He lives in Los Angeles. In 2002, Simon and Schuster announced that he would finish the work of his friend, the late Kay Thompson, on her children's book *Eloise Takes a Bawth,* the last in a sequence of *Eloise* books.

See *Contemporary American Dramatists,* New York, 1994 (with an erroneous item about Crowley's death in 1991); C. Barnes, *"The Boys in the Band,"* New York Times, April 15, 1968; B. Beyette, "A Tranquil Place Where Work Is Far from the Pits," *Los Angeles Times,* May 6, 1993; M. Crowley, *Three Plays by Mart Crowley,* Los Angeles, 1996; D. W. Dunlap, "In a Revival, Echoes of a Gay War of Words," *New York Times,* June 9, 1996; W. Franklin, "A 'Hart to Hart' Chat with Mart Crowley," *The Advocate,* September 18, 1980; R. Kramer, "A Play of Words about a Play," *New York Times,* October 31, 1993; G. Raymond, "Return of the One-Man *Band,"* Out Magazine, June 1996; R. Reed, "Breakthrough by 'The Boys' in the Band," *New York Times,* May 12, 1968; J. Tallmer, "Artist in Residence," *New York Post,* June 27, 1968; and *Who's Who In the Theatre,* 17th ed., Detroit, 1981.

Jon Fraser

CUKOR, George Dewey (1899–1983), film and theater director, was born in New York City, the son of Victor and Helen (Gross) Cukor, Hungarian Jews. In 1917, he joined the Army Training Corps and after the war endured a period of unemployment until he was hired as the assistant stage manager of a Chicago production of *The Better 'Ole.* After some minor theatrical experiences in Toronto in 1920, Cukor organized a stock company for the Lyceum Theatre in Rochester, New York. Following seven years running the Lyceum company, he found his way back to New York City as manager of the Empire Theatre. Here he had the opportunity to supervise productions featuring Jeanne Eagels, Laurette Taylor, and Ethel Barrymore, thus developing his skills in dealing with star actresses. This ability would serve him well in Hollywood.

In 1929, following Hollywood's transition to sound, Cukor was hired as dialogue coach for *River of Romance* (based on Booth Tarkington's play *Magnolia*) and *All Quiet on the Western Front* (1930) before he was given the opportunity to direct *One Hour with You* (1930). He proved to be too inexperienced, so the film's producer, Ernst Lubitsch, took over the direction and reshot most of what Cukor had done. After a few other films, including *The Royal Family of Broadway,* based on the George S. Kaufman and Edna Ferber play, he scored a minor success with *Tarnished Lady* (1931), starring **Tallulah Bankhead.** In 1932, he moved from Paramount to RKO, where he immediately scored successes with *What Price Hollywood?* and *A Bill of Divorcement.* The latter featured John Barrymore and was the screen debut of Katharine Hepburn, who would work with Cukor on nine subsequent movies.

Cukor's homosexuality was well known in Hollywood circles, but it was never publicized during the golden years of his career, roughly between 1932 and 1955. Many of his contemporaries credited him with "performing a vital function in the annals of Hollywood's gay life" (Levy, 49) in that he created a civilized gay society. However, with moral turpitude clauses in studio contracts in that era, he was extremely vulnerable and realized the necessity of disguise. His discretion seems to have resulted from his arrest as part of actor William Haines's gay entourage in Hollywood at the beginning of his career, although the incident was hushed up at the time. Nonetheless, Cukor was never dishonest about his sexuality. When one studio mogul asked him if he was, in fact, a homosexual, he answered, "Dedicated."

Following *A Bill of Divorcement,* Cukor forged a reputation for himself as a director of "prestige" films who was adept at getting outstanding performances from leading ladies. *Dinner at Eight* (1933), based on Kaufman and Ferber's play, was his first runaway hit as a director and his first film at MGM, where he worked frequently for the remainder of his career. With *Little Women* (1933), starring Hepburn, he established himself as the premiere director of literary adaptations. *Little Women* was followed by *David Copperfield* (1935), a David O. Selznick production.

The success of *David Copperfield* was followed by the greatest failure of Cukor's career, despite the fact that it was his favorite film: *Sylvia Scarlett,* starring Hepburn and Cary Grant, in 1936. Unsophisticated audiences were shocked by the sexual ambiguity of Hepburn's character, a young woman who "passes" as a man for much of the picture.

The failure of *Sylvia Scarlett* did not significantly harm the careers of Cukor, Hepburn, or Grant, and this threesome would work together again on *Holiday* (1938) and *The Philadelphia Story* (1940). Cukor filled out the decade of the 1930s directing *Romeo and Juliet* (1936), *Camille* (1937), *Free to Live* (1938), *Unconventional Linda* (1938), *Zaza* (1939), *The Women* (1939), and *Susan and God* (1940), among others.

In 1938–39, Cukor spent almost a year preparing the epic *Gone with the Wind* (1939), but when star Clark Gable expressed to producer David O. Selznick his discomfort with a "woman's director," Cukor was removed from the picture and replaced with Victor Fleming. Despite this setback, Cukor continued for nearly three decades as one of Hollywood's most distinguished directors. Among his later films were such memorable features as *A Woman's Face* (1941), *Gaslight* (1944), *A Double Life* (1947), *Adam's Rib* (1949), *Born Yesterday* (1950), *Pat and Mike* (1952), and the Judy Garland remake of *A Star Is Born* (1954), which numerous critics have dubbed his "flawed masterpiece." Few of his later projects matched the critical or commercial success of many of his earlier works, although *My Fair Lady* (1964), based on the stage musical, was an exception.

Homosexual issues rarely surfaced in obvious ways in Cukor's movies, largely due to his discretion. However, in the post-Stonewall era, he "became really open about his homosexuality" (Levy, 150), although by then his career was slowing down. The importance of Cukor's sexuality to his work is difficult to assess, but as one biographer notes, homosexuality was not "the be-all and end-all of his life, but a significant impulse, and a window offering fresh light on him and his career" (McGilligan, 349).

See J. Bernardoni, *George Cukor: A Critical Study and Filmography,* Jefferson, N.C., 1985; G. Carey, *Cukor and Co.,* New York, 1971; R. Flamini, *Scarlett, Rhett, and a Cast of Thousands,* New York, 1975; P. B. Flint, "George Cukor, 83, Film Director, Dies," *New York Times,* January 26, 1983; R. Haver, *A Star Is Born: The Making of the 1954 Movie and*

Its 1983 Restoration, New York, 1988; G. Lambert, The Making of Gone with the Wind, Boston, 1973; G. Lambert, On Cukor, New York, 1972; E. Levy, George Cukor, Master of Elegance, New York, 1994; R. E. Long, George Cukor: Interviews, Jackson, Miss., 2001; W. Mann, Behind the Screen: How Gays and Lesbians Shaped Hollywood, 1910–1969, New York, 2001; P. McGilligan, George Cukor: A Double Life, New York, 1991; R. V. Tozzi, "George Cukor," Films in Review, February 1958; and K. Tynan, "George Cukor," Holiday, February 1961.

James Fisher

CUNNINGHAM, Merce (1919–), dancer and choreographer, was born in Centralia, Washington. In the late 1930s, he attended the Cornish School (now Cornish College of the Arts) in Seattle, where he began studying dance with Bonnie Bird. He left Cornish in 1939 to join the Martha Graham Dance Company (Cohen-Stratyner, 218).

Cunningham's experiences at Cornish were especially significant in the development of his aesthetic; there he began seriously studying modern dance technique, and in 1938 he met **John Cage,** a composer and accompanist for Bird's dance classes (Snyder, 37). A few years later, Cunningham and Cage became lifelong partners and collaborators, changing the face of modern dance by insisting that the music and the dance did not necessarily have to go together: sounds and physical movements exist independently and should be appreciated for their own sakes (Klosty, 11). Cunningham has listed Cage among the artists to whom he feels "close in spirit" (Cunningham, 1968, n.p.).

Cunningham has been one of the most influential innovators in the world of modern dance, "chang[ing] the way people dance and the way people see dancing in the same way that Picasso and the cubists changed the way people painted and the way people saw painting" (Dalva, 179). In 1953, Cunningham formed the Merce Cunningham Dance Company (Cohen-Stratyner, 218). During this time, he worked with various artists, including composers David Tudor and Christian Wolff, and painters Robert Rauschenberg and Jasper Johns. At various stages, the company included dancers Remy Charlip, Carolyn Brown, Viola Farber, Valda Setterfield, and Chris Komar (Klosty, 11–17). Cage was the company's musical director until 1968 (Brown, 19) and served as its musical adviser until his death in 1992.

Cunningham developed a choreographic technique using chance procedures. The first Cunningham composition that utilized the chance technique was Sixteen Dances for Soloist and Company of Three (1951). He tossed pennies in order to determine the order of solos, duets, and quartets. Later, in 1953, he made *Suite by Chance,* using chance methods to determine as many elements as possible in the dance (Klosty, 12–13). In *Dime a Dance* (1953), the audience played a significant role in the way the performance was organized, as Cunningham began to experiment with "open form." When the piece was first performed, audience members paid a dime to pick cards from a deck, thus determining the sequence of the performance's events (13).

Cunningham developed techniques that focused on bodily movements independent from the constraints placed on bodies by the rhythms and forms of music. For the most part, during the 1950s and 1960s dance critics and audiences failed to appreciate Cunningham's "nonnarrative dancing" techniques. Photographer James Klosty described the reception of Cunningham's early work, observing that "the whitest of 'white' ballets was still about music in some sense, still about the great ongoing affair between dancer and orchestra or dancer and piano. . . . But the music at Cunningham performances was new and usually experimental. It was difficult to listen to" (12). Cunningham's works in the 1950s and 1960s included *Fragments* (1953), *Galaxy* (1956), *Nocturnes* (1956), *Aeon* (1961), *How to Pass, Kick, Fall, and Run* (1965), and *Rain Forest* (1968) (Vaughan, 218–22).

Cunningham has also staged Events, which consist of sections of previously choreographed dances and dances still in rehearsal that are rearranged into a new sequence. The first Event took place in 1964 in Vienna. The Company has performed more than 500 Events, each usually lasting about ninety minutes, with no intermission. The Cunningham repertoire and the infinite number of possible arrangements ensure the uniqueness of each Event (Anderson, 95). In addition, Events have been performed in a variety of nontraditional spaces such as gymnasiums, museums, and lofts (96). Cunningham has claimed that Events "'allow for, not so much an evening of dances, as the experience of dance'" (qtd. in Anderson, 95).

For most of his career, Cunningham has attempted to reconcile individuality and community. He has said that his choreography "'deal[s] with a different idea about how people can exist together. How you can get along in life, so to speak, and do what you need to do, and at the same time not kick somebody else down in order to do it'" (qtd. in Shetley, 73). His work reveals a sense of disenchantment with the modern and postmodern worlds, but at the same time it celebrates a "vision of human possibility" (73).

In the 1970s, Cunningham began experimenting with video and took some time off from working with the company to produce *Un jour ou deux*

(1973) for the Paris Opera Ballet (Brown, 31; Vaughan, 222). He returned to New York and choreographed numerous dances for his own company, including works for video, such as *Westbeth* (1974), *Video Triangle* (1976), part of *Event for Television,* and *Fractions* (1977) (Vaughan, 222–23).

Cunningham worked steadily throughout the 1980s, and the company continues to perform its dance pieces around the world. He explored the contrasts between age and youth in *Quartet* (1982) and *Pictures* (1984) and has continued to choreograph dances about support and community (Dalva, 183). His interest in technology has also continued: he has used computer software to create dances (Young, F7).

John Cage died in 1992 after suffering a stroke while he was preparing evening tea for himself and Cunningham (Kostelanetz, "Second Preface," xvii). Some critics have faulted Cage and Cunningham for their refusal to speak publicly about their personal relationship, arguing that, at least to a certain degree, they were closeted (Gill, 31–32). However, even though they never spoke publicly about their homosexuality, the two lived openly together as lovers. *Architectural Digest* visited the couple's New York loft in 1988, noting that they had begun "sharing their lives" after Cage's separation from his wife in the early 1940s (Gruen, 272). Those who have worked with Cunningham often describe him as an intensely private person uncomfortable with public attention. Carolyn Brown, a dancer who spent over twenty years with the Cunningham Dance Company, has written that his need for "seclusion" is so overwhelming that he refuses "to reveal any more about himself than that which he willingly offers. One must always meet him on *his* terms; anything else is an encroachment on his territorial rights to privacy" (19). Cage and Cunningham exhibited a commitment to each other in both their public and private lives. As Jill Johnston, former dance critic for the *Village Voice* has argued, Cunningham without Cage "would be like the Bible without God" (Kostelanetz, "Twenty Years," 15).

See J. Anderson, "Dances about Everything and Dances about Some Things," in *Merce Cunningham: Dancing in Space and Time,* edited by R. Kostelanetz, Chicago, 1992, 95–100; C. Brown, untitled essay in *Merce Cunningham,* edited by J. Klosty, New York, 1975, 19–31; B. N. Cohen-Stratyner, "Cunningham, Merce," in *Biographical Dictionary of Dance,* New York, 1982, 218–20; R. Copeland, "Dancing for the Digital Age: Merce Cunningham's 'Biped,'" in *Society of Dance History Scholars: Conference Proceedings,* edited by the Society of Dance History Scholars, Baltimore, 2001, 23–28; R. Copeland, "Ballet, Modern Dance, and Modernity," *Dance Theatre Journal* 16, no. 2 (2000): 42–47; R. Copeland, "Dancing for the Electronic Age: Merce Cunningham and the Contemporary Technology," *Carion* 5 (1999): 7–20; M. Cunningham and J. Lesschaeve, *The Dancer and the Dance,* London, 1999; M. Cunningham, in *Changes: Notes on Choreography,* edited by F. Starr, New York, 1968; N. Dalva, "The Way of Merce," in *Merce Cunningham: Dancing in Space and*

Time, edited by R. Kostelanetz, Chicago, 1992, 179–86; E. Farnsworth, "A Conversation with Merce Cunningham," *Ballet Review* 27, no. 4 (winter 1999): 21–23; W. Fetterman, "Merce Cunningham and John Cage: Choreographic Cross-Currents," *Choreography and Dance* 4, no. 3 (1997): 59–78; J. Gill, *Queer Noises: Male and Female Homosexuality in Twentieth-Century Music,* Minneapolis, 1995; R. Greskovic, "Merce Cunningham," in *Fifty Contemporary Choreographers,* edited by M. Bremser, London, 1999, 72–77; J. Gruen, "*Architectural Digest* Visits John Cage and Merce Cunningham," *Architectural Digest,* November 1988; J. Klosty, introduction to *Merce Cunningham,* edited by J. Klosty, New York, 1975, 11–17; H. Koegler, "Lifelong Companions," *Neue Zeitschrift für Musik* 155, no. 5 (September 1994): 29–31; R. Kostelanetz, "Second Preface," in *John Cage, Writer: Previously Uncollected Pieces,* edited by R. Kostelanetz, New York, 1993, xvii–xviii; R. Kostelanetz, "Twenty Years of Merce Cunningham's Dance," in *Merce Cunningham: Dancing in Space and Time,* edited by R. Kostelanetz, Chicago, 1992, 15–20; L. Kuhn, "Cunningham + Cage," *Ballet Review* 26, no. 3 (fall 1998): 80–98; J. Mackrell, "The Variety Is Endless," *Dance Now* 7, no. 1 (spring 1998): 3–8; V. Rimmer, "Collaborations between Dance and Technology as a History of the Present," in *Society of Dance History Scholars: Conference Proceedings,* edited by the Society for Dance History Scholars, Baltimore, 2001, 111–15; V. Shetley, "Merce Cunningham," *Raritan* 8, no. 3 (winter 1989): 72–90; E. J. Snyder, "Chronological Table of John Cage's Life," in *John Cage,* edited by R. Kostelanetz, New York, 1970, 36–41; D. Vaughan, *Merce Cunningham: Creative Elements,* Amsterdam, 1997; D. Vaughan, "Chronology of Works by Merce Cunningham," in *Merce Cunningham: Dancing in Space and Time,* edited by R. Kostelanetz, Chicago, 1992, 214–27; D. Vaughan and M. Harris, *Merce Cunningham: Fifty Years,* New York, 1997; A. Wesemann, "Merce Cunningham," *Ballet International,* November 2001, 8–9; and J. Young, "Tuning into His Influence," *Austin American-Statesman,* February 2, 1996.

Krista L. May

CUSHMAN, Charlotte Saunders

CUSHMAN, Charlotte Saunders (1816–76), actress, was born on July 23, 1816, in Boston. She grew up a self-described tomboy in a middle-class merchant family. The family struggled financially during her late adolescence and was supported primarily by her mother, Mary Eliza, who took in boarders. Through the aid of family and friends, Cushman was trained as a singer and attracted the attention of James Maeder, the musical director of the Tremont Theater. She began her artistic career at the age of nineteen as the Countess Almaviva in a performance of Mozart's *Marriage of Figaro* in Boston. Maeder then invited her to sing with his wife, Clara Fisher, in New Orleans. However, that early operatic engagement proved disastrous for Cushman, ending her professional singing career, for her ability proved unequal to its supposed potential. On the advice of James Caldwell, the manager of New Orleans' St. Charles Theater, Cushman turned to acting. Her first performance was as Lady Macbeth on April 23, 1836. Highly regarded in this initial run, the role remained one of her most commended throughout her career.

Cushman's early success led to various engagements in New York and

Albany, and she eventually secured a contract as a stock actress at the Park Theater in New York City. By then, she had taken over financial responsibility for her mother, sister, and brothers, her father having receded from the family picture. In 1837, she first performed what became one of her most popular roles, that of Meg Merrilies in an adaptation of Sir Walter Scott's *Guy Mannering.* Her depiction of the haggard old gypsy woman never failed to excite audiences. In 1839, she added Nancy Sykes (from *Oliver Twist*) to her list of famous roles. She excelled at strong, complex character parts and avoided the role of ingenue. A large, robust woman with a rich, resonant voice, she had a commanding presence. She once confided to a friend: "I long to play a woman of strong ambition, who is at the same time very wily and diplomatic, and who has an opportunity of a great outburst when her plans are successful—in short, a female Richelieu" (Marston, 77). Not finding suitable artistic challenges in female characters, Cushman turned to the first of many male roles, Romeo in Shakespeare's *Romeo and Juliet,* in 1837. In all, she would play nearly forty different male characters, including Hamlet and Cardinal Wolsey, though her portrayal of Romeo would elicit the most extensive praise. Acclaimed throughout her career for the sensuality of her Romeo, it is not difficult to conjecture that her sexuality contributed to her success in portraying the desiring subject opposite various actresses.

Early in her career, Cushman met Rosalie Sully, and the two became intimate friends, often exchanging material tokens of affection. However, Cushman's profession took precedence over personal matters, and after a turn as manager of Philadelphia's Walnut Street Theater in 1842–43 her talent brought her to the attention of William Macready, who suggested that she go to England to improve her skills. During the voyage to England, Cushman wrote of Sully often in her diary, including a passage that describes her as "thinking of dear Rose for more than an hour, speaking to her,—calling on her in the most endearing manner and hoping for an answer—I only saw her lips move to kiss me! and almost sprang up from my berth at the fair thought of my usual reply to that sweet Expression from her" (November 14, 1844). Sully died before Cushman's triumphant return to the United States, but by then another young woman had taken her place in her affections. The poet Eliza Cook met Cushman while she was taking London by storm, performing Meg Merrilies, Bianca in *Fazio,* and Romeo opposite her sister Susan's Juliet. An adoring fan, Cook wrote poems to Cushman, praising her acting and declaring undying love.

While in England, Cushman's performance of Romeo at London's Haymarket Theater, more than any other role she played, sealed her fame.

The London critics were ecstatic. The playwright James Sheridan Knowles called it "a triumph of pure genius" (228). Cushman was complimented for her masculine appearance and christened the best Romeo London had seen in years. With no real professional training, she had become the first great tragedienne of the United States, introducing a more natural, energetic style of acting than had previously been known to nineteenth-century audiences. She quickly became the toast of London and was sought out by high society. Her talent brought financial security, as well as the apparently welcome duty of supporting family and friends. In 1849, she returned to New York a celebrated actress with two new characters in her repertoire: Queen Katharine in Shakespeare's *Henry VIII* and Claude Melnotte in *The Lady of Lyons.*

Just before her return, Cushman met Matilda Hays, who was five years her junior. Hays was a novice seeking the coaching of an established actress and played the female leads to Cushman's male roles. She also became Cushman's intimate companion, causing a considerable stir among Cushman's other friends and acquaintances. Elizabeth Barrett Browning was dismayed at their Boston marriage. Hays remained with Cushman for nearly seven years, but the demands she placed on Cushman's time and energy severely strained their relationship. Ultimately, Hays left Cushman, who by then had retired to Rome, and returned to England.

Actually, Cushman ended her career several times. Her first farewell performance came in 1852, at the age of thirty-six, after which she established a salon of sorts for female artists in Rome. Women such as Harriet Hosmer, Margaret Foley, Sara Jane Clarke, Kate Field, Florence Freeman, Edmonia Lewis, Anne Whitney, and Anne Brewster all benefited from Cushman's support. However, financial misappropriation by her business manager forced her return to the stage in 1857. While still in Rome, at the age of forty, Cushman met the woman who would become her devoted life companion, the forty-year-old sculptress Emma Stebbins. In *Charlotte Cushman: Her Letters and Memories of Her Life,* Stebbins chronicles their first meeting: "It was in the winter of 1856–57 that the compiler of these memoirs first made Miss Cushman's acquaintance, and from that time the current of their two lives ran, with rare exceptions, side by side" (100). They lived together for the last twenty years of Cushman's life. In a letter to members of her family, Cushman wrote of Stebbins: "I love her very much, she is the finest nature I have ever been thrown in contact with, the very truest and dearest of human beings and I want you both to love her" (Charlotte Cushman Papers, I, 298). Cushman's talent allowed her to amass a sufficient fortune for a second retirement, again to Rome and England, in 1858. She came to the stage once more in 1860, as the Civil War began, and made brief appearances in 1863, accompanied always by Stebbins. The two returned to the United States for good in the fall of 1870 and established a residence in Cushman's native Boston, with a large summer house in fashionable Newport.

Less than a year after meeting Stebbins, Cushman made the acquaintance of another woman who would remain a part of her life. Emma Crow was nineteen when Cushman visited St. Louis, seeking the financial advice of the young woman's father, Wyman Crow. Emma became infatuated, and the voluminous letters Cushman wrote to her reveal a passionate and frankly sensual attraction between the two. Although Stebbins remained Cushman's life partner, Crow enjoyed a privileged position in her affections. This triangle was further complicated in 1860, when Crow married Cushman's adopted son, Edwin Charles Cushman, or Ned (Cushman had adopted her sister Susan's child because Susan's second husband refused to raise a child by her previous marriage). Ned was not an advantageous match. He was immature, with few prospects for success. Letters reveal that Cushman only planned the match between Crow and Ned so that the two women could maintain a close relationship. These letters also reveal jealousies between Crow and Stebbins, which Cushman skillfully navigated and forestalled, carefully managing them just as she did her career and reputation.

Despite Cushman's multiple and obviously intimate relationships with women, her sense of propriety prevented any suspicion of scandal in her own life. She was highly regarded, both by those in the theater and by those outside it. Her friends included Macready and Fanny Kemble, and she acted with the best and brightest talents that England and the United States had to offer, including **Edwin Forrest** and Edwin Booth. At home in Boston, Philadelphia, and New York, she socialized with the likes of Henry Wadsworth Longfellow and counted William Henry Seward, the secretary of state under Abraham Lincoln, as a trusted friend and adviser. During her initial London triumph, she made lasting friendships with the Carlyles and Brownings, and she enjoyed the acquaintance of women writers such as Julia Ward Howe and Geraldine Jewsbury.

Cushman was diagnosed with breast cancer in 1869, and, although an operation that year removed most of the tumor, she remained weak and in almost constant pain. While work was her greatest contentment, in her later years she increasingly performed less demanding oral readings. During the 1874–75 season, she gave several emotional farewell performances to wildly enthusiastic and adoring crowds on the East Coast. When she last walked onto the stage on May 15, 1875, at Boston's Globe

Theater, where she played Lady Macbeth, her career had come full circle. Her final performance was a reading in Easton, Pennsylvania, the following month. Charlotte Cushman died on February 18, 1876. Her obituary notice in the *New York Tribune,* written by William Winter, attests to her reputation. He writes: "The greatness of Charlotte Cushman was that of an exceptional, because grand and striking personality, combined with extraordinary power to embody the highest ideals of majesty, pathos, and appalling anguish. She was not a great actress merely, but she was a great woman" (qtd. in Stebbins, 295). Cushman's memory faded into obscurity after her death, partially because a stigmatized lesbian identity became attached to women in society who followed her example and cultivated independent lives and careers that included female companionship.

See L. Barrett, *Charlotte Cushman: A Lecture,* New York, 1889; S .S. Cole, "Charlotte Cushman," in *Notable Women in the American Theater: A Biographical Dictionary,* edited by A. M. Robinson, V. Mowry Roberts, and M. S. Barranger, New York, 1989, 185–88; C. Cushman, Diary of 1844–45, Rare Books and Manuscripts Division, Butler Library, Columbia University, New York; Charlotte Cushman Papers, Manuscript Division, Library of Congress, Washington, D.C.; C. E. Clement, *Charlotte Cushman,* Boston, 1882; F. E. Dudden, *Women in the American Theater: Actresses and Audiences, 1790–1870,* New Haven; James T. and Annie Fields Collection, Huntington Library, San Marino, CA; Folger Shakespeare Library, Washington, D.C.; Theatre Collection, Harvard University Library, Cambridge; Hoblitzelle Theatre Collection, University of Texas, Austin; J. S. Knowles, "Things Theatrical," *Spirit of the Times,* July 4, 1846, 228; J. Leach, *Bright Particular Star: The Life and Times of Charlotte Cushman,* New Haven, 1970; J. Markus, *Across an Untried Sea: Discovering Lives Hidden in the Shadow of Convention and Time,* New York, 2000; W. Marston, *Our Recent Actors,* vol. 2, Boston, 1888; L. Merrill, *When Romeo Was a Woman: Charlotte Cushman and Her Circle of Female Spectators,* Ann Arbor, 1999; E. R. Mullenix, "Acting between the Spheres: Charlotte Cushman as Androgyne," *Theatre Survey* 37, no. 2 (1996): 22–65; S. F. Parrott, "Networking in Italy: Charlotte Cushman and 'The White Marmorean Flock,'" *Women's Studies* 14 (1988): 305–38; Robinson Locke Scrapbooks, New York Public Library, New York; Seward-Cushman Correspondence, University of Rochester Library, Rochester, New York; E. Stebbins, *Charlotte Cushman: Her Letters and Memories of Her Life,* Boston, 1878; and D. Walen, "'Such a Romeo as We Had Never Ventured to Hope For': Charlotte Cushman," in *Passing Performances: Queer Readings of Leading Players in American Theater History,* edited by R. A. Schanke and K. Marra, Ann Arbor, 1998, 41–62.

Denise A. Walen

de ACOSTA, Mercedes (1893–1968), playwright, poet, novelist, and screenwriter, was born in New York City. In her lifetime, she published three volumes of poetry—*Moods* (1919), *Archways of Life* (1921), and *Streets and Shadows* (1922); two novels—*Wind Chaff* (1920) and *Until the Day Break* (1928); and two plays—*For France* (1917) and *Sandro Botticelli* (1923). She wrote ten additional plays, but even though two of these—

Jacob Slovak and *Jehanne d'Arc*—received professional productions, none was published until Robert A. Schanke's *Women in Turmoil: Six Plays by Mercedes de Acosta* appeared in 2003. She completed two film scripts—*East River* (1931) for Pola Negri and *Desperate* (1932) for Greta Garbo; they were not produced and remain unpublished.

Until the age of seven, de Acosta was convinced that she was a boy. Her mother called her "Rafael," dressed her in Eton suits, and encouraged her to play boys' games. When she was sent to a convent school to learn "feminine ways," she befriended two lesbian nuns and stood guard in the corridors while they stole some privacy.

When de Acosta was about twenty years old, **Elisabeth Marbury,** a theatrical producer and the doyenne of Sapphic Broadway, assumed the role of matchmaker and introduced her to several available women. One was the dancer **Isadora Duncan.** Another was the exotic and sensual Russian actress **Alla Nazimova.** In *Moods,* her first book of poems, de Acosta explores her mysterious desire for women. She became notorious for walking the streets of New York in mannish pants, pointed shoes trimmed with buckles, tricorn hat, and cape. Her pale white face, thin red lips, and jet black hair slicked back with brilliantine prompted **Tallulah Bankhead** to call her Countess Dracula.

In spite of the confusion she was feeling over her same-sex romances, in 1920, to please her mother and maintain at least a semblance of propriety, she married Abram Poole, a handsome and wealthy portrait painter who had studied in France and Germany. That same year she published her first novel, *Wind Chaff,* the story of a young girl who struggles with her sexual identity. Certainly adding to de Acosta's personal torment was meeting the young, attractive, and ambitious actress **Eva Le Gallienne.** Because de Acosta was married, their five-year relationship was hidden and very discreet. In two more books of poetry, *Archways of Life* (1921) and *Streets and Shadows* (1922), de Acosta reveals the private thoughts and anxieties she was experiencing. Perhaps because she was a closeted woman living in shadows and feeling marginalized, she had an overwhelming yearning to commit to a woman.

Instead she began writing plays for Le Gallienne. The first, *Sandro Botticelli* (1923), focuses on Simonetta Vespuci, who is beloved by all of Florence but has remained chaste and aloof to all men until she meets the handsome Botticelli. When he rejects her, the enraged Simonetta runs from his art studio into the pouring rain, becomes ill, and dies. Ironically, a likeness of Botticelli's painting *The Birth of Venus,* which was used in the final scene of the play, was painted by de Acosta's husband. The play closed after twenty-four performances at the Provincetown Playhouse.

De Acosta next wrote *The Mother of Christ* and *Jehanne d'Arc*. Her personal life informed her portrayal of Joan—the character in the play begs to be saved from an arranged marriage and is ridiculed for wearing men's clothing. Voices in a crowd scene accuse her of trying to be a man and call her a sexless woman. At one point, Joan explains: "We are each one of us chained to something. Each one of us in a different way. I have my battles too" (*Jehanne* manuscript, M. de Acosta Collection). American newspapers from coast to coast announced the play's 1925 opening in Paris, and *Theatre Magazine* ran photos of the sets along with detailed descriptions. The critics, however, were appalled by the dazzling scenery and lighting, which overwhelmed the script. Plans for London and Broadway productions were quickly dropped. As de Acosta and Le Gallienne sailed back to New York, they were aware that both their public and private partnerships were finished.

De Acosta quickly turned to a play she had been writing for several years, *Jacob Slovak*. Like her earlier work, her own life experiences served as fuel for the story of a young Jewish man who encounters prejudice. Just ten days after a successful Off-Broadway tryout in 1927, the Shubert Brothers changed the title and moved the production to a Broadway house. But, when they were threatened with a lawsuit by another author who claimed the new title—*Conflict*—was his, they closed the production. The next year it was revived in London, with John Gielgud and Ralph Richardson starring in their first production together. Although reviews were consistently favorable, audiences questioned the play's relevance. They would not admit, just a few years before the Holocaust, that persecution of Jews existed.

When de Acosta returned to New York, she continued writing. Her novel *Until the Day Break* centers on a married woman, like herself, who is confused about her sexual longings: "It's something in me, something struggling for expression that I don't understand" (de Acosta, *Until the Day Break,* 24). And, like de Acosta, the main character rejects a life of domesticity, leaves her husband, and embarks on a career in the theater.

Although de Acosta showed great promise as a writer in the early 1920s, the temper of the times had changed. During the latter part of the decade, a public reaction set in against licentiousness. Outrage against portrayals of lesbianism in the Broadway production of *The Captive* (1926) and in Radclyffe Hall's *The Well of Loneliness* (1928) convinced de Acosta that she could never write so openly again. The prevailing homophobia silenced her; her publishing days were over.

Hoping to find a community more accepting of her sexuality, de Acosta moved to Hollywood, where she began a lifelong infatuation with Greta Garbo. They vacationed, sunbathed in the nude, and even lived together for a short time. But it was an unpredictable and stormy relationship. After a film script she wrote for Garbo—*Desperate* (1932)—was rejected because the glamorous actress would have been seen wearing pants for over half the film, de Acosta's life and career became a series of disappointments and rejections. A passionate affair with **Marlene Dietrich** ended suddenly when the actress decided to marry. In 1935, de Acosta's husband of fifteen years sued for divorce. She fell in love with **Ona Munson,** the actress who played Belle Watling in *Gone with the Wind,* but their affair lasted only a year. Later she managed a six-year relationship with Poppy Kirk, the daughter of a Philadelphia diplomat. But since Poppy was married their affair was clandestine, and Poppy eventually decided to live permanently with her husband.

Throughout the 1940s, 1950s, and 1960s, de Acosta's health deteriorated. She suffered a nervous breakdown, fell into a severe state of depression, and contemplated suicide. Her major undertaking was an autobiography, *Here Lies the Heart,* which finally appeared in 1960. Although she discusses all her female friends with only veiled reference to their sexual orientation, readers were often outraged by the implications. Because royalties from the book were meager, she was forced to sell her family jewels and move into a tiny, two-room apartment in New York City. Old lovers such as Marlene Dietrich lent her money. Her only visitors in the end were "Les Girls," young women hoping they would be introduced to Garbo. When he learned of her death, Cecil Beaton wrote in his diary: "I am . . . sorry that she should have been so unfulfilled as a character. In her youth she showed zest and originality. She was one of the most rebellious and brazen of Lesbians" (qtd. in Vickers, 281).

See M. de Acosta, *Moods,* New York, 1919; M. de Acosta, *Wind Chaff,* New York, 1920; M. de Acosta, *Archways of Life,* New York, 1921; M. de Acosta, *Streets and Shadows,* New York, 1922; M. de Acosta, *Until the Day Break,* New York, 1928; M. de Acosta, *Here Lies the Heart,* New York, 1960; M. de Acosta Collection, Rosenbach Museum and Library, Philadelphia; R. A. Schanke, *Eva Le Gallienne: A Bio-Bibliography,* Westport, Conn., 1989; R. A. Schanke, "Say What You Will about Mercedes de Acosta," in *Staging Desire: Queer Readings of American Theater History,* edited by K. Marra and R. A. Schanke, Ann Arbor, 2002, 81–104; R. A. Schanke, *Shattered Applause: The Lives of Eva Le Gallienne,* Carbondale, Ill., 1992; R. A. Schanke, *"That Furious Lesbian": The Story of Mercedes de Acosta,* Carbondale, Ill., 2003; R. A. Schanke, *Women in Turmoil: Six Plays by Mercedes de Acosta,* Carbondale, Ill., 2003; and H. Vickers, *Loving Garbo: The Story of Greta Garbo, Cecil Beaton, and Mercedes de Acosta,* New York, 1994.

Robert A. Schanke

DEAN, James Byron (1931–55), actor, was born in Fairmount, Indiana, on February 8, 1931, and died in a car accident on the way to a racing event in California on September 29, 1955. At the time of his death at the age of twenty-four, he had performed two major roles on Broadway, acted in several television dramas, and performed leading roles in three major motion pictures.

In New York, he performed in N. Richard Nash's *See the Jaguar* (1952) and Augustus Goetz's adaptation of André Gide's novel *The Immoralist* (1954), while also working regularly in live television drama. In Hollywood, he filmed *East of Eden* (1955), *Rebel without a Cause* (1955), and *Giant* (1956). Only *East of Eden* reached release before his death.

Dean grew up in Fairmount with his aunt and uncle, Ortense and Marcus Winslow, with whom he was sent to live after the death of his mother, Mildred, in 1940. He discovered acting through Adeline Nall, the drama teacher at Fairmount High School. After graduation, he went to California to live with his father, Winton, and attended the University of California, Los Angeles, for one year. In October 1951, he left for New York to pursue a professional career in acting, with the primary aim of auditioning for the Actors Studio.

Ironically, Dean did not audition for the Actors Studio, the premier school for "Method" acting, until he met Christine White in the office of his agent, James Deacy, nearly one year after his arrival in New York (Dalton, 80). White was writing an original scene for her own audition for the Actors Studio. Dean offered to help her refine the scene and audition with her. They were two in a class of fifteen accepted at the studio that year.

Dean, as it turned out, attended very few classes. His first scene was for a class with Lee Strasberg, who critiqued his work severely. As a result, Dean never performed before the class again. He said to his roommate, Bill Blast, "If I let them dissect me, like a rabbit in a clinical laboratory or something, I might not be able to produce again. For chrissake, they might sterilize me!" (Dalton, 92).

In his first Broadway show, *See the Jaguar,* which opened in December 1952, Dean was featured in the nonspeaking role of Willy Wilkens. Although the play received mixed reviews upon its opening, Dean gained positive notices. Nash said of Dean's performance, "He brought a great richness of the part. [His acting] was deep down and quite beautiful" (qtd. in Hyams, 61). *See the Jaguar* closed after only five performances, but on the basis of his reviews James Deacy was able to secure steady work for him in television.

The next phase of Dean's career is highlighted primarily with television credits, although he did a small number of workshop productions Off-Broadway. He returned to Broadway for Goetz's stage version of Gide's *The Immoralist,* which opened on February 8, 1954, starring Geraldine Page and Louis Jourdan. Dean played the role of the homosexual houseboy, Bachir. He was dissatisfied with *The Immoralist* from the beginning. In a letter to Barbara Glenn, a girlfriend at the time, he stated: "This is the most boring dull cast and show I have ever seen" (Hyams, 92). He had conflicts with the director and the producers throughout the rehearsal process. The play opened to good reviews in the pre-Broadway tryouts in Philadelphia and later to a positive critical reception in New York. But Dean's conflicts were not resolved, and on opening night he gave two weeks notice. The resignation followed a verbal conflict between him and Mann, the director, but probably he had other reasons for leaving the show. Hyams states in his biography, *James Dean, Little Boy Lost,* that Deacy, Dean's agent, "probably sensed the play's ultimate failure, and [believed that] the role of a conniving homosexual was not auspicious for Jimmy's future type casting" (94). Hyams also notes that by the time of Dean's resignation Deacy had already arranged for a screen test for the Warner Brothers' film *Battle Cry.* In brief, "Jimmy did not leap from *The Immoralist* into open air" (94). Meanwhile, screenwriter Paul Osborne and director Elia Kazan attended a performance of *The Immoralist.* As a result, Kazan invited Dean to interview for the role of Cal Trask in Osborne's new adaptation of John Steinbeck's novel *East of Eden.* Kazan called Osborne after the interview and said, "James Dean [is] Cal" (96).

East of Eden began shooting in May 1954 and was completed in August. Warner Brothers announced on January 4, 1955, that Dean would have the lead in *Rebel without a Cause.* When the film finished shooting on May 25, Dean was already rehearsing scenes for *Giant.* He began shooting the film on June 3, 1955 and finished on September 24. The purchase of the Porsche 550 Spyder in which he would die had been finalized three days earlier. On September 29, Dean crashed into the side of Donald Turnupseed's 1950 Ford Tudor and died within minutes.

Dean's sexual activity is revealed in most biographical research written since the 1980s. His relationships with Pier Angeli, Ursula Andress, Barbara Glenn, and Arlene Sachs are well documented (Riese, 19, 21, 212, 472). Of these "straight" relationships, those of substance seem to have been with Pier Angeli and Barbara Glenn. Both women ended their relationship with Dean to marry other men.

Dean had an intimate relationship with his pastor, Dr. James DeWeerd, which began in his senior year of high school and "endured for many years" (Hyams, 20). Hyams described this relationship as "experimental" (79). He also makes reference to an "opportunistic" relationship between Dean and Rogers Brackett, the director of the radio show *Alias Jane Doe* in 1951 (79). Evidently, Dean exchanged sexual favors for a place to live, Hollywood contacts, and friendship (37). Interviews with Barbara Glenn (75) and Arlene Sachs (86) reveal that Dean's relationships included many brief homosexual encounters, and Kenneth Anger, in *Hollywood Babylon II* (1984), describes a lifestyle that included "anonymous sex, beatings, boots, belts, and bondage scenes" (135). Dean himself once said in reference to his sexuality: "Well, I'm certainly not going through life with one hand tied behind my back" (Riese, 239).

See K. Anger, *Hollywood Babylon II,* New York, 1984; D. Dalton, *James Dean, The Mutant King,* San Francisco, 1974; B. Hoskyns and D. Loehr, *James Dean, Shooting Star,* London, 1989; J. Hyams, *James Dean, Little Boy Lost,* New York, 1992; and R. Riese, *The Unabridged James Dean: His Life and Legacy from A to Z,* Chicago, 1991.

Richele Pitalo

DeLARVERIÉ, Stormé (1920–), singer and male impersonator, was born in Louisiana and grew up in New Orleans. In 1939, Danny Brown and Doc Brenner began producing drag shows in a Miami gay nightclub (the Jewel Box), calling their productions the Jewel Box Revue. By 1942, Doc and Danny began limited tours of the show, first playing gay bars and then "straight" clubs and theaters. The revue toured the country continuously for more than thirty years, advertised as "Twenty-five Men and a Girl," featuring "The World's Foremost Femme-Mimics." From 1955 to 1969, the "girl" of the show was Stormé DeLarverié.

DeLarverié began her performing career in the 1940s as Stormy Dale, a big band singer. The daughter of an African American mother and a white father, Stormy's publicity photographs from this period reveal a statuesque, slender woman with curly, shoulder length hair. But as the emcee of the Jewel Box Revue she appeared in male clothing. While members of the audience were trying to locate the "real" woman among the drag queens (a gimmick later used by the musical *La Cage aux Folles,* 1983), few thought to question the sex of the few performers in the cast who were dressed as men. Most editions of the revue contained a number, "A Surprise with a Song," in which DeLarverié revealed her true identity to the audience. During her fourteen years with the Jewel Box Revue, she not only performed with the troupe but occasionally served as its stage manager and musical arranger.

Most of the men in the Jewel Box Revue appeared in drag, mimicking the voice, mannerisms, and aura of a particular female star. DeLarverié, on the other hand, remarked that she was always herself: "All I did was cut my hair" (qtd. in Parkerson, *Stormé*). She insists that Stormy Dale and Stormé DeLarverié sang and moved the same way; it was only the context that changed. Most reviewers spoke of DeLarverié's baritone voice, instead of calling her a contralto, disregarding the truth of her sexual body.

Soon after she began to sing with the Jewel Box Revue, DeLarverié began to dress in male clothing, offstage as well as on. This presentment of conflicting gender codes often prompted confusion on the part of the viewer. "Some say sir and some say ma'am. . . . It makes no difference to me" (qtd. in Parkerson, *Stormé*). An intensely private person, she stymied interviewers who attempted to pin down her ethnicity, her gender preference, or her sexual orientation. Elizabeth Drorbaugh remarks: "Much about Stormé is hidden (and kept private by those who have known and worked with her), and her efforts to shroud facts in gauzy references may have been an attempt to keep the inquiring gaze off her and on the show" (128). Acknowledging the difficulty of living outside binary coding (black/white, male/female, straight/lesbian), DeLarverié told Michelle Parkerson that her favorite expression was "It ain't easy being green" (*Stormé*).

None of the reviews of the Jewel Box Revue discusses Stormé's ethnicity. In her 1987 film, *Stormé: The Lady in the Jewel Box,* Parkerson argues that male impersonation is often seen as threatening, as a woman is appropriating the costume, voice, and manner of power and privilege. "This power shift is especially disconcerting when embodied by a black woman" (qtd. in Pisik, n.p.). One way of diffusing this perceived threat is not to acknowledge it, not to see it. For the reviewers (who were mostly Caucasian), DeLarverié was invisible: as a woman in disguise, she was not a referent to the drag queens; as an African American she was racially inferior; and she was a woman in a production that invited the audience to "Meet the BOY-OLOGICAL EXPERTS!" Sometimes the invisibility was deliberate. *Harper's Bazaar* refused to print a portrait of DeLarverié that was part of "The Full Circle," a photo and text project by Diane Arbus (November 1961).

During the 1980s and 1990s, DeLarverié worked as a bouncer for various lesbian bars in New York City: "I see a lot of things in my position as bouncer—but please don't call me that. At the Cubbyhole and the Fat Cat, I consider myself a well-paid babysitter of my people, all the boys and girls" (qtd. in Als, 31).

See H. Als, "Love in the Afternoon," *Village Voice,* June 28, 1988; W. Avery, *Female Impersonation,* New York, 1971; E. Drorbaugh, "Sliding Scales: Stormé DeLarverié and the

Jewel Box Revue," in *Crossing the Stage,* London, 1993, 120–43; M. Parkerson, "Beyond Chiffon: The Making of Stormé," in *Blasted Allegories: An Anthology of Writings by Contemporary Artists,* edited by B. Wallis, New York, 1987, 375–79; M. Parkerson, *Stormé: The Lady in the Jewel Box,* film/video, 1987; B. Pisik, "In Search of a Lost Legacy," *Washington Blade,* May 1, 1987; and L. Senelick, *The Changing Room: Sex, Drag, and Theatre,* New York, 2000.

Bud Coleman

de WOLFE, Elsie. See Marbury, Elisabeth.

DIETRICH, Marlene (1901–92), actress, singer, and entertainer, was born Marie Magdalene Dietrich in the small city of Schoneberg, Germany. Her father, Louis Erich Otto Dietrich, a distant figure in Marlene's life, died when she was not yet six. Consequently, it was her mother, Elizabeth Josephine (neé Felsing), who exerted the most influence on her daughter's early life. From her mother, Marlene learned discipline, industry, and the ability to disguise her feelings. As her biographer, Steven Bach, suggests, her early training to conceal her emotions was "something very much like acting" (20). In later years, Marlene would partially credit her German discipline and her mother's strict upbringing for her success (Schell); however, she was not strict about facts that she wished to ignore. She listed her birth date as 1904 and failed to acknowledge that she had an older sister, Elisabeth.

Marlene attended school at Weimer in 1919, where she studied classical violin. This led to her first job, playing in an orchestra that accompanied silent films (Bach, 42). Eventually, she worked as an actor with Max Reinhardt, appearing as the Widow in his 1922 Berlin production of *The Taming of the Shrew* (480). She went on to play Hippolyta in *A Midsummer Night's Dream* (1924), Toinette in *The Imaginary Invalid* (1924), and Hypatia Tarleton in *Misalliance* (1928) (Streif). Dietrich's early theatrical career in Berlin included over twenty-five professional stage productions, and she also acted in film and cabaret.

In 1923, Marlene married Rudi Sieber. The next year she gave birth to their only child, Marie Elizabeth Sieber. Marlene and Rudi's marriage lasted until his death in 1976, but it quickly turned unconventional when Dietrich became romantically involved with others. She frequented "Berlin's lesbian bar scene" and established a persona that was both glamorous and male (Spoto, *Blue Angel,* 38).

In 1929, a young director, Josef von Sternberg, was searching for an actress to play Lola in what was to become the first German talkie, *Der*

Blau Engel. In Dietrich, he found the "bewitching indifference" and intense sexuality that was crucial for the role (Spoto, *Blue Angel,* 56). *The Blue Angel,* filmed in both German and English, became the turning point of Dietrich's career. Throughout her life, she would credit von Sternberg for her initial success and for teaching her how to shape her image. Together they made the seven movies that launched her into film stardom.

After *The Blue Angel*'s U.S. release, Dietrich emigrated to the United States and moved to Hollywood. Between 1930 and 1944, she starred in nineteen films, playing a variety of parts. Her life in Hollywood both professionally and personally was rich and varied. She had many lovers, both male and female. She often became involved with her leading men, but she was also attracted to women. Several authors have chronicled her relationship with the writer **Mercedes de Acosta,** a liaison that she pursued openly. Some letters written by Dietrich to de Acosta preserved in the de Acosta Collection of the Rosenbach Museum and Library in Philadelphia certainly prove that the two women enjoyed a romantic relationship for a short time in the 1930s.

Dietrich had come of age in the world of 1920s Berlin, and her affairs with women thus began in a climate much more tolerant than that of Hollywood in the 1930s. This change of locale, however, apparently did not curtail Dietrich's same-sex pursuits, nor did she try to hide them. Costar Maximilian Schell once stated that Marlene was "totally open about her homosexual relationships" (Spoto, *Blue Angel,* 278). And Dietrich's personal secretary, Bernard Hall, quoted the star as saying: "When you go to bed with a woman, it is less important. Men are a hassle" (265).

Dietrich not only crossed sexual boundaries but transgressed gender definitions and wrote her own dress code. She preferred trousers, and often appeared in smart, mannish outfits. She found men's clothes more comfortable, but undoubtedly she also realized that cross-dressing complemented her androgynous image. Josef von Sternberg played up Dietrich's androgyny—particularly in the film *Morocco.* He remarked that he wanted "to touch lightly[!] on a lesbian accent"(Spoto, 1985, 41).

Dietrich's ability to manipulate her gender into an essential part of her image is a fact that has never been called into question, but her bisexuality has. In a recent interview in the *Advocate,* Maria Riva, Dietrich's daughter, responded to inquiries regarding her mother's cross-dressing and bisexuality. Riva confirmed that Dietrich's wearing of men's clothes was intended to add to her mystique. However, she refused to confirm that her mother had had an affair with Mercedes de Acosta or Greta Garbo; instead she bantered that her mother may have found Garbo "beautiful, perhaps—but intelligent? Hardly" (Stockwell, 68).

Marlene Dietrich's proficiency at capitalizing on her image brought her a remarkably successful career. One critic stated that she "gained her fame through a combination of good looks, good timing, wartime gallantry, unerring professionalism and an indefinable star quality" (Garber, 25). In 1944, Dietrich demonstrated her gallantry and star quality by performing with Danny Thomas for U.S. troops. Soldiers were enthralled with the star. Dietrich, who had become a U.S. citizen in 1939, was later awarded the Medal of Freedom for her war efforts. Her experiences in singing for the troops provided at least partial impetus for a later one-woman show.

From 1946 to 1952, Dietrich resurrected her film career. Then in 1953 she began performing solo in Las Vegas. One biographer notes: "Cinema represents only a portion of her working life, and a minor one. It is as a cabaret star that she sustained her career" (Baxter, 197). She toured her one-woman show, *Marlene Dietrich,* from 1960 to 1975. The act consisted of a series of songs and costume changes designed to play on the famous Dietrich persona. She toured internationally and appeared on Broadway in 1968–69; remarkably, fueled by the devotion of audiences all over the world, the show propelled her into legend. By 1975, however, her career and health were declining. She became plagued by incessant physical ailments and falling ticket sales. On September 29, 1975, while performing in Sydney, Australia, at Her Majesty's Theatre, her touring career ended when she fell and shattered her left femur. She retired to her Paris apartment and lived in seclusion until her death in 1992. She did make one last cameo appearance in the film *Just a Gigolo,* and she allowed Maximilian Schell to make a biographical documentary in which only her voice is heard, while she remains unseen; the only images of Marlene observed in the documentary are a parade of shots from her films and legendary concerts.

Alfred Hitchcock said of Dietrich: "Marlene was a professional star, she was also a professional cameraman, art director, editor, costume designer, hairdresser, make-up woman, composer, producer and director" (*Sight and Sound,* 26). She controlled every aspect of her public image both onstage and off. Her live performances and film work have left the vivid imprint of a star who captured the attention and admiration of millions. According to Steven Bach: "Marlene Dietrich—the legend and artifact—was one of the most disciplined and sustained creative acts of the twentieth century" (xi).

See S. Bach, *Marlene Dietrich: Life and Legend,* New York, 1992; J. Baxter, "Marlene Dietrich," in *International Dictionary of Films and Film Makers: Actors and Actresses,* edited by James Vinson, Chicago, 1993, 3: 196–97; M. Dietrich, letters from Dietrich to Mercedes de Acosta, Rosenbach Museum and Library, Philadelphia; M. Dietrich, *Marlene,* translated by Salvator Attanasio, New York, 1989; M. Garber, "Strike a Pose," *Sight and Sound,* September 1992; R. A. Schanke, *"That Furious Lesbian": The Story of Mercedes de Acosta,* Carbondale, Ill., 2003; M. Schell, *Marlene,* documentary film, 1983; D. Spoto, *Blue Angel,* New York, 1992; D. Spoto, *Falling in Love Again: Marlene Dietrich,* Boston, 1985; M. Streif, "Marlene: Meik's Tribute to The Goddess of the Century," <http://www.ivnet.co.at/streif/index.htm>, accessed November 4, 1997; A. Stockwell, "Dish from Dietrich's Daughter," *The Advocate,* January 22, 2002; H. Vickers, *Loving Garbo: The Story of Greta Garbo, Cecil Beaton, and Mercedes de Acosta,* New York, 1994.

Amy Cuomo

DODSON, Owen (1914–83), writer, director, and teacher, was born on November 28, 1914, in the Flatbush section of Brooklyn, New York, the youngest of nine children, to Nathaniel and Sarah Dodson. While the family struggled to survive, Nathaniel Dodson enjoyed a place among the vanguard of educated African Americans and served as press agent for Booker T. Washington. Although both parents died before Owen was thirteen, they instilled in him a pride of penmanship and proper manners and steeped him in the teachings of the Bible. After distinguishing himself in numerous speech contests in high school, Dodson entered Bates College in 1932, supported by an Urban League scholarship.

In response to a challenge from Professor Robert George Berkelman, Dodson composed a sonnet per week during his four years at Bates, and in 1936 he won a Maine State Poetry Contest and was published in the *New York Herald Tribune.* Active in theater as an actor and director while at Bates, he also wrote short plays, but his love for poetry was foremost and bound him to his closest friends. Another poet at Bates, Priscilla Heath, fell in love with him, and for a short time they were engaged to be married. James V. Hatch, in his biography *Sorrow Is the Only Faithful One,* indicates that the engagement may have been broken off due to Dodson's homosexual orientation, something he kept private throughout his life.

As a black student at an overwhelmingly white college, Dodson's awareness of his racial identity increased at Bates, and this, along with his lifelong support of humanist values, would become his chief social concern as an artist. By the time he entered the Yale Drama School in 1936, he was determined to use his talents and education to promote African American theater.

At Yale, Dodson emerged as a promising young playwright, writing verse drama with language and themes drawn largely from African American culture. The first of these, *Divine Comedy,* was produced at Yale in 1938. Another play, *Garden of Time,* adapted from *Medea* to illustrate

Owen Dodson, probably in the late 1960s, at Howard University. (Courtesy of the Billy Rose Theatre Collection, New York Library of the Performing Arts.)

racial relations in the South, won second place in a national contest sponsored by Stanford University.

In 1938, Dodson accepted a position at Spelman College in Atlanta, where his work as a director greatly impressed the school's most distinguished resident, W. E. B. DuBois. This production experience helped to prepare Dodson for his later, considerable success in directing. In 1941, after teaching briefly at the Hampton Institute in Virginia, he enlisted in the navy. While in the service, he wrote and staged short plays with patriotic themes.

Shortly after a medical discharge due to asthma in October 1943, Dodson received a Rosenwald Fellowship to write and stage a pageant, *New World A-Coming,* a celebration of the role played by African Americans during the war. Produced at Madison Square Garden on June 26, 1944, as part of the Negro Freedom Rally, the show played to some twenty-five thousand spectators and proved both a popular and a critical success.

Dodson's first book of poetry, *Powerful Long Ladder,* was published in 1946 by Farrar and Strauss and included poems previously published in numerous periodicals, from *Mademoiselle* to *Phylon.* His poems range greatly in style and subject matter (e.g., slavery, war, love, and dancing), but humanism and hope are clearly present, as in the fourth stanza of

"The Precedent": "Eventually the broken tree / Will be restored again / And the songs will cut the smoke / With sweetness, and all will/ Prosper with Men."

Dodson resumed his work in academic theater in 1947, when he joined the faculty of Howard University. During the next twenty-three years, he helped to develop the drama department at Howard into one of the most exciting and prominent in the country. One of his early productions, Ibsen's *The Wild Duck,* so impressed a Norwegian diplomat, Fredrik Haslund, that he initiated a plan to take the production to Norway. The resulting tour took place the next year and included performances in Sweden, in Denmark, and at several American military bases in Germany.

Many of the artists who received training at Howard during Dodson's tenure later became famous and influential figures in professional theater (Gordon Heath, Debbie Allen, Ted Shine, and Leroi Jones [Amiri Baraka], to cite but four). His training of young black artists counts as one of the most significant of his contributions to American theater. The role Howard's drama department played in the development of black theater during the 1950s has often been underrated due to the greater attention paid to the more radical black theater movement of the 1960s, a movement not embraced by Dodson, who remained a humanist to the end. Hatch's acclaimed biography of Dodson helps restore to him and the other Howard faculty members their due.

In addition to his directing and teaching duties, Dodson continued to write. *Boy at the Window,* his first novel, was published in 1951. It tells the story of a boy living in Brooklyn in the 1920s, drawing heavily on the author's childhood experiences in a neighborhood of mixed cultures and races. Robert Bone, in his critique of the novel, notes that a dramaturgical sensibility prevails, for "one can almost see the curtain coming down on certain scenes" (187). **W. H. Auden,** whom Dodson had befriended at Yale and one of his many lifelong friends, gave him use of his Italian villa in 1952, when Dodson, on sabbatical, sought a place to work on a second novel. A Guggenheim fellowship for the project helped to defray expenses.

Dodson's later years at Howard, and the years that followed, brought increasing hardship. Heavy drinking impaired his personal and professional relationships to the point of failure in many cases. This was perhaps linked, more than can ever be known, to the intolerance of homosexuality in his time and to the anguish of a duplicitous and cramped life in the closet. His departure from Howard on disability retirement seems to have resulted as much from the drinking as from arthritic pain, for which he underwent a series of treatments, including hip replacements. He continued to write, read poetry, direct shows, teach, and receive honors (from Bates an honorary doctorate).

In 1974, Dodson moved into an apartment on West Fifty-first Street with his sister Edith. Until her death in 1983, Dodson and his sister enjoyed a close and loving relationship, which was great comfort to a man who had long suffered from loneliness. None of his intimate relationships had formed a lasting bond. Alcohol and acute physical pain strained his relationships, and death took from him one after another of his friends. The proper manners he had learned as a child suited his affable and gentle way with people, endeared him to countless students and fellow artists, and brought discipline and form to his work. They may also have worsened his chances of fostering intimate relationships. But Dodson rarely spoke of such things. He died at home on June 21, 1983.

See R. Bone, *The Negro Novel in America,* New Haven, 1965; O. Dodson, *Powerful Long Ladder,* New York, 1946; N. L. Grant, "Extending the Ladder: A Remembrance of Owen Dodson," *Callaloo,* 20 (summer 1997): 640–45; J. V. Hatch, *Sorrow Is the Only Faithful One: The Life of Owen Dodson,* Urbana, 1993; B. L. Peterson Jr., "The Legendary Owen Dodson of Howard University: His Contributions to the American Theatre," *The Crisis,* 86 (November 1979): 373–78; and C. H. Rowell, "An Interview with Owen Dodson," *Callaloo,* 20 (summer 1997): 627–39.

Eric Wiley

DUBERMAN, Martin Bauml (1930–), playwright, historian, critic, and essayist, was a respected professor of history and an award-winning author when he made his successful debut as a playwright with *In White America* in 1963. An anthology of authentic historic documents presented in a manner reminiscent of the Federal Theater's Living Newspaper productions, *In White America* reflected both his academic interest in black American history and his commitment to civil rights reform. Duberman later noted: "Though I hardly knew it at the time, involvement with the black struggle was serving as a channel (not a substitute) for working my way into an awareness of my own oppression" (*Cures,* 63). As he became involved in the gay rights movement and struggled to understand and accept his homosexuality, he abandoned the nonfiction format for plays that examined issues of male sexual identity.

Born in New York City, Duberman experienced an early infatuation with the theater when as a teenager he played George in a summer stock tour of *Our Town.* Rather than pursuing a career as an actor, however, he embarked on a strenuous academic path, earning an undergraduate history degree at Yale, followed in quick succession by both an M.A. and a

Ph.D. in history from Harvard. After five years as an assistant professor at Yale, he joined the history department at Princeton University in 1962 and rapidly advanced to a full professorship.

Duberman's specialty at Princeton was nineteenth-century American history, with a concentration on the role of blacks in the development of the country, and *In White America* allowed him to give theatrical shape to historical texts. The documents, diaries, speeches, and public records compiled by Duberman comprise a panoramic view of two hundred years of black American life, from slave ship arrivals to desegregation battles in the South, and include such diverse voices as those of Thomas Jefferson, W. E. B. DuBois, Ku Klux Klan members, numerous slaves, and a black schoolgirl seeking classroom integration in Little Rock, Arkansas. With a racially mixed cast of six and a spare, presentational production, *In White America* opened Off-Broadway in the fall of 1963, at the crest of the civil rights movement, and gained near unanimous acclaim. It was praised as "a flaming editorial, a record of the Negro's agony and a witness to his aspirations . . . filled with indignation" (Taubman, C26). The play's New York run of five hundred performances and its numerous subsequent productions in both the United States and Europe attest to its social and cultural currency. Indeed, the play was later acknowledged as "not only a considerable achievement in its own right, but [one which] also set the tone for much subsequent black theatre" (Simon, 56).

In White America won for Duberman the 1963–64 Vernon Rice Drama Desk Award, but its success was not to be repeated by any of his subsequent plays. His historical research, however, brought him acclaim throughout the rest of the decade. Among other books, his historical biographies *Charles Francis Adams, 1807–1886* (1962) and *Charles Francis Adams* (1966) were particularly well received, with the former winning the Bancroft Prize, and the latter a National Book Award nomination. Duberman also contributed essays and theater criticism to the *Partisan Review* and *Show* magazine during this time.

Eventually Duberman became disenchanted with traditional historical research methodologies and began to take a more subjective approach to his subjects, and his 1972 study of the experimental Black Mountain College in North Carolina served as a vehicle for his own public outing. His plays likewise began to mirror many unresolved issues concerning his sexuality. (He spent the better part of the 1960s in both private and group therapy, unsuccessfully attempting to alter his sexual orientation.) Several of the plays share common characteristics: many are duologues between sexually liberated, streetwise young men and older, possibly closeted academicians, and all examine the construct of masculinity. The one-act *Metaphors* (1968) takes the form of an admissions interview between a prospective student and a Yale University administrator, with a strong homoerotic undercurrent. *The Colonial Dudes* (1969), which is similarly structured though less overtly gay, was presented under the auspices of the Playwright's Unit of the Actors Studio. *The Recorder* and *The Electric Map,* a pair of two-character plays produced Off-Broadway in 1970 under the collective title *The Memory Bank,* were further variations on this template.

For Duberman, 1971 proved to be a benchmark year. Theatrically, it began inauspiciously with *Soon,* a rock musical for which Duberman provided the book adaptation, which opened and promptly closed on Broadway. Later that year he left Princeton to accept an appointment at Lehman College and the Graduate Center of the City University of New York (CUNY) as Distinguished Professor of History. He also became a member of the New Dramatists, where several of his plays would be given workshop productions and where *Payments* (1968), a full-length play about a male hustler, was first performed. Duberman later described the play, written in 1968, as "an exercise in homophobia" in which every gay character exhibits "varying forms of self-destruction and self-pity" (*Cures,* 91). In this, he drew a parallel between *Payments* and *The Boys in the Band,* which he had famously panned in the *Partisan Review* when it opened in 1968. By 1971, however, he was no longer seeking to change his sexual orientation through therapy, and he was slowly becoming involved in the gay rights movement, which he had previously supported in theory only. He later observed about his personal progress that "it was my playwriting and my experiences in the theater that did the most to fuel the advance" (212). *Payments,* despite its homophobic strain, explored homosexuality more candidly than any of Duberman's previous plays, and it served to "out" him as a gay playwright.

The remainder of Duberman's playwriting career was dominated by revivals of his early works, while his new plays enjoyed little success. New Dramatists presented an evening of three Duberman one acts in 1972: *Metaphors, The Colonial Dudes,* and a new play, *The Guttman Ordinary Scale.* The program was repeated for a commercial run at the John Drew Theater in East Hampton, New York, later that year. The Manhattan Theater Club presented *Metaphors* and *The Colonial Dudes* together under the umbrella title *Inner Limits* in 1973. *Metaphors,* along with **Lanford Wilson**'s *The Madness of Lady Bright,* was also chosen by San Francisco's gay theater company, Theater Rhinoceros, as its opening attraction in 1977.

The New Dramatists workshop also produced a new, full-length Duberman play, *Elagabalus,* in 1973. The play's protagonist, the androgynous Adrian, is a romanticized ideal for the rejection of the stifling armor of societally imposed masculine roles. Indeed, *Male Armor,* the title of an anthology of seven Duberman plays written between 1968 and 1974, was chosen as a reference to Wilhelm Reich's theory of "character armor." As Duberman noted in an introduction, each play explores "the devices we use (which then use us) to protect ourselves from our own energy, and especially from our sexual energy: the strategies that help us grow a skin—and then keep us in it" (xii).

Visions of Kerouac, an examination of the life of Beat poet Jack Kerouac and his relationship with Neal Cassady, is Duberman's most recent work for the theater. Originally commissioned for a 1976 bicentennial season of American plays at the Kennedy Center for the Performing Arts in Washington, D.C., it was withdrawn by Duberman when the management expressed discomfort with its portrayal of sexual tension between the two men. Incorporating key sections of the poet's work, *Visions of Kerouac* combines historical research with the theme that continued to engage Duberman's imagination as a playwright: the limitation of emotional expression allowed males in American culture. After a workshop production, again courtesy of New Dramatists, the play opened Off-Off-Broadway at the Lion Theatre Company late in 1976 to mixed reviews and played only a short time. A Los Angeles production the next year received far better critical response but still managed only an abbreviated run.

Duberman's spotty record as a playwright stands in sharp contrast to his successes in other fields. In the 1970s and 1980s, he emerged as a forceful and eloquent spokesperson for gay and lesbian issues. He was a founding member of the Gay Academic Union, was an originating board member of the National Gay Task Force, and served on the advisory board of the Lambda Legal Defense Fund. His activism strongly influenced his academic life, and in 1991 he founded and served as executive director of the Center for Lesbian and Gay Studies (CLAGS) at the CUNY Graduate Center, the first university research center devoted to the study of gay and lesbian subjects. In 1995, the center established the Martin Duberman Fellowship in Lesbian and Gay Studies. His historical research now focused on documenting the history of oppression experienced by gay and lesbian Americans. *About Time: Exploring the Gay Past* (1986) and *Hidden from History: Reclaiming the Gay and Lesbian Past* (1989), which he coedited, combine historical documents and oral histories. *Stonewall* (1993) is an oral history of participants in the 1969 Stonewall Riots. Duberman's 1989 biography of the black singer, actor, and activist Paul Robeson shares a theme with his gay and lesbian social histories, "that one's personal triumphs . . . cannot be entirely personal when, against your will, you are representative of a group denied their basic liberties" (Cole, 16). In two memoirs, *Cures: A Gay Man's Odyssey* (1991) and *Midlife Queer: Autobiography of a Decade* (1996), Duberman combined social history with autobiography, paralleling his personal struggle out of oppression with the social and political strides made by gays and lesbians in this country.

Ironically, Martin Duberman, a gay icon of activism and academic achievement, had his greatest success as a playwright with *In White America,* the one play that did not touch on gay issues. His other plays nonetheless remain a brilliant gay man's examination of his sexual conflicts during a period when society was slowly coming to terms with homosexuality. For this reason, the plays of Martin Duberman demand consideration alongside his other writings as part of our gay literary heritage.

See K. Berney, ed., *Contemporary American Dramatists,* London, 1994; C. B. Cole, "Pulling Down the Ivory Tower: An Interview with Martin Bauml Duberman," *New York Native,* April 29, 1991; M. Duberman, *Cures: A Gay Man's Odyssey,* New York, 1991; M. Duberman, *Male Armor: Selected Plays, 1968–1974,* New York, 1975; M. Duberman, *Midlife Queer: Autobiography of a Decade,* New York, 1996; "Martin Duberman" Clipping Files, Billy Rose Theatre Collection, New York Public Library for the Performing Arts; L. Mass, "Excavating Time: Martin Bauml Duberman Talks about Gay History, the Sexual Revolution, Sex Phobia, and His New Book, *About Time,*" *New York Native,* December 22, 1986; J. Simon, "Out of the Closet," *New York,* February 2, 1970; and H. Taubman, "Theater: Living Editorial," *New York Times,* November 1, 1963).

Kevin Winkler

DUNCAN, Isadora (Angela Isadora) (1877–1927), dancer, choreographer, teacher, and author, is described by the dance scholar Ann Daly as the "major source" of American modern dance, a charismatic innovator who established the agenda by "defining the terms and literally setting the practice in motion" (x). Born in San Francisco, Duncan left school at the age of fifteen to help support her mother and siblings by teaching social dance. When she was eighteen, in 1895, shortly after traveling to Chicago to seek work as a dancer, she joined Augustin Daly's theater company and relocated to New York, where she danced small roles and toured with the troupe to London.

In 1898, she quit Daly's company and began offering salon recitals in New York, adding elements of the Delsarte technique and principles of women's dress reform to interpretive dances of literary sources such as *The Rubaiyat* of Omar Khayyam. In the following year, she performed similar

recitals in London, where she successfully gained the patronage of prominent artists and society matrons. She also began studying Greek and
Roman antiquities at the British Museum and incorporated this imagery
into her dances. She moved to Paris in 1900 to teach and there made the
acquaintance of another dancer, **Loie Fuller,** who was performing her
visual spectacles at the Universal Exposition. Late in 1901, Fuller invited
Duncan to join her troupe of female dancers. She traveled with them to
Leipzig, Munich, and (in 1902) Vienna, where she made her debut. It was
the first of a series of artistic triumphs in Austria, Hungary, Germany,
and France that would bring her international acclaim and notoriety.

Duncan left the troupe shortly after her Vienna debut, but her affiliation with Fuller is significant because of her exposure to the lesbian environment cultivated by Fuller and her entourage. In her autobiography,
My Life, Duncan describes Fuller as surrounded by "a dozen or so beautiful girls . . . alternately stroking her hands and kissing her" (94).
Although Duncan gives no indication of the extent of her involvement
with the entourage and, moreover, indicates surprise at "this extreme
activity of expressed affections, which were quite new to me," she fondly
describes the environment as having "an atmosphere of such warmth as I
had never met before" (95). This confession is frequently omitted from
biographical accounts of her association with Fuller.

Duncan's first book, *Der Tanz der Zukunft* (1903), became an influential manifesto for the modern dance movement. In this text, she expresses
a strong desire to open a school of dance, a dream realized in the following year in the Grunewald suburb of Berlin, with the assistance of her
elder sister Elizabeth. This endeavor was to be the first of several attempts
by Duncan to establish permanent schools of dance in Paris, Italy,
Athens, New York, San Francisco, and, most successfully, Moscow, where
she achieved her biggest solo and group successes between 1921 and
1924. Her original German pupils, who later received international
recognition as the Duncan Dancers (nicknamed "The Isadorables"),
would be instrumental in teaching the "Duncan method" after Isadora's
accidental death by strangulation in 1927.

Duncan's long-term heterosexual affairs with Hungarian actor Oscar
Beregi, stage designer and theorist Edward Gordon Craig (the father of
Duncan's daughter Deidre), millionaire sewing machine heir Paris Singer
(the father of Duncan's son Patrick), and pianists Walter Morse Rummel
and Victor Seroff are well documented by her biographers and Duncan
herself, as are her numerous other sexual escapades and her stormy marriage to the (possibly bisexual) Russian poet Sergei Esenin in 1922. From
the vantage point of 1926, however, as she was writing *My Life,* her

assessment of her lovers is revealing. She describes her companions as "artists and dreamers" who were "more or less neurasthenic and either sunk in deepest gloom or buoyed up to sudden joy by drink." She concludes by stating: "I suppose all my lovers had been decidedly feminine" (345).

Duncan scholars and biographers have done relatively little serious investigating of her romantic liaisons with women. Of central importance is her involvement with poet, playwright, and screenwriter **Mercedes de Acosta,** a lesbian artist who counted among her many lovers **Eva Le Gallienne**, Greta Garbo, and **Marlene Dietrich.** In *Here Lies the Heart,* de Acosta details her first meeting with Duncan on a beach in Amagansett in 1916, an encounter that resulted in a lasting friendship (78–81). De Acosta was instrumental in persuading Duncan to write *My Life* and assisted her financially during the last years of her life. A collection of erotic letters and poetry de Acosta received from Duncan is housed in the Mercedes de Acosta archive in Philadelphia's Rosenbach Museum and Library. These documents appear to substantiate allegations of Duncan's bisexuality (Dillon, 350–51; Daly, 170; Madsen, 10).

Other evidence, much of it fragmentary, points to Duncan's lesbian leanings. Biographer Alex Madsen, for example, makes note of Duncan dancing in the Paris gardens of the wealthy American lesbian Natalie Barney (47). Duncan's longtime friend, the cosmetics and perfume entrepreneur Mary Desti, recounts an anecdote concerning Isadora being solicited by a lesbian prostitute in Paris (130–31). And Victor Seroff, as a final illustration, maintains that almost all the members of Duncan's 1926–27 entourage were lesbians (392–95). Also to be taken into consideration is Duncan's own writing about homosexuality. In addition to discussing Loie Fuller, in *My Life* Duncan recalls counseling two male Turkish lovers in 1914, concluding with the comment: "I believe the highest love is a purely spiritual flame which is not necessarily dependent on sex" (285).

The relationship between Duncan's bisexuality and the production and reception of her dancing is an area that has received little critical attention. Daly, however, begins to forge some significant connections between Duncan's affair with de Acosta and the writing of *My Life* (249). Similar considerations might prove profitable with regard to Duncan's final concerts, which were staged during the same time frame or shortly afterward.

While her highly publicized affairs, news of her out of wedlock children (as well as the children's tragic deaths in 1913), and sensationalized reports of her marital difficulties with Esenin inevitably impacted spectator response to Duncan's dancing and her work as a teacher, most contemporary scholars and contemporaneous critics downplay sexuality in Duncan's dancing. Instead they echo Duncan's own insistence that she created images stripped of eroticism and concentrated on constructing the female dancing body as "natural," chaste, classical artwork. With knowledge of her bisexual orientation, however, it may be possible to expand this view by exploring the homosocial dimensions of, for example, Duncan's dancing in the salons of wealthy patrons for primarily female spectators, her impact on female spectators in her public concerts, her pedagogical work with primarily female students, and her friendships with Eleanora Duse, Eva Le Gallienne, Ruth Mitchell, and particularly Mary Desti, whom de Acosta describes as worshiping Duncan "to such an extent that in a curious way she had taken on some essence of Isadora" (80). Such explorations might shed new light, as well, on Duncan's choice of the musical compositions, physical imagery, and subject matter from which she assembled her dances.

Reassessment may expand our appreciation of Duncan's considerable achievements in modern dance practice, theory, and education, adding another critical lens through which one of the twentieth century's most innovative and subversive artists may be viewed.

See F. Blair, *Isadora: Portrait of the Artist as a Woman,* New York, 1986; A. Daly, *Done into Dance: Isadora Duncan in America,* Bloomington, Ind., 1995; M. de Acosta, *Here Lies the Heart,* New York, 1975; M. Desti, *The Untold Story: The Life of Isadora Duncan, 1921–1927,* New York, 1929; M. Dillon, *After Egypt: Isadora C. Duncan and Mary Cassat,* New York, 1990; D. Duncan, C. Pratl, and C. Splatt, eds., *Life into Art: Isadora Duncan and Her World,* New York, 1993; I. Duncan, *Duncan Dancer,* Middleton, Conn., 1965; I. Duncan, *My Life,* New York, 1927; I. Duncan, *The Art of Dancing,* New York, 1928; P. Kurth, *Isadora: A Sensational Life,* New York, 2001; G. McVay, *Isadora and Esenin,* Ann Arbor, 1980; A. Madsen, *The Sewing Circle: Hollywood's Greatest Secret–Female Stars Who Loved Other Women,* New York, 1995; B. O'Connor, *Barefoot Dancer: The Story of Isadora Duncan,* Minneapolis, 1994; V. Seroff, *The Real Isadora,* New York, 1971; and F. Steegmuller, ed., *Your Isadora: The Love Story of Isadora Duncan and Gordon Craig,* New York, 1974.

Jay Scott Chipman

ELTINGE, Julian (William Julian Dalton) (1886–1941), female impersonator, was born in the Boston suburb of Newtonville, Massachusetts. His father was rarely able to find or keep well-paying jobs and was frequently absent, traveling the country to make his fortune. Subsequently, Eltinge's mother encouraged him to take small roles in local stock companies as a means of earning extra income. Because of the puritan underpinnings of Boston society, young girls were often banned from playing on the stage, thus opening those roles to young boys. Eltinge became a specialist in playing girls. As he aged, he continued to play female parts, though the time came when he was playing roles that could legally be played by women. He then embarked on an adult career as a female impersonator.

Choosing to make one's livelihood in this manner was not socially acceptable, and Eltinge created numerous stories to explain why he was in this profession. The story that received the most public play was that Eltinge had been discovered by Lillian Russell, that day's most popular entertainer, while he was performing in drag at a Harvard Hasty Pudding show. Then, as now, all the roles in the annual production are played by men, and men in drag is an integral element of the show. This story— entirely false—was perfectly conceived to provide the most cover for Eltinge. There was no more prestigious university. The Hasty Pudding show was renowned for college lads dressing in drag in a kind of demon- stration of high spirits. And, of course, being "discovered" and "forced" to go on performing professionally was a page right out of Horace Greeley.

Eltinge played small-time vaudeville until he made a successful New York debut in 1904. His act consisted of a series of songs, each sung by a different female type. He would appear as "The Bride," retire from the stage for no longer than ninety seconds, and return as "The Bathing Beauty." This character would be succeeded by "The Siren-Vampire," "The Gibson Girl," Salome, or even Carmen. For each song, he appeared in a different costume and wig. It was during this period that George M. Cohan hired him to costar in a new edition of the Cohan and Harris Min- strels. For two years, Eltinge toured with the company, not only per- forming his vaudeville turns but also playing—in drag and blackface— the one-act play that concluded the production.

In 1911, Eltinge opened on Broadway in a musical-play, *The Fascinat- ing Widow.* This was followed by *The Crinoline Girl* (1914) and *Cousin Lucy* (1915, with music by Jerome Kern). All of these plays, like Eltinge's later movies, had the plot requirement of a man dressing as a woman. His character would have to disguise himself, make numerous costume changes, and be revealed at the end. Touring domestically and interna- tionally, the shows made Eltinge so rich and famous that a Broadway the- ater was built and named after him. (It still stands on Forty-second Street, now called the Empire.)

What was unique to Eltinge was that he did not perform a burlesque or caricature of women—as had been the general practice up to that time—but played women truthfully and as objects of desire, not ridicule. He was skilled enough to take advantage of his more feminine attributes and to disguise his masculine ones. His makeup was perfect. His nails were highly polished. A natural mimic, he learned to walk and sit and pose as various types of women would. His few attempts at performing as a man in men's clothing were failures. Even those few scenes at the beginnings and endings of his plays were considered less satisfactory than the main portion, when he appeared in drag.

Eltinge's commercial success was based both on his very real ability at female impersonation and on society's very real fascination with his crossing of gender boundaries. Public intrigue with his gender bending enabled him to extend his popularity and influence with his own nationally distributed magazine, which ran articles on such topics as the application of makeup and the reasons why women should take up boxing as a means of exercise. The *Julian Eltinge Magazine* also featured his line of cold cream and other beauty aids, along with many other commercial products. He often boasted that he made more money than the president of the United States.

Although Eltinge was fiercely discreet about his private life, information has surfaced in recent years about a relationship he had of some duration with a male sportswriter that threatened to become scandalous (Senelick, "Lady and the Tramp," 30). In his own day, many critics believed that his career was an abomination and that he was a freak. Percy Hammond called him "ambisextrous." Burns Mantle said that female impersonators inspired in him "a longing for a shotgun and an unwritten law." Eltinge was often forced to defend himself, usually protesting that he was merely an actor playing a part, much like an actor playing a murderer.

More than critical hostility, time proved to be Eltinge's greatest enemy. As he aged and grew more stout—and as women's wear changed from long, bustled dresses to short flapper outfits—his career declined. Also society turned more and more against cross-dressing and displays of what some considered to be homosexual behavior. States and municipalities passed laws outlawing female impersonation, even on the stage. In the 1930s, Eltinge was forced to perform his vaudeville act in nightclubs, where he would stand in front of a rack of women's clothes, display an outfit, and then perform that female characterization while still in his tuxedo.

At the time of his death, he was rehearsing for an "old time vaudeville" show at a New York City nightclub. Having played the bride but never having married, he was survived by his mother.

See J. Eltinge, "From the Player's Point of View, Why I Do It," *Chicago Tribune,* December 11, 1910; P. Kellar, "Making a Woman of Himself," *Green Book,* December 1909; B. Mantle, *Chicago Tribune,* September 20, 1908; W. Sage, "Oh, Horrors! Julian's

Real Name is Bill Dalton," *Cleveland Leader,* February 4, 1912; L. Senelick, *The Changing Room: Sex, Drag and Theatre,* New York and London, 2000; L. Senelick, "Lady and the Tramp: Drag Differentials in the Progressive Era," in *Gender in Performance: The Presentation of Difference in the Performing Arts,* edited by L. Senelick, Hanover and London, 1992, 26–45; A. Slide, *Great Pretenders,* Lombard, Ill., 1986; J. Walton, "As Men Practice Beauty Culture," *Woman Beautiful,* November 1908.

Lee Alan Morrow

ENGEL, Lehman (A. Lehman Engel) (1910–1982), teacher, composer, conductor, author, and lecturer, was born in Jackson, Mississippi, the only child of Ellis and Juliette Lehman Engel. He began playing piano by ear at about the age of seven and began formal lessons when he was ten. He later studied at the Cincinnati Conservatory, the Cincinnati College of Music, and the University of Cincinnati. In 1929, during his third year at the university, he conducted the premiere of his first opera, *The Pierrot of the Minute,* a musicalization of a play by Ernest Dowson.

Engel moved to New York City at the age of nineteen to study composition with Rubin Goldmark. After meeting **Aaron Copland** and other composers, he helped form the Young Composer's Group. Despite the effect of the stock market crash, his family was able to support him, including his studies at the Juilliard School of Music Graduate School (1930–33).

Before Engel graduated from Juilliard, he was working professionally. In 1932, he began a collaboration with the great modern dance choreographer Martha Graham, for whom he eventually composed five works. He was also the musical director of Kurt Weill's children's opera, *Der Jasager* (Grand St. Playhouse, 1933).

The Broadway debut of an Engel composition occurred in 1934, when he composed new music (replacing the original score) for Sean O'Casey's *Within the Gates.* At the request of the Federal Music Project, a subsidiary of the Work Projects Administration (WPA), he formed the Madrigal Singers in 1936, a group that performed for the next four years. Concurrently, he also worked for the Federal Theatre Project, composing music for T. S. Eliot's *Murder in the Cathedral* (1936) and writing incidental music for two productions of the WPA's Children's Theatre unit. Engel has the distinction of being the conductor for the first "performance" (the final dress rehearsal before an invited audience) of **Marc Blitzstein**'s *The Cradle Will Rock,* (Maxine Elliott Theatre, 1937). On the day of its scheduled opening, the government blocked the musical's run, so director Orson Welles presented the show without an orchestra, with cast members singing their roles from the auditorium in a hastily rented theater

Lehman Engel in his early sixties, from the dust jacket of his book, *Their Words Are Music: Lyrics and Lyricists* (1975). (Photo by Fred Plaut, courtesy of the Billy Rose Theatre Collection, New York Public Library for the Performing Arts.)

twenty blocks away. (In 1960, Engel had the satisfaction of conducting a full revival of *The Cradle Will Rock* at City Center.) Also, during the WPA years Engel, along with Aaron Copland, Marc Blitzstein, and **Virgil Thomson,** formed Arrow Music Press, which was dedicated to publishing and distributing the work of American composers. He served as the president of this firm for the twenty years of its existence.

At the age of twenty-five, Engel conducted Paul Green and Kurt

Weill's *Johnny Johnson* (1936) for the Group Theatre. In 1938, he composed the incidental music for Maurice Evans's uncut *Hamlet,* directed by
Margaret Webster, the first of twelve productions directed by Webster
for which Engel composed a score. In 1939, he conducted the premiere of
The Little Dog Laughed, with music and lyrics by Harold Rome; he would
subsequently conduct all the Rome musicals.

In 1938, Engel met one of the loves of his life, nineteen-year-old
Montgomery Clift. He wrote: "I had never met so lively and vital a boy.
. . . For several years Monty and I went to the theatre, museums, and took
trips together. He made everything seem exciting" (*This Bright Day,*
108). But during a trip to Mexico in 1940 Clift became very ill and
returned to the United States alone, diagnosed with amoebic dysentery:
"Our careers drove wedges between us, and our meetings—always warm
and friendly—became less and less frequent. . . . He looked to me for
advice, and years later, after World War II, although I seldom saw him,
he continued to depend on me when he needed to make a decision" (111).
The last time they saw one another was in 1954, when Engel was called
in to mediate an altercation between Clift and the cast of the Phoenix
Theater's revival of *The Seagull.* Clift died in 1966 at the age of forty-six.
Engel would write in his autobiography: "His young laughter and enthusiasm and taste are unforgettable" (112).

During World War II, Engel served in the U.S. Navy (1942–46), rising to the rank of lieutenant, first as leader of the Great Lakes Naval
Training Station's symphonic concert band and then as chief composer of
the navy's film division. He wrote that he left the service with a new
respect for men, having overcome the "terror" of groups of men he had
endured throughout his teen years (*This Bright Day,* 147). Among his
inner circle of friends, he made no secret of his sexual orientation, but he
did not discuss the subject in his autobiography, *This Bright Day* (1974).

After his discharge, Engel returned to Broadway, conducting Harold
Rome's *Call Me Mister.* He was also in demand as a composer of incidental music for plays, writing for Uta Hagen's *Saint Joan* (1951) and the Old
Vic's *Measure for Measure* (1957) and serving as musical adviser for *A
Streetcar Named Desire* (1947). He received a total of two Tony Awards and
two Tony nominations for his musical direction. (A Tony Award for Conductor and Musical Director was awarded from 1949 to 1964.)

Engel's discography lists over eighty recordings, including many
musicals, eighteen operettas for the *Reader's Digest* series, Charles Ives's
67th Psalm—the first recording of Ives's music by a major label—and solo
recordings by such artists as Bing Crosby, Mary Martin, and Ezio Pinza.
One of his significant gifts to American theater was setting up studio

recordings of Broadway shows, which prior to that time had never been recorded in their entirety (i.e., *Oh, Kay!, On Your Toes, Brigadoon,* and *Porgy and Bess*).

Although Engel had composed the incidental music for thirty-eight plays, wrote four operas, and conducted over one hundred Broadway orchestras, his most important legacy to American theater was as a teacher. After presenting a two-hour lecture in March 1961, he was approached by several people, who asked if they might meet again. Engel agreed, but took the invitation further, devising a method for the study of musical theater. Supported by Broadcast Music, Inc. (BMI), he developed a two-year curriculum for composers and lyricists.

The New York BMI Workshop was a safe place for writers to fail. It provided an environment for experimentation and a forum for analysis among peers deeply concerned with creative problems and techniques— a place to educate would-be theater "craftsmen." Engel's legacy continued throughout the BMI Workshops in Nashville and Toronto, the Lehman Engel Musical Theater Workshop in Los Angeles (which took over its own management in 1979), and the New Turners Workshop in Chicago (est. 1984), directed by one of Engel's students. He was also director of the musical department of the American Musical and Dramatic Academy (AMDA) from 1962 to 1966.

Engel's greatest achievement is the continued existence of the philosophy and methodology of the workshop. After his death in 1982, Ed Kleban, Alan Menken, and Maury Yeston "discussed what would be the best memorial for this great man of the theatre. We concluded that nothing would be more fitting than to keep his work going" (qtd. in "BMI–Lehman Engel"). This ongoing legacy moved William B. Kennedy to suggest that Lehman Engel should be called "the man who taught Broadway" (261). Engel died at his home in Manhattan of cancer at the age of seventy-one.

Engel is the author of *Renaissance to Baroque* (1931), *Music for the Classical Tragedy* (1953), *Musical Shows: Planning and Producing* (1957), *The American Musical Theater* (1967), *Words with Music* (1972), *Getting Started in the Theater* (1973), the autobiography *This Bright Day* (1974), *Their Words Are Music* (1975), *The Critics* (1976), *The Making of a Musical: Creating Songs for the Stage* (1977), and *Getting the Show On* (1983). With funding from the National Endowment for the Humanities, his last project was collecting oral histories pertaining to American musical theater.

See "BMI–Lehman Engel Musical Theatre Workshop: 25 Years Young," *BMI Music-World* 9 (1986): 48–49; L. Engel, *This Bright Day,* New York, 1974; L. Engel, "A Place to Fail," *BMI MusicWorld* 3 (1980): 22–24; W. B. Kennedy, "Rhyme and Reason: An

Evaluation of Lehman Engel's Contribution to the Criticism of Musical Theatre," Ph.D. diss., Kent State University, 1987; C. Mather, "The Engel Musical Theatre Workshops: A Network for Musical Writers," M.A. thesis, University of Colorado, Boulder, 1994; and G. Stern, "Where Is the Next Generation of Musical Creators?" *Back Stage,* February 6, 1987, 1A, 22A.

Bud Coleman

FIELD, Ron (Ronald) (1934–89), dancer, choreographer, and director, was born in New York City. By the age of eight, he was appearing on Broadway with Gertrude Lawrence in *Lady in the Dark,* marking "the start of a long apprenticeship which gave him a wider experience of the popular dance vocabulary than any stager other than [Bob] Fosse" (Steyn, 12). Although Field's career peaked prematurely and he never attained the status of Broadway dance innovators such as Fosse, Jerome Robbins, or **Michael Bennett,** his versatility and efficiency made him one of the busiest choreographers in show business for three decades. A survey of his work also reveals a number of interesting gay touchstones in an otherwise thoroughly mainstream career.

After being the first male dance student enrolled at New York's High School of the Performing Arts, Field spent more than a decade as a quintessential "gypsy," alternating work in stage musicals, nightclubs, and television. He performed on Broadway in *Carnival in Flanders* (1953) and *Kismet* (1954) (beginning an influential association with choreographer Jack Cole), danced on over three hundred television variety show broadcasts, and toured the nightclub circuit with Cole's dance troupe. During this period, he began to choreograph, and he staged dozens of musicals in summer stock.

In 1962, after mounting elaborate casino revues in Paris and Beirut, and at New York's Latin Quarter, Field produced a showcase of his dances at the Ninety-second Street YMCA, which resulted in his being hired to choreograph an Off-Broadway revival of *Anything Goes* (1962). That success led to his first Broadway show as a choreographer, *Nowhere to Go but Up* (1962), a fast flop but one in which his choreography made a strong impact and earned him a Tony Award nomination.

The songwriting team of John Kander and Fred Ebb, with whom Field had worked on a nightclub act for Liza Minnelli, encouraged producer-director Harold Prince to hire him to choreograph their new musical, *Cabaret* (1966). Based on **John Van Druten**'s play, *I Am a Camera,* and **Christopher Isherwood**'s *Berlin Stories, Cabaret* eliminated the homosexuality of the protagonist (who was based on Isherwood himself), through whose eyes the story is seen, and involved him in a conventional heterosexual romance. It was Field's cabaret numbers, however, that projected the ambivalent sexuality and decadent glamour of the musical's Weimar era setting. *Cabaret* included what was to become Field's signature dance number, "The Telephone Song," a comically sexy routine featuring angular, dislocated movements that showed Jack Cole's influence. He received the Tony Award for Best Choreography for the 1966–67 Broadway season.

After a modestly successful reteaming with Prince, Kander, and Ebb for *Zorba* (1968), Field made his debut as director-choreographer with *Applause* (1970), a musical version of the film *All About Eve,* starring Lauren Bacall as Margo Channing. Working with an undistinguished book and score and a star who had never sung or danced, Field created a slick, lightning-paced show in which all the elements, including the scenery, seldom stopped moving. The reviews fully acknowledged his accomplishment: "The real key to the show's success may be Ron Field. . . . He charges the production with a rampant, almost indiscriminate energy that makes everything buzz with excitement" (Bunce, 4). A solid hit, *Applause* won Field two Tony Awards, for direction and choreography and placed him at a new pinnacle of success.

Applause was also one of the gayest Broadway musicals to be produced up to that time, as it was set in a hothouse Broadway milieu rife with gay characters and situations. In Duane Fox, Margo's hairdresser-confidant, it features one of the first openly gay musical comedy characters who is not the target of derisive comedy. Margo spends her opening night dancing in a Greenwich Village gay bar decorated with images of queer culture icons such as Judy Garland, Mae West, a leather-clad Marlon Brando, and assorted male beefcake photos. Among the male and female "gypsies" who make up *Applause*'s chorus, the men clearly identify with and envy the stardom of Margo and Eve Harrington, and scenes set in a theater district bistro are not markedly different in tone from the gay bar sequence. When nudity is fleetingly presented, it is male bodies that are on display. In an interview with a gay journalist, Arthur Bell, Gene Foote, a dancer in the show, remarked on Field's casting of *Applause,* noting that "if you see someone who turns you on, you'll probably want to work with him. A lot depends on the choreographer. . . . in *Applause,* the majority of the dancers were good-looking and gay" (Bell, 10).

In 1971, Field embarked upon his most ambitious Broadway effort, the first full-scale revival of the 1944 musical *On the Town,* the product of a legendary collaboration among **Leonard Bernstein**, Betty Comden, Adolph Green, and Jerome Robbins. If *Applause* had marked his entrée into the circle of successful director-choreographers, *On the Town* was intended to confirm his place alongside Champion, Fosse, and Robbins himself as a Broadway auteur: a visionary who not only directs and choreographs but whose overall production concept is the dominant creative force. Field was particularly expansive during *On the Town*'s preproduction. In an interview with *After Dark* magazine, he spoke candidly about his sexuality, noting: "I've been able to adjust to anything. Even homosexuality, which I really thought that a lot of people would hate a lot. I guess I thought I would too—when I was less secure I spent a lot of time going to analysts" (Zadan, 40).

On the Town proved to be a major failure, and, most damagingly for Field, it generated some of his worst critical notices, nearly all of which compared him unfavorably to his predecessor, Robbins. It halted Field's momentum as a director-choreographer, and his career never fully recovered. His remaining theater credits form a mere coda to his earlier successes. *King of Hearts* (1978) had only a brief run and was the last Broadway show to carry the credit "Directed and Choreographed by Ron Field." As a choreographer only, he was nominated for a Tony Award for *Rags* (1986), but it closed in one weekend. Ironically, his biggest success during this period was a musical that did not even list his name. Field revamped the direction and choreography for a chaotic pre-Broadway tour of the musical *Peter Pan,* starring Sandy Duncan, and brought it into New York to great acclaim in 1979.

If his career on Broadway was checkered, Field nonetheless remained in demand as a solid professional who could, and would, stage almost anything. He was one of the most sought-after choreographers on television for awards shows and star specials—one highlight being the acclaimed *Baryshnikov on Broadway* (1980). He also became well known for his skill in mounting large-scale spectacles, most prominently the gargantuan opening and closing ceremonies of the 1984 Olympics in Los Angeles.

On a more intimate scale, Field directed and choreographed an act for Chita Rivera in 1974 that immediately set a new standard for cabaret performance. Described as "a synthesis of Las Vegas and Fire Island" (Gavin, 307), the act consisted of song and dance numbers from Rivera's Broadway shows interspersed with gay-tinged specialty material such as "Trash," a song featuring a "who's who" list of camp figures, and patter between Rivera and her two male dancers, much of it filled with gay slang and innuendo. The act was a sensation, and its popularity proved to be surprisingly broad, doing as much to bring camp humor and sensibility to a wide audience as did the more audacious Bette Midler. Field's death on February 6, 1989, was variously attributed to neurological impairment from brain lesions and AIDS (Maychick, 35).

See A. Bell, "Homosexuality," *Playbill* 10 (January 1973): 8–11, 40–41; A. Bunce, "Bacall and Booth: Broadway Ladies' Day," *Christian Science Monitor,* April 6, 1970; B. Cohen-Stratyner, *Biographical Dictionary of Dance,* New York, 1982; Ron Field Clippings File, Billy Rose Theatre Collection, New York Public Library for the Performing Arts; Ron Field Scrapbook, Dance Collection, New York Public Library for the Performing Arts; J. Gavin, *Intimate Nights: The Golden Age of New York Cabaret,* New York, 1991; D. Maychick, "Broadway Beat," *New York Post,* March 16, 1989; *Notable Names in the American Theater,* Clifton, N.J., 1976; M. Steyn, *London Independent,* February 13, 1989; and C. Zadan, "Haworth, Hayworth: A Mistake Is a Mistake," *After Dark,* 14 (November 1971): 36–40.

Kevin Winkler

FITCH, (William) Clyde (1865–1909), playwright and director, was born in Elmira, New York, to William Goodwin Fitch, a captain in the Union army, and Alice Clark, a Maryland belle. Fitch attended Hartford Public School in Connecticut and Holderness School in New Hampshire before entering Amherst College in 1882, where his theatrical interests blossomed. Following his 1886 graduation, he moved to New York City determined to become a playwright. His breakthrough success came in 1889 with *Beau Brummell,* which he created as a star vehicle for Richard Mansfield. In 1892, he began his longtime association with Charles Frohman by crafting an adaptation of a French farce, *The Masked Ball,* for **Maude Adams** and John Drew. After he began directing his own work in 1898, Fitch quickly became, in Frohman's words, "the leading producer of plays" for the Theatrical Syndicate. His stock-in-trade was witty, sumptuously appointed social comedies that focused on fashionable upper-class women and catered to the legitimate theater's increasingly female dominated audience. During the season of 1900–1901, Fitch had four original plays running simultaneously on Broadway. The ensuing years, however, saw his most critically acclaimed plays: *The Girl with the Green Eyes* (1902); *The Truth* (1907); and, for this playwright, an atypical heroic melodrama, *The City* (1909). In all, Fitch wrote sixty-two plays: thirty-six original works, twenty-one adaptations, and five dramatizations of novels. With an annual income in excess of $250,000 at the height of his career, he became one of the nation's first dramatist millionaires.

The enormous commercial success and social regard Fitch ultimately earned did not come to him easily. From his early youth, his peers targeted him with epithets of "sissy boy" and "effeminate molly coddle," chiding him mercilessly for his sartorial flamboyance, seemingly affected manners and speech, and falsetto voice (Phelps, 142–44). Fitch's eccentric style continued at Amherst, where, in addition to ruffling the community with his dandiacal wardrobe, he painted the walls of his fraternity room with a floral frieze, exhibited an extensive doll collection, and scented the air with mounds of potpourri in cut crystal bowls. Most notoriously, he engaged in frequent female impersonation. While this was not in itself anomalous in formal dramatic productions at the then all male Amherst College, he far exceeded the conventional parameters of the behavior. Indeed, the blossoming of his theatrical talents occurred chiefly through his attempts to create new venues, scripts, roles, costumes, and settings for female characters. Fitch himself preferred to play the ingenue, which he did repeatedly not only in main stage productions but also in the less formal fraternity sketches he devised and the more impromptu performances he gave at patio tea and cocktail parties. In addition, he expertly dressed and directed his colleagues in female as well as male role types for College Dramatics productions, chiefly Restoration and eighteenth-century comedies. By his sophomore year, he had distinguished himself as Amherst's premier theatrical impresario (Marra, "Transvestite," 22–26).

Many of Fitch's contemporaries, especially the more derisive ones, following the sexologists' logic of inversion, assumed that his nonnormative gender behavior signaled nonnormative sexual behavior, and imputed that he had more than a "hint of lavender" about him (Carnevale-Kanak, 34). Throughout the twentieth century, however, scholars have either ignored the issues of Fitch's gender and sexual identities or dismissed them as irrelevant to assessments of his work. Letters recently brought to light from archives indicate that Fitch may in fact have experienced homosexual as well as transvestite impulses. It has long been established that after college, when he began to make annual trips to England and Continental Europe, he made the acquaintance of Oscar Wilde. In *The Stranger Wilde* (1994), Gary Schmidgall analyzes correspondence between the two men preserved in the Clark Library in Los Angeles as evidence that they were lovers during the years 1889–91. For example, Fitch wrote to Wilde: "Oh! You adorable creature! You *are* a great genius. And oh! such a sweet one. Never was a genius so sweet so adorable. . . . And I— wee I—I am allowed to loose the latchet of yr shoe. Am bidden tie it up—and I do, in a *lover's knot!* . . . You are my sight, and sound, and touch. Yr love is the fragrance of a rose—the sky of a summer—the wing of an angel—the cymbal of a cherubim. . . . (176)." The two also exchanged coded homoerotic pet names such as Oscar's for Clyde, "little

Brown-eyed Fawn" (178). Referring to Wilde's "The Portrait of Mr. W. H.," which is about Shakespeare's love for the child actor Willie Hughes, Fitch called the story *"great—and fine"* and declared *"I believe in Willie Hughes"* (176). Wilde inscribed a copy of *The Happy Prince* for Fitch with the line "Faery-stories for one who lives in Faery-Land" (154).

If Fitch expressed sexual exhilaration in his correspondence with Wilde, he exhibited considerable anxiety and reticence about "certain temperaments of men for the not ordinary sexual enjoyment" in his correspondence with another friend, DeWitt Miller, in 1891. He argued that revelation of these proclivities "would ruin the reputation of many men living and dead who had fought hard against their temptations and done all in their power to make up for their secret life. . . . I believe this temperament belongs to them, and they are answerable for it to God (who perhaps is *also* answerable to them) and not to the world who would condemn and damn them" (qtd. in Schmidgall, 443). Fitch asked that Miller destroy the letter, a request that, as the document's presence in the New York Public Library attests, he did not honor. Given his personal connection to the accused, Fitch's need to hide his sexuality likely was exacerbated by Wilde's 1895 criminal trials. While rumors of his proclivities persisted during his lifetime, no further documentary "proof" has been found. Neither was Fitch seriously linked to another specific partner, though journalists who chronicled his activities repeatedly pointed out that he traveled with a male companion and kept menservants in constant attendance. Voyeuristic society page coverage continually construed the baroque lavishness of his lifestyle and wardrobe as eccentric and effeminate.

In light of the existing evidence, it can be argued that Fitch's nonnormative gender and sexual identifications both proved instrumental in the development of his artistic work. His first major professional playwriting success, *Beau Brummell* (1889), the story of the Georgian dandy, may be seen, if not as a tribute to Wilde himself, at least as a tribute to the sartorial styles for which he and Wilde shared a predilection. Given that *fairy* was a term then in circulation meaning "invert," it is significant that Fitch published his own collection of fairy tales, *The Knighting of the Twins,* in 1891, with the last one—"The King's Throne," dated "Bushey, Herts. September 1889"—dedicated "To Oscar Wilde" (Schmidgall, 154). Seven months after Wilde's *Picture of Dorian Gray* was published in *Lippincott's Magazine* (July 1890), Fitch, too, published a novel in *Lippincott's.* This was his only novel, and it is markedly darker in tone than his plays. Entitled *A Wave of Life,* the novel depicts the destructive passion between two lovers, who are each betrothed to someone else. Their illicit, irrepressible affair rends the social fabric, and the resulting tragedy and guilt drive them to suicide. Although the lovers are ostensibly heterosexual, the young heroine can be read as Fitch in another ingenue role, and her older paramour, a tall man of artistic temperament with long, wavy hair and a moustache, can be seen as a conflation of Fitch and Wilde (Oscar was tall with long wavy hair, artistically inclined, and eleven years older than the considerably smaller, mustached Clyde). The fictional couple's experience reflects the fears about uncontrollable sexual desire and public revelation that Fitch expressed in his correspondence of the same period.

The impact of Fitch's gender and sexual identities on his artistic work continued in the contemporary, female-centered urban social comedies for which he became most famous and wealthy. Fitch found a legitimate outlet for his transvestism in the professional theater where he could vicariously impersonate women as a playwright and physically impersonate them as a director of his own work. Playing the female characters himself in rehearsal and then instructing actresses to copy him became his signature directorial method. Testimonials to the success of his efforts abound. Leading actress **Elsie de Wolfe** declared: "Fitch knows women better than they know themselves." Likewise, Amelia Bingham commented about his staging of *The Climbers:* "Could the entire first act of the play—which you will remember is dominated by women characters—have been played by Mr. Fitch, it would have scored such a success as New York rarely knows. Not a woman of us could approach him in look, manner, and, above all, voice" (qtd. in Marra, "Transvestite," 29).

As reflected in the titles of many of his plays—for example, *My Girl Jo (Her Great Match), The Girl and the Judge, The Girl with the Green Eyes,* and *Girls*—Fitch specialized in creating a particular type of womanhood, the newly emergent national ideal of femininity iconized across a wide range of contemporary media and labeled the American Girl. Through the transformation of merely human females into living embodiments of this dominant cultural deity, he became known as the "Maker of Actresses" and launched the careers of numerous leading ladies of the period, including **Maude Adams,** Ethel Barrymore, Maxine Elliott, and Clara Bloodgood. Working with such actresses, Fitch exploited the many opportunities his profession afforded him to fetishize the feminine ideal and thereby obliquely express his sexuality. He not only directed his actresses to copy his impersonations, but he personally dressed them in the most fashionable costumes, styled their hair, applied their makeup, fixed their nails, and showcased them in ornate sets filled with sumptuous real furnishings and objets d'art. This self-disguising deployment of style, baroque fantasy, and sensuous detail aligns Fitch aesthetically as well as sexually with Wilde and problematizes traditional assessments of his work according to the standards of social realism (see, e.g., Meserve, 161–65).

While making expert use of these artistic outlets, Fitch, like his former lover, could not escape the darker demons of dominant cultural degradation of his sexuality. Fetishizing the American Girl, scion of what was deemed most beautiful and virtuous in U.S. culture, may also have been a means of overcoming the personal feelings of sickness and sinfulness he confided in his correspondence with DeWitt Miller. The fervid, workaholic pace at which he drove himself, against the advice of doctors and friends and long after his wealth and success could well have afforded him a respite, suggests the workings of such a compensatory dynamic. His biographers report that "he was often rehearsing two plays at a time, writing on another, and planning ahead with managers for a fourth and fifth" (Moses and Gerson, *Clyde Fitch and His Letters,* 209). His unwillingness to slow down, even when a severe health condition called for surgery, contributed to his death from a ruptured appendix in Chalon-sur-Marne in the autumn of 1909. He was forty-four years old and, like Wilde, dead before his time.

See J. A. Carnevale-Kanak, "Clyde Fitch and His Reception by the American Periodical Press," Ph.D. diss., Fordham University, 1978; Clyde Fitch Collection, Amherst College Special Collections and Archives, Amherst, Massachusetts; and Clyde Fitch Letters, 1890–1904, New York Public Library. Fitch's letters to Wilde are quoted in their entirety in Milissa Knox, *Oscar Wilde: A Long and Lovely Suicide,* New Haven and London, 1994, 151–53. See also K. Marra, "Clyde Fitch's Too Wilde Love," in *Staging Desire: Queer Readings of American Theater History,* edited by K. Marra and R. A. Schanke, Ann Arbor, 2002; K. Marra, "Clyde Fitch, Transvestite *Metteur-en-Scene* of the Feminine," *New England Theatre Journal* 3 (1992): 15–37; W. Meserve, *An Outline History of American Drama,* New York, 1994; M. J. Moses and V. Gerson, eds., *Plays by Clyde Fitch,* 4 vols., Boston, 1915; M. J. Moses and V. Gerson, eds., *Clyde Fitch and His Letters,* Boston, 1924; W. L. Phelps, *Essays on Modern Dramatists,* New York, 1921; and G. Schmidgall, *The Stranger Wilde: Interpreting Oscar,* New York, 1994.

Kim Marra

FONTANNE, Lynn. See Lunt, Alfred.

FORREST, Edwin, (1806–72), actor, is usually considered to be the first star born and trained in the United States. Born in 1806 to a nontheatrical Philadelphia family, he had no formal training as an actor but developed an interest in the stage at an early age, submitting himself to a rigorous physical regimen of exercise and tumbling, inspired by circus performers, that nurtured both his famously "Herculean" physique and his lifelong obsession with physical culture. After he and his brother organized an amateur Thespian Club, he made his 1817 debut, cross-dressed, as a fill-in for an absent ingenue at the Southwark Theatre—a fact that seems to have caused all of his biographers considerable anxiety.

After sporadic Philadelphia appearances, Forrest set out for four years of exhausting stock actor work in traveling troupes in the Midwest and South. After working his way up to leading actor status, he made his New York debut in 1826 as Othello at the Bowery Theatre. He was an instant success, and the managers of the Bowery immediately increased the twenty-eight dollars a week stipulated in his contract to forty dollars a week. Before long, he was acknowledged as one of the great actors of the age, and he toured England and France as well as the United States. His financial success outstripped that of any other American actor.

Forrest was best known for his interpretations of Lear, Othello, Richard III, and Macbeth and for fostering native drama with a series of competitions for American playwrights. He bought and produced the prizewinning plays and allowed the authors no royalties, even though these native plays in his repertory rivaled Shakespeare in popularity. Prizewinners included John Augustus Stone's *Metamora* (1829), Robert Montgomery Bird's *The Gladiator* (1831) and *The Broker of Bogota* (1834), and Robert Conrad's *Jack Cade* (1835), all of which featured Forrest in his favorite role, that of a manly democrat and opponent of oppression. Another regular role was Damon in John Banim's *Damon and Pythias* (1821), a play set in Rome that related remarkable love and devotion between two men. In addition to spotlighting Forrest's radically democratic political convictions, all of the native plays featured elaborate costuming designed to show off his masculine physique and feats of strength and agility.

Forrest's reputation depended on his large audience of working-class supporters: the upper and middle classes were alienated by his increasingly hostile rivalry with English actor William Macready, which led to the Astor Place Opera House riot (1849), and by his scandalous public divorce that same year from his English wife Catherine Sinclair. Embittered after he was found guilty of adultery (with "burly" actress Josephine Clifton) and ordered to pay alimony, Forrest continuously appealed the decision, and became an increasingly virulent misogynist, in his letters referring to marriage as the "invention of the devil" and women as "swindlers" and "whores."

After his divorce, Forrest's closest relationship was with his lifelong friend James Oakes, a Boston merchant. Forrest labeled the bedchamber across from his own in his Philadelphia mansion "Oakes's room," and Oakes hosted Forrest whenever the actor played Boston. Forrest's official biographer, William R. Alger, relates that his Philadelphia mansion displayed portraits of Oakes in four rooms. Oakes cared for Forrest as his health worsened and was left an annuity of $2,500 a year in his will. While biographers have ignored or discounted suggestions that the men were lovers, Forrest and Oakes clearly had a more passionate relationship than Forrest and his wife. Forrest's letters to Oakes report on his engagements, finances, and health in intimate detail. He continually invites Oakes to join him on vacations and business trips, and the two men refer occasionally to a common fantasy in which they move together to Cuba, to "live and die there amid the warm breath of fragrant fruits and flowers" (Forrest, letters to James Oakes, January 17, 1870, folder 4, quoted with the permission of the Princeton University Libraries). Oakes, for his part, often began his letters to Forrest with "My noble Spartacus" (Moses, 312) and closed with even more effusive affection, in one early letter signing, "Command my services to the fullest extent in anything and in everything. For I am, from top to bottom, inside and out, and all through, forever yours" (qtd. in Alger, 626). In a letter to the sculptor Thomas Ball, who had been commissioned to make a statue of Forrest, Oakes explained that "For more than forty years I have known this man with an intimacy not common among men. Indeed, our friendship has been more like the devotion of a man to the woman he loves than the relations usually subsisting between men" (632).

As might be expected, the intensity of the relationship was easily acknowledged by early biographers, and downplayed by later ones, as the possibility of a homosexual relationship became an issue. Alger relates that "whenever they met after a long separation, as soon as they were alone together they threw their arms around each other in a fond embrace with mutual kisses after the manner of lovers in our land or of friends in more tropical and demonstrative climes" (627). Moody, in the most recent biography, feels compelled to assert that "there are no grounds for believing that their relationship was unnatural" (345).

In a letter that has been ignored or misread by every biographer, Forrest relates to Oakes that his leading lady, Lillie Swindlehurst, had asked him "if *we* are married as you told her—which is the Woman" (Forrest, letters to James Oakes, March 29, 1866, folder 4). Moody mistakenly reads "we" as referring to Forrest and Swindlehurst (358), when it is clear that it refers to Forrest and Oakes. In a subsequent letter, Forrest declares that he will tell Lillie "that either of us is quite likely to *turn to* a Woman, when it is desirable" (Forrest, letters to James Oakes, April 3, 1866, folder 4). The ambiguity of "turn to" demonstrates the sexual ambiguity that seems to have disturbed all of Forrest's biographers, who were constantly driven to make hyperbolic claims about his masculinity and virility. The fact that Forrest, even in his most misogynist phases, seems to have been continually attracted to and involved with women sexually has given commentators the ability to rationalize or ignore his clearly superior love and passion for Oakes.

The anxiety about Forrest's sexuality grows out of his work as well. Hard-pressed to account for a career so intently focused on valorizing masculine power, the male physique, and close bonds between men, critics have typically read him as hypermasculine, more willing to create him as a parody than as bisexual or sexually ambiguous. But Forrest's sexuality is perhaps best compared to that of Walt Whitman (who was a fan of Forrest): both men fostered ambiguity and sexual inclusiveness through the construction of the self as representative, while clearly being most compellingly drawn to masculine attributes of mind and body. Forrest's selection of manly roles, his attraction to plays with gladiatorial or Roman settings, and his love for physical culture can all clearly be read as part of a male-centered aesthetic. But his fervently democratic politics and his constant attempts to play the part—on- and offstage—of protector of the oppressed can also be illuminated further when they are considered in relation to his sexual inclusiveness, directing attention to the ways in which nineteenth-century ideals of manly virtue are dependent on the incorporation of feminine principles, even as they seem to devalue women.

In 1872, while on what would be his final stage tour, Forrest was stricken with pneumonia in Boston. Oakes nursed him back to health and then spent much of the summer with him in Philadelphia. Physically unable to perform onstage, Forrest embarked that autumn on a reading tour that was received by the public with politeness but lukewarm interest. He returned to Philadelphia to gather his strength but died on December 12, 1872. Oakes arrived immediately to supervise all preparations and dress Forrest's body for burial. As he contemplated the body of his dead friend, Oakes later wrote to Alger that "it seemed to me that my body was as cold as his and my heart as still. The little while I stood at his side, speechless, almost lifeless, seemed an age. No language can express the agony of that hour, and even now I cannot bear to turn my mind back to it" (Alger, 834).

See W. R. Alger, *Life of Edwin Forrest,* 2 vols., Philadelphia, 1877; L. Barrett, *Edwin Forrest,* Boston, 1881; Edwin Forrest, letters to James Oakes, Manuscripts Division, Department of Rare Books and Special Collections, Princeton University Libraries,

CO721; Edwin Forrest, diary of trip abroad, Harvard Theatre Collection, Harvard University; G. Harrison: *Edwin Forrest,* Brooklyn, 1889; L. Merrill, "'Appealing to the Passions': Homoerotic Desire and Nineteenth-Century Theater Criticism," in *Staging Desire: Queer Readings of American Theater History,* edited by K. Marra and R. A. Schanke, Ann Arbor, 2002, 221–61; R. Moody, *Edwin Forrest: First Star of the American Stage,* New York 1960; M. Moses, *The Fabulous Forrest,* Boston, 1929; J. Rees [Colley Cibber], *The Life of Edwin Forrest,* Philadelphia, 1874; G. Strand, "'My Noble Spartacus': Edwin Forrest and Masculinity on the Nineteenth-Century Stage," in *Passing Performances: Queer Readings of Leading Players in American Theater History,* edited by R. A. Schanke and K. Marra, Ann Arbor, 1998, 19–40.

Ginger Strand

FOSTER, Stephen (Collins) (1826–64), composer, was born in Pittsburgh, on July 4, 1826. Since his younger brother James died as an infant, Foster, the ninth of ten children of William Barclay Foster and Eliza Clayland Tomlinson Foster, remained the baby of his family. As his many songs about home and family suggest, his happiest experiences and most emotionally intimate relationships appear to have occurred within the context of his family. His father was something of a ne'er-do-well; consequently, after an idealized early childhood Foster's life was a long slide of downward economic mobility.

Foster was educated at several schools and by tutors. He was not a diligent student, and his family regarded him as a dreamer. In 1846, he went to work as a bookkeeper at his brother Dunning's business in Cincinnati, while writing songs in his spare time. In 1850, encouraged by his early success with songs such as "Oh, Susanna," he left the business world, returned to Pittsburgh, married, and devoted himself to a songwriting career full time. In the early 1850s, his career prospered, but professional setbacks, the failure of his marriage, and apparent alcoholism contributed to an early death. Foster died in 1864 as a result of a bizarre accident in which a fall resulted in a serious cut to his throat.

The first American to make a career as a full-time popular songwriter, Foster composed 189 songs during his brief life. He so authentically captured the American spirit in his songs that many of them, such as "Camptown Races," came to be regarded as folk songs, with the composer's identity forgotten. Foster wrote most of his songs for either performance on the minstrel stage or performance within the context of the Victorian parlor. He achieved prominence as a songwriter for what he called his "Ethiopian" songs, which were written for the minstrel stage with lyrics in a black dialect. Raucous comedy and mockery of African Americans characterized the early-nineteenth-century minstrel stage. Foster helped

Stephen Foster, probably in his early thirties, from *The American Weekly,* August 7, 1855. (Courtesy of the Billy Rose Theatre Collection, New York Public Library for the Performing Arts.)

change that by infusing the genre with nostalgia and moral implications through songs such as "Uncle Ned," "My Old Kentucky Home," and "The Old Folks at Home." His influence resulted from a special arrangement with the Christy Minstrels, one of the most successful minstrel troupes in the nation, in which he permitted the company to perform his songs prior to their publication as sheet music. As a child, Foster had occasionally attended an African American church with a family servant, which perhaps accounts for his authentic black music idiom. William Austin suggests that a friend, the abolitionist Charles Shiras, may have influenced the sympathetic attitude toward slaves that Foster discloses in his music. In addition to minstrelsy stage presentations, songs such as "Jeanie with the Light Brown Hair," "Come Where My Love Lies Dreaming," and "Beautiful Dreamer" became popular home entertainments, furnishing families in nineteenth-century America an abundant source of musical pleasure. Foster derived most of his income from the royalties generated from the sale of sheet music. His reliance on performances in the parlor for his livelihood may explain why, over the course of his career, his Ethiopian songs came to resemble the parlor songs.

Stephen Foster epitomizes those nineteenth-century figures whose sexuality disappears behind the limits that Victorian propriety placed on discussions of physical intimacy. John Tasker Howard's biography, *Stephen Foster: America's Troubadour* (1934), suggests that Foster did not have a typical man's sexual interest in his wife. Since Foster's niece had a strong influence on that book, it is not surprising that there is no mention of possible homosexuality. Current nonfiction works, such as the *Gay Almanac* (1996), identify Foster as homosexual but fail to provide the sources on which the assertion is based. Peter Quinn's novel, *Banished Children of Eve* (1995), and Noel Tipton's play, *Dear Friends and Gentle Hearts* (1996), portray Foster as homosexual. Quinn depicts him that way because he believes it makes emotional sense within the narrative. Tipton attributes both Foster's creativity and his unhappiness to homosexuality. Both authors admit that they have no clear evidence on which to base their speculations. An early identification of Foster as homosexual occurs in Ian Whitcomb's *Irving Berlin and Ragtime America* (1987) in which the author reports "rumors he'd turned pansy" but cites no source for the rumors. Ken Emerson's biography *Doo-Dah: Stephen Foster and the Rise of American Popular Culture* (1998) extensively examines the factual evidence before concluding that Foster never achieved an adult sexuality of any persuasion.

The failure of Foster's marriage; his alcoholism; the gentle, dreamy, feminine nature of much of his music; and some close male friendships all serve to fuel speculation about his sexual identity. Discontinuities in the narrative of Foster's life result in part from his family's destruction of some records. Deane Root, curator of the Stephen Foster Collection in Pittsburgh, asserts that Morrison Foster, Stephen's older brother, destroyed records that might have proved embarrassing to the family (telephone interview with the author, October 1996). This erasure may point to a concealed homosexual identity; Ken Emerson maintains that it is impossible to prove or disprove repressed sexuality.

Given his intention to forge a career as a songwriter, Foster's choice to marry Jane McDowell, a rather conventional, bourgeois woman with no interest in music, proved unfortunate if not disastrous. Their one child was born almost exactly nine months after the marriage. Several subsequent separations suggest a desire on Foster's part to escape from the marriage, an idea reinforced by the absence of any indication that the relationship achieved consistent emotional or physical intimacy.

Foster forged close relationships with men outside the family unit, at least two of which merit examination. Beginning in 1845, he formed a special friendship with Charles Shiras; together with some friends, they established a club called the "Five Nice Young Men." Foster set the words of one of Shiras's poems to music ("Annie My Own Love") and reportedly composed music for a production of a play by Shiras, although no known record of the music exists. As mentioned earlier, Shiras may have influenced Foster's attitude toward African Americans.

In 1862, at the age of thirty-six, while separated from his family and living alone in New York, Foster developed a friendship with twenty-year-old George Cooper, who would write lyrics for twenty-one of Foster's songs. This professional collaboration was unique in Foster's career. Foster usually wrote his own lyrics, and other than Cooper he used no individual lyricist more than three times. Howard reports that Foster called Cooper "the left wing of the song factory" (Howard, 318). Emerson and others report that Cooper and Foster met in the back room of a Bowery grocery store that Foster frequented when drinking. Was this clandestine drinking establishment some kind of 1860s gay bar or just a cheap and private place to drink? Emerson believes that Foster served as a mentor for Cooper, while Cooper functioned as something of a caregiver for Foster. Howard and others report that after what would prove to be Foster's fatal accident Cooper was the person summoned by the hotel chambermaid to care for him. Cooper took Foster to Bellevue Hospital and kept his family apprised of his condition. Is that mentor-caregiver relationship, a not uncommon one of the October-May sort, a clue to a more intimate one?

An interrogation of Foster's music yields no clues of an overt sexual identity. That there are no songs of sublimated sexual longing is not surprising, given the Victorians' reluctance to discuss anything sexual. Foster's admission in a letter to E. P. Christy that "I find I cannot write at all unless I write for public approbation and get credit for what I write" suggests that he was unlikely to write songs that might run counter to a middle-class sense of propriety. The unreal and idealized character of the women in his songs perhaps confirms that he had no adult, mature knowledge of women. Susan Key posits that the authorial voice in his songs frequently expresses a nostalgic longing for the past by one who is stuck in an alien present. This may suggest that Foster's inability to accept his emotional and/or sexual feelings about men resulted in alienation from his state of sexual awareness while he clung to nostalgia for a past in which he was not yet sexually aware.

To speculate that Stephen Foster was a homosexual sheds an intriguing light on the narrative of his life. However, since the modern gay identity was constructed in the last decade of the nineteenth century, some thirty years after Foster's death, it is unlikely that he ever thought of himself as gay. He had homophilial friendships, and the absence of proof of a genital expression of sexuality need not lead one to presume heterosexuality. However, given the limitations of our knowledge resulting from partial erasure of the record, any current definitive identification of the sexuality of Stephen Foster must remain speculative.

See W. W. Austin, *"Susanna," "Jeanie," and "The Old Folks at Home": The Songs of Stephen C. Foster from His Time to Ours,* Urbana, Ill., 1975; C. Elliker, *Stephen Collins Foster: Guide to Research,* New York, 1988; K. Emerson, *Doo-Dah: Stephen Foster and the Rise of American Popular Culture,* New York, 1998; *The Gay Almanac,* New York, 1996; J. T. Howard, *Stephen Foster, America's Troubadour,* New York, 1934; S. Key, "Sound and Sentimentality: Nostalgia in the Songs of Stephen Foster," in *American Music* 13 (summer 1995): 2, 145–46; E. F. Morneweck, *Chronicles of Stephen Foster's Family,* Pittsburgh, 1944; and I. Whitcomb, *Irving Berlin and Ragtime America,* New York, 1987.

Stephen Berwind

FULLER, Loie (Marie Louise Fuller) (1862–1928), dancer, lighting innovator, choreographer, and filmmaker, was born in Fullersburg, Illinois. This revolutionary artist, the first to present a full evening of solo dance, is also recognized as a pioneer in lighting design. Fuller choreographed over 135 dances, most of them group works for her all-female company, the Loie Fuller Dancers.

Isadora Duncan was very impressed with this "luminous vision" in performance: "What an extraordinary genius! No imitator of Loie Fuller has ever been able even to hint at her genius! . . . She was one of the first original inspirations of light and changing color" (95).

The great Ruth St. Denis agreed with this assessment, adding, "I personally feel that Loie Fuller has been neglected. She brought appurtenances—lights and veils—to dance and where would I be, pray, without my lights? where would Isadora have been without her simple lighting effects? where would the theatre dancers of today find themselves without Loie's magnificent contributions?" (qtd. in Terry, 30).

Fuller did not receive formal dance training as a child; rather, she took singing lessons. She began her professional acting career at the age of fifteen when she was cast as the soubrette in a touring pantomime spectacle of *Aladdin.* Thereafter, Fuller performed with several stock companies, produced a play she had written, toured with Buffalo Bill (1883), and sang in musical burlettas at New York's Bijou Theatre (1886–89).

Fuller introduced her first choreographed "silk" dance, presented with her own lighting design, in the New York extravaganza *Uncle Celestin* (1892). By manipulating the fabric of a voluminous skirt in *The Serpentine Dance,* she became the hit of the show. Within weeks of her debut in New York, she was plagued by a problem she would have to face for the rest of her life—imitators. In 1892, she sued Minnie Renwood for infringement of her copyright, but the court refused protection because the dance did not tell a story and so did not fall within the meaning of a "dramatic composition" as defined in the Copyright Act.

With a repertoire of new dances, Fuller traveled to Europe and made her Parisian debut at the Folies Bergère on November 4, 1892; taking the city by storm, her initial engagement ran for more than three hundred performances. The French critics dubbed her "La Loie" and "La Creatrice," positioning her work in the context of art nouveau and symbolism. While she awed such greats as Andre Levison, Baudelaire, and Rodin and was immortalized by many visual artists, it was Stéphane Mallarmé who announced Loie Fuller as the personification of symbolist ideals (Sommer, 394).

Fuller designed her own dance costumes, many of which incorporated hundreds of yards of silk. Utilizing the effects of air currents and gravity, she manipulated her fabric into an endless catalog of abstract shapes. Dubbed the "Fairy of Light," her costumes often contained pole extensions, which dramatically enlarged her silhouette, thus creating a large surface on which to display her experiments with electric light. For *Fire Dance,* Fuller had a hole cut in the stage and covered it with a large plate of glass. With lighting coming from underneath the stage, she appeared to float in space, engulfed in yards of silk and vibrant color. Her dancers were invisible in *Radium Dance* (1904), as the audience saw only the moving patterns created by designs painted on their costumes with phosphorescent paint.

After four years in Paris, Fuller returned in triumph to New York, where she commanded a salary in vaudeville double that of Lillian Russell. But Paris is the city that loved her and the city she was to call home for over thirty years. In 1900, Henri Sauvage built a beautiful theater for her at the Paris Universal Exposition.

When Isadora Duncan met Loie Fuller in 1898, she was taken aback by the sight of the older dancer surrounded by a "dozen or so beautiful girls," who were "alternately stroking her hands and kissing her," but nevertheless she was happy to accept the terms of a tour that Fuller arranged for her (94). One night in Vienna one of the members of the Fuller entourage made either direct advances to Isadora or tried to strangle her—Duncan's account of the incident kept changing—and Isadora refused to continue with the tour (98).

Beginning around 1898, Fuller began a relationship with Gabrielle Bloch in what was commonly known to be a sexual relationship. This partnership attracted attention since "Gab" was sixteen years younger than Loie and always dressed in men's clothing. In her autobiography, *Fifteen Years of a Dancer's Life* (1913), Loie devotes an entire chapter to her partner.

> For eight years Gab and I have lived together on terms of the greatest intimacy, like two sisters. . . . [H]er voice is of velvet, her skin and locks are of velvet, her eyes are of velvet and her name ought to be *Velours*. If one could compare her to a living creature a boa constrictor would be most appropriate, for her movements are like those of a snake. There is nothing sinuous, nothing rampant about them, but the *ensemble* of her motions suggests the suppleness of the young adder. (250–51)

Although the two women did not always live together, they nurtured a relationship that lasted more than thirty years until Fuller's death in 1928. Bloch—who adopted the name Gab Sorere around 1920—took control of the Loie Fuller Dancers upon Fuller's death and kept the company performing for another ten years.

While performing in Bucharest in 1902, Fuller had the occasion to meet another important woman in her life, the crown princess of Romania, later to become Queen Marie Alexandra Victoria. The two struck up a friendship and organized many benefits for war charities. As Clare de Morinni reports, there were "innumerable scandalous rumors concerning the Queen and the dancer" (50). In their extant correspondence (1912–27), Loie's letters are effusive and adoring, while the queen's are warm but reserved.

Despite her fame, Fuller lived modestly, as the technical demands of her productions were costly; *Fire Dance,* for example, required fourteen electricians. When she toured America in 1910, her company included fifty French electricians.

After the war, Fuller's public performances became infrequent. No longer young and now quite heavy, she confined her appearances to benefits and special occasions. For her war relief work, she received military decorations from France, Belgium, and Romania. Her last professional engagement was in London in 1927; the following year she died of pneumonia at the age of sixty-six.

Fuller liked to say that she could see music. Her concept of choreography was that of music visualization: "I try to follow the musical waves in the movements of the body and the colors" (qtd. in Sommer, 390).

Debussy is said to have remarked that her dance to his *Nocturnes, Nuages, Fêtes, and Sirènes* permitted him to "hear" his music for this first time (Thompson, 172).

Many critics share the opinion of Mario Amaya that Fuller's artistic contributions were restricted to innovations in lighting and costume design and that she used these elements "to hide a lack of talent," since "she could not dance brilliantly" (34). Recognized while she was alive as a pioneer of stage lighting, Fuller fully exploited the technical and artistic possibilities of electric light and even referred to her dancers as "instruments of light" (qtd. in Morinni, 51).

Fuller began using young women in group pieces in the late 1800s and established a school for their training in 1908. Since Loie's choreography and concept of dance was not centered on a technique, the pedagogy of the school was not that of a traditional ballet academy. Rather, she wanted to encourage the girls to retain their natural gifts of inherent, unaffected movement.

Although her choreography was not based on codified patterns of movement, Fuller nevertheless can be seen as a genius in her unique combinations of existing forms. She took the nautch dance and the skirt dance (long popular in vaudeville) and transformed them into studies of movement and color. By greatly increasing the size of the costume, Fuller took the emphasis off the female form, which became almost invisible amid all the yards of fabric. Although they worked independently, Loie Fuller and Isadora Duncan were instrumental in offering a new vision of a woman who was neither virginal nor a temptress but was able to move with freedom and power. Barefoot, sans bra, and sans corset, this new woman was realized with a complexity of character far beyond the scope of stage presentations of female characters in nineteenth-century ballets. And by manipulating her body using technology Fuller's work predates the experiments of many performance artists by decades.

See M. Amaya, "The Little Genius of Montmarte," *Dance and Dancers* 12 (April 1961): 18–21, 34; R. Current and M. Current, *Loie Fuller: Goddess of Light,* Boston, 1997; C. De Morinni, "Loie Fuller: The Fairy of Light," *Dance Index* 1:3 (March 1942): 40–51; I. Duncan, *My Life,* New York, 1927; L. Fuller, *Fifteen Years of a Dancer's Life,* Boston, 1913; "Loie Fuller," New York Public Library Dance Collection at Lincoln Center; S. Sommer, "Loie Fuller's Art of Music and Light," *Dance Chronicle* 4 (1981): 389–401; O. Thompson, *Debussy: Man and Artist,* New York, 1940; W. Terry, "The Legacy of Isadora Duncan and

Ruth St. Denis," *Dance Perspectives* 5 (winter 1960): 5–60; and J. Townsend, "Alchemic Visions and Technological Advances: Sexual Morphology in Loie Fuller's Dance," in *Dancing Desires,* edited by J. Desmond, Madison, 2001.

Bud Coleman

GRANGER, Farley (Farley Earle Granger II) (1925–), actor, was born July 1, 1925, in San Jose, California. He made his film debut in 1943 in *The North Star* at the age of seventeen, and he soon completed another film (*The Purple Heart,* 1944) before serving a two-year stint in the Special Services of the Armed Forces. Soon after his discharge, he signed a contract with Samuel Goldwyn, who lent him out to other studios. One of his first films was Arthur Hitchcock's *Rope* (1948). Granger was the only principal player who accepted the role when it was first offered; Cary Grant and **Montgomery Clift** turned down their roles—ultimately taken by James Stewart and John Dall—because of the threat to their images (Russo, 94). Granger and Dall were playing a gay couple.

The story was based on the Leopold and Loeb murder case: two young men kill a friend as an intellectual exercise. Granger played a passive, nervous pianist, who turns to Dall for leadership and assurance. James Stewart played a teacher, whose teachings they had misinterpreted (and who, in an earlier draft, had been a role model for them) (Spoto, 305). Although not very successful, the film remains of interest because it is presented in one uninterrupted take (actually eight ten-minute takes) and because of the subtle relationship between Granger and Dall.

By the time *Rope* had begun filming, Granger—known as "Farfel" to his friends—had entered a gay relationship of his own. He was living with playwright **Arthur Laurents,** who was brought in to polish the script of *Rope.* Laurents and Granger had met on Laurents's first day in Hollywood and had flirted at Gene Kelly's house before cementing what was to be a four-year relationship (Laurents, 80–81, 92, 122; Kramer, 53).

Granger's second film with Hitchcock was *Strangers on a Train* (1951). He played a tennis pro who becomes involved in a homosexual psychopath's (played by Robert Walker) bizarre plan to kill the tennis pro's wife and then have the tennis pro kill his own father. Granger's skills at tennis were called on in the film, as was his "passive" homosexuality: he was the object of the psychopath's plan and affections. Laurents later recalled that Granger reported it was Walker's idea to play his character as a homosexual (Russo, 94); this may have been true, but nothing in a Hitchcock film was unplanned. That relationship was an essential yet unspoken part of the film. Hitchcock biographer Spoto writes: "Walker is Granger's 'shadow,' activating what Granger wants, bringing out the dark underside of Granger's potentially murderous"—and sexual— "desires" (328).

Both films were made during a time of rigorous censorship. The homosexual relationships are played not in words but in the subtext—looks, a subtle gesture, an indefinite inflection. Russo notes in *The Celluloid Closet* that the murderers in both films believed themselves to exist "outside the culture," thus "able to deny explicit homosexuality while at the same time reinforcing specific stereotypes" (94–95). Such elite effetes helped Hollywood "define gays as aliens" in the 1950s (94).

By this point, Laurents and Granger had split up, and Granger took up (at least temporarily) with a dancer, James Mitchell, who had played Dream Curly in the original production of *Oklahoma!* (Laurents, 287).

Granger's next major film had him playing a handsome dandy with cruel ways, the abusive ballet master in the musical *Hans Christian Anderson* (1952). He raised star **Danny Kaye**'s closeted ire and envy and was deprived of his only song because of it (Gottfried, 177).

As the Hollywood studio system fell apart in the 1950s, so did Granger's film career. His association with Hitchcock had given him a reputation for horror, and his subsequent films have such lurid titles as *Something Creeping in the Dark, The Slasher, Kill Me My Love,* and *The Co-ed Murders.*

Set on improving himself (and his career), Granger moved to New York in the mid-1950s and studied acting with **Sanford Meisner,** Stella Adler, and Lee Strasberg. His commercial theater appearances included originating the role of Fitzwilliam Darcy in *First Impressions,* the musical version of *Pride and Prejudice* (1959, ninety-two performances). He also played roles in two revivals of musicals at the New York City Center: as the King in *The King and I* (1960) and as sardonic, alcoholic best friend Jeff Douglas in *Brigadoon* (1961). None of these roles stretched Granger's talents; his characters were handsome, haughty, and/or not what they seemed.

He subsequently joined **Eva Le Gallienne**'s National Repertory Company in the mid-1960s, playing leading roles in *The Seagull, The Crucible, Hedda Gabler, Liliom, Ring Round the Moon,* and *She Stoops to Conquer.* Yet no one came calling for Granger's talents, or if they did he turned them down. He eventually returned to California and semiretired.

In the mid-1970s, he appeared as a guest star on such prime time television shows as *Kojak* and *The Six Million Dollar Man* (he had made TV appearances in the 1950s as well). He later played continuing roles on the daytime soap operas *One Life to Live* (1976–77) and *As the World Turns* (1986–88) but has otherwise kept out of the public eye.

Granger's life and career evince the contradictions and goal of comfort seen in the careers of other gay performers. Although Laurents recalls him stating: "I never thought there was anything wrong with being gay" (154), he publicly escorted young women while they were together (Kramer, 53). Granger has granted many interviews to people writing stories about those he worked with in his career (Alfred Hitchcock, Frank Loesser, Danny Kaye, Eva Le Gallienne), and he even appeared on-screen in *The Celluloid Closet* (1996), but he has remained quiet about himself. His two Hitchcock films contained homosexual subtexts from which he did not shy. Yet when Larry Kramer brought up Granger's affair with Arthur Laurents in an interview for *The Advocate* Laurents said: "I don't know whether he'll be pleased to have that appear in print" (53). His disappearance from the national scene starting in the mid-1960s and his reluctance to discuss himself indicate the desire for a comfortable, private life—away from questions. His early career provided an image of gays when few were available, and his later silence bespeaks the public illusion so many are fearful of breaking. Together they express the possibilities and plight of a gay performer on the national scene.

See M. Gottfried, *Nobody's Fool: The Lives of Danny Kaye,* New York, 1994; "Granger, Farley," in *The Biographical Encyclopaedia and Who's Who of the American Theatre,* edited by W. Rigdon, New York, 1966, 497; "Granger, Farley," in *International Motion Picture Almanac,* edited by B. Monush, 66th ed., New York, 1995, 137; L. Kramer, "His Brilliant Career," *The Advocate,* May 16, 1995, 49–56; A. Laurents, *Original Story By: A Memoir of Broadway and Hollywood,* New York, 2000; V. Russo, *The Celluloid Closet: Homosexuality in the Movies,* rev. ed., New York, 1987; and D. Spoto, *The Dark Side of Genius: The Life of Alfred Hitchcock,* Boston, 1983.

Jeffrey Smart

GUILFOYLE, Paul (1902–1961), stage and screen actor and television director, specialized in self-loathing and alienated characters. From 1925 to 1934, he played an assortment of lepers, dope fiends, drunkards, handicapped youths, and weak-willed homosexuals in such Broadway productions as *The Green Hat* (1925), *Box Seats* (1928), *Zeppelin* (1929), *Penny Arcade* (1930),*This One Man* (1930), *Six Characters in Search of an Author* (1931), and *Jayhawker* (1934).

In 1935, he went to Hollywood, where he played supporting roles in many films, often with a tragic demise, including *The Crime of Dr. Crespi* (1935), *Winterset* (1936), *Stage Fright* (1938), *The Grapes of Wrath* (1940), *White Savage* (1943), *Mighty Joe Young* (1949), and *White Heat* (1949).

Paul Guilfoyle, in his twenties as an actor in New York. (Photo by Paul Stone-Raymor, courtesy of the Billy Rose Theatre Collection, New York Public Library for the Performing Arts.)

During the next decade, Guilfoyle directed over one hundred television episodes for such series as *Lawman, Science Fiction Theater, Highway Patrol,* and *Sea Hunt.*

Born in Jersey City, New Jersey, Guilfoyle as a young man heard about a scholarship competition at New York's School for the Theater (on Lexington Avenue), and he decided to audition. The three judges (Elsie Ferguson, George Arliss, and Frank Craven) chose him as one of two winners. After distinguishing himself as best student in the nine-month course, Guilfoyle was chosen to play in the traveling company headed by the school's vice president, Walter Hampden. As one of the actors in the road production of Ibsen's *Ghosts,* Guilfoyle was scouted by a Broadway stage manager. By 1925, he was making his Broadway debut opposite Katharine Cornell and Leslie Howard in Michael Arlen's *The Green Hat,* directed by **Guthrie McClintic.** About his stint in that production's role of a sniveling invert, Gerald Marsh, he said: "Since that time managers have been able to see me only in morbid character parts, and I'm afraid I'll have to go on playing them if I want to work" ("In the Current Broadway Panorama," 1929). Guilfoyle's authenticity in the "outsider" character roles that made up his acting career undoubtedly stemmed in part from his sense of alienation as a homosexual. According to Kaier Curtin, his foster son, the young actor was seduced (presumably willingly) by Guthrie McClintic, who had a reputation for pursuing neophyte actors and crew members (Harbin, interview, 1996).

In Hollywood, Guilfoyle continued to lead a secret gay life, as he had in New York. To disguise his homosexuality, he had entered into a sham marriage, as did many gay actors. Guilfoyle's lesbian wife was a musical theater actress, **Kathleen Mulqueen,** who had performed on Broadway in *Molly Darling* (1922), *Sally, Irene, and Mary* (1925), *Tomorrow* (1928), and other productions, before her marriage. Guilfoyle and Mulqueen, who were both acting on Broadway throughout the 1920s and early 1930s, went to the same parties with the same theater crowd and were "Broadway buddies." They moved to Hollywood in 1935, and Guilfoyle secured a film contract with the RKO studio. They had a son, Anthony, who was a Down syndrome baby. By the late 1930s, Guilfoyle had become an alcoholic, but he was able to overcome his addiction by joining the motion picture branch of Alcoholics Anonymous (AA); he remained an active charter member until a year before his death in 1961. He became such an effective speaker at his AA meetings that he appeared as guest speaker for other AA groups throughout California and Texas. He was "so good at it" that "Joan Crawford, shy about an appearance at an AA meeting, began lengthy personal and phone consultations with him, which she credited with sobering her" (Harbin, interview, 2002).

In 1945, Guilfoyle and Mulqueen became foster parents to Kathleen's cousin, Kaier Curtin, when Curtin's mother sent him to Kathleen (at the age of fourteen) to escape his father's alcoholic binges. Guilfoyle did not disguise his homosexuality from his foster son, who was gay himself, though an innocent who did not fully recognize his sexual identity. Nor did Guilfoyle lead Curtin into sexual activity; rather, he assumed a protective fatherly role (Harbin, interview, 1996).

Guilfoyle, like other gay men in Hollywood, had constantly to be on his guard against police entrapment (which often took place in public toilets) and blackmail. Nevertheless, he was entrapped by police in a "North Hollywood park bench encounter," and his arrest on a "morals charge" was featured prominently in local newspapers. According to Curtin, this happened in the late 1940s and Guilfoyle was blackmailed in another situation in the next decade. Criminals posing as policemen entrapped him in a sexual encounter with a teenager (the son of one of the men had been used as "bait"). They agreed to keep the scandal out of the papers for a price of sixty thousand dollars. Guilfoyle somehow managed to raise the money, but the experience was a nightmare that would not go away; personally and professionally he never regained his balance. When in 1961 the blackmailers made further demands, Guilfoyle committed suicide in despair. His obituary reported his death as a "heart attack" (Harbin, interview, 1996).

See "In the Current Broadway Panorama," *New York Times,* February 10, 1929; B. J. Harbin, interviews with Kaier Curtin, September 4 and 22, 1996, and May 17, 2002; "Paul Guilfoyle, Actor, 58, Dies," *New York Times,* June 30, 1961; A. E. Twomey and A. F. McClure, *The Versatiles,* New York, 1969; and E. M. Truitt, *Who Was Who on Screen,* New York, 1983.

Hamilton Armstrong

HAMILTON, Nancy (1909–85), lyricist, writer, and actress, was born in Sewickley, Pennsylvania, and attended Smith College. There she directed and appeared in *The Mikado, The Chocolate Soldier,* and *Caesar and Cleopatra.* In her senior year, 1930, as president of the Dramatic Association, she wrote and directed a topical revue, *And So On.* She had received special permission from the president of this women's college to hire men to play in the show's orchestra. On opening night the audience was scandalized when it was discovered that Hamilton had incorporated many of the men into onstage scenes.

After graduation, Hamilton moved to New York, where she was hired as Katharine Hepburn's understudy in *The Warrior's Husband.* The following year, she joined the company of *New Faces of 1934,* a revue for which she provided over half of the sketches and song lyrics—many of which were reworkings from *And So On.* *New Faces* introduced Imogene Coca and Henry Fonda to Broadway and also made Hamilton's talents well known. Her two most popular numbers were an imitation of Hepburn in a sketch Hamilton wrote, "Katharine Hepburn Gets in the Mood

Nancy Hamilton in her review *One for the Money* (1939). (Photo by Vandamm Studio, courtesy of the Billy Rose Theatre Collection, New York
Public Library for the Performing Arts.)

for '*Little Women*'" (a movie Hepburn had recently made) and an acerbic
song of her own entitled "I Hate the Spring."

Beatrice Lillie so liked "I Hate the Spring" that she incorporated it
into her nightclub act, where its success prompted her to hire Hamilton
to provide material for her radio appearances. (Lillie also had Hamilton
write a dramatization of *Mary Poppins* for her, a project that never came to
fruition.)

After *New Faces,* Hamilton appeared as Miss Bingley in the 1935 Broadway production of *Pride and Prejudice.* She then devoted herself to writing sketches and lyrics for three revues: *One for the Money* (1939), *Two for the Show* (1940), and *Three to Make Ready* (1946). These Broadway revues featured such performers as Alfred Drake, Gene Kelly, Betty Hutton, and Ray Bolger. (In 1972, portions of them were revived Off-Broadway as *One for the Money.*)

Katharine Cornell's general manager, Gertrude Macy, was so taken with Hamilton's impersonation of Eleanor Roosevelt in *One for the Money* that Macy arranged a meeting between Cornell and Hamilton. Even though Cornell was married to **Guthrie McClintic,** she and Hamilton became lovers. During World War II, Hamilton served as wardrobe mistress in order to accompany Cornell on her USO tour of *The Barretts of Wimpole Street.* After McClintic died in 1961, Hamilton and Cornell were able to live together and did so until Cornell's death in 1974.

During their years together, although Cornell had officially retired, she narrated two documentary films produced by Hamilton. One, *This Is Our Island,* was about Martha's Vineyard, where they kept a home. The other, *Helen Keller in Her Story,* won an Academy Award as Best Documentary in 1955.

In an interview conducted shortly before she met Cornell, Hamilton referred to herself as a "gay and chatty bachelor girl" with a "boyish haircut" who has beer for breakfast, loves Barbara Stanwyck movies, and considers herself to be "the feminine Noël Coward" (Bald, n.p.). Her obvious desire to keep her relationship with Cornell private led Hamilton to refuse interviews after they joined their lives.

While Hamilton's work is mostly minor, some endures. Perhaps her most lasting contribution is the lyrics to "How High the Moon," a song written with Morgan Lewis, her longtime collaborator. It is easy to see them as paying tribute to Cornell's love.

> The darkest night would shine
> If you would come to me soon,
> Until you will,
> How still my heart,
> How high the moon!

See W. Bald, "Bachelor Girl Makes Good on Broadway," *New York Post,* April 19, 1946; T. Mosel, *Leading Lady,* Boston, 1978; and H. Pringle, "Her Own Best Bet," *Colliers,* April 13, 1940, 11, 46–47.

Lee Alan Morrow

HART, Lorenz ("Larry" Milton) (1895–1943), lyricist and librettist, was born to German Jewish immigrant parents in Manhattan, attended Columbia University, and translated German-language stage works before partnering with composer Richard Rodgers to become one of the premiere creators of musical theater, generating an unrivaled string of successes in the late 1930s. Together, Rodgers and Hart created shows that were witty, tuneful, and experimental in their use of source material. In spite of this success, Hart experienced such self-loathing that he drank himself into an early grave.

Hart's self-loathing stemmed from a handful of liabilities. He was short (4'10"), misshapen (his head was too large for his body), unreliable, an alcoholic, and a homosexual. Although he acted on his homosexual desires, he loathed them: he was inept at lovemaking (Nolan, 238) and could not remain in bed with a sex partner (Marx and Clayton, 224). His friend, agent, and pimp, Milton "Doc" Bender (a dentist by trade), hosted orgies, where Hart was always an invited guest, and connected him with a series of anonymous male sexual partners, usually unemployed chorus boys (116). Balancing these proclivities were Hart's family and Richard Rodgers.

Rodgers was Hart's antithesis: stable, sober, methodical, and solidly middle to upper middle class in his outlook. Rodgers, only sixteen when he met Hart, learned about theater from him and confessed to his "reverence" for the erudite, energetic lyricist (R. Rodgers, 27). One friend suggested what the twenty-three-year-old Hart felt for the talented, earnest family friend: "Poor Larry. What a shame he had to fall in love with Dick" (Nolan, 19). Rodgers tolerated Hart's drinking and absences, looking out for his partner, but he could endure only so much. Prone to anger, Rodgers resorted to locking Hart in rooms to get work out of him on more than one occasion (Hart, 41; Nolan, 206). As Hart's lyrics reveal— "When you're not around to scold me, / Life's a bitter cup" (D. Hart and R. Kimball, *Lyrics,* 150)—the combination of acceptance and anger became addictive.

When Rodgers and Hart met in 1919, they began writing together immediately. They collaborated on two shows for Columbia University and wrote others for amateur societies around town. An early break of writing songs for *Poor Little Ritz Girl* (1920) secured their alliance with Lew Fields, who would produce many of their shows in the late 1920s, and with his son Herbert, who would write many of their librettos. One final amateur show, this time for the understudies and bit players at the Theatre Guild, resulted in *The Garrick Gaieties* (1925), a sensational success ("Manhattan" and "Sentimental Me" were in the score) that launched Rodgers and Hart on their professional careers.

Their next show, *Dearest Enemy* (1925), came from their own ideas about the legendary Mrs. Murray, who detained British soldiers during the Revolutionary War, allowing General Washington to escape. Herbert Fields wrote the libretto for this show, as he did for *The Girl Friend* (1926), *Peggy-Ann* (1926), and *A Connecticut Yankee* (1927), their biggest hit of the 1920s, based on Mark Twain's novel and featuring such songs as "My Heart Stood Still" and "Thou Swell." By 1931, Rodgers and Hart had written for the New York and London stages twelve other musicals, which included such songs as "I've Got Five Dollars," "A Ship without a Sail," "Ten Cents a Dance," and "Dancing on the Ceiling."

Anecdotes about Hart's sexuality from the 1920s are few. The most overt references to gay life are found in his earliest professional lyrics. In "Manhattan," he has the couple singing that they will "starve together, dear, / In Childs" (D. Hart and R. Kimball, 33). Several Childs restaurants in the theater district were established meeting places for gays in the 1920s and 1930s. In other lyrics, movie he-men do needlework and "talk like sissies" (143). In *The Girl Friend,* the number "What Is It?" asks explicitly the gender role question of the day: "A she or he?" (67).

After the crash of 1929, Rodgers and Hart went to Hollywood to compose and write for films. Their best, *Love Me Tonight* (1932), featured Jeanette MacDonald and Maurice Chevalier as a princess and tailor falling in love. Another ambitious project, *Hallelujah! I'm a Bum* (1933), for Al Jolson, failed at the box office, not because of their score but due to the public's waning interest in Jolson. Hart also wrote new lyrics for Ernst Lubitsch's film *The Merry Widow* (1934), again with MacDonald and Chevalier. They wrote songs for other films, but the material was often dropped by the time the film was released.

The earliest stories confirming Hart's homosexuality center on his life in Hollywood. He attended parties with **Tallulah Bankhead** and William Haines (Marx and Clayton, 171) and followed the nightclub career of drag performer Jean Malin (170). The impression is that Hart ran wild in heady, hedonistic Hollywood—far from whatever restrictions he felt in New York City. It is from Hollywood, too, that we have the report of Hart's only statement acknowledging his homosexuality. While there, he came under a blackmail threat; he confided in one friend that "his mother would die if she thought her son was homosexual" (190–91). As one acquaintance recalled: "In those days it wasn't an open and acknowledged thing. . . . [Hart] felt permanent guilt because he was a homosexual" (190).

Although they were well paid, the indolent life and unfulfilling work in Hollywood did not suit Rodgers. Rodgers and Hart left Hollywood for a New York theater scene blighted by the Depression. Their first work was on Billy Rose's mammoth production *Jumbo* (1935), which became a smash hit. Their score, which included "The Most Beautiful Girl in the World" and "My Romance," made them bankable and enabled them to pursue their own projects.

Their next show, *On Your Toes* (1936), originated from their idea and book, polished by director George Abbott. Rodgers's "Slaughter on Tenth Avenue" ballet was balanced by Hart's clever lyrics to "Glad to Be Unhappy," "It's Got To Be Love," and "There's a Small Hotel." The same production team returned later in the year with *Babes in Arms* (1936), again based on a Rodgers and Hart idea. The production won raves for its youthful cast and perhaps the most memorable of all Rodgers and Hart scores, including "My Funny Valentine," "Johnny One Note," "I Wish I Were in Love Again," and "Where or When."

They next collaborated with George S. Kaufman and Moss Hart on *I'd Rather Be Right* (1937), which spoofed President Franklin Roosevelt. Rodgers and Hart managed to produce only "Have You Met Miss Jones?" out of a show dominated by Kaufman and Hart's satire. Their Hungarian fantasy *I Married an Angel* (1938) told of a banker who did just that. The show was heralded for its sophisticated comedy, its score (featuring the title song and "Spring Is Here"), and its brilliant cast: Dennis King, Vera Zorina, Walter Slezak, and Hart's favorite actress, Vivienne Segal. In the same year, Rodgers and Hart generated the first musical adaptation of Shakespeare, *The Boys from Syracuse* (from *A Comedy of Errors*), in a version directed by Abbott. The show had "Falling in Love with Love," "This Can't Be Love," "Sing for Your Supper," and a featured role for Hart's brother Teddy as one of the twin servants.

After such success, many felt Rodgers and Hart deserved a slump. The college musical *Too Many Girls* (1939) featured Desi Arnaz and "I Didn't Know What Time It Was." In *Higher and Higher* (1940), servants masqueraded as wealthy folk; the enduring song was "It Never Entered My Mind." Then Rodgers and Hart had their two greatest successes.

Pal Joey (1940) is the most frequently revived of Rodgers and Hart shows, thanks to its mature character analysis and its score, which included "I Could Write a Book," "Bewitched, Bothered, and Bewildered," and pastiche nightclub numbers. Their daring story featured a not too bright nightclub singer (Gene Kelly) and the woman who kept him (Vivienne Segal). By *Jupiter* (1942) was the longest running of all Rodgers and Hart shows. Ray Bolger headed a cast of mannish Amazons, timid men, and lusty Greeks. "Ev'rything I've Got" reflects the combative nature of the story, while "Nobody's Heart (Belongs to Me)" reveals its softer side.

On his return to New York in 1935, Hart's attraction to men became fairly common knowledge, if not spoken of openly (D. Rodgers, 111). His increasing wealth made him a frequent party giver and an easy touch. Yet, while surrounded by festive hangers on, Hart was an intensely lonely man. His primary homosocial relationship remained with Rodgers. He turned away from his work—even as their success grew—and sought Rodgers's personal attention by becoming more drunk and absent. Rodgers reactively pulled away from Hart, finally choosing a new creative partner in Oscar Hammerstein II. Hammerstein, of course, took Rodgers up on the offer when Hart nixed the idea that became *Oklahoma!* (1943). Hart's descent continued. The death of his mother one month after the opening of *Oklahoma!* especially loosened his ties to the respectable people who were holding him together.

After *Oklahoma!* Rodgers returned to Hart to update and revise *A Connecticut Yankee* (1943) for the war era, enlarging the role of Morgan Le Fay for Vivienne Segal. Her "To Keep My Love Alive" attests to Hart's continuing lyric-writing prowess. However, once his work was finished he began drinking heavily. He contracted pneumonia on the show's rainy opening night and died a week later.

References to gay life are found only in the secondary rank of Hart's songs and form a small portion of the more than six hundred songs he wrote. Only rarely did he pen a line that twits heterosexual expectations with a gay subtext. Even when he did, these lines are sung by women, masking the threat. An Amazon in the gender-reversed *By Jupiter* sings out "a sailor has a boy in every port" (D. Hart and R. Kimball, 284–85). An abandoned young woman sings, "I was a queen to him. / Who's goin' to make me gay now?" (152). Significantly, this is the only time Hart used the word *gay* when a homosexual subtext could be posited; all other uses rely on the conventional meanings "merry," "quick," or "colorful." Unlike Cole Porter or Noël Coward, Hart did not surround himself with homosexual artists onstage or behind the scenes or revel in the thinly veiled lyrics that earned Porter his coterie audience.

Hart's experiences as a homosexual and his perceptions of life found subtle expression in his lyrics: love is physical, from the strike of the first infatuating look to the physical symptoms created by longing and dish-throwing fights. The majority of these references are sung by men. Hart's preference for attractive, stupid men is also found in his lyrics. The overall picture of men in love—not too bright but decidedly corporeal—

reflects a distinct homosexual underworld of brief sexual encounters where good looks are desired and conversations are limited. Hart's loneliness, self-abasement, and self-pity—which resulted from his resistance to his homosexuality—are funneled through the lyrics given to female characters. By channeling his experiences and feelings into "appropriate" staged representations of male and female, Hart's understanding of his divided nature becomes overt even as he buries it in a heterosexual context.

See J. Clum, *Something for the Boys: Musical Theater and Gay Culture,* New York, 1999; D. Hart, *Thou Swell, Thou Witty: The Life and Lyrics of Lorenz Hart,* New York, 1976; D. Hart and R. Kimball, eds., *The Complete Lyrics of Lorenz Hart,* New York, 1986; S. Marx and J. Clayton, *Rodgers and Hart: Bewitched, Bothered, and Bedeviled,* New York, 1976; F. Nolan, *Lorenz Hart: A Poet on Broadway,* New York, 1994; D. Rodgers, *A Personal Book,* New York, 1977; R. Rodgers, *Musical Stages: An Autobiography,* New York, 1975; M. Secrest, *Somewhere for Me: A Biography of Richard Rodgers,* New York, 2001; and J. Smart, "Lorenz Hart: This Can't Be Love," in *Staging Desire: Queer Readings of American Theater History,* edited by K. Marra and R. A. Schanke, Ann Arbor, 2002, 167–93.

Jeffrey Smart

HEIDE, Robert (1939–), actor, playwright, and cultural historian, spent his childhood in Irvington, New Jersey. After studying theater at Northwestern University's School of Speech, he moved to New York and entered what he has described as a time of creative experimentation with periods of disillusionment. In addition to studying with Stella Adler, Uta Hagen, and Harold Clurman, he was a production assistant at The Living Theatre and performed at the American Shakespeare Festival in Stratford, Connecticut, under the direction of John Houseman. Heide was also a member of **Edward Albee**'s Playwrights Group at the Van Dam Theatre. His first play, *Hector,* was presented in 1961 by The Living Theatre at the Cherry Lane Theater; subsequently, Lee Paton (noted for introducing Ionesco's plays to the United States) staged *Hector* and *West of the Moon* Off-Broadway at New Playwrights in Greenwich Village. Written specifically for New Playwrights, *West of the Moon* concerns a hustler who attempts to seduce a religious young man whom he meets when the two seek shelter in a Christopher Street doorway during a sudden rainstorm. One of the first plays to deal openly and positively with gay sexuality, it elicited harsh criticism, with the reviewer in *Theatre Arts Magazine* suggesting that Heide should "break his typewriter over his hands." Heide was so shaken by the reaction that he wondered whether he should write for the theater again.

Shortly after this experience came Heide's "illumination": "A first visit

Robert Heide in his twenties when he was writing plays for Caffe Cino. (Courtesy of Robert Heide.)

to the Divine Shrine—the mad mythic mystical Caffe Cino" (Heide, *At War*, 73). Having seen the production at New Playwrights, **Joe Cino** encouraged Heide to write for the Caffe, a tiny coffeehouse generally considered to be the birthplace of the Off-Off-Broadway movement. Heide recalls Cino saying to him: "I think it's about time you wrote that existentialist play. But make it a play for blond men. You know what I mean, Heide. It's time to get off your ass and write it. *Now*" (Heide, "Magic Time," 30). The resulting play was *The Bed*, which initially played at a benefit to help restore Caffe Cino after it burned on March 5, 1965. Given a regular run when the coffeehouse reopened, it was revived on several occasions, ultimately playing about 150 performances at the Caffe Cino. Set in a bed, the play concerns two men whose relationship is beginning to crumble because of too much boredom, alcohol, and drug abuse. *The Bed* was made into a movie by Andy Warhol (his first experimental split-screen film), but disputes over ownership of the film forced it off the market after a brief run at the Cinemateque in New York; subsequently, Warhol spliced parts of it into *Chelsea Girls*. The film of *The Bed* in its entirety has been restored by the Museum of Modern Art. Heide also wrote the Warhol scenario *Lupe* for Edie Sedgwick and appeared in two Warhol films alongside Jack Smith: *Dracula/Batman* and *Camp*.

Heide has suggested that he became known as Cino's "resident existentialist" because he usually carried with him a copy of either Sartre's *Being and Nothingness* or Heidegger's *Being and Time*, but his work reflects basic ontological concerns. In his introduction to Heide's *Moon, Village Voice* critic Michael Smith comments: "Robert Heide is preoccupied with the experiences of alienation and pointlessness and transmits them with exquisite intensity. His characters make contact only when they panic" (47). Anthologized in two collections (*The Off Off Broadway Book* and *The Best of Off Off Broadway*) and printed as an acting script, *Moon* was the most successful of Heide's Cino plays. In addition to several runs at Cino, the Cherry Lane Theater, the Manhattan Theater Club, and numerous theaters and universities in America and abroad, it was revived in 1993 (in a twenty-fifth anniversary production) at the Theatre for the New City in a space named for Joseph Cino.

Heide's produced and published plays also include *At War with the Mongols* (premiered at Brecht West, New Brunswick, New Jersey), *Why Tuesday Never Has a Blue Monday* and *Statue* (both premiered at Cafe LaMama), and *American Hamburger, Tropical Fever in Key West,* and *Crisis of Identity* (all three premiered at Theatre for the New City). He has also worked with New York Theatre Strategy, which produced his *Suburban*

Tremens. He is currently working on a play about the Factory days of Andy Warhol.

Heide is an authority on American popular culture and in collaboration with his longtime companion John Gilman (who appeared in some of the original productions of Heide's plays) has written *Mickey Mouse: The Evolution, the Legend, the Phenomenon; Box-Office Buckaroos—The Cowboy Hero from the Wild West Show to the Silver Screen; Disneyana—Classic Collectibles 1928–1958; O' New Jersey;* and *Greenwich Village,* the latter being part tour guide, part history, and part cultural study. In an unpublished interview conducted by the author on December 18, 1997, in Greenwich Village, where Heide still resides, he suggested how his sexual orientation has influenced his work.

> It gave me a deeper outsider's view of the world around me. . . . I could see behind the facade of defensive attitudes because of having to exist in a kind of secret identity—I always searched what was going on underneath. In theater it was the subtext that always interested me more than what was actually being said on the surface. I had more or less a mistrust of words in the usual sense. (interview by the author, December 18, 1997)

See D. Gordy, "Joseph Cino and the First Off-Off Broadway Theater," in *Passing Performances: Queer Readings of Leading Players in American Theater History,* edited by Robert A. Schanke and Kim Marra, Ann Arbor, 1998, 303–23; R. Heide, "*Moon,*" in *The Best of Off Off Broadway,* edited by M. Smith, New York, 1969, 47–70; R. Heide, *At War with the Mongols,* in *New American Plays,* edited by W. Hoffman, vol. 4, New York, 1971, 71–90; R. Heide, "Magic Time at the Caffe Cino," *New York Native,* May 6, 1985; R. Heide, *Greenwich Village,* New York, 1995; and Review of "The Bed," *Village Voice,* July 23, 1964.

Wendell Stone

HERMAN, Jerry (Gerald) (1933–), composer and lyricist, was born in New York City, the only child of Harry Herman, who owned a children's summer camp, and Ruth (Sachs) Herman, a musician who taught voice and piano. The family moved to Jersey City, New Jersey, while Jerry was still a child. There the six-year-old learned to play piano by ear; wisely, his mother encouraged him "without making it seem like a chore, such as making me take daily lessons" (Wershba, n.p.). When Herman saw his first musical, *Annie Get Your Gun,* starring Ethel Merman, he was dazzled by the talent of the show's creator, Irving Berlin, who became a great influence on his work.

However, after graduating from Henry Snyder High School, Herman chose not to pursue his passion for music; he enrolled at the Parsons School of Design in New York in order to train as an interior designer. While there he sold his first song for two hundred dollars and decided to make his passion his profession. Transferring to the University of Miami in Coral Gables, Florida, he majored in drama and worked in all aspects of theatrical production. During this period, when he was still in his teens, he came out. His mother, who had died some years before, never knew, although Herman claims that "she would have gone to Fire Island with me; she was that kind of a terrific swinging lady"; he told his father, and "it did not change a thing." The large university and drama department, where there were many gays, provided a supportive atmosphere for a young gay man during the early 1950s (Newman, 84).

Herman received his bachelor's degree in 1953 and moved to New York, where he made his living writing special material for such performers as Ray Bolger, **Tallulah Bankhead,** and Hermione Gingold and playing piano in cocktail lounges. He made a modest Off-Broadway debut in 1954 with the intimate revue *I Feel Wonderful,* which closed after forty-nine performances. In 1958, he convinced the owner of the nightclub in which he was playing to stage his revue *Nightcap.* It ran for four hundred performances and was followed by another popular Off-Broadway revue, *Parade,* in 1960.

The next year, Herman achieved his first success (and Tony nomination) on Broadway with *Milk and Honey,* which followed the adventures of three tourists in Israel and captured the spirit of the young nation. After the failure of his next show, *Madame Aphrodite,* Herman bounced back with the unqualified hit *Hello Dolly!* which opened on January 16, 1964. Based on **Thornton Wilder**'s play *The Matchmaker* and set in 1898, the musical tells the story of Dolly Levi, a New York marriage broker who manages to catch one of her clients for herself. With Gower Champion as director and Carol Channing as Dolly, *Hello Dolly!* made stage history on several counts: it captured ten Tonys, including one for best musical and one for Herman's score; it accumulated the greatest number of consecutive performances (2,844) of any musical prior to 1970, when it closed; and it became the only musical in recent history to have simultaneous productions on Broadway when the second, with an all-black cast headed by Pearl Bailey, opened on Broadway in 1967. The title song became one of the biggest hits of the decade: at least seventy versions of it have been recorded in America, and with a change in lyrics—"Hello, Lyndon"—it became the theme of Lyndon Johnson's presidential campaign.

In 1966, another Herman hit, *Mame,* appeared on Broadway. Centered around yet another strong, forceful "grande dame," the show relayed in music the oft-told tale of the adventures of Patrick Dennis's eccentric, freewheeling Auntie Mame, who had been played in the original production by Angela Lansbury. Here, too, the principal song was the title number, although "If He Walked into My Life" enjoyed some popular success as well. *Mame* received a Tony for best musical and a Grammy for best original cast album.

For the next seventeen years, the success that pervaded *Hello Dolly!* and *Mame* eluded Herman. *Dear World* (1969), *Mack and Mabel* (1974), and *The Grand Tour* (1979) all completed their tenure on Broadway with mediocre runs. It was not until 1983, when *La Cage aux Folles* opened, that a Jerry Herman show again enjoyed blockbuster status on the Broadway stage. It contained all the ingredients for success that Herman had employed previously: glamour and glitz, a showstopping tune, and the presence of a grande dame to hold it all together. Only this time the grande dame was a man, the glamour and glitz shone from a chorus line of drag queens, and the showstopping tune, "I Am What I Am," became the unofficial anthem of the gay rights movement. Based on a French play, which was adapted for the musical stage by Harvey Fierstein, *La Cage aux Folles* was the first Broadway musical to openly portray a homosexual relationship, although it went beyond that relationship to explore universal themes of the importance of commitment, loyalty, and self-pride. Herman has claimed that the score was the easiest he has written, perhaps because it hit so close to home; he is quite open about his own sexuality, claiming that it has never been a big issue in his life: "I've always just lived my life" (qtd. in Newman, 84). When *La Cage aux Folles* won six Tonys, including those for best musical and best score, Herman attended with his lover and business partner, Marty Finkelstein, who died of AIDS in 1990. Herman first realized that the musical was a universal hit, for both homosexuals and heterosexuals, when he sat behind an elderly man and woman at a tryout in Boston. When Gene Barry began to sing "Song in the Sand," the man took the woman's hand in his own, and they slowly put their heads together. Herman cried, knowing at that moment that "we had something universal" (85).

Since *La Cage aux Folles,* several revues of Herman's songs have appeared, including *Jerry's Girls* (1985), *The Best of Times* (1998), and *An Evening with Jerry Herman* (1998). Herman supervised the return of *Hello Dolly!* to Broadway in 1995 and has written for television while indulging his second passion, architecture: he has designed twenty-seven houses and lives in a Bel-Air, California, home that he has turned into a private retreat. Herman, who discovered that he was HIV positive in

1985, has organized countless fund-raisers and participated in numerous events, such as the Los Angeles gay pride parade, to combat the disease that claimed the life of his lover.

In a time when musical theater was moving from the "cockeyed optimism" of a Rodgers and Hammerstein show to the hard-edged bite of a Sondheim production, Herman injected the musical with his own brand of realistic optimism, born of his belief in the universality of love regardless of sexual preference. In his memoir *Showtune,* he writes:

> Early in my career people used to put me down for writing upbeat songs—as if the feelings I put into them were not genuine. It has taken me the better part of my lifetime to make people understand that I write the way I feel, and that these sentiments are honest. We all have to write from our own life experience and be true to those feelings. I can't help writing melodic showtunes that are bouncy, buoyant, and optimistic. That's me. And I am what I am. (267)

Criticized for what has been called crass commercialism, Jerry Herman nevertheless has created some of the most popular songs of the musical stage and proved that mainstream musical audiences can look beyond sexuality to see and hear only love.

See I. Borger, "Jerry Herman in Bel-Air: Off Broadway with the Composer and Lyricist," *Architectural Digest,* November 1995; J. Clum, *Something for the Boys: Musical Theater and Gay Culture,* New York, 1999; D. M. Flinn, *Musical! A Grand Tour,* New York, 1997; K. Ganzl, *The Encyclopedia of Musical Theatre,* 2d ed., New York, 2001; O. L. Guernsey Jr., ed., *Broadway Song and Story: Playwrights/Lyricists/Composers Discuss Their Hits,* New York, 1985; J. Herman, with M. Stasio, *Showtune,* New York, 1996; T. S. Hischak, *Word Crazy: Broadway Lyricists from Cohan to Sondheim,* New York, 1991; A. Lamb, *150 Years of Popular Musical Theater,* New Haven, 2000; J. L. Newman, "Inside Herman's Head," *The Advocate,* June 29, 1993; B. Weinraub, "Celebrating His Music and Precious Life Itself," *New York Times,* July 26, 1998; Joseph Wershba, *New York Post,* January 26, 1962; and M. Wolf, "Musical Man Humming Along," *Variety,* October 9, 1995.

Judith A. Sebesta

HINDLE, Annie (ca. 1847–?), male impersonator of the American variety stage, was born in England, adopted at the age of five, and put onstage to sing love songs to a working-class audience. As she grew older, she continued to perform and traveled to London, where she expanded her repertoire. According to a *New York Sun* reporter: "One day, half in jest, she put on a man's costume and sang a rollicking ditty about wine, women,

Annie Hindle in her "makeup," circa 1870s. (Courtesy of the Harvard Theatre Collection, Houghton Library, Harvard University.)

and the races. A shrewd manager who listened to her saw a new field for her. In a week, Hindle was a 'male impersonator,' and all London was talking about the wonderful and minute accuracy of her mimicry" ("Stranger Than Fiction," n.p.). In 1867, a theatrical manager, Tony Pastor, brought Hindle to the United States as the first "out and out 'male impersonator' New York's stage had ever seen." Hindle's success as a male impersonator continued as she toured the variety circuit in New York, earning as much as $150 per week, a sum equal to that of popular male comic singers of the time. Her success was also measured in "mash" notes.

> It is a fact that this dashing singer was the recipient of as many "mash" notes as probably ever went to a stage favorite in this country. Once she compared notes with H. J. Montague, that carelessly handsome actor at whose shrine so many silly women had worshipped, but Hindle's admirers far outnumbered his, and they were all women, strange as that may seem. ("Stranger Than Fiction," n.p.).

Hindle would return the "strange" affection she received from women when she found the "loving wife so gentle and so kind" of which she sang in "Have You Seen My Nellie?" but first she married a man, fellow actor Charles Vivian, in September 1868. This abusive marriage was not to last more than a few months. As Hindle herself told the *Sun* reporter, "He lived with me . . . several months—long enough to black both my eyes and otherwise mark me; yet I was a good and true wife to him" (n.p.). Hindle and Vivian never officially divorced, but after parting in Denver, Colorado, the two never met again. Fortunately, Hindle's second marriage proved to be much more successful. In June 1886, the cross-dressed Annie Hindle married one of her dressers, Annie Ryan, in a ceremony conducted by a minister and attended by the female impersonator Gilbert Saroney. When the minister was questioned about the "strangest romance" between Hindle and Ryan, he replied: "The groom gave me her—I mean his—name as Charles Hindle and he assured me that he was a man. The bride is a sensible girl, and she was of age. I had no other course to pursue. I believe they love each other and that they will be happy" ("Stranger Than Fiction," n.p.).

Annie Hindle and Annie Ryan then retired to a small cottage in Jersey Heights, New Jersey, which Hindle had built using her savings from her career as a male impersonator. When Ryan died in 1891, Hindle said that the loss of her wife meant the loss of "the best of her life." It is not known when Annie Hindle died, but she was survived by a legacy of male impersonators, as her success prompted an entire line of women to enter the field of male impersonation, copying the Hindle style onstage and, for some, offstage as well.

See F. Graham, *Histrionic Montreal,* New York, 1902; L. Senelick, *The Changing Room: Sex, Drag, and Theatre,* New York, 2000; L. Senelick, "The Evolution of the Male Impersonation on the Nineteenth-Century Popular Stage," *Essays in Theatre* 1:1 (November 1982): 31–44; and "Stranger Than Fiction," *New York Sun,* December 21, 1891.

Sherry A. Darling

HOFFMAN, William M. (1939–), playwright, grew up "genuinely poor" after being born in New York City on April 12, 1939, the child of Eastern European immigrants. His father, Morton, was born in Bialistok, and his mother, Johanna (Papiermeister), was born in Latvia, bringing a multi-lingual environment to their home in the Inwood section of Manhattan. As a young boy, William heard German, Yiddish, Polish, and Russian spoken in his home, and he developed a lifelong love for language. This took him to the Inwood branch of the New York Public Library, where he began reading authors such as **Gertrude Stein** and Sigmund Freud in elementary school: "I loved to choose books by the way they were bound. I read 'avant-garde' literature before I read the classics" (interview with the author, July 15, 1996). His favorites were Stein's "Four Saints in Three Acts" and Ezra Pound's "Cantos." "None of the people in the world of Freud, Stein, and Pound lived in a cramped, peeling basement apart-ment to the right of the garbage cans, as I did" (*New York Native,* June 3, 1985, 39). By junior high school, he was arguing the merits of Freud with his older brother.

"I grew up very unconventionally, where learning was encouraged but no one was learned." Indeed, neither of his parents had a formal educa-tion, but he describes them as "terrific, crazy, very gifted people . . . wildly ahead of their time" (interview with the author, July 15, 1996). Morton was a caterer in the fashion and diplomatic communities of New York; Johanna, though frequently ill, owned a costume jewelry shop (the contents of which Hoffman still owns). Their families had been killed by the Nazis during the Holocaust, a fact that influenced much of Hoffman's future work.

Morton wanted his son "to study boxing and ballet," but after being rejected by the High School of Performing Arts William entered the Bronx High School of Science, where he studied biology (and "was terri-ble at it"). From there, he entered City College of the City University of New York, where he began as a biology major but quickly switched to English and finally Latin, graduating with honors in 1960. He fell in love with the classics at City College, and when, in a Latin class text, he came across the ancient phrase "Julius Caesar, Queen of Egypt," his "life was forever altered. I knew that gay was okay because it was okay two thou-sand years ago" (interview with the author).

After college, he stumbled into book publishing, working first as an editorial assistant for Barnes and Noble. In 1961, he began to work for Hill and Wang, starting as an assistant editor and eventually becoming an associate editor in 1967 (*Contemporary Dramatists,* 304–6): "I was a good editor, but I felt like a bathroom attendant. I found it degrading."

He had no image of himself as a writer and describes himself as a "ne'er-do-well" at the time. He never went to the theater, which he found boring. "If I had any love of anything with words, it was poetry. It wasn't theater" (interview with the author).

During this period, Hoffman lived on the Upper West Side of Manhattan with his lover, the composer John Corligliano. It was at a large party in their home that they met **Lanford Wilson** and Michael Powell, who had just moved to New York from Chicago. Corligliano knew of a coffee shop in Greenwich Village, the Caffe Cino, where he suggested Wilson go to have his plays produced. Wilson and Hoffman became involved, causing Hoffman to break up with Corligliano and move to Greenwich Village. Hoffman fell in love with Caffe Cino and especially the works of Wilson. He became the editor of the American Plays series for Hill and Wang, but with all of his new friends writing he felt left out. He wrote a short story, all in dialogue, which Wilson said was really a play, and it was produced at Caffe Cino in 1965 as *Thank You, Miss Victoria* (published in Hoffman, *New American Plays 3*). Reflecting on the Caffe Cino period, Hoffman said: "I didn't think of myself as a playwright. I still don't." He wanted to write plays "that keep *me* awake," experimental plays, because "realistic theatre bored me." He wrote *Good Night, I Love You* (directed by Marshall Mason, 1966); *Saturday Night at the Movies* (1966, published in Poland and Mailman); *Spring Play* (directed by Marshall Mason at La Mama and starring Harvey Keitel, 1967); *Three Masked Dances* (1967); *Incantation* (1967); and *Uptight* (1968). In 1969, he wrote a play whose title, *XXX,* is unspoken (as Hoffman put it, "way before Prince adopted an unspoken sign for his name"). It translated the life of Jesus into a dance step, and Hoffman describes it as "new without being arty" (interview with the author, July 15, 1996). *XXX* was published in Smith. Hoffman also acted in plays by **Robert Patrick** during the 1960s.

Working with a group of actors in 1970 at the Old Reliable Theatre Tavern in the East Village, Hoffman's next work, *A Quick Nut Bread to Make Your Mouth Water* (published in Owens), had a structure based on a recipe in a box of flour. But the play was about "goodness," continuing his interest in spiritual themes. Looking back at these early works collectively, Hoffman said: "These were tentative stabs in my exploration of why there was a Holocaust. My family had been murdered, and I was working up the courage to deal with that, but I didn't know that . . . during that period . . . they all had to do with goodness: how can there be evil if God is good?" (interview with the author). The style was presentational and unconventional for the time, with characters constantly breaking the "fourth wall," and no scene changes or transitions. Subject matter dictated style, and therefore style changed from play to play. The big influence on Hoffman's writing, however, remained Lanford Wilson ("he led the way"), especially his *Balm in Gilead.*

The 1970s was a fruitful decade for Hoffman's explorations. He wrote several plays that were produced in New York, including *Luna* (1971); *From Fool to Hanged Man* and *The Children's Crusade,* both in 1972; *Gilles de Rais* (1975); and *Combury* and *Shoe Place Murray,* both cowritten with Anthony Holland (the former produced in New Haven, 1977, the latter produced in San Francisco, 1978), both published in Hoffman, *Gay Plays.* He also wrote teleplays for CBS, including "Notes from the New World: Louis Moreau Gottschalk," with Roger Englander, in 1976; "The Last Days of Stephen Foster," which aired in 1977; and "Whistler: Five Portraits," which aired in 1978. He also wrote two musicals, "A Book of Etiquette" (described by Hoffman as "the Marx Brothers meet Emily Post") and "Gulliver's Travels" (based on the Swift novel). Both were produced in New York in 1978 with music by John Braden.

His efforts earned him a MacDowell Colony Fellowship in 1971; a Colorado Council on the Arts and Humanities Grant, Carnegie Fund grant, and PEN grant in 1972; a Guggenheim Fellowship (which took him to France to do research on *Gilles de Rais* in 1974); and two grants from the National Endowment for the Arts in 1975 and 1976.

In the early 1980s, Hoffman's friends began to die of a new and mysterious virus that seemed to target gay men. He wanted to spread the word about the disease, soon to be called AIDS, and began writing scenes for a new play, which he presented in a workshop at the Circle Repertory Company. Eventually, Hoffman's brother would suggest the title "As Is," which comes from the world of antiques, where you buy something "as is." The play was produced by The Glines (a gay theater company) and Circle Repertory, directed by Marshall Mason, and opened on March 10, 1985. It was a hit and soon moved uptown, making it the first AIDS play on Broadway. The play was nominated for a Tony Award and won Obie and Drama Desk awards for best play of the year. *As Is,* published by Random House, in 1985, opened in London in 1987.

Hoffman began work on a number of other projects almost simultaneously with *As Is* in the early 1980s. These included another play with Anthony Holland entitled *The Cherry Orchard, Part II* (now called *After the Orchard*), the beginnings of what is now called *Riga,* and some collaborative work with John Corligliano on an opera. The Houston Grand Opera wanted to commission an opera, and the collaborators suggested *La Mere Coupable,* the third in Beaumarchais's trilogy of plays, two of which were already famous operas. Neither Hoffman or Corligliano had read the play, but they tried to sell the idea. ("It was Napoleon's favorite play. That says a lot!" says Hoffman sarcastically [interview .with the author, July 15, 1996].) Eventually, it was James Levine, musical director of the Metropolitan Opera in New York, who commissioned the work for the company's centennial. Rarely in the Met's history had a new opera been commissioned, so when *The Ghosts of Versailles* opened on December 19, 1991, it created a sensation in both the theater and opera worlds. It had taken its creators over a decade to complete.

Riga, written and presented in a workshop at the Circle Repertory Company during the late 1980s and early 1990s, continues Hoffman's struggle with moral and spiritual questions. It is a multimedia play about the Holocaust and the murder of Hoffman's family and asks the questions "Why worship a god who allows this?" and "How do you go on after that?" Originally scheduled for a full production in 1995, Circle Repertory abruptly abandoned the project in 1996 for what Hoffman describes as internal political reasons. While looking for another venue, Hoffman began work on a new musical.

"I've really wanted my work to say something. I don't think of it as propaganda. Art can offer practical solutions in the real world. I don't see a division between art and politics" (interview with the author). William Hoffman lives in New York City.

See *Contemporary Theatre, Film and Television,* vol. 1, Detroit, 1984; *Contemporary Dramatists,* 5th ed., Detroit, 1993; *Christopher Street,* June 1978; W. Hoffman, *As Is: A Play,* New York, Random House, 1985; W. Hoffman, ed., *Gay Plays,* New York, 1979; W. Hoffman, ed., *New American Plays 3,* New York, 1970; *New York Native,* March 11–24, 1985; *New York Native,* June 3, 1985; *Now: Theater der Erfahrung;* R. Owens, ed., *Spontaneous Combustion: Eight New American Plays,* New York, 1972; A. Poland and B. Mailman, eds., *The Off-Broadway Book,* Indianapolis, 1972; and M. Smith, ed., *More Plays from Off-Off Broadway,* Indianapolis, 1972.

Jon Fraser

HOPWOOD, Avery (James) (1882–1928), playwright, was born on the west side of Cleveland, Ohio, to James and Jule Pendergast Hopwood, dealers in wholesale and retail provisions. A studious boy from an early age, Hopwood preferred reading and writing to playing baseball or "painting the town red on a Saturday night." He was a Phi Beta Kappa graduate of the University of Michigan (1905), where he wrote short fiction for the university literary magazine and was chapter scribe for the Phi Gamma Delta social fraternity (the Fijis). His first play, *Clothes,* a social thesis drama, was written during his senior year in response to an article he had read in

the alumni magazine by drama critic Louis Vincent DeFoe, "The Call for the Playwright," which described the vast fortune in royalties to be earned from writing a few good plays.

After graduation, he took a job as a cub reporter for the *Cleveland Leader* and headed for New York City. There he met seasoned playwright and play reader for the Shuberts, Channing Pollock, who helped craft *Clothes* (1906) into a successful vehicle for the actress Grace George. Ability, hard work, and luck had paid off quickly for Hopwood. His next two solo efforts, however, *The Powers That Be* (1907) and *This Woman and This Man* (1909), also social thesis dramas, met with little success. Luck found him again, though, when a popular mystery writer, Mary Roberts Rinehart, invited him to collaborate with her on a dramatization of her successful novel *Seven Days* (1909). This preposterous farce scored a solid hit, and, true to the promise of "The Call for the Playwright," the royalties from the production brought Hopwood a small fortune. Having found a lucrative voice and facility for amusement, he turned from serious drama and devoted the remainder of his career primarily to writing comedies and farces. His talent for creating funny situations and snappy dialogue immediately caught the attention of David Belasco, who commissioned him to write a vehicle (*Nobody's Widow,* 1910) for Blanche Bates. Musical comedy star Marie Cahill also ordered up a piece (*Judy Forgot,* 1910), custom built for her rapid patter. But these successes were followed by miserable failures with *Somewhere Else* (1913), an operetta with music by Gustav Luders, and a play for Grace George, *Miss Jenny O'Jones* (1913). Discouraged, Hopwood threatened to give up playwriting in favor of his early passion, fiction, but within two years he was back on Broadway with two smart comedies of the recently popular bedroom variety, *Sadie Love* (1915), starring Marjorie Rambeau, and the hugely popular *Fair and Warmer* (1915), starring Madge Kennedy. Critic George Jean Nathan, after seeing another of his risqué concoctions, *Our Little Wife* (1916), praised him for having "a quick eye to the crazy-quilt of sex humours and a keen vision to the foibles of the cosmopolite." Hopwood was soon crowned the "King of Bedroom Farce," a distinction he eschewed but had earned and one that was very close to his own life.

Avery Hopwood's bedroom was not like that of the younger generation of heterosexuals who populated his plays. The romping frivolity of his stage work gave way to a darker, painful life often spent far from the Great White Way. Not only was he "King of Bedroom Farce," but he was the "Recluse of the Rialto." Typical of the time, his homosexuality was shadowed and not openly discussed in the press, although the theatrical community knew. As a satirical sketch in the musical revue *Keep Kool*

(1924) depicts, "nancified" young men were at home in his world. Regrettably, very few of Hopwood's personal papers survive; the bulk of them, including his daybooks, which were in the hands of a childhood girlfriend, were destroyed in 1975, in part to keep his sexuality secret. Hopwood himself did not accept his homosexuality. First introduced to the scene by Carl Van Vechten in the early teens, he had an ongoing, tempestuous, and often physically abusive (to Hopwood) relationship with a young playwright, John Floyd (1900–1962). Thirteen years his junior, Floyd's passport application indicates that he had known Hopwood from an early age when both lived in Cleveland. Floyd eventually had one successful play on Broadway himself, *The Wooden Kimono* (1926), no doubt due to Hopwood's guidance. Van Vechten's daybooks, thanks to the scrupulous transcriptions of scholar Bruce Kellner, shed further light on Hopwood's relationship with Floyd and other young men. It is seductive to speculate that Hopwood acted out his sexual repressions through his bedroom farces or projected himself through the personae of his leading ladies, and perhaps he did, but the work itself palled on him. He was often observed at his openings with the air of a minister officiating at a funeral. According to **Gertrude Stein,** Hopwood was a favorite in her circle during the early days because he was charming and gentle as a lamb; in the "latter days . . . the lamb turned into a wolf" (Stein, 70).

The height of Hopwood's career came in 1920, when he achieved the additional distinction of having four plays running concurrently on Broadway: *The Gold Diggers* (1919, starring Ina Claire and Bruce McRae), which gave birth to the spectacular gold digger movie musicals of the 1930s; *Ladies' Night (In a Turkish Bath)* (1920, written with Charlton Andrews and featuring Doris Kenyon and Charles Ruggles); *Spanish Love* (1920, written with Mary Roberts Rinehart and featuring William Powell); and the still-popular mystery-thriller *The Bat* (1920, also written with Rinehart). After 1920, however, Hopwood became increasingly dissatisfied with his career in the theater, and mainly doctored plays, such as *Getting Gertie's Garter* (1921, written with Wilson Collison and starring Hazel Dawn) and *The Best People* (1924, written with David Gray), or adapted popular foreign hits, such as *The Demi-Virgin* (1921, starring Hazel Dawn), *Little Miss Bluebeard* (1923, starring Irene Bordoni), *The Alarm Clock* (1923, starring Bruce McRae), *The Harem* (1924, starring Lenore Ulrich), and *Naughty Cinderella* (1925, starring Irene Bordoni). His other plays include *Double Exposure* (1918), *The Girl in the Limousine* (1919, written with Wilson Collison and featuring Charles Ruggles), *Why Men Leave Home* (1922), and *The Garden of Eden* (1927, starring Miriam Hopkins).

Between 1915 and 1925, Hopwood's farces ran an average of 168 performances each, compared to the average run of 91 performances for all other farces during the same period. Combined, all of Hopwood's plays ran a total of 4,932 performances in New York, or an average of 206 performances each—this at a time when 100 performances still ensured a profitable hit. In addition, his plays were performed around the world and in countless stock companies across America. At least twenty of his scripts were made into motion pictures. Hopwood amassed a fortune on the theory that the drama was a "democratic art" and that the playwright was not the "monarch, but the servant of the public." He admitted that he wrote for Broadway, "to please Broadway." As a result, his plays turned greater profits than any other playwright's of the day. Hopwood was a master at giving theatergoers what they wanted: cleverly built plays that presented characters whose breezy dialogue typified the attitudes of the time. He came to realize, however, that his axiom, "the voice of the public should be considered the voice of the gods," was destroying him (Haberman, 278). Lacking sufficient versatility to free himself from the formulae that had made him a success and tormented by the nature of his sexual identity, Hopwood's life deteriorated into a self-indulgent masquerade characteristic of the cynical gaiety of the times. At the age of forty-six, after too much food and drink and a liaison with a young soldier, cocaine and alcohol abuse induced a fatal heart attack while he was swimming at Juan-les-Pin on the French Riviera. He died almost instantly, leaving an estate worth well over one million dollars. "The Call for the Playwright" had indeed paid off—in royalties.

Because Hopwood's talents were applied to popular drama, as distinct from the literary drama, during the period of innovation of the 1920s, his plays and career have been almost totally eclipsed. Today he is chiefly remembered on the campus of his alma mater as the benefactor of the prestigious Avery Hopwood and Jule Hopwood Creative Writing Awards—awards that encouraged such writers as Betty Smith, Marge Piercy, John Ciardi, and Arthur Miller, to name but a few. Dissatisfied with his own contribution to writing, he wished to encourage in others, in the words of the bequest, "the new, the unusual, and the radical." Hopwood had always wanted to write good fiction, "something," he once told a newspaper reporter, "which an intelligent man can sit down and read and think about." Although he worked on such a book throughout his career, he only succeeded in completing a rough draft, which disappeared shortly after his death. Rumored to be a "devastating theatre exposé," the work was uncovered in 1982 (Bell, n.p.). It is a semiautobiographical novel that sheds significant light on Hopwood's sexuality, self-destructive behavior, and successful career and the reasons why he wanted to encourage young writers.

See the Archie Bell Folder, Literature Department, Cleveland Public Library; Letters from Hopwood, Avery Hopwood Papers, Department of Rare Books and Special Collections, University of Michigan Libraries; Mary Roberts Rinehart Collection, Hillman Library, Special Collections, University of Pittsburgh; and the Gertrude Stein Collection, Beinecke Rare Book and Manuscript Library, Yale University. Copies of Hopwood's unpublished plays and his novel are housed in the Avery Hopwood Papers, Department of Rare Books and Special Collections, University of Michigan Libraries; and the Billy Rose Theatre Collection, New York Public Library, Lincoln Center. Newspaper clippings were consulted in the Robinson Locke Collection, Billy Rose Theatre Collection, New York Public Library, Lincoln Center. A collection of dramatic reviews and biographical materials, compiled by Arno L. Bader, are housed in the Department of Rare Books and Special Collections, University of Michigan Libraries. See also A. Bell, "Devastating Theatre Expose, Avery Hopwood's Last Work," *Cleveland News,* March 11, 1929, n.p.; L. Haberman, "American Farce on Broadway, 1914 to 1950," Ph.D. diss., Stanford University, 1959; J. Sharrar, *Avery Hopwood: His Life and Plays,* Ann Arbor, 1998; G. Stein, *The Autobiography of Alice B. Toklas,* New York, 1933; G. Stein, *Everybody's Autobiography,* New York, 1937; A. B. Toklas, *What Is Remembered,* New York, 1963; Mary Roberts Rinehart, *My Story,* New York, 1948; *New York Times,* July 2, 1928; and *Variety,* July 2, 1928.

Jack F. Sharrar

HUGHES, James Mercer Langston (1902–67), playwright and lyricist, was

the son of a frustrated actress and went to the theater often while growing up in Kansas, Ohio, and Mexico. He achieved early fame as a poet of the Harlem Renaissance, however, and he remains best known for verse and prose inspired by his experience as an African American, his involvement in the civil rights movement, and his travels to Africa, Spain, Cuba, and the Soviet Union. Still, Hughes returned to the theater periodically throughout his life, and his legacy includes more than thirty-five plays, operas, and scripts for radio and film; he also founded African American theaters in New York, Chicago, and Los Angeles. In a wide range of theatrical styles, these works reflect Hughes's ear for the rhythms of everyday speech and his respect for ordinary characters who meet injustice with extraordinary feeling.

The subject of Hughes's sexuality has been controversial and seems likely to remain so. Although he admitted to a few visits to female prostitutes (Rampersad, 1:46) and to sexual encounters with men during his stints as a sailor (77), Hughes's most obvious sexual "preference" was for discretion. One biographer sees in him a textbook case of the homosexual with a domineering mother and distant father (Berry, 6); another judges Hughes "asexual" because the poet refused to discuss his sex life even with friends (Rampersad, 1:289). Still, Hughes was fluent in traditional gay codes: he alluded to Plato and Walt Whitman in flirtatious letters to one male suitor (69), and more than once he equated his kind of "loneliness" with that of homosexual friends (Berry, 94, 150). By the 1960s, he remained unmarried and was generally seen in the company of attractive young men. His Harlem neighbors assumed he was gay, and he apparently made no effort to challenge that impression (Rampersad, 1:335, 338).

As a young man, Hughes hoped to create a new form of theater, its content based on African American experience and mythology and its form taken from black vernacular speech and folk songs (Smalley, viii–ix). To this end, he wrote *Mule Bone: A Comedy of Negro Life* with Zora Neale Hurston in 1930, but the two authors quarreled over personal matters before the comedy could be staged. (*Mule Bone* received its belated premier at New York's Lincoln Center in 1991.) Instead, Hughes's first Broadway production was *Mulatto* in 1935. The play was a great commercial success—in its day the longest running production by an African American—but a terrible disappointment for the playwright. *Mulatto*'s white producer rewrote the text, adding highly sensationalist elements, and then listed himself as coauthor in order to reduce Hughes's royalties; on opening night, neither the playwright nor any of the black members of the company were invited to the after-show party (Rampersad, 1:312–14).

Hughes looked beyond Broadway, seeking a more hospitable climate for the truly African American theater he hoped to create. *Little Ham,* produced in 1936 by the Gilpin Players of Cleveland, was the first of several comedies in which Hughes explored urban, "Negro" stereotypes for the benefit and amusement of black audiences. Back in New York, but very Off-Broadway, Hughes founded the Harlem Suitcase Theater with his political review *Don't You Want to be Free?* in 1938. Typically, however, such efforts offered minimal financial compensation, and for most of his life he toured the country giving lectures and poetry readings; these events proved to be his longest-running and perhaps most lucrative "theatrical" endeavors.

Hughes often acknowledged his artistic debt to music, especially gospel and the blues, and some of his greatest dramatic successes were operas. In 1947, he contributed lyrics to Elmer Rice's book and Kurt Weill's music for the Broadway opera *Street Scene,* which is still performed in opera houses around the world. When New York's City Center premiered *Troubled Island* in 1949, with a libretto by Hughes and music by William Grant Still, it was the first production by a major American company of an opera by African Americans (Rampersad, 2:166). The following year saw the New York premier of *The Barrier,* Hughes's musical adaptation of *Mulatto,* with a score by Jan Meyerowitz. Eventually, Hughes found what was perhaps his truest dramatic voice in the form of gospel musicals such as *Simply Heavenly* (which opened Off-Broadway in 1957 before moving to the 48th Street Playhouse), *Black Nativity* (1961), and *Tambourines to Glory* (1963).

If Hughes's poetry and fiction only rarely broach the subject of same-sex attraction, his plays are yet more circumspect: even his comedies, with their colorful pantheons of urban characters, lack open or obvious gays. Overt references to homosexuality were hardly acceptable on the American stage during the decades when Hughes was writing plays; it may be necessary and fair to apply what Gregory Woods calls "gay reading strategies" (127) to an analysis of Hughes's texts. One such tactic is to examine style: *Little Ham*'s disturbing but hilarious take on minority stereotypes seems to reflect a camp sensibility and tone. Another strategy is to deconstruct the content of the plays: Woods argues that Hughes's recurring theme of miscegenation is a metaphor for the "forbidden love" (homosexuality) more central to the author's experience. In fact, when Hughes finally created an openly homosexual character in a 1963 short story, he pitted queer son squarely against homophobic father, just as his earlier play, *Mulatto,* set mixed-race son against racist father. At the very least, it can be said that Langston Hughes functioned comfortably and often in gay social circles and that most who knew him thought him sexually "different" in some sense or another. Read in light of such biographical information, Hughes's dramatic works offer unique insights and pleasures to gays and lesbians of all races.

See G. H. Bass and H. L. Gates Jr., eds., *Mule Bone: A Comedy of Negro Life,* New York, 1991; F. Berry, *Langston Hughes: Before and Beyond Harlem,* Westport, Conn., 1983; A. Borden, "Heroic 'Hussies' and 'Brilliant Queers': Genderracial Resistance in the Works of Langston Hughes," *African American Review* 28, no. 3 (fall 1994): 333–46; T. A. Mikolyzk, *Langston Hughes: A Bio-Bibliography,* Westport, Conn., 1990; A. Rampersad, *The Life of Langston Hughes,* vol. 1: *1902–1941, I, Too, Sing America,* New York, 1986; A. Rampersad, *The Life of Langston Hughes,* vol. 2: *1941–1967, I Dream a World,* New York, 1988; W. Smalley, Introduction to L. Hughes, *Five Plays by Langston Hughes,* Bloomington, 1968, vii–xvii; G. Woods, "Gay Re-readings of the Harlem Renaissance Poets," *Journal of Homosexuality* 26, no. 2–3 (fall 1994): 127–42.

William MacDuff

HUTCHINSON, Josephine (1904–98), actress, was born in Seattle. At the age of sixteen, she won a scholarship to **Maurice Browne**'s School of Acting. She made her film debut in 1917 in *The Little Princess,* which starred

Josephine Hutchinson as Alice in *Alice in Wonderland*. (Photo courtesy of Robert A. Schanke.)

Mary Pickford, and her stage debut in 1920 in *The Little Mermaid* at Seattle's Metropolitan Theatre. In 1922, she moved to New York and played a bit part in *The Hairy Ape* at the Provincetown Playhouse. During a three-year stint with the Ram's Head Players of Washington, D.C., she married the grandson of Alexander Graham Bell. Her husband, Robert W. Bell, was the director of Washington's Anderson-Milton School of

Theatre. In 1925, she returned to New York to appear in a Broadway production of *The Bird Cage.*

In December 1926, while appearing on Broadway in *The Unchastened Woman,* she was invited by **Eva Le Gallienne** to join the Civic Repertory Theatre. Her mother, Leona Roberts, was already a member of the acting company. Since she had not created much of a stir among the critics, her meteoric rise to stardom was surprising. Perhaps because of Le Gallienne's romantic interests in the slender, fragile, petite redhead with the delicate, cameolike face, Hutchinson soon was assigned major roles. During the next nine years, she appeared in the Civic's productions of *Twelfth Night, The Cradle Song, The Good Hope, Hedda Gabler, John Gabriel Borkman, Peter Pan, The Sea Gull, The Three Sisters, Camille,* and *Alice in Wonderland.*

Soon after she moved into Le Gallienne's apartment above the theater in 1927, rumors escalated about their lesbian relationship. When Hutchinson and her husband met reporters for the *New York Times* outside the stage door one night, they admitted they were living apart but that "their relations were entirely cordial" (*New York Times*).

Attempts to keep the relationship hidden were shattered when Hutchinson's husband sued for divorce in 1930, complaining to the press that he never had a chance to have lunch with his wife since she was with Le Gallienne "morning, noon, and night. If my wife had not joined Miss Le Gallienne," he charged, "this would not have happened" (*New York Daily News*). From coast to coast, the press did all it could to expose the relationship. Headlines in the *New York Daily News* read "Le Gallienne Shadow Actress Is Divorced," *shadow* being a euphemism for *lesbianism.* The *New York Daily Mirror* proclaimed "sex in the office."

Although Hutchinson remained with Le Gallienne for five more years, the relationship was not the same. Le Gallienne pursued other women, and Hutchinson, wanting the relationship to continue, became the perfect enabler. Finally, in 1934, while touring with *Hedda Gabler* and *A Doll's House,* Hutchinson announced that she was leaving the Civic Repertory and Le Gallienne for a film career. She signed a long-term contract with Warner Brothers. Her last recorded stage appearance was in *The Shining Hour* at the Berkshire Playhouse in 1936.

Her first film was with Dick Powell in Mervin LeRoy's *Gentlemen Are Born.* When the film was released, the critics, aware of her lesbian relationship with Le Gallienne, complained that her romantic scenes seemed false; she did not know how to kiss. Among her other film appearances were roles in *The Life of Louis Pasteur* (1935), *The Son of Frankenstein*

(1939), and Hitchcock's *North by Northwest* (1959). During the Golden Age of Television in the 1950s, she appeared in several TV dramas.

Hutchinson's nearly eight years with Le Gallienne were apparently her only diversions with lesbianism. She was married two more times—to talent representative James Townsend in 1935 and actor Staats Cotsworth in 1972. But clearly, the time of her greatest success as an actress was the years with the Civic Repertory Theatre, dubbed by George Jean Nathan "the Le Gallienne sorority" (122).

See Civic Repertory Theatre Collection, Beinecke Library, Yale University; E. Le Gallienne, *At 33,* New York, 1934; G. J. Nathan, "The Theatre," *American Mercury* 14 (May 1928): 122; *New York Daily Mirror,* July 9, 1930; *New York Daily News,* July 8, 1930; *New York Times,* February 29, 1928; J. R. Parish and W. T. Leonard, *Hollywood Players: The Thirties,* New Rochelle, 1976; R. A. Schanke, *Eva Le Gallienne: A Bio-Bibliography,* Westport, Conn., 1989; and R. A. Schanke, *Shattered Applause: The Lives of Eva Le Gallienne,* Carbondale, Ill., 1992.

Robert A. Schanke

INGE, William Motter (1913–73), playwright, born in Independence, Kansas, became one of theater's foremost interpreters of Midwestern American life at the mid–twentieth century. The fifth and youngest child in his family, he grew up close to his mother, Maude Sarah, and distant from his father, Luther Clayton, who worked as a traveling dry goods salesman. Inge spent his formative years in Kansas, a state and region that was to furnish the setting and character of his best dramas. His novel, *My Son Is a Splendid Driver* (1971), a memoir disguised as fiction, provides a good glimpse of his early years. His nephew, Luther Clayton Inge, calls it the "nearest" thing he's seen to an Inge autobiography.

Like most homosexuals of homophobic eras, Inge kept his private life a secret from all but his most intimate friends, and information about his sexual relationships and short- or long-term partners is virtually nonexistent. Barbara Baxley, one of Inge's closest friends, reported in an interview that he was uncomfortable with his sexuality and did not want to be gay. He longed for a family home, and he and Baxley seriously considered marriage. Her greatest regret about her friendship with Inge is that they did not marry. Clearly, however, her understanding of homosexual orientation is based on the traditional theories and beliefs of the 1950s, especially the idea that sexual identity is a matter of choice and that any homosexual can be changed by the right woman. At any rate, Inge's homosexuality was undoubtedly a major cause of unhappiness in a life that was frequently unhappy.

Called Billy as a child, Inge demonstrated his interest in theater at an early age. His older sister Helene took elocution lessons, and Billy sat in the room where she practiced, frequently learning the short pieces faster than his sister. He was noted for his recitations, and he especially enjoyed the praise he received from adults following his performances. As a child of eleven, he organized a group of neighborhood children to produce a series of theatricals held in a barn behind the Inge house. Several family photographs depict Inge cross-dressing as a child. On one occasion, dressed as an old lady, he met his sister and mother on the street, completely fooling them. A photograph of Inge dressed as the little old woman can be found in the William Inge Collection at Independence Community College, Independence, Kansas.

By his teen years, Inge had established a pattern of making no close friendships that would persist throughout his life. His parents' unhappy marriage, which he viewed largely from his mother's point of view, and his mother's smothering love may have been contributing factors in developing this personality trait. In *My Son Is a Splendid Driver,* Joey, the Inge persona, talks about his "compulsion to be excluded from any personal relationship that looked to be binding."

Leaving home in September 1930 to attend the University of Kansas in Lawrence represented a major turning point in Inge's life because it was his first break from his family. An English major, he participated in campus theatrical events. Professor Allen Crafton taught him the fundamentals of the well-made play. Crafton's lack of interest in experimental theater was perhaps to some degree passed on to Inge, who, though never an innovator in dramatic form, demonstrated a mastery of dramatic craftsmanship. His goal after graduation was to move to New York and become a professional actor. In the summer before his senior year, he toured with a Toby company (a popular melodramatic tent show, featuring the character Toby) and experienced firsthand the difficulty of making a living as an actor during the Depression. The actors were frequently paid by barter and considered themselves lucky to make five dollars a week.

Upon his graduation from the university, Inge had neither the motivation nor the funds to go to New York and instead followed his older sister Helene to graduate school at George Peabody College in Nashville, Tennessee. He wrote his thesis on David Belasco and the age of photographic realism in American theater, a topic that in retrospect provides an interesting preview of his later work as a playwright. But before completing his degree requirements at Peabody Inge suffered a major clinical depression, the first of many that occurred throughout his life. Unable to function, he left school without a degree and returned to Independence to live with his parents. That summer he took a job with a road crew, and the long, hard days of physical labor helped him to regain a normal sleep pattern and emerge from his illness. He then moved to Wichita, where he worked for almost a year as a radio announcer for KFH. He began to consider teaching as an alternative career, and he accepted a job to teach English and drama in Columbus, Kansas, for the 1937–38 school year. He returned to dramatics for the first time in two years, and he had a remarkably productive year as a teacher and director. In the summer of 1938, he returned to Peabody to complete his master of arts degree. At the end of the summer, through a chance meeting, he was hired for a position at Stephens College in Columbia, Missouri, where he taught from 1938 to 1943.

While at Stephens, Inge worked with the celebrated American actress **Maude Adams,** who had also taken a teaching position there. His dreams of an acting career ended, and his interest in writing was kindled. At Stephens, he began to make trips to Kansas City to see a psychiatrist, as well as weekend trips to Saint Louis to escape the small town atmosphere in Columbia. He also began drinking heavily for the first time; he was to battle alcoholism for the rest of his life.

During a trip to Saint Louis, Inge met Reed Hynds, a critic for the *Saint Louis Star-Times.* Hynds was about to be drafted, and Inge, who was ineligible for the draft for reasons that are unclear, approached the editor with writing samples and received the position as replacement critic.

In 1944, Inge met and interviewed **Tennessee Williams** prior to the pre-Broadway tryout of *The Glass Menagerie.* The meeting was one of the most important of his life; they became friends, and, inspired by Williams, Inge began writing a play. Spoto and Loverich consider it likely that the two men had a brief sexual affair; at any rate, they remained friends until Inge's death.

In a burst of creative energy during the first months of 1945, Inge wrote his first play, *Further off from Heaven,* which contained material that he would later rework into two of his most successful plays, *Come Back Little Sheba* and *Dark at the Top of the Stairs.* Between then and his departure for New York in 1949, he would write the early sketches that eventually were developed into *Picnic, Bus Stop,* and *Splendor in the Grass.*

In 1946, Reed Hynds returned from the war to reclaim his job, and Inge returned to teaching, this time at Washington University. A heavy drinker the entire time he was in Saint Louis, he first sought help in coping with his addiction from Alcoholics Anonymous in 1948. During this period, Williams introduced him to Margo Jones, who produced *Further off from Heaven* as part of the opening season for her new Dallas Theater Center. Jones became an important personal and professional supporter.

Williams also introduced Inge to his agent, Audrey Wood. Not interested in *Further off from Heaven,* Woods nevertheless encouraged him to continue writing. When she read his next play, *Come Back Little Sheba,* she accepted him as a client and persuaded the Theatre Guild to produce the play. The period between a successful September tryout at the Westport Playhouse in Connecticut in 1949 and the Broadway opening in 1950 was stressful for Inge; he lost control over his drinking, was housed in a sanatarium in Greenwich, and was allowed out only under supervision. *Come Back Little Sheba* became a critical and popular success on the stage and later in film (Shirley Booth won both a Tony and an Oscar for her performance as Lola). Each of Inge's next three plays, *Picnic* (1953), *Bus Stop* (1955), and *Dark at the Top of the Stairs* (1957), enhanced his artistic reputation; he became securely established, along with Tennessee Williams and Arthur Miller, as one of the three most important living dramatists in America at midcentury.

Inge did not find success to be the pleasure that he expected. He continued to undergo psychoanalysis; his unresolved drinking problem and his ambivalent feelings about his homosexuality were major factors. In the early 1950s, he wrote a series of one-act plays, which employ themes related to his analysis. *The Strains of Triumph* implies his disappointment with success. The gay characters in *The Boy in the Basement* and *The Tiny Closet* suggest that he no longer felt compelled to disguise homosexuality in his art. But he waited until 1962, well after the death of his parents, before publishing these plays. After his mother's death, characters with homosexual tendencies appear more frequently in his plays. In a preface to the single volume of his four hit plays published in 1958, he reveals that unhappiness and psychoanalysis accompanied his success.

In November 1958, *Harper's* carried a cover story entitled "Men-Taming Women of William Inge," by Robert Brustein, which posited that despite his success Inge represented a mediocre imitation of Tennessee Williams, that his plays offer preachy endorsements of family life and love, and that his female characters dominate the males through symbolic emasculation. Inge, deeply wounded by this critical attack, never quite recovered from it.

As America entered the decade of the 1960s, with civil, social, and artistic revolutions disrupting the nation, Inge, as an artist, could not manage to create works that suited current tastes. Probably it was a mistake for him to believe that he needed to do so; Tennessee Williams found himself in a similar artistic struggle. Inge's last three Broadway plays failed: *A Loss of Roses* (1959), *Natural Affection* (1963), and *Where's Daddy?* (1966).

During the early 1970s, Inge had numerous brief hospitalizations in attempts to treat his addictions and depression. Baxley and Williams urged Helene to commit him until his treatment had positive results. Inge entered Westwood Hospital on June 1, 1973, and signed himself out against medical advice on June 5. In the early hours of June 6, he stepped into his new Mercedes in the closed garage of his Hollywood Hills home, started the car, and committed suicide through carbon monoxide poisoning.

Although Inge left no suicide note, he did leave a play that suggests his mental state during his last years. *The Love Death* deals with a writer who takes pills to commit suicide, then makes a series of telephone calls to his mother, agent, friend, and critic while he awaits death. In reviewing a 1975 Off-Off-Broadway production of the play, Harold Clurman called it "an open confession of the author's anguish."

See R. Brustein, "The Men-Taming Women of William Inge," *Harper's,* November 1958; A. McClure, *William Inge: A Bibliography,* New York, 1982; G. Millstein, "The Dark at the Top of William Inge," *Esquire,* August 1958; B. Shuman, *William Inge,* New York, 1989; R. Voss, *A Life of William Inge: The Strains of Triumph,* Lawrence, 1989; and A. Wertheim, "Dorothy's Friend in Kansas: The Gay Inflections," in *Staging Desire: Queer Readings of American Theater History,* edited by K. Marra and R. A. Schanke, Ann Arbor, 2002, 194–217.

Stephen Berwind

ISHERWOOD, Christopher William Bradshaw (1904–86), playwright, screenwriter, translator, and writer of fiction and nonfiction, was born into an upper middle class family in Cheshire, England. His life experiences formed the basis of his writings, which included collaborations on several plays. His most famous work, *The Berlin Stories* (1946), inspired two successful and influential dramatic treatments.

Analyses of Isherwood's sexuality and career stress his childhood and family influences. Until he was twenty-four years old, his mother, Kathleen, obsessively chronicled his life in a manuscript entitled "The Baby's Progress." Capt. Frank Isherwood died on a French battlefield in 1915. But his father's love of stories, music, and art had already made a strong impression on his son. Isherwood later chronicled his parents' lives in *Kathleen and Frank.*

In 1919, Isherwood attended Repton (a public school) with **W. H.**

Auden and Edward Upward. The three became lifelong friends and influenced each other's writing careers. At this time, he also started writing the journals that later became *Lions and Shadows.* He briefly attended Corpus Christi, Upward's Cambridge college, from 1923 to 1925. In *Christopher and His Kind,* Isherwood says it was here that he "at last managed to get into bed" with a man. "This was due entirely to the initiative of his partner, who, when Christopher became scared and started to raise objections, locked the door, and sat down firmly on Christopher's lap. I am still grateful to him" (3).

In December 1925, Isherwood met Auden again. This time their companionship included sex, a physical relationship that continued until 1939. In 1929, the year after Isherwood's first novel was published, he traveled to see Auden in Berlin. The two collaborated on *The Enemies of a Bishop,* an unproduced play about two men in disguise causing sexual havoc.

Isherwood traveled extensively during this period, sometimes with Auden. They continued their collaborations. In their verse dramas, Isherwood worked on the plot and the prose sections. They wrote three more plays: *The Dog Beneath the Skin* (1936), *The Ascent of F6* (1938), and *On the Frontier* (1938). All premiered in England to moderately favorable receptions. In 1947, a production of *The Dog Beneath the Skin* appeared at New York's Cherry Lane Theatre, but none of the other plays made much of an impact in the United States.

In 1939, Isherwood and Auden emigrated to the United States, where they went their separate ways. Dissatisfied with New York, Isherwood moved to California. He met Swami Prabhavananda and joined the Vedanta Society, which led to the books *An Approach to Vedanta* (1963) and *My Guru and His Disciple* (1980). Theatrical figures intrigued by Vedanta included **Tennessee Williams** and Greta Garbo. Both also became Isherwood's friends.

Isherwood settled into his adopted country and became an American citizen in 1946. His occupations included screenwriting and teaching American customs to refugees. In 1951, he worked with two young writers to dramatize "Sally Bowles," from *The Berlin Stories,* as a play. But, as with Isherwood's later attempt to musicalize it, the project was completed by someone else.

Oddly, Isherwood's most notable contribution to American theater is as source and protagonist for two shows he did not write. Gay playwright **John Van Druten** adapted *The Berlin Stories* as the play *I Am a Camera* (1951) and called the protagonist Christopher Isherwood. This almost asexual person functions as narrator and character in a play that focuses on

Sally Bowles and other friends in the desperate world of prewar Berlin. Although there is no mention of homosexuality, Van Druten comically emphasizes the character of Isherwood's lack of sexual interest in the two attractive women in the play.

Cabaret, with book by Joe Masteroff and songs by John Kander and Fred Ebb, premiered in 1965. This version emphasized the horrors of nazism and added two romances to the plot. The Isherwood character (now called Clifford Bradshaw) loses some of his detachment and has an affair with Sally. But Sally and her abortion were no longer the focus of sexual interest. Instead, the sexually ambiguous Master of Ceremonies (played by Joel Grey) mesmerized audiences and reviewers.

Isherwood's other theatrical work included an adaptation of George Bernard Shaw's *The Adventures of a Black Girl in Search of God* and a play adaptation that he and Don Bachardy wrote of *A Meeting by the River* (1967). These were produced at the Mark Taper Forum in 1969 and 1972, respectively. *A Meeting by the River* failed at the Palace Theater on Broadway in March of 1979.

But it is as master of ceremonies to his own life that Isherwood is best remembered. His many autobiographical and semiautobiographical works use various devices to reveal and yet keep himself distant. He often uses "William Bradshaw" and other pseudonymous characters and writes about "Christopher" in the third person instead of the first. He inserts a disclaimer that "Christopher Isherwood" in *The Berlin Stories* is a "convenient ventriloquist's dummy." All of these devices keep the reader unsure of what has been revealed.

Isherwood eventually revealed his homosexuality in *Kathleen and Frank* (1971), his biography of his parents. Both this book and the autobiographical *Christopher and His Kind* (1976) give the public personal information about himself. Yet both books still seem dispassionately observant, as if he is writing about an intimate acquaintance. Edmund White wrote that Isherwood's *A Single Man* (1964) "is the founding text of modern gay fiction" (White, 3).

Despite his initial reluctance to discuss his own sex life in his books, almost all of Isherwood's writings have homosexual characters and themes. And in his private life he did not disguise his homosexuality. He lived with several men before settling down with Bachardy in 1953. In an interview about his homosexuality, published in 1973, he said: "I never felt I was concealing it, as far as my own life and my own relations with other people were concerned." In 1981, Isherwood was diagnosed with prostate cancer. Don Bachardy took care of him during his final years and was with him when he died on January 4, 1986.

See J. J. Berg and C. Freeman, eds., *The Isherwood Century: Essays on the Life and Work of Christopher Isherwood,* Madison, WI, 2000; K. Bucknell, ed., *Christopher Isherwood, Diaries: 1939–1960,* New York, 1997; R. Davenport-Hines, *Auden,* New York, 1995; B. Finney, *Christopher Isherwood: A Critical Biography,* New York, 1979; J. A. Fryer, *Isherwood: A Biography of Christopher Isherwood,* London, 1977; R. W. Funk, *Christopher Isherwood: A Reference Guide,* Boston, 1979; C. Isherwood, *Christopher and His Kind,* New York, 1976; C. Isherwood, *The Berlin Stories,* New York, 1945; C. Isherwood and K. Bucknell, eds., *Lost Years: A Memoir, 1945–1951,* London 2001; J. Lehmann, *Christopher Isherwood: A Personal Memoir,* New York, 1987; "No Parades," *New York Times Book Review,* March 25, 1973; P. Parker, *Isherwood,* London, 2004; J. Van Druten, *I Am a Camera,* New York, 1952; S. Wade, *Christopher Isherwood,* New York, 1991; and E. White, "Tale of Two Kitties: How Christopher Isherwood was Defined by his Mother and His Lover," *Times Literary Supplement,* no. 5279 (June 4, 2004), 3–4.

Christine Mather

JANIS, Elsie

JANIS, Elsie (Elsie Jane Bierbower) (1889–1956), actress and vaudeville entertainer, was born in Columbus, Ohio. Her mother, Jennie Cockrell Bierbower, put her on stage at the age of four; she made her debut with the James Neil Stock Company at the Great Southern Theatre. Elsie's father did not approve, so Jennie divorced him rather than deny her daughter the opportunity for a stage career. To an even greater degree than Rose and Louise Hovick in the more famous case later chronicled in the musical *Gypsy,* mother and daughter embarked on a trouper's life that thwarted the traditional bounds of female domesticity and heterosexual marriage. Until Jennie's death, neither became romantically involved with men, and both sought emotional and professional sustenance chiefly from other women, primarily each other but also well-positioned role models such as **Elisabeth Marbury** and **Elsie de Wolfe.** Janis, in turn, would support a younger generation of more overtly lesbian theater professionals.

Driven by her archetypal stage mother, Janis's talent became quickly evident, no more so than in her ability to instantly photo- and phonographically imitate others. By nature a tomboy, she readily impersonated male as well as female personalities. Her first career break came on Christmas Day 1898, when she was invited to perform at the White House for President and Mrs. McKinley, who were old acquaintances from Columbus. This performance allowed Jennie to publicize Janis's appearances as "Recited for the President," which led to more and better bookings.

After almost six years in vaudeville, Jennie signed Janis to head a musical play touring group, the Aborn Brothers Company, which enabled Janis to play characters in scenes instead of simply imitating others. The two years spent with the company gave Janis the rudimentary acting skills necessary to make her Broadway debut as the star of *The Vanderbilt Cup* (1906). She was a sensation, and her $1,000 weekly salary made her the most highly paid sixteen year old in America.

The decade leading up to World War I was spent on Broadway and touring nationwide in a succession of musicals: *The Hoyden* (1907), *The Fair Co-Ed* (1909), *The Slim Princess* (1911), *The Lady of the Slipper* (1912), *Miss Information* (1915), *The Century Girl* (1916), and *Miss 1917*. *The Fair Co-Ed* found Janis for the first time performing in male drag. (She had always imitated males as well as females, but this was the first time she actually wore male clothing onstage.) *Miss Information* brought Janis to Broadway in a new guise, that of lyricist, as she wrote lyrics for Jerome Kern's music.

Also during this prewar period, Janis saw her only play produced on Broadway (*A Star for a Night,* 1911), published her first book (*Love Letters of an Actress,* 1912), and made her London debut (in *The Passing Show of 1914*). Her London appearance, in which she sang "Florrie was a Flapper" in full male evening dress, playing a man commenting on a girl he had known, won her the adoration of the young lesbian actress **Eva Le Gallienne,** who became part of Janis and Jennie's intimate circle and whose career they helped advance by arranging numerous employment opportunities. In 1915, Janis appeared in her first silent films, making four within six months (*The Caprices of Kitty, Betty in Search of a Thrill, Nearly a Lady,* and *'Twas Ever Thus*). Early film history is often obscure, but *Betty in Search of a Thrill,* directed by Janis, is perhaps the first film directed by a woman. Certainly it is the first time one woman not only directed but also wrote, produced, and starred in a single film.

During World War I, Janis was one of the only female entertainers allowed to tour the front line camps in France. She and Jennie traveled from camp to camp in a chauffeur-driven Cadillac. Some camps would have built a stage on which Janis would perform for thousands of gathered soldiers. At other times, the car would simply stop and Janis would climb on top to sing, dance, and tell jokes. She gave hundreds of shows and was given dozens of nicknames, including "The Playgirl of the Western Front," "The Lady of the Smiles," and "The Sweetheart of the AEF." Much of her appeal lay in her girl next door nature; ever the tomboy, she engendered not the sexual passions of a soldier's pinup girl but the comforting charms of a soldier's kid sister. Her mother's unflaggingly severe chaperoning also helped ensure that Janis moved into adulthood with little contact with men as anything other than platonic friends.

However, these wartime performances marked a critical turning point in Janis's life. She had put her Broadway career on hold, placed herself in physical danger, and become an adult. Up to this time, she had let her mother take care of all the business and management decisions so that she could focus on performing. The war experience and greater maturity brought her the self-confidence to take more control over her own life and career. This transformation was noticed by many. After the war, Maurice Chevalier came to consider her "the most independent woman in show business" (Ringgold and Bodeen, 22).

Janis's first postwar performances were in a show that re-created her wartime work (*Elsie Janis and Her Gang in a Bomb-Proof Revue,* 1919–20).
The cast consisted of men and women who had been soldiers, nurses, or other overseas war personnel. Janis billed herself as director, following **Rachel Crothers** as a female pioneer in this area. Over the next decade, Janis made her debut in Paris (performing in French); published several novels and collections of stories, essays and poetry; and ventured to Hollywood, where she made several more silent films. She was befriended by the infamously bisexual Edmund Goulding, with whom she wrote of feeling "something 'sympathique'" and to whom she gave a job as a writer for her first David O. Selznick picture, *A Regular Girl* (1919) (Mann, 91). Beginning with *Behind the Lines* (1926), she moved on to talking films. Not relinquishing her musical past, she also played Kay in the Los Angeles production of Gershwin's *Oh, Kay!*

But, for all its seeming variety, Janis's postwar career stagnated in repeated tours of productions based on her wartime entertainments (*It's All Wrong,* 1920; *Elsie in Paris,* 1921; *Elsie Janis and Her Gang in a New Attack,* 1922; and *Clowns in Clover,* 1928). In 1929, she announced her retirement from the stage and channeled her talents and ambitions primarily into the even more masculine-identified enterprises of writing, directing, and producing for stage and screen. She wrote music and lyrics, scripts and dialogue, and, with *Paramount on Parade* in 1930, became the first woman to produce a talking picture.

That same year Janis's mother died, and within a matter of months she married Gilbert Wilson, a man sixteen years her junior. There are indications that this was a "bearded" arrangement that signaled not only Janis's final emergence from her mother's chaperoning but a reversal of their star-making dynamic, as she attempted in fierce motherly fashion to manage her husband's acting career much as Jennie had managed hers. Although his talent was far more limited, his good looks and Janis's connections helped get him cast as a chorus boy in Noël Coward's revue *Set to Music* (1934). He never ascended to theatrical greatness, but he did become one of Coward's party companions. Janis also socialized independently, appearing at one gathering clad in male riding attire on the arm of the notoriously libidinous actress Marilyn Miller.

Moving between New York and Hollywood during the Depression, Janis struggled to keep her career going with various projects. She was production supervisor for *New Faces of 1934,* a revue that introduced to Broadway Henry Fonda and Imogene Coca. Also in the cast was **Katharine Cornell**'s eventual lesbian companion, **Nancy Hamilton,** whose career Janis was helping to bolster. Later in 1934, Janis became the first woman announcer on nationwide radio. She made an unsuccessful attempt to return to Broadway in 1939 in the short-lived *Frank Fay's Vaudeville* and acted in a final movie, *Women in War* (1941), in which she played a nurse in France in World War II. Her husband was drafted and spent five years overseas. When he returned, their marriage became more formally one of convenience, as they did not divorce but no longer lived together.

Janis underwent a sort of religious conversion after surviving a car accident, and she began attending church regularly. Dedicating herself to good works, she went daily—for more than fifteen years—to veterans' hospitals to read to the old soldiers, help them write letters, or sing a few of the old songs. Every few years she would be coaxed into the public eye, performing on radio with Dinah Shore (a World War II soldier's sweetheart) or at a navy base with Bob Hope (who took from Janis the job of nonstop soldiers' entertainer).

When Janis died in 1956, at her bedside was Mary Pickford, an old friend from their days as child stars in turn of the century vaudeville. Although Janis had been out of the public eye for almost three decades, her obituary appeared on the front pages of newspapers throughout the world. She had been one of the most famous women in the world during World War I, and she had not been forgotten. Her funeral was attended by many Hollywood stars but also by hundreds of soldiers, who, wearing their old uniforms, gave her a final salute.

See E. Le Gallienne, *At 33,* New York, 1934; E. Le Gallienne, *With a Quiet Heart,* New York, 1953; E. Janis, *The Big Show,* New York, 1919; E. Janis, *So Far, So Good!* New York, 1932; W. J. Mann, *Behind the Screen: How Gays and Lesbians Shaped Hollywood, 1910–1963,* New York, 2001; L. Morrow, "Elsie Janis," Ph.D. diss., Northwestern University, 1988; L. Morrow, "Elsie Janis: A Comfortable Goofiness," in *Passing Performances: Queer Readings of Leading Players in American Theater History,* edited by R. A. Schanke and K. Marra, Ann Arbor, 1998; M. Pickford, *Sunshine and Shadow,* New York, 1955; and G. Ringgold and D. Bodeen, *Chevalier: The Films and Career of Maurice Chevalier,* Secaucus, N.J., 1973.

Lee Alan Morrow

JOFFREY, Robert (1928–88), choreographer, dancer, artistic director, and teacher, was born Anver Bey Abdullah Jaffa Khan in Seattle on December 24, 1928 (or possibly 1930), to an Italian mother and an Afghan

Robert Joffrey in the early 1960s. The photo appeared in *Current Biography*, November 1967. (Courtesy of the Billy Rose Theatre Collection, New York Public Library for the Performing Arts.)

father, the latter a successful restaurateur. Best known as founder and artistic director of the Joffrey Ballet, one of the premier dance companies in America, Joffrey was also an acclaimed choreographer and dance instructor. His popular, innovative approach to dance introduced new audiences to the art and allowed new choreographers, such as Twyla Tharp and William Forsyth, the opportunity to work with a prominent company. His many honors included the Dance Magazine Award (1964), the Capezio Award (1974), the Handel Medallion of the City of New York (1981), and an appointment by President Carter to the National Council of the Arts (1977).

Joffrey's passion for dance began early. Although his first lessons, at the age of eight, were in tap and ballroom dancing, within two years he was taking private ballet lessons on a daily basis. His first interest in dance was encouraged and financed by a man, known as Uncle Marcus Joffrey, who sometimes lived with the family and whose influence over "Bobby" was profound. Sasha Anawalt, in her biography, *The Joffrey Ballet: Robert Joffrey and the Making of an American Dance Company,* notes that "people who remembered Marcus Joffrey, including his nephew Naim Shah, believe that he was homosexual" (Anawalt, 25). Perhaps this generous benefactor provided a positive, homosexual role model for the young dancer, who became sexually involved, at seventeen, with a young man who was to become his lifelong companion and collaborator, Gerald Arpino. Uncle Marcus's presence might also help to explain what appears to have been the family's "wholesome attitude of acceptance" (37) toward the boy's homosexuality. When Joffrey met Arpino in the fall of 1945, an intimate bond soon formed between them that would last a lifetime. Born Gennaro Peter Arpino on January 14, 1923, the youngest in a large Italian family on Staten Island, Gerald, or Jerry, as he came to be called, left college in 1942 to enter the U.S. Coast Guard Reserve, abandoning his plans for medical school. After being detached to Seattle in 1945, he paid a visit to Mrs. Joffrey, with whom his mother had been acquainted in Italy, and so met her son and, with him, developed a passion for ballet. Arpino and Joffrey soon became inseparable; their friendship developed into a sexual relationship, and dance became a shared way of life. Joffrey and Arpino, who was a novice, began to study in 1945 with Mary Ann Wells, the teacher who best prepared Joffrey for a professional career and after whose eclectic and knowledgeable approach to dance he fashioned his own. In 1948, after living and studying together for three years, Joffrey and Arpino moved to New York City.

Although they ceased to be lovers after their first year in New York, Joffrey and Arpino continued to live together until Joffrey's death in 1988, a total of forty-three years, which encompassed Joffrey's entire adult life. They collaborated throughout their decades together, and when Joffrey died Arpino succeeded him as artistic director of the Joffrey Ballet. The domestic partnership between the two men had its practical side, with Arpino doing most of the household chores, but it was firmly grounded in the couple's emotional intimacy. Jonathan Watts, who lived with the two dancers during the 1950s, later recalled: "I believed them to have a perfect relationship the way married couples perhaps become better friends than they are lovers" (Anawalt, 62). Anawalt, in describing the manner in which Joffrey combined a promiscuous lifestyle with his relationship with Arpino, noted that "he always had Arpino, plus usually one principal lover . . . and many one-night sex partners" (62).

In 1949, Joffrey performed as a soloist with Roland Petit's Ballets de Paris, making his New York professional debut. He studied at the School of American Ballet and also with Alexandra Fedorova. During the next four years, he studied American modern dance (especially Martha Graham's work) at the Gertrude Schurr–May O'Donnell studio and performed as a soloist in O'Donnell's company, but an injury forced him to retire as a dancer in 1953. He taught at the American Ballet Theater School and New York's High School of the Performing Arts, where he developed his own choreography; he also founded his own school, the American Ballet Center, which later became the Joffrey Ballet School. Successful work as a choreographer led to his appointment in 1957 to the position of resident choreographer for the New York City Opera, where he worked for five years.

Joffrey's childhood dream of starting his own dance company was realized in 1954 with the founding of the Robert Joffrey Ballet Company, whose productions were so popular with the critics and the public that he was invited to London the following year to stage two of his ballets for Marie Rambert's company. In 1956, with Arpino as its principal choreographer, he founded the Robert Joffrey Ballet. Touring eleven states in its first year, the company brought ballet to new audiences and established for itself an unusually popular base of support. The company owed its survival chiefly to Joffrey's extraordinary determination and energy, for which he became well known; he required throughout his adult life only four to five hours of sleep each night.

In 1962, Rebekah Harkness, a Standard Oil heiress, extended generous financial support to the young company and enabled it to tour overseas. When Harkness withdrew her support two years later, after failing to gain the degree of control over the company that she desired, Joffrey lost the majority of his dancers and had to assemble a new troupe. His perseverance kept the organization solvent until it received a major grant from the Ford Foundation, followed by funding from other major contributors, including the Andrew W. Mellon Foundation, the National Endowment for the Arts, and Philip Morris. In 1966, the Joffrey Ballet became the resident dance company at New York's City Center Theatre on West Fifty-fifth Street, and it achieved considerable success at this location.

The company emerged in the mid-1960s as one of the leading new dance companies in America. While Joffrey devoted himself to the direction of the company, Arpino choreographed, though Joffrey occasionally presented new work of his own. Cover stories in *Time* and *Life* magazines featured Joffrey's most famous work, *Astarte* (1967), a rock ballet in mixed media, described in *Time* as "a wild, whirling riot of sight and sound" (Kennedy, 45). Dance critic Jennifer Dunning has written of the erotic aspect of *Astarte,* which drew widespread attention to the piece: "Mr. Joffrey made exotic—and erotic—use of the popular technology of the time, with a film of the ballet's two dancers projected on a billowing screen as the dancers moved sensuously before it" (39).

Homoerotic elements were more prominent in Arpino's choreography than in Joffrey's, although Arpino repeatedly objected to the suggestion that such motifs characterize his work, perhaps to protect the company's image at a time when homoeroticism could stigmatize dancers and jeopardize funding and public support. Arpino's all-male *Olympics* (1966) featured a sensuous pas de deux of wrestlers: "While one man stood in a wide-legged plie, the other straddled him. They pushed and pulled up and down in slow motion until the straddling man swivelled his pelvis in direct alignment with the standing man's pelvis" (Anawalt, 218). Arpino's sexually charged *The Relativity of Icarus* (1974) created a scandal, drawing large audiences as well as charges that the choreographer had indulged in pornographic representations (Hanna, 231). Both Joffrey and Arpino eschewed public identification with homosexuality, but their work routinely appeared to celebrate it.

Under Joffrey's guidance, the Joffrey Ballet became noted for work commissioned from new choreographers. He had an exceptional ability to recognize potential among young choreographers, in whose work he looked for signs of a distinctive, personal style. Often, as with Twyla Tharp's *Deuce Coupe,* works by new choreographers generated tremendous publicity and critical enthusiasm for the Joffrey Ballet. The opportunity Joffrey gave to Tharp and other women was especially rare at the time. In her recollection of working with the Joffrey Ballet, Tharp notes in her autobiography that male dancers were "not used to taking orders from a woman, for in 1970 you could count on the fingers of one hand the number of female choreographers who'd been allowed to create ballets in the twentieth century" (179).

In 1983, the Joffrey Ballet became the first dance company to maintain bicoastal headquarters, adding the Music Center in Los Angeles to its New York City Center base. Nancy Reagan, the president's wife, was instrumental in obtaining the Los Angeles site; Ron Reagan, her son, was a member of the company in the fall of 1982. The additional location and Reagan's membership in the company brought publicity and much-needed corporate funding to the company.

Joffrey was found to be HIV positive in 1985, and he began to take the drug AZT the same year. He chose not to disclose his condition to the public, and when he died of AIDS-related illnesses on March 25, 1988, the cause of death was given in the press as "liver, renal and respiratory failure" (Dunning, 1). His last months were devoted to the completion of two ballets, on which he labored after his deteriorating health prevented him from seeing his company perform.

See S. Anawalt, *The Joffrey Ballet: Robert Joffrey and the Making of an American Dance Company,* New York, 1996; W. Como, "Robert Joffrey: A Remembrance," *Dance* 62 (June 1988): 56; J. Dunning, "Robert Joffrey, Fifty-Seven, Founder of the Ballet Troupe, Is Dead," *New York Times,* March 26, 1988; J. L. Hanna, *Dance, Sex, and Gender,* Chicago, 1988; R. Kennedy, "The Theater: Dance, the Great Leap Forward," *Time,* March 15, 1968, 44–48; R. Philip, "Robert Joffrey, 1930–1988," *Dance* 62 (June 1988): 52–56; and T. Tharp, *Push Comes to Shove: An Autobiography,* New York, 1992.

Eric Wiley

JONES, Robert Edmond (1887–1954), scene designer, director, and essayist, is credited with introducing the principles of the European New Stagecraft into the commercial American theater with his designs for Harley Granville-Barker's 1915 production of Anatole France's *The Man Who Married a Dumb Wife.* Through the 1920s, he continued to adapt the theories of Adolph Appia and Edward Gordon Craig and to lead the vanguard of scenic artists whose emphasis on mood and simplification sought to release the American stage from the stranglehold of Belascoesque realism.

In addition to expressing his aesthetic credo through design, Jones wrote numerous articles; published an influential book, *The Dramatic Imagination* (1941); and presented a lecture series, all of which gave voice to his poetic concept of theater and his quasi-mystical approach to life. In a lecture entitled "Curious and Profitable," he articulated his belief in the dual nature of human existence: "At the root of all our living . . . is a consciousness of our essential duality. . . . Life . . . is a never ending dialogue between the outer self and the inner self which together make up our dual nature" (qtd. in Unruh, 77–78). This duality, this dynamic between the inner and outer selves, emerges from both the life and work of Robert Edmond Jones.

Born in Milton, New Hampshire, Jones was the son of Fred Jones, a farmer, and Emma Cowell Jones, a retired concert pianist. Having little aptitude for farming, the sensitive young Jones cultivated skills in drawing and the violin. His artistic nature and a physical limp naturally set him apart from the other members of Nute High School in Milton, "where he figured that he is not as other boys" (Sergeant, 41).

Entering Harvard in 1906, however, afforded Jones the opportunity to pursue many of the activities that had become his passion: designing posters, sets, and costumes for Harvard theatricals, playing the violin in the university orchestra, and devouring theater and dance performances in the Boston area. He graduated in 1910 but stayed at Harvard for the next two years, where he had an undistinguished career as a graduate assistant in the Fine Arts Department.

Jones moved to New York after his departure from Harvard and had a short-lived career designing costumes for the theatrical producers Ray Comstock and Morris Gest, but he eventually found himself living on park benches. It was during this low period of his life that he renewed his friendship with the political activist John Reed, who was also a member of Harvard's class of 1910. Through Reed and art patron Mabel Dodge, Reed's companion at the time, money was raised in the name of the "Robert E. Jones Transportation and Development Company," which allowed him to study informally at Max Reinhardt's Deutsches Theatre in Berlin in 1913 until the outbreak of World War I. It was during this European trip that he became immersed in the theories and techniques of the New Stagecraft, which sought a unified evocation of mood and atmosphere. As the American prophet of the New Stagecraft, Jones would strive to create a poetic rather than a prosaic theater.

Upon his return to America, the young designer began an association with the Stage Society of New York, and it was under its auspices that his work gained wider exposure. An exhibition of the work of new American designers sponsored by the Stage Society included Jones's concepts for *The Merchant of Venice;* as a result of his entry, he was commissioned to design the sets and costumes for the above-mentioned production of *The Man Who Married a Dumb Wife.*

The fledgling Broadway producer Arthur Hopkins was so impressed with Jones's translation of the European principles that he hired him to design sets for his 1915 production of *The Devil's Garden.* This was the beginning of a collaboration between the two men that spanned three decades and numbered forty-seven productions, including John Barrymore's *Richard III* (1920) and *Hamlet* (1922), Lionel Barrymore's *Macbeth* (1921), and the premiers of Eugene O'Neill's *Anna Christie* (1921) and *The Hairy Ape* (1922). The Jones-Hopkins productions were among the most instrumental in assuring that the ideas and techniques of the New Stagecraft gained currency on the commercial American stage.

Bobby Jones was not an artist to be confined to any one theatrical style or venue, however, for his work encompassed both the established and the experimental. From the back room of the Washington Square Bookshop, which was used for the 1914 inaugural production of the Washington Square Players (which presented Lord Dunsany's *The Glittering Gate*), to the Metropolitan Opera House for Nijinski's 1916 *Til Eulenspiegel;* and from Hutchins Hapgood's living room, which served as his backdrop for the two one-act plays that launched the Provincetown Players in the summer of 1915, to Lewisohn Stadium, the site of the New York City Shakespeare Tercentenary Celebration featuring Percy Mackaye's *Caliban by the Yellow Sands* (1916), Robert Edmond Jones's designs began to transform the American stage.

During the 1920s, under the auspices of the Experimental Theatre, Inc., which was formed from the original Provincetown Players and overseen by the artistic triumvirate of Robert Edmond Jones, Eugene O'Neill, and Kenneth MacGowan, Jones had an opportunity to meld his design theories with his emerging skills as a director in such productions as *Desire under the Elms* (1924) and *The Great God Brown* (1926).

In 1932, he briefly held the post of art director at Radio City Music Hall, where his primary responsibility was to create the visual aspects of its inaugural program. That was also the year in which he began his ten-year association with the Central City Opera House summer season in Central City, Colorado. He also served a short stint in Hollywood working on color designs for *Becky Sharp* (1934) and *The Dancing Pirate* (1936), but theater was to be the medium of his success. Although the volume of his work began to diminish somewhat during the 1930s and into the 1940s, he continued designing for Hopkins, the Theatre Guild—most notably for *The Iceman Cometh* (1946) and *A Moon for the Misbegotten* (1947)—the Metropolitan Opera Association, and others.

In 1933, at the age of forty-five, Jones married Margaret Huston Carrington. Carrington, Walter Huston's sister, was the widow of a wealthy businessman and patron of the arts. After an injury ended her operatic career, she developed and taught a vocal training technique. John Barrymore had sought out her rigorous training program in preparation for his Shakespearean debut for the Jones-Hopkins *Richard III*. Carrington succumbed to cirrhosis of the liver in 1942.

With the revival of *The Green Pastures* in 1951, Jones's long and illustrious career as a designer came to a close. After a prolonged period of illness, he died in his hometown of Milton, New Hampshire, on November 26, 1954.

Upon his death, the *New York Times* obituary referred to Jones as "one of the most influential forces in the development of the modern American theatre" ("R. E. Jones," n.p.). While his public life as a designer, director, and essayist is openly available, the private life of this "most influential force" is frequently shrouded in mystery and secrecy. His papers and correspondence, which are housed at Harvard University, apparently have been expunged of virtually all personal references. One must look to his "public" life and work to unravel the private person behind the public mask.

Jones's ambivalence about his identity is revealed in Elizabeth Sergeant's study of the artist: "The truth is that even the intimate friends of this innovator scarcely know how he looks, for his looks, like his personality and his achievement in the theatre, are constantly being formed and reformed out of the mutable substance of the times" (37). Even his clothing functioned as "a disguise, of course; a man of the theatre must have various layers" (38).

Jones's fascination with the layering of the true self behind the mask is evident throughout his design career and ranged from the literal exploration of masks in *The Great God Brown* to more metaphorical manifestations in such work as *Macbeth* and *Desire under the Elms*. For example, as Dana Sue McDermott argues, his much-maligned design for *Macbeth* (1921) was the first example of abstract symbolism in the commercial American theater and was, not coincidentally, a result of the designer's personal experience with psychoanalysis.

> When the curtain rose, the audience was confronted by the first open-space use of a Broadway stage. With black drapes and selective lighting Jones created a void rather than a set. Into this black hole came abstract grey fragments and shafts of light. For the witches' scenes three large silver masks loomed over the void with white light streaming from the eyes. (113)

This visual manifestation of the duality between the inner and outer selves, the struggle within a man's soul, is graphically depicted in Jones's use of light and shadow; his utilization of abstract design mirrors the torments of the character's mind.

With these tools of his trade, Jones explored his own duality. While his homosexuality has been acknowledged by many who knew him (see Davis), Jones took great pains to hide behind the veneer of heterosexual respectability. Just as his scenery "stands out in memory . . . but always with something held back" (Sergeant, 44), Jones attempted to reconcile the New England puritan with the worldly man of the theater. The masks, both literal and metaphorical, of his own devising gave expression to the duality of his nature, the dynamic between the inner and outer selves.

See F. Davis, interview with author, New Hampshire Farm Museum, Milton, N.H., June 2001; M. Gorelik, "Life with Bobby," *Theatre Arts,* May-June 1955; L. Grobel, *The Hustons,* New York, 1989; R. E. Jones, *The Dramatic Imagination,* New York, 1941; M. D. Luhan, *Movers and Shakers,* New York, 1936; D. S. McDermott, "The Void in *Macbeth:* A Symbolic Design," in *Themes in Drama 4: Drama and Symbolism,* edited by J. Redmond, Cambridge, U.K., 1982, 113–25; R. Pendleton, *The Theatre of Robert Edmond Jones,* Middletown, Conn., 1958; J. Peterson, "'Not as Other Boys': Robert Edmond Jones and Designs of Desire," in *Staging Desire: Queer Readings of American Theater History,* edited by K. Marra and R. A. Schanke, Ann Arbor, 2002, 338–64; "R. E. Jones Is Dead; Stage Designer, 67," *New York Times,* November 1954; E. S. Sergeant, *Fire under the Andes: A Group of Literary Portraits,* Port Washington, N.Y., 1927; and D. Unruh, ed., *Towards a New Theatre: The Lectures of Robert Edmond Jones,* New York, 1992.

Jane T. Peterson

KALLMAN, Chester (1921–75), librettist, was often discounted during his lifetime as the mere boy toy of a famous writer, and in fact he was an unrepentant wastrel who dabbled at writing poetry and music criticism. Without him, however, one of the few internationally acclaimed modern operas might never have been written.

Born and educated in Brooklyn, Kallman was still a teenager when he met thirty-two-year-old **W. H. Auden** at a poetry reading in 1939, yet the two made a marriage based on the high regard each had for the intellect and talent of the other. Auden brought selfless devotion to the union; Kallman's dowry included good looks, a quick wit, and an encyclopedic knowledge of popular and classical musical theater (Carpenter, 259–61). Although Kallman was monogamous for only a short period and punished Auden's jealousy by ending their sexual relations entirely in 1941 (Farnan, 57), their relationship would prove to be long-lived and fruitful.

For most of the 1940s, the two men lived in Manhattan, where, while Auden supported him financially, Kallman pursued his twin passions for "rough trade" and opera. It may be that Kallman's tempestuous romantic encounters with straight-identified men found their perfect artistic expression in the tragic heroines of musical drama. Certainly, his true vocation was that of opera queen: he doted on backstage gossip, sometimes claimed that the controversial soprano Kirsten Flagstad was his "mother" (Farnan, 100), and frequently entertained Auden's famous friends by acting out the plots of obscure musical plays.

If Auden found Kallman's sexual adventures disturbing and eventually even dangerous (Farnan, 202–6), he was quickly converted to his partner's taste for opera. So when Igor Stravinsky asked for a libretto based on Hogarth's pictures of "The Rake's Progress," Auden turned to Kallman for assistance. In many ways, the text they wrote together mirrors their relationship: like Kallman, the hero, Tom Rakewell, pursues a series of vices while his beloved Anne follows behind, like Auden, ever adoring and forgiving. The story is more than autobiography, however, and its most complex character—a bearded woman whom Tom marries instead of his true love—awaits a fuller critical analysis of its transsexual implications; in 1950, Tom's inclination toward gender ambiguity over traditional femininity, albeit temporary, was deemed so disturbing that the New York City Opera declined to produce the premiere (Mendelson, xxiii). *The Rake's Progress* did open in Venice in 1951, however, and it has been performed throughout the world; it is often mentioned as the prime example of twentieth-century neoclassicism.

Auden and Kallman completed a second libretto for Stravinsky, but the composer never set the text to music. Instead the poets adapted *The Magic Flute* for a television broadcast in 1956 and repeated this success with *Don Giovanni* in 1959. They were also attached for brief periods to projects that, without them, would become the Broadway musicals *Man of La Mancha* and *Cabaret*.

On his own, Kallman wrote one original libretto (*The Tuscan Players*) for composer Carlos Chávez. Although he opposed the translation of librettos on the ground that vocal music is best served by its original language, Kallman reasoned that if translation must be done it ought to be done well (Farnan, 191). To this end, he wrote English versions of numerous operas, which were performed and/or published throughout the 1950s. For much of that decade, Kallman and Auden spent summers on the island of Ischia off the coast of Italy. There they met a young German composer, Hanze Werner Henze, with whom they wrote *Elegy for Young Lovers* (first performed in 1961) and *The Bassarids* (1966). Although neither opera repeated the success of *The Rake's Progress,* each has enjoyed more than one major production and recording.

After 1958, Austria replaced the Mediterranean as the couple's summer home, and in 1963 Kallman began to winter without Auden in Greece, an apparent attempt to assert his independence (Carpenter, 408). To Kallman, however, independence all too often meant idleness, and by 1968 Auden had agreed that the two should adapt *Love's Labour's Lost* with composer Nicolas Nabokov, primarily so that Kallman would have something to do (428). It was the last collaboration that they would see onstage. W. H. Auden died in 1973; only fifteen months later, Chester Kallman drank himself to death at the age of fifty-four.

See M. Bronski, *Culture Clash: The Making of Gay Sensibility,* Boston, 1984; H. Carpenter, *W. H. Auden: A Biography,* London, 1981; R. Craft, "The Poet and the Rake," in *W. H. Auden: A Tribute,* edited by S. Spender, New York, 1975; D. J. Farnan, *Auden in Love,* New York, 1984; R. Giddings, "Engaging an Audience: Auden and the Idea of Opera," in *W. H. Auden: The Far Interior,* edited by A. Bold, Totowa, N.J., 1985; E. Mendelson, ed., *W. H. Auden and Chester Kallman: Libretti and Other Dramatic Writings by W. H. Auden, 1939–1973,* Princeton, 1993; and C. Osborne, *W. H. Auden: The Life of a Poet,* New York, 1979.

William MacDuff

KAYE, Danny (David Daniel Kaminski) (1913–87), entertainer, was born in Brooklyn on January 18, 1913, into a Jewish family with a "doting—too doting" mother and a father who "kept his emotional distance" (Gottfried, 17, 19). The young Kaye tried to break into vaudeville, but he found more permanent, if seasonal, employment as a tummler in the summer retreats in the Catskills (*tummler* is a Yiddish word meaning "fun maker"). Kaye entertained the guests but also led them in sing-alongs, mock excursions, and such. This talent—combined with his skillful dancing, fine singing voice, and talent for acting—kept him out of vaudeville and its pigeonholes, but it ultimately raised him to the heights of sui generis entertainer.

That rise was assisted by partnering with Sylvia Fine. They met while working on a one-night uptown revue. Fine, instantly smitten with Kaye, began writing material for his unique talents. Her songs relied on "sexually ambiguous" material—roles with secret identities or playing in drag (Gottfried, 48). Her "Anatole of Paris" is about a hatmaker who "shriek[s] with chic" and confides "I hate women." A summer's engagement at Camp Tamiment turned into *The Straw Hat Revue* (1939), which played for eleven weeks on Broadway. Kaye married Fine in early 1940. No one recalls him being especially in love with her. The two quickly cobbled together a nightclub act. Thanks to Kaye's tummler training and personal brilliance, he became the hot ticket in New York.

Kaye's first big opportunity came from Moss Hart. In a "subtle flirtation," Hart "coyly" told Kaye, "If I ever write another revue, it would only be because you could be in it" (Gottfried, 55). In fact, Hart wrote a part for him in his next musical, *Lady in the Dark* (1941), that of fey fashion photographer Russell Paxton. Kaye's representation was not mincing but dynamic. His recorded performance from that show—the material leading up to the star-making, tongue-twisting, full-speed "Tchaikov-sky"—reveals no lisping or effeminacy except for one short falsetto whoop.

After six months of *Lady in the Dark,* Kaye jumped into the lead of **Cole Porter**'s musical *Let's Face It!* (1941). Porter's material for Kaye included the song "Farming," wherein George Raft's bull is described as "gay," and "Let's Not Talk about Love." During the run of *Let's Face It!* Kaye began a serious affair with costar Eve Arden. He eventually broke up with Arden and remained married to Fine—out of a sense of loyalty to the woman who had helped create his performing persona. Over the years, Kaye had many affairs with women—Gwen Verdon (Gottfried, 167), Shirley MacLaine (MacLaine, 278–83), and perhaps even Princess Margaret (Gottfried, 159). There were interludes with less famous women as well. The usual beginnings of these affairs were abrupt—escalating from introduction to sexual advance quickly, taking the women by surprise (251, 281, 290, 299, 310–12).

In 1943, Kaye signed a five-year contract with Metro-Goldwyn-Mayer. These early pictures established Kaye's screen persona, which Fine helped shape with musical and specialty acts for him. *The Secret Life of Walter Mitty* (1947) typifies these characters: one side is mild, shy, and passive, while the other is brilliant, talented, and charismatic. Kaye was a nonman in man's roles, playing each side well but never generating sparks with his leading women.

Kaye briefly separated from Fine after the birth of their only child in 1947. He played London's Palladium and was a smash hit. As difficult and aloof as he could be offstage, he was open, loving, and loved onstage.

It is uncertain where and when Kaye met Sir Laurence Olivier—Hollywood in 1940 (Spoto, 211) or London in 1947 (Gottfried, 139–40). Clearly, however, they met and got along famously. Kaye brought out the music hall in Olivier, and the two performed together at parties and benefits (with Olivier's wife, Vivien Leigh). Kaye gave Olivier infantile nicknames—"Lally" or "Lala" (Spoto, 211). After he returned to Hollywood in 1949, the Oliviers arrived for their own film projects. Kaye's behavior became intrusive: he showed up unannounced at their house (they had rented a home next door to him), got himself invited to any function where the Oliviers were expected, threw them parties of his own, and traveled with Olivier to Nöel Coward's Caribbean home (Spoto, 228–30; Gottfried, 167–68). In short, Kaye and Olivier were having an affair.

Although Gottfried dismisses many of the stories surrounding the Kaye-Olivier relationship as rumors (see 192–95), he cannot deny its existence. Olivier wrote a letter to former wife Leigh in 1961, "weakly describing as merely transitory and unimportant the sexual intimacy between himself and Kaye" (Spoto, 230). Kaye made an "unprompted" statement late in life that "I've never had a homosexual experience in my life. I've never had any kind of gay relationship. I've had opportunities, but I never did anything about them" (Gottfried, 323). Gottfried accepts this at face value even after relating duplicitous stories about Kaye "forgetting" insults to others (319) or faking the length of his recovery from a torn ligament in his leg during his final Broadway show (300). If Kaye could lie about these matters, why not about his relationship with Olivier?

The lie about homosexual relations is but one sign of his ambivalence toward the subject. During the filming of *Hans Christian Anderson* (1952), Kaye was alternately "solicitous or remote" with gay costar **Farley Granger** and demanded that Granger's one musical number in the score be given to him—which it was (Gottfried, 177). Granger later wondered if Kaye's erratic and remote treatment "might have had a homosexual element about it; and guilt" (178).

The affair with Olivier seems to have ended with Leigh's mental breakdown in 1953. Kaye stayed by Olivier's side to help as best he could, but his presence merely aggravated Leigh more. The friendship was terminated when Kaye was billed to appear in Olivier's Chichester Theatre Festival in 1967 and did not show up (Gottfried, 271).

Meanwhile, Kaye had been under contract with Paramount. *White Christmas* (1954) features Kaye and costar Bing Crosby in drag lip-synching "Sisters." (Kaye had previously done an impersonation of cabaret singer Kay Thompson "so uncanny" that some people thought it was her [Gottfried, 168].) His next picture, *The Court Jester* (1955), is his best, allowing his physical, verbal, and musical abilities full sway amid a cast of experts. But the film was a flop—it only grossed $2.2 million of its $4 million expense. Kaye's subsequent movie career dwindled and died.

Kaye attempted a career on radio and television but failed because, unlike Jack Benny or Burns and Allen, Kaye had no unique comic persona (distinct from his movie characters) on which to hang entertainment. However, as a spokesman for the United Nations agency UNICEF and as a children's entertainer—never patronizing, his antics clearly crossing language barriers—Kaye became loved and his place in American culture as "an entertainer" was secured.

After an erratic performance in Richard Rodgers's musical *Two by Two* (1970), Kaye became preoccupied with his hobbies. His appearances thereafter were rare: he played Captain Hook and Gepetto in two TV specials, and he played a Holocaust survivor in the TV movie *Skokie* (an even rarer serious role). He received a Kennedy Center honor in 1984, but by this time health problems were overcoming him. He died on March 3, 1987, at the age of seventy-four.

Kaye's contradictory moods—open and giving onstage, snide and morose off—are typical of many performers who find safe outlets for personal expression on the stage (Olivier was another such performer). Kaye's personal life, however, compounds this ambiguity: a Brooklyn Jew who strove to eliminate traces of both from himself and a bisexual whose sexual urges were inappropriately or infrequently expressed. The fact that ambiguity became part of Kaye's performances is worthy of deeper consideration. Was Fine's choice of ambivalent subject matter conscious or not? Were Kaye's dexterous gestures a cover for limp-wristedness? Did Hollywood's casting of Kaye in ambiguous roles signify its inability to categorize a bisexual? Did his identification as a children's entertainer safely place him in a nonsexual environment? In an era in which so many successfully hid their private lives or turned public lies into personal acceptance, Kaye's ambiguous public and private behavior suggests that "nobody's fool" was working hard at fooling himself.

See M. Gottfried, *Nobody's Fool: The Lives of Danny Kaye,* New York, 1994; S. MacLaine, *My Lucky Stars: A Hollywood Memoir,* New York, 1995; and D. Spoto, *Laurence Olivier: A Biography,* New York, 1992.

Jeffrey Smart

KELLY, George Edward (1887–1974), playwright, was born at the Falls of Schuykill, Philadelphia, the second youngest of ten children, to John Henry and Mary Costello Kelly, hardworking Irish Catholics. The Dobson Carpet Mills (1851–1927) employed and exploited the large Irish Catholic settlement in the Falls area, and nearly all of the Kelly children, one by one, as they reached the employable age of nine, went to work there. George quit school in the fourth grade and went to work. By young adulthood, he was dreaming of an escape from his oppressive environment.

George's older brother, Walter (1873–1939), went into vaudeville at the turn of the century, became a headliner by 1902 as the "Virginia Judge," and in his late years, with vaudeville's demise, performed in movies and on New York's legitimate stage. Undoubtedly, his brother's example as an international vaudeville star encouraged George in 1910, at the age of twenty-three, to secure an acting job, barnstorming across the country in *East Lynne.* From 1911 to 1914, Kelly gained additional

stage experience acting in national touring companies of *The Virginian,*
Live Wires, and *The Common Law.*

In 1915, Kelly entered vaudeville, acting in Paul Armstrong's *Woman*
Proposes, and within a year he was writing and acting in his own sketch,
Finders Keepers, on the Keith-Orpheum circuit. After one year in the army
(1917), he wrote, directed, and toured several of his own sketches
(1918–22), including *The Flattering Word, Poor Aubrey, The Weak Spot,*
Smarty's Party, Mrs. Ritter Appears, Mrs. Wellington's Surprise, and *One of*
Those Things (Hirsch, 11). Kelly developed *Mrs. Ritter Appears* into his
first full-length Broadway play, retitled *The Torch Bearers* (1922) and *Poor*
Aubrey into his second New York success, *The Show-Off* (1924).

Kelly's years in vaudeville informed both plays, but *The Torch Bearers,*
which required the skillful manipulation of many characters making
entrances, exits, stage business, and theatrical "points," reveals more
tellingly than any of his later plays his confident mastery of vaudeville
craftsmanship. Moreover, critics recognized in the play a moral passion
and literary skill that elevated the piece above the conventional and
familiar comedies and farces that made up the majority of Broadway's
190 new productions in that season (Mantle, 18). *The Torch Bearers* satirizes the pose and pretension that Kelly believed had begun to dominate
the little theater movement. He clearly condemns those community
members (primarily women) who love being displayed *in* the art rather
than the art itself, about which they know nothing. Some critics questioned the severity of Kelly's condemnation of these naive players, for
whom his rather stern judgment seems to exceed their crime. Ten plays
by Kelly were to open on Broadway between 1922 and 1946; all of them
depict to some degree his uncompromising expectations for human conduct and his austere, puritanical judgment of those who fall below the
mark.

Kelly's second play to open on Broadway, *The Show-Off,* although
nominated for the Pulitzer Prize, failed to win, but his third, *Craig's Wife*
(1925), gained the award. *The Show-Off,* the greatest critical and popular
success of all his plays, presents the domestic relationships of a middle-
class Philadelphia suburban family. In the play, Kelly's Aubrey Piper, a
show-off and braggart who possesses no particular skills or talents but
expects fortune to drop in his lap, can be read as representative of a generation indifferent to traditional American values, lacking respect for
work, integrity, or social responsibility. Aubrey's ludicrous presence per-
vades Mrs. Fisher's house as the curtain falls, suggesting a Chekhovian
change in the social order.

Kelly's third full-length play, the prizewinning *Craig's Wife,* brought the author eminent critical respectability, establishing him as one of America's foremost dramatists and placing him in the ranks of previous Pulitzer Prize recipients such as Eugene O'Neill and Sidney Howard. *Craig's Wife,* which depicts in the title role an asexual, female predator who marries Walter Craig for the purpose of subjugating him and possessing his house, led to Kelly's being labeled a misogynist, a criticism of his portrayal of women that persisted throughout his life. Walter Craig, decent, generous, and responsible, becomes the innocent victim of Harriet, who has methodically alienated her husband's friends, isolated Craig from any influence but her own, and secured and preserved the museum-like orderliness of her house. For Kelly, Harriet represents "the modern woman," who, faced with the realities of getting ahead in the world, has dropped romantic notions about men and is cynically viewing "marriage as a means of insuring . . . food, shelter, and clothes" (qtd. in Hirsch, 68). *Craig's Wife* (originally subtitled *A Drama of the Changing Social Order*) continues the exploration of shifting generational values begun in *The Show-Off,* which Kelly further developed with variations in all of his produced plays.

Arthur H. Lewis argues that George Kelly's homosexuality influenced his harsh depiction of female characters, whose various sins against males or social codes bring them retribution, and he refers to a critical essay on Kelly written for *The Nation* by Joseph Wood Krutch for support (the essay appeared on November 13, 1929; Lewis mistakenly identifies the date as September 20, 1929).

> Hate seems to be the real source of [Kelly's] inspiration, and one is almost inclined to suspect that behind the harshness of his attitude lies some personal experience which would have to be known before one could entirely understand [his] vehemence. . . . He has idiosyncratic standards of judgment and he distributes rewards and punishments according to some personal canon of poetic justice which leaves the spectator less satisfied than vaguely resentful. (qtd. in Lewis, 110)

Foster Hirsch believes that Kelly viewed women as "aesthetic objects" to be deployed in his art. For his study on Kelly, he gained an extensive personal interview with the playwright at his Sun City, California, home in 1971. Alert, articulate, and cooperative, Kelly talked readily about his work but never permitted the interview to become personal. William Weagly, Kelly's companion of many decades, appeared briefly in the kitchen doorway during the interview, but Kelly did not introduce him (Hirsch, interview with author, April 13, 1996).

Newsweek published a brief description of George Kelly a year before Hirsch's interview, and, adhering to the decorum of the time, conventionally identified Weagly merely as "an aging private secretary named William" ("Where Are They Now?" 12). Probably George Kelly and Bill (as he called him) became lifetime partners in the early 1930s, although one story puts the year of their meeting as early as 1919 (Lewis, 126, 128). Weagly (b. 1896), nine years younger than Kelly, may have been a bellhop at New York's Concord Hotel (another story goes), when Kelly, who had a suite there, chose him privately as his lover and publicly as his valet, secretary, and traveling companion (126). Weagly, "slightly built, plain-looking, [and] unsophisticated," was schooled by Kelly in the social graces. The two entertained stylishly as cohosts at home and dined at the tables of friends and the famous (including visits to George's niece, Princess Grace of Monaco). But the Kelly family in Philadelphia never accepted the Kelly-Weagly relationship as anything other than one of master and servant. There Weagly came not as a guest but as George's valet and secretary, "and was treated as such, [and] ate in the kitchen with the hired help or didn't eat at all" (126).

After the award-winning *Craig's Wife,* Kelly's next play was awaited with high expectation, but *Daisy Mayme* (1926) met a modest critical and public reception. The play, like *Craig's Wife,* is about a struggle for the domination and control of a man and his house. For the rest of Kelly's career, critics implied that the playwright never quite fulfilled the artistic potential that his first three plays had promised. At the same time, they recognized (in seasons when over two hundred new productions were the norm) that his plays were more literate and provocative than most.

Although Burns Mantle chose Kelly's fifth play, *Behold the Bridegroom* (1927), for his annual collection of the ten best of the season, the production failed with critics and the public. Of all his plays, *Behold the Bridegroom* demonstrates most emphatically Kelly's refusal to "compromise with his puritan conscience or make any effort to hide his contempt for contemporary morality" (Krutch, "Austerity," 241).

With the productions of his last five plays, Kelly's artistic prominence continued to decline. Krutch's comment on *Maggie the Magnificent* (1929) that it "commands respect without awaking enthusiasm" captures in a few words the critical attitude that persisted throughout the rest of Kelly's career. *Maggie the Magnificent,* like *Behold the Bridegroom,* examines integrity of character; here the "ugly disorder in the soul of an uncultivated mother is contrasted with the character of a daughter whose sheer determination lifts her out of the mess in which she was reared" (Krutch, "Drama," 564). Kelly next turned his energies to *Philip Goes Forth* (1931), which takes up the playwright's views of the sacred high calling of the theater arts and those practitioners who delude themselves into believing that they have enough talent to contribute. The subject was explored to better advantage in Kelly's first produced play, *The Torch Bearers. Philip Goes Forth,* without any zestful comic action to inflate it, sank quickly on Broadway. Five years later, Kelly returned with *Reflected Glory* (1936), which featured the irrepressible **Tallulah Bankhead** in her first major New York role, that of an actress torn between choosing a career or marriage. In a characteristic Kelly move, she chooses art and sacrifices romance. Although Bankhead's performance gave the critics amusing copy for their reviews, the play failed.

Kelly's last two plays, *The Deep Mrs. Sykes* (1945) and *The Fatal Weakness* (1946), completed his Broadway career. *The Deep Mrs. Sykes* features Ralph, the son of Mr. and Mrs. Sykes, who has fallen in love with Mrs. Taylor and wishes to leave his own wife. In an unromantic conclusion, Ralph's father delivers a long sermon, urging his son to remain in his loveless marriage, which is precisely what he himself has done. Although all of Kelly's plays demonstrate to some extent his cynical view of marriage, this one strongly pronounces it. His last produced play, *The Fatal Weakness,* featured the stylish actress Ina Claire as Mrs. Espenshade, the wife of a man who is secretly having an affair. She is also the mother of a married daughter who has lost all common sense in her wish to become a sophisticated "modern." Mrs. Espenshade, for whom romance no longer exists in her marriage, compensates by attending the weddings of beautiful young people, about whom she fantasizes in vaguely romantic ways. The play offers a satiric view of the sanctity of marital relationships.

In early May 1974, George Kelly, in fragile health and having decided that he preferred to die publicly with the Philadelphia Kellys rather than privately with his companion of a lifetime, left William Weagly in their Sun City home and flew east to spend his last days with a niece in Bryn Mawr, Pennsylvania. His relationship with Weagly over the years had evolved into what the public had long defined it, one of employer and employee, rather like some longtime marriages in which the passion is gone but a bond remains. But for the playwright, at the end of his life, in choosing between Weagly and the Kellys, the family bond was the strongest.

George Kelly died on June 18, at the age of eighty-seven, the last surviving member of his siblings. William Weagly, it is said, came to the funeral in Philadelphia, but he was not seated in front among the Kelly family of mourners. Instead, he "sat weeping in a back pew at St. Bridget's" (Lewis, 129).

See B. Mantle, ed., *Best Plays of 1922–23,* Boston, 1923; B. J. Harbin, "George Kelly, American Playwright: Characters in the Hands of an Angry God," in *Staging Desire: Queer Readings of American Theater History,* Ann Arbor, 2002, 126–44; F. Hirsch, *George Kelly,* New York, 1974; G. E. Kelly, Theatre Collection, Free Library of Philadelphia; J. W. Krutch, "Drama: George Kelly," *The Nation,* November 13, 1929; J. W. Krutch, "The Austerity of George Kelly," *The Nation,* August 30, 1933; A. H. Lewis, *Those Philadelphia Kellys,* New York, 1977; W. McGarry, "Oh, for a Million Mothers Like Mary Kelly!" *American Magazine,* September 1925; "Where Are They Now?" *Newsweek,* February 2, 1970; and R. M. Thomas Jr., "George Kelly, Playwright, Dies, Won Pulitzer for *Craig's Wife,*" *New York Times,* June 19, 1974.

Billy J. Harbin

KOUTOUKAS, H. M. (Haralimbus Medea) (1947–), playwright and performer, was born on June 4, 1947, in Endicott, New York. Koutoukas wrote, directed, starred in, and produced more than 150 productions, many of which contributed to the "brilliant senselessness" ("Off-Off-Academia," 23) that eventually became the style recognized as Off-Off-Broadway theater in the 1960s and 1970s. He has been deemed the "quintessential Off-Off-Broadway dramatist" (Smith, 324), and his work was performed in coffeehouses, churches, lofts, art galleries, concert halls, and movie theaters and as private entertainments for the wealthy. During the 1960s, he was associated with the Caffe Cino, which many consider to have been the birthplace of gay theater. There plays by such gay and gay-friendly luminaries as Doric Wilson, **William M. Hoffman,** Tom Eyen, John Guare, and Sam Shepard were performed. Randy Gener described the scene in a retrospective in 1994: "The Caffe's misfit, boho, theatrical-fringe status jibed with the displacement of being a sexual other" (5). Koutoukas was also associated with the Electric Circus and Judson Church and was a founder of the Chamber Theater Group. He received an Obie Award in 1966 for his numerous Off-Off-Broadway contributions that season.

Gerald Rabkin, writing in the *Soho Weekly News,* once defined the theatrical style he called "Koutoukasian" as being "a torrent of imagery, both verbal and visual, clustering around themes of loss, hallucination, falling apart, disconnecting—and carrying on in spite of it all" (51). More succinctly, however, Koutoukas was considered the "last of the aesthetes" (Faber, n.p.), and he may best be remembered as the inventor of "camp" (Poland and Mailman, 534). With baroque wordplay and go-for-

Harry Koutoukas at the LaMama Experimental Theatre Club, March 1965. (Photo courtesy of James D. Gossage and the Billy Rose Theatre Collection, New York Public Library for the Performing Arts.)

broke performances, his style was flamboyantly romantic, idiosyncratic, sometimes self-satirizing, and full of private references and inside jokes. He often wrote in verse, and his characters and situations displayed a highly fanciful imagination and an elaborately refined sensibility, worshiping glitter, glamour, beauty, and magic long before they came into fashion.

Koutoukas did "just about everything there is to do in the theater from the magnificent to the unmentionable" ("Off-Off-Academia," 23). One of his first plays, *Tidy Passions,* involved the survivors of a nuclear experiment and had Nöel Coward, Virginia Woolf, several witches, a dying dove, Narcissus, and Jean Harlow as characters. A casting call in 1967 for *View from Sorrentino,* a play about Queen Isabella, called for "one trained panther, a male-female dwarf chorus that can tap dance, and a sort of rough Dietrich-type male impersonator. Freaks of all kinds are also wanted but they must be able to sing and/or dance" ("Only Those of You," n.p.). Among his most notable works was *Medea,* an adaptation of the Greek drama in which the action is set in a laundromat and the title character is played by a man. *Christopher at Sheridan Squared,* a hallucinatory documentary about Greenwich Village, involved the statue of General Sheridan and three mad queens looking for a cat, one of whom was played by actor/writer Harvey Fierstein. Indeed, Koutoukas's personal life has often been seen as being as mythical as his productions. Fierstein was once Koutoukas's houseboy, "my general organizational clutter coordinator" (Heide, n.p.), and Koutoukas has suggested that Fierstein used his life as a model for the central character in his early play *In Search of the Cobra Jewels.*

Along with the changing economic nature of Off-Off-Broadway, Koutoukas's output also diminished in the late 1970s and early 1980s. He reemerged in the mid-1980s when he presented his students, the School for Gargoyles, in his play A *Hand Job for Apollo.* Legend also has it that "when Harry Koutoukas became pregnant, it was **Charles Ludlam** who was born," or so Roderick Faber reported in the *Village Voice* in 1975 (n.p.). Whether or not Koutoukas was "the immaculate conceptive progenitor" does not matter much, or so Faber related; what mattered were the "radioactively gay genetic mutations in the line of descent" that were passed down from one to the other (n.p.). Ironically, Koutoukas joined the Ridiculous Theatrical Company after Ludlam's death and won acclaim for his performances in the company's revivals, most notably as the evil Baron de Varville in *Camille,* playing opposite Everett Quinton. Two of Koutoukas's one acts were presented by the Ridiculous Theatrical Company under the title *When Lightning Strikes Twice* in 1991, starring

Everett Quinton and directed by Eureka. In 2003 he received the Robert Chesley Award for lesbian and gay playwriting.

See R. Faber, "The Godfather of Glitter Still Wears Gold," *Village Voice*, November 24, 1975; R. Gener, "Back to the Cino: Remembering the Café Where Gay Theater Came Out," *Village Voice*, June 21, 1994; R. Heide, "All about Harry," *New York Native*, October 29, 1990; "Off-Off-Academia," *Village Voice*, November 17, 1975; "Only Those of You," *Village Voice*, September 28, 1967; A. Poland and B. Mailman, eds., *The Off Off Broadway Book*, New York, 1972; G. Rabkin, "Footnotes in the Sand," *Soho Weekly News*, April 20, 1978; M. Smithy, "Christopher at Sheridan Squared," *Village Voice*, November 25, 1971; M. Smith, "H. M. Koutoukas," in *Contemporary American Dramatists*, edited by K. A. Berney, London, 1994, 323–25; and W. Stone, *Caffe Cino: the Birthplace of Off-Off-Broadway*, Carbondale, 2005.

Jameson Currier

KRAMER, Larry (1935–), playwright, novelist, screenwriter, film producer, and activist, was born into a middle-class Jewish family in Bridgeport, Connecticut. The family relocated to Washington, D.C., when he was seven years old, and it was there during the boom years of World War II and its aftermath that Kramer's love of theater and his struggles to recognize and accept his homosexuality began. A childhood dominated by an abusive father and an alternately clutching and self-centered mother provided grist for Kramer's dramatic mill. These painful memories— along with an account of his college years at Yale, where he received a bachelor of arts degree in English literature in 1957, flirted with suicide, and was pressured into analysis by an older brother intolerant of his budding sexuality—form part of the plot of *The Destiny of Me* (1992), a drama favorably compared by some critics to the memory plays of **Tennessee Williams** and Eugene O'Neill. In the same year as the Stonewall riots, Kramer achieved his first success as producer and writer of *Women In Love* (1969), a film adaptation of the D. H. Lawrence novel about sexual politics between two English couples. Critics were divided over its frank depiction of sexuality, and some questioned the film's fidelity to the source material; nevertheless, Kramer's screenplay was nominated for an Academy Award. Even though the film resonates with overtones of bisexuality and includes a homoerotic nude wrestling match between the male leads (cited by Vito Russo in his filmography for *The Celluloid Closet*), Kramer admits to having lived a semicloseted existence while working in the film industry (Smith, 42).

Kramer stumbled with two follow-up projects: his screenplay for the 1971 musical remake of *Lost Horizon* was derided in some quarters as so bad as to merit status as a camp classic; and his initial effort at playwriting, *Four Friends* (originally titled *Sissies Scrapbook*), opened Off-Broadway in 1975 to unanimous critical pans and expired after one performance. He again hinted at his sexuality by making one of the Yale graduates who comprise the title's quartet a gay man with a lover, although critics still seemed uncertain of his sexuality. For example, Martin Gottfried noted that "Kramer is the remarkable playwright who can write homosexual love scenes as well and as convincingly as heterosexual ones" (46).

With the publication of his first novel, *Faggots* (1978), and the tumultuous reception accorded it by both the gay and straight communities, Kramer presented himself to the world as a self-identified gay male. (Indeed, he later affirmed in the introduction to *The Destiny of Me* that his homosexuality "as unsatisfying as much of it was for so long, has been the single most defining characteristic of my life" [3].) *Faggots* satirizes the gay sexual revolution that followed in the wake of Stonewall. Through the eyes of the author's alter ego, Fred Lemish, the reader is treated to a dissection of the promiscuity and lack of commitment rampant in the gay ghettos of Greenwich Village and Fire Island during the 1970s. Although it was intended as a morality tale in the style of Evelyn Waugh, the best seller's bitter humor "earned Kramer the wrath of a number of gay critics," who instead saw it as a setback for gays' hard-won sexual freedom (Dlugos, 58).

Thus began an ongoing battle between Kramer and certain factions of the gay community. In *Faggots,* he begins to develop his controversial themes, namely, the necessity for gay self-examination and sexual responsibility. All of his subsequent writings and political activities reflect these concerns, as he seeks a vision of a gay identity that defines and explores "ourselves as part of a culture that isn't merely sexual but that includes Plato, da Vinci, Michelangelo, Proust, Melville, and many others" (Smith, 44).

The emerging AIDS epidemic supplied Kramer with a worthy cause on which to test out his ideas and also provided him with the great subject that has since dominated both his writing and his life. Indeed, except for his 1988 comedy *Just Say No,* a satirical indictment of sexual hypocrisy among the political elite, the remainder of his dramatic output has presented the disease in strictly autobiographical settings.

In the summer of 1981, frightened by the mysterious (and then unnamed) illness afflicting gay men, Kramer gathered some of his friends in his Greenwich Village apartment to lay the foundation for what would evolve into one of the most influential AIDS-related organizations—the Gay Men's Health Crisis (GMHC). The budding activist also contributed fiery political writings to publications such as the *Village Voice* and the

New York Native. (These articles, along with his speeches, were anthologized in a 1989 volume, *Reports from the Holocaust.*) Kramer lashed out at society's slow response to what he predicted would be a catastrophic health crisis, choosing the Reagan and Koch administrations and the *New York Times* as special targets for his angry rhetoric. Moreover, he again clashed with segments of the gay community over their failure to heed his prophetic warnings: "Every gay man who is unable to come forward now and fight to save his own life is truly helping to kill the rest of us. . . . How many of us have to die before *you* get scared off your ass and into action?" (*Reports from the Holocaust,* 45–46).

Kramer's zeal in the battle for AIDS awareness, particularly regarding gay sexual activity in the midst of an epidemic ("I am sick of guys who can only think with their cocks" [*Reports from the Holocaust,* 46]), led to disputes with his GMHC compatriots, and he was forced out of the organization. Objective details of this bitter split are chronicled in gay journalist Randy Shilts's *And the Band Played On.* Kramer, however, subjectively transformed this experience into what arguably may be his masterwork. *The Normal Heart* presents another authorial alter ego, Ned Weeks, as he battles what he perceives as bureaucratic indifference to and gay intransigence in the face of AIDS, while simultaneously suffering the loss of his lover to the disease. Kramer's powerful polemic, produced in April 1985 by Joseph Papp at his Public Theater, shares the distinction with **William Hoffman**'s gentler, more intimate *As Is* (produced only a month earlier) as being one of the first plays to dramatize AIDS for a mainstream audience. The drama stunned both audiences and jaded critics. According to Shilts, even the notoriously homophobic critic John Simon admitted "that he left the play weeping" (556). To date, *The Normal Heart* is the longest-running play ever staged at the Public Theater and has received hundreds of productions worldwide. Viewed by many as "a touchstone in the literature of AIDS," it helped to pave the way for the many AIDS plays that followed in its wake (Specter, 60). In 2004, a revival of *The Normal Heart* was produced at New York's Public Theatre and received generally positive reviews.

After splitting with GMHC and discovering that he was HIV positive himself, Kramer founded another, more militant AIDS organization in 1987, the year in which he was honored with an Arts and Communication Award from the Human Rights Campaign Fund. Founded on the principles of civil disobedience and fueled by the author's celebrated temper, the AIDS Coalition to Unleash Power (ACT UP) took to the streets, waging a kind of urban guerrilla warfare to demand more government funding for AIDS research and easier access to promising drug trials. Since its inception, ACT UP has expanded to include chapters worldwide, yet its founder, not wishing "to repeat the GMHC experience," withdrew from active participation as the organization grew in prominence (Kramer, *Reports from the Holocaust,* 139).

The author once more fashioned personal demons into artistic fuel. In *The Destiny of Me,* a companion piece to *The Normal Heart,* an AIDS-infected Ned Weeks finds himself at odds with the activist organization that he founded and also at the mercy of the very governmental and medical agencies that he has so vehemently denounced. Kramer juxtaposes the political with the personal, as a desolate Ned confronts the ghosts of his past. Through encounters with Alexander, his younger self, Ned tries to make peace with himself in relation to his family, his homosexuality, and his AIDS. The play, which won an Obie, enjoyed an Off-Broadway run of close to two hundred performances and was a finalist for the 1993 Pulitzer Prize.

In recent years, Kramer's health has declined due to his HIV infection and a serious bout of hepatitis B, which required him to have a liver transplant in 2001 (Specter, 61). While no longer a high-profile activist, he continues to write and is nearing completion of perhaps his most ambitious work to date, *The American People.* An epic novel that Kramer calls "a history of America," it spans hundreds of years and examines, among other issues, politics, religion, homosexuality, and AIDS (Mass, 332–33).

In *The Destiny of Me,* Ned, confronted by the horrors of the AIDS epidemic, laments that he "wanted to be Moses but I only could be Cassandra" (87). In truth, Ned's creator may be both: "To his critics, he is arrogant, self-promoting, irrationally angry and rude, cruel, deluded, double-dealing, and possibly deranged. To his admirers he is an Old Testament prophet whose early warnings to the gay community about sexual profligacy and AIDS now read as eerily prescient" (Shnayerson, 231). In whatever light one examines him, Larry Kramer must be seen as a major contributor to both the canon of gay dramatic literature and the ongoing dialogue of AIDS awareness.

See T. Dlugos, "Larry Kramer," *Christopher Street* 12 (February 1979): 58–60; M. Gottfried, "Review of *Four Friends,*" *New York Post,* February 18, 1975; L. Kramer, *The Destiny of Me,* New York, 1993; L. Kramer, *Just Say No,* New York, 1989; L. Kramer, *Reports from the Holocaust,* New York, 1989; L. Kramer, *The Normal Heart,* New York, 1985; L. Kramer, *Faggots,* New York, 1978; L. Mass, "Interview with a Writer," in *We Must Love One Another or Die: The Life and Legacies of Larry Kramer,* edited by L. Mass, New York, 1997, 319–85; V. Russo, *The Celluloid Closet,* New York, 1987; R. Shilts, *And the Band Played On,* New York, 1988; M. Shnayerson, "Kramer vs. Kramer," *Vanity Fair,* October 1992; D. Smith, "The Cry of 'the Normal Heart,'" *New York,* June 3, 1988; M. Specter, "Public Nuisance," *New Yorker,* May 13, 2002; and S. Trosky, ed., *Contemporary Authors,* vol. 126, Detroit, 1989.

Ray Schultz

LAUGHTON, Charles (1899–1962), actor, director, and producer, was born in Scarborough, England, at the Victoria Hotel, which was owned by his parents, Robert and Elizabeth Laughton. Successful in business, they sold the Victoria and purchased the elegant Pavilion Hotel. Extremely busy, the Laughtons left their three boys to their own devices. One amusing account tells of "a chambermaid discovered trapped in the linen cupboard, while Charles, swathed in sheets, declaimed" (Callow, 3).

A staunch Catholic, Elizabeth sent Charles to Stonyhurst, a strict Jesuit school, where Charles's young psyche was embedded with a deep sense of guilt. Later his most vivid memory of Stonyhurst was of a Jesuit who told him that if he sinned he would "be punished through all eternity. . . . Do you know what eternity is? It is as if this world were a steel globe and every thousand years a bird's wing brushed past that globe— and the time it would take for that globe to wear away is all eternity." This guilt "easily attached itself to his desire to make love to men" and caused "a sense of not being right in the world, of not deserving what the world has to offer" (Higham, 5). It is perhaps this overwhelming sense of guilt that made Charles's life so painful and his art compelling, especially when he played characters who were overcome by shame or ostracized from society by virtue of some physical and/or psychological dysfunction.

After serving a year with the Royal Huntingdonshire Regiment during World War I, Laughton took refuge in amateur theatricals with the Scarborough Players. This led him, at twenty-four, to leave the family business and enroll in the Royal Academy of Dramatic Art. Upon graduation, he launched a career that catapulted him to fame on the London stage, playing over thirty roles between 1926 and 1936.

His first notable role was Solyony in Chekhov's *The Three Sisters* (1926). Others were the gangster boss, Perelli, in *On the Spot* (1930), the murderous William Marble in *Payment Deferred* (1931), and Lopakhin in *The Cherry Orchard* (1933). During rehearsals for *Payment Deferred,* he was forced to confess his homosexuality to his wife, Elsa Lanchester. He had brought a young man home for a sexual encounter one evening when Elsa was not home. The next evening, when Laughton returned home, the young man was waiting for him, asking for money. Laughton refused, a policeman intervened, and the young man was arrested. Realizing that he would be required to appear in court, Laughton confessed to Elsa. She told him it was "perfectly all right . . . I understand" (qtd. in Higham, 24). In court, Laughton received only a warning for misguided generosity, and his name was not mentioned in the press.

Elsa may well have "understood," for she had lived a rather Bohemian life and counted a number of London's homosexual elite among her friends. She says that they never spoke of the incident nor his homosexuality again. They stayed together out of a sense of duty, each taking lovers while maintaining the facade of their marriage and the reality of their friendship.

Laughton's taste in men tended toward the masculine, lean, handsome, and young. His first meaningful relationship was with David Roberts, a handsome young actor whom Laughton met in 1941. Their relationship lasted ten years, until 1950, when Laughton was performing in *The Cherry Orchard* in England. Although Laughton was not in love with him, Roberts provided him with emotional support and made him feel physically attractive. After their relationship ended, Roberts remained friends with Laughton and served as a pallbearer at his funeral. In 1959, while at Stratford-upon-Avon, Laughton met Bruce Ashe and fell in love for the first time. Ashe was a classically proportioned photographer's model and aspiring actor. When the season ended, he accompanied Laughton to Italy for the filming of *Under Ten Flags* (1960). Their relationship lasted until Laughton's death three years later.

After Laughton confessed his homosexuality to Elsa, they continued rehearsing *Payment Deferred,* which opened to rave reviews for Laughton. Probably, Laughton had incorporated the reality of his confession into his portrayal of Mr. Marple. The review in the *Star* reported that "there was a moment when, thinking his wife had discovered his secret, he collapses into hysteria. The sight of the quivering, blubbering wretch aroused mingled feelings of disgust and pity" (Callow, 39). This performance provided the vehicle by which Laughton and Elsa would first travel to the United States.

Broadway producer Gilbert Miller was so impressed with Laughton's performance that he signed the couple to appear in the New York production. Although it opened to excellent reviews, *Payment Deferred* proved too dispiriting for Depression audiences and closed after three weeks. Next Laughton repeated his 1928 London success as Hercule Poirot in the New York production of *Alibi.* Despite ovations for Laughton, it also closed after forty performances, and the couple returned to London.

Soon after they resettled in England Laughton was offered a long-term contract with Paramount, and in 1932 he portrayed the cruel, jealous Commander Sturm in *The Devil and the Deep.* He played the character as a man bordering on insanity, who drives his wife (**Tallulah Bankhead**) to adultery (with Gary Cooper). The *New York Times* called his performance an "outstanding histrionic contribution" (Callow, 52). He was well on his way to fame in the United States. Laughton's star status as a character actor in films was firmly secured by his portrayal of the title role in *The Private Life of Henry VIII*. His impulsive, confident, robust performance earned him his only Academy Award.

Laughton appeared in fifty-three films, forty-one of them made in the United States. He is remembered best for three roles: Henry in *The Private Life of Henry VIII;* Captain Bligh in *Mutiny on the Bounty* (1935), which earned him an Academy Award nomination; and Quasimodo in *The Hunchback of Notre Dame* (1939). He also received an Oscar nomination for his performance as Sir Wilfred Robarts in *Witness for the Prosecution* (1957).

Laughton became known for his portrayal of sullen, anguished, self-loathing characters who are alienated from society. These feelings were inextricably tied to Laughton's own self-image as fat and ugly, and, too, he was deeply "tortured by his homosexuality" (Higham, 109). His intensity was often labeled overacting; it is, indeed, a larger-than-life style of acting, full of theatricality and exaggerated behavior.

Laughton's style piqued the interest of Bertolt Brecht. Further, the actor had a gift for text, and from 1943 to 1946 he and Brecht prepared an English-language version of *The Life of Galileo* (1938), which opened July 30, 1947, in Los Angeles. Local reviews were positive, but the national ones were discouraging. Despite this, plans proceeded for a production in New York; Laughton's performance was poorly reviewed, although large and enthusiastic audiences turned out. The theater was booked for only two weeks, however, and the production was forced to close.

The last twenty years of Laughton's life were less productive than his earlier career, but certainly his many remarkable accomplishments throughout his life distinguished him as an artist: his concert reading tours produced with Paul Gregory (*Don Juan in Hell, John Brown's Body*); his artistic collaboration with Brecht; his stage production of *The Caine Mutiny Court-Martial;* his season at Stratford-upon-Avon; and his unforgettable film roles, such as Captain Bligh, Henry VIII, and others.

In 1951, Laughton and Gregory produced a concert reading tour of *Don Juan in Hell,* taken from Shaw's *Man and Superman.* Laughton directed and played the Devil, with Charles Boyer as Juan, Cedric Hardwicke as Statue, and **Agnes Moorehead** as Dona Ana. Known as the Drama Quartet, the tour was an enormous success in Los Angeles and New York and in regional engagements across the country, especially at universities.

After this success, Laughton and Gregory organized a reading tour of *John Brown's Body* (1953). Once again, Laughton employed his skill with text, adapting Stephen Vincent Benet's poem for the stage. The company consisted of Tyrone Power, **Judith Anderson,** and Raymond Massey, all playing multiple roles, with Laughton as director. Performances in New York and on the road sold out.

The Caine Mutiny Court-Martial (1954), Herman Wouk's best-selling novel, became Laughton and Gregory's third project together. They initially asked Wouk to adapt the novel for a staged reading, but eventually they decided that the piece warranted a fully staged production. They hired Dick Powell, a film and television actor/director with no experience in theater, to direct and Henry Fonda to play Lieutenant Greenwald. Within the first two weeks of rehearsal, it became clear that Powell was inadequate for the task, and Laughton took over as director. By his own admission, Laughton's behavior in rehearsals was brutal and at times cruel. To make matters worse, he cut the four-hour script down to two and a half hours, upsetting the actors (including Fonda), whose roles were diminished substantially. The tension was so great between Fonda and Laughton that the former is reported to have called the latter a "fat, ugly, faggot" (Callow, 232). Nonetheless, the production became an enormous success. Fonda received ovations each night, and Laughton's direction was hailed for its austerity, integrity, and restraint, qualities that were benchmarks of a Laughton production. Of the seven plays he directed, *The Caine Mutiny Court-Martial* was arguably Laughton's greatest triumph.

The same did not prove true of his only venture into directing for film, *Night of the Hunter* (1955). It starred Robert Mitchum as the murderous Preacher, Shelley Winters as his victim, and Lillian Gish as the woman who rescues Winters's children from the clutches of Preacher. Laughton transferred his aesthetic taste and simplicity of style to the film, producing an expressionistic effect that was lyrical and haunting. Although critics recognized *Night of the Hunter* as a work of notable artistry (compared to the usual Hollywood fare), it failed at the box office. Laughton was heartbroken that the public did not appreciate the film. It was his last great project in the United States.

His final project of note was the fulfillment of a lifelong ambition to play Lear in *King Lear* at Stratford-upon-Avon in 1959. In repertory, he also played Bottom in *A Midsummer Night's Dream.* He spent nearly a year preparing for Lear, traveling to Stonehenge to drink in the atmosphere as he studied the role and discussing it with the director, Glen Byam Shaw. His interpretation ran contrary to the traditional thunderous madman, typified at that time by Olivier. Laughton's Lear was "subdued, gentle, ruminatory" (Higham, 216). His portrayal was not well received in the press, but the public supported the production; *A Midsummer Night's Dream* received a similar critical and public reception.

After *King Lear,* Laughton's health deteriorated drastically. Once home in the United States, he suffered with gall bladder problems, followed by a heart attack. When he recovered sufficiently, he began filming *Advise and Consent* (1962), directed by Otto Preminger. Laughton played Seab Cooley, the homophobic southern senator, with subtlety, "creat[ing] a character at once sly and childlike, devious and amusing, ruthless and charming" (Higham, 226). Ill throughout filming, Laughton nevertheless later attempted a reading tour with Bruce Ashe but had to be hospitalized after a fall in the bath. Doctors discovered cancer, which soon became pervasive. Laughton was flown home and died in Los Angeles on December 15, 1962.

See S. Callow, *Charles Laughton: A Difficult Actor,* London, 1987; K. Carter, "Lear's Terrible Journey: Charles Laughton at Stratford, 1959," *New Theatre Quarterly* 4 (November 1988): 315–20; C. Higham, *Charles Laughton: An Intimate Biography,* Garden City, N.Y., 1976; E. Lanchester, *Elsa Lanchester Herself,* New York, 1983; and M. C. Mills, "Charles Laughton: Adaptation of *The Night of the Hunter,*" *Film Quarterly* 16, no. 1 (1988): 49–57.

Lionel Walsh

LAURENTS, Arthur (1918–), playwright and director, was born July 14, 1918, in Brooklyn, New York. After receiving a bachelor's degree in English from Cornell University in 1937, he returned to the city to work briefly in nightclub revues and then on several radio plays. In 1941, he was drafted into the U.S. Army and was soon writing for military training films and radio programs. His research among the wounded for one of his radio dramas developed into the subject matter for his first Broadway play, *Home of the Brave* (1945), a psychological drama that centers on the hysterical paralysis of a Jewish soldier.

In 1947, Laurents moved to Hollywood and wrote the screenplay for *The Snake Pit* (1948), another story featuring insanity (Kramer, 52). His next assignment was polishing the script of Alfred Hitchcock's *Rope* (1948). *Rope* is unique for being presented in one uninterrupted take (actually eight ten-minute takes). The story, based on the Leopold and Loeb murder case, centers on two homicidal homosexuals. Although Hitchcock's treatment was "indirect," it was clear enough to frighten **Montgomery Clift** away from one of the roles, which was later cast with John Dall (Spoto, 305). **Farley Granger** played the pianist of the twosome. By the time filming began, Granger and Laurents were living together (Laurents, 122). Their affair lasted four years (Kramer, 53).

During the Hollywood blacklistings, which he calls "seminal in my life" (Kramer, 50), Laurents left Hollywood for New York, where he wrote *The Time of the Cuckoo* (1952), starring Shirley Booth. This tale of a spinsterish schoolteacher trying to accept love during a Venetian vacation is Laurents's most successful straight play. It was filmed in 1955 as *Summertime*, with Katherine Hepburn, and was transformed into the musical *Do I Hear a Waltz?* in 1965.

In the mid-1950s, Laurents turned to the stage work that over the next fifteen years would define his career. He also embarked on a relationship that would define his personal life. On January 10, 1957, *A Clearing in the Woods* opened. This psychological drama of one woman confronting her earlier selves did not last long on Broadway. However, Tom Hatcher, a good-looking, well-built, blond from Oklahoma was cast as "The Boy." Hatcher, who was twenty-six, and Laurents, thirty-eight, had already begun their still ongoing relationship, of which Laurents said in 1995: "He is more to me than he ever was, and I'm happier than I ever was" (Kramer, 56). Hatcher later played the role of Schuyler Grogan in Laurents's *Invitation to a March* (1960) before retiring from acting to become a contractor (Laurents, 408).

Laurents's next project had been bandied about in discussions with Jerome Robbins and **Leonard Bernstein** before Laurents got the idea of setting Robbins's update of the Romeo and Juliet story against a background of urban gangs (Loney, 36). This became *West Side Story* (1957). It was Laurents who invited **Stephen Sondheim** to write the lyrics for the piece (Sondheim had previously auditioned for him). Laurents and Sondheim became friends and worked together on five more projects over the next fifteen years, both musicals (*Gypsy, Anyone Can Whistle,* and *Do I Hear a Waltz?*) and straight plays (Sondheim wrote incidental music for *Invitation to a March* and *The Enclave*).

Although they had had a falling out during *West Side Story,* Robbins insisted that Laurents write the book for his next project, which was based on the memoirs of Gypsy Rose Lee. Laurents felt "too grand" for such "trash" until he heard one woman say: "My first lover was Gypsy Rose Lee's mother" (Kramer, 54). As he learned more about Gypsy Rose Lee and her mother—both lesbians, according to Laurents—he became more interested and eventually focused the story on Mama Rose. Highly successful, *Gypsy* (1959) is heralded for its strong drama, just as *West Side Story* is for its riveting dance.

Laurents next wrote *Invitation to a March* (1960). This fairy tale of a play featured a bride who falls asleep at a convention and finds her Long Island prince in a shorter man (Laurents himself is short). Laurents directed for the first time, because "there was a great paucity of directors" (Raymond, 22). He claimed: "If I direct and it fails, at least it will have been closer to what I meant . . . and I'd rather blame myself" (Loney, 34).

Laurents had met David Merrick during *Gypsy,* which Merrick produced. Now that he was a proven director, Merrick hired him to direct the musical *I Can Get It for You Wholesale* (1962), which is now best known for introducing Barbra Streisand as Miss Marmelstein.

Laurents wore the director and librettist hats for *Anyone Can Whistle* (1964), an absurdist-influenced musical that ran only nine performances but is legendary for the cast album of Sondheim's score. Laurents's second original libretto was for *Hallelujah, Baby!* (1967), which garnered him a Tony Award. Laurents's book followed a black woman (played by Leslie Uggams) and her two lovers (one black, one white) through the panorama of musical styles and racism from the turn of the century to the 1960s, while the leading characters did not age.

Laurents got the idea for *The Way We Were* while looking at Barbra Streisand, to whom he was pitching another movie (Laurents, 247–48). Streisand would star in the film with Robert Redford. Both the film (1973) and the novel (1972) call on Laurents's background at Cornell and during the McCarthy era in Hollywood.

In 1973, Laurents went to London to direct a revival of *Gypsy* with Angela Lansbury playing Rose. He doctored the script slightly to show the maturation of Gypsy in her strip sequence, a task he says he only perfected in the 1989 revival (Laurents, 392). The production was well received, especially Lansbury's performance, and moved to Broadway on September 23, 1974.

On November 15, 1973, *The Enclave,* written and directed by Laurents, opened Off-Broadway. In this play, one man, leading his friends into an enclave to protect themselves from the city, reveals his homosexuality and watches his friendships disintegrate. The potential for parallels with Laurents's own life and relationships seems obvious. The play's lead and his boyfriend are forty and twenty-four years old, respectively; Laurents and Hatcher have a twelve-year age difference and were approximately the same ages when they met. The leading role's homosexuality was known but unspoken of by his friends; Laurents's homosexuality was known to his friends but not acknowledged by the press. However, these and other parallels in *The Enclave* have not been commented on, not even by Laurents in his autobiography.

His next Hollywood screenplay, *The Turning Point* (1977), starring Anne Bancroft and Shirley MacLaine, had been suggested by his onetime romantic partner and longtime friend Nora Kaye (a former ballet dancer) and was directed by her husband, Herbert Ross. Set in the world of ballet, the inclusion of homosexual material had been planned by Laurents but was mostly excised by the director and cast (Russo, 227–30).

Laurents's greatest success as a director, and his most overt affiliation with a gay project, came with *La Cage aux Folles* (1983). He was "eager" to work with librettist Harvey Fierstein (who was just coming off his successful *Torch Song Trilogy*) and composer/lyricist **Jerry Herman** ("Laurents, Arthur," 223). Laurents threw every theatrical trick he knew into the production. He says of the highly successful musical: "I thought that to have two men sing a love song and hold hands and kiss onstage in a musical was a big step. . . . At the end of every performance, straight people would get up applauding two men dancing together into the sunset. I thought that was a big accomplishment" (Kramer, 55).

In 1989, Laurents directed another revival of *Gypsy,* this time with Tyne Daly, whom he preferred of the three leading ladies. In 1991, he wrote and directed *Nick & Nora,* a noted flop. A subplot of this "Thin Man" musical mystery involved a lesbian bookkeeper. The collapse of *Nick & Nora* freed Laurents to work on several plays. In 1995, *Jolson Sings Again,* about theater people facing the betrayal of the McCarthy era, played at the Seattle Repertory Theatre. It was during this production that Laurents was unintentionally outed by *New York Times* columnist Frank Rich. Laurents later revised *Jolson Sings Again* for a 1999 George Street Playhouse production in New Brunswick, New Jersey. Also in 1995, *The Radical Mystique,* which was based on the infamous cocktail parties for militant racial causes of the late 1960s, played at the Manhattan Theatre Club. It featured a young man discovering his sexual identity after witnessing the Stonewall Riots (Raymond, 21).

Laurents's plays have not endured as well as his musical librettos. His straight plays show his talent for writing three-dimensional characters and fully realized theatrical creations. His best plays are marked by strong female voices (Shirley Booth in *The Time of the Cuckoo* and Celeste Holm and Eileen Heckart in *Invitation to a March*). As he notes in his autobiography, this should come as no surprise: "It's men that homosexual men can have trouble writing" (Laurents, 411). However, Laurents has always considered himself a "social playwright" ("Laurents, Arthur," 220); his need to *tell* what should be said—instead of demonstrating it—leads to the most disappointing moments in his scripts. On the other hand, his librettos are noted for their mature approach to an often juvenile form; his direct messages are served well in the broad strokes required for adumbrated dialogue. Also he usually works with the best composers available, and their music draws continued productions.

Laurents's ability to direct is more often lauded than his writing. He regularly unites all elements of the production—music, voice, setting, movement, and picturization—to create vibrant dramatic moments. The understanding of structure and character honed in his writing assists in drawing out fully human characterizations. His ability to find new or underutilized talent—Jane Fonda in *Invitation to a March,* Lansbury in *Anyone Can Whistle,* George Hearn in *La Cage aux Folles*—signifies an astute eye and ensures his lasting influence.

A very sexual man—his first gay experience was at thirteen and he was more interested in quantity of partners than quality for many years—Laurents struggled with his homosexuality in psychotherapy, keeping it out of his play *Heartsong* (1946) and claiming that he would have excluded it as a subtext from *Home of the Brave* (Laurents, 65, 53). At the same time, he accepted his homosexuality and is proud of how "truthfully" it was treated in his first movie, *Rope* (131). There are biographical aspects of his work to explore (particularly in *The Enclave*), as well as thematic obsessions, such as the figure of the complicated, boyish blond (i.e., the major in *Home of the Brave,* the disillusioned artist in *Time of the Cuckoo,* the characters played by Hatcher, and Robert Redford's Hubbell in *The Way We Were*). Laurents has identified his own recurrent themes as discovery, acceptance, prejudice, and betrayal (4)—themes with which any homosexual can empathize. Although he struggled with it, he has never denied his homosexuality. He wrote that, even while carrying on physical relationships with women, "I didn't believe the ability to have sex with a woman made me heterosexual" (55). Homosexuality's impact on his life—his relationship with Hatcher and his friendships—and his working relationships with gay men is clear. However, it is also clear that the media ignored this man's personal life until 1995, denying many a role model whose mainstream career unashamedly included gay material.

See L. Kramer, "His Brilliant Career," *The Advocate* 681 (May 16, 1995): 49–56; A. Laurents, *Original Story By: A Memoir of Broadway and Hollywood,* New York, 2000; "Laurents, Arthur," in *Current Biography Yearbook, 1984,* edited by C. Moritz, New York, 1984, 220–23; G. Loney, "Arthur Laurents Is High on Comedy," *After Dark* 6 (November 1973): 34–36; G. Raymond, "Arthur Laurents: Back to the Future," *Theatre Week,* June 26, 1995; V. Russo, *The Celluloid Closet: Homosexuality in the Movies,* rev. ed., New York, 1987; and D. Spoto, *The Dark Side of Genius: The Life of Alfred Hitchcock,* Boston, 1983.

Jeffrey Smart

Le GALLIENNE, Eva (1899–1991), actress, director, producer, author, and translator, was born in London. Her parents traveled in the popular artistic circles of the day, and Eva quickly developed a taste for literature and the arts. Her father was an intimate of Oscar Wilde. As the marriage of her parents disintegrated, she moved with her mother to Paris, where they lived alongside free-spirited expatriate women such as Edith Wharton, **Isadora Duncan,** and **Gertrude Stein** in the area that was later labeled "the left Bank of Lesbos." Inspired by the performances of Sarah Bernhardt, she studied acting at the Royal Academy of Dramatic Arts and made her acting debut in London in 1914.

The next year she sailed for New York. In 1918, while performing in a company with Ethel Barrymore, she formed her first important lesbian relationship with the notorious actress **Alla Nazimova** and moved into an apartment at the famous Algonquin Hotel. From 1920 to 1925, her name was in lights, and there were larger than life photos of her on billboards as she toured the country in *Not So Long Ago, Liliom,* and *The Swan.* She was the darling of the media, providing interviews about her beauty secrets, advertising products, and modeling the latest fashions.

While she was projecting heterosexuality in the media, she was engaged in a five-year relationship with **Mercedes de Acosta.** She starred in two of de Acosta's plays—*Sandro Botticelli* in New York and *Jehanne d'Arc* in Paris. Neither was successful. Le Gallienne's reviews began to describe her acting as "cold and intellectual," code words from disapproving male critics over her masculine behavior onstage at a time when frilly femininity was still the expected mode.

Rejected by the Actors' Theatre when she asked it to produce Ibsen's *The Master Builder* with herself in the role of Hilda Wangel, she struck out on her own and mounted a production with lesbian Gladys Calthrop as designer. Reviewers were dazzled by her ultramasculine performance as she toured the country with the play.

Heady with success, at the age of twenty-seven and at the height of her fame, this daunting and determined maverick turned her back on stardom and dared to challenge the male-dominated Broadway system of long runs, high prices, and typecasting. Supported by wealthy patrons such as Otto H. Kahn and the reclusive lesbian Alice De Lamar, she established America's first classical repertory theater, the Civic Repertory Theatre (1926–35). Associated with her theater was a school for apprentices, whose students included Robert Lewis, Burgess Meredith, Arnold Moss, Howard da Silva, John Garfield, May Sarton, and J. Edward Bromberg.

Her Civic Repertory Theatre enjoyed tributes from leading critics of the day. Robert Benchley insisted that "one ought to go there about once a month just to recapture the feeling of theatregoing" (36). At the end of the first season, she had filled her theater to an average 78 percent capacity and had produced six out of eight critical successes. She won a listing for two years on *Nation* magazine's Roll of Honor and a cover photograph on *Time* (November 25, 1929). By her third season, she was playing to 91 percent capacity. During the company's ten years, she staged thirty-seven plays in New York and toured the most successful ones during the summer. The most popular offerings included *Hedda Gabler, Peter Pan, Romeo and Juliet, Camille, The Cherry Orchard, Alice in Wonderland,* and *The Cradle Song.* Her production of Chekhov's *The Three Sisters* was New York's English-language premiere.

Her popularity took a turn in the 1930s. With her focus on the classics, especially on the plays of Ibsen, she limited her following. She had been honored from coast to coast for her commitment to noncommercial drama, but by 1935 Americans, caught in the Great Depression, were more interested in contemporary social commentary.

Theatergoers had also become more aware of her lesbianism. She had begun a relationship with Civic actress **Josephine Hutchinson** in the late 1920s. When newspapers across the country got wind of "Josie's" divorce from her estranged husband, they reported that he had named Le Gallienne as correspondent. Although it was not true, the damage was done. Influential and homophobic critic George Jean Nathan dubbed the Civic Repertory Theatre "the Le Gallienne sorority" (122) while countless cruel jokes and rumors began to circulate about activities at the theater.

In 1937, **Margaret Webster** moved into Le Gallienne's professional and private life. Along with **Cheryl Crawford,** the troika of lesbians founded the American Repertory Theatre in 1946. Le Gallienne starred in *Henry VIII, What Every Woman Knows, John Gabriel Borkman,* and *Alice in Wonderland,* directing the latter two shows as well. Although it received considerable financial support and strong testimonials from Broadway luminaries, the company could not withstand union demands, the high cost of producing plays in repertory, and the many complaints over its play selection. The accusations of communism leveled at both Webster and Crawford hurt ticket sales.

Le Gallienne's life and career went steadily downhill. In 1951, her relationship with Margaret Webster ended, and, except for sporadic successes, her theater career was over. When not acting or directing, she turned her energies to translating the plays of Ibsen and the tales of Hans Christian Andersen, as well as writing a biography of Eleonora Duse and her own autobiography. In the summers, she often taught acting at Lucille Lortel's White Barn Theatre in Connecticut. One of her young students was Peter Falk. During long stretches of inactivity, she turned to alcohol for escape.

In 1957, Le Gallienne appeared as Queen Elizabeth in Tyrone Guthrie's production of *Mary Stuart,* which was a stunning success. The attention brought her television roles and a five-year affiliation with the National Repertory Theatre (1961–66), where she either acted in or directed the great plays of Shakespeare, Ibsen, Chekhov, Sheridan, Molière, Schiller, and Euripides. Instead of performing in New York, the company toured the country, performing at colleges and universities and in civic auditoriums. In 1968, she joined the APA-Phoenix Theatre for one season, performing in *Exit the King* and directing *The Cherry Orchard.* Between 1957 and 1975, the once prominent actress appeared in only 117 Broadway performances.

Le Gallienne returned to Broadway in 1975 with Ellis Rabb's revival of *The Royal Family.* Although it was intended for only a two-week engagement at Washington's Kennedy Center, the successful production went on to the Brooklyn Academy of Music, Broadway, a twenty-three-week national tour, and finally a television special.

Her range of acting was remarkable. She went from the classic *Trojan Women* to the contemporary *Exit the King,* from the sentimental *Liliom* to the psychological complexity of *Ghosts,* from the romanticism of *Camille* to the realism of *Hedda Gabler,* and from the fantasy of *Peter Pan* to the operatic bravado of *Mary Stuart.* She was selected by nationally known director Lee Strasberg as a "vivid example of what American actors are capable of" (qtd. in Wasserman, 6).

Intent on making her characterizations appear realistic, she carefully plotted their logical development in the play. Constant attention was given to maintaining her technical skills of vocal control and bodily movement. But when rehearsing and performing her acting was dependent on her concentration. She tried to think and listen as the character, often including pauses to draw the audience into her thought process.

When she directed, she always read the play to the company at the first rehearsal, making no attempt to act it out but rather to set the tone. This was followed by several full-company readings, until the meanings were understood and the actors had clear ideas about their characterizations. Only then did they begin to explore on the stage. Her most vital function as a director was building an ensemble, one in which each actor was important and in which all worked as a harmonious unit. Rather than direct as a dictator imposing her ideas, she looked on rehearsals as a collaborative effort. She had clear concepts not only of the characters but of all technical elements, from the lighting to the smallest prop.

Behind her public role as a famous actress, director, and producer, Eva Le Gallienne led a private life troubled by her personal struggle with lesbianism. For more than fifty years, she lived in shadows. Like many lesbians of her generation, she viewed herself as a man trapped in a female body. Because she was unwilling to hide behind a convenient marriage or to camouflage her relationships in order to boost her career, her sexuality became a nemesis that created her great need for privacy.

Acting was a way of publicly expressing her personal feelings. She could reveal her soul when she performed. Some have said that her struggle with her sexuality drained her creative energy; others have said it was the very source of it. Regardless, it profoundly influenced her art, coloring her selection of scripts, casting choices, management decisions, style of acting, and ultimately her critical reception.

Burgess Meredith has remarked that in the 1920s Le Gallienne was regarded as a "Young Goddess, an inspiration." The high royalty of the American theater consisted of five people—**Katharine Cornell**, Helen Hayes, **Alfred Lunt, Lynn Fontanne,** and Eva Le Gallienne. "To have a role in one of their plays was more than a privilege," he stressed. "It was a kind of knighthood" (*New York Times,* June 16, 1974).

During her long career, she earned a Tony Award for lifetime achievement (1964), an Emmy for her role in a television broadcast of *The Royal Family* (1977), the American National Theatre and Academy's (ANTA) National Artist Award (1977), and an Oscar nomination for Best Supporting Actress in the film *Resurrection* (1980). At the age of eighty-two, she received another Tony nomination for her performance in *To Grandmother's House We Go* (1981). She did not win, but the *New York Times* paid tribute: "She has no equal on Broadway. It is easy to fall in love all over again with Eva Le Gallienne, her face, her voice, her poise, and her beauty" (*New York Times,* January 16, 1981). In 1986, President Ronald Reagan awarded her the National Medal of the Arts. When *American Theatre* magazine celebrated the silver anniversary of the nonprofit theater movement in America, they featured Le Gallienne and proclaimed that her efforts in the 1920s, 1930s, and 1940s "presaged a changing role for the theatre a generation in advance." Along with Tyrone Guthrie, John Houseman, and Zelda Fichandler, she was credited with being one of the theater artists who "played a part in shaping America's nonprofit theatre" (Zeisler, 5).

See R. Benchley, "Early Christmas Flopping," *New Yorker* 6 (December 15, 1930), p. 36; Billy Rose Theatre Collection of the New York Public Library; Civic Repertory Theatre Collection, Beinecke Library, Yale University; E. Le Gallienne, *At 33,* New York, 1934; E. Le Gallienne, *With a Quiet Heart,* New York, 1953; G.J. Nathan, "The Theatre," *American Mercury* 14 (May 1928), p. 122; R.A. Schanke, *Eva Le Gallienne: A Bio-Bibliography,* Westport, CT, 1989; R.A. Schanke, *Shattered Applause: The Lives of Eva Le Gallienne,* Carbondale, IL, 1992; R. A. Schanke, *"That Furious Lesbian": The Story of Mercedes de Acosta,* Carbondale, 2003; R.A. Schanke, "Images of Eva Le Gallienne: Reflections of

Androgyny," *Theatre Survey* 34 (November 1993), 43–53; H. Sheehy, *Eva Le Gallienne: A Biography,* New York, 1998; D. Wasserman, "Developing an American Acting Style," *New York Theatre Review,* II (February 1978), p. 6; P. Zeisler, "Toward Brave New Worlds," *American Theatre* 3 (November 1986), p. 5; *New York Times* (June 16, 1974) and (January 16, 1981). Many letters written over a five-year period by Le Gallienne to Mercedes de Acosta are located in the de Acosta Collection, Rosenbach Museum and Library, Philadelphia, PA.

Robert A. Schanke

LUDLAM, Charles (1943–1987), playwright, actor, director, and designer, was a multidimensional, prolific artist responsible for founding and growing one of the nation's most unique theater enterprises, The Ridiculous Theatrical Company. He was born on April 12, 1943, in Floral Park, New York. Social, cultural, and familial conditions all conspired to shape the artist at the earliest age: his mother lost him at the Mineola Fair, where he aimlessly wandered into a Punch and Judy show, followed by a freak show, "where he saw armless black dwarves painting pictures with their toes" (Samuels, *Complete Plays,* x); the Catholic Church, with its high religious ritual and pageantry, was a prominent force in the Ludlam family; and a movie theater sat directly across the street from his family's home. Ludlam was encouraged to explore his vivid imagination as a child, producing backyard and basement plays and vignettes with other neighborhood children.

Known as a rebel and outcast throughout high school, Ludlam's first real exposure to theater came in the form of an apprenticeship at a summer stock company, the Red Barn Theater, in 1958. There he was exposed to the often frantic, haphazard, and chaotic experience theater can be. He pursued his newfound interest in the theater by traveling to New York and seeing a variety of theatrical entertainments, from the commercial to the avant-garde to the experimental. One such company of the latter type, The Living Theatre, proved to be such a significant influence and motivator for Ludlam that at the age of seventeen he founded his own avant-garde company, the Student's Repertory Theater in Northport, New York.

Ludlam enrolled at Hofstra University (1961–65), where as an acting major he met great resistance from the faculty. He was simply too outrageous and informed, and "his acting was excessive" (Samuels, *Complete Plays,* xi). Two significant milestones in his career grew out of this experience: first, as a result of being an unwanted actor, he turned to writing and directing and wrote his first full-length play, *Edna Brown;* and, second, he explored his sexual identity as a homosexual man. Shortly after graduating from Hofstra, he left for New York City as a young gay playwright and actor wanting to explore and create new theatrical forms.

Collaborating with fellow absurdists John Vaccaro and Ronald Tavel (who had founded their own theater, Play-House of the Ridiculous), Ludlam performed his first stage role, Peeping Tom, in *The Life of Lady Godiva* in 1966. This production was "a self-conscious mix of high and low culture, an anarchic, psychosexual phantasmagoria filled with camp, drag, pageantry, grotesquerie and literary pretension" (xi) that defined Ludlam's style of theater for the next twenty years. The significant influence of this production on Ludlam and his future as a playwright, director, actor, and designer cannot be overestimated. At this juncture, only one theatrical element was missing from Ludlam's creative mix, and that was soon added when he performed his first drag role in *Screen Test* for the Play-House of the Ridiculous. Searching for good, innovative, *ridiculous* material, Vaccaro approached him; Ludlam, in turn, created his first *ridiculous* venture, *Big Hotel* (1966), a sweeping comic melodrama that cartooned the lives of the people who occupy a big hotel. During the production of his second play for the Play-House, *Conquest of the Universe* (1967), Ludlam and Vaccaro engaged in a conflict that ultimately drove Ludlam from the company and inspired him to start his own, The Ridiculous Theatrical Company.

Ludlam's new company found its first home at Tambellini's Gate (a movie theater) on the lower east side of Manhattan, but like so many fledgling theater companies, the troupe continually traveled from venue to venue seeking a permanent home. The company's first theatrical venture, a double bill of *When Queens Collide* and *Big Hotel,* drew limited audiences (and consequently made insufficient money for a growing theater company). Ludlam supported himself (and often his company) by working in a health food store and doing occasional guest shots on a popular television show, *Candid Camera.* The company exhaustively continued to work, producing one Theater of the Ridiculous play after another, such as *Whores of Babylon* (1969), *Turds in Hell* (1969), and *The Grand Tarot* (1969), but it never received the critical or audience attention it so desperately needed to survive. All of that would change with the small, modest production of *Bluebeard* in 1970.

Based on H. G. Wells's *Island of Dr. Moreau,* the plot revolved around a "mad vivisectionist in search of a third sex, obsessed with the creation of some 'new and gentle genital'" (Samuels, *Complete Plays,* xiv). Produced in a gay bar in Manhattan's Greenwich Village, *Bluebeard* caught the attention of critics, which in turn brought the audiences forward. Within days of its opening, The Ridiculous Theatrical Company had its first critical and financial success and began negotiations for a European tour, which would eventually be funded in part by the New York State Council on the Arts, the National Endowment for the Arts, and a Guggenheim playwriting fellowship. *Bluebeard* established the standard for most of Ludlam's work thereafter, gaining awards, endowments, fellowships, critical acclaim, and an audience that grew from a predominantly homosexual base to a completely heterogeneous group.

Although plays such as *Eunuchs of the Forbidden City* (1971) and *Corn* (1972) broadened Ludlam's appeal to a larger audience, the unqualified success of *Camille* (based on Dumas fils' *La Dame aux Camelias*) in 1973, resulted in five hundred performances over seven years. Ludlam's play incorporated all that he was renowned for: drag, high comedy, poignant melodrama, satire, detailed literary references, gender politics, clever manipulation of language and image, makeshift stage presentation, sexual frolic, and a plethora of acting styles. The success of *Camille* would sustain Ludlam's company for many years, allowing him to present other Ridiculous classics, such as *Hot Ice* (1974), *Stage Blood* (1975), and *Caprice* (1976), a play that satirized the fashion industry, presented a variety of unapologetic homosexual characters, and introduced Ludlam's longtime companion, Everett Quinton, to the New York theater crowd.

During the late 1970s and early 1980s, Ludlam and his company produced play after play, experience after experience, and secured a permanent home at One Sheridan Square in the heart of Manhattan's Greenwich Village. Ludlam was sought after by producers, lyricists, directors, theater companies, colleges, and universities for his innovative, experimental vision. He taught commedia dell'arte and playwriting at several colleges, wrote books for Broadway musicals, constructed puppet shows for children, conducted European and national tours of his company's work, and continued writing, creating such Ridiculous classics as *Der Ring Gott Farblonjet* (1977), *The Ventriloquist's Wife* (1978), *Utopia Incorporated* (1978), *The Enchanted Pig* (1979), *Reverse Psychology* (1980), *Galas* (1983), *How to Write a Play* (1984), *Medea* (1984), and *The Artificial Jungle* (1986), to name only a few. But nothing before or after would equal the success of his Ridiculous comic masterpiece, *The Mystery of Irma Vep,* which, according to Richard Connema, "has probably played in every regional theatre in this country and the UK since it was first presented by The Ridiculous Theatrical Company in 1984."

Ludlam died on May 28, 1987, from complications of AIDS at the age of forty-four.

See M. Banham, ed., *Cambridge Guide to World Theatre,* Cambridge, 1988; K. A. Berney, ed., *Contemporary American Dramatists,* London, 1994; R. Brustein, *Theatre of*

Revolt, Boston, 1962; R. Connema, *"The Mystery of Irma Vep,* A Delirious Lampoon of a Gothic Thriller," *San Francisco,* www.talkinbroadway.com, accessed July 18, 2004; J. W. Dorff, *Gender and Performance: An Introduction to Female Impersonation in the West,* Providence, 1986; *Gay and Lesbian Literature,* Detroit, 1994; M. Hawkins-Dady, ed., *International Dictionary of Theatre,* vol. 2: *Playwrights,* Detroit, 1994; D. Kaufman, *Ridiculous: The Theatrical Life and Times of Charles Ludlam,* New York, 2002; P. J. Kaye, ed., *National Playwrights Directory,* Waterford, Conn., 1981; C. Ludlam, *The Complete Plays,* New York, 1989; B. Milman and A. Plard, *The Off Off Broadway Book,* New York, 1972; *Notable Names in the American Theatre,* edited by Walter Rigdon, Clifton, N.J., 1976; S. Samuels, "Charles Ludlam: A Brief Life," in Charles Ludlam, *The Complete Plays,* edited by S. Samuels and E. Quinton, New York, 1989, ix–xx; S. Samuels, ed., *Ridiculous Theater: Scourge of Human Folly, the Essays and Opinions of Charles Ludlam,* New York, 1992; S. Sherman, "Charles Ludlam," *Theater* 25 (1994); M. Smith, *The Best of Off Off Broadway,* New York, 1969; A. Wilcox, *Charles Ludlam on Commedia Dell' Arte, the Ridiculous, and Anything Else That Comes to Mind,* Billy Rose Theatre Collection, Lincoln Center Library for the Performing Arts, New York; *Writers Directory,* 11th ed., Detroit, 1994.

Gary Garrison

LUNT, Alfred David, Jr. (1892–1977), and Lynn Fontanne (Lillie Louise) (1887–1983), actors, were the most famous married acting couple in the American theater in the central decades of the twentieth century. Lynn Fontanne, born in Woodford, Essex, ten miles outside of London, began her theatrical career in England, and came to the United States in 1916 as a member of the company run by Laurette Taylor and Hartley Manners. She left the Taylor-Manners company and began her career in New York, achieving her first major success in the title role of Kaufman and Connelly's *Dulcy* in 1921. Alfred Lunt, born and raised in Milwaukee, studied at Carroll College in Wisconsin and Emerson College in Boston. While in Boston, he began performing professionally. After working for several years on tour, he achieved his first major success in the New York theater in 1919 in the title role of Booth Tarkington's *Clarence.* Lunt and Fontanne met that year and were married in 1922. They had their first success onstage as a couple in 1924 in Molnar's *The Guardsman,* and from 1928 through their final triumph in the 1958 production of Dürrenmatt's *The Visit* they appeared onstage exclusively as a team. Among their other successes were Anderson's *Elizabeth, the Queen* (1930), Coward's *Design For Living* (1933), Shakespeare's *The Taming of the Shrew* (1935), Sherwood's *Idiot's Delight* (1936), Giraudoux's *Amphitryon 38* (1937), and Sherwood's *There Shall Be No Night* (1940).

Historical evidence about the Lunts' personal lives is largely circumstantial. Extremely protective of their privacy, they rarely discussed their emotional attachments even in their private letters. The press depicted them as a happily married couple, and reviews of their productions frequently cited their marriage offstage as the source of their brilliant rapport onstage. A series of articles that appeared in the 1940s in popular magazines such as the *Ladies Home Journal* and *Vogue* showed them not in New York but at home on their Wisconsin farm and described how they shunned the lively social scene of New York in favor of quiet evenings together. This image of idyllic heterosexuality was picked up and solidified in all of the biographies of the Lunts, by George Freedley (1957), Maurice Zolotow (1965), and Jared Brown (1986).

Although Brown's exhaustive biography largely adopts this idealized image, it is clear from the evidence he provides, and from information he omits, that Lunt and Fontanne were not simply a happily married couple who happened to be actors. They were both difficult and moody people, who fought with each other frequently and could be cruel to other members of their companies. Lunt was particularly troubled and wrestled frequently with depression. Despite the articles emphasizing their life at home on the farm, they participated actively in the New York social scene. Many of their closest friends were prominent members of New York's elite gay circles, particularly Noël Coward, Carl van Vechten, and **Alexander Woollcott**. And, contrary to the image of unsullied heterosexuality, rumors persisted throughout their careers that they regularly engaged in homosexual relationships. These rumors never blossomed into scandal, but they recurred frequently, especially in New York tabloid newspapers at the height of the Lunts' careers in the 1930s.

Brown strenuously denies that there was any truth to these rumors, but his only evidence is that he was unable to find anyone willing to confirm the stories (395). Brown does, however, offer many stories that undermine the view of the Lunts generated by the press. For example, he recounts a story told by Coward from the years prior to the Lunts' marriage in which the three young performers plotted their futures together: "Lynn and Alfred were to be married. That was the first plan. Then they were to become definitely idols of the public. That was the second plan. Then, all this being successfully accomplished, they were to act exclusively together. This was the third plan" (79). In other words, the Lunts viewed their marriage as a practical career move, a picture in sharp contrast to the romantic image offered by the press and the biographers. A highly ironic mock interview of the Lunts, published by the lesbian author **Djuna Barnes** in *Theatre Guild Magazine,* also strongly implies that their marriage was a performance done largely for public show.

The most concrete evidence that the Lunts engaged in same-sex relationships comes from early in their lives, before they became known to the public. Lunt had a close childhood friend named Ray Weaver. Brown documents letters written by Lunt to Weaver in which he refers to Weaver as "dearest boy," "honey," and "my hero of delight." Brown also quotes Weaver as remarking that as teens he and Lunt never dated women and that they "were a world unto themselves" (26). In the years during which Fontanne performed with the Taylor-Manners company, according to Brown and Zolotow, she developed a close and emotional relationship with Taylor. Taylor, who according to many stories engaged in lesbian affairs with her husband's knowledge, became the dominant personality in Fontanne's early career. She brought Fontanne into her home on weekends and became intensely jealous when Fontanne began to see Lunt romantically. Shortly after the Lunts' marriage, Taylor broke with Fontanne. Brown offers no evidence that Lunt engaged in a serious relationship with a woman prior to his marriage. Fontanne was engaged briefly to a man in London, but they rarely saw each other, and Brown doubts the seriousness of the affair. These anecdotes, the Lunts' close relationship with gay friends, and the implications of evidence such as Coward's story and the Barnes article, cannot "prove" the rumors that Lunt and Fontanne had same-sex relationships or that their marriage was not based on affection. This evidence does, however, indicate that the idealized image of the Lunts was an illusion of the press and that they were not only familiar with same-sex relationships but were actively involved in New York's lively gay subculture in the 1920s and 1930s.

In the first decade and a half of their careers together, the Lunts regularly appeared in plays that defied sexual norms. This fact is notable because there began in New York at this time a major crackdown on all public expressions of "deviant sexuality." In 1927, the police closed a production of *The Captive,* a play depicting lesbian characters, and prevented Mae West's progay play *The Drag* from coming to Broadway. The following years saw a substantial increase in antigay bar raids, with the names of those apprehended often published in the newspapers. Within this atmosphere of repression, the Lunts regularly sought productions with homosexual content. Fontanne in 1928 starred in the first production of O'Neill's *Strange Interlude,* which Lunt called "a six-day bisexual race" (Brown, 167); at about the same time, the couple planned a production of *Twelfth Night,* never staged, which would have emphasized the homoerotic implications of Orsino's attraction to Viola/Cesario (Hewitt, 98). The Lunts, then, not only used their marriage as a career move; under the protection of their public perception as a married couple, they tested the boundaries of sexual expression onstage in a period of increasing anti-gay repression.

The Lunts' most significant production in the early 1930s, and their most daring test of sexual norms, was *Design for Living,* written by Noël Coward specifically for himself and the Lunts. In Coward's play, both Otto (Lunt) and Leo (Coward) are in love with Gilda (Fontanne) and, more importantly, with each other. After a series of mix and match relationships, at the end of the play the three reject traditional marriage and set up a ménage à trois. Many critics of the original production expressed discomfort with the play's defense of "deviant" sexuality, but they assumed in their reviews that Otto and Leo were just close friends. But, as George Chauncey documents, gay audience members at the time were fully aware of the sexual nature of the relationship depicted in the play (288). Coward includes clear autobiographical allusions in the play; he even inscribes his own name into his character's, backward. It is probably going too far to read the play strictly as autobiography, and there is no evidence to suggest that either Lunt or Fontanne had sexual relations with Coward. Brown recounts, however, that the three had pondered this production for over a decade and that each previous version of the play involved a defense of nonnormative sexuality (204–5). It is likely, then, that the play's ardent speeches in defense of sexual bohemianism reflected the views of both Coward and the Lunts.

After the 1930s, the Lunts became progressively less daring in their portrayal of sexual relationships and more protective of their image as a happily married couple. Although they had no children of their own, they also began to serve as parental figures for several young actors, most notably the closeted **Montgomery Clift.** In 1940, they appeared as husband and wife in Robert Sherwood's *There Shall Be No Night;* the nineteen-year-old Clift played their son. The Lunts virtually adopted Clift, taking him into their home and advising him on his career. They even gave him a photograph of themselves signed "From your *real* mother and father" (Brown, 290). According to Clift's biographer, Patricia Bosworth, Lunt feared that if Clift's homosexuality became known it would destroy his career in the relentlessly growing antigay atmosphere of New York in the 1940s. Bosworth relates that Lunt advised Clift to leave his male lover and marry actress Phyllis Thaxter. According to Clift's lover, Lunt told Clift: "Well, y'know Noël Coward's an exception. You can't ordinarily be a pansy in the theater and survive" (Bosworth, 82). It was at this time that most of the articles depicting the Lunts at home on their Wisconsin farm appeared, though the couple continued to associate closely with Coward and their other gay friends. In the 1940s, as the Lunts moved into their fifties, and as antigay public sentiment increased, the couple altered their desire to test societal sexual boundaries, choosing instead to encourage the idealized image of themselves as a married couple.

The joint careers of Alfred Lunt and Lynn Fontanne, then, reflect significant changes in the Broadway theater in the middle of the twentieth century. In the 1920s and early 1930s, Broadway permitted a large degree of sexual license, even encouraging depictions of homoeroticism, as Chauncey documents in a movement he calls the "pansy craze" (301–30). Under the protection of their public marriage, the Lunts were able to experiment with homosexuality onstage and, in *Design For Living,* speak directly to a gay audience. In the late 1930s and early 1940s, this open atmosphere shut down. The Lunts stopped their experimentation, retreated firmly into their public image of idealized heterosexuality, and encouraged young gay performers to follow their lead. Broadway would not see a similar openness until the Lunts had come to the end of their long, productive lives.

See S. Abel, "Staging Heterosexuality: Alfred Lunt and Lynn Fontanne's Design for Living," in *Passing Performances: Queer Readings of Leading Players in American Theater History,* edited by R. A. Schanke and K. Marra, Ann Arbor, 1998, 175–96; D. Barnes, "Lord Alfred and Lady Lynn: An Interview to Prove That Marriage Is No Hindrance to Art," *Theatre Guild,* March 1930; P. Bosworth, *Montgomery Clift: A Biography,* New York, 1978; J. Brown, *The Fabulous Lunts: A Biography of Alfred Lunt and Lynn Fontanne,* New York, 1986; G. Chauncey, *Gay New York: Gender, Urban Culture, and the Making of the Gay Male World, 1890–1940,* New York, 1994; G. Freedley, *The Lunts,* London, 1957; B. Gill, "The Perfectionists," *New Yorker,* October 13, 1986; A. Hewitt, "Repertory to Residuals: Reflections on American Acting since 1900," in *The American Theatre: A Sum of Its Parts,* New York, 1971; Alan Hewitt Papers, Dartmouth College Library, Hanover, N.H.; A. Moats, "Mr. and Mrs. Alfred Lunt," *Ladies Home Journal,* December 1940; Lunt Papers, State Historical Society of Wisconsin, Madison; W. Morehouse, "Lynn Fontanne and Alfred Lunt, of Genesee, Wisconsin," *Vogue,* May 1940; M. Peters, *Design for Living: Alfred Lunt and Lynne Fontanne: A Biography,* New York, 2003; and M. Zolotow, *Stagestruck: The Romance of Alfred Lunt and Lynn Fontanne,* New York, 1965.

Sam Abel-Palmer

MARBURY, Elisabeth (1856–1933), theatrical agent and producer and **de Wolfe Mendl, Elsie** (Ella Anderson) (1865–1950), actress, designer and interior decorator. Marbury was born in New York City to Francis Ferdinand Marbury, a successful lawyer made famous by the *Marbury v. Madison* case, and Elizabeth McCoun Marbury, a prominent socialite. Growing up, Elisabeth spent summers on the Oyster Bay estate her mother inherited, where she met Theodore Roosevelt. Her Presbyterian father tutored her in the classics at home and in his law offices until she was sent away to "a fashionable girl's school, the name of which is not known" (Marbury, 10). Although her parents tried to mold her according to Victorian standards of proper womanhood, Marbury persisted in her inclination toward independence and a business career. At the age of twenty-five, she undertook her first capitalist venture—as a poultry farmer. During these years of her youth, she was also cultivating her interest in theater as an audience member at professional productions and as a participant in amateur charity productions at various fashionable venues.

It was during an amateur production for the opening of swank Tuxedo Park in 1886 that Marbury met the actress **Elsie de Wolfe.** Within a few months, the two had entered into a "Boston marriage," which endured for more than forty years and was the primary love relationship in both women's lives. De Wolfe was the daughter of a doctor, Stephen de Wolfe, and his wife, Georgiana Copeland, who had immigrated to New York from Nova Scotia in 1857. Considered newcomers, the de Wolfes were not easily accepted into the insular world of New York's landed gentry. Elsie had to work her way in with her acting ability and studied flare for fashion and style. The combination of de Wolfe's talents and Marbury's blue-blood connections enabled the two women, as a couple, to traffic in the highest social circles and eventually to host the internationally renowned Marbury and de Wolfe Sunday salons at their jointly owned homes in New York and Paris. But more than these social connections the women's shared love and lifestyle provided a crucial support base from which each could defy conventional feminine role expectations and pioneer lucrative professions. Dubbing them "bachelor girls," "bosom friends," or "those fair inseparables," the press avidly chronicled their joint activities, both factual and rumored. Public knowledge of Marbury and de Wolfe's connection as well as their deep mutual devotion impacted a wider range of social relations that galvanized crucial developments in their respective careers.

Two years into their relationship, the partners culminated their amateur theatrical careers with a charity production of Marbury's script, *Contrast,* which showcased a resplendent de Wolfe and for which Marbury lined up the supporting cast, arranged publicity, printed playbills, and secured a high-profile performance space, Daniel Frohman's Lyceum Theatre, then known as the premier "society house." Frohman was so impressed that he urged Marbury to take up theatrical management on a more permanent basis, and she forsook her chickens to incubate Frances

Hodgson Burnett's dramatization of *Little Lord Fauntleroy*. De Wolfe impressed Charles as well as Daniel Frohman and was offered acting lessons from David Belasco.

While with de Wolfe in Paris in 1890, after a business associate for the European tour of *Fauntleroy* had deserted her and absconded with her savings, Marbury developed the idea of becoming foreign authors' American representative. Bolstered by her lover's support and encouragement, she found the gumption to contact Victorien Sardou, president of the French Society of Dramatic Authors, and ask for an interview. Marbury made such an impression that she gained not only Sardou's business but that of the entire membership of his organization. When they returned to New York, Elisabeth Marbury Enterprises opened its first offices and sold production rights to Charles Frohman for the American premiere of Sardou's *Thermidor*. Marbury also convinced Frohman to cast de Wolfe in the title role for her professional acting debut. Within a few years, Marbury had expanded her clientele to include such writers as Oscar Wilde, George Bernard Shaw, James M. Barrie, and **Clyde Fitch**. She also made it a special cause to support women in the profession. Among her clients were Frances Hodgson Burnett, Jeanette Gilder, Edith Wharton, and **Rachel Crothers**. With her help, some of these women, notably Crothers and Maxine Elliott, were able to move into the even more masculine-identified theatrical occupations of directing and producing. Her theatrical agency grew to wield such influence that in 1911 *Metropolitan Magazine* proclaimed her "the fourth estate of the dramatic world."

Following the professional acting debut that Marbury had arranged for her, de Wolfe, with her partner's continuing support and assistance, worked as an actress for fourteen years. Her emotional limitations onstage prevented her from becoming a star of the first magnitude, but she found a niche as the "clotheshorse" of the "Frohman stable of stars," drawing audiences with the Parisian fashions she imported and the costumes and sets she designed. Her reputation for arbiting fashion burgeoned, and she reinforced her stage displays with prescriptive periodical literature, such as her 1901–2 series for the *New York Evening World* entitled "How to Dress by the Best-Dressed Yankee Actress." The stage-acting vocation ultimately proved unsatisfying, however, and after two embarrassing failures in the fall of 1904 she determined to retire but feared being unable to support herself. Pained by her partner's shame and depression, Marbury suggested that she capitalize on her greatest talents and hire herself out to their wealthy friends to do for others' homes what she had done for their houses and so many of Frohman's stages—remake them in the latest fashion. Coincidentally, Marbury was on the board of the newly erected but yet undecorated Colony Club, the first private club exclusively for women, and she garnered the unproven de Wolfe the endorsement of the board and architect Stanford White. The result was a historic, career-making first commission. In a matter of months, de Wolfe went from being an actress of mediocre talent to high society's consummate professional decorative expert, and she rapidly gained business on both sides of the Atlantic.

The social circle that formed the Colony Club brought Anne Morgan, the third daughter of financier J. P. Morgan, into Marbury and de Wolfe's intimate circle. Reading the diaries Anne Morgan began keeping in 1903, Alfred Allan Lewis argues that she fell in love with Marbury but that Marbury, while flattered by and welcoming of the younger woman's ardor, remained primarily devoted to de Wolfe. The three women cohabited at the Villa Trianon, a summer mansion famously refurbished by de Wolfe in Versailles, and were dubbed the "Versailles Triumvirate." Marbury inspired Morgan to defy her father and pursue an alternate vision of independent life for women. She, and to a lesser extent de Wolfe, became role models for Morgan's own career as an activist and for her subsequent romantic and socially influential partnership with Anne Vanderbilt.

World War I proved to be a divisive as well as traumatic experience for the Versailles Triumvirate. All participated heroically in the relief effort from their vacation home. However, de Wolfe's ties to France intensified through the experience while Marbury became increasingly obligated to her business in New York and Morgan became more involved in other social causes. Marbury's biographer, R. Strum, suggests that these strains in the primary relationship between Marbury and de Wolfe provided a major impetus for Marbury to enter the next phase of her theatrical career, that of producer as opposed to play broker and agent. As the producer of her own shows, Marbury could hire her clients as writers and performers, and, most importantly, she could hire de Wolfe to design the shows and thereby distract her from the war (198).

Out of this relational dynamic came a revolutionary entertainment genre, the so-called "intimate musical." Marbury went into partnership with F. Ray Comstock and Lee Shubert to manage the 299-seat Princess Theater at 104 West Thirty-ninth Street. In this space, she implemented her vision of a small-scale "light opera" with a coherent script, songs organically related to the story, individualized chorus members, and domestic-scale design elements suited to de Wolfe's interior decorating talents. Total expenditures for each production were not to exceed

$7,500, a drastic downsizing from the $50,000 cost of contemporary Broadway extravaganzas such as the Ziegfeld Follies. The combined talents of the lovers and a book by Jerome Kern and Guy Bolton resulted in an entertainment known as the Princess Musical, which eschewed the overt sensuality and ostentation associated with full-scale musicals and presented, according to the *New York Mirror,* "pretty girls dressed in fashionable frocks, with an atmosphere of smartness and refinement and daintiness, with delightful and tinkly tunes and with youth as the keynote."

As to occupying de Wolfe's focus and keeping her in New York, the Princess Musicals were at best only temporarily successful. From 1915 to 1918, six "intimate musicals" were produced at the Princess Theatre, but Marbury and de Wolfe directly participated only in the first two. By the time the third, *Go to It,* went into production, personal and global conflict precluded both women's participation in mounting this example of the revolutionary form they had created and led to the end of Marbury's producing career.

These developments precipitated changes in the partners' lifestyle whereby de Wolfe lived most of the year in Versailles and joined Marbury in New York for three to four months in the fall. De Wolfe's biographer, J. S. Smith, suggests that it may have been in part to fill the void of the time separated from Elsie that Marbury turned to politics, assuming a leadership role in the Democratic Party for the next fifteen years and contributing instrumentally to her friends Franklin and Eleanor Roosevelt's installation in the White House (190–97). In a social climate increasingly informed by sexologist vilification of intimate same-sex relations, the partners' postwar living arrangement continued until Marbury's death, even after de Wolfe, always concerned with appearances, entered into a marriage of convenience at the age of sixty with a titled British diplomat, Sir Charles Mendl. Following the settlement of Marbury's estate, of which she was the principal beneficiary, de Wolfe lived out her years primarily in France with an interval in Hollywood during World War II.

See A. A. Lewis, *Ladies and Not-So-Gentle Women,* New York, Viking, 2000; E. Marbury, *My Crystal Ball,* London, 1923; K. Marra, "A Lesbian Marriage of Cultural Consequence: Elisabeth Marbury and Elsie de Wolfe, 1886–1933," in *Passing Performances: Queer Readings of Leading Players in American Theater History,* edited by R. A. Schanke and K. Marra, Ann Arbor, 1998, 104–28; J. S. Smith, *Elsie de Wolfe: A Life in the High Style,* New York, 1982; and R. Strum, "Elisabeth Marbury, 1856–1933: Her Life and Work," Ph.D. diss., New York University, 1989, an exhaustively researched volume citing the manifold archives and secondary sources in which material on Marbury and de Wolfe can be found.

Kim Marra

McCLINTIC, Guthrie. See Cornell, Katharine.

McCULLERS, Carson (1917–1967), playwright and novelist, was named for her grandmother, Lula Carson Waters. Her rejection of her first name, Lula, early in her career symbolizes her ambivalence toward her regional origins, where compound names were common, and the female body in which she had been born.

Born on February 19, 1917, in Columbus, Georgia, McCullers had the rare advantage of a mother who "had been alerted by the oracles that her firstborn would be unique" (Carr, 3). Consequently, Marguerite Waters Smith prepared her daughter from infancy for her exceptional positioning in life, remarking on her genius to all visitors and deciding when McCullers was six that she deserved a piano. On the day the piano was delivered, McCullers shocked her parents by playing "Yes, Sir, That's My Baby" and "Yes, We Have No Bananas" without any known previous contact with the keyboard. In fact, in her autobiography McCullers confesses that she had been practicing the two tunes in secret elsewhere, but her facility for inventing melodies made it quickly evident that she was a gifted musician (Savigneau, 34).

Confirmed in her belief that her daughter was a genius, Marguerite established a lifelong obsession with McCullers that riddled their relationship until Marguerite's death in 1950. McCullers accepted her genius and believed it was what made her odd as she plodded through the school system, dedicating the important hours in her day to piano practice and writing. Her high school classmates found her eccentric in her long white shirts, knickers (which even the boys didn't wear), and dirty tennis shoes. She was ridiculed for her straight hair and bangs, which she cut herself (Carr, 30) and was self-conscious of her gangly height of five feet, eight inches.

From childhood, McCullers was determined to become a concert pianist. She studied first with Mrs. Kendrick Kierce and thereafter with Mary Tucker, a woman for whom she developed an adolescent passion and with whom she chose to study after graduating from high school. During this period, she also read voraciously, as she had since early childhood, challenging herself with Greek philosophy, European works in translation, and the classics of British and American literature. When Mrs. Tucker was forced to leave Columbus in 1934 because her husband had been transferred, McCullers responded by announcing that she had decided to become a writer, not a pianist. According to Virginia Spencer Carr, the shock of this separation was later translated into a novel and then a play, *The Member of the Wedding* (36). For Josyane Savigneau, however, the break between the two women (which lasted fifteen years) was caused by McCullers's decision not to be a musician and simply represented the end of her childhood (55). McCullers's development as an artist had already encountered a major setback in 1932 when she became seriously ill with what was misdiagnosed as pneumonia and was in fact rheumatic fever, which damaged her heart and caused the many strokes that eventually debilitated and killed her.

With the loss of Mary and music, McCullers had no motivation to stay in Columbus, so she announced that she would go to New York to study music at Juilliard and writing at Columbia. Two family heirlooms were pawned to pay her passage (Robinson, Roberts, and Barranger, 613). After her arrival, a misplaced trust in new friends resulted in the loss of her money and perversely caused her to choose Columbia over Juilliard and, obviously, writing over music. She studied with Dorothy Scarborough and Helen Ross Hull at Columbia and returned to Columbus in the summer of 1935. While there, she experienced a shock: her first view of Reeves McCullers, who "was the most beautiful man I had ever seen. . . . I was eighteen, and it was my first love" (Savigneau, 62).

That summer a romance began for Reeves and Carson, resulting in their marriage in 1937, divorce in 1941, remarriage in 1945, divorce in 1950, and reunion in 1951. From the moment of their meeting, "with their identical tastes and reciprocal seduction, there was between the two young people a deep and . . . irrational bond, a bizarre twinning that no one ever really understood" and that was both inescapable and disastrous, ending with Reeves's suicide in 1953 (Savigneau, 64). Both were writers by ambition, and they agreed that they would alternate years for writing and earning a living. In the first year of their marriage, Carson had already started her first novel, *The Heart Is a Lonely Hunter,* and by 1940 she was the toast of the New York literary scene.

Professionally, McCullers's success was phenomenal. True to the predictions of her mother, she had proven herself a wunderkind, a child genius. At the age of twenty-three, she was "boyish-looking, dressed in Reeves's shirt and dark man-tailored corduroy jacket . . . [with] the wondering look of a sixteen-year-old. . . . Both the book and the person took New Yorkers by storm" (Carr, 98).

Her first book was followed by a second, written in two months, *Reflections in a Golden Eye* (1941), and a third, *The Member of the Wedding* (1946), the first of her works to be dramatized. Challenged by a critic that her novel contained no drama, McCullers started the adaptation when she was visiting **Tennessee Williams** on Nantucket Island, a meeting arranged sight unseen. Pancho Rodriguez, Williams's companion, described their first view of McCullers.

> Here before us stood the Genius. Sparkling eyes, the softest Southern voice I had ever heard, shy and almost trembling. She couldn't talk. Tennessee embraced her and I kissed her and immediately we knew we were going to like each other. She was so plain and unassuming, yet warmth and affection oozed out of her as if from an inexhaustible fountain (Carr, 272).

Comforted by being part of a threesome—a pattern she repeated throughout her life—McCullers created a play that eventually earned her over a million dollars on Broadway, opening on January 5, 1950, and running for 501 performances. She was awarded the New York Drama Critics Circle Award and the Donaldson Award, as well as the Gold Medal from the Theatre Club, Inc., as the best playwright of the year (Robinson, Roberts, and Barranger, 616).

Her subsequent plays were not so successful. *The Square Root of Wonderful* opened on Broadway on October 30, 1957, and ran for 45 performances, primarily due to advance ticket sales. A musical version of *The Member of the Wedding,* produced Off-Broadway, ran for 20 performances in May 1971. *The Ballad of the Sad Café,* dramatized by **Edward Albee,** closed on Broadway after 123 performances. *Reflections in a Golden Eye* was made into a film in 1967, directed by John Huston, and *The Heart Is a Lonely Hunter* was released as a film in 1968. Two additional films were made of her work: *A Rock. A Tree. A Cloud.* (1981) and *The Ballad of Sad Café* (1991).

The pattern of love that seemed to characterize McCullers is emblematized through her relationship with her husband. She was tortured by romantic passions but seemed to be repelled by their sexual expression. Apart from infatuations with women throughout her life, the attachment in her early twenties that was the most troubling involved a young Swiss woman, Annemarie Clarac-Schwarzenbach, whom McCullers met in a bar after *The Heart Is a Lonely Hunter* had been successfully published. Annemarie was a beautiful androgyne whom Thomas Mann had once told "if you were a young man, you would be extraordinarily beautiful" (Savigneau, 97). In Annemarie, McCullers saw one of the "doubles she was constantly seeking" (95), as they claimed to love each other "like brothers." The last time McCullers saw Annemarie, "she kissed me. It was the first and the last kiss that we ever had" (McCullers, "Illumination"). When Annemarie died in 1942 in a bicycle accident, McCullers felt that her youth—and perhaps her heart, or at least part of it—had died.

McCullers's sexuality has been discussed by those who disdain her lesbian or bisexual orientation and those who do not. There is ample evidence to argue either way because she clearly sustained a long and tortured relationship with her husband and she clearly enjoyed romantic infatuations with a number of powerful and beautiful women. However, in all of her writings she speaks only of the emotional aspects of loving members of her own sex, never the physical. It seems that she was sentimentally drawn to women because they were less different from her than men and therefore less sexual. In fact, she had a similar infatuation with one man, her doctor, Robert Myers, who was "exempted" from sexuality because of professional ethics (Savigneau, 99), but her attraction to him is yet another example of her need for sexless infatuations, which were more probable with women than with men.

In her works, sex is almost always associated with shame, repulsion, and violence, of which her relationship with Reeves seemed to be a manifestation. For her, eroticism produces horror while love produces beauty, and beauty does not exist in sex (McCullers, "Illumination"). She identified early in life as an androgyne: a female in male clothes and with male habits (she was an inveterate smoker and drinker from adolescence). She possessed an assertiveness and ambition atypical of her period to establish herself in a male-dominated art form. She never learned the arts of housekeeping and maintained servants until the day she died.

The basis for identifying Carson McCullers as a lesbian or a bisexual is limited to her own idealization of her relationships with women and her passionate adoration of Annemarie. To say that she was sexually active as a lesbian is to refute the evidence her stories tell of characters whose loneliness prevents them from ever finding fulfillment in love. It is possible that the physical gap she put between herself and those she loved was the divide that prevented her from escaping her own loneliness. She died on September 29, 1967, after a massive stroke.

See V. Carr, *The Heart Is a Lonely Hunter,* New York, 1975; C. McCullers, "Illumination and Night Glare," unpublished memoirs, Austin: University of Texas; C. McCullers, *The Heart Is a Lonely Hunter,* Boston, 1940; C. McCullers, *Reflections in a Golden Eye,* Boston, 1942; C. McCullers, *The Member of the Wedding,* Boston, 1947; A. Robinson, V. Roberts, and M. Barranger, eds., *Notable Women in the American Theatre,* New York, 1989; and J. Savigneau, *Carson McCullers: Un coeur de jeune fille,* Paris, 1995.

Lynne Greeley

MCNALLY, Terrence (1939–), playwright, was born in Saint Petersburg, Florida, but grew up in Corpus Christi, Texas. Born into a family of native New Yorkers, McNally was early exposed to the theater when his parents took him at the age of seven to a production of *Annie Get Your Gun,* starring Ethel Merman. The McNally household engaged in frequent outings to the theater, thereby developing the playwright's appreciation for and fascination with the art form that he would not explore personally until many years later.

In 1956, McNally attended Columbia University in New York, majoring in English and graduating Phi Beta Kappa. He left New York in 1960 on a Henry Evans Traveling Fellowship (an award won in a creative writing class), taking up residence in Mexico and writing his first play. Although the play was never produced, it caught the attention of Molly Kazan (Elia Kazan's wife), a veteran of the Actors Studio, who recognized the potential in McNally's writing. Kazan offered McNally a job as a stage manager for the studio, and he returned to New York to educate and indoctrinate himself in the professional theater. He was offered work shortly thereafter tutoring John Steinbeck's family throughout their excursions in Europe.

McNally's first significant recognition as a playwright came in 1962 when he was awarded the Stanley Award for the best original play at the New York City Writer's Convention. The play, *This Side of the Door,* went through numerous revisions and eventually appeared in production as *And Things That Go Bump in the Night.* McNally was awarded a Rockefeller Foundation grant to produce this play in 1964, and, together with works by Arthur Kopit, was scheduled to receive his first professional production at the Tyrone Guthrie Theater sponsored by the University of Minnesota in Minneapolis. Controversy quickly enveloped both playwrights' work when the university canceled the double bill as an offering for its season ticket holders, deeming it in poor public taste. Kopit withdrew his one acts from production in protest, but McNally, though embittered over the censorship, was determined to realize the production on which he had worked so long and hard. *And Things That Go Bump in the Night* opened on February 4, 1964, at the Guthrie to an audience full of curious spectators and critics, who were there to experience the controversy as much as the play.

While *And Things Go Bump in the Night* met with mostly unfavorable reviews, the production of the play is significant for several reasons: McNally succeeded in having a production at a reputable regional theater, critics became aware of the work of the fledgling playwright, the New York theater producer Theodore Mann committed to producing it in New York (Royale Theater, April 1965), and McNally created his first homosexual character, Clarence, for the stage.

McNally had gathered enough critical attention with *Bump* to win a Guggenheim Fellowship in 1966. He spent that year exploring his craft as a writer. When the 1967 theater season began, he had his second major production, *Tour,* a short play (one of a series he would write on the subject of Vietnam) included in an evening of theater pieces grouped under the title *Collision Course* at the Mark Taper Forum.

In the following year, McNally created seven new short plays: *Sweet Eros, Botticelli, Witness, Noon* (as part of a trilogy by three playwrights entitled, *Morning, Noon and Night*), *Cuba Si!, Bringing It All Back Home,* and the long-running Off-Off-Broadway success, *Next.* The popularity of *Next* was completely unexpected by the playwright. Originally presented by Lucille Lortel in 1967 at the White Barn Theater in Westport, Connecticut, a revision was produced at the Berkshire Theater Festival in August 1969. The New York production opened at the Greenwich News Playhouse on February 10, 1969, and ran for an unprecedented 707 performances. Noted for its biting satire of gender issues, this play became a turning point in McNally's career, as critics and audiences alike grew to appreciate his sharp wit, raucous comedy, and serious undertones of pain and oppression. He ended his already successful year with a second Guggenheim Fellowship, which allowed him to work freely on his craft and indulge in promoting his work. From the 1967 collection of work, *Noon* is particularly meaningful for its sympathetic portrait of Kerry, a gay male who answers a personal advertisement with blind optimism and refuses to believe (against all evidence) that his solicitor may not be interested in him. Kerry's experience is contextualized with those of various neurotic heterosexuals who likewise have answered the ad. For Kerry, the play ends with neither affirmation nor denial of his desire.

In the 1970s, McNally continued to innovate and accumulate an even more diverse body of work. Although many considered the melancholic *Where Has Tommy Flowers Gone* (1971) to be his most serious and important work to that date (MacNichols, 79), the outrageous dark comedy *Bad Habits* (1971) brought him critical acclaim, financial reward, and widespread audience appeal. The whimsical, aristocratic folly of the gay couple, Hiram Spane and Frances Tear, in the act entitled *Ravenswood* added much comic momentum to the already zany antics of life in a sanatorium. That year *Bad Habits* won the Hull-Warriner Award for 1973–74 and an Obie Award and ran for 126 performances at the Booth Theater.

The success of *Bad Habits* quickly gave way to the failure of *Whiskey*

(1973), which closed after only seven performances. McNally rebounded quickly with an outrageous farce set in a gay bathhouse called *The Ritz*. Originally called *The Tubs* for its production at the Yale Repertory Theater, the play was revised and brought to Broadway at the Longacre Theater in January 1975. Replete with a variety of types (and stereotypes) of gay men on the sexual prowl, *The Ritz* ran for four hundred performances in a commercial theater for a predictably heterocentric audience.

The decade of the 1980s brought one very significant association that would influence McNally's writing career well into the 1990s: the Manhattan Theater Club. McNally "had become one of the blessed writers; he had found a home in the Manhattan Theater Club. . . . I say Blessed because for a playwright, belonging to a trusting theater only generates more work (John Guare, in McNally, *15 Short Plays,* ix)." The Manhattan Theater Club subsequently produced the majority of McNally's most critically acclaimed plays: *It's Only a Play* (1986), *Frankie and Johnny in the Claire de Lune* (1987), *Andre's Mother* (1988), *Lisbon Traviata* (1989), *Lips Together, Teeth Apart* (1991), *A Perfect Ganesh* (1993), and the wildly successful *Love! Valour! Compassion!* (1994). Although McNally has never publicly discussed his homosexuality (**Lanford Wilson** outed him in *The Advocate* in 1987), it is interesting to note that four of these seven plays are constructed around the lives of gay male characters (*Andre's Mother; Lisbon Traviata; Lips Together, Teeth Apart;* and *Love! Valour! Compassion!*) and deal either directly or indirectly with issues of gay culture (AIDS, relationships, stereotypes).

McNally's *The Wibbly, Wobbly, Wiggly Dance That Cleopatterer Did,* which was produced at Naked Angels in March of 1993, is thematically consistent with these four plays. In 1995, McNally combined an innovation of style, structure, and content with his personal passion for opera in a theatrical portrait of opera diva and gay icon Maria Callas in *Masterclass.* In 1997, the production of his *Corpus Christi,* a controversial modern adaptation of the life of Jesus in which Jesus and his disciples are gay, elicited bomb and death threats, protests, walkouts and endless (and often unkind) editorials in the mainstream press focusing on McNally, the producing organization, the Manhattan Theatre Club, and members of its board of directors. Bending from the weight of the political maelstrom that surrounded its anticipated opening, the Manhattan Theatre Club initially canceled the production but relented when high-profile playwrights (such as Tony Kushner) threatened to boycott it with future work.

Aside from being an accomplished playwright, McNally has had several significant and successful collaborations in musical theater, including the book for *The Full Monty* (2000); the book for *Ragtime,* a collaboration with Stephen Flaherty and Lynn Ahrens, which won a Tony (1998); the book for *Kiss of the Spider Woman,* with John Kander, composer, and Fred Ebb, lyricist, which also won a Tony (1992); and the book for *The Rink,* with Kander and Ebb (1984). McNally continues to live and write in New York City.

See K. A. Berney, ed., *Contemporary American Dramatists,* London, 1994; J. L. DiGaetani, *A Search for a Post-modern Theatre: Interviews with Contemporary Playwrights,* New York, 1991; *Contemporary Authors, New Revision Series,* Detroit, 1981; *Contemporary Literary Criticism,* Detroit, 1987; *Gay and Lesbian Literature,* Detroit, 1994; E. Kay, ed., *International Authors and Writers Who's Who,* Cambridge, U.K., 1993; P.J. Kaye, ed., *National Playwrights Directory,* Waterford, Conn., 1981; J. MacNichols, *Twentieth-Century American Dramatists,* Detroit, 1981; F. N. Magill, *Critical Survey of Drama,* Pasadena, 1994; *McGraw-Hill Encyclopedia of World Drama,* New York, 1984; T. McNally, "Theater Isn't All on Broadway," *New York Times,* April 28, 1974; T. McNally, *Three Plays,* New York, 1980; T. McNally, *15 Short Plays,* New York, 1994; *Notable Names in the American Theatre,* edited by Walter Rigdon, Clifton, N.J., 1976; G. Perkins, ed., *Benet's Reader's Encyclopedia of American Literature,* New York, 1991; and *Love! Valor! Compassion!* Playbill, Manhattan Theater Club, 1993.

Gary Garrison

MEISNER, Sanford (1905–97), teacher, actor, and director, was born on August 31, 1905, in the Greenpoint section of Brooklyn, New York. He was the firstborn child of Herman and Bertha (Knoepfler) Meisner. His father was a manufacturer. The Meisners, both Jews, had emigrated from Hungary. She arrived as an infant, he as a teenager. They fled the anti-Semitism of Brooklyn and moved to the Bronx immediately after Sanford's birth. His brother Jacob was born here. Jacob died of bovine tuberculosis soon afterward. "The death of my brother," said Meisner, "was the dominant emotional influence in my life from which I never. . . escaped" (*Current Biography,* 1991, 396).

Another brother, Robert, and a sister, Ruth, were born later. In his childhood, signs of Meisner's future career as an acting coach and director emerged. Using his cousins and other neighborhood children as actors, he would direct *tableaux vivantes* based on news footage of the battle fronts of World War I. Even then he was considered a visionary and autocrat. He told *American Film* in 1983 how he managed to take control of his actors, "because if they didn't do what I wanted them to, I would practically kill them" (78). He graduated from Erasmus Hall High School in Brooklyn in 1923. He then enrolled at the Damrosch Institute of Music (now the Juilliard School of Music) in 1924. He spent only one year at the institute to study piano. He was married in 1940 to Peggy

Sanford Meisner in Clifford Odets's *Golden Boy* (1937). (Photo by Alfredo Valente, courtesy of Richard Valente and the Billy Rose Theatre Collection, New York Public Library for the Performing Arts.)

Meyer; they were divorced in June 1947. In December of the same year, he married Betty Gooch. This marriage ended in 1958. Meisner never married again but remained with longtime companion James Carville until the time of his death. Meisner was not interested in discussing his personal life with either the press or his students. Though much is speculated, little is publicly known about his long and intimate relationship with Carville. As a punctuation to his life, and perhaps as his first "out-ing," *American Theatre* prepared an obituary for Meisner that included the following sentence: "Meisner is survived by his longtime companion, James Carville" (33).

Sanford Meisner began his career acting in productions at the Theatre Guild, where he won a scholarship. A musician friend introduced him to **Aaron Copland,** and through Copland he was introduced to Harold Clurman. Clurman, in turn, introduced him to Lee Strasberg. "Strasberg had a great, uplifting influence on me," Meisner wrote in *Sanford Meisner on Acting.* "He introduced me to quality actors and artists of various kinds, and this helped enormously to solidify my emotional needs. I learned from him. I solidified my natural tastes and inclinations with his help" (*Current Biography,* 1991, 396). It was through Strasberg that Meis-ner became an original member of the Group Theatre. Meisner made his first stage appearance with the group as a Farmhand in *They Knew What They Wanted* (1924). He subsequently appeared in Group Theatre pro-ductions of *Garrick's Gaeities* (1925), *The Doctor's Dilemma* (1927), *Marco Millions* (1928), *Volpone* (1928), *The House of Connelly* (1931), *1931* (1931), *Night over Taos* (1932), *Men in White* (1933), *Gold Eagle Guy* (1934), *Awake and Sing* (1935), *Waiting for Lefty* (1935), *Paradise Lost* (1935), *The Case of Clyde Griffiths* (an adaptation of the novel *An American Tragedy,* 1936), *Johnny Johnson* (1936), *Rocket to the Moon, Awake and Sing* (1939), and *Night Music* (1940). His performances received consistently positive critical notice. He directed *The Time of Your Life* in New York City and appeared in *The Cold Wind and the Warm* (1958).

Meisner spent a couple of years in Hollywood. While there, he made his film debut as Phil Stanley, the prosecuting attorney in *The Story on Page One* (Fox, 1959), followed by a scheming psychoanalyst in the screen adaptation of F. Scott Fitzgerald's *Tender is the Night* (Fox, 1962). His last role, as the syndicate boss in Elaine May's *Mikey and Nicky* (1976), was a difficult experience that discouraged him from acting and sent him back to his first love, teaching.

Meisner began teaching method acting at the Neighborhood Play-house School of Theater in 1935 and served as head of the school from 1936 to 1958. He left in 1958 after a creative dispute with the school's administrators. After this, he held many other teaching and directing jobs. He moved to Hollywood to become the director of the new talent division of Twentieth Century-Fox (1959–61). He set up a training pro-gram for the studio's contract players. But soon he became disenchanted with the political infighting of studio executives, and he returned to New York at the end of this contract in 1961.

He briefly headed the Department of Drama at the recently founded American Musical and Dramatic Theatre Academy (1962–64). Finally, he returned to his former position at the Neighborhood Playhouse School of Theater in 1964. The two-year program, which Meisner designed at the playhouse, included courses in speech and vocal production, singing, stage movement, dance, fencing, and makeup, as well as acting. Even after his health began to deteriorate, Meisner took all first-year students through weeks of exercises to develop spontaneity and concentration before turning them over to acting instructors he had trained himself. He took a large departure from Strasberg's teaching methods in developing his own system. He, like his good friend Stella Adler (another Strasberg detractor), created a unique but derivative technique. He stated in an interview with *Yale Theater* in 1977:

> My approach is a hell of a lot healthier than Strasberg's. I think he takes an introverted person and introverts him further. It's like wearing three overcoats. I'm always trying to encourage truthful behavior related to the situation. All of the training up to the point where it has to do with the creation of a character has to do with my basic premise: what you do doesn't depend on you—it depends on what the other fellow does. (38)

During his more than fifty years as a teacher in New York and Hollywood, his students included actors Elizabeth Ashley, Barbara Baxley, James Broderick, Suzanne Pleshette, Jo Van Fleet, James Caan, Tammy Grimes, Eli Wallach, Grace Kelly, Gregory Peck, Steve McQueen, Joel Grey, Maureen Stapleton, Tony Randall, Lorne Greene, Louise Lasser, Diane Keaton, Joanne Woodward, Jon Voight, and Robert Duvall. He also worked with directors, choreographers, and playwrights, such as Bob Fosse, Sydney Pollack, Horton Foote, and David Mamet.

In 1987, Meisner, along with Dennis Longwell, compiled his theories on teaching acting into a text entitled *Sanford Meisner on Acting.* In it, the director Sydney Pollack, who once worked as Meisner's assistant, wrote a tribute to Meisner in an introduction to the book, stating,

> I believe there are only a few people who can really teach the technique of acting. Most are well read and intelligent, and confuse their ability to theorize and intellectualize about the subject with an ability to cause real growth in an actor. There are almost no good books on acting. This is one of the best. I envy all of you who may be discovering Sandy for the first time (69).

Meisner dedicated his book to his companion James Carville. In 1994, a second text, *The Sanford Meisner Approach,* written by a former student, Larry Silverberg, featured a moving preface written by Horton Foote.

In August 1990, a Public Broadcasting documentary on Meisner's approach to acting, "Sanford Meisner: The Theatre's Best Kept Secret," was reviewed favorably in *Variety.* Sydney Pollack noted: "Meisner had an indelible impact on several generations of performers during his forty year plus career." The tribute included observations from several of Meisner's famous students. Gregory Peck, with a smile, called his training, "two years of stress and strain—almost unrelieved." Lee Grant explained that Meisner, like all good teachers, was "God to his students." Eli Wallach called him "autocratic," while Mary Steenburgen described him as "wonderfully funny, and terrifying as ever—he's just like an old lion."

Meisner and Carville also cofounded the Meisner/Carville School of Acting on the Caribbean island of Bequia in 1985. In 1995, he opened the Sanford Meisner Center for the Arts in North Hollywood with Carville and another colleague, Martin Barter. He gave his last performance at the age of ninety on the NBC television series *ER.* In 1990, as a testament to his achievements, he received the Public Service Award from President George H. W. Bush.

In his late years, Meisner suffered many physical ailments. He wore thick glasses as a result of multiple operations for cataracts and detached retinas in both eyes. Even more debilitating were the two operations he sustained for cancer of the larynx, which left him completely without a voice. During this time, he was also hit by a truck while crossing the road. As a result, both his left femur and hip had breaks in three places. Reconstructive surgery helped him to continue to walk. Sanford Meisner died in February 1997 at the age of ninety-one. According to the *New York Times,* on February 4, 1997: "The Neighborhood Playhouse is still in operation, along with the Meisner/Carville School of Acting (his companion, James Carville was the co-founder) and the Sanford Meisner Center of the Arts, both in North Hollywood."

Meisner received commendations from Presidents Clinton, Bush, and Reagan. He was honored by California Governor Pete Wilson and was named "Humanitarian of the Year 1990" by the Washington Charity Awards. Upon his death, *Backstage West* newspaper dedicated its February 12, 1998, issue to Meisner and his world-renown "Meisner Technique."

Arthur Miller once said of Meisner, "He was been the most principled teacher of acting in this country for decades now, and every time I am reading actors I can pretty well tell which ones have studied with Meisner. It is because they are honest and simple and don't lay on complications that aren't necessary" (http://www.themeisnercenter.com/meisner-Bio.html).

See *American Film,* spring 1983; *American Theatre,* April 1997; *Backstage West,* February 12, 1998; *Current Biography,* April 1991; *Current Biography,* April 1997; *Los Angeles Times,* February 5, 1997; *New York Times,* February 4, 1997; S. Meisner, *Sanford Meisner on Acting,* New York, 1987, www.themeisnercenter.com/meisnerBio.html, accessed June 30, 2004; *Notable Names of American Theatre,* edited by W. Rigdon, 1976; L. Silverberg, *The Sanford Meisner Approach,* Lime, N.H., 1997; *Variety,* August 22, 1990; *Washington Post,* February 16, 1997; and *Yale Theater,* spring 1977.

Daniel-Raymond Nadon

MENKEN, Adah Isaacs (1835–69), actress, was best known for her seemingly "naked" wild ride while strapped to the back of a real horse in the sensational stage play *Mazeppa.* Menken was more of an entertainment personality than an acting talent. She possessed shimmering eyes and a spectacular figure and embraced the flamboyant image of the nineteenth-century Bohemian artist throughout her short life. With an audacious and assured calculation, she cultivated both an enigmatic biography and sexuality, encouraging conjecture about her past and speculation about her current involvements. Menken entered into four short, tempestuous marriages, which served her professional advancement and enhanced her scandalous reputation. She also demonstrated a passion for women that exceeded mere gastronomic companionship.

Menken's birth date has generally been accepted to be June 15, 1835. She was born near New Orleans as Ada Bertha Theodore (she did not add the *h* to Ada until her first marriage), and not as Delores Adios Fuentes, daughter of a Presbyterian minister, a popular myth she encouraged about her background. She also claimed an unproven Jewish ancestry. Her father died when she was several years old, and her mother remarried a man named Josephs, who died when Menken was a teenager. It was to support her mother that she probably began her work as a teacher at this time, but her theatrical debut soon followed.

Adah Menken and her sister Josephine made their stage debuts in dancing roles in 1853 at New Orleans' French Opera House, then toured Mexico, Texas, and Cuba. From about the ages of nineteen to twenty-one, Adah studied and taught languages (she had an impressive command of Hebrew, Spanish, French, and German) and embarked on her second career as a poet. Sometime between 1856 and 1858, she married Alexander Isaac Menken in Texas, with whom she lived for only a brief time, but whose name she retained for the remainder of her career (with a slight variation, as she added an *s* to Isaac).

The Menkens returned to New Orleans, where Alexander began to promote his wife's career, and Adah made her acting debut in 1858 in *The Lady of Lyons,* followed by appearances in *Fazio, The Soldier's Daughter,* and *A Lesson for Husbands.* She was praised not only for her beauty and grace but for the range she demonstrated in these dramatic and comic pieces. In Nashville, she first essayed Shakespeare, as Lady Macbeth opposite James E. Murdoch.

In the summer of 1858, Menken embarked on a successful run at Wood's Theatre in her husband's home town of Cincinnati. She was warmly received by the local Jewish community, particularly for her performance in *The Jewess.* Then, in Dayton, Ohio, she attempted her own cross-gender rendition of Jack Sheppard's life, her first excursion into male roles, which would quickly prove to be her most popular characters. Her postperformance activities also set a career pattern, as she became embroiled in the first of numerous scandals. Menken accepted the dinner invitation of members of the Dayton Light Guards, who bestowed on her the honorary title of captain, which she thought particularly suitable in light of her newfound specialty roles in male dress. Her husband was appalled, and this began the disintegration of their marriage.

After a divorce granted by a rabbi, Menken returned to the stage in 1859, this time making her first appearance in New York as the Widow Cheerly in *The Soldier's Daughter.* Later that year she married boxer John Heenan, although she did not realize that she had not been legally divorced from her first husband. A series of misfortunes followed, including a public scandal over the legality of the marriage, the deaths of her infant son and her mother, Adah and John's separation in 1860, and their divorce in 1862.

Amid all of this, Menken made her historical first ride as Mazeppa in the equestrian spectacle of that name, igniting her career and quite literally catapulting her into international fame. In 1861, when she was in her mid-twenties, she took on the role of Cassimir, or Mazzepa, in the melodrama based on Lord Byron's poem. She became identified with this role, her most popular during the remaining seven years of her life. In playing a young man who is sent to death lashed to the back of a horse because of love for a woman, the exposure of her female form in a flesh-colored bodysuit gave her the semblance of nudity, and the gender-bending spectacle proved to be provocative, daring, occasionally injurious, and always financially rewarding. This led to a series of "Protean comedy" roles in which the sailor's uniform in *Black-Eyed Susan* and the military dress in *The French Spy,* though "male" costuming, actually served to reveal her shapely body.

In 1863, Menken married for a third time, to writer Robert Henry Newell. They divorced in 1865. She was well into a pregnancy at her fourth marriage ceremony, to James Paul Barclay, in the following year. Throughout her last several marriages, Menken had spent a good deal of time traveling and performing, from San Francisco to London and Paris, entertaining and becoming acquainted with the leading writers and artists of the day. Her final marriage was no exception, as she again left her husband just a few days after the wedding to go to Paris. There she gave birth to a son, met George Sand and Alexandre Dumas (*pere*), and, in August 1868, died at the age of thirty-three. She was buried in Paris.

Evidence in Menken's own writings and other contemporary accounts indicates that she had romantic and possibly sexual relationships with several women, including the "Queen of Bohemia" Ada Clare and writer Aurore Dudevant, better known as George Sand, whom Menken idolized. Sand, well known as a bisexual, and Menken, both short haired and cigar smoking, shared a predilection for men's sartorial accoutrements during their frequent public dining excursions in Paris. Despite a thirty-year age difference, contemporaries certainly thought that their relationship was lesbian, not merely literary. More recently, one of Menken's biographers, Wolf Mankowitz, maintains that her writings do not register homosexual desire, while Samuel Edwards, who wrote about George Sand's life, argues that Sand and Menken may have had a lesbian affair. If Sand and Menken did have more than the typical female friendship, it was an extremely brief affair, for Menken died only a year and a half after they met. No correspondence between the two seems to have survived, and Sand's own letters to others include only a few references to seeing the young performer onstage and meeting her. Menken, on the other hand, whom Samuel Edwards notes was "usually circumspect in her language," referred to Sand as "my darling George" in letters to friends and once gushed, "she so infuses me with the spirit of life that I cannot bear to spend an evening apart from her" (249). Reviewing this evidence, Renee Sentilles finds that "in fact Sand and Menken had probably met only briefly and socially" (271). But Sentilles cites letters Menken wrote to Hattie Tyng in 1861 and 1862 in which she confessed "I have had my passionate attachments among women, which swept like whirlwinds over me, sometimes, alas! Scorching me with a furnace-blast, but generally only changing and renewing my capabilities for love. I would 'have drunk their souls as it were a ray from Heaven'—have lost myself and lived in them. . . ." (153–54).

There are conflicting reports regarding the nature of Menken's relationships with a number of men. Some biographers have tried to link her to Walt Whitman and dwell on the brief liaisons with Dumas *pere* and Algernon Swinburne. This latter "affair" with the homosexual British poet was most likely neither a hetero- nor a conventionally "sexual" relationship; she was perhaps another one of his "whipping ladies." Thus, the kind of "mistress" she may have been to the masochistic Swinburne was probably not what polite society imagined.

Menken demonstrated, as do present-day celebrities, a proficiency in exploiting and obfuscating her sexuality for sensational effect. Her gay Bohemian life merged with an uncanny ability to upstage her contemporaries. Onstage she simultaneously blurred and revealed her sexuality, exposing more of her body than perhaps any other female performer had in a legitimate venue while ostensibly essaying male characters. Offstage she reveled in a good deal of gender slippage as well, smoking cigars, dressing in male clothing, and frequenting gambling establishments and brothels. She was extremely savvy about what would pique public interest, and, like Madonna's flirtation with a pansexual appeal, she traded on her following of both genders. Critically, she was one of the first personalities to use and appreciate the value of the photo opportunity. However, despite her careful manipulation of the press and a series of publicity stunts, Menken remains a cipher in many ways; deliberately evasive regarding her real name, background, and other biographical facts, she constructed a mysterious past she may not have had.

See L. Adler, "Adah Issacs Menken in *Mazeppa*," in *Women in American Theatre*, edited by F. E. Dudden, New York, 1987, 81–87; A. Auster, *Actresses and Suffragists*, New York, 1984; N. Barnes-McLain, "Bohemian on Horseback: Adah Isaacs Menken," in *Passing Performances: Queer Readings of Leading Players in American Theater History*, edited by R. A. Schanke and Kim Marra, Ann Arbor, 1998, 63–79; T. Davis, *Actresses as Working Women: Their Social Identity in Victorian Culture*, London, 1991; S. Edwards, *George Sand: A Biography of the First Modern, Liberated Woman*, New York, 1972; C. Johnson, *American Actress: Perspective on the Nineteenth Century*, Chicago, 1984; W. Mankowitz, *Mazeppa: The Lives, Loves, and Legends of Adah Issacs Menken*, New York, 1982; and Menken Portfolio, Players' Collection, Billy Rose Theatre Collection, New York Public Library; and R. M. Sentilles, *Performing Menken: Adah Isaacs Menken and the Birth of American Celebrity*, Cambridge, 2003.

Noreen C. Barnes

MOOREHEAD, Agnes (Robertson) (1900–1974), actress, is most immediately remembered as Endora, the meddlesome witch and mother-in-law in the television series, *Bewitched*. Her career, however, spanned many decades. She appeared mostly in supporting roles in 29 stage productions, 61 movies, 72 television shows (in addition to over 150 episodes of *Bewitched*), 161 radio appearances, and multiple recordings.

Born in Clinton, Massachusetts, to a clerical father and an artistic mother, Moorehead was undoubtedly imbued with a certain Victorian respect for keeping up appearances and being good. She reportedly sang in church at age three and carried a Bible to the rehearsals of *Bewitched.* "My life," she claimed, "has been ruled by beliefs" (Bowers, 299).

The Moorehead family moved to Hamilton, Ohio, in 1904 and to Saint Louis, Missouri, in 1912, where Agnes joined the Saint Louis Municipal Opera Company. At the urging of her father, she attended Muskingham College, an institution founded by her uncle, and completed graduate work at the University of Wisconsin. As she studied for her master's degree in English, she taught high school and worked in summer stock for five years. In 1926, she appeared on radio as the "Girl Baritone" (Kear, 3) and auditioned for the American Academy of Dramatic Arts (AADA) in New York City. She did not have the conventional prettiness required for romantic leads. Her nose was slightly aquiline, and the irregular proportioning of her face was subject to distortion when lit for that purpose, a factor that later served to her benefit but prevented her as a young actress from being cast in leading roles.

After graduating from AADA in 1929, Moorehead was cast in bit parts on Broadway or in the touring companies of productions such as *Marco Millions, Courage, Soldiers and Women, Scarlet Pages, Candle Light,* and *All the King's Horses.* Eventually, she was chosen as a member of the company at the Mercury Theatre, where she worked with Orson Welles in his first production, *Julius Caesar.* Such a stage career provided a meager living, forcing her to return to radio, where her "looks didn't limit her choices[s]" (Hadleigh, 180). As a radio actress, she read many roles, including leads, and worked as many as seven shows a day—sometimes going on cold (*TV Guide,* August 24, 1968). She was the foil for well-known comedians, including Fred Allen, Bob Hope, Bert Lahr, and Ed Wynn (Kear, 7). She eventually performed in "The March of Time," impersonating over forty women, including Eleanor Roosevelt, who, after hearing and meeting Moorehead, announced that she was "the only woman that I'll allow to do [my] impersonation" (*TV Guide,* July 17, 1965, 25). One reviewer noted that Moorehead could "control her voice as expertly as a radio engineer can control sound" (*Time,* 57).

From ages forty-one to seventy-four, Moorehead worked continuously onstage, in film, and on television, but she is best remembered by the public for her characterizations in films, ranging from *Citizen Kane* (1941) to *Hush, Hush, Sweet Charlotte* (1964). Perhaps her most notable stage performance was as Dona Ana in a concert reading presentation of *Don Juan in Hell,* taken from Shaw's *Man and Superman.* The acclaimed company, called the First Drama Quartet, also featured **Charles Laughton** (who directed as well), Charles Boyer, and Sir Cedric Hardwicke. The 1951 production was a remarkable success in Los Angeles, New York, and regional engagements across the country, including many universities. To a greater extent than any of her other work, the production convinced critics and public alike of Moorehead's exceptional skills as an actress.

Moorehead also toured extensively throughout the United States in a one-woman show, called alternately *An Evening with Agnes Moorehead, That Fabulous Redhead,* and *Come Closer, and I'll Give You an Earful.* Produced originally in 1954 with the encouragement of Orson Welles, the show was continually revived and revised with updated monologues until 1970.

Moorehead's sexual identity has been a source of controversy. In the publicity propagated by her studios, she was portrayed as the perfect housewife and mother (even though both her marriages ended in divorce) and was photographed in poses of domesticity with her husband and her cat. But the alternative press represented her differently. In periodicals such as the *New York Post,* the *NYQ, The Advocate,* the *Southern Voice,* and *Out/Look,* Moorehead was identified as a lesbian (White, 111). Paul Lynde, who publicly insinuated a relationship between Debbie Reynolds and Moorehead, asserted: "The whole world knows Agnes was a lesbian— I mean classy as hell, but one of the all-time Hollywood dykes" (*Out/Look,* 26). Other sources claim that Moorehead was intimate with a number of lady friends when she first arrived in Hollywood, but the information was kept "within the show biz family. . . . When one of her husbands was caught cheating, so the story goes, Agnes screamed at him that if he could have a mistress, so could she" (Hadleigh, 179).

Contradicting the gossip, Debbie Reynolds flatly denied Moorehead's lesbianism, arguing that Aggie wouldn't know the meaning of the word *lesbian* (241). Reynolds, who met Moorehead during the filming of *How the West Was Won* (1963), allegedly threatened to sue her ex-husband Eddie Fisher should he include the story of her friendship with Moorehead in his autobiography (White, 111).

Moorehead's obsession with privacy fueled the controversy. "My work anyone can see. I never really cared to share anything with the public . . . besides my work" (Hadleigh, 192). Her stage, movie, and television characters were "Nurses, secretaries, career women, nuns, companions, housekeepers, [and aunts, who] connote, not a lesbian identity, but a deviation from heterosexualized femininity" (White, 94). In one of her last interviews, she confessed: "I think for most people there's more fear of life [than death] . . . and of exploring or feeling everything one would like to. It's an unavoidable truth: fear of life closes off more opportunities for us than fear of death ever does" (Hadleigh, 194). Moorehead died in 1974 of lung cancer.

See R. Bowers, "Agnes Moorehead Thinks Acting Is More a Matter of Magic than of Craft," *Films in Review,* May 1966; B. Hadleigh, *Hollywood Lesbians,* New York, 1994; L. Kear, *Agnes Moorehead: A Bio-Bibliography,* Westport, Conn., 1992; *Out/Look,* 6 (fall 1989); D. Reynolds, *Debbie: My Life,* London, 1988; "She Doesn't Need Glamour," *Holly-wood,* October 1942; *Time,* September 10, 1945; *TV Guide,* July 17, 1965; *TV Guide,* August 24, 1968; and P. White, "Supporting Character: The Queer Career of Agnes Moorehead," in *Out in Culture: Gay, Lesbian, and Queer Essays on Popular Culture,* edited by Corey K. Creekmur and Alexander Doty, Durham, 1995.

Lynne Greeley

MOORE, Robert (1927–84), director and actor, was born in Detroit, Michigan, and as a teenager moved to Washington, D.C., where he later attended Catholic University after a year's stint in the navy. While still in college, he made his debut on Broadway (as Brennan Moore) in Jean Kerr's short-lived *Jenny Kissed Me* (1949). Following the play's demise, Moore returned to school and later spent many years as a journeyman actor and director in stock and regional theaters. He served as president of Washington's University Players touring repertory company and was resident director at both the Olney Theatre in Maryland and the Royal Poinciana Playhouse in Palm Beach, Florida. He directed countless star revivals of plays and musicals in stock and made his directorial debut in New York with an Off-Broadway production of *The Ticket-of-Leave Man* in 1961.

Moore returned to Broadway in 1964 as understudy for Alan Alda in *The Owl and the Pussycat* and then enjoyed a two-year run in a supporting role in the hit comedy *Cactus Flower.* In 1967, he was featured in **Edward Albee**'s *Everything in the Garden,* also on Broadway, and it was during this run that **Mart Crowley**, a friend from Catholic University, moved in with Moore and asked him to direct a play he had recently completed, *The Boys in the Band.* Presented first as a workshop production at the Playwrights Unit in Greenwich Village, Crowley's comedy-drama was set at a birthday party in a Manhattan apartment attended by a group of gay male friends. A straight interloper, the college roommate of the host, becomes the catalyst for a series of revelations and confessions. The response to the workshop production was so enthusiastic that financing for a commercial transfer was secured, and on April 14, 1968, *The Boys in* the Band* opened at Off-Broadway's Theatre Four, eventually playing a three-year run.

More than a year before the Stonewall Riots and at a time when media images of gays were either nonexistent or wildly homophobic, Crowley's characters were a revelation by virtue of their visibility. He was rightfully criticized for the play's gallery of stereotypes (the lisping queen interior decorator, the self-loathing host, the moronic, muscled hustler), but he also drew complex, troubled characters who were less concerned with hiding or eliminating their homosexuality than with simply getting along in an often hostile world. David Rothenberg, the press agent for the play, later remarked: "We were no longer the secondary characters, a sick joke, or a pathetic friend. We were the reason for the play, and we discovered that our emotions could be shared by a larger audience" (11). Moore's seamless direction of a play told in real time was hailed by virtually every reviewer, with many obviously relieved to find a disciplined hand at the service of such flamboyant material. Typical was *Variety*'s favorable mention: "The bitchiness, outrageous wisecracking and outlandish situations are handled deftly by the director" ("Shows Abroad," 70). Other critics were quick to laud his "discernment and discretion" (Clurman, 52) and "controlled and sensitive staging" (Oppenheimer, 33).

The overwhelming success of *The Boys in the Band* immediately shifted Moore's career equation from actor who directs to director who acts. His breakthrough may have come with a play that was daring and provocative in its subject matter at the time, but his tastes were squarely in the mainstream and his later directing career was devoted to solidly commercial projects. While many of *Boys'* cast members suffered career repercussions from playing gay characters, no such taint applied to its director. Moore immediately signed to direct the new Neil Simon, Burt Bacharach, and Hal David musical, *Promises, Promises* (1969), produced by David Merrick—as heterosexual and mainstream a project as he could have chosen.

Although Moore was later described as "openly gay" (Murray, 77), he was also the product of a less forthcoming era and resolutely refused to discuss his personal life or empathize too enthusiastically with homosexuality—even as it was depicted in his career-making vehicle. A *New York Times* interview after the opening of *Promises* duly noted that the director of two hit shows "shares a two-bedroom apartment with two male stage managers" (Klemesrud, D1) but did not pursue his campy description of *Promises* as "my butch musical" (D6). Discussing *Boys*, Moore flatly stated, "As far as I know, everyone in 'Boys' is straight. . . . Besides, 'Boys' isn't about homosexuality; it's about self-destruction" (D6).

Promises was followed by another Neil Simon smash, *The Last of the Red Hot Lovers* (1969), giving Moore the rare distinction of having three simultaneous hits in New York. (He also won back-to-back Tony nominations in both the musical and play categories, along with a Drama Desk Award for his *Boys* direction.) Moore, however, continued to think of himself as an actor and, indeed, turned down the chance to direct the film version of *Boys* in order to take a role in Otto Preminger's film, *Tell Me That You Love Me, Junie Moon* (1970). Ironically, the role Moore chose over the *Boys* film was that of a gay paraplegic whose homosexuality is "cured" by a tryst with a prostitute.

Moore returned to directing on Broadway with several star vehicles: Maureen Stapleton won a Tony under his direction in Neil Simon's *The Gingerbread Lady* (1970); he was the last in a series of directors for the troubled musical *Lorelei* (1974), an update of *Gentlemen Prefer Blondes* for Carol Channing; and he guided Lynn Redgrave in *My Fat Friend* (1974) for a short run. He also began a successful career as a film and television director, and, as with his stage work, his choices were safely commercial. He directed numerous episodes of the sitcom *Rhoda;* a made for television film, *Thursday's Child* (1974); and a television adaptation of **Tennessee Williams**'s *Cat on a Hot Tin Roof* (1976) starring Natalie Wood and Laurence Olivier. Moore's professional relationship with Neil Simon provided his entry into feature film directing, and he served as a proficient and accommodating director for three Simon vehicles: the all-star comedy spoof, *Murder by Death* (1976); a less successful follow-up, *The Cheap Detective* (1978); and the film adaptation of Simon's autobiographical play, *Chapter Two* (1979).

By this time, Moore had once again returned to Broadway with two long-running hits: Ira Levin's murder mystery-comedy *Deathtrap* in 1978 (with a now mundane gay lovers plot twist); and the Neil Simon, Marvin Hamlisch, and Carol Bayer Sager musical *They're Playing Our Song* in 1979. His last directing credit was a typical Moore show: the expensive, star-powered musical *Woman of the Year,* with Lauren Bacall, in 1981.

Moore died May 10, 1984, at the age of fifty-six in New York City, with his obituaries listing cause of death as pneumonia or simply, "after a brief illness." Harry Haun, writing in *Playbill* in 1993, noted that AIDS had claimed not only five original cast members of *The Boys in the Band,* but a coproducer, Richard Barr, and the director, Moore, a cruel irony for the collaborators on this landmark play about the lives of gay men.

See H. Clurman, "Comedy about Tragedy," *New York,* May 6, 1968; H. Haun, "On the Aisle," *Playbill* 93 (November 1993): 46; J. Klemesrud, "He Promises to Beat the

Band," *New York Times,* January 5, 1969; Robert Moore Clippings File, Billy Rose Theatre Collection, New York Public Library for the Performing Arts; R. Murray, *Images in
the Dark: An Encyclopedia of Gay and Lesbian Film and Video,* Philadelphia, 1994; *Notable
Names in the American Theater,* edited by W. Rigdon, Clifton, N.J., 1976; G. Oppenheimer, "On Stage: 'Boys in the Band,'" *Newsday,* April 15, 1968; D. Rothenberg, "A Life
in the Theater: The Boys in 'The Boys in the Band,'" *Center Stage.* April 1989; and "Shows
Abroad: 'The Boys in the Band,'" *Variety,* February 19, 1969.

Kevin Winkler

MORGAN, Agnes Bangs (ca. 1880–1976), director and playwright, was
born in LeRoy, New York. She received an A.B. in 1901 and an A.M. in
1903 from Radcliffe, where she studied playwriting and play production
with George Pierce Baker. In the spring of 1903, Baker offered students
in his English 39 (a class in dramatic literature) the opportunity to write
a play rather than an essay. After the submission of her play, Morgan and
two other women were selected by Baker as the nucleus of his first English 47 class in playwriting. Baker sent the three to England, France,
and Germany from June 1903 to January 1904 to study production practices and plays. Morgan was the only one to complete the tour and return
to Cambridge for the first offering of English 47, a pioneering course in
playwriting. Since the course did not offer production training until
1912, when it became the 47 Workshop, Morgan turned to the Idler
Club to direct her two plays. On leaving Radcliffe, she went to New York
to work in the professional theater, translating and adapting plays from
the French repertoire, writing her own plays, and becoming one of the
first women to make a professional career as a director on the American
stage. She earned 100 to 250 dollars per play and supplemented her
income with secretarial work.

Morgan maintained professional contact with Baker throughout her
years in New York. She wrote to him in 1909 about **Helen Arthur,**
whom she had recently met and who was to be her lifelong partner, stating that Arthur believed in her writing and was helping to get her produced. Arthur introduced Morgan to the Henry Street Settlement on
New York's Lower East Side, founder Lillian Wald, and the Lewisohn sisters, Alice and Irene. The Lewisohns, Arthur, and Morgan began collaborating on theater productions at the settlement in 1912 with a play on
the impending Russian Revolution, and in 1915 they began full seasons
at the Neighborhood Playhouse, which had been built by the Lewisohns
a few blocks from the settlement. The four women served as the producing staff: Morgan was director and specialist in literature, Arthur was

business manager and lawyer, Alice Lewisohn was actress and director, and Irene Lewisohn was dancer and choreographer. The Neighborhood Playhouse repertoire stands out among New York's little theaters for its eclecticism: it produced social realist plays, classics of world dramatic literature, and a genre the producing staff termed lyric drama, which welded music, dance, and visual effects with the spoken word. In the early years, Morgan directed such plays as Bernard Shaw's *Captain Brassbound's Conversion,* Lord Dunsany's *A Night at an Inn* and *The Queen's Enemies,* Robert Browning's *Pippa Passes,* Serafin and Joaquin Alvarez Quinteros' *Fortunato* and *A Sunny Morning,* the miracle play *Guibour* starring Yvette Guilbert, and original plays such as Violet Pearn's *Wild Birds.* She frequently codirected with Alice Lewisohn, who prior to her collaboration with Morgan had no professional directing experience. In 1920, the Neighborhood Playhouse supplemented the amateur players with a professional company. Morgan directed Galsworthy's *The Mob* with the new professionals in the lead roles and the amateurs in minor parts and as the mob, a format that set the tone for future Playhouse productions. In later years, she adapted, directed, and published the Indian classic *The Little Clay Cart* and directed such plays as *The Harlequinade* and *The Madras House* by Harley Granville-Barker and *The Lion Tamer* by Alfred Savoir. In 1922, the Neighborhood Playhouse made its annual private spoof of its own work and that of the Broadway season into a public event. Called *The Grand Street Follies* and written and directed by Morgan, the revue was offered to the public each spring beginning in 1922. The *Follies* was the Neighborhood's greatest financial success, extending its run further into the summer each year. Morgan adapted, wrote, and directed plays full time for the Neighborhood Playhouse at a salary of 75 dollars per week for twelve years.

When the Playhouse dissolved in 1927, Morgan, Arthur, and several of the actors and designers formed the Actor-Managers, Inc, a producing organization that lasted until 1940, offering more editions of *The Grand Street Follies* as well as new plays. Morgan was stage director and Arthur executive director. Among Morgan's productions with Actor-Managers were *Maya,* by Simon Gantillon, in February 1928 at New York's Comedy Theater, which was shut down for its sympathetic portrayal of a prostitute; and Morgan's own play, *If Love Were All,* which was written under the pseudonym Cutler Hatch. In the 1930s, Morgan directed for summer stock in Newport, Bar Harbor, Ann Arbor, and Mount Kisco; at universities such as Barnard College; and for the Popular Price Unit of the Federal Theater Project. She occasionally wrote and directed her own plays, such as *Grandpa,* which was produced at the Newport Casino Theater. On December 10, 1939, Helen Arthur died, ending the two women's artistic and personal partnership after three decades.

In 1940, Agnes Morgan became associate director of the Paper Mill Playhouse in Millburn, New Jersey. At the Neighborhood Playhouse, she had rarely been involved in the production of musical plays and lyric dramas except for her *Grand Street Follies,* but at the Paper Mill she was to embrace the musical form for the next thirty years. The theater established a permanent company, which played supporting and chorus roles while stars were hired as leads. By the 1940s, a regular ten-month season of eight productions running five to six weeks each was standard, and Morgan regularly worked fourteen-hour days. Frank Carrington, director of the Paper Mill Playhouse in New Jersey, and Morgan codirected *Papa Is All* for the Theater Guild in 1941 and brought their production of *I Killed the Count* to a Shubert house on Broadway in 1942. But for the most part their activities were confined to artistic direction and staging in Millburn. In 1970, at the age of ninety, Morgan was still working full time at the Playhouse but needed a cane to navigate the stairs. She died in California on May 25, 1976, having retired from the Paper Mill Playhouse in 1972 and moving to a retirement home in Loma Linda with her sister. The Paper Mill Playhouse burned on January 14, 1980, after a work lamp exploded on stage; doubtless many records of Agnes Morgan's contributions to American theater were lost to history in that fire.

See George Pierce Baker folder of correspondence with Agnes Morgan, Harvard Theatre Collection, Harvard University, Cambridge; D. F. Benardete, "The Neighborhood Playhouse in Grand Street," Ph.D. diss., New York University, 1949; M. N. Blood, "The Neighborhood Playhouse from 1915 to 1927: A History and Analysis," Ph.D. diss., Northwestern University, 1993; A. L. Crowley, *The Neighborhood Playhouse: Leaves from a Theater Scrapbook,* New York, 1957; S. Hennigan, "Women Directors: The Early Years," in *Women in American Theater,* edited by H. K. Chinoy and L. W. Jenkins, rev. ed., New York, 1987; A. B. Morgan, "How English 47 Started," *Radcliffe Quarterly* (February 1961): 13–14; Agnes Morgan folders of clippings and programs, Billy Rose Theatre Collection, New York Public Library for the Performing Arts at Lincoln Center, New York; and Agnes Morgan folder of clippings and alumnae information cards, Radcliffe College Archives, Cambridge.

Melanie Blood

MULQUEEN, Kathleen (Catherine) (1901–91), musical comedy actress, was born in Philadelphia. Because her mother had died in childbirth, Kathleen was reared by her father's spinster sister and educated at a convent day school in Philadelphia. Her mother's German relatives were affluent brewers and bankers, who lived in Allentown, Pennsylvania, where Kathleen, throughout her childhood and adolescence, spent her summers.

Kathleen Mulqueen, circa 1959, in costume for the grandmother role in the TV series *Dennis the Menace*. (From the collection of Kaier Curtin.)

While a teenager, Mulqueen met "the love of her life," Hazel Dawn (b. 1891), an actress with whom she remained intimate but platonic friends for nearly half a century. When Dawn was starring on Broadway in *The Pink Lady* in 1911 (Mantle and Sherwood, 441), Mulqueen wrote her "such a charming mash note" that the actress invited the young fan to visit her backstage in her dressing room. For more than forty years thereafter, Mulqueen became "an almost familial figure, another younger sister, not only in Hazel Dawn's life, but in that of her husband and her two children" (Kaier Curtin [Mulqueen's foster son], interview with the author, May 17, 2002).

At sixteen, Mulqueen was spotted by a Broadway talent scout when she made her stage debut in the chorus of a musical in Allentown. She went on to chorus lines and ingenue roles in New York. On September 1, 1922, she opened (under the name Catherine Mulqueen) in *Molly Darling,* a musical comedy starring Jack Donahue. Three years later she was starring as Irene in Eddie Dowling's revival of his musical comedy *Sally, Irene, and Mary* (which he cowrote with Cyrus Wood and first presented on Broadway in 1922). In this production, the actress began using the name Kathleen Mulqueen (Kaier Curtin, interview with the author, May 17, 2002; Mantle, 446).

Called by one critic "The most beautiful girl on Broadway," Mulqueen performed in musical pieces in New York, across the country on road tours, in stock company dramas, and on the vaudeville circuit. She appeared in *Kosher Kitty Kelly* (1925), *The White Sister* (1927), and *To-Morrow (1928),* among many others (Kaier Curtin, interview with the author, May 17, 2002).

Meanwhile, **Paul Guilfoyle** (1902–61), a talented, young, gay actor, had made his Broadway debut at the age of twenty-three in Michael Arlen's *The Green Hat,* opposite leading stars **Katharine Cornell** and Leslie Howard and directed by **Guthrie McClintic.** Guilfoyle made a positive impression in his first Broadway role and went on to perform in at least six additional Broadway productions between 1928 and 1934. Mulqueen met Guilfoyle in the 1920s when both were acting in New York, attending the same parties, and running around with the same theater crowd. They became "Broadway buddies." Both were young, attractive, and talented, and they "made a charming couple, right out of a Noël Coward comedy, seemingly lovers, particularly witty, erudite, popular, and sophisticated" (Kaier Curtin, interviews with the author, September 2 and 4, 1996, and May 17, 2002).

At the age of thirty, and still a maiden lady, Mulqueen "became increasingly uncomfortable at her family's concern about her 'unnaturally' long-term friendship with Hazel Dawn." Curtin believes pressure from her father partly motivated Mulqueen impulsively to elope in 1931 with a reporter from the *New York Times,* "a cliche stage door Johnny, who overwhelmed her by flooding her dressing room every night with flowers." "On that disastrous honeymoon," Mulqueen confessed to her foster son, "I realized immediately that I had made an error in judgment and soon shipped myself off to Cuba to obtain a quickie divorce" (Kaier Curtin, interview with the author, May 17, 2002).

Her sudden divorce may have "made her Catholic family even more suspicious about her sexual predilection, so Kathleen decided to marry her longtime, social 'beard' and good time Broadway buddy, Paul Guilfoyle." She was well aware that Guilfoyle "had been sexually involved with a series of gay lovers but naively believed that he would change and settle down, perhaps even become celibate and satisfied enough, as she would be, with a compatible 'marriage of true minds'" (Kaier Curtin, interview with the author, May 17, 2002).

Hazel Dawn, who was living in retirement in Beverly Hills after a successful film career, encouraged Mulqueen and Guilfoyle to come to Hollywood, where, like many other stage actors during the Depression, they might find work in motion pictures. The couple moved to Los Angeles in 1935. Guilfoyle fortunately secured a long-term contract at RKO Studios, where he made some twenty-five films over the next fifteen years. In the 1950s, he directed more than 150 television shows, including episodes of *Highway Patrol* and *Sea Hunt*. But by the late 1930s, he had become an alcoholic, in part, perhaps, because he was leading a double life; he was secretly an active homosexual but publicly a married man. Also he suffered from depression over the birth of his and Kathleen's child, Anthony, who was afflicted with Down syndrome. He joined Alcoholics Anonymous, where he met and became friends with other Hollywood actors, all of whom helped each other to remain sober.

Kathleen, aware of her husband's sexual adventures, "was worried sick that he might be arrested." Los Angeles "was a hotbed of homophobic entrapment before, during, and after World War II," and Guilfoyle was caught in the late 1940s in a police dragnet operation. The shocking report of his arrest appeared on the front page of the *Los Angeles Times*. Both Guilfoyle and Mulqueen withdrew socially in humiliation. As a consequence of the scandal, he was "blackballed" and never again appeared on the screen. "What saved Kathleen's sanity during the long period when Paul was unemployable was an unexpected chance to resume her acting career with a bit part in the film *Marty*." Thereafter, she was cast in numerous small character roles in films and on television, including a continuing role as the grandmother in the comedy series *Dennis the Menace* (Kaier Curtin, interviews with the author, September 4 and 22, 1996, and May 17, 2002).

At the end of the 1950s, Guilfoyle was again entrapped in a compromising situation. This time he was blackmailed. Afraid to even tell his wife, rather than resorting to his old habit of alcohol—but unable to cope—he became addicted to codeine. He became irrational and unpredictable and so distressed his retarded son that Kathleen insisted that he move out of the house. Despair and humiliation overwhelmed him, and in June 1961 he committed suicide. Kathleen Mulqueen "never again spoke of Paul Guilfoyle, either in bitterness or in compassion" until the AIDS epidemic hit in 1981–82. "Thank God, he's not alive," she said. "He'd be one of the first to come down with it" (Kaier Curtin, interviews with the author, September 4 and 22, 1996, and May 17, 2002).

It was not until her ninetieth birthday that Kathleen Mulqueen admitted that she had been a closeted lesbian all of her life. "Because of those Irish nuns and my Catholic, old maid aunt, I was brought up to believe that sex was dirty. That may be why I never acted upon whatever attraction I might have unconsciously had to women. I never had a lesbian friend [that I was aware of]. Even when aware that certain women were rather butch, I thought them only to be asexual tomboys, whose obvious masculinity was particularly unattractive to me. I would have wanted no more to do with them than with men, all of whom I found sexually repugnant. Had I only had the courage to follow my natural inclination when infatuated with such feminine and beautiful stars as Hazel Dawn!" Kathleen Mulqueen died at the age of ninety in 1991, in a Canyon County retirement community in California (Kaier Curtin, interview with the author, May 17, 2002).

See B. Mantle, ed., *Best Plays of 1924–25,* Boston, 1925; B. Mantle, ed., *Best Plays of 1928–29,* New York, 1929; B. Mantle and G. P. Sherwood, eds., *Best Plays of 1909–1919,* New York, 1943; B. Mantle, ed., *Best Plays of 1922–23,* Boston, 1923; and "Paul Guilfoyle, Actor, 58, Dies," *New York Times,* June 30, 1961.

Billy J. Harbin

MUNSON, Ona (1906–55), actress, was born in Portland, Oregon. She danced in New York as a child, learned ballet, and performed in vaudeville. Her first major success was singing "Tea for Two" and "I Want To Be Happy" in a traveling company of the musical *No, No, Nanette* in 1925. She took over the role on Broadway the next year. She appeared with Joe E. Brown in *Twinkle, Twinkle* and with Ed Wynn in *Manhattan Mary.* In 1928, she sang "You're the Cream in My Coffee" in *Hold Everything!* which starred Bert Lahr and Victor Moore. In the mid-1930s she played Regina in **Alla Nazimova**'s national tour of Ibsen's *Ghosts.* Her last stage performance was in the New York City Center production of *First Lady* in 1953.

She is best remembered, however, for her work in Hollywood. Following her film debut in *Going Wild* (1930), she played opposite Edward G.

Robinson in *Five Star Final* (1931), one of the year's ten best films and an Oscar nominee for Best Picture. She went on to play Rhett Butler's drinking pal, Belle Watling, in *Gone with the Wind* (1939); a depraved and coldly venomous whorehouse madam in Josef von Sternberg's *Shanghai Gesture* (1941); and featured roles in *The Cheaters* (1945) and *The Red House* (1947). After a major dispute with her studio about the roles she was assigned, her career disintegrated.

While carefully concealing her bisexuality with two "lavender" marriages—to actor-director Eddie Buzzell and designer Eugene Berman—and with a romance with director Ernst Lubitsch, she had affairs with women. One was with "Dorothy A.," perhaps a reference to film director Dorothy Arzner (Ona Munson File, March 1, 1940, and October 13, 1944). Munson was a member of "the sewing circle," a term originated by Alla Nazimova for a clique of lesbians and bisexuals who socialized in Hollywood (Madsen, 14–15).

Just weeks after meeting playwright **Mercedes de Acosta** in 1939, she confessed, "I long to hold you in my arms and pour my love into you" (Ona Munson File, February 26, 1940). Munson rented a new Los Angeles duplex with her mother but told de Acosta there were "completely separate quarters and entrances so that you can visit me any time of day or night without even being seen" (February 20, 1940). In little more than a year, guilt ridden over her bisexuality and fearful that she would be exposed, Munson severed their relationship. Although she admitted that they had "shared the deepest spiritual moment that life brings" and "created an entity as surely as though [we] had conceived and borne a child," she refused to see de Acosta again (qtd. in Vickers, 76).

She gained weight, suffered from depression, and lived much of the time as a recluse in Paris. In 1955, she was found dead in her New York apartment with a suicide note that read: "This is the only way I know to be free again. . . . Please don't follow me" (*New York Times*).

See A. Madsen, *The Sewing Circle: Female Stars Who Loved Other Women,* New York, 1995; Ona Munson File, Mercedes de Acosta Collection, Rosenbach Museum, Philadelphia; *New York Times,* February 12, 1955; R. A. Schanke, *"That Furious Lesbian": The Story of Mercedes de Acosta,* Carbondale, Ill., 2003; and H. Vickers, *Loving Garbo: The Story of Greta Garbo, Cecil Beaton, and Mercedes de Acosta,* New York, 1994.

Robert A. Schanke

NAZIMOVA, Alla (Adelaide Leventon) (1878–1945), actress, was born in Yalta. When she was sixteen, she joined an amateur dramatic society and subsequently studied under Vladimir Nemirovich-Danchenko, who was later to become Stanislavsky's partner at the Moscow Art Theatre. After graduation in 1899, she began acting in the provinces, and there she met Paul Orlenev. They toured Russia with Evgeny Chirikov's *The Jew,* known in this country as *The Chosen People.* But when the pro-Jewish play was censored and they feared possible arrest, she and Orlenev fled to Berlin, London, and then America. On March 22, 1905, they began a year of headline-making performances in New York, Chicago, and Boston. Although the media lauded this intriguing and seemingly married duo, the couple was advised to offer no correction, for their supposed marriage would serve as a convenient cover for their illicit relationship.

When Orlenev and the company returned to Russia to escape creditors, Nazimova remained in New York, having signed a five-year contract with Lee Shubert. After learning English in six months, she opened in the title role of *Hedda Gabler* in November 1906, adding *A Doll's House* two months later and *The Master Builder* the next year. Dozens of articles appeared in major publications, poets penned tributes, and artists painted her portrait. Her fame reached such heights that in 1910 the Shuberts remodeled their 39th Street Theatre and renamed it Nazimova's 39th Street Theatre.

She fascinated her critics with her ability to physically transform herself into widely diverse characters and became known as "the witch of makeup" (*Cleveland Leader*). She hid behind masks in her private life as well and in a letter warned her sister: "Do not confide . . . about anything. . . . I am a mystery for the Americans and that is my biggest advertisement." "One must always be at a pitch and 'acting,'" she confided (Alla Nazimova LC Collection, 1908 and 1912). "Nazimova doesn't live except in the imagination of the public" (Nazimova Interview with Viola Justin, no title, *New York Evening Mail,* n.d.). She submerged herself completely in her roles, and even family members recognized that in her private life she actually became the character of her current play.

The Shuberts, aware of her bisexuality, attempted to dismantle the rumors by creating an image of a dangerous, seductive siren. The roles they gave her to perform in such plays as *The Comet* and *Bella Donna* were more than just strong-willed women; they were neurotic, bizarre, exotic characters of temperamental extremes who created for Nazimova the image of a femme fatale. Theatergoers found her fiery personality, lurid acting, and sinuous beauty electrifying. Her reputation soared, but her fame soon turned to infamy.

Hoping to change her image, she broke her contract and chose to present in vaudeville the antiwar drama *War Brides* (1915). Her acting in the role of a young mother whose husband and brothers have been killed in a senseless war was so successful that Lewis J. Selznick produced a film version and paid her $30,000 for thirty days' work (Spears, 125–27). Her costar was Charles Bryant, a handsome Englishman who had been her male lead in *Bella Donna*. For the next fourteen years, she promoted the rumors that the two were married. Like Orlenev ten years earlier, however, Bryant was a cover whom she hoped would conceal her private life. At the very time of her "lavender" marriage to Bryant, she began an affair with the eccentric **Mercedes de Acosta.**

In 1918, she moved to Hollywood and signed an extraordinary film contract with Metro Pictures that granted her a special production unit as well as approval of stories, directors, and casts. With a guarantee of $13,000 per week with raises, it made her one of the first Hollywood superstars.

She was delighted with what Hollywood had to offer, not only the financial security but also the freedom to pursue her sexual interests more aggressively. At her mansion, The Garden of Alla, she became the doyenne of the lesbian community. Among the intimates at her scandalous house parties, which she called "sewing circles," were such lesbian protégées as Dolly Wilde, Jeanne Acker, June Mathis, and Natacha Rambova. The weekend soirees became so notorious that journalists began hinting of her androgyny. Two of her female lovers at the time were **Eva Le Gallienne** and Dorothy Arzner.

After three consecutive film failures in 1920, she selected *Camille* as her next vehicle and Rudolph Valentino as her leading man. In their scenes together, the usually sensual Nazimova appears aloof, cold, and sexless. Hints of lesbian affection are everywhere. Nazimova's character holds and caresses another woman. Four times they kiss on the mouth. When a man tries to break them up, her character insists: "Take your hands off. She is too good for you." The public was so appalled that Metro terminated her contract, and her role as a Hollywood superstar ended. Desperate to resume her career and continue the sexual freedom she had enjoyed in Hollywood, she invested all her assets in filming *A Doll's House* and *Salome*. The latter was a surreal, expressionistic production with a supposedly all gay cast. Although United Artists promoted it as "an orgy of sex and sin" (Spears, 148–49) with hints of nudity, viewers found it rather innocuous. It wiped out Nazimova's savings and destroyed what was left of her credibility.

Faced with financial ruin, she resurrected once again her image as a dangerous, seductive witch and returned to Broadway in *Dagmar*. When that did not succeed, she returned to vaudeville. Eventually, she joined Eva Le Gallienne's Civic Repertory Theatre in New York City, where she starred in sixty-four sold-out performances of *The Cherry Orchard* (1928).

A true comeback, her acting was praised for its truthfulness and sincerity. In 1930, she joined the prestigious Theatre Guild and starred in its productions of *A Month in the Country, Mourning Becomes Electra,* and *The Good Earth.* Plaguing her during these brighter years, however, was a frightening lawsuit against her with a fine of $30,000 for the wrongful death of a woman hit by her car. To meet her expenses, in 1935 she directed and starred in her own versions of *Ghosts* and in the following season revived *Hedda Gabler,* which played successfully both in New York and on tour.

Her newfound fame was cut short. In late 1938, she underwent major surgery for breast cancer. She returned to Hollywood. But because there was little demand for a sixty-year-old dramatic actress she accepted small roles in such films as *Escape* (1940), *The Bridge of San Luis Rey* (1944), and *In Our Time* (1944). She lived in a spartan apartment above a garage at her former Hollywood estate. Her partner for her last seventeen years was Glesca Marshall, an actress she had met at the Civic Repertory Theatre.

See C. Ashby, "Alla Nazimova and the Advent of the New Acting in America," *Quarterly Journal of Speech* 45 (April 1959): 182–88; *Cleveland Leader,* April 20, 1908; G. Lambert, *Nazimova: A Biography,* New York, 1997; L. O. Lewton, *Alla Nazimova: My Aunt,* Ventura, Calif., 1988; Alla Nazimova Collection, Glesca Marshall Library of Visual Arts, Springer Opera House, Columbus, Ga.; Alla Nazimova Collection, Library of Congress; Alla Nazimova files, Billy Rose Theatre Collection, New York Public Library for the Performing Arts; R. A. Schanke, "The Legend of Alla Nazimova," *Central States Speech Journal* 29 (spring 1978): 36–43; R. A. Schanke, "Alla Nazimova: 'The Witch of Makeup,'" in *Passing Performances: Fuller Readings of Leading Plays in American Theater History,* edited by R. A. Schanke and K. Marra, Ann Arbor, 1998; R. A. Schanke, *"That Furious Lesbian": The Story of Mercedes de Acosta,* Carbondale, 2003; and J. Spears, *The Civil War on the Screen and Other Essays,* South Brunswick, N.J., 1977.

Robert A. Schanke

O'NEIL, Nance (Gertrude Lamson) (1874–1965), actress, was born on October 5, 1874, in Oakland, California. In the summer of 1893, "an awkward, undeveloped girl" went to the Alcazar Theatre, then under the management of McKee Rankin, with a letter of introduction from Peter Robinson, the dramatic critic of the *San Francisco Chronicle.* "Here is a young friend of mine who wants to go on the stage. Kindly discourage her." (Porter, 529). Nevertheless, Rankin, who would become her longtime manager, hired Gertrude to play minor roles at the Alcazar. He began grooming her for a career in the theater by changing her name from Gertrude Lamson to Nance O'Neil, combining the names of Nance (Anne) Oldfield, the eighteenth-century British comedienne, and Eliza O'Neil, the famous tragic actress of the seventeenth century.

By the close of 1897, O'Neil had made her New York debut, gaining positive critical notice from the critics for her performances at the Murray Hill Theatre in *East Lynne* and *True to Life.* Several New York critics saw great potential and predicted that soon Nance O'Neil would be one of America's foremost tragediennes. After such a promising debut, the press was surprised when, instead of capitalizing on O'Neil's success, Rankin arranged for a world tour that would last nearly three years, taking her from Honolulu to Cairo and back again. This tour, taken between 1900 and 1903, was central to O'Neil's legend; for years, she would capitalize on her successes in foreign lands and her reputation as an independent and adventurous explorer. Her company, which included the young Lionel Barrymore (who later married Rankin's daughter) and D. W. Griffith, arrived in South Africa just as the Boer War was ending. The company played in Capetown, Kimberley, and a number of towns on the African coast before moving on to Cairo, where O'Neil was the first American woman to be invited to play at the Khedival, Egypt's national theater. She was also the first American woman to climb to the top of the great pyramid of Cheops.

Despite foreign successes, financial troubles plagued the company and Rankin was constantly embroiled in legal battles concerning money owed to actors, authors, and producers. There were also rumors that he and his young star were sexually involved. In 1903, W. S. Cleveland, manager of the Cleveland Theatre in Chicago, brought suit against O'Neil and Rankin to recover advance expenses for her performances in that city. Cleveland testified that O'Neil had been hypnotized by Rankin and that without his spell she had no talent or independent personality of her own; rather, she owed her entire professional persona to the conjuring of a sinister Svengali. In the public imagination, O'Neil's relationship with Rankin kept slipping into the realm of the unnatural and the bizarre; either she was sexually involved with him, violating feminine decorum, or she was literally out of her mind, controlled by his hypnotic spell. Perceptions of O'Neil's transgressive heterosexuality coupled with accusations of a bizarre insanity may well have prepared the discursive soil in which the later accusations of a pathological lesbianism would take root.

Some of the blame for these accusations may also lie in O'Neil's choice of repertoire, which included many independent women who refused to adhere to societal constraints. When she played roles such as Lady Macbeth, Elizabeth I, Magda, or Hedda Gabler, the negative reviews often gave equal criticism to the actress and the women she essayed to represent.

O'Neil reached the zenith of her popularity during the 1904–5 Boston season. It was there that she met Lizzie Borden, the woman who twelve years earlier had been found not guilty of the murder of her father and stepmother in a trial that had captured the attention of the nation. In 1905, a provocative newspaper item appeared in papers across the country announcing that Lizzie Borden was writing a play for her "warm personal friend" Nance O'Neil (Spiering, 208). Unfortunately, no record of that play is left, but the imagination reels with the possibilities.

During O'Neil's two year stay in Boston, Lizzie paid her legal expenses in several law suits; the reclusive Lizzie even accompanied O'Neil into the courtroom for moral support. After one of the suits had been settled, Lizzie rented a house in the resort town of Tyngsboro so that "she and Nance's company could enjoy a week-long house party." According to those who had been in neighboring cottages, "it was not a noticeably quiet and sober time" (Spiering, 208). Later, when O'Neil decided to buy a summer home in Tyngsboro, Lizzie helped her with the down payment (Spiering, 206; Lincoln, 16). Rumors that the two were involved in a lesbian relationship began to circulate. After one all-night party given for O'Neil and her company at Lizzie's home in Fall River, Emma, Lizzie's sister, left the house and never spoke to Lizzie again.

It is unclear how or when the two women parted company, but by 1906 the bank had foreclosed on O'Neil's Massachusetts home and no more money was forthcoming from Lizzie ("Nance O'Neil Faces Poor Debtor Action"). Perhaps the article that reported Lizzie's playwriting aspirations had placed O'Neil in an awkward position and she, or Rankin, had found it wise to distance herself from someone so notorious. A review of O'Neil's performance as Lady Macbeth in Boston in 1906 was very different in tone from the initial critical praise.

> Miss O'Neil's Lady Macbeth is quite worthy a place in the repertoire of an actress who is a woman of genuine talent, blemished though it undoubtedly has been, either by unskillful training, or *personal perverseness.* ("Tremont Theatre," emphasis added)

There is no explanation as to what the actress's "personal perverseness" might have been, but clearly it was not just Rankin being criticized this time. O'Neil had clearly alienated this reviewer in some way that was not related to her performance. Had her multiple court appearances or her relationship with the acquitted ax murderess ruined her credibility in the eyes of the Boston press? It is hard to say. In any event, her popularity was quick to fade. In November 1906, the actress, who the year before had been all the rage, held a benefit performance to raise money—it was sparsely attended ("Nance O'Neil Benefit"). Four days later, she was in court facing a poor debtor action ("Nance O'Neil Faces Poor Debtor Action"). When she left her home in Tyngsboro, she told a reporter that the New Englanders she had hoped would embrace her had turned judgmental and cold.

O'Neil never recaptured the popularity of her early days in Boston, and despite an attempt by the Shuberts to revitalize her career she was eventually reduced to playing vaudeville, sharing the bill with Miss Kitty, the juggling equestrienne ("Nance O'Neil's First on Vaudeville Bill"). In 1908, she finally split with Rankin, who by this time, according to one critic, was "so fat, he can't act for he can hardly move . . . [and] his voice is so covered from fat and whiskey that he is not intelligible" (Beasley, n.p.). O'Neil had been offered a position in David Belasco's company, and she jumped at the chance to leave her longtime manager. She had a few successes with Belasco, particularly in the role of the spinster Odette in *The Lily,* but her career never regained momentum.

As an unmarried woman working in the theater, O'Neil was vulnerable to intense public scrutiny. In order to escape public censorship, she maintained a difficult balance throughout her career between cherishing her independence and distancing herself from the emancipatory discourse of the New Women. In 1916, at the age of forty-two, she married a former costar, Alfred Hickman. It is unclear why she chose to marry late in her life; perhaps in the waning years of her career she craved a more orthodox existence. Or perhaps by 1916, when relations between women were becoming increasingly stigmatized, she wished to put rumors of her lesbian past to rest once and for all. In any event, Hickman was central to O'Neil's career in its later years. He was her professional collaborator and director; together they adapted the plays of the Spanish playwright Benavente for American audiences, unfortunately without much critical success. Denying rumors of a separation in 1925, O'Neil referred to Hickman as "the dearest and best of pals and collaborators" ("Nance O'Neil Longs for Lighter Roles"), but some evidence of disappointment in marriage can be read in the essay she penned for the magazine *Theatre* in 1920, after four years of wedlock.

Domestic convenience, which has held so many unloved women in the biting chains of their imprisoned souls, seems a great price to pay for very little . . . tradition has made women cowardly. Still, the freedom of all the Magdas of the world has been worthwhile, if only to enlarge the scope of a woman's emotional conquest of her own soul. (O'Neil, "Unloved Woman," 516)

O'Neil and Alfred had no children, and she never remarried after her husband's death. She died in 1965 at the age of ninety. There was no mention of Lizzie Borden in her obituary.

See Nance O'Neil File, Billy Rose Theatre Collection, New York Public Library for the Performing Arts at Lincoln Center; and Nance O'Neil File, Harvard Theatre Collection, Harvard University (hereafter NOF, Harvard). See also D. Beasley, "The Nance O'Neil Company and the Shuberts in 1908," *The Passing Show* (newsletter of the Shubert Archive), spring 1992; V. Lincoln, "Whatever Became of Lizzie Borden?" *Playbill,* October 11, 1967; "Lizzie Borden, Who with Her Sister Was Acquitted of Murder, Is Now an Author," June 5, 1905 (NOF, Harvard); "Nance O'Neil Benefit," May 22, 1906 (NOF, Harvard); "Nance O'Neil Faces Poor Debtor Action," May 26, 1906 (NOF, Harvard); "Nance O'Neil's First on Vaudeville Bill," October 1907 (NOF, Harvard); "Nance O'Neil Longs for Lighter Roles," December 20, 1925 (NOF, Harvard); N. O'Neil, "The Unloved Woman on the Stage," *Theatre,* June 1920; C. Porter, "Boston Discovers Miss Nance O'Neil," *The Critic,* June 1904; F. Spiering, *Lizzie,* New York, 1984; and "Tremont Theatre: Macbeth," unidentified article (NOF, Harvard).

Jennifer Jones Cavenaugh

PATRICK, John (Groggan) (1905–95), playwright and screenwriter, was born in Louisville, Kentucky, on May 17, 1905, with the surname Groggan, which he later dropped. He died, a suicide, in 1995. He grew up in orphanages and set off on his own at the age of fifteen. Studying at Our Lady of the Holy Cross College in New Orleans and at Harvard and Columbia universities, Patrick began his career by turning out scripts for NBC radio in San Francisco from 1933 to 1936. His lucky break came one day in Manhattan's Central Park, where he ran into an actor friend who invited him to attend a cocktail party. There he met the wife of an actor who was busy in Hollywood. The wife wanted her husband back in New York, and she persuaded a wealthy friend to invest in Patrick's play so that her husband could return for the role. That play, Patrick's first, *Hell Freezes Over* (1935), which was also Joshua Logan's first directing assignment on Broadway, was a gloomy tale of seven survivors of a dirigible crash at the South Pole who meet their fates through gangrene, suicide, exposure, and murder. The curtain fell as the last survivor waited to die of starvation. It ran for twenty-five performances and prompted the critic George Jean Nathan to suggest that the author be "tossed into the Hollywood ashcan" (Vallance, 16). Twentieth Century-Fox promptly offered Patrick a job. "In other words," he later joked, "having a bad play on Broadway qualified you as a picture writer" (Oliver, 34).

In Hollywood, Patrick cowrote twenty-four scripts in two and a half years, most of them B movies for Fox, including vehicles for Jane Withers (*The Holy Terror,* 1937), Dolores Del Rio (*International Settlement,*

John Patrick, forty-seven, in the year that his play *Lo and Behold!* opened (1952). (Courtesy of the Billy Rose Theatre Collection, New York Public Library for the Performing Arts.)

1938), the Dionne quintuplets (*Five of a Kind,* 1939), and Peter Lorre (*Mr. Moto Takes a Chance,* 1939). Convinced that he had mastered his craft, he moved to Boston and wrote two more plays, one of which, *The Willow and I,* had a brief Broadway run in 1942. In the same year, he joined the American Field Service, serving as an ambulance driver with the British in North Africa, Syria, India, and Burma. While en route to the United States from Burma he wrote in twelve days (on toilet paper because paper was scarce) his only autobiographical play, *The Hasty Heart.* Produced on Broadway in 1946, *The Hasty Heart* also brought Patrick his first success. Set in a military hospital camp, it concerns a fiercely proud and independent Scot who discovers he is dying and is finally able to make friends with the other inmates. The film version (scripted by Ronald MacDougal) was made in England in 1949 and starred Ronald Reagan and Patricia Neal. With the profits from *The Hasty Heart,* Patrick bought a farm in Suffern, New York, named it "Hasty Hill," and installed every modern convenience. When he applied to the local authorities for an extra power line, their continual negligence so angered him that he armed himself with a chain saw and threatened to cut down an elm tree on the lawn of the power company's president.

Such anger also extended to rehearsals of his work, where Patrick referred to his outbursts as "anger that I have to generate and use as a whip to drive myself" (Vallance, 16). His next two plays, *The Story of Mary Seurat* (1947), which starred Dorothy Gish, and *The Curious Savage* (1950), were flops, though the latter went on to contribute almost $700,000 to the author's income from regional productions during his lifetime. His biggest success came in 1953 when actor-producer Maurice Evans, who had long owned the rights to Vern Sneider's novel *Teahouse of the August Moon,* asked Patrick to write the stage adaptation of the fictional story of the U.S. Army's effort to establish a democracy in a village on Okinawa during World War II. Evans himself wanted to play the central character of the wily interpreter Sakini, but Evans and Patrick were soon battling over the show's conception and characters. Evans eventually decided against playing Sakini, and David Wayne was cast in the part of the lovable rogue who is constantly confiding in the "lovely ladies, kind gentlemen" of the audience, with John Forsythe as the American captain. Patrick also feuded with the director, Robert Lewis, who wanted to change some dialogue, and hostilities did not end with the show's triumphant opening at the Martin Beck Theater in October 1953. Although the play was praised by Brooks Atkinson in the *New York Times* as "not only amusing, but enchanting, and perhaps illuminating as well" (qtd. in Pace, B17), when Evans arrived for the first-night party he found a glass of champagne hurtling through the air to shatter on the wall behind him. "Fortunately," he said later, "the attacker was not armed with a chainsaw" (Vallance, 16). The play won the Pulitzer Prize, the Tony, the New York Critics Circle Award, the Aegis Club Award, and the Donaldson Award. It ran for 1,027 performances on Broadway and was produced in more than thirty countries. The film version, written by Patrick and starring Marlon Brando and Glenn Ford, lacked the play's lightness and simplicity but was nonetheless successful.

In 1953, Patrick returned to Fox. Hollywood had nominated him for an Oscar in 1946 for his original screenplay for *The Strange Love of Martha Ivers,* a film noir starring Barbara Stanwyck, and he had written the story for *Framed* (1947), a typical 1940s thriller of a rover (Glenn Ford) duped by a beautiful blonde (Janis Carter). A succession of big budget movies followed in the 1950s: *The President's Lady* (1953), with Charlton Heston as Andrew Jackson and Susan Hayward as his wife, and two gigantic Cinemascope hits, *Three Coins in the Fountain* (1954), about three American office girls finding romance in Rome, and *Love Is a Many Splendored Thing* (1955), from Han Suyin's autobiographical novel of a Eurasian girl's ill-fated affair with an American war correspondent. At MGM, he adapted Philip Barry's *The Philadelphia Story* into a musical, *High Society* (1956), which starred Bing Crosby, Frank Sinatra, and Grace Kelly, and he won the Screen Writers Guild award for his witty screenplay for *Les Girls* (1957), about three showgirls who tell a jury their own version of their relationship with their male partner, who was played by Gene Kelly in his last screen musical. Patrick also adapted James Jones's sprawling novel *Some Came Running* (1958) and Paul Osborne's play *The World of Suzie Wong* (1961). His final film credits were *Gigot* (1962), with Jackie Gleason as a deaf-mute; *The Main Attraction* (1963), a musical drama; and *The Shoes of the Fisherman* (1968), a lengthy version of Morris L. West's novel about a Russian pope.

Patrick wrote about sixty plays, most of which championed the good guy who remained tenacious while fighting off evil forces. Many are popular with repertory companies, particularly *Everybody Loves Opal* (1962), a favorite of middle-aged actresses. An ill-fated musical version of *Teahouse of the August Moon,* entitled *Lovely Ladies, Kind Gentlemen,* ran for only two weeks on Broadway in 1970.

For some years, Patrick lived with a longtime companion at his farm, which he proclaimed maintained his sense of values. "If things go well, I go to work at the typewriter," he once said. "If not, I get out the tractor" (Vallance, 16). According to one of the British newspaper accounts of his death, the lack of success in his later years did not contribute to his suicide, "Nor was his homosexuality ever a problem. He had a companion living with him for a long period, and was always lively and amusing company" (Bergan, 17). Later Patrick also lived on a former sugar plantation in St. Thomas, where one of his neighbors was Robert Ludlum. Patrick filed suit against Ludlum for stealing his idea for the popular novel *The Road to Gandolfo,* which involves kidnapping the pope. The two settled out of court in 1994. In 1980 in St. Thomas, Patrick met two schoolteachers, Brad Strauman and Steve Rehl, who eventually became like family to him. Strauman and Rehl moved to Florida with Patrick four years before his death. "I think the fact that old age was catching up to him was more than he could handle," Strauman told the *Palm Beach Post* about the author's suicide on November 7, 1995 (Lomartire, 1A). At the age of ninety, Patrick was found dead with a plastic bag over his head at an assisted living facility in Delray Beach, Florida, where he had lived for two years. A poem he had written entitled "A Suicide Note" was found at his side: "I won't dispute my right to die; / I'll only give the reasons why; / You reach a certain point in time / When life has lost reason and rhyme" (1A).

See R. Bergan, "An Old Stager," *The Guardian,* October 10, 1995; G. Bordman, *American Musical Theatre,* New York, 1978; H. Erstein, "Playwright Recalls Heyday in Theater," *Palm Beach Post,* September 11, 1994; R. Gardner, "Playwright Holds His Audience Dear," *Sun-Sentinel,* September 2, 1994; P. Lomartire, "'August Moon' Playwright John Patrick Takes His Life," *Palm Beach Post,* November 9, 1995; M. Oliver, "John Patrick, Playwright, Screenwriter, Won Pulitzer," *Los Angles Times,* November 10, 1995; E. Pace, "John Patrick, Pulitzer Winner for 'Teahouse,' Is Dead at 90," *New York Times,* November 9, 1995; T. Vallance, "Obituary: John Patrick," *The Independent,* December 4, 1995; and "Suit against Novelist Is Settled Out of Court," *New York Times,* December 12, 1994.

Jameson Currier

PATRICK, Robert (Robert Patrick O'Connor) (1937–), playwright, director, and actor,

was born on September 27, 1937, in Kilgore, Texas. His father, Robert Henderson O'Connor, found migrant work as an oil field worker and electrical lineman. The family traveled throughout the Southwest in the Depression era during Patrick's youth; he attended twelve different schools in one year due to the continual movement. The only constant was the pop culture media—radio, records, films, and magazines—that the young Patrick eagerly absorbed and which he credits with forming his artistic aesthetic.

As a child, Patrick concocted amateur theatricals with his playmates and also drew comic books and wrote verse. He attended Eastern New Mexico University for two years, taking theater and English classes, and then joined the U.S. Air Force in San Antonio. He lasted through eight weeks of basic training but was discharged when his homosexual orientation became evident. Because he felt there must be something wrong with him because he did not seem to fit in anywhere, he sought help at the New Mexico State Mental Hospital in Las Vegas. Kept under observation for exactly two weeks, the doctors told him there was nothing wrong that a move to a large city wouldn't cure. As Patrick says: "I was kicked out of the Air Force for being gay and out of the mental hospital for being sane" (interview with author, November 1995).

Through friends, Patrick became involved in a summer stock company in Maine, where he learned stagecraft. In 1961, after the season ended, he took a Greyhound bus to Manhattan. In his first hour in New York, he followed a Salvation Army band to Greenwich Village, where he noticed an attractive young man. Following the boy, Patrick was led to a small coffeehouse on Cornelia Street, the Caffe Cino—the seminal Off-Off-Broadway theater. The boy turned out to be John Dodd, the theater's lighting designer. Patrick began to hang out at the Cino, doing odd jobs and working as the doorman. He also took temporary typing jobs—including one filling out autopsy forms—as the major source of his income. He reveled in the furtive New York gay scene and has written of his experiences: "Bars and baths prospered. . . . Anonymous sex was the rule because people who couldn't face themselves couldn't face each other" (*Untold Decades,* xv).

Buoyed by the creative example set by such fledgling playwrights as Sam Shepard and **Lanford Wilson,** who staged their first plays at the Cino, Patrick tried his own hand at composition. His initial effort, *The Haunted Host,* was originally rejected, unread, by the Caffe's producer, **Joe Cino,** until the other playwrights staged a protest on Patrick's behalf. The play, which Patrick admits was loosely based on the relationship between Cino and one of the Caffe's hangers-on, is about a gay playwright who exorcises the ghost of his dead lover when a straight boy, the lover's spitting image, invades his apartment. Patrick cast himself in order to get the play on, intending to use the stage name, Robert Patrick, as actor and his real name, Bob O'Connor, as playwright. The names were inadvertently switched on the program, however, and his plays have been produced under that nom de plume ever since.

The Haunted Host was a success in its initial run, and it has also received numerous major revivals, most notably with Harvey Fierstein performing his first nondrag role, in 1975. Patrick wrote a half dozen plays for the Cino, till it closed in 1968, and then moved his site of operations to Norman "Speedy" Hartman's Old Reliable Theatre Tavern, where he was to become the most produced playwright of Off-Off-Broadway. He was so prolific that scripts for at least twenty of the plays he wrote during that period have been lost; he also quips that if he'd been more sexually active he might not have written so many plays. *Camera Obscura, Joyce Dynel* (winner of the Show Business Award for Best Off-Off-Broadway Play of 1968–69), *Mercy Drop,* and *The Arnold Bliss Show* were some of his early successes; about a third of his early plays, Patrick estimates, had overtly gay content.

In 1973, Patrick left New York disgusted with the stagnation and overcommercialization of Off-Off-Broadway, and began traveling widely to promote his own plays and theater in general. With money derived from royalties on a year-long run of *The Haunted Host* at the Drama Shelter in Chicago (of which he was vice president), he traveled to Britain. The success of his play *Kennedy's Children* (which was partly based on his

Cino experiences) in London in 1974 led to international acclaim and the Glasgow Citizens' Theatre World Playwriting Award. The New York production, directed by Clive Donner and starring Shirley Knight, also enjoyed considerable success and toured widely. *Kennedy's Children* was subsequently translated into a dozen languages and performed worldwide.

In 1976, Patrick became affiliated with the International Thespians Society, an organization dedicated to bringing theater to school-age children worldwide, writing extensively about his experiences and publishing his new work in its *Dramatics* magazine. He has said: "I thought how wonderful I would have felt if some famous person had come around talking to us when I was in high school. I wanted to be the kind of person I wish I had met" (interview with author, November 1995). He received the society's Founders Award in 1980 for his services "to theater and to youth."

Among Patrick's other successful gay-themed plays are *T-shirts* (1976); *Michaelangelo's Models* (1981), subtitled *An Historical Romantic Fantasia; Blue Is for Boys* (1983), the first play about gay teenagers, in recognition of which two consecutive Manhattan Borough presidents declared Blue Is for Boys weekends in New York in 1983 and 1986; *The Trial of Socrates* (1986), the first gay play produced by the city of New York; *Untold Decades* (1988), seven one acts, each set in a separate decade from the 1920s through the 1980s, which showed the changes in gay culture through the ages; *Un-tied States* (1990), an ambitious compendium of fifty brief scenes, each set in a different state of the union; *Evan of Earth* (1991), an AIDS comedy; and *Bread Alone* (1993), about a gay teacher's influence on a closeted student. His major nongay plays include *Play-by-Play* (1975), *Mutual Benefit Life* (1978), and *My Cup Ranneth Over* (1980).

In 1986, Patrick began work on a 460-page novel called *Temple Slave* about his (fictionalized) early experiences at the Cino and elsewhere, which was completed and published in 1994. In 1996 he received the Robert Chesley Award for Lesbian and Gay Playwriting. He has also completed a sequel about his subsequent adventures in the theater entitled *Echo.* He now lives in Los Angeles and continues his prolific output and commitment to gay theater. Among his recent projects are television screenplays for *High Tide* and *Robin's Hoods,* a 1930s-style shipboard romantic musical commissioned by the Denver Center Theater; *All At Sea,* for which he contributed the script, lyrics, and music; and a musicalization of *Blue Is for Boys,* subtitled *The Bugger's Opera.*

See D. Crespy, *Off-Off-Broadway Explosion,* New York, 2003; K. Furtado and N. Hellner, eds., *Gay and Lesbian American Plays,* Metuchen, N.J., 1993; W. Hoffman, ed., *Gay*

Plays: The First Collection, New York, 1979; R. Patrick, *Mercy Drop and Other Plays,* New York, 1979; R. Patrick, *Temple Slave,* New York, 1994; R. Patrick, *Untold Decades,* New York, 1988; A. Poland and B. Mailman, *The Off Off Broadway Book,* New York, 1972; and *Robert Patrick's Cheep Theatricks,* New York, 1972.

Douglas W. Gordy

PIERCE, Charles (ca. 1926–1999), male actress, has been called "La Superba of Transvestivania" and hailed as "undoubtedly the top femme impersonator in U.S. showbiz" (Cart., 93). In a career spanning five decades and encompassing virtually all media and performance venues, Pierce has taken the most clichéd female impersonator trope—donning the gowns and hairstyles of flamboyant, often aging movie actresses—and spun it into zany, high-camp reflections on the duality of gender. His "basic persona [as] a kind of glamorous, haggard Auntie Mame who wears sleek evening gowns and makes fast, worldly chitchat," served not only as a springboard for a VIP list of gay icons (Bette Davis, Gloria Swanson, Joan Crawford, Katharine Hepburn, and Mae West most prominently) but allows him to "reveal himself, commenting on the gay life, on transvestism and the pain behind it" (Durbin, 109). In comparing Pierce's work to that of two other gay artists, one critic observed: "[Nöel] Coward and [Somerset] Maugham both attempt to mask their profoundest feelings in realistic conventions, while Pierce's impersonations take us deeper into the true nature of his sexuality" (Wetzsteon, 90).

A disc jockey and radio announcer by the age of sixteen in his hometown of Watertown, New York, Pierce migrated to the West Coast after high school and attended the Pasadena Playhouse. He later acted and stage managed in summer stock and Off-Broadway plays and performed as a monologist at San Francisco's Chi Chi Club.

Influenced by female impersonator Arthur Blake, who performed in a tuxedo (full drag being illegal at that time), Pierce began performing his female film star impressions at private parties in Los Angeles. He later noted: "The original premise of my act was to take a dramatic actress and make them [*sic*] do an act in a nightclub" (*New York Post,* Davis, 63). His career as a female impersonator was launched on September 28, 1954, at the Club LaVie in Altadena, California, north of Los Angeles. At first, he performed in a tuxedo or black trousers and turtleneck, not only in observance of the law but also for convenience of packing and traveling. His first drag appearance and the genesis of his later, elaborately costumed act, came in 1955 at Miami Beach's Echo Club, where he rolled up his pants and donned a dress over his male attire for a performance.

Pierce's reputation over the next two decades was established largely on the West Coast, where his iconoclastic performances—combining elements of stand-up comedy, song and dance, improvisation, puppetry, and dramatic acting—gained him further acclaim. A series of successful club engagements in San Francisco culminated in a record-breaking six-year run at the Gilded Cage. Pierce's comedy routines and one-liners—particularly those involving imaginary feuds between Bette Davis and Joan Crawford or **Tallulah Bankhead** entered the lexicon of contemporary gay humor. Bette on Tallulah: "She had the only blood test in town that came back with an olive!" Bette on Joan: "We must speak good of the dead. She's dead? Good!" Many of Pierce's notices of the period, particularly in the nongay press, reflect a matter-of-fact homophobic response to the gay camp sensibility of his act: "Pierce is, down under, tenderloin, gay bar dirty and a lot of his camp homo material will go right past straight ringsiders" (Hard., 88). Nevertheless, his popularity moved beyond a core gay audience, and he became a particular favorite of theater professionals.

In 1970, *The Charles Pierce Review,* a short film featuring cabaret footage of the star, appeared on a double bill with a soft-core porn film, *Meat/Rack,* at a Manhattan gay male theater. In 1971, Pierce was cast as Helen, the mother, in an otherwise "straight" production of a play entitled *Geese* at San Francisco's Encore Theatre. In 1974, Pierce brought his gallery of impressions to new venues and extended the scope of his work as a "male actress." First, he performed in concert at Los Angeles's Dorothy Chandler Pavilion. He then starred as Margo Channing in a San Francisco production of *Applause,* a musical adaptation of the film *All about Eve,* with Pierce in the role created first on screen by Bette Davis and later in the musical by Lauren Bacall. His performance as Margo was particularly noteworthy as a dramatic characterization within the scope of a conventional production rather than as a comedic drag impersonation.

The year was capped by the star making his long-delayed New York debut when *The Charles Pierce Show* opened Christmas night at the Top of the Gate. The widely praised show was eventually extended for a five-month run and earned Pierce an Obie Award. *New York Times* critic Clive Barnes raved: "What he does is to caricature these ladies with slashing histrionic flashes of insight" (25). In commenting on Pierce's now legendary Bette Davis impersonation, he observed: "What you see is not a playback of Bette Davis . . . but the living equivalent of an Al Hirschfeld cartoon" (25). Pierce also introduced a delightful new highlight of his act, "The Living Dolls," in which his head (crowned with a variety of wigs and headdresses) was placed atop puppets, whose limbs he manipulated.

Following this success, British impresario Harold Fielding presented Pierce in his London debut at the Fortune Theatre, where the *London Observer* compared the American-born impersonator to British drag star Danny LaRue: "Mr. Pierce is quite free of the single-track hypocrisy of Danny LaRue whose humour consists of nudging you about how butch he really is" (Cushman, 23). During this period, Pierce also brought his drag characterizations to commercial television with appearances on several popular dramatic and situation comedy series.

By the 1980s, Pierce had become a fixture on the New York/Los Angeles/San Francisco nightclub and concert circuit, and he began humorously billing many of his appearances as "farewells." His performances during this period were captured in the 1988 video release *Charles Pierce at the Ballroom.* Pierce's final "farewell" nightclub appearances took place throughout 1988, and at year's end he appeared in a high-profile supporting role as Bertha Vanation in the film version of Harvey Fierstein's long-running play *Torch Song Trilogy.*

Following the death of Bette Davis in 1989, Pierce was deluged with requests to return to nightclubs and revive his most popular impersonation, and another round of appearances resulted. By now, his career had seen the pre-Stonewall world of marginalized, camp, theatrical presentation give way to a postliberation acceptance of gay humor and performance. Far from marking him obsolete, the mainstreaming of gender illusion in popular culture brought Pierce new cachet as the grand dame of drag. Always pragmatic, and uncomfortable with elaborate theorizing, he explained his art simply: "I'm a stand-up comic in an evening gown . . . some people prefer 'impersonator' . . . illusionist or 'star impressionist.' I don't care, although my own personal favorite is 'male actress'" (*New York Post,* Ervolino, 21). During the 1994 Stonewall Celebration, writer and drag artiste Charles Busch hosted *Dressing Up!*— a "who's who" of drag—at Town Hall in New York. Charles Pierce's reception that night, by both the audience and his younger colleagues, was an outpouring of affection, pride, and respect for one of the best-loved and most admired practitioners of a frequently dismissed theatrical art.

Charles Pierce died of cancer at his home in Toluca Lake, California, on May 31, 1999.

See C. Barnes, "Stage: Women, Wittily," *New York Times,* January 29, 1975; Cart., "One-Man Show," *Variety,* November 19, 1986; R. Cushman, "Charles Pierce Review," *London Observer,* November 9, 1975; C. Davis, "On Stage Pierce Is Something Else," *New York Post.* June 18, 1982; K. Durbin, "Female Impersonators: The Great Escape," *Village Voice,* February 25, 1975; B. Ervolino, "Pierce Encore Is a Sure Bette," *New York Post,* March 27, 1990; K. Garfield, "Charles Pierce: A Legend Steps from Stage to Screen," *The Advocate,* January 31, 1989; J. Hammond, "So Many Women, So Little Time: An Interview with Charles Pierce," *New York Native,* October 17, 1988; Hard., "Charles Pierce Review," *Variety,* August 4, 1971; F. M. Moore, *Drag! Male and Female Impersonators on Stage, Screen, and Television: An Illustrated World History,* Jefferson, N.C., 1994; Charles Pierce Clippings File, Billy Rose Theatre Collection, New York Public Library for the Performing Arts; and R. Wetzsteon, "Private Wives: The Disguises of Sex," *Village Voice,* April 28, 1975.

Kevin Winkler

PLATT, Livingston (1874–?), designer, is perhaps best known for his set and costume designs for Margaret Anglin. They collaborated on many productions, including four plays by Shakespeare that toured the United States (1913–14); three were presented in repertory in New York. These productions represented a significant introduction of the New Stagecraft to the American stage. Mary Henderson, for one, cites Platt as one of the first to bring home from Europe the ideas and practices of the new movement (202). Platt and Anglin continued their collaboration with a series of revivals of Greek plays, and Platt designed on Broadway through 1933. Despite his achievements, he remains an obscure figure in American theater history.

Livingston Platt was born in 1874 in Plattsburgh, New York, a member of the family for whom the town is named. *Theatre* (August 1915, 83) reported that he was a talented painter, studied abroad, and exhibited his paintings at the Paris Salon. After deciding that stage design was his chief interest, he moved to Bruges, Belgium, and in 1903 he began work in a theater there.

In 1911, Mrs. Lyman Gale engaged Platt to design for the Toy Theatre in Boston, where, according to the *New York Dramatic Mirror* (May 29, 1913), he accomplished "scenic miracles." Feinsod says that the thirty-four plays he designed there "contributed significantly to stage simplification in the American theatre" (109). From there, Platt went to Boston's Castle Square Theatre. Recognizing manager John Craig's energetic force in theater, the *New York Dramatic Mirror* observed that "by far the most daring of Mr. Craig's ventures is his recent appointment of Livingston Platt as scenic designer of the Castle Square." Once there, Platt designed *The Comedy of Errors, Hamlet,* and *A Midsummer Night's Dream* (*Theatre,* August 1915, 83). During this period he also assisted George Pierce Baker in the setting and lighting of plays produced by Baker's Harvard Workshop (Kinne, 180). In 1913, Margaret Anglin saw Platt's *Comedy of Errors* (Platt said of the set: "I had only a cyclorama lit in hot yellow, a single sail showing above a wall of yellow" [*Theatre,* April 1916,

Livingston Platt, in about 1914, the year he designed Margaret Anglin's Shakespearean season. (From *Theatre*, August, 1915. Courtesy of the Billy Rose Theatre Collection, New York Public Library for the Performing Arts.)

219]) and engaged him to design four Shakespearean productions: *The Taming of the Shrew, Twelfth Night, As You Like It,* and *Antony and Cleopatra.* The *New York Dramatic Mirror* reported: "Miss Anglin believes he [Platt] is to become our Gordon Craig or Max Reinhardt" (June 18, 1913).

In the years that followed, the reviews of Anglin's productions usually included praise of Platt's scene designs. John LeVay, her biographer, quotes the *New York Times* on *Twelfth Night* in Anglin's Shakespeare season of 1913–14: "As for the setting . . . it is impossible to speak with anything but the greatest enthusiasm" (147). LeVay also quotes Clayton Hamilton's *Vogue* (May 1914) review of the same season, which mentions the beauty of Platt's design as well as its practicality for touring: "In the *Shrew,* for example, [Platt] suggests the gorgeous richness of the Renaissance in scenery so light in structure it may be shifted in ten seconds and packed without damage in a traveling trunk" (150–51). Platt not only designed the Anglin productions, but he seems usually to have been present for their mounting. For a 1925 summer production of *Electra* in Saint Louis, Anglin arrived to find Platt and her company awaiting her. However, Anglin's stage manager, Jerome Collamore, writing to her biographer, John LeVay, in 1985, said that Platt was sometimes distracted from production work, such as during the mounting of *Hippolytus,* by his interest in an attractive young man. Platt remained a friend of Anglin and of her husband, Howard Hull, long after he had stopped designing plays for her. Hull, in a letter to his wife, described his own role as host and server of drinks during the visits of Platt and friends as "watering the pansies" (private collection of LeVay).

Platt gave to the young **Alfred Lunt,** who had been acting at the Castle Square, a letter of introduction to Margaret Anglin, for whom Lunt had a great admiration. Anglin invited Lunt to join her company of *Beverly's Balance* (which Platt had designed) in 1915 (Brown, 66–67), and he remained for additional productions. Later that year he appeared with her in *Iphigenia in Aulis, Electra,* and *Medea.* In his biography of the Lunts, Jared Brown notes that for a silent role in *Electra,* as the leader of a procession, Anglin asked that Lunt suggest decadence "bordering on the obscene." Brown says that at the next rehearsal Lunt "entered with his arms draped suggestively around two young boys, all of them drunk and all of them made up with painted fingernails and toenails" (69). Maurice Zolotow describes the same incident but adds that "Alfred gilded his hair and his nipples, painted his fingers and toenails red and draped vine leaves in his hair" (45). He describes the "assistant deviates" as having the same makeup. Neither Brown nor Zolotow mentions Platt, but since, as

Brown says, "Lunt's benefactor, Livingston Platt, was hired to design the properties, costumes, and stage machinery" (68), surely Lunt asked Platt for advice or perhaps Platt insisted on giving it. Sam Abel cites the scene as evidence that Lunt "knew enough about sexuality between two men to evoke homoerotic images, and to perform them in public" (183). The older Platt probably knew more.

Platt did not, apparently, give up everything for the New Stagecraft. In 1919, he designed a production praised by David Belasco that celebrated the hundredth anniversary of the founding of the Methodist missions. *The Wayfarer,* a "mammoth religious spectacle," was staged in New York's Madison Square Garden (Kahan). In 1926, **George Kelly,** one of the most distinguished playwrights on Broadway (he had that year won the Pulitzer Prize for *Craig's Wife,* produced in the previous season), chose Platt to do the sets for his next three plays: *Daisy Mayme* (1926), *Behold the Bridegroom* (1927), and *Maggie the Magnificent* (1929). Both Livingston Platt and George Kelly were homosexuals. That Kelly engaged Platt to design three plays over a four-year period suggests that they knew, or came to know, each other very well, but neither Platt nor Kelly left records of their relationship.

Mary Henderson notes that "From 1923 to 1933, Platt designed six or seven plays a year" (203). In some years, there were more. Orville Larson calculated that Platt designed sixteen plays in 1927, ten in 1932, and nine in 1933, his last year of recorded productions (297). Henderson singles out *Dinner at Eight* (1932) as having "a most stylish set, all done in Art Deco. A turntable stage used almost cinematically effected rapid changes of scene" (203).

Platt disappeared from the theater, and some thought from life, in 1933. The *New York Times* reported on October 19 of that year that "Joseph P. Bickerton, Jr., Platt's attorney, a well-known theatrical lawyer, had received a note from his client saying that there was no need to represent him in court, as he would be dead." The court date, the *Times* noted, was "to answer a charge of impairing the morals of a minor." The exact nature of the charge is not clear. LeVay believes that Platt was charged with homosexual soliciting but was acquitted. Whatever Platt had in mind when he wrote to Bickerton, according to LeVay, Platt did not commit suicide but "spent a couple of years painting in Belgium" and then returned, "heavily bearded," to New York (Collamore). Margaret Anglin told Jerome Collamore that Platt, once in New York, moved in with the dancer-choreographer Edwin Strawbridge, who died in 1957 (*New York Times,* October 31, 1957; Collamore, letter to LeVay, n.d.). Platt's date and place of death are not known.

See S. Abel, "Staging Heterosexuality," in *Passing Performances: Queer Readings of Leading Players in American Theater History,* 1998, edited by R. A. Schanke and Kim Marra, Ann Arbor, 1998, 175–96; G. Bordman, *American Theatre: A Chronicle of Comedy and Drama, 1914–1930,* New York, 1995; J. Brown, *The Fabulous Lunts,* New York, 1986; J. Collamore, letters in the private collection of John LeVay; A. Feinsod, *The Simple Stage,* New York, 1992; M. C. Henderson, *Theater in America,* New York, 1996; G. Kahan, "*The Wayfarer,* an American Religious Pageant," *Players,* April-May 1972; W. P. Kinne, *George Pierce Baker and the American Theatre,* Cambridge, Mass., 1954; O. K. Larson, *Scene Design in the American Theatre from 1915–1960,* Fayetteville, Ark., 1989; J. LeVay, *Margaret Anglin: A Stage Life,* Toronto, 1989; H. K. Moderwell, *The Theatre of Today,* New York, 1923; *New York Times,* "Strawbridge Dead, Led Child's Theatre," October 31, 1957; and M. Zolotow, *Stagestruck,* New York, 1965.

Joseph Kissane

PORTER, Cole (1891–1964), composer and lyricist, was born in Peru, Indiana, the only child of Kate (Cole) Porter, daughter of one of central Indiana's wealthiest families, and Samuel Fenwick Porter, the shy druggist whom she had married. Kate and her wealthy father, J. O. Cole, became the dominant influences in the young Cole Porter's life. He was raised in as regal an environment as rural Indiana could afford and educated privately in literature, French, dancing, piano, and violin. Despite his grandfather's objections, Kate sent Cole to Worcester Academy in Massachusetts in 1905. He rarely returned to Indiana. He graduated from Worcester in 1909 and entered Yale University in the fall of that year.

The slender and gregarious freshman became one of the best-known members of his class. He gravitated almost at once to a group of upperclassmen who were very much like himself: wealthy, homosexual, and devoted to theater, music, and wit. Cole's lifelong friendships with **Monty Woolley** and Leonard Hanna date from this period. Charles Schwartz, who in 1977 published the first honest biography of Porter, speculates that his homosexual activities may have begun in his first year at Yale or that he may simply have continued and expanded a hidden way of life that he began at the all-male Worcester Academy. Porter took steps to gain proximity to the Yale football team: he was elected cheerleader and chairman of the football song selection committee and composed five "fight songs" that have become Yale classics. Porter wrote more than three hundred songs while at Yale, most of them for original musicals staged by his fraternity (Delta Kappa Epsilon) or the Yale Dramatic Association.

After his graduation from Yale in the spring of 1913, Cole obeyed his grandfather and enrolled in Harvard Law School, but he soon changed his registration to the music school and applied himself modestly to a program in theory and harmony. In 1915, two songs that he had written for Yale shows were incorporated into the Broadway musicals *Hands Up* and *Miss Information.* Neither show was commercially successful, but Porter's work had by this time attracted the interest of **Elisabeth Marbury,** a wealthy socialite and lesbian who was influential in the Broadway scene as an agent and producer. Marbury arranged for Porter to collaborate with his former Yale classmate Lawrason Riggs on a Broadway musical called *See America First*—a satire of patriotic musicals and devised in the same rollicking, farcical style that had delighted the Yale students. The show opened on March 28, 1916, but ran for only fifteen performances.

Porter's penchant for inventive autobiography only grew in the confused environment of World War I. What he actually did after the failure of *See America First* was to take a Manhattan flat and enjoy the city's social scene until July 1917, when he sailed to France as part of a "relief mission" organized by socialite Nina Larre Smith Duryea, whom he served as personal assistant. Porter lived alone in Paris in a comfortably furnished home on the Place Vendôme. The myth of his war years is far more glamorous. He told various versions of this story over the years, the main theme being that he was so distraught over the failure of his first Broadway show that he fled to France and immediately signed up with the French Foreign Legion. On other occasions, he told interviewers that he was a member of the regular French army or that he had been part of the American Aviation Forces in France. Charles Schwartz's search of French and American military records showed that, in spite of Porter's frequent appearance on the streets of Paris in the uniforms of various branches of the military, and of various ranks, he had never been a member of any army anywhere.

While in Paris, Porter met Linda Lee Thomas, a wealthy socialite known for her exquisite taste and manners. The two struck up a friendship at once, and on December 18, 1919, they were married in Paris. They saw in one another the perfect match: Porter adored Linda's elegance and wealth at a time when he was dependent on his grandfather's allowance; she found in Porter a witty and youthful companion (she was eight years his senior) who made no sexual demands. Brendan Gill, who knew them both, acknowledged the frequently voiced theory that Linda was a lesbian, but he thought it more likely that Linda had simply had enough of "the sexual side of marriage" because of the sexual sadism of her former husband (Gill, xv). Whatever the facts of her sexuality, she and Porter were devoted companions for the rest of their lives. Porter's sexuality was certainly no secret from his wife. Both were open-minded, sexually liberated people who enjoyed one another's company. Linda's many friends, a majority of whom were gay or lesbian, soon became Cole's friends, and beginning as early as 1920 the Porters spent much of their lives traveling around the world or entertaining in the company of gay men such as Nöel Coward, Jack Wilson, Howard Sturges, and Monty Woolley and lesbians such as Elsa Maxwell, Anne Morgan, **Elsie de Wolfe,** and Elisabeth Marbury.

As in his lyrics, so often built around a series of double entendres, Porter constructed his life in layers: the private facts kept just for an insider's coterie behind a public mask of conventionality and sentimental romance. The doubleness was not simply facilitated by the media but was nearly forced on gays and lesbians before Stonewall. By the time Porter had achieved prominence as one of America's leading theatrical composers in the 1930s, virtually everyone in show business knew that he was a homosexual. Yet not one word was published or broadcast about his sexual identity until Brendan Gill included the subject in a biographical essay in the *New Yorker* in 1971—seven years after the composer's death. The height of heterosexual media fantasy was in the bizarre spectacle of *Night and Day,* the 1946 Warner Brothers film "biography" that presented Cary Grant playing Cole as a wounded war hero, Alexis Smith portraying Linda Thomas as a volunteer army nurse, and Monty Woolley as himself, yet a self somehow transformed into a heterosexual law professor. During his later years, when the film began to be shown on television, Porter was said to roar with laughter at its absurdities. Still he collaborated wholeheartedly in the project, approving the script and casting, as well as negotiating a $300,000 payment for the rights to what was supposed to be his life story (Schwartz, 215).

By the time of the release of *Night and Day* in 1946, Porter was at the top of his profession as a composer and lyricist for theater and film. His sophistication and skill developed greatly during the 1920s as he wrote songs for vaudeville-style reviews such as *Greenwich Village Follies* (1924) and *Paris* (1928). His reputation as a witty artist was bolstered by such songs as "Let's Do It" (1928), "Let's Misbehave" (1927), "I've Got a Crush on You" (1929), and "You Do Something to Me" (1929). He proved his talent for ballads with songs such as "What Is This Thing Called Love?" (1929), "Love for Sale" (1930), and "Night and Day" (1932). His first smash hit came in 1934, in his collaboration with Howard Lindsay and Russel Crouse on the Guy Bolton and P. G. Wodehouse story for *Anything Goes.* This show launched Porter's long association with Ethel Merman, whom he considered the outstanding stage singer of his time. In addition to the title song, which became something of a Porter signature tune, his score included such songs as "I Get a Kick Out of You," "You're the Top," and "Blow Gabriel Blow." The composer followed up this success with memorable songs for some forgettable shows: "Begin the Beguine" and "Just One of Those Things" for *Jubilee* (1935), "It's De-Lovely" for *Red, Hot and Blue!* (1936), "At Long Last Love" for *You'll Never Know* (1938), and "My Heart Belongs to Daddy" for *Leave It to Me* (1938). During the 1930s, Porter also began his long relationship with Hollywood, completing scores for such films as *Born to Dance* (1936) and *Rosalie* (1937).

The income from Porter's songs, shows, and films added to his and Linda's already ample fortune. Porter had inherited income-producing forest lands, gas fields, and coal mines when his grandfather died in 1923. These multiple incomes allowed the Porters to live in very high style, dividing their time between a vast suite on the Lido, a series of fabulous Renaissance palaces in Venice, two adjoining apartments at the Waldorf in New York, and—beginning in the 1930s—a rented estate in Hollywood. The Porters were forced to give up their home in Venice as the result of a 1927 police raid on their home, the Palazzo Rezzonico, in which a group of local teenaged boys were discovered dressed up in Linda's clothing and parading before Porter and several gay friends. The incident would have simply been overlooked, as were Porter's many other violations of public mores, except that one of the boys was the son of Venice's chief of police (Schwartz, 77).

This incident is misleading with regard to Porter's sexual preferences. He typically sought out mature, rugged-looking men, preferably sailors or truck driver types. Through confidential interviews with Porter's friends after the composer's death, Schwartz assembled a good deal of information about his sexual activities. Although he obviously enjoyed the company of other wealthy gay men (Hanna, Woolley, Sturges, Coward, and Wilson), he seems rarely to have developed sexual relationships with men of his own economic class. Porter and Woolley made frequent use of pimps, who supplied men of whatever race and type were desired. These would appear at the door of the pair's hotel suite discreetly dressed as delivery men (Schwartz, 115).

The hardest part of Porter's life began in 1937, when his legs were crushed in a horseback riding accident, leaving him in constant pain. The right leg was amputated in 1958. Porter also suffered a string of failed Broadway shows in the 1940s, and show business insiders began to whisper that the accident and its aftermath had ruined his talent. These rumors were put to rest with the gigantic success of *Kiss Me Kate* in 1948 and the moderate success of *Can-Can* (1954) and *Silk Stockings* (1955). Porter was troubled by chronic depression from 1950 to 1951 and was treated with electrical shock therapy. After Linda's death in 1954 (from emphysema), he found work difficult. He retreated in the later 1950s to his nine-room apartment on the thirty-third floor of the Waldorf Towers in New York or to his country estate near Williamstown, Massachusetts. Guests often described Porter in this late period as a host who would drink to excess before dinner and then sit silent and staring until his valet would put him to bed at ten o'clock (Clarke, 341). He died from the combined effects of emphysema and kidney failure on October 15, 1964.

The loneliness and ill-health of Porter's last years were in stark contrast to the conviviality and pleasure that had comprised the first fifty years of his life. The freedom that he and his circle enjoyed as a result of wealth allowed them to live gay and lesbian lives that were relatively unrestrained by social mores. Only a thin veneer of heterosexuality, epitomized by the many marriages, such as that between Cole and Linda, was necessary to provide cover in the wider public sphere. With his wealth and influence, Porter could cruise the streets of Manhattan in his convertible in search of willing sailors with little fear of the arrest or harassment that would have threatened people of lesser means. Wit, irony, and double meanings comprised not just the matter of Porter's songs but also the means of living at once a life and a pseudolife.

See G. Clarke, *Capote: A Biography,* New York, 1988; B. Gill, "A Biographical Essay," in *Cole,* edited by R. Kimball, New York, 1971, ix–xix; J. Howard, *Travels with Cole Porter,* New York, 1991; R. Kimball, *The Complete Lyrics of Cole Porter,* New York, 1983; C. Marowitz, "In the Depths on the 90th Floor: The Down Side of Cole Porter's High Life," *Theater Week,* June 24, 1991; W. McBrien, *Cole Porter: A Biography,* New York, 2000; C. Schwartz, *Cole Porter: A Biography,* New York, 1977; and S. Smith and S. Stoddard, "Night and Day: The Difference between Cole Porter's Life and the Movie about Him," *Show Music* 7 (winter 1991–92): 37–42.

Mark Fearnow

RAINEY, "Ma" (Gertrude Pridgett) (1886–1939), blues singer and stage performer, was born in Columbus, Georgia, the second of five children, including a younger sister, Malissa Pridgett Nix, with whom she is often confused. She made her stage debut at age fourteen in the Bunch of Blackberries Revue, and soon began to perform throughout the South in tent shows, adding blues to her repertoire as early as 1902. At the age of eighteen, she married dancer, comedian, and singer William "Pa" Rainey, who was several years her senior. They toured as a song and dance team for many years with several black minstrel shows, including a stint from 1914 to 1916 with Tolliver's Circus and Musical Extravaganza as "Rainey and Rainey, Assassinators of the Blues."

As the popularity of blues increased, and as her fame spread, she began heading her own act, billed as "Madame Gertrude Rainey." Although she is known primarily as a blues singer, she also sang popular and novelty songs, wrote blues songs, performed comedic sketches, and danced. She toured throughout the South with many troupes, most notably the Rabbit Foot Minstrels. Black minstrel shows at this time included a variety of acts, including singers, dancers, comedians, and even contortionists, with the headliner appearing at the end.

In 1923, Rainey left minstrelsy, went to Chicago, and recorded the first of many sessions with Paramount Records. While "Bad Luck Blues" was her first actual recording, "Moonshine Blues" was the first Ma Rainey recording released and promoted by Paramount. In 1924, she recorded eighteen songs, three with Louis Armstrong: "Jelly Bean Blues," "See See Rider," and "Countin' the Blues." Her style was characterized by an earthy, "down home" quality that sharply contrasted with the smoother but paler styles of previously recorded blues singers such as Lucille Hegamin and Ethel Waters. Her rich, throaty contralto moaned, groaned, growled, and wailed. Paul Oliver wrote that she had "one of those voices you never forget—particularly for singing the blues" (130). Her records were extremely popular with her longtime southern fans, both black and white, and found an entirely new market with northern blacks. Paramount began sending her on tours of the Theatre Owners' Booking Agency (TOBA) circuit, which ran through major cities in both the South and the Midwest. Rainey was promoted as the "Mother of the Blues," and the "Gold Neck Woman of the Blues," due to a necklace made of gold coins that she often wore while performing. Based in Chicago, she was not a Harlem regular, but she did appear in New York at the Lincoln Theatre in 1923 and 1926, and possibly in 1924 and 1925, when she had traveled to New York to record. From 1924 to 1928, she was wildly popular, almost constantly touring the TOBA circuit, playing independent engagements, or recording. By this time, her revue included her adopted son Danny, "The World's Greatest Juvenile Stepper," who sang, danced, and did female impersonations. Those who knew Ma Rainey characterize her as generous, easygoing, and warmhearted. Lionel Hampton, whose bootlegger uncle introduced him to Rainey as a boy, said: "I used to dream of being in Ma Rainey's band because she treated her musicians so wonderfully, and she always bought them an instrument" (Albertson, 76).

A consummate performer, she held audiences in the palm of her hand. Even **Bessie Smith,** who was reportedly hotly jealous of other blues singers and rarely attended performances of any kind, went to see Ma

Rainey in 1925 when both singers were appearing in Birmingham, Alabama. Although Smith appeared at the start of her career with one of Rainey's shows, both women denied the widespread rumor that Rainey had kidnaped Smith from her Chattanooga home and "taught" her to sing the blues.

Rainey was a large woman, with coarsely straightened, unruly hair and gold caps on many of her teeth. Her size and dark complexion differed greatly from the standard of beauty in her time, but her personality and enormous talent won both fans and hearts. One of her trombone players, in an interview with writer Sandra Lieb, said: "Yes, she was ugly. But I'll tell you one thing about it: she had such a lovely disposition, you know, and personality, you forget all about it. She commence to lookin' good to you" (Lieb, 8). She had a preference for young men, called "pig meat" in those days, and indulged her taste for women with her chorines. She was surprised by the police once in Chicago just as a drinking party with several of her chorines had turned intimate. She spent the night in prison, and the next morning Bessie Smith paid her bail.

Guitarist Sam Chatmon, in another Sandra Lieb interview, states: "I believe [Ma] was courtin' Bessie . . . the way they'd talk. . . . I believe one or the other of them was the man, the other one was the girl. . . . I believe Ma Rainey was the one, was cuttin' up like the man. . . . If Bessie'd be 'round, if she'd get to talkin' to another man, [Ma would] run up. She didn't want no man to talk with her" (Lieb, 18).

Rainey authored two songs about same-sex relations: "Prove It on Me Blues," about lesbianism ("It's true I wear a collar and a tie / Like to watch while the women pass by / They say I do it, ain't nobody caught me / They sure got to prove it on me"); and "Sissy Blues," about losing her man to another man ("Last night I dreamed I was far from harm / Woke up and found my man in a sissy's arms. . . . Some are young, some are old / My man says sissies got good jelly roll. . . . Now all the people ask me why I'm all alone / A sissy shook that thing and took my man from home").

After 1928, interest in the blues waned nationally, and Paramount stopped recording Ma Rainey, although it did continue to release her records until 1930. Her show toured the TOBA circuit until 1930, when, for lack of funds, she joined Boisey de Legge's Bandanna Babies. When TOBA closed in 1930, a victim of the Depression, Rainey fell back on black minstrelsy. She toured with tent shows until 1933, when her sister Malissa died, and then retired from performing, returning to Columbus to operate two theaters she had acquired during happier financial times. In 1939, she died of heart disease and was buried in the family plot at Porterdale Cemetery in Columbus.

The title "Mother of the Blues" is an appropriate one for Ma Rainey, for she is perhaps the only, and certainly the earliest, link between "the male country blues artists who roamed the streets and back roads of the South, and their female counterparts, the so-called 'Classic Blues' singers" (Albertson, 26). Unquestionably, Ma Rainey was instrumental in shaping the style, sound, and attitude of the blues.

See C. Albertson, *Bessie,* New York, 1972; S. Lieb, *Mother of the Blues: A Study of Ma Rainey,* Amherst, 1981; P. Oliver, *Conversation with the Blues,* New York, 1965; and D. Stewart-Baxter, *Ma Rainey and the Classic Blues Singers,* New York, 1970.

Melissa Hillman

ROSENTHAL, Jean (Eugenia) (1912–69), lighting and scene designer, theatrical supplies wholesaler, and consultant for illumination and architectural projects, is described by biographer and friend Lael Wertenbaker as "a pioneer in the art and craft of lighting design, [and a] historical figure in her field recognized for her particular creative genius" (Rosenthal and Wertenbaker, vii). Her proficiency and artistic skill facilitated Rosenthal's collaboration with many leading twentieth-century theater practitioners, including John Houseman, who in his memoirs remarked that "with [Jean] at my side, there were no physical or technical difficulties I did not feel confident of overcoming" (351).

The daughter of two physicians who had emigrated from Romania to New York City, Rosenthal received an unconventional early education that began at the Ethnical Cultural School in the Bronx, continued at William Finke's Manumit School in Pawling, New York, and concluded with high school graduation at the Friends' Seminary in Manhattan. Turned down by colleges to which she had applied, in 1929 Rosenthal enrolled at the Neighborhood Playhouse School of the Theatre, where she studied all aspects of performance and production and served as technical assistant to faculty member Martha Graham, initiating a lifelong collaborative friendship. At the encouragement of George Pierce Baker, in 1930 Rosenthal matriculated at Yale, where she studied lighting design with Stanley McCandless and gained practical experience at the Yale Drama Workshop.

Rosenthal began her professional career at age twenty-one as a technical assistant with Federal Theater Project Number 891, where she became closely acquainted with producer John Houseman and director Orson Welles. When Houseman and Welles were fired from the project following the controversy surrounding the production of **Marc Blitzstein**'s *The Cradle Will Rock,* Rosenthal (who played a key role in the event) joined them in 1937 as technical director for the Mercury Theatre venture. In both of these early positions, she gained additional practical experience in lighting design and a reputation for being able to light difficult spaces with whatever instruments were at hand, no matter the quality or quantity.

These experiences, along with the professional contacts she cultivated, helped Rosenthal to secure a series of prestigious positions. Most notably, perhaps, she designed the lighting and provided technical assistance for fifty-three of Martha Graham's modern dance productions, a collaboration that lasted thirty-seven years. When Lincoln Kirstein and George Balanchine formed the Ballet Society in 1946, Rosenthal was hired as technical supervisor and lighting designer, positions she retained when the venture was rechristened the New York City Ballet in 1948 and which she held until 1957. She designed again for Houseman from 1953 to 1957 at the American Shakespeare Festival in Stratford, Connecticut, and served from 1957 until her death in 1969 as lighting designer and technical consultant for the Dallas Civic Opera. Other significant assignments included designs for the American Ballet Theatre, New York City Opera, Lyric Opera of Chicago, Metropolitan Opera, and in the 1950s and 1960s numerous Broadway plays and musicals, including *Cabaret, Carousel, Fiddler on the Roof, Hello Dolly, The Sound of Music,* and *West Side Story.*

In 1940, just as her artistic talents were consistently beginning to be in demand, Rosenthal cofounded Theatre Production Service (TPS), a successful mail-order wholesale business for theatrical supplies and design consultant services. In 1958, she formed Jean Rosenthal Associates, an enterprise devoted to consultation on major theater and architectural projects at educational, civic, and commercial facilities. Both of these businesses allowed her to share her knowledge and expertise in considerably broader theatrical and cultural contexts.

The issue of Rosenthal's sexuality is challenging, mainly because she placed a high value on her personal privacy. Wertenbaker foregrounds this trait in her description of Rosenthal in the preface to *The Magic of Light* by calling attention to Rosenthal's "warmth, which reserved to itself a deep personal privacy and never invaded yours." She characterizes this, along with Rosenthal's vitality, courtesy, and "the provocative originality of her mind" as factors that made her such a cherished friend (Rosenthal and Wertenbaker, v). One consequence of this valuation of privacy, however, is that Rosenthal's personal and sexual life is deliberately obscured or omitted from her own writing and, out of courtesy or lack of details, from the work of those writing about her. It is conceivable that Rosenthal cultivated this veil of privacy because, working in the male-dominated field of lighting design and technology, she perceived it as a necessity for gaining maximum cooperation from those she supervised. "My only real weapon in the battle for acceptance," she notes in *The Magic of Light,* "was knowledge" (35).

Rosenthal never married, though this fact, too, receives no mention in any accounts of her work. She does occasionally tease the reader, however, with a comment such as "Sometimes I have lived alone and sometimes shared my apartment," but then she offers no details (Rosenthal and Wertenbaker, 26). Other sources fill in some of the gaps and reveal that she shared long-term domestic living arrangements with two women. Winthrop Sergeant, in a 1956 *New Yorker* profile story, mentions that she was sharing an apartment with Nananne Porcher (58). Porcher, hired in the early days of TPS, is described by Wertenbaker as having become Rosenthal's "invaluable stage manager for ballet and opera" (and later resident lighting designer for the American Ballet Theatre and president of Jean Rosenthal Associates) (Rosenthal and Wertenbaker, 25). Wertenbaker also mentions that Rosenthal "shared a house with Marion Kinsella" (an independent artist and sculptor, Rosenthal's on-the-job lighting assistant, and the artist who illustrated *The Magic of Light*) on Martha's Vineyard, Rosenthal's favorite retreat from the stresses of work and the city (v, viii). The relationship is not defined further, but it is implied that Kinsella was Rosenthal's primary caregiver following a cancer operation in 1968 (viii).

Rosenthal's inclusion in this volume can be further justified because of the homosocial nature of her many collaborations. Whenever possible she surrounded herself with women as work partners. In addition to Porcher and Kinsella, the other cofounders of Theatre Production Service were "two able, talented women graduates of the Yale Drama Workshop, Helen Marcy and Eleanor Wise" (Rosenthal and Wertenbaker, 24). Houseman notes this particular aspect of Rosenthal's work when remembering the days at the Mercury Theatre, commenting that all technical matters "were handled by Jean Rosenthal and her flock of female assistants" (150). Additionally, in Rosenthal's own writing, she limits her descriptive examples to her collaborative projects involving women. Most notably among these is Martha Graham, about whom she writes: "To do one or two works for Martha a year was a part of my life and a renewal of my own internal spirit" (Rosenthal and Wertenbaker, 131).

Other than one unpublished dissertation and two recent essays, very little has been written about Jean Rosenthal's contributions to the advancement of stage lighting practice. Nor have her designs been evaluated in terms of spectatorship, partially due to a continuing dearth of critical technical assessment vocabularies. Given Rosenthal's deeply felt sentiments about the women with whom she collaborated and the homosocial and overtly lesbian implications of a preference for female work partners, as well as those of a female lighting designer providing illumination for a female star performer (such as Martha Graham), Jean Rosenthal's career and designs offer a productive avenue for examining the sexual dimensions of women's artistic and workplace collaborations.

See M. Boone, "Jean Rosenthal's Light: Making Visible the Magician," *Theatre Topics* 7, no. 1 (1997), 77–92; J. Chipman, "A Lifetime in Light: Jean Rosenthal's Careers, Collaborations, and Commitments to Women," in *Staging Desire: Queer Readings of American Theater History*, Ann Arbor, 2002, 365–89; A. Chujoy, *The New York City Ballet*, New York, 1953; J. Houseman, *Unfinished Business: A Memoir*, London, 1986; L. Leatherman, *Martha Graham: Portrait of the Lady as Artist*, New York, 1966; J. Rosenthal and L. Wertenbaker, *The Magic of Light: The Craft and Career of Jean Rosenthal, Pioneer in Lighting for the Modern Stage*, Boston, 1972; M. Sesak, "The Lighting Designs of Jean Rosenthal," Ph.D. diss., Ohio State University, 1976; and W. Sergeant, "Profiles: Please, Darling, Bring Three to Seven," *New Yorker*, February 4, 1956, 57–58.

Jay Scott Chipman

SAVOY, Bert (1888?–1923), vaudevillian and female impersonator, was born Everett McKenzie. Before the turn of the century, he began his career in show business as a "chair dancer" in a curio museum in Boston. (Chair dancing is an eccentric form of dance in which the performer uses a chair as a partner.) He performed twelve shows a day for six dollars a week.

For many years, Savoy drifted across the United States, often ending up stranded when a producer skipped town without paying the entertainers. Savoy performed at honky-tonks throughout the mining towns of Montana, California, and even Alaska. Although virtually nothing is known about the impetus, it was during this period that he gave up his chair for women's clothing.

By 1913, Savoy had returned to the East Coast, along with a woman he had married in Chicago. She managed a boardinghouse in Hell's Kitchen (an immigrant neighborhood on New York City's west side) while Savoy tried to get theatrical work. He met Jay Brennan, another out of work vaudevillian, on a Broadway trolley car, and they decided to form an act. (Savoy and his wife were divorced in 1922.)

Within three years, the act of Savoy and Brennan had made the big time, with Brennan as the sophisticated yet dandified straight man and Savoy as the gabby, dirt-dishing woman, dressed to kill in jewelry, low-cut gown, and gigantic picture hat. The act skirted the edge of the vulgar and risqué, with repeated sexual inferences. Unlike most other female impersonators of the time, Savoy never removed his flame-red wig at the end of the performance to remind the audience that he was indeed a man. (Several theatrical historians believe that Mae West's persona was heavily influenced by Savoy.)

Savoy's ability to coin catchphrases was well noted. "You must come over" was transformed by Mae West into "You must come up and see me sometime." Savoy's "You don't know the half of it, dearie" was immortalized by the Gershwins in their "You Don't Know the Half of it, Dearie, Blues." Some historians have proposed that Savoy's onstage dialogue was "a somewhat laundered version of the *patois* of the homosexual subculture" (Senelick, 37).

There appears to be agreement between Savoy's two main scholarly biographers—Senelick and Slide—that he was homosexual. Of course, many homosexual men marry women, and many heterosexual men are quite flamboyant. In Savoy's case, his private sexuality remains an area for further research. Undoubtedly, as Senelick points out, Savoy in his act mined deeply the cultural idiosyncracies of the homosexual underground. Was his knowledge firsthand?

Once again, as with so many artists from this period, Savoy positioned himself as a liaison between that shadowy homosexual world that was slowly beginning to emerge and the public, mainly heterosexual audience. His performances introduced the minority subculture to the majority and as such helped to make important first steps in de-demonizing the minority milieu.

Savoy and Brennan appeared in two editions of the Ziegfeld Follies, four editions of the Greenwich Village Follies, and such other shows as *Miss 1917, Hitchy-Koo,* and *Cinderella on Broadway.* During World War I, he was invited by Irving Berlin to coach the soldier actors in *Yip Yip Yaphank* who were playing female roles.

In 1923, at the height of his fame, Bert Savoy was killed by a lightning bolt while walking on a beach on Long Island. Also killed was Jack Vincent, a "chorus man," who was walking alongside. The rumor, reported in *Variety,* was that the lightning struck immediately after Savoy commented: "Mercy, ain't Miss God cutting up something awful!"

See L. Senelick, *Gender in Performance: The Presentation of Difference in the Performing Arts,* Hanover, N.H., 1992; and A. Slide, *Great Pretenders: A History of Female and Male Impersonation in the Performing Arts,* Lombard, Ill., 1986.

Lee Alan Morrow

SHAWN, Ted (Edwin Myers Shawn) (1891–1972), dancer, choreographer, educator, and author, was born in Kansas City, Missouri. Known as the "Father of American Modern Dance," Shawn's list of pioneering achievements is remarkable: first internationally known American male dancer; choreographer of the first all-dance moving picture (*The Dance of the Ages*, 1913); first male dancer to be listed in *Who's Who in America;* first American dancer to be awarded an honorary degree by an American college (Springfield College, 1936); first to form an all-male dance company; and first to build a theater designed and used only for dance.

Partially paralyzed when he was eighteen years old after an attack of diphtheria, Shawn was determined to walk again. In 1910, while studying for the Methodist ministry at the University of Denver, he enrolled in a ballet class. He not only regained the use of his legs, but he quickly developed into a stunning performer. After moving to Los Angeles and establishing his own dance studio, he began to tour with Norma Gould, performing exhibition ballroom dance. In 1914, he met the great concert dancer Ruth St. Denis (1877–1968); he was immediately attracted to her personally and to her choreographic style. Ted Shawn married Ruth St. Denis on August 13, 1914, at New York's City Hall, five months after they met. The union was not made public because Ruth felt marriage was fatal to a woman's career; nevertheless, the truth was discovered six months later when "Ruth St. Denis Marries the Most Beautiful Man in the World" flashed across the Associated Press wire.

The two founded the Denishawn School in Los Angeles in 1915, the first dance academy in America to produce a professional company. A second studio, the Denishawn House in New York City, opened in 1927. Indicative of their popularity, St. Denis and Shawn were included in the first series of color photographs published in *National Geographic* (1916). The Denishawn Dancers, with a repertoire of works choreographed by Shawn and St. Denis, toured the United States, Europe, and Asia until 1931. Famous students of Denishawn include Jack Cole, Martha Graham, Doris Humphrey, Pauline Lawrence, and Charles Weidman. (The company did not perform in 1917–22, while Shawn served in the military, and after his discharge, when he pursued a career in vaudeville.)

The Denishawn aesthetic featured various "primitive" dance forms, ballet, and several Asian dance traditions, eventually including modern German dance as well. Shawn felt that "The art of dance is too big to be encompassed by any one system, school or style. On the contrary, the Dance includes every way that men of all races, in every period of the world's history, have moved rhythmically to express themselves" (qtd. in Terry, 67). While Denishawn has been criticized for appropriating ethnic materials for its "exotic" appeal, Shawn and St. Denis can be credited with educating their students and audiences about other traditional forms of dance at a time when ballet was the only recognized form in the West.

In 1950, Shawn defended his eclecticism.

Critics have hurled the words "eclectic" and "hybrid" at me as if they were devastating and destructive critical "bombs" and have been annoyed because I have refused to be eliminated by these weapons. On the contrary, I have always glorified in the word "eclectic," for it means choosing of the best, and using everything that is good, regardless of the source from which it comes—and also not being classifiable as belonging to any one "school" (Shawn, B2).

Over six feet tall and weighing 175 pounds, Shawn often exhibited his striking physique clad only in the briefest of costumes. While he did not possess the ideal dancer's body—he was big and husky, and his personal style owed more to raw power than finesse, he was a commanding presence on the stage. Denishawn student Jane Sherman recalls:

He was gorgeous to look at, and to everybody he came across like a house afire. . . . [Audiences] were just overwhelmed by his personality. Any films you see of him now show him when he was already an old, fat man, and you must not judge by them what he was and could do. In his prime, he was just fantastic (qtd. in "Determined," 24).

Ruth's constant infidelities, her refusal to bear him children, and his weariness of being treated as her inferior led to many conflicts in the marriage. The final rift came when the two fell in love with the same man and "Ted Shawn won the wooing contest" (Terry, 10). While Ruth and Ted never legally divorced, they separated in 1930 and lived apart for the rest of their lives. While Shawn approved of the Greek model of the husband with a wife and a male lover, he was unable to make this a reality in his own life (14).

In the 1932–33 academic year, Shawn taught some five hundred men who were training to be physical education teachers and/or coaches at Springfield College in Massachusetts. On March 21, 1933, he presented in Boston his first all-male concert with students from these classes. He realized that his success in modern dance had not yet created opportunities for other men in dance, so he came to the conclusion "that something drastic should be done to restore masculine dancing to its ancient and rightful prestige and legitimate dignity" (qtd. in *San Francisco Performances*, 8). In the summer of 1933, Shawn invited eight men to live and train at Jacob's Pillow, a hundred-year-old farm in the Berkshire Hills of Massachusetts that he had bought in 1930, to prepare for a tour he had booked for the fall. In the middle of the Depression, promoting any kind of dance was a risky venture, but to market something new—an all-male modern dance company—seemed foolhardy. The only American modern dance company with male dancers was the Humphrey-Weidman company, and Charles Weidman had been trained by Shawn. At this point, the companies of Martha Graham, Helen Tamiris, and Hanya Holm were composed only of women.

Life at Jacob's Pillow was not easy. In addition to taking dance class and learning choreography, the men built their own cabins, raised the food they ate, and did what they could to provide creature comforts to a place without indoor plumbing, electricity, or a telephone. Before the company left on tour, it began to open some rehearsals to the public. For seventy-five cents, local patrons could listen to Shawn talk about dance, watch his attractive troupe of scantily clad dancers perform, and be served tea by these college boys (now wrapped in white terry robes). Life on the road was scarcely easier. Traveling by car, the first tour (1933–34) racked up 23,000 miles and 111 performances.

For the next six years, the company (Ted Shawn and His Men Dancers) lived, trained, and presented their work each summer at Jacob's Pillow before embarking on tours that took them across the United States, Canada, Cuba, and England. Though new to dance, Shawn's men were accomplished athletes in competitive sports (pole vault, wrestling, football, basketball, swimming, track, and so on). Using the raw material of sports movement, a great deal of Shawn's choreography was aggressively "masculine," showcasing his dancers as laborers, athletes, and warriors. When the armed services called for his dancers, Shawn dissolved the company in 1940; they had performed over 1,250 times in 750 cities for more than a million people.

Besides Shawn, the other star of the company was his lover, Barton Mumaw (ca. 1912–2001). After Barton finished his tour of duty in the U.S. Army, Shawn began to groom his partner as a solo artist. While various critics hailed Barton as the "American Nijinsky," he did not possess the presence to command an entire evening by himself. Even before the two severed their personal relationship in 1948, Barton danced in musicals on Broadway and on the road (among them, *Annie Get Your Gun* and *My Fair Lady*). Following Shawn's death in 1972, Mumaw committed himself to keeping his legacy alive by teaching classes and workshops across the country. It is an image from Mumaw's performance of *BOureé*, which he choreographed, that was fashioned into the weather vane at Jacob's Pillow: a male dancer, standing on one leg, arching back with his other leg and two arms open in a large expansive gesture to the sky.

Shawn initiated the Dance Festival at Jacob's Pillow in 1933, with the summer "Tea" performances by his Men Dancers. In 1940, he sold Jacob's Pillow to a nonprofit corporation that would operate a summer dance school and festival run by Shawn. When the Ted Shawn Theatre was completed in 1942, Shawn launched his "University of Dance," which was dedicated to broadening the dance education of dancers and audiences alike. This venue, which seats five hundred, was the first theater in America to be designed exclusively for dance. As its impresario, Shawn introduced American audiences to the Royal Danish Ballet, the National Ballet of Canada, Scotland's Celtic Ballet, Ballet Rambert, and other international companies and soloists.

Tirelessly active as a choreographer, lecturer, author, and producer, Shawn continued to dance until he was in his seventies. In 1957, he was awarded the Capezio Dance Award and the Knighthood in the Order of Dannebrog, conferred on him by King Frederick IX of Denmark. Ted Shawn died January 9, 1972, in Orlando, Florida, shortly after his eightieth birthday.

"Papa" Shawn has been called the father of American modern dance, even though very little of his choreography (more than two hundred pieces) has been performed since his death. Rather, his significant contributions include popularizing the male dancer in American modern dance, establishing a successful international dance festival, justifying a place for dance at the university level, and extensive writings on dance history and pedagogy. According to critic Clive Barnes: "Shawn did not merely enrich American dance—he was one of the people who created it" (36).

Shawn's many publications include *Ruth St. Denis: Pioneer and Prophet* (Los Angeles, 1920); *Gods Who Dance* (New York, 1929); *The American Ballet* (New York, 1926); *Fundamentals of a Dance Education* (Girard, Kan., 1937); *Dance We Must* (Pittsfield, Mass., 1940); *How Beautiful upon the Mountain: A History of Jacob's Pillow* (n.p., 1944); *Every Little Movement: A Book about François Delsarte* (Pittsfield, Mass., 1945); *Thirty-three Years of American Dance* (Pittsfield, Mass., 1959); and *One Thousand and One Night Stands* (Garden City, N.Y., 1960).

See C. Barnes, "Shaper of the Dance," *New York Times,* January 10, 1972; M. Campbell, "Spotlight on Dance," *Johper,* May 1972; "Determined," *New Yorker,* September 23,

1991; J. Dunning, "Dance 'by Men, for Men and about Men,'" *New York Times,* October, 22, 1991; "On Jacob's Pillow," *Time,* July 25, 1955; "Men Dancers: The Ted Shawn Legacy," *San Francisco Performances 1992–1993 Season,* 8; T. Shawn, "The Dance: All Good," *New York Times,* July 16, 1950; C. Schlundt, *The Professional Appearances of Ted Shawn and His Men Dancers,* New York, 1967; and W. Terry, *Ted Shawn: Father of American Dance,* New York, 1976.

Bud Coleman

SHORT, Hassard (1877–1956), designer and director, was one of the most sought-after stagers of musicals and revues on Broadway for over thirty years. Variously referred to as "Broadway's master magician" and the "master of color and movement," he is credited with numerous innovations of lighting and stagecraft, and he was associated with some of the most high profile successes of his era. Yet today his name is mostly unknown. This may be because his accomplishments did not fall neatly into clearly defined roles. While he is described as a "stager," he generally did not direct book scenes or sketches, nor was he a choreographer in the manner of one who devises dance steps. He was credited with designing lights (and sometimes sets and costumes), but these were done to enhance his musical staging and he never contributed designs for a show he did not stage. Possibly, his name has faded because he led an unusually low profile private life. The diminutive Short (always called Bobby) was, according to a profile written in the 1930s, "soft spoken," "diffident," and "regarded by many as cold and unsociable" (Morehouse, n.p.) It is likely that this "cold and unsociable" manner was cultivated to distract attention from his personal life. His homosexuality was known within a small circle of associates, but it would have been unthinkable for him to be more open about his personal life, given the social climate of the time.

Hubert Edward Hassard-Short was born into a family of landowners in Lincolnshire, England. As a teenager, he left school to seek a life on the stage. His first stage appearance took place in London in 1895, and he was brought by producer Charles Frohman to the United States in 1901. Short enjoyed a journeyman career which included a few films, but he was typecast as "silly-ass Englishmen" (qtd. in Sederholm, 48) in roles sometimes known as "Hassard Short parts." These included the foppish Algernon Peppercorn in the premier of Somerset Maugham's *Smith* in 1910.

Short began augmenting his acting career by staging the Lamb's Club *Gambols,* annual benefit productions. However, it was his staging of an all-star fund-raising show during the Actors Equity strike of 1919 that brought him notice. With little more than a bare stage and a brick wall, Short devised ingenious lighting effects for artfully deployed crowds of

Hassard Short at about the time of Irving Berlin's *As Thousands Cheer* (1933), which Short staged. (Photo by Vandamm Studio, courtesy of the Billy Rose Theatre Collection, New York Public Library for the Performing Arts.)

actors. He staged three more of these Equity shows and then moved immediately on to major Broadway assignments. Among his notable successes of the next decade were the intimate *Music Box Revues* (1921, 1922, 1923), with scores by Irving Berlin; his own *Ritz Revue* (1924), with Charlotte Greenwood; *Greenwich Village Follies* (1925); and Jerome Kern's *Sunny* (1925), starring Marilyn Miller.

From the beginning of his directing career, Short established complete authority over his productions and was known for his time-efficient approach to rehearsals. As a "staging director," he mounted the production numbers and "routined" the show, deciding the placement of all scenes, sketches, songs, and production numbers. His multifaceted contributions were reflected in his billing, which was usually a variation on "Staged and lighted by Hassard Short" but was often much grander. For Franz Lehar's *Frederika* (1937), his billing stretched to "Entire production, including settings, costumes, and lighting executed under the personal supervision of Mr. Short."

A triumvirate of successful musical revues in the early 1930s contained some of Short's most significant innovations. In *Three's a Crowd* (1930), he eliminated the footlights along the edge of the stage and hung a light bridge along the front of the balcony. The breathtaking "Body and Soul" number could not have been staged to such effect without this repositioning of lighting instruments. Against a background of black drapes, with the vocalist lit only by a pin spot, traveling spotlights caught the dancers—first their heads and upper torsos, then their legs and feet—giving the impression of disembodied faces and limbs.

The Band Wagon, with Fred and Adele Astaire, the next year featured a revolving stage devised by Short to hold a merry-go-round. (He would use revolves—sometimes several at once—in later productions.) He utilized stage elevators to striking effect to move both actors and scenery, often in full view of the audience. Short sought new ways to light drapes, scrims, mirrors, and curtains to dramatic effect. The highlight of *The Band Wagon* was his staging of "Dancing in the Dark," featuring dancers dancing with their own reflections in a swirl of mirrors and colored lights.

As Thousands Cheer (1933), with a score by Irving Berlin and sketches by Moss Hart, contained one of Short's masterpieces of lighting. The show, which used newspaper headlines of the day as its framework, ended its first act with the stunning "Easter Parade," presenting a stage full of actors, dancers, singers, and children all bathed in the monochromatic palette of a rotogravure page. While the stage pictures he created were sumptuous, they were done with economy, taste, and attention to detail and stood in contrast to the elaborate, often garish revues of Ziegfeld and others.

The always impeccably attired Short frequently traveled to Europe looking for ideas and inspiration, and newspaper notices remarked on his departures or returns, often with Hart or the Berlin family. However, none mentioned that he traveled with his companion, Billy Ladd, a slender chorus boy with bleached blond hair. Mrs. Irving Berlin later remarked that Bobby and Billy's "was the happiest marriage of the group" (qtd. in Bach, 90). Short's shunning of publicity means that there is little information about Billy Ladd or their relationship. During the production of *As Thousands Cheer,* there was great difficulty in finding an actor who resembled the prince of Wales for a sketch to be directed by Hart. Finally, a handsome young man named Thomas Hamilton was discovered. When Short enthused that he would personally spend as much time as necessary to coach him, "Billy Ladd pointed out coolly that directing the actors was Moss's job." (109).

The successes continued throughout the 1930s: Berlin's *Face the Music* (1932), Jerome Kern's *Roberta* (1933), and **Cole Porter**'s *Jubilee* (1935), with another signature Short staging of "Begin the Beguine," which featured a series of panels resembling palm trees that moved to reveal a nightclub with evocative lighting. In 1934, he staged the large-scale operetta *The Great Waltz* at the gargantuan Center Theatre, complete with turntables, fireworks, a company of 140 performers and, for the finale, an orchestra rising on an elevated platform up to the stage, where it then revolved to the tune of "The Blue Danube."

Short continued to work into the early 1950s. His later successes included *Lady in the Dark* (1941), with a score by Kurt Weill and a book by Moss Hart, for which Short created a series of imaginative dream sequences; and *Carmen Jones* (1943), Oscar Hammerstein II's contemporary adaptation of Bizet's opera. For this, Short devised boldly color coded sets, costumes, and lights to reflect the dominant emotions of each of its four acts. Following *My Darlin' Aida* (1952), another adaptation of an opera, this time transferring Verdi's *Aida* to the American Civil War, Short retired to the South of France, where he died four years later. His will named a William B. Strahlman Jr. as sole beneficiary, but there were no survivors. As one obituary noted: "Mr. Short was a bachelor."

See S. Bach, *Dazzler: The Life and Times of Moss Hart,* New York, 2001; S. Leiter, *The Great Stage Directors: 100 Distinguished Careers of the Theater,* New York, 1994; W. Morehouse, "Broadway after Dark," unidentified article in the Hassard Short Clippings File, Billy Rose Theatre Collection, New York Public Library for the Performing Arts; and J. Sederholm, *The Musical Directing Career and Stagecraft Contributions of Hassard Short, 1919–1952,* Detroit, 1974.

Kevin Winkler

SMITH, Bessie (1894–1937), blues singer and stage performer, was born in Chattanooga, Tennessee, into desperate poverty, one of seven children. Both her parents had died by Smith's ninth birthday, leaving Viola, the eldest daughter, to raise the rest. Smith sang on the street for change, accompanied by her brother, Clarence, on guitar. Clarence landed a job as a dancer and comedian with a traveling minstrel show in 1912 and arranged for an audition for Bessie, who was hired as a chorus girl. That this show also featured **Ma Rainey** is probably the root of the groundless rumor that Rainey kidnaped Smith and "taught" her to sing the blues. A few months later, Smith was in the chorus of another troupe, also featuring Ma Rainey, which toured throughout the South. She was dismissed from this troupe because Irvin C. Miller, the producer, felt that she "did not meet my standards as far as looks were concerned." The standard of the day was expressed in slogans for shows such as "Sepia Toned Lovelies" and Miller's own "Glorifying the Brownskin Girl." To put it plainly, Bessie was too black (Albertson, 27).

By 1913 or 1914, Smith was singing at Atlanta's "81" Theatre, training chorus girls there during the day. The "81" was part of the Theatre Owner's Booking Association (TOBA), the major black vaudeville circuit, and by 1918 Smith was touring with Pete Werley's Florida Blossoms and the Silas Green show. By 1922, she had achieved some measure of fame among blues fans in the South and Northeast after having moved to Philadelphia and performed in cabarets there and in Atlantic City.

In 1923, she made her first records for Columbia in New York, "Down Hearted Blues" and "Gulf Coast Blues." In April, she signed a contract for twelve more "sides" (recordings). Smith's records sold exceptionally well, and she toured extensively to packed houses. Her fame grew rapidly, and she was soon commanding $1,500 a week for appearances. Of course, she was expected to bring an entire show with her, and all her dancers, musicians, and crew members had to be paid out of her salary. Still she was able to keep most of the money and soon after moved her family to Philadelphia.

From 1923 to 1930, Smith enjoyed remarkable financial, popular, and critical success. She recorded and toured almost constantly and even appeared in a short film, *St. Louis Blues,* wherein she sang the title song and acted. (Although rumor has it that the film was lost or banned due to controversial content, it actually played frequently between 1929 and 1932.) She recorded with Louis Armstrong, Fletcher Henderson, James P. Johnson, and a young Coleman Hawkins among many others.

By 1930, however, the popularity of the blues had tapered off, and the Depression had taken a bite out of record and ticket sales. Although her career began to slow almost to a halt, she relied on Richard Morgan, her bootlegger lover (who was also Lionel Hampton's uncle), and managed also to eke out a living touring and occasionally recording for a low-end label. In February 1936, she was hired to replace an ill Billie Holliday (who counted Smith as one of her influences) at New York's Connie's Inn, a former Harlem hot spot that had recently moved to Broadway and Forty-eighth, the most prestigious booking she had had in years. Smith capitalized on her good fortune by presenting an all new repertoire featuring popular swing-style songs and was held over until April. Her career experienced a revival, and she began a lively schedule of appearances throughout New York and Philadelphia. There were plans not only to record her again at Columbia but also for her to appear in a Hollywood film. Unfortunately, these plans never materialized. Bessie Smith was killed in a car accident on September 26, 1937.

The circumstances of Smith's death are surrounded by many controversial rumors. Popular legend states that she bled to death because she was first taken to a white hospital and was refused treatment. Another legend, popularized by **Edward Albee**'s play *The Death of Bessie Smith,* states that she died because the doctor on the scene was more interested in a pretty young nurse than his famous patient. Neither of these stories are true. Smith and Richard Morgan set out for Darling, Mississippi, from Memphis early on the morning of September 26. Their car struck a truck parked half on the side of the road, half in the southbound lane. Shortly afterward, Dr. Hugh Smith and his friend Henry Broughton approached the scene on their way to Memphis for a fishing trip. Dr. Smith found Bessie Smith lying in the middle of the road, her right arm nearly torn off but with the major arteries intact: "What that boils down to is that hemorrhage from the arm did not cause Bessie Smith's death" (Albertson, 223). Her entire right side had been severely crushed. Broughton called for an ambulance. After a few minutes, with no ambulance in sight, the doctor began to remove the fishing gear from his back seat to prepare to take Smith to the hospital himself. Before this was completed, however, another car, traveling at about fifty miles an hour, barreled into Dr. Smith's car and shoved it into Bessie Smith's. A young white couple, obviously drunk, was now added to the list of patients. Fortunately, neither of the passengers had critical injuries, but now they were all forced to wait for the tardy ambulance. It finally arrived, and, according to Willie George Miller, the ambulance driver, Smith was taken immediately to a black hospital, the G. T. Thomas, where she died of shock and internal injuries (223).

Smith's personal life was rocky at best. As a young girl she married a man named Earl Love, only to see him die a few months into the marriage. Her next marriage, in June 1923, was to a night watchman, Jack Gee. Their stormy relationship continued for many years, despite, or perhaps because of, their many separations. Gee was apt to surprise Bessie while she was on tour, more often than not in a rage over her infidelity, despite his own. He was known to beat her publicly. She had many affairs with both men and women, and possibly she had a sexual relationship with Ma Rainey. From 1926 to 1927, Smith had an affair with Lillian Simpson, one of her chorines. Although she was able to hide this relationship from Jack, he caught her (just days after Lillian had left the show) in a compromising situation with another of her chorines. She narrowly escaped him by herding her entire entourage out of Detroit in the middle of the night.

Bessie Smith, a rare artist, managed to transgress nearly every aspect of the rigid female gender role of her era without sacrificing her career (in itself a transgression) or her popularity. Rough, irresponsible, uncouth, and a heavy drinker, she was frequently involved in physical fights over slights, real or imagined. She cared nothing for niceties. She often left a town before her contracted run was finished; sometimes she would never show up at all. A fun-loving partygoer, she sought out relaxed, "down home" parties, eschewing show business soirees. Generous to a fault, despite the notoriously low pay her troupes received, she often lavished gifts or money on those she felt were in need.

Most importantly, she was enormously, intoxicatingly talented. She influenced innumerable singers and musicians, not only in her era but down to the present day. The indelible voice of the "classic blues," she was, by all accounts and without controversy, the greatest blues singer who ever lived.

See E. Albee, *The Death of Bessie Smith,* New York, 1960; C. Albertson, *Bessie,* New York, 1972; P. Oliver, *Bessie Smith,* New York, 1959; P. Oliver, *The Story of the Blues,* New York, 1969; and D. Stewart-Baxter, *Ma Rainey and the Classic Blues Singers,* New York, 1970.

Melissa Hillman

SONDHEIM, Stephen (1930–), composer and lyricist, is widely regarded as the most important and influential figure in the contemporary musical theater. His choice of challenging subjects, his sophisticated and complex melodies, and above all the bracing intelligence and dazzling wordplay of his lyrics have dramatically extended the boundaries of the musical, creating a unique lyric theater. Sondheim's career can be divided into three distinct periods: the early years, matching lyrics to the music of Broadway veterans and experimenting with concepts he would later more fully explore; his collaboration in the 1970s with producer-director Harold Prince on a series of Broadway musicals that brought a new peak of artistry and daring to the form; and, finally, a move toward increased experimentation, in which he developed his work in regional and institutional theaters. This final period also saw a lionization of Sondheim as the last great Broadway composer still active.

Sondheim was born in New York City and at the age of ten, following his parents' divorce, moved with his mother to a farm in Doylestown, Pennsylvania. Their neighbors included the family of Oscar Hammerstein II, the celebrated lyricist and librettist. Hammerstein became a surrogate father for the boy and strongly encouraged his interest in musical theater. He later set him on a rigorous course of writing assignments, which Sondheim has acknowledged as a crucial period in his development as a writer.

After studying music at Williams College, Sondheim studied theory and composition with noted avant-garde composer Milton Babbitt. Following a brief sojourn in California writing scripts for the *Topper* television series (1953), Sondheim, at the age of twenty-five, wrote his first score for a Broadway musical, the unproduced *Saturday Night.* He then put his ambition to compose both words and music on hold while he contributed lyrics to Leonard Bernstein's music for *West Side Story* (1957) and to Jule Styne's for *Gypsy* (1959). These back-to-back hits, which featured Sondheim lyrics for such popular and enduring songs as "Somewhere," "Tonight," and "Everything's Coming up Roses," firmly established him as a major player in Broadway musical theater.

In 1962, he realized his goal of writing both music and lyrics with *A Funny Thing Happened on the Way to the Forum,* which used characters and situations from the comedies of Plautus, the third-century B.C. Roman playwright. *Forum* was a truly comedic musical, and it contains Sondheim's funniest score. The original production, which starred Zero Mostel, played nearly a thousand performances (the record for a Sondheim show).

Two disappointing projects followed. For the satirical *Anyone Can Whistle* (1964), Sondheim wrote his most ambitious score to date, and its sophisticated interweaving of dialogue, music, and dance hinted at approaches he would later develop more fully. The chaotic production was a nine-performance flop, but *Whistle* has achieved cult status through its original cast album. Sondheim then inexplicably accepted the assignment of supplying lyrics to the music of Richard Rodgers for *Do I Hear a Waltz?* (1965). However, the warm relationship Sondheim had enjoyed with mentor Oscar Hammerstein was not to be repeated with the late Hammerstein's distinguished partner, and their uneasy collaboration resulted in a lackluster show that had only a brief run.

This failure commenced a fallow period for Sondheim, in which his only produced work was the score for an original television musical, *Evening Primrose,* (1966). He returned with *Company,* (1970), the first of several ambitious and influential musicals created in partnership with Harold Prince. Prince may have been Sondheim's ideal collaborator: the producer-director and the composer-lyricist both believed that the Broadway musical could accommodate a wide range of social, cultural, and political issues, and they were determined to establish it as a serious theatrical genre. *Company,* a series of vignettes on the state of marriage and urban life, dispensed with the linear plotting of the Rodgers and Hammerstein musical plays; Sondheim's glittering, edgy songs *commented* on the action to a greater degree than they advanced it. *Company* brought a truly contemporary sensibility to the Broadway musical and is justifiably considered a landmark show.

Almost immediately after *Company* opened, the team embarked upon *Follies* (1971), an ambitious examination of the death of idealism in the post–World War II era told through the story of the reunion of a group of retired showgirls. Sondheim wrote what amounted to two complete scores: songs for the contemporary scenes, in his usual trenchant style, and an entire catalog of pastiche period songs for which he wrote in, and commented on, the style of Sigmund Romberg, Jerome Kern, Irving Berlin, the Gershwins, and others. *Follies'* relentlessly unsentimental look at marriage and lost values proved to be the antithesis of the nostalgia craze that was sweeping popular culture at the time, and the lavish show's large opening costs resulted in its closing after a year with the loss of its entire capitalization.

The next Sondheim-Prince show was the elegant *A Little Night Music* (1973), adapted from the Ingmar Bergman film *Smiles of a Summer Night* and graced with a score written entirely in variations on three-quarter time. A warmer, more romantic musical than their last two outings, the show was a popular hit and won Sondheim his third Tony Award in a row for Best Score (following *Company* and *Follies*). The score's ballad, "Send in the Clowns," also proved to be a genuinely popular song outside the context of the show, a rarity for Sondheim, who is frequently accused of not writing "catchy" or "hummable" songs.

During this period, Sondheim made the first of several periodic contributions to films, composing the music for *Stavisky* (1974) and coauthoring the screenplay for the murder mystery *The Last of Sheila* (1973).

He later wrote the score for *Reds* (1981) and supplied songs for *The Bird-cage* (1996) and *Dick Tracy* (1990), one of which, "Sooner or Later," won the Academy Award for Best Song.

After contributing additional lyrics to Prince's new version of *Candide* (1974) and writing the score for an adaptation of Aristophanes' *The Frogs* (1974) at the Yale Repertory Theatre, Sondheim composed a sophisti-cated hybrid of Broadway and Eastern music for *Pacific Overtures* (1976), which examined the Westernization of Japan following the 1852 arrival of Commodore Perry. The show's subject matter and restrained, cerebral quality made it a tough sell, particularly in the year of *A Chorus Line,* and it closed after fewer than two hundred performances. It was followed by one of the team's most acclaimed works, *Sweeney Todd* (1979), based on the Victorian melodrama about a murderous barber obsessed with revenge on a harsh and unjust society. Interestingly, Sondheim responded to the bloodcurdling subject matter with a richly melodic score com-prised of arias, duets, and extended choral sequences. So continuous was the music that *Sweeney Todd* was dubbed an opera by many. Prince's gar-gantuan production was similarly operatic in size, and *Sweeney Todd* became the first Sondheim score to enter the opera repertory.

Following the high-profile failure of the team's final show, *Merrily We Roll Along* (1981), Sondheim withdrew from the commercial sphere. Changes in Broadway economics had made the prestigious but commer-cially risky Sondheim-Prince musicals less viable; *Company* and *Night Music* had been their only profitable shows. Perhaps inevitably, Sondheim moved to the nonprofit arena, where he developed a musical in workshop at Off-Broadway's Playwrights Horizons. *Sunday in the Park with George* (1984), a look at the life and work of the painter George Seurat, marked his first show with playwright-director James Lapine, his most frequent post-Prince collaborator. Only after all parties were satisfied, did *Sunday* move to a Broadway house, where it won Sondheim the Pulitzer Prize for Drama.

Lapine's background was exclusively in noncommercial theater, and the Sondheim-Lapine musicals, with their fluid, free-flowing construc-tion, have a significantly different texture than the Prince productions. Sondheim's scores likewise moved away from traditional Broadway "numbers" and toward continuous, through-composed pieces.

Sondheim and Lapine's two other musicals, *Into the Woods* (1987), a reexamination of fairy tale plots and characters, and *Passion* (1994), a chamber musical that deals with obsessive love and features a continuous score of intimate solos and duets, were also developed at institutional the-aters before their Broadway transfers. *Assassins* (1990), which explores the characters and motivations of a gallery of presidential murderers, played only a limited engagement at Playwrights Horizons—the first Sondheim show not to be produced on Broadway. When it was revived on Broadway in 2004, it won five Tony Awards, including Best Revival of a Musical. Sondheim developed his non-musical-comedy thriller, *Getting Away with Murder* (written with *Company*'s librettist, George Furth), at a regional theater before its brief 1996 Broadway run.

By this time, the Sondheim "cult" (see Kaplan) was in full swing, driven by its gay male contingent. With no comparable talents on the horizon to succeed him, Sondheim increasingly loomed as one of an endangered species: the last in a line of American composers and lyricists whose work in Broadway musicals had defined and elevated popular songwriting in the twentieth century. The idolatry therefore took on a fervor earlier artists never experienced in their lifetime. Sondheim was suddenly everywhere. There were numerous recorded compilations of his music; jazz interpretations of his scores; opera company productions; Broadway revivals; the premiere of an unproduced musical, *Saturday Night;* drama anthologies; a Best Song Academy Award for "Sooner or Later," from *Dick Tracy* (1990); a gala seventieth birthday tribute at the Library of Congress; a quarterly publication devoted to everything Sondheim; and even Sondheim on the Internet (www.sondheim.com). A series of high-profile, one-time-only Sondheim tributes took on legendary status: "Sondheim: A Musical Tribute" (1973); "*Follies* in Concert" (1985); "Sondheim: A Celebration at Carnegie Hall" (1992); and concert stagings of *Anyone Can Whistle* (1995) and *Sweeney Todd* (2000) were all-star events verging on hysteria, with large numbers of gay men in attendance. In 2002, the John F. Kennedy Performing Arts Center in Washington produced an unprecedented Sondheim celebration. The ten-million-dollar, summer-long festival of his works took on the appearance of a sacred pilgrimage for Sondheim devotees from around the world and served to acknowledge him as America's greatest living musical theater composer.

Throughout his career, Sondheim—never married and frequently compared to Robert, the enigmatic, unmarried central character of *Company*—has declined to discuss his personal life, although that did not deter the National Museum and Archive of Lesbian and Gay History from listing him in its Guide to Notable Gay and Bisexual Men (National Museum, 63). Those who seek some hint of Sondheim's sexuality in his work often point to the unflattering portraits of married life in *Company, Follies,* and *Merrily,* the celebration of nonconformity in *Whistle;* the gay anthem status of such songs as "I'm Still Here," "Some People," "The Ladies Who Lunch," and "I Never Do Anything Twice," the latter from the film *The Seven-and-a-Half Percent Solution* (1976); and the bisexual portrayal of one of the husbands in the 1996 London revival of *Company* (presumably with Sondheim's approval). Only during interviews surrounding the opening of his musical *Passion* did Sondheim allude to his personal life, admitting that he was in love but offering no further information. His discretion was respected by the openly gay composer, Ned Rorem, who, according to interviewer Lawrence D. Mass, would not discuss Sondheim because he "refused to comment on the homosexuality of living, closeted figures in the music world" (qtd. in Mass, 96). Others had no such qualms. In a 1995 interview with **Arthur Laurents,** a frequent Sondheim collaborator, conducted by writer **Larry Kramer,** both men made references to Sondheim's homosexuality (Kramer, 54–55).

See J. Gordon, *Art Isn't Easy: The Achievement of Stephen Sondheim,* New York, 1992; M. Gottfried, *Sondheim,* New York, 1993; M. Kakutani, "Sondheim's Passionate 'Passion,'" *New York Times,* March 20, 1994; J. Kaplan, "The Cult of Saint Stephen Sondheim," *New York,* April 4, 1994; L. Kramer, "His Brilliant Career," *The Advocate,* May 16, 1995; L. Mass, "A Conversation with Ned Rorem," in *Queering the Pitch: The New Gay and Lesbian Musicology,* edited by P. Brett, E. Wood, and G. Thomas, New York, 1994, 85–112; E. McMurray, ed., *Contemporary Theatre, Film, and Television,* vol. 11, Detroit, 1994; C. Michenor, "Words and Music—by Sondheim," *Newsweek,* April 23, 1973; National Museum and Archive of Lesbian and Gay History, *The Gay Almanac,* New York, 1996; F. Rich, "A Musical Theater Breakthrough," *New York Times Magazine,* October 21, 1984; S. Schiff, "Deconstructing Sondheim," *New Yorker,* March 8, 1993; M. Secrest, *Stephen Sondheim: A Life,* New York, 1998; *The Sondheim Review,* Chicago, summer 1994– ; and C. Zadan, *Sondheim and Co.,* rev. ed., New York, 1989.

Kevin Winkler

STEIN, Gertrude (1874–1947), playwright and critic, was born in Allegheny, Pennsylvania, and raised in Oakland, California. When both her parents died while she was still a minor, an older brother arranged a lifelong income for Stein that gave her considerable freedom relative to most women of her era. She put that freedom to good use. She studied under psychologist William James at Harvard and advanced to medical school at Johns Hopkins, though she left the latter without a degree partly to escape a romantic triangle involving two other women (Blackmer, 682). She moved to Paris in 1903 and devoted herself to writing fiction; although some of her earliest efforts use traditional narrative techniques, she very quickly determined to do new things with prose (Souhami, 63) and was to become, along with James Joyce, one of the leading lights of modernist literature.

In 1907, Stein met Alice B. Toklas. It is reported that Toklas heard bells upon encountering Stein's genius, but this is only reported by Stein herself. What is certain is that the two women formed a successful life partnership and were seldom separated during the next forty years; because so much of Stein's writing is literal or thinly disguised autobiography, Stein and Toklas became one of the most famous couples of the twentieth century. Their rented rooms at 27 Rue de Fleurus in Paris served as a salon to the turn of the century avant-garde (including, most notably, painters such as Pablo Picasso, Georges Braque, and Henri Matisse) and as the symbolic center of the American expatriate community (including Ernest Hemingway and F. Scott Fitzgerald) that arose after World War I.

Although Stein often attended plays and operas as a girl, she lost interest in the popular stage and always considered herself an outsider relative to the world of the theater. She claimed to have given up going to plays entirely by the time she began to write them (Stein, 111). As such, it is not surprising that her early dramatic efforts toss aside even the most basic assumptions about the nature and purpose of the theatrical medium. In 1913, she wrote her first play to commemorate the hubbub of voices and phrases she had overheard at a dinner party. The result, ironically entitled *What Happened, a Play,* abandons plot and character in favor of atmosphere and whimsical play with language. Though an early work, *What Happened* would prove typical in many respects. Stein rejected plausible narratives and carefully motivated character actions, calling these elements the stuff of newspapers and everyday gossip (118). (Not that she disdained gossip in private life—it was daily fare at 27 Rue de Fleurus.)

Moreover, Stein complained that traditional dramatic illusions are counterfeit and remote and proposed to treat the stage as a "landscape" of the spoken word (125). Although her plays are set in a sort of continuous present, they are never really static in the theater. Instead, the spectator is provoked to mentally explore the world onstage, substituting this contemplative but genuine (and contemporary) action for the recounting of imaginary (and past) events.

Stein wrote numerous short plays, but she is best known in the theater for her three full-length opera librettos. The first, *Four Saints in Three Acts,* was written for composer **Virgil Thomson** in 1930 but was not produced until 1934 (after its libretto had been reworked somewhat by Thomson's friend Maurice Grosser). It was the first Stein play that she would see onstage; she was sixty years old. *Four Saints in Three Acts* has four acts and more than two dozen saints; the text repeatedly refers to itself ("How many saints are there in it?" it asks) and ultimately seems to be about the nature of language and the process of writing. Produced and directed by John Houseman with an all-black cast, it became not only an extraordinary commercial success for an opera on Broadway but the critical event of its season (Souhami, 201).

Despite the success of *Four Saints* and Stein's growing fame as a writer of prose, no other of her plays received a major production in her lifetime (although some of her prose and verse pieces were set to music and performed). Stein wrote *Dr. Faustus Lights the Lights* for composer Gerald Berners in the late 1930s, but Berners didn't get around to writing the music before war broke out in 1939, making the prospect of a production unlikely. As a result, he resigned from the project and, though music is sometimes added to productions, *Dr. Faustus* remains without an "official" score. The libretto borrows elements from the Faust plays by Marlowe and Goethe, but it offers modern technology (electric lights) as the knowledge for which the title character sells his soul. Stein's version is more concerned with its heroine, however, who is named both "Marguerite Ida" and "Helena Annabel" and may represent the complexity of female identity or even two women who function practically as one.

In October 1945, Stein began another libretto for Virgil Thomson entitled *The Mother of Us All;* the text concerns Susan B. Anthony and her struggle for female emancipation (although the opera is by no means a literal representation of historical events). The work may be read as autobiography in significant ways (Brinnin, xiv): like Stein herself, "Susan B." finds her own faithful companion in "Anne." Unfortunately, Stein never heard a note of the music Thomson wrote to accompany her words.

Stein's death from cancer on July 27, 1946, did not diminish her place in modern culture, including the theater. *The Mother of Us All* received its premier at Columbia University in May of the following year; *Dr. Faustus* appeared at the Cherry Lane Theatre in 1951 (with incidental music by Richard Banks). Her plays and theories proved central to the rise of the American theatrical avant-garde of the 1950s and 1960s, when *Dr. Faustus* and some of Stein's shorter pieces were rethought and revived by The Living Theatre and the Judson Poets' Theatre in New York City. In the 1970s, Stein's influence reached a new generation of artists and spectators through the experimental work of directors Richard Foreman and Robert Wilson (Marranca, xxv); in early February 1996, Wilson's new production of *Four Saints in Three Acts* began an international tour from the stage of the Houston Grand Opera. In one sense, even Stein's playwriting continues posthumously: her life and literature provide the raw materials for dramatic adaptations such as Leon Katz's *The Making of Americans* (1973) and for periodic monodramas performed by actresses such as Pat Bond and Pat Carroll.

See C. E. Blackmer, "Gertrude Stein," in *The Gay and Lesbian Literary Heritage: A Reader's Companion to the Writers and their Works, from Antiquity to the Present,* edited by C. J. Summers, New York, 1995, 681–86; J. M. Brinnin, introduction to G. Stein, *Selected Operas and Plays of Gertrude Stein,* Pittsburgh, 1970, ix–xv; J. Grahn, *Really Reading Gertrude Stein: A Selected Anthology with Essays by Judy Grahn,* Freedom, Calif., 1989; B. Knapp, *Gertrude Stein,* New York, 1990; B. Marranca, introduction to G. Stein, *Last Operas and Plays,* edited by C. Van Vechten, reprint, Baltimore, 1995, vii–xxvii; D. Souhami, *Gertrude and Alice,* San Francisco, 1991; G. Stein, *Lectures in America,* reprint, New York, 1975; G. Stein and Alice B. Toklas, *Baby Precious Always Shines: Selected Love Notes between Gertrude Stein and Alice B. Toklas,* edited by K. Turner, New York, 1999; L. Wagner-Martin, *"Favored Strangers": Gertrude Stein and Her Family,* New Brunswick, N.J., 1995; S. Watson, *Prepare for Saints: Gertrude Stein, Virgil Thomson, and the Mainstreaming of American Modernism,* Los Angeles, 1995.

William MacDuff

TERRY, Megan (1932–), playwright and director, was born in Seattle, Washington, to Joseph Duffy Jr. and Marguerite Cecelia (Henry) Duffy; she later changed her name to reflect her Welsh heritage. Her early theatrical education was in stage design at the Banff School of Fine Arts at the University of Alberta, Edmonton, and she received a bachelor's degree from the University of Washington, Seattle, in 1956. Terry moved to New York that year, and in 1963 she became a founding member of the New York Open Theater (1963–73), along with Joseph Chaikin and **Jean-Claude van Itallie.** She was also a founding member of the New York Theater Strategy (1971), the Women's Theater Council (1971), and the Women's Forum of NYC (1972).

It was at the Open Theater that she wrote *Comings and Goings, Calm Down Mother,* and *Keep Tightly Closed in a Cool Dry Place.* The form being developed by Terry in these plays used a technique referred to as "transformations," which takes the realities of the action and transforms them into other realities throughout the play. This innovative form, which broke with the psychological realism of the time, eschewing traditional gender roles and linear structure, loosened the oppressive hold of traditional forms of drama and strongly influenced the work of practitioners such as Eric Overmeyer, Maria Irene Fornes, and Suzan Lori-Parks. Terry's experimentation with form, begun with her three early works, culminated in her creation of *Viet Rock: A Folk War Movie* (1966), originally produced at the La Mama Experimental Theater. A masterpiece of radical artistic and political expression, both in form and in content, *Viet Rock* was produced extensively across America for the next decade; it was frequently taken up by university theater groups, which produced the piece with a missionary passion in virtually every state in the union.

In 1970, Terry won the Obie (Off-Broadway) Award for her play *Approaching Simone,* about the French philosopher Simone Weil, who starved to death protesting the rule of the Nazi regime in Germany. The playwright chose Weil as the subject for her play because she considers her a "great intellectual of the century" and "one of the greatest theological thinkers" of all time. Like Weil, who fought against totalitarianism at one of its most historically pernicious moments, Megan Terry's work embodies her lifelong battle, in words and deeds, against totalitarianism in any form. Weil's example influenced Terry in all spheres of her life and art, and she acknowledges that through Weil she finally achieved an education. Moreover, what is learned by the process of rehearsal, "the effort of attention" needed, and "the practice of making [the rehearsal] new everyday" Terry found in her study of Weil, who tried to do the same in her practice of saying the Lord's Prayer everyday (interview with author, July 11, 1996).

According to Terry, a primary impetus for the work at the Open Theater was that "we felt theater we were looking at was about manners, about trying not to spill drinks, or learning how the upper class did it." Most of the drama being done in New York seemed to be European in origin or influence, and she and the other Open Theater members wanted to create a uniquely American theater: "What the Open and Chaikin wanted to do was strip away the baggage" and create a theater "where American actors could play heroic." The energy, talent, and chemistry of the Open Theater empowered the members: "We knew we were going to change the world. When I wrote *Viet Rock,* I wanted to stop the war. We felt we had the power to do it, because we were Americans. We had the American Revolution as precedent." Ironically, Terry and other Open Theater members were interviewed, followed, tape-recorded, and photographed by the FBI and CIA during this time, probably because their work was considered subversive or dangerous (interview with the author).

Terry met Joanne Schmidman, who was to become her lifetime personal and professional partner, at Boston University, where she had been asked to write a two-hundredth anniversary commemorative play (*Approaching Simone*) for the school. Terry and Chaikin needed "a strong person to play Simone. [But] they kept bringing [into auditions] blond people training for soaps." Terry decided that improvisations might reveal an actress of power, and among the performers she chose Schmidman to participate. Joseph Chaikin saw her perform and put her immediately into the Open Theater company. Terry recalls that "everyone else had to crawl over glass for six months" to get in, but Schmidman had so impressed Chaikin with her talent that she was accepted at once. In 1970,

Schmidman joined the Open Theater in what was to be its last three years. Since the theater operated only six months each year, in the summers Schmidman founded and ran the Magic Theater in Omaha, Nebraska, during breaks from her work in New York. Terry joined Schmidman permanently in Omaha in 1974, and the two have been together since that time.

The political and artistic ground covered by Terry and Schmidman at the Magic Theater since the 1970s is immense, but the myriad subjects covered in their works have many common threads. Often the subjects are closely tied to the concerns of their immediate community in Omaha, are about the suppression of freedoms and the destructiveness of totalitarianism, or are explorations of the personal psyche's relationship with self-awareness or the world at large in a technological age. Among their works are *American King's English for Queens* (1978), about "how colloquial usage and career specific language can be used to include or exclude"; *Kegger* (1982), about underage alcohol use and abuse; *Sleazing toward Athens* (1986), about earning versus learning and the price being charged young people for the acquisition of knowledge; *Body Leaks* (1990), about self-censorship; and *Belches on Couches* (1993–94), about the "evolutionary possibilities for the American couch potato" (publicity materials, Omaha Magic Theater, 1996).

Seminal influences on Terry as an artist are popular culture materials such as comic books, radio, advertising, and TV; fine arts such as the work of the antirealistic painters; the lighting of Adolphe Appia and Gordon Craig; Meyerhold; and Antonin Artaud. Terry read Artaud at the age of seventeen, and his observation that "you don't have to feel that it's all been done" propelled Terry's playwriting forward. She continues to write plays, developing new forms and raising old and new questions. For her, "content dictates the form" (interview with the author).

Her work as an artist coincides with her personal life. The collaboration with her personal and professional partner, Joanne Schmidman, has been one of the most fruitful in America's post–World War II theater. For over two decades at the Magic Theater, they have tackled controversial issues, raised significant questions, and invented new modes of theatrical expression. They work as a team, with Schmidman as the director of Terry's works. Terry sees Schmidman as an "advocate of the playwright," and she believes that her work makes a stronger statement because of this partnership.

Terry considers the expression of sexuality to be a right afforded to individuals in a free society. Her own sexual orientation is an inextricable part of her identity and inextricably linked to her work, and she perceives it as one of the many individual freedoms of choice and expression that inform her art.

See "Contemporary Women Artists: A Panel Discussion," in *Images of the Self as Female: the Achievement of Women Artists in Re-envisioning Feminine Identity,* edited by K. N. Benzel and L. Pringle De La Vars, New York, 1992, 247–60; J. Breslauer and H. Keyssar, "Making Magic Public: Megan Terry's Traveling Family Circus," in *Making a Spectacle: Feminist Essays on Contemporary Women's Theatre,* edited by L. Hart, Ann Arbor, 1989, 169–80; E. Diamond, "(Theoretically) Approaching Megan Terry: Issues of Gender and Identity," in *Art and Cinema 3,* New York, 1987; H. Keyssar, "Megan Terry: Mother of American Feminist Theatre: An Introduction to Plays of Contemporary British and American Women," in *Feminist Theatre, An Introduction to Plays of Contemporary British and American Women,* New York, 1985, 53–76; J. Larson, "Public Dreams: A Critical Investigation of the Plays of Megan Terry, 1955–1986," Ph.D. diss., University of Kansas, 1986; "Megan Terry," in *Interviews with Contemporary Women Playwrights,* edited by K. Betsko and R. Koenig, New York, 1987, 377–401; and M. Terry, "Who Says Only Words Make Great Drama?" *New York Times,* November 10, 1968.

Lisbeth Herer

THOMSON, Virgil (1896–1989), composer and critic, was born on November 25, 1896, in Kansas City, Missouri. A musical prodigy as a child, he attended Kansas City Junior College from 1914 until he entered the army in February 1917. In college, he formed a group of intellectuals like himself; they called themselves the Pansophists and devoted themselves to reading and discussion. Thomson was almost expelled from the school for publicly reading selections from the *Spoon River Anthology;* he was saved by the testimony of the president of the Pansophist's sister society, the Anons, that the young women had been warned ahead of time that the material would be presented (Hoover and Cage, 22).

After the war, Thomson entered Harvard University, where he was introduced to the works of two people who would have a profound influence on his compositions: the French composer Eric Satie, whose music would find a sympathetic mirror in many of Thomson's own compositions, and **Gertrude Stein,** whose *Tender Buttons* inspired him to begin setting portions of it to music.

At Harvard, he met Maurice Grosser (1903–86), an artist and author, who would eventually help Thomson to shape libretti into tableaux that facilitated their staging. The relationship between Grosser and Thomson would be the longest of the composer's life, an on and off relationship as lovers and friends that was continually shifting (Tommasini). Thomson lived with the artist at different times and credited Grosser's companionship as inspiring his steady compositional flow (Thomson, 83).

In 1921, Thomson toured France as a member of the Harvard Glee

Virgil Thomson, May 6, 1947, on the eve of the premier of *The Mother of Us All*. (Photo by Irving Haberman, courtesy of the Billy Rose Theatre Collection, New York Public Library for the Performing Arts.)

Club, but when the singing group returned home he remained in Paris for a year. During his stay, he studied composition with Nadia Boulanger, the famous teacher who worked with the majority of the twentieth century's foremost composers. He returned to Harvard in 1922 to finish his degree. There he organized the American premiere of Satie's cantata *Socrate* and was church organist at King's Chapel in Boston.

Thomson returned to Paris in 1925 and remained until 1940, becoming one of the so-called lost generation—a phrase he abhorred (Trilling). In 1926, he met Gertrude Stein and won her friendship when after their first meeting he sent her a musical setting of one of her pieces. Although Stein knew almost nothing about music, she was pleased, and the two became friends. They soon began collaborating on what was to become their first opera, *Four Saints in Three Acts*. Stein turned the libretto over to Thomson and gave him free license to cut it as he saw fit. Not only did he retain anything, but he set everything in the text to music, including her stage directions (Interview by author with Tommasini, January 28, 1997). The piece premiered in Hartford, Connecticut, on February 8, 1934, directed by a young John Houseman. It was subsequently produced on Broadway; after a run of forty-eight performances, it went on to establish performance records worldwide.

Their second collaboration, *The Mother of Us All,* is an opera much less abstract in terms of plot and language. The work premiered at Columbia University on May 7, 1947, eleven months after Stein's death from cancer. The opera centers on Susan B. Anthony, showing her anachronistically onstage with such historical characters as Daniel Webster, John Quincy Adams, Andrew Johnson, and Lillian Russell. While *The Mother of Us All* did not achieve the immediate success of *Four Saints in Three Acts,* it subsequently became popular with opera companies worldwide.

Thomson's third opera, *Lord Byron,* has a libretto by Jack Larson (who played Jimmy Olsen on the *Superman* television series). Initially staged in 1972 by John Houseman, the piece has never equaled the acceptance of Thomson's earlier works; nevertheless, the composer always had a great fondness for it (Rockwell).

Thomson was a prolific composer and wrote musical portraits of his acquaintances throughout his career, usually for solo piano. The subject would sit for the portrait, just as one would for a painter. He also composed the music for several films, among them *Louisiana Story* (1948), for which he was awarded the only Pulitzer Prize ever awarded for a film score. He created music for *Filling Station* (1938), a work commissioned for Ballet Caravan. From 1940 to 1954, as music critic of the *New York Herald Tribune,* he became one of the most significant and influential critical voices in American music.

Thomson's compositions fall broadly into two types: those influenced by Satie, which are found primarily in his earlier music and throughout his orchestrations; and those that reflect the American music of his youth—patriotic, gospel, hymns, and folk music. His decision that *Four Saints in Three Acts* should be sung entirely by a cast of African American singers was revolutionary in 1934. Both operas with Stein contain a male and female narrator; the association with the composer and librettist is made quite clear in *The Mother of Us All,* where they are named Virgil T. and Gertrude S.

In general, Thomson's characteristic musical style intertwines short phrases with abundant native inspiration (above all, the Baptist hymns and the white and black folk music that he grew up hearing) into patterns full of repetition. His music anticipated both minimalism and the eventual return to a diatonic musical style. He also anticipated the movement toward simplicity, accessibility, and the blends of cultivated music with vernacular inspiration that would become a mainstay of much twentieth-century music. In his critical writings, he championed living American composers and helped to shape the American operatic style: simple, understandable settings of the text.

Virgil Thomson died on September 30, 1989, three weeks shy of his ninety-third birthday.

See K. Hoover and J. Cage, *Virgil Thomson: His Life and Music,* New York, 1959; W. Koestenbaum, *The Queen's Throat: Opera, Homosexuality, and the Mystery of Desire,* New York, 1993; R. Marx, jacket notes for *The Mother of Us All,* New World Records, NW 288/289, 1977; J. Mellow, *Charmed Circle: Gertrude Stein and Company,* New York, 1974; J. Rockwell, "Virgil Thomson, Composer, Critic, and Collaborator with Stein, Dies at 92," *New York Times,* October 1, 1989; V. Thomson, *Virgil Thomson,* New York, 1966; D. Trilling, "An Interview with Virgil Thomson," *Partisan Review* 47 (1980): 544–58; and A. Tommasini, *Virgil Thomson: Composer on the Aisle,* New York, 1997.

Don Whittaker

VAN DRUTEN, John (1901–57), playwright, novelist, and stage director, was born in London on June 1, 1901. Educated at London's University College School between 1911 and 1917, Van Druten then studied law at the University of London before becoming a solicitor in 1923. He taught law at the University College of Wales between 1923 and 1926, beginning his playwriting career during this time. His first produced play, *The Return Half,* was staged with modest success in 1924 at the Royal Academy of Dramatic Art.

In 1926, Van Druten decided to devote himself to writing full time and emigrated to America (he became a U.S. citizen in 1944). Once firmly established in America, he began a successful career as a dramatist that would span nearly thirty years. Only a few playwrights have achieved the level of popular success on both sides of the Atlantic that Van Druten attained between the mid-1930s and the early 1950s. Often compared to nineteenth-century playwright and actor Dion Boucicault, whose plays also addressed the concerns and tastes of both British and American audiences, Van Druten similarly became known as a first-rate craftsman of well-made plays of character and comedies of manners. His earliest dramas were in the "problem play" mode, as in the case of *After All* (1929), which criticized a rather typical upper middle class English family that falls into disrepute due to its inability to face up to its economic decline.

John Van Druten in about 1932, when his play *There's Always Juliet* opened on Broadway. (Courtesy of the Billy Rose Theatre Collection, New York Public Library for the Performing Arts.)

These first works were often subject to censorship. *Young Woodley* (1925) was refused a license by the lord chamberlain because its subject matter focused on a schoolboy's love for a teacher's wife. It was performed in America first, serving as an inspiring forerunner of Robert Anderson's highly successful *Tea and Sympathy* (1953) a generation later.

Van Druten's maturing works shifted the focus more to character than theme, as exemplified by *There's Always Juliet* (1932), *The Distaff Side* (1933), and *Old Acquaintance* (1940). All of these feature strong-willed women characters, a Van Druten specialty, and, like his other works of the era, they have often been compared favorably to Anton Chekhov's plays. Late in his career, Van Druten experimented with comic potboilers, most lucratively with *Bell, Book, and Candle* (1950). However, it was during the last fifteen years of his career that his most representative plays were written. These frequently examined changing sexual mores. *The Damask Cheek* (1943), cowritten with Lloyd Morris, places a young British woman in staid New England, where she creates a scandal by approving of sex outside of marriage. *The Voice of the Turtle* (1943) also depicts a strong young woman who rejects outmoded social conventions. A highly proficient adapter of the works of others, Van Druten had a great success with *I Am a Camera* (1951), based on **Christopher Isherwood**'s stories. In this work, Van Druten more pointedly addressed sexual matters in the decadent early days of Nazi Germany through the story of free-spirited Sally Bowles and her tempestuous affair with a bisexual writer, Chris, who was based on Isherwood himself. *I Am a Camera* evolved into the musical drama *Cabaret,* an acclaimed Broadway success, in 1966. Van Druten's other outstanding dramatic adaption, *I Remember Mama* (1944), a long-running Broadway success that spawned a film version and a perennial radio and television drama, was based on Kathryn Forbes's recollections of her Norwegian family and her beginnings as a writer.

Along with his stage work, Van Druten also wrote several screenplays, including *Night Must Fall* (1937), *The Citadel* (1938), *Johnny Come Lately* (1943), and *Gaslight* (1944). He worked on the screen versions of a few of his own plays, including *Young Woodley* (1930), *Old Acquaintance* (1943), and *The Voice of the Turtle* (1948). He wrote several novels and memoirs, all of which were received respectfully, and he also directed on Broadway, most notably several of his own plays and the original production of Richard Rodgers and Oscar Hammerstein's *The King and I* in 1951.

Living in an era when his sexual orientation, if known, would have ruined his hopes of commercial success, Van Druten, a lifelong bachelor, veiled his homosexuality behind the strong but troubled women characters of his plays, much as **Tennessee Williams** did in his earliest works. His manner was often described by interviewers and critics as "mild," and in his autobiography, which was published shortly after his death, he betrayed his sexuality only by recalling some "close friendships with several nameless young men" and the pain of his "mildness" when he recalled that "I was bullied at school, tormented by wrist-twisting, and by the gibes and ridicule of masters and recruit-squad sergeants in the O.T.C. . . . The only weapon which it seemed could serve me against them was the weapon of the tongue" (*The Widening Circle,* 18). In a book on the process of playwriting, he wrote: "A play recommending homosexuality, or taking a tolerant view of it (not regarding it as a form of sickness), would be hard of acceptance. That may not last forever. If the author has a firm conviction on the subject, a firm and basic desire to write that play, then he should do so" (*Playwright at Work,* 48). Van Druten envisioned a theater he could not be part of, and apparently his own convictions were not strong enough to lead him to write a play taking a "tolerant view" of homosexuality, perhaps because he placed a high value on the approval of an audience that was not, in his time, prepared to accept such a play.

Following treatment for a heart ailment, Van Druten died in his sleep on December 19, 1957, in Indio, California. His obituary in the *New York Times* described him as "a gentle man who wrote gentle plays."

See "John Van Druten, Playwright, Dead," *New York Times,* December 19, 1957; J. Van Druten, *The Way to the Present: A Personal Record,* New York, 1938; J. Van Druten, *Playwright at Work,* New York, 1953; and J. Van Druten, *The Widening Circle,* New York, 1957. Most of Van Druten's novels and plays are in print. No significant critical studies have been published on his work.

James Fisher

van ITALLIE, Jean-Claude (1936–), playwright, was born on May 25, 1936, in Belgium to Hughes and Marthe (Levy) van Itallie on the eve of World War II. His mother, who was Jewish, and his father, who was part Jewish, chose not to have the boy circumcised in order to hide his heritage from the Nazis. Reflecting on that choice sixty years later, van Itallie has said metaphorically that his life's work has been "to uncover the truth about myself" (interview with the author, December 31, 1996).

Following the German invasion in 1940, the family escaped to France and went on to Spain and Portugal before finally taking a Japanese ship to the United States. Van Itallie's first home in the United States was the Taft Hotel in New York City, but the family soon moved to Forest Hills when Hughes went to work on Wall Street ("Jean-Claude van Itallie," 6–8).

Jean-Claude van Itallie at his farm in Massachusetts in 2002.
(Courtesy of Jean-Claude van Itallie.)

In 1942, another son, Michael, was born to the van Itallies, and the
family moved to the posh suburb of Great Neck, New York, where they
were to remain during van Itallie's childhood and adolescence. He
attended the public schools there, and performed in productions by the
Junior Players, the high school drama club. He became a U.S. citizen in
1952 and the next year went to Deerfield Academy in Massachusetts to

finish his senior year of high school. He was admitted to Harvard University in 1954 and became a history and literature major. He was active in theater during his college years and wrote his senior thesis on "The Pessimism of Jean Anouilh." After receiving a bachelor of arts degree from Harvard in 1958, he did graduate study in the television and film program at New York University (*Contemporary Dramatists,* 671–73).

He moved to Christopher Street in Greenwich Village in 1960. In the next few years, he would publish a short story, "Francois Yattend," in the *Transatlantic Review,* where he was editor until 1963; work as a researcher for the television network CBS; and become engaged, briefly, to Tania Leontov, a high school friend.

He calls the death of his mother from a brain tumor in 1963 as "the most tragic experience in my life" (*Other Stages,* 4). But it was during that same year that his career as a writer blossomed. Gordon Rogoff introduced him to Joseph Chaikin, who formed the Open Theater that year, and van Itallie began attending workshops there. While their relationship was first and foremost professional, Chaikin and van Itallie soon became lovers, forming an intimate bond, both as lovers and later as friends (interview with the author). The first public performance by the Open Theater, in December 1963, included van Itallie's one-act play *From an Odets Kitchen.*

During the same month, van Itallie's one act *War* was produced by the Barr-Wilder-Albee Playwrights Unit at the Vandam Theatre. In an interview years later, he would say: "*War* is probably my most evidently 'gay' play. But I hope that my gay van Itallie brothers and sisters are moved by what moves me and that whatever plays I have written are for them and especially for them, too" (*Christopher Street,* 21).

Van Itallie was a playwright-in-residence with the Open Theater from 1963 to 1968, with the "trust and intimate tension" of his romance with Chaikin fueling his work (interview with the author). During this time, he wrote numerous short pieces, including what became known as "The Doris (Day) Plays," a series of wacky comedies about Hollywood, including *Almost Like Being* and *I'm Really Here* (*Contemporary Dramatists,* 673). The themes that emerged in his works involved the American political and social landscapes and the forces that cause individuals to behave violently or withdraw from society altogether, and he found what Robert Brustein calls "the truest poetic function of the theatre, which is to . . . invent metaphors which can poignantly suggest a nation's nightmares and afflictions" (*Contemporary Authors,* 674).

His best-known work during this period is *America Hurrah,* a group of three one-act plays: *Interview* (formerly called *Pavanne*), *TV,* and *Motel: A*

Masque for Three Dolls. The latter was directed by Michael Kahn with dolls created by Robert Wilson and presented along with *Interview* at Café LaMama ETC in 1965. The show moved Off-Broadway to the Pocket Theatre the next year, when *TV* was added, under the direction of Chaikin, van Itallie, and Jacques Levy and ran for 640 performances. When the Royal Court Theatre in London chose to produce the play, the lord chamberlain refused to grant a license, causing the producers to change the Royal Court into a private club, where the show was successfully produced in 1967. Van Itallie won an Outer Circle Critics Award and the Vernon Rice Award for *America Hurrah* that same year.

His theater writing was supported during this time, in part, by a grant from the Rockefeller Foundation, as well as from his work in television. Between 1964 and 1966, he wrote eleven adaptations for the CBS television series *Look Up and Live,* as well as half a dozen original scripts for the program from 1963 through 1969.

The fervent period of the 1960s ended with another successful collaboration with Joseph Chaikin in *The Serpent: A Ceremony.* This one act, which van Itallie says is a product of his intimate relationship with Chaikin, first opened in Rome at Teatro degli Arte in 1968 before being produced in Cambridge, Massachusetts, at Loeb Drama Center in 1969 and finally produced Off-Broadway by the Open Theater at the Public Theatre in May 1969 (interview with the author). van Itallie won an Off-Broadway award (an Obie) for the piece, which uses the Book of Genesis to explore themes about the human condition.

Van Itallie considers the 1960s to have been "an exciting time of revolt and reformation," which he used during the 1970s when he wrote new versions of the classics, a period he considers "a time of retrenchment" (*Contemporary Dramatists,* 672). During that decade, he adapted Chekhov's *The Sea Gull* (1973), *The Cherry Orchard* (1977), *Three Sisters* (1979), and *Uncle Vanya* (1983), as well as Euripides' *Medea* (1979). But he also wrote important original works, including *Mystery Play,* which was produced at the Cherry Lane Theatre Off-Broadway and then revised and retitled *The King of the United States,* with music by Richard Peaslee, in 1973. In a review of the production in the *New York Times,* Mel Gussow wrote that "van Itallie is revealed as one of the most astute theatrical commentators on the indelicacies and indecencies in the American social and political scene" (Gussow, 21). He collaborated with **Megan Terry** and Sam Shepard on a play called *Nightwalk* (1973) and with Joseph Chaikin and Richard Peaslee on *A Fable* (1975). He won the first of his two Guggenheim fellowships in 1973 (the other was awarded in 1980), and was awarded an honorary doctorate from Kent State University in 1977.

Van Itallie began to explore Buddhism in college and became a follower of the Tibetan lama Chogyam Trungpa, Rinpoche, in the early 1970s. This exploration found its way into his work, especially during the next decade, when he wrote *Naropa* (1982) and, more significantly, *The Tibetan Book of the Dead; or, How Not to Do It Again* (1983), both plays with music by Steve Gorn.

The 1980s also saw the production of three one acts in an evening entitled *Early Warnings*, including *Bag Lady* (written and originally produced in 1979), *Sunset Freeway,* and *Final Orders* (1983). In this decade, which brought the pain of Joseph Chaikin's stroke in 1984 and, of course, the AIDS crisis, he wrote *The Traveler* (1987) about Chaikin's stroke, which was produced in Los Angeles, Leicester, and London that year. As Chaikin recovered, van Itallie wrote a performance piece for his friend called *Struck Dumb,* which was produced in both Los Angeles (1989) and New York (1991). *Ancient Boys,* inspired by the death of his friend the puppeteer Robert Anton of complications from AIDS, was produced in Boulder, Colorado (1990), and at LaMama ETC in New York (1991).

The 1990s have continued to be productive for van Itallie. In 1993, he adapted Mikhail Bulgakov's banned 1940 novel, *Master and Margarita,* for a production at Theatre for the New City in New York. He completely revised his adaptations of the Chekhov plays, which were published in 1995.

The American Music Theatre Festival and the Houston Grand Opera cocommissioned an opera of van Itallie's *The Tibetan Book of the Dead,* with music by Ricky Ian Gordon, which was presented in both Philadelphia and Houston in the summer of 1996 (*Village Voice,* 68–69). The prolific writer has also begun his memoirs, which, along with his journals, may comprise three volumes when finished. Drawing on these writings, he created a performance piece about his childhood and "coming out" as a gay man, *Guy's Dreamin',* which had its first performances in Boston and at LaMama ETC in New York in 1996. Two years later, another one-man show, *War, Sex, and Dreams,* premiered at LaMama ETC to favorable reviews. In 2002, van Itallie completed his latest play, *The Enlightenment.* His book on playwriting, *The Playwriting Workbook,* was published in 1997. Grove Press issued his anthology, *America Hurrah and Other Plays* in 2001. He also conducts workshops all over the country in which "spiritual and artistic practices meet" because he feels that spiritual life and artistic life are, "in a deeper sense, the same thing" (interview with the author).

Van Itallie's career has included writing for the theater, film, and television, as well as directing and acting in the theater and teaching at some of the nation's finest universities. An article in the *New York Times* states that he "identifies himself not only as an artist, but equally as a Tibetan Buddhist, an antinuclear activist, a teacher and a homosexual." (Harris, B5). Jean-Claude van Itallie lives on his farm in Massachusetts, which is now run by the Shantigar (meaning "Peaceful Home") Foundation, and in New York City.

See *Christopher Street,* June 1978; *Contemporary Authors,* New Revision Series, vol. I, Detroit, 1981; *Contemporary Dramatists,* 5th ed., London, 1993; M. Gussow, review of *The King of The United States, New York Times,* November 23, 1974; W. Harris, "Plays Are For Questions, Not Answers," *New York Times,* May 23, 1993; "Jean-Claude van Itallie," special issue of *Serif* (Kent, Ohio), 9, no. 4 (winter, 1972); *Other Stages,* May 17, 1979; J.-C. van Itallie, *America Hurrah and Other Plays,* New York, 2001; J.-C. van Itallie, *The Playwriting Workbook,* New York, 1997; and *Village Voice,* July 9, 1996. See also the van Itallie's Web site, <http://www.vanitallie.com>, accessed June 28, 2004.

Jon Fraser

VIDAL, Gore (Eugene Luther Vidal) (1925–), essayist, novelist, playwright, and screenwriter, was born in West Point, New York, to Eugene and Nina Gore Vidal. The family moved shortly after his birth to Washington, D.C. Living there with his maternal grandparents, Vidal discovered literature and history as he read books to his blind grandfather (Thomas P. Gore, an Oklahoma senator) from the elder statesman's library. In 1935, Vidal's parents divorced. Shortly thereafter, Nina married Hugh D. Auchincloss Jr. and moved her son to the Auchincloss's family estate in Virginia.

For the next four years, Vidal attended St. Alban's school in Washington, where he boarded during the week, and it was during these years that he had his first sexual experiences. At St. Alban's, Vidal met James "Jimmie" Trimble (1925–45), who he later came to regard as his "other half, reconstituting the original male that Zeus had split in two" (Vidal, *Palimpsest,* 23 and 31). By his own reckoning, young Gene's short-lived love affair with Trimble represented the single merging of his sexual and emotional life. A prominent theme in his memoirs and at least one novel, Vidal's love affair with Trimble has haunted him ever since.

Although Vidal admits sexual consummation with both genders, he has steadfastly refused to label his sexual identity. He notes that his experience has been "largely with males" (Wieder, 39) but rejects whatever label is proposed, saying: "I don't think you need a word for it" (Mitzel and Abbott, 53). His refusal of a sexual identity has sociopolitical ramifications. As he has explained: "To be categorized is, simply, to be enslaved. Watch out." Later in the same interview, he compromises: "Anyway, I accept no labels about myself other, perhaps, than failed revolutionary" (Wieder, 38 and 39).

Vidal continued his education in New Mexico for a year, where he renamed himself from Eugene to Gore, and then entered the Exeter Academy in September 1940. John Knowles was in the class behind him, and Gore became the model of Brinker in Knowles's *A Separate Peace* (1959). After graduating in 1943, and rather than attending Harvard, as his father wished, he joined the army. Thus, his formal education ended with high school. He was initially stationed in Colorado and then served with the Army Transport Service in the Aleutian Islands. During his military tenure, he completed his debut work (*Williwaw,* 1946), the first of six novels published during the next five years. His third book (*The City and the Pillar,* 1948) would later become known as the "father of contemporary homosexual fiction" (Dick, 31). Dedicated to Trimble, the novel chronicles the adventures of an ordinary young man from his first idyllic same-sex affair through his travels in the gay world.

In the early 1950s, Vidal continued to write fiction (publishing some works under the pseudonym Edgar Box) and began his relationship with Howard Austen. According to Vidal, they have remained companions for forty-five years: "As the relationship is not sexual . . . I do my best to observe my own law: no sex with friends if you want to keep the friend" (Wieder, 40). He wrote and adapted works for television beginning in 1954, and later in the decade he worked for MGM under contract, adapting **Tennessee Williams**'s *Suddenly Last Summer* for the screen.

In the late 1950s, he began writing for the stage. While Vidal has written in most literary genres, he claims that no form comes easier than others, nor does he have a preference: "It's all the same" (Stanton and Vidal, 65). However, he was attracted to the theater for economic reasons: "I should never have been drawn to playwriting had it been possible to live by prose" (Vidal, *Visit,* xxii). In 1957, his first stage work, *Visit to a Small Planet,* adapted from his own teleplay, ran on Broadway for over three hundred performances. *The Best Man* (1960) followed, opening in the same year in which Vidal suffered the first of two defeats running for the U.S. Congress. *The Best Man* became his longest-running play, with over five hundred performances. In it, two candidates vie for an unspecified party's nomination, and one blackmails his opponent (William Russell), who must weigh the morality of a counterattack by publicizing his married antagonist's rumored homosexuality. Although neither character becomes the chosen candidate, and Russell refuses to reveal the gay gossip about his opponent, Vidal hints at the destructive consequences for a politician in even a merely rumored homosexual encounter. Nevertheless, gay innuendo is simply a plot detail and not a central theme in the work. *The Best Man* was topical in that presidential election year but "quite easily dated in its appeal and comprehensibility" (Parini, 129). In 1964 Vidal wrote the screenplay, which starred Henry Fonda. During the 2000 presidential election, the play was revived on Broadway and praised for its relevance.

Vidal's future dramatic projects never matched *The Best Man* in popularity. In 1962, *Romulus* (an adaptation of Friedrich Duerrenmatt's *Romulus the Great*) had only seventy performances, while *Weekend* (1968) and *An Evening with Richard Nixon* (1972) both had less than thirty. Thus, when his pieces were no longer profitable, Vidal ceased to write for the stage. As his success with playwriting faded, he reestablished himself as a writer of fiction through his historical novels *Washington, D.C.* (1967), *Burr* (1973), and *1876* (1976), as well as his tale of transsexualism, *Myra Breckinridge* (1968). In the 1980s and 1990s, he continued to produce novels (*Lincoln* in 1984 and *Hollywood* in 1990) and increasingly concentrated on essays, many of which are collected in his *United States: Essays, 1952–1992* (1993). As an essayist, he assesses a wide variety of subjects, ranging from history to modern politics sexual mores, and literature. Since the late 1960s, he has maintained his primary residence in Italy.

Though unlikely to be remembered for his plays, Gore Vidal's significance as an intellectual and critic demands attention. In his 1981 essay "Pink Triangle and Yellow Star," he warns against the growing conservative movement, "whose kindly voice is that of Ronald Reagan," and cautions minorities such as gays, blacks, and Jews to form a unified front or risk obliteration (*United States,* 611). He must be admired for his courage in publishing works such as *The City and the Pillar* at a time when public discussion of homosexuality was taboo and for his outspoken, thought-provoking essays. By refusing to label his sexual identity, he anticipated multiculturalism and gender issues, which are finally gaining attention and scholarly respectability in the academy.

See B. Dick, *The Apostate Angel: A Critical Study of Gore Vidal,* New York, 1974; J. Mitzel and S. Abbott, *Myra and Gore,* Dorchester, Mass., 1974; J. Parini, ed., *Gore Vidal: Writer against the Grain,* New York, 1992; R. J. Stanton and G. Vidal, eds., *Views from a Window: Conversations with Gore Vidal,* Secaucus, N.J., 1980; G. Vidal, *Palimpsest: A Memoir,* New York, 1995; G. Vidal, *United States: Essays, 1952–1992,* New York, 1993; G. Vidal, *Visit to a Small Planet,* Boston, 1957; and J. Wieder, "Vidal on Vidal," *The Advocate,* October 31, 1995.

Mark Zelinsky

WEBB, Clifton (1889 or 1891–1966), dancer, singer, and actor, was born Webb Parmalee Hollenbeck in Indianapolis, Indiana, the son of an ambitious stage mother and a father who was a railway ticket clerk (Mann, 251). A versatile performer, Webb had already enjoyed a long and prominent stage and revue career by the time he became a screen star in his fifties. He was also noted "in show-business circles for being unabashedly padlocked to his mother's apron strings and an uncloseted homosexual" (Parish and Leonard, 665).

Webb's mother, Mabelle, transferred her own unrealized theatrical yearnings to her son early on, teaching him "to recite and dance before company," an influence that infuriated her husband, Jacob Hollenbeck (Holland, 196). When Clifton was three, Mabelle spirited him off to New York. Some suggest that Jacob tracked them down and continued to visit, while other accounts state that "Clifton never again saw his father after that" (Mann, 252). At any rate, the couple eventually divorced, and Jacob was to remain an insignificant and ultimately exiled figure in both of their lives. By contrast, Mabelle became Clifton's best "pal" (Holland, 195), and he lived with her all her life. According to press reports: "Their relationship . . . bordered on the incestuous," almost to the point where they could "be seen as husband and wife" (Mann, 250–51).

In New York, Mabelle enrolled Clifton in music, dancing, and acting school, where at the age of seven, having attracted an agent's attention, he won an audition at Palmer Cox's Children's Theatre. The outcome was his stage debut (1900) as "Cholly" in *The Brownies,* using the stage name Webb Raum in accordance with his mother's remarriage to a man named Green Raum, whom she later divorced (Mann, 252). For four seasons, he "flitted around in his part as a fairy" (Holland, 196), and several children's plays followed, including *Oliver Twist, The Prince and the Pauper,* and *The Master of Charlton Hall.*

After outgrowing such roles, Webb developed into "quite the artistic young teenager" (Parish and Leonard, 666), studying painting with Robert Henri and opera with Victor Maurel and being tutored in several languages. He held an art exhibition at the age of fourteen and learned to play piano well enough to begin composing concertos at sixteen—about the time he changed his name to Clifton Webb, purportedly because his mother had been taken by the name of Clifton, New Jersey, while passing through there (Mann, 253). In 1906, Webb made his operatic debut with Boston's Aborn Opera Company in *Mignon;* he subsequently appeared in *La Bohème, Madame Butterfly,* and several other productions, until the emergence of the dance craze prompted him to abandon opera in favor of making "a reputation as a dancer" (Parish and Leonard, 666).

He did so with great success. In his Broadway debut (1913) in *The Purple Road,* whose cast included his mother, Webb's effeminate performance drew much laughter, and he was quickly noted for his originality. He was paired for a while with a ballroom dancer, Bonnie Glass, and then briefly with Mae Murray, but his most successful teamwork would be in the 1920s with former Ziegfeld Follies showgirl Mary Hay. Usually playing droll, effeminate roles, Webb gained attention through club and vaudeville shows as well as Broadway performances in *Dancing Around* (1914) and Jerome Kern's *Love O' Mike* (1917), in which he was noted for "some exuberant dancing" (*New York Times,* January 16, 1917). Soon he was establishing a reputation in Europe, playing London in *Fun at the Phayre* (1921) and *Phi-Phi* (1922) and Paris (in 1923) at Les Acacias, a club that belonged to his friend Elsa Maxwell. Webb's return to Broadway for a leading role in *Meet the Wife* (1923) fulfilled his desire to be known as more than a dancer and launched his fame as a comic actor; one critic wrote that he, "stepping out of his dancing shoes, also supplies a good deal of amusement" (*New York Times,* November 27, 1923).

During the next few years, Webb made a brief but inconsequential foray into silent movies, with roles in *Polly with a Past* (1920), *Heart of a Siren* (1925), and *New Toys* (1925). But his stage career was prospering, first with Marilyn Miller in the smash hits *Sunny* (1925) and with Gertrude Lawrence in *Treasure Girl* (1928), then with Libby Holman in *The Little Show* (1929). The latter featured a rousing apache dance along with Holman's famous "Moanin' Low" number, which Webb directed. He and Hay also headlined at the Palace in January 1929. "By the mid-Twenties, Webb was one of Broadway's highest paid stars" (Mass, 254), and his performance in *Three's a Crowd* (1930) earned high praise from critic Brooks Atkinson, who described Webb as "at the top of his form," a dancer who was "a pliant figure of postures and rhythms." Atkinson called the "Body and Soul" dance in *Three's a Crowd* "a thing of black magic," (*New York Times,* October 26, 1930), while *Theatre* noted that this extraordinary number "has made him one of the most sought after song-and-dance men in town (23)." Similar adulation followed for *Flying Colors* (1932), but Webb's greatest success came with the Irving Berlin and Moss Hart show *As Thousands Cheer* (1933), in which Webb impersonated such celebrities as John Rockefeller, Noël Coward, and Ghandi to great acclaim. By 1933, Atkinson could write: "It is almost impossible to produce a smart revue without putting Clifton Webb into it somewhere" (*New York Times,* October 15, 1933).

As Webb's fame grew, so did the gossip about him. He lived with his mother on an estate in Greenwich, Connecticut, and at the Park Lane

Hotel in New York City, along with a black French poodle named Ernest and a parrot, Goo-Goo, which was notorious for insulting guests, much to Webb's delight (Block, 810). Although Webb was often linked romantically with leading ladies, "he was the subject of much speculation concerning assorted homosexual affairs," which he "took little effort to conceal" (Parrish and Leonard, 667). In fact, Holland speculates that the movie mogul Louis B. Mayer feared promoting as a romantic star someone "so widely suspected of being a homosexual" (Holland, 195), even though he had lured Webb to Hollywood in 1935 at a salary of $3,000 a week. Webb remained there for eighteen months doing virtually nothing but swimming and vacationing, as the proposed film, *Elegance,* based on the life of the dancer Maurice, dissolved due to star discord (Joan Crawford) and story problems. Holland suggests that the project was finally abandoned because of Mayer's concern over Webb's image. When Webb ended the siege by returning to New York, he said: "The only thing I can really chide the movie industry for is its negligent attitude toward the actor's chief assets—time and talent" (Parish and Leonard, 667).

The ensuing decade brought Webb continued success on the New York stage, including performances in such classics as *The Importance of Being Earnest* (1939), *Blithe Spirit* (1941)—which provided him with his longest run, 650 performances (Parish and Leonard, 667–68)—and *Present Laughter* (1946), as well as *And Stars Remain* (1936) and *You Never Know* (1938), the latter written by his good friend **Cole Porter.** After *The Man Who Came to Dinner* opened in the fall of 1939, with **Monty Woolley,** Webb was cast as the acidic Sheridan Whiteside for the touring version, in which he remained for a year and a half.

In 1944, Webb's career took yet another turn. Performing *Blithe Spirit* in Los Angeles, he was spotted by director Otto Preminger, who persuaded Darryl Zanuck to cast him as Waldo Lydecker in the film version of Vera Caspary's best-selling novel *Laura.* Zanuck resisted, protesting Webb's effeminacy (he said Webb "flies"), but Preminger argued that Webb's offstage mannerism did not carry over into his performances (Parrish and Leonard, 668). Zanuck relented, and the movie was an enormous hit, earning Webb his first Academy Award nomination for Best Supporting Actor (he lost to Barry Fitzgerald for *Going My Way*). A second nomination came two years later for his role as the acerbic Elliott Templeton in the film adaptation of Somerset Maugham's *The Razor's Edge* (1946), which Holland considers the movie that "came closest to showing the real Clifton Webb" (193). Director Edmund Goulding in fact "encouraged the very gay Clifton Webb to play his character the same way" in this film (Mann, 177), marking him as one of many gay actors who would "infuse their celluloid character with personal temper" (8). Indeed, Webb was considered by many to be icy and haughty, and this film certainly established the bitchy, egocentric, and sharp-tongued screen persona that became his trademark.

After this cinematic triumph, Webb returned to New York for the last time, to star in *Present Laughter,* and then in 1948, permanently ensconced in Hollywood, he was catapulted to major stardom as Mr. Belvedere in *Sitting Pretty,* in which he "stole the picture." This performance earned him his third Academy Award nomination, this time as Best Actor, although Laurence Olivier won as Hamlet (Mann, 255). With its famous scene of Webb dumping oatmeal on a baby's head, *Sitting Pretty* generated a pair of sequels, neither quite as successful: *Mr. Belvedere Goes to College* (1949) with Shirley Temple, and *Mr. Belvedere Rings the Bell* (1951). Both films continued to showcase "his 'flippantly arrogant' personality" (Mann, 255). In subsequent films, including *Cheaper by the Dozen* (1950), *Mr. Scoutmaster* (1953), and *The Remarkable Mr. Pennypacker* (1954), the "avowed bachelor" Webb, as the press often referred to him, was ironically cast as a family man. He also played roles in *For Heaven's Sake* (1950), *Elopement* (1951), *Dreamboat* (1952) with Ginger Rogers, and *Stars and Stripes Forever* (1952), in which he played bandleader John Philip Sousa. Webb's own personality reasserted itself in *Titanic,* in which he played a snobby expatriate, as well as in the hilarious *Woman's World* (1954) and *Boy on a Dolphin* (1957). His homosexuality "informed both reel and real-life personas," notes Mann. "It's impossible to separate Webb's offscreen star persona—urbane, caustic, arch, and decidedly homosexual—from his screen roles . . . [for] Clifton was always playing himself" (256, 249).

Having settled on the West Coast for good, Webb and his mother moved into a house on North Rexford Drive, which Webb continually renovated to make it a "dream home." Their neighbors included Mickey Rooney, Boris Karloff, and **Marlene Dietrich** (Parish and Leonard, 669). He became renowned for his scintillating witticisms, which "only increased his reputation as the waspish duenna of Hollywood" (669). Throughout his life, Webb and his mother continued to travel, logging over three dozen trips to Europe.

In October 1960, Webb was devastated by the death of his mother at the age of ninety. His grief and tears have become legendary, and his friend Noël Coward, who called him "the world's oldest orphan," reportedly told him over the phone to stop wailing or "I shall be forced to reverse the charges" (Holland, 204; Parish and Leonard, 673). Webb never really recovered from the loss of his mother, from whom he had always been inseparable. He remained secluded and miserable for the rest of his life, making only one more film, *Satan Never Sleeps* (1962), which was poorly received and revealed the terrible aging he had undergone. In October 1966, he died at his home of a heart attack.

Webb's undaunted acceptance of his homosexuality, supplemented by his obsessive relationship with his mother, no doubt nurtured his screen career, as he played priggish and polished characters much like himself. These personas also helped him to armor himself "against the world with an acidic exterior" (Parish and Leonard, 665). Webb left both a stage and screen legacy, having spent nearly half a decade as a renowned song and dance man on Broadway and going on to achieve major Hollywood stardom with nearly two dozen films.

See M. Block, ed., *Current Biography,* New York, 1943; G. Bordman, ed., *The Oxford Companion to American Theatre,* New York, 1984; L. L. Holland, "Clifton Webb," *Films in Review,* April 1981; W. J. Mann, *Behind the Screen: How Gays and Lesbians Shaped Hollywood, 1910–1916,* New York, 2001; *New York Times,* January 16, 1917; *New York Times,* November 27, 1923; *New York Times,* October 26, 1930; *New York Times,* October 15, 1933; J. R. Parish and W. T. Leonard, *The Funsters,* New York, 1979; A. Slick, *The Encyclopedia of Vaudeville,* Westport, Conn., 1994; and *Theatre,* March 1931.

Karen C. Blansfield

WEBSTER, Margaret (1905–72), Anglo-American director, actor, producer, and writer, was born in New York City at 260 West 59th Street while her father, Benjamin Webster III, accompanied by her mother Mary Louise ("May") Whitty, was on tour from London with the William Brady-Grace George Company. Her parents returned with their new daughter to 31 Bedford Place, London, where they resided for the next thirty-three years.

As the daughter of well-known professional actors, "Peggy," as she was known to family and friends, grew up in the world of the commercial theater. She was educated at the Burlington School for Girls and during the war years at Bradley Wood House in Devonshire and Queen Anne's School in Reading. She excelled in languages, literature, and history to the degree that her teachers at Queen Anne's proposed her for a university scholarship to Oxford or Cambridge. Dame May Whitty intervened to preserve the theatrical career of the fifth generation of Websters, who had made their reputations on the London stage as actors, managers, and dancing masters. Conceding to her parents' wishes, Peggy received her formal training as an actor at the Etlinger Dramatic School, where her parents taught. She was forever sanguine about her career choice and often quipped that her parents objected "to my stage career with the usual insincerity of theatrical parents" (*Celebrity Register,* 814).

Peggy's childhood and adolescent years as an "only" child were spent with her parents' professional friends and in the company of three strong-willed, accomplished women: May Whitty, Sybil Thorndike, and Edith Craig. Her celebrity mother was known as a "petite, doe-eyed beauty," Sybil Thorndike as one of the great classical actresses of her day, and Edith Craig as the "Bohemian" daughter of the renowned actress Ellen Terry. These women directed Peggy's life, early career, and developing sexuality. May Whitty and Sybil Thorndike guided her career, but Edith Craig demonstrated a life of twin devotions to her aging mother and her female lover, Christopher St. John (née Christabel Marshall). Craig was Peggy's first acquaintance with a woman who lived an alternative lifestyle that was accepted by the theatrical community as little more than an oddity.

Peggy's adolescent weight problems—at nineteen, she was five feet, four inches tall and weighed 140 pounds—relegated her to theatrical roles as aunts, spinsters, and chorus members in the provincial companies where she practiced her early craft: first with the Casson-Thorndike Company, where she made her professional debut in 1924 as a chorus member in *The Trojan Women;* then with J. B. Fagan's Oxford Players; the Ben Greet Shakespeare Company; and, finally, Lilian Baylis's Old Vic. Peggy emerged from the chaotic obscurity of touring companies onto the stage of the Old Vic in the 1929–30 season. After a year of playing minor roles in a company with John Gielgud as the rising star, she declined to renew her contract with the Old Vic and returned to her parents' West End world. There, after many disappointing months, she played in lengthy runs with Sir Martin Harvey in *The Devil's Disciple* and in John Gielgud's productions of *Musical Chairs* and *Richard of Bordeaux.* Between these productions, she made her directing debut in 1934 with Shake-speare's *Henry VIII,* in which she directed eight hundred women in an outdoor production for the British National Federation of Women's Institutes in Kent. Peggy had found her true artistic place in the theater, but it would take several years and an ocean voyage before she would be a stage director of international importance.

Actor Maurice Evans, a friend from her Etlinger schooldays, salvaged her career from minor parts in West End comedies. Evans telephoned from New York City to invite her to direct him in a series of Shakespeare plays on Broadway. Faced with the very realistic dilemma of finding no American directors to whom he could entrust his new career as a Shake-spearean leading actor, Evans summoned his friend from London. Peggy's directing experience was limited to showcases and Sunday matinees, but her acting experience in Shakespeare, even in minor roles, was extensive. Evans's choice of Peggy minimized his risks. With one of the aggressive young male directors (Orson Welles, John Houseman, or even John Gielgud), he risked losing control not only of the productions but of the leading roles he envisioned for himself. By accepting his offer to direct *Richard II,* Peggy changed the direction of her life and her career. She returned to the city of her birth in 1937 to become, almost overnight, the leading director of Shakespeare on Broadway and to submerge herself into a lesbian culture that would include other leading theater artists. She would be associated with men, such as actor Maurice Evans and composer **Lehman Engel,** as friends and colleagues throughout her life but never as sexual partners.

The 1940s were Peggy's halcyon days. Following the unprecedented 1937 success of the first Evans-Webster production, they staged four more Shakespeare plays in the next decade: *Hamlet; Macbeth; Henry IV, Part I;* and *Twelfth Night.* For the Theatre Guild, Peggy played opposite **Alfred Lunt** and **Lynn Fontanne** in *The Sea Gull* and directed **Tennessee Williams**'s first full-length play, *Battle of Angels.* The climax of her career came with the 1943 production of *Othello,* in which she and Paul Robeson defied stage and social conventions by introducing the first African American actor to Broadway in the title role. In the face of hostile predictions of doom for Peggy's decision to use an interracial cast—Robeson as Othello, Uta Hagen as Desdemona, José Ferrer as Iago, and Peggy herself as Emilia—the production broke all box office records for a Shakespeare play, with 296 performances followed by a national tour. Throughout, Peggy had argued the paramount importance of the black actor to the play's "credibility and to the validity of every character in it" (Webster, *Shakespeare without Tears,* 178). Although some critics expressed reservations about Robeson's technical skills in speaking verse, the overriding importance of his Othello as a racial event of the first magnitude overwhelmed their concerns. The production was an unprecedented success, and Peggy was hailed the "high priestess of Shakespeare" (Barnes, n.p.).

Peggy's personal life had settled into a closeted relationship, essential for the time, with actress **Mady Christians,** whom Peggy had cast as Gertrude opposite Maurice Evans's Hamlet. They shared New York apartments and a cottage on Martha's Vineyard and joined friends for weekends in Connecticut. **Eva Le Gallienne,** who was shortly to become Peggy's lover, owned a house in Weston, Connecticut, where with producer **Cheryl Crawford** the three women eventually planned a new enterprise to be called the American Repertory Theatre (ART).

In the 1945–46 season, the three women opened the nonprofit ART on Columbus Circle. It lasted only two years. At the outset, they misjudged the severity of the New York theatrical scene and the permissiveness of postwar America. Critics found their play selections ill-advised for popular tastes, and unrelenting union demands inflated production costs. In addition, Peggy and Cheryl Crawford soon became objects of charges from the political Right that they were "communist sympathizers." The fact that Peggy had directed a Soviet play on Broadway, had employed a "known communist," Paul Robeson, and worked as a fund-raiser for organizations sympathetic to the Soviet cause during the war years brought her before Joseph McCarthy's House Un-American Activities Committee in 1953. By that time, ART had been defunct for six years. Moreover, Peggy's parents died within fourteen months of one another in Hollywood, where May Whitty had become a film star at the age of seventy. Peggy was now bereft of her beloved companions of forty-three years.

In 1950, Peggy's name appeared in *Red Channels,* a booklet compiled by the FBI listing communist sympathizers in the entertainment industry. This publication was the official beginning of the decline and marginalization of Peggy's career. Although she appeared before the McCarthy committee three years later and was exonerated, her career was permanently "undermined, if not ostensibly broken" (Webster, *Don't Put Your Daughter on the Stage,* 273). Eva Le Gallienne had also broken off their relationship during the political frissons out of concern for her own career and exposure.

Following the Red-baiting days of the 1950s, Peggy found herself isolated among her women friends and segregated from the Broadway power brokers. Moreover, the theater was changing in England and America, where Peggy continued to work sporadically, and she was no longer sought by producers for her artistic skills and creative insights. She found refuge from a changing Broadway and the infamous "blacklist" with Jean Dalrymple's New York City Center Theatre Company, where Peggy directed plays by Shakespeare and George Bernard Shaw. Employment also emerged from an unexpected corner. Rudolf Bing, the new general manager of the Metropolitan Opera Company in 1950, was determined to improve the production values at the Met by hiring such accomplished stage directors as Alfred Lunt, Garson Kanin, Tyrone Guthrie, and Peggy Webster. Peggy staged seven operas for the Metropolitan Opera Company and the New York City Opera over a period of ten years before poor health and disaffection with the limitations of operatic staging turned her from this path. She had also settled once again into a lifestyle that included living and working on two continents. Sometime in 1955, she met British novelist Pamela Frankau, and they formed a relationship that would last until the novelist's death in 1967.

Engaged in what she called "transatlantic schizophrenia," Peggy criss-crossed the Atlantic directing at the Shakespeare Memorial Theatre at Stratford-on-Avon, at the Old Vic, and on the West End (Webster, *Don't Put Your Daughter on The Stage,* 290). In the United States, she gave solo performances, delivered lectures and readings on college campuses, accepted term professorships, and traveled to South Africa and Australia for the U.S. Department of State. She wrote over forty articles for magazines and newspapers and published a family history (*The Same Only Different,* 1969) and an autobiography (*Don't Put Your Daughter on the Stage,* 1972).

Suffering from colon cancer in her final years, she directed her last successful Broadway production (*The Aspern Papers*) in 1962, starring old friends Maurice Evans and Wendy Hiller. From a wealthy friend, Bostonian Jane Brundred, she inherited a small fortune, which she used to pay her medical expenses. She spent her last days at St. Christopher's Hospice in Sydenham, England, and died there on November 13, 1972. Her ashes were interred behind a plaque in St. Paul's Church, Covent Garden, on the East wall next to her parents' marker.

Peggy Webster pioneered many firsts in the American theater over the forty-five years of her professional career and was celebrated with distinguished awards and seven honorary degrees. Despite the social, political, and artistic marginalization that she experienced at midcareer, she was one of the first women to establish herself as a stage director and actress both in England and the United States. When Brooks Atkinson saw what was to be her final Broadway performance as an actress in *The High Ground,* he called her "the ablest woman in our theatre" (Atkinson, n.p.). Eva Le Gallienne eulogized her distinction with these words: "It is rare for a woman to succeed in this difficult field. She must be quite exceptionally talented to overcome the ingrained prejudices, the skepticism and distrust that stand in her way" (*New York Times,* November 26, 1972).

See B. Atkinson, *New York Times,* February 21, 1951; Howard Barnes, *New York Herald Tribune,* October 20, 1943; M. Barranger, *Margaret Webster: A Life in the Theater,* Ann Arbor, 2004; *Celebrity Register 1959,* New York, 1959; E. Le Gallienne, *New York Times,* February 21, 1951; E. Le Gallienne, *New York Times,* November 26, 1972; M. Webster, *Shakespeare without Tears,* New York, 1942; M. Webster, *The Same Only Different: Four Generations of a Great Theatre Family,* New York, 1969; and M. Webster, *Don't Put Your Daughter on the Stage,* New York, 1972.

Milly S. Barranger

WESNER, Ella (1847–1917), American variety hall performer and male impersonator, began performing at age nine with her sister Mary. In her twenties, she joined the initial ballet of *The Black Crook* at the Eagle Theatre in New York. Her fame came when she donned male garb and the mannerisms of a dashing dandy. According to Wesner's agent, T. Allston Brown: "In 1870—when she was in the ballet I loaned her some of my male attire and put her on for a trial performance at Tony Pastor's . . . She was an instant success" (Brown). A dresser for **Annie Hindle,** the forerunner of this genre, Wesner modeled her own act after Hindle, who did not contest this copy, and the two often played to the same houses. Wesner's new venture proved to be very successful, and she is said to have earned as much as two hundred dollars a week at the height of her fame for her portrayals of dandies, drunks, and military men.

Wesner worked for Tony Pastor in his resident company in New York and as part of his national and European touring companies. A *Theatre Comique* review of Wesner's act states: "Ella Wesner, brave and dashing, threw vital sparks into the house" (Odell, 328), and another review cites her as "the beau ideal of male impersonators" (116). Wesner's characters included the cigarette-puffing Captain Cuff, Tom Vapid, and a drunken dandy who falls asleep in the barber's chair. She wore her hair in the same fashion as Annie Hindle, and, like Hindle, her clothes included the short waistcoat and watch chain. She was often photographed wearing a pinky ring, tugging on a glove, and holding either a riding crop or a slim walking stick.

Fashioning her private life after Hindle, who married one of her female dressers, Wesner, too, was apparently attracted to women. She never married, and her only reported romance, as cited by the *New York Sun,* was with Josie Mansfield, a woman whose lover, Edmond Stokes, served a prison sentence in Sing Sing for shooting another of her male lovers, Jim Fisk. It was after this shooting and Stokes's subsequent sentencing that Mansfield and Wesner traveled together to England and Europe and presided over a louche salon at the Cafe American in Paris. Wesner was not to remain abroad for long, however, and she returned to the United States alone in the spring of 1873 to be part of Tony Pastor's national summer tour.

Wesner continued to perform through the decades of the 1870s, 1880s, and 1890s, appearing in the theatrical listings as late as 1893, though by this time as a "sinking celebrity." According to her *Variety* obituary, she was stricken with paralysis in 1902 while appearing at Tony Pastor's. She spent the last three years of her life at the Home for Incur-

Ella Wesner, "the beau ideal of male impersonators." (Courtesy of the Harvard Theatre Collection, The Houghton Library, Harvard University.)

ables in New York City under the care of the Actors' Fund. She died at the age of seventy-six on November 11, 1917. At her request, she was buried in men's clothing.

While she was not first in the line of male impersonators, Ella Wesner was by far the most influential, expanding the male impersonation act by adding quick-change costumes and the title of "Character Vocalist," which set the precedence for further growth in this genre. Her popular career earned her the titles of "England's Pride!" and "America's Favorite!" and like Annie Hindle, she served as a role model for other performers of male impersonation to follow.

See T. A. Brown, ALS Manuscript File, Harvard Theatre Collection, Harvard University; "Ella Wesner Lies in Man's Garb," *New York Times,* November 14, 1917; "Miss Ella Wesner," *New York Clipper,* November 30, 1872; "Obituary: Ella Wesner," *Variety,* November 16, 1917; G. C. Odell, *Annals of the New York Stage,* vol. 9, New York, 1937; L. Senelick, *The Changing Room: Sex, Drag and Theatre,* New York, 2000; L. Senelick, "The Evolution of the Male Impersonator on the Nineteenth-Century Popular Stage," *Essays in Theatre* 1, no. 1 (November 1982): 31–44; and "Stranger Than Fiction," *New York Sun,* December 27, 1891.

Sherry A. Darling

WILDER, Thornton (1897–1975), playwright and novelist, was born in Madison, Wisconsin, where he spent the first nine years of his life. In 1906, he lived for six months in Hong Kong, where his father, Amos, a newspaper editor, was appointed to the post of consul general. He returned to the United States with his mother, Isabella, and his sisters and brother and settled in Berkeley, California, until 1910, when he joined his father in Shanghai. He returned to Berkeley in 1912 without having seen any Asian theater on either trip to China, but throughout his childhood he had immersed himself in Western theater, making up plays to be acted by his friends, sisters, and himself. Wilder saw stock plays and road shows at Ye Liberty Theatre in Oakland and at the Greek Theatre in Berkeley. In Berkeley, he saw **Maude Adams** in *As You Like It,* Sarah Bernhardt in *Phedre,* and Sidney Howard in *The Countess Cathleen.* At Berkeley High School, one of his first stage efforts was a sketch he wrote in 1913, *The Advertisers,* in which he played "Mr." Lydia Pinkham (the nineteenth-century feminist who made a fortune selling her home remedy for various ailments). While in high school, Wilder also began writing his brief, epigrammatic "three-minute plays," which were published in 1928 as *The Angel That Troubled the Waters,* created in the belief, as he says, "that beauty is the only persuasion." These plays display his concern with form and reveal his "personal passion for compression." As Wilder explained in the preface to this work: "No idea was too grandiose for me to try and invest it in this strange discipline." Wilder's first efforts stylistically foreshadow the theatricalism of his later major plays.

Wilder began his undergraduate education at Oberlin College, where he won a prize for his essay "The Language of Emotion in Shakespeare." His references to other writers reveal his familiarity with world drama. He points out that great plays do not need the detailed stage directions that modern writers use; such directions are often included to hide the fact "that the scant text reveals the deepest distress." This may be seen as Wilder's summons to revitalize the anemic dramatic literature of his day, a literature that often settled for startling, theatrical effects on the stage, disguising the drama's weak text.

After military service during World War I, Wilder resumed his education at Yale. A passionate theatergoer, he began reviewing plays he saw in New Haven, Stamford, and Hartford, cities in which Broadway-bound plays were regularly tested. He eventually contacted the drama critic of the *Boston Evening Transcript,* H. T. Parker, and showed him his work. For the next two years (1918–20), the newspaper published Wilder's reviews; his assessment of the commercial theater of the day provides hints of the innovative directions that his own art would take.

During his senior year at Yale, Wilder's full-length play, *The Trumpet Shall Sound,* was published serially in the *Yale Literary Magazine* (October 1919–January 1920). An allegory of divine justice and mercy, and staged by the American Laboratory Theatre in New York in 1926, the play received the first professional production of any of his works. Reviews were negative, and it closed after only thirty performances. Prior to the opening of *The Trumpet Shall Sound,* Wilder's first novel had been published, *The Cabala* (1926), and during the next decade he wrote three additional novels: *The Bridge of San Luis Rey* (which received the Pulitzer Prize for 1927), *The Woman of Andros* (1930), and *Heaven's My Destination* (1935).

Meanwhile, Wilder was studying the work of contemporary theater artists, such as directors Jacques Copeau, Michael St. Denis, and Max Reinhardt and dramatists Luigi Pirandello and André Obey, among others. Their stagecraft helped Wilder find his unique style (often called theatricalism) and inspired him to begin work on his second collection of one-act plays, *The Long Christmas Dinner and Other Plays in One Act* (1931). He also translated and adapted André Obey's *Lucrece* (1932) and Ibsen's *A Doll's House* (1937) for Broadway production.

Our Town (1938), Wilder's most popular and acclaimed play, fused the theatricalism and allegorical themes of earlier pieces. Writing about daily life, love, marriage, and death in Grover's Corners, an imaginary New Hampshire village, in the early years of the twentieth century, he evoked the universal truths of people in all times and places. The play was awarded the Pulitzer Prize, making Wilder the only American to receive that honor in both fiction and drama.

The Merchant of Yonkers (1938), Wilder's adaptation of Nestroy's *Einen Jux will er sich Machen* (1842), set in Yonkers and New York City in the 1880s, is catapulted into action by the determination of its principal characters to break out of their provincial and boring workaday existence to lead more adventuresome lives in the big city. Although the production failed, Wilder's later version, *The Matchmaker* (1954), gained exceptional success on Broadway, with Ruth Gordon in the title role. A decade later, **Jerry Herman** and Michael Stewart adapted the play into the long-running musical *Hello, Dolly!* (1964).

Prior to serving in World War II, Wilder wrote the screenplay of *Shadow of a Doubt* (1942) for director Alfred Hitchcock, and in the same year his epic allegory, *The Skin of Our Teeth,* appeared on Broadway. Indebted to James Joyce's *Finnegan's Wake,* the play features the Antrobus family and their maid, Sabina, of Excelsior, New Jersey, who survive the Ice Age, the Flood, and a major war by "the skin of their teeth." Just as the human race is in danger of annihilation, the world of the theater is also seen to be precarious, with sets collapsing and actors becoming ill or recalcitrant about performing. For this play, Wilder received his third Pulitzer Prize. This was followed by his fifth novel, *The Ides of March* (1948).

Wilder's final full-length play, *The Alcestiad* (1954), was produced in Edinburgh under the title *A Life in the Sun.* Constructed like a Greek tetralogy, *The Alcestiad* has three acts, each focusing on separate actions, and is followed by a satyr play, *The Drunken Sisters.* The plot of *The Alcestiad* covers thirty years, from the marriage of Alcestis and Admetus to her death, and presents a major theme of self-sacrifice as an expression of love. Though not well received at its premiere in Edinburgh, subsequent productions in Switzerland and Germany fared better. In the mid-1950s, Wilder began to collaborate with composer Louise Talma on an operatic version of *The Alcestiad,* which was first performed in 1962 in Frankfurt, Germany, to a mixed critical reception. Two years previously, Wilder's libretto for composer Paul Hindemith's operatic score of *The Long Christmas Dinner* premiered in Mannheim, Germany, to positive reviews.

Wilder's final plays consist of two cycles, *The Seven Ages of Man* and *The Seven Deadly Sins,* begun in the 1950s. Two plays from the first cycle (*Infancy* and *Childhood*) and four plays from the second (*Someone from Assisi,*

The Drunken Sisters, Bernice, and *The Wreck on the Five-Twenty Five*—which depict, respectively, lust, gluttony, pride, and sloth) were published during his lifetime. Several other plays written by Wilder have neither been produced nor published.

In his final years, Wilder returned to the novel, writing *The Eighth Day* (1967) and *Theophilus North* (1973). He died at home in Hamden, Connecticut, in 1975. Posthumously, *American Characteristics and Other Essays* (1979), *The Journals of Thornton Wilder, 1939–1961* (1985), and *The Collected Short Plays of Thornton Wilder,* vols. 1 and 2 (1997–98), which contain the extant plays from the two cycles, were published.

Throughout his life, Wilder recoiled from revealing his sexual identity. As a man born in the late nineteenth century and coming of age in the early twentieth, he did not believe in autobiographical soul baring or self-celebration. Instead, he preferred the persona of the kindly bachelor who had little time for romantic, sexual attachments (Castronovo, 13). Wilder did experience the pleasures and regrets of a number of same-sex relationships but was reluctant to speak about homosexuality, even among close friends with whom he shared the predilection, such as **Gertrude Stein** and Alice B. Toklas (Castronovo, 20; Stein, 55–56). For his biography of Wilder, Gilbert Harrison interviewed Samuel Steward, who attested to having had a sexual liaison with Wilder in the 1930s. Harrison writes that "the sexual act was so hurried and reticent, so barren of embrace, tenderness, or passion, that it might never have happened. Steward felt that for Thornton the act was literally 'unspeakable'" (166). Such accounts indicate that his homosexuality was a great burden to Wilder and that any physical encounters he did experience were brief, awkward, and left him discomforted and probably remorseful. Many who knew him believed that he was asexual (167).

A glimpse of Wilder's views of sexual relationships can be gleaned from his work. Although romantic love figures prominently, sexual encounters are not depicted. Wilder's own lack of interest in heterosexuality, as well as his Victorian views of sexual behavior, prevented him from writing about the subject in any explicit way (Simon, 64). "I'm not interested in the adulteries of dentists," he stated. Rather, as a dramatic poet he was interested in the metaphoric implications of his work and avoided graphic or literal depictions of passionate or sexual behavior. Undoubtedly, too, Wilder, like most homosexuals who lived in homophobic eras, shielded his private behavior from public scrutiny, fearing personal or professional humiliation. Michael Gold's savage attack on Wilder (1930), in which he all but called him a homosexual, was devastating to the playwright (266–68). Nevertheless, while he sees avoidance of sexuality in Wilder's penchant for the poetic, metaphorical, and allegorical, critic Peter G. Christensen also finds subtextual invocations of same-sex desire in some of Wilder's novels, for example, in the love between the brothers Esteban and Manuel and between the Abbess and her young convert Pepita in *The Bridge of San Luis Rey* (1927), and in the sympathetic treatment of Caesar and Catullus in *The Ides of March* (1948).

Leon Edel has called Wilder America's "only great novelist who could be at the same time a supreme playwright" (Blank, 1). Wilder's rejection of realism and his innovative experiments in epic forms and nonrealistic styles represent his efforts to return to the scenic simplicity and profound poetic humanism of theater's ancient beginnings.

See M. Blank, ed., *Critical Essays on Thornton Wilder,* New York, 1995; M. Blank, D. Hunyadi Brunauer, and D. G. Izzo, eds., *Thornton Wilder: New Essays,* West Cornwall, CT, 1999; D. Castronovo, *Thornton Wilder,* New York, 1986; P. Christensen, "Thornton Wilder's Defence of Homosexuality in *The Ides of March,*" *Orbis Litterarum* 50 (1995): 289–303; M. Gold, "Wilder: Prophet of the Genteel Christ," *New Republic* 64 (1930): 266–68; D. Haberman, "Preparing the Way for Them: Wilder and the Next Generations," in *Critical Essays on Thornton Wilder,* edited by M. Blank, New York, 1996, 129–37; G. Harrison, *The Enthusiast: A Life of Thornton Wilder,* New Haven and New York, 1983; L. Simon, *Thornton Wilder: His World,* New York, 1979; G. Stein, *Dear Sammy: Letters from Gertrude Stein and Alice B. Toklas,* edited by S. M. Seward, Boston, 1997; T. Wilder, *The Collected Short Plays of Thornton Wilder,* vols. 1–2, New York, 1997–98; T. Wilder, *Thornton Wilder: Journals, 1939–1961,* New Haven, 1985; T. Wilder, *American Characteristics and Other Essays,* New York, 1979; T. Wilder, "The Trumpet Shall Sound," *Yale Literary Magazine,* December 1919, January 1920, February 1920, and March 1920; and T. Wilder, "The Language of Emotion in Shakespeare," *Oberlin Literary Magazine,* May 1916.

Martin Blank

WILLIAMS, Tennessee (Thomas Lanier Williams III) (1911–83), playwright, short story writer, novelist, screenwriter, essayist, and poet, was born in Columbus, Mississippi, the first son of Edwina Estelle Dakin Williams, the daughter of an Episcopalian minister, and Cornelius Coffin "C. C." Williams, a traveling salesman. Given his father's career, young Tom, along with his mother and older sister Rose, spent his first eight years in his maternal grandparents' rectories. With C. C. an infrequent visitor, the Reverend Walter Dakin became a father figure to his grandchildren, exposing Tom to the works of Homer, Milton, Shakespeare, and Poe.

In 1916, Williams, a rambunctious toddler, contracted diphtheria and remained immobilized for many weeks. During her son's convalescence, "Edwina devoted herself entirely to him," reading him Dickens and

Shakespeare (Leverich, 42). "During this period of illness and solitary games, my mother's overly solicitous attention planted in me the makings of a sissy, much to my father's discontent," Williams recalled in his memoirs (11–12). This disease not only shaped his personality but also marked the end of an idyllic childhood.

In 1918, just as Tom was fully recovered, C. C. secured a managerial position with the International Shoe Company and moved his family to Saint Louis. The move proved traumatic for Tom, and "he was ridiculed for his Southern accent, for his smallness, and for being a sissy" (Hayman, 9). A third child, Dakin, was born in 1919, but the next decade brought increasing tension between Williams's parents (they would legally separate in 1946). C. C. became an increasingly heavy drinker, and this was later accompanied by womanizing. His style collided with that of the ever more puritanical and sexually repressed Edwina, and the two became polarized in a symbiotic response to the other. Rose slipped into mental instability, later accusing her father of sexual abuse, which may, in part, explain why she was lobotomized in 1943. Tom coped with the heightened family strife by escaping through his writing.

Williams's first published works were essays and short stories, which appeared while he was a teenager; his first plays were mounted by amateurs after his college career had begun. His higher education included studies at three colleges and was interrupted several times during the course of eight years, but he graduated from the University of Iowa in 1938. It was in Iowa City during the fall of 1937 that his "first and last and only consummated sexual affair with a woman" occurred; the liaison was sustained for several months until she "dismissed [him] in favor of a new stud" (Williams, 43–45). By December 1938, he was in New Orleans, a city that not only became prominent in much of his work but also turned out to be the birthplace of the name "Tennessee"; while in the Crescent City, he began submitting scripts under that now famous name.

In early 1939, the budding playwright entered a period of almost constant travel, accompanied by a series of odd jobs. In June of that year, he recorded details about his first homosexual encounter, calling it a "rather horrible night," but by July he had found an evening with another gentleman "too perfect and complete" to risk continuing the relationship (Devlin, 2000, 174; Leverich, 308, 311). That summer he also attracted agent Audrey Wood's attention, beginning a professional relationship that lasted until 1971. Through her representation, Williams's first professional production, *Battle of Angels* (1940), was mounted, but it closed during Boston tryouts. Williams returned to his itinerant wanderings, writing regularly and devotedly all the while.

Wood obtained a screenwriting contract for her struggling client at MGM in 1943, and this proved to be a major turning point. After the studio declined his screenplay "The Gentleman Caller," Williams rewrote it for the stage, calling it *The Glass Menagerie* (1945). The play catapulted him from obscurity to the forefront of American culture. It ran for over 550 performances, becoming "one of the most performed and most anthologized [plays] in modern theatre history, translated into more than thirty languages, universal in its appeal" (Roudané, 27).

With *A Streetcar Named Desire* (1947), Williams solidified his position among the world's top playwrights. The drama ran for over 850 performances, eventually winning the Pulitzer Prize, making a star of Marlon Brando, and transforming the way our culture viewed the male, thanks to the character of Stanley Kowalski, who was the eroticized object of desire rather than Blanche or Stella. Further, the staging marked the first of four theatrical teamings between Williams, Elia Kazan, and Jo Mielziner: "There can be no doubt that their creative collaboration was among the most important of the twentieth-century theatre" (Murphy, 164).

The year proved to be significant in Williams's personal life also because he met Frank Merlo (1921–63), who moved in with the playwright in 1948, establishing the longest romantic attachment Tennessee would ever enjoy. By most accounts, Merlo was reliable and even tempered, creating order and stability around Williams, thereby allowing the latter to work and leaving the day-to-day details of existence to his partner. Merlo was also confident and direct about his sexuality. The pair was out among Williams's family, and Grandfather Dakin was a frequent visitor to the couple's Key West home. In a famous anecdote from the early 1950s, studio executive Jack Warner asked Merlo what he did: "Without change of expression and in a loud, clear voice, Frank replied, 'I sleep with Mr. Williams'" (Williams, 168).

By the late 1940s, Tennessee was entering a period of sustained creative output and burgeoning popularity. *Summer and Smoke* (1948) ran for over one hundred performances but remains perhaps more significant thanks to the 1952 Circle in the Square revival—a production some credit as marking the start of the Off-Broadway movement. *The Rose Tattoo* (1951) received over three hundred performances and won Williams his sole Tony. Perhaps his most ambitious and underrated work, *Camino Real* (1953), enjoyed sixty showings. Nearly seven hundred performances and a second Pulitzer were garnered by *A Cat on a Hot Tin Roof* (1955). The reworking of *Battle of Angels, Orpheus Descending* (1957), lasted less than seventy showings, but *Sweet Bird of Youth* (1959) ran for nearly four hundred performances and *The Night of the Iguana* (1961) ran for nearly three hundred. No one dominated Broadway from 1945 to 1961 like Williams, but as the 1960s started some critics began to accuse him of repeating his themes and characters. His next Broadway production, *The Milk Train Doesn't Stop Here Anymore* (1963), had fewer than seventy performances, and for the rest of his life not one of his new plays produced on Broadway approached *Milk Train*'s run.

As his professional fortunes declined, so did his private world. Although the partnership between Williams and Merlo became increasingly unstable in the early 1960s, the latter's death from lung cancer proved to be a devastating blow. Williams later wrote: "After Frank's death, no one was able to help me out of the almost clinical depression into which I sank" (228). His use of alcohol and drugs increased, and his artistic output declined, despite his ongoing habit of writing each morning. In 1969, his condition became so alarming that his brother committed him to a Saint Louis mental hospital.

Williams began the new decade by becoming one of the first out celebrities. When asked by David Frost in a January 1970 television interview if he'd had homosexual experiences, he famously replied: "I don't want to be involved in some sort of a scandal, but I've covered the waterfront" (Devlin, 146). His retort was greeted with laughter and applause from the studio audience—and this a mere six months beyond Stonewall. When *Small Craft Warnings* (1972) appeared Off-Broadway, Williams, perhaps in an effort to generate ticket sales, made his acting debut as Doc. The play also deserves special note for being the first in which Williams depicts openly gay and bisexual characters (Quentin and Bobby) onstage. A highly autobiographical drama about Williams's first stay in New Orleans, *Vieux Carré* (1977) also featured two openly homosexual characters (Nightingale and the Young Writer), but it had only six Broadway performances, while *Clothes for a Summer Hotel* (1980), the much anticipated reunion of Williams, Geraldine Page, and José Quintero, the trio that made the revival of *Summer and Smoke* such a hit, received only fourteen Broadway performances.

He continued writing plays in the remaining years of his life, and his new works continued to be produced, but the halcyon days would not return while he was alive. Restlessly traveling during the final months of his life, Williams was found dead in his suite at the Elysée Hotel in New York City on February 25, 1983. "*Elysée* translates as the 'mythical paradise of the dead'" (Leverich, 1), but the playwright sometimes joked that the hotel should be called "the easy lay" ("Tennessee Williams"). Fittingly, Williams, who battled between sensuality and spirituality, raised by parents personifying the conflict, and creating characters in this mold, died in a place with a striking duality in name and function.

During the 1980s, as queer studies and minority readings were gaining greater acceptance, some gay critics continued to denigrate Williams's works as those of a self-loathing homosexual as evidenced by so many of his gay characters remaining dead and unseen. David Savran brilliantly silences such criticism by arguing that Williams's works are strategically radical given the context of the 1940s and 1950s: "Williams was able to protect this homosexual subject from 'the torrent of lies and distortions' that overwhelms him on the commercial stage only by displacing him, or by not allowing him to speak, since the only language he was permitted to speak was the very one that ensured his abjection and his marginalization" (110). Savran's analysis is not only far more fruitful than those of opposing critics, but it also suggests how vital Williams's dramas were to the development of gay characters on the American stage. Put simply, gay characters were not allowed to speak from the commercial stage until the post-Stonewall era.

In a rediscovered play, *Not about Nightingales* (1938), Williams did place a gay character onstage, known simply as the Queen. Set in a prison, the Queen exhibits a humanity and tenderness absent from the sadistic warden and prison guards. While the Queen hardly commands the play's focus, the character hints at Williams's radical dramaturgy. Predictably, the work was not staged during his life but was a critical and commercial success in both London and New York in 1998 and 1999. The Broadway production ran for 125 performances and received several Tony nominations, including that for Best "New" Play. Finally, the post-Stonewall, post-AIDS, American commercial theater was prepared for Williams's onstage gay characters.

One could argue that Williams's objectification of the male formed the foundation of our contemporary culture's emphasis on the "cut" male body that is popular in contemporary film, television, and advertising. In play after play, males such as Stanley Kowalski, Brick Pollitt, Val Xavier in *Orpheus,* Chance Wayne in *Sweet Bird,* and the Reverend Shannon in *Night of the Iguana* bound and prone in a hammock (see Roudané, 148, for a production photo of the moment in its erotic splendor), form the locus of desire. Williams celebrated the male form unlike any other pre-Stonewall playwright. His commercially successful plays were made into Hollywood films and television movies; thus, his vision reached an even wider audience. Although his most significant contributions to world culture are undoubtedly his plays, he wrote many short stories (among them "The Mysteries of the Joy Rio" [1941], "One Arm" [1945], and "Two on a Party" [1952]) with gay characters and themes, as well as a novel that focuses on homosexual desire.

Donald Windham, who met Williams in 1940, reports: "I've never known anyone who accepted being homosexual more" ("Tennessee Williams"). Windham's observation suggests a man who embraced his sexuality and artfully translated fierce forbidden passions to the stage during a time of culturewide homophobia, creating a body of work that ranks among the greatest and most internationally renowned in the canon of American drama.

See A. Devlin, ed., "Conversations with Tennessee Williams," Jackson, Miss., 1986; A. Devlin and N. Tischler, eds., *The Selected Letters of Tennessee Williams,* vol. I: *1920–1945,* New York, 2000; R. Hayman, *Tennessee Williams: Everyone Else Is an Audience,* New Haven, 1993; L. Leverich, *Tom: The Unknown Tennessee Williams,* New York, 1995; B. Murphy, *Tennessee Williams and Elia Kazan: A Collaboration in the Theatre,* Cambridge, U.K., 1992; M. Roudané, *The Cambridge Companion to Tennessee Williams,* Cambridge, 1997; D. Savran, *Communists, Cowboys, and Queers: The Politics of Masculinity in the Work of Arthur Miller and Tennessee Williams,* Minneapolis, 1992; "Tennessee Williams: Wounded Genius," 1998, A&E Television Networks, 50 min.; J. Tharpe, ed., *Tennessee Williams: A Tribute,* Jackson, Miss., 1977; and T. Williams, *Memoirs,* Garden City, N.Y., 1975.

Mark Zelinsky

WILSON, Lanford (1938–), playwright, often labeled as the "Populist Playwright" and the "American Poet of Loss and Endurance," was born into a very poor family in Lebanon, Missouri, on April 13, 1937. His parents divorced when he was five. Wilson moved with his mother to Springfield, Missouri, while his father moved west to San Diego. Six years later, Wilson moved once again to a farm in Ozark, Missouri, with his mother and new stepfather. He became interested in theater while in high school after seeing a touring production of *Brigadoon.* He was charmed by the idea of a medium that could visually create a live, mythical, magical city. Between pursuing his interests in arts and sports and waiting tables to help support his family, he began reading about the theater, seeing plays, and relishing the classics of dramatic literature. But as Wilson matured to a young adult, the need to regain a sense of family (lost with his parents' divorce) overrode all other interests. In 1955, at the age of seventeen, he left Missouri for California to reconcile with his father.

The year in California was a bitter disappointment. An earnest but failed attempt to establish a relationship with his father encouraged Wilson to move to Chicago, where he took a job as a commercial artist at an advertising agency. Because of his estrangement from his father, his relationship with his mother strengthened tremendously during this time. Although he claims never to have been "in the closet," he says he "never really published any kind of pronouncement" for fear of his mother's reaction (Frank, 33). His work in Chicago lasted for six years, long enough to recapture his interest in theater. At the Downtown Center of the University of Chicago, he took a playwriting class and decided at the end of his first project that he was meant to be a playwright.

Wilson moved to New York in 1962, and his long awaited introduction to theater in New York City clearly did not meet his expectations: "I expected to see *Long Day's Journey into Night* playing next to *Death of a Salesman* playing next to *Hamlet.* I saw everything—*Bye Bye Birdie* and *Do Re Mi*—such a lot of crap" (Allen, 30). Acquaintances told Wilson of the legendary Caffe Cino, whose defiantly "out" proprietor, **Joe Cino,** encouraged and supported new playwrights and plays and offered a special haven to gay theater artists. Strolling in Greenwich Village one night, Wilson's curiosity led him to the stage of "carpet covered milkcrates" at Caffe Cino and a production of a slightly altered version of Ionesco's *The Lesson.* After the performance, Wilson was introduced to Cino, who warmly invited him to submit a sample of his writing, and, although Cino was unimpressed with Wilson's *Home Free,* a friendship formed that gave new creative energy to the struggling playwright. Wilson's creative efforts at Caffe Cino totaled eleven plays, including *Home Free, So Long at the Fair, Ludlow Fair,* and *The Madness of Lady Bright,* a play that broke performance records Off-Off-Broadway by running an impressive 250 performances and was Wilson's first significant homosexual-themed play, focusing on the tortured life of a transvestite.

Wilson's association with Cafe LaMama provided the next significant step in his career. His first production with LaMama's eccentric producer, Ellen Stewart (known for her eclectic taste in playwrights), was on January 30, 1964. The bill consisted of *Home Free* and *Trespassing,* both written and directed by Wilson. More important to his career was his first collaboration with director Marshall Mason on his first full-length play, *Balm in Gilead* (1965), a play that chronicles an aimless gang of drug dealers, pimps, gay boys, lesbians, prostitutes, and others found in a diner on any given night on upper Broadway. Wilson's career would thrive for many years because of the invaluable artistic collaboration that developed out of his relationship with Mason during this production, partly due to the discovery of similar artistic sensibilities and perhaps the strong kinship they developed based on their mutual sexual orientation. His second full-length play, *The Rimers of Eldrich,* premiered at LaMama in July 1966.

Wilson was given an introduction to Broadway in 1969 with a production of *Gingham Dog,* an unrelentingly brutal depiction of a soured interracial relationship. The production closed after five performances. In less than a year, an Off-Broadway production of *Lemon Sky* was equally unsuccessful. Wilson took a one-year hiatus from writing but in the interim began work with Cino and LaMama comrades Marshall Mason, Tanya Berezin, and Rob Thirkield on renovating a pornographic movie house into a theater space, known first as Circle Theater and later as the Circle Repertory Company. Wilson's close association with his friends at Circle Rep formed a bond between playwright and company that would eventually evolve into one of the great Off-Broadway theaters that thrived in New York through the 1970s and 1980s.

In 1972, Wilson wrote his first play to be staged by Circle Rep, *The Great Nebula in Orion,* a poignant and painful character study of two women, one a bitter, lonely lesbian. Further encouraged by the security of friends and a company of known actors at Circle Rep, he then began constructing *Hot'L Baltimore,* the landmark play that would finally establish him as one of America's premier playwrights. *Hot'L Baltimore* opened Off-Off-Broadway on January 27, 1973, moved to Off-Broadway on March 22, and won the New York Drama Critics Circle Award for Best American Play, the Outer Circle Critics Award, and an Obie Award for Best Off-Broadway Play. Wilson's reaction to the success of *Hot'L Baltimore* fell between "Jesus Christ, do you believe the reaction to this?" and "Uh, where the hell have you been, folks?" (qtd. in Sibley, 79).

Wilson followed *Hot'L Baltimore*'s success with an incredibly diverse group of plays: *The Mound Builders* (1975), *Serenading Louie* (1975), and *Brontosaurus* (1977). He would not repeat his critical success again until Circle Rep's production of *Fifth of July* (1977), the first dramatic installment of the Talley Trilogy, which includes *Talley's Folly* and *Talley and Son. Fifth of July* is significant for its honest depiction of a comfortable gay relationship between the two central characters, Ken and Jed. Although many of his plays feature gay characters, Wilson was particularly unsettled to learn that *Fifth of July* was not included in a then recent collection of gay plays. The rationale given in the introduction of the book stated that "we [gay people] are not accepted as fully as those characters depicted in *Fifth of July*" (qtd. in Frank, 33).

Talley's Folley was awarded the Pulitzer Prize in Drama and became a Broadway hit in the 1980 theater season. *Talley and Son* opened to unfavorable reviews on a double bill with Paul Osborne's *Tomorrow's Monday* in October 1985. Wilson's account of emotional exposure to a nuclear accident in *Angels Fall* (1982) and a translation of Chekhov's *Three Sisters*

(1984) were moderately successful, but *Burn This* (1987), his searing comic drama of obsessive, volatile lust, moved from Off-Broadway (Theater 890) to a very successful run on Broadway. Again Wilson constructs his gay male character, Larry, with great affection and compassion, contextualizing the normalcy of Larry's life in the chaos of his heterosexual roommate's life. Wilson's next play, an extended one act titled *The Redwood Forest,* opened and closed on Broadway quickly in April 1993.

In the Signature Theatre Company's season of 2002–3, Wilson was given a very successful restrospective of his career. Productions of his *Fifth of July* and *Burn This* received notable critical receptions, with two New York premieres of *Book of Days* and *Rain Dance* appearing in the second half of the season. Wilson continues to live and write in New York City and Sag Harbor and continues his affiliation with many of the Circle Rep theater artists through a newly formed theater company, Circle East.

See J. Allen, "Portrait: Lanford Wilson," *Life,* June 1980; G. A. Barnett, *Lanford Wilson,* Boston, 1987; K. A. Berney, ed., *Contemporary American Dramatists,* London, 1994; J. R. Bryer, ed., *Lanford Wilson: A Casebook,* New York, 1994; M. Busby, *Lanford Wilson,* Boise, 1987; A. Dean, *Discovery and Invention: The Urban Plays of Lanford Wilson,* London, 1994; G. Flatley, "Lanford Is One 'L' of a Playwright," *New York Times,* April 22, 1973; L. Frank, "Intersecting with Success," *The Advocate,* August 13, 1983; I. Herbert, ed., *Who's Who in the Theatre,* 17th ed., Detroit, 1981; E. Kay, ed., *International Authors and Writers Who's Who,* Cambridge, U.K., 1993; *McGraw-Hill Encyclopedia of World Drama,* New York, 1984; Prentice Hall General Reference, *Legends in Their Own Time,* New York, 1994; A. Sainer, *Contemporary Dramatists,* New York, 1978; W. J. Sibley, "Lanford Wilson," *Interview,* August 1983; *Who's Who in Entertainment,* 2d ed., Wilmette, Ill., 1992; and *Writers Directory,* 11th ed., Detroit, 1994.

Gary Garrison

WOOLLCOTT, Alexander Humphreys (1887–1943), drama critic, actor, and playwright, was born when his mother was forty and suffered a chromosomal defect that led to reduced testosterone output. This, in turn, reduced his secondary sexual characteristics: although he sported a mustache, his face was smooth and his body generally free of hair; his skin was soft; he retained a plumpness about the hips; his voice remained high pitched; and his hands and feet were tiny (Teichmann, 23, 38). To complement and compound his nature, he was raised by women, encouraged in his idiosyncracies by the commune in which he lived, and became bookish, keeping apart from a masculine world (his father was largely absent).

He nonetheless quickly determined to live in the public arena. In high school, Woollcott became a book reviewer for the *Philadelphia Telegraph.* He attended Hamilton College in upstate New York, graduating in

1909. In that all-male preserve, Woollcott's oddities stood out and earned him regular tossings into the campus fountain. He did not retreat but aggressively assumed a leadership role on campus. He became editor of the literary magazine and founded the dramatic society, in which he claimed all of the leading women's roles for himself (Teichmann, 45).

Transvestism at male colleges for dramatic purposes was common in that day, but it had deeper resonance for Woollcott. He had himself photographed in women's clothing and appears stately and aloof, with little sign of artifice. He attended parties in drag, even printing up cards with "Alexandra Woollcott" on them (Teichmann, 45). Curious to understand his difference, Woollcott read Krafft-Ebing's *Psychopathia Sexualis,* but he preferred the biological explanations found in Havelock Ellis's *Sexual Inversion* (44). In later years, posing in a snood, he would be "Aunt Aleck," "one of his favorite roles" (Hoyt, 255).

Upon graduation, Woollcott briefly worked at a bank, where he soon contracted mumps. Although today the damaging effect of mumps on male sexual prowess has been disproved, common knowledge in 1909 presumed that it debilitated a man. Woollcott's physician, unaware of his chromosomal defect, declared him a victim of the mumps, and Woollcott used it as an excuse and smoke screen for the rest of his life (Teichmann, 53–54).

After he had recovered, Woollcott applied to the *New York Times* and began work there as a reporter. His reporting prowess and his dramatic demeanor earned him the position of dramatic critic in 1914. At the *Times,* he improved the lot of dramatic critics everywhere. First, he ended the practice of critics soliciting theater managers for advertising. Second, he broke the influence of managers on the content of reviews. In 1915, when he voiced his dislike for a Shubert production entitled *Taking Chances,* the Shuberts physically barred him from attending their next production. In response, *Times* publisher Adolph Ochs got an injunction against the Shuberts and refused to run their ads in his paper. Although the courts ruled in favor of the Shuberts, they caved in to pressure and allowed Woollcott in their theaters. Newspapers across the nation supported the case, circulation for the *Times* increased, and Woollcott's reputation was enhanced considerably as a reviewer (he now merited a byline) and public figure (Chatterton, 67–82).

Woollcott joined the army as a medical orderly in 1917 and soon became a reporter for the newly founded *Stars and Stripes.* He returned to the *Times* in 1919 to discover that the secondary drama critic (and soon his assistant) was George S. Kaufman. Woollcott worked at the *Times* until 1922, when he moved to the *New York Herald* for two thousand dollars per month (his salary at the *Times* had never paid more than four hundred dollars a month). When the *Herald* was sold to the *Tribune* in 1924, Woollcott worked briefly for the *Sun* (an afternoon paper) before moving in 1925 to the *New York World,* where he remained until 1928.

This period marked Woollcott's mature style; he was not as "cream puff" as he had been before the war but assessed the good and bad in the production, vacillating between overwhelming praise and vicious vituperation. It was, however, the era of the wit, as Woollcott's place as a founder and member of the Algonquin Roundtable demonstrates. Brooks Atkinson (who followed Stark Young, Woollcott's successor at the *Times*) has pointed out the difficulty in writing memorable praise; the critic who condemned cleverly, however, would be quoted constantly. Woollcott was quoted constantly. His eccentric personal dress augmented his celebrity; he wore a cape on opening nights and escorted a young lady— usually an actress. He was unafraid of confrontation—his position and his acid tongue kept him secure; he could leave the theater, write a review, then show up at the opening night party to tell author and director how bad the play was.

In 1928, Woollcott left daily newspaper reviewing to become a freelance author, writing for magazines, and in 1929 he began the radio career that would enshrine his place in the American public's favor as the "Town Crier." Rather than displaying the sharp tongue known to his colleagues, Woollcott's radio persona presented for his audiences a literate confidante, weaving stories about whatever topic took his interest. This familiar and benign persona served him on lecture tours as well.

Woollcott maintained his connection to the theater. With George S. Kaufman, he wrote two plays: *The Channel Road* (1929), based on a story by de Maupassant, and *The Dark Tower* (1933), a murder mystery calling on his fascination with criminals. The public was fascinated by neither; both plays failed. Woollcott also "acted" on the professional stage—if behaving in a character patterned on oneself can be called acting. S. N. Behrman wrote for him the character of "Sig," Harold Sigrift, given to lying on a sofa and spouting acid remarks, in *Brief Moment* (1931). An expanded version of this character appeared with the name of Binkie in Behrman's play *Wine of Choice* (1938).

Woollcott's most enduring contribution to dramatic literature emerged after two years of nagging his friends Kaufman and Moss Hart to write a play for him. Instead, they wrote a play *about* him, *The Man Who Came to Dinner* (1939). The play captured Woollcott's domineering ways, his scathing wit, his sentiment, and his need to be surrounded by friends. Woollcott refused to play it at first, declaring that he would have "no mask to hide behind" (Teichmann, 261); the role was played on Broadway by **Monty Woolley** and in the Chicago company by **Clifton Webb**. Woollcott finally agreed to play the part in the Los Angeles company in 1940. Unfortunately, he suffered a heart attack, which ended the run. After his recuperation, the cast regathered in the East in December 1940 and the production ran through the following summer.

The rest of Woollcott's life was dominated by concerns for his health and the onset of World War II. He suffered another heart attack during a broadcast debate on Germany. He died on January 23, 1943, soon after his fifty-sixth birthday.

Clearly, Woollcott's peers thought of him as a homosexual. He was caricatured as mincing into the trenches carrying a single rose (Teichmann, 78) and was called "Louisa M. Woollcott" (88), "a faint homosexual mosquito" (270), and "a fag but nobody ever caught him" (54)—all of which never failed to arouse his ire. The only sexual stories in print are of the briefest encounters, one of which connected him with a female prostitute "who needed a few minutes of rest" (54, 130). Contrasting this is the embarrassing confession to Anita Loos that he "had always wanted to be a girl" and that "All my life I've wanted to be a mother" (157–58). After these admissions, he avoided Loos for the rest of his life.

While no evidence of male sexual liaisons exists, his long association with selected younger men (Jo Hennessey, Richard Carver Wood, and Dr. Frode Johnson), bespeak of homosocial bonds if not downright mothering by Woollcott. Indeed "mother" may have been the safest role for Woollcott and is evidenced in his arrangements of many of his friends' weddings (the Herbert Rosses, Helen Hayes to Charles MacArthur, and Irving Berlin to Ellin McKay) and his gatherings of friends for strictly regulated vacations at Neshobe Island in Vermont.

Because he was part of the Algonquin Roundtable, more attention needs to be paid to Woollcott's unique voice in shaping modern America. Although two critical books on his work exist, neither examines his contradictory, extreme personality in light of his homosexuality—the sentimental (feminine) side he allowed only the distant public to see, the waspish, defensive (masculine) attacks he used with his friends, or the steely determination forged from the fiery conflicts between the two that drove him to make his own course in public life.

See M. Burns, *The Dramatic Criticism of Alexander Woollcott,* Metuchen, N.J., 1980; W. Chatterton, *Alexander Woollcott,* Boston, 1978; E. Hoyt, *Alexander Woollcott: The Man Who Came to Dinner,* New York, 1968; and H. Teichmann, *Smart Aleck: The Wit, World, and Life of Alexander Woollcott,* New York, 1976.

Jeffrey Smart

WOOLLEY, Monty (Edgar Montillion) (1888–1963), director and actor, was born in New York in the old Hotel Bristol (Fifth Avenue and Forty-second Street), one of several owned or managed by his father, William Edgar Woolley. When Monty was three, his father leased the legendary Grand Union Hotel in Saratoga Springs, where the likes of Lillian Russell, Diamond Jim Brady, and Victor Herbert spent the racing season. Woolley's stern father and indulgent mother provided him and his only sibling, James (1882–1958), with a privileged upbringing. In adolescence, he toured Europe with his parents, prepared for college at the Mackenzie School in Dobbs Ferry, and entered Yale with the class of 1911.

Woolley's family background was not unlike that of **Cole Porter,** whose wealthy grandfather controlled the purse strings and whose devoted mother, acting as liaison between the two, managed to satisfy Cole's every financial need. By the time Porter entered Yale in 1909, Woolley had become a dominant figure in its social fraternities and the Dramatic Association (of which he was president in his last year). Within a short time of their meeting, Woolley became Porter's confidant and close friend and remained so throughout both their lives. Both were homosexuals (though never lovers), precocious, literate, and socially ambitious; both had an infectious, even outrageous sense of humor. Charles Schwartz's biography, *Cole Porter,* reveals the pleasure they took in each other's company, talents, and humor over a period of half a century, and it provides as well candid accounts of their homosexuality and pursuit of partners.

Woolley graduated with the bachelor of arts in 1911, but he stayed on at Yale to gain a master's degree (1912) and then went to Harvard, where he earned another master's (1913) under George Lyman Kittredge. During the Mexican expedition of 1916, he enlisted in the army. He soon received a lieutenant's commission and in 1918 spent eight months in France. Whenever he could obtain military leave, he partied in Paris with Cole Porter, who had moved there in 1917.

After the war, Woolley settled in New York and gained experience as a stage manager for Brock Pemberton and Arthur Hopkins (Irving Drutman). But the directing jobs he hoped to secure never materialized, and in 1923 he gratefully accepted a faculty position at his beloved Yale University, where for the next four years he lectured on drama and directed undergraduate productions in the Dramatic Association. In 1927, however, he resigned from Yale because the university had selected George Pierce Baker (rather than Woolley) to direct a newly endowed experimental theater on campus; in response to what he considered Yale's lack of confidence in his work, he returned to New York to pursue work in the professional theater.

In 1929, Porter asked Woolley to direct *Fifty Million Frenchmen* (with a book by Herbert Fields); the show became Porter's first Broadway triumph. Its success reflected on Woolley, too, and he thereafter directed several productions in New York, including Howard Dietz's *The Second Little Show* (1930), Porter's *The New Yorkers* (1930), Rodgers and Hart's *America's Sweetheart* (1931), Vernon Duke's *Walk a Little Faster* (1932), and Porter's *Jubilee* (1935).

Although *Jubilee* contained some of Porter's most memorable songs, the $150,000 production failed, which may in part account for Woolley's decision to turn from directing to acting. In the next year, he achieved critical and public recognition in the showy supporting role of the ballet impresario in the Broadway hit *On Your Toes,* which led to a two-year contract with the movie studio Metro-Goldwyn-Mayer.

The film industry had become rampantly homophobic, especially after the establishment of the Production Code in 1934 (Chauncey, 353), and the depiction of homosexuality was forbidden except as an object of derision or contempt. Once in Hollywood, Woolley was quickly stripped of his wit and distinctive individuality and became a target of ridicule. In his first film, *Live, Love, and Learn* (1937), he was required to lose his trousers as he was simultaneously doused with a bucket of water (Othman, 46). During the two years of his contract (1937–39), he acted minor roles in fifteen films, ranging from *Nothing Sacred* (1937) to *Dancing Co-ed* (1939), becoming increasingly "humiliated, disgusted, and desperate" (44). But his fortunes changed when George S. Kaufman and Moss Hart offered him the leading role of Sheridan Whiteside in *The Man Who Came to Dinner.* The production, which opened on Broadway on October 16, 1939, became the hit of the season. Woolley's success in the role elevated him to stardom as a performer and to celebrity as a personality.

During his two seasons with the production, Woolley lived most of the time at the Astor Hotel in a single room, "which was usually a horrid welter of letters, linen, and empty bottles." His only necessities, he said, were "a bed, a bathroom, and a telephone" (Maloney, 29). None of the interviews printed in the months following the show's success mentioned that Woolley was living with a homosexual companion, Cary Abbott, who had joined him sometime in 1939. Abbott, identified in the press as Monty's "courier-secretary-traveling companion" (Beebe), was the son of a distinguished Cheyenne banking family; he had graduated with Monty in the Yale class of 1911. After joining Woolley, Abbott remained his partner for the rest of his life; he died prematurely of lung cancer at the actor's home at Saratoga Springs in 1948 at the age of fifty-eight (*The Saratogian,* October 5, 1948).

Meanwhile, Warner Brothers had bought the screen rights to *The Man Who Came to Dinner* for $350,000. The film became a popular success, and Woolley's bellowing, wasp-tongued, literate, and strangely appealing depiction of Whiteside established him as a movie star. He received many subsequent film offers and never returned to the stage. He was nominated for an Academy Award as Best Actor in *The Pied Piper* (1943) and for Best Supporting Actor in *Since You Went Away* (1944). In 1946, he had the unique distinction of playing himself in the Warner Brothers' fictionalized version of Cole Porter's life, *Night and Day.* The scripted characters and their relationships had little resemblance to the truth. No hint of the homosexuality of Porter, Woolley, or any of their circle was permitted to emerge.

After the completion of the film *Life Begins at 8:30* (1942), Woolley had bought a modest new house in Saratoga Springs. Woolley, then fifty-four, and Abbott, fifty-two, made it their permanent home. After many years of living in hotel rooms and in the public eye, the domestic retreat in Saratoga represented a long-sought private sanctuary where Woolley and Abbott could spend the rest of their lives, among friends, family, and a community that had known Woolley since childhood.

Woolley and Abbott commuted to Hollywood when a film project emerged, and upon its completion they hurried home to Saratoga. Although their Saratoga retreat provided them with an escape from the celebrity-seeking press and public, their "private sanctuary" did not actually permit them to abandon the disguise of their homosexual partnership. Abbott was still identified publicly as Woolley's secretary, and only among their inner circle of friends and family was their sexual partnership known.

After Abbott's death in 1948, Woolley continued to make a few films, completing his last one (*Kismet*) in 1955 at the age of sixty-seven. On April 6, 1963, Monty Woolley, suffering heart problems, was admitted to the Saratoga Springs Hospital; he was transferred on April 8 to the Albany Hospital, where he died on May 6. For posterity, Woolley's achievements as a director and actor are minor but indelible. The *New Yorker* stated that if he had done nothing else in life "the delight and solace" he brought to Cole Porter would have justified his existence (Maloney, 25). But to give Woolley his due, his unique talents in theater and films received exceptional critical and public recognition. That his peers in the film industry nominated him for Academy Awards as Best Actor and Best Supporting Actor in the 1940s testifies to the artistic distinction he was able to gain in an industry that initially had ridiculed his talent. Woolley's lifetime need to shield his socially forbidden private life from a probing public eye surely brought him a sensitive perception and understanding of individuals such as himself, real or fictional, accounting in part for his appealing depictions of the irascible wits who attract attention and yet deflect private probing.

See L. Beebe, *New York Herald Tribune,* November 9, 1941; G. Chauncey, *Gay New York: Gender, Urban Culture, and the Making of the Gay Male World, 1890–1940,* New York, 1994; *Current Biography,* New York, 1940; I. Drutman, "The Town Crier Plus Whiskers," *New York Herald Tribune,* October 15, 1939; R. Kimball, ed., *Cole,* New York, 1971; N. Poirer, *New York Post,* April 9, 1963; R. Maloney, "Profiles," *New Yorker,* January 20, 1940; F. C. Othman, "The Beard That Talks Like a Man," *Saturday Evening Post,* September 4, 1943; *The Saratogian,* October 5, 1948; *The Saratogian,* August 2, 1949; *The Saratogian,* May 6, 1963; C. Schwartz, *Cole Porter,* New York, 1977; Monty Woolley File, Billy Rose Theatre Collection, New York Public Library of the Performing Arts.

Billy J. Harbin

Listing by Occupation

Composers, Lyricists, and Librettists

Leonard Bernstein
Marc Blitzstein
Paul Bowles
John Cage
Al Carmines
Aaron Copland
Lehman Engel
Stephen Foster
Nancy Hamilton
Lorenz Hart
Jerry Herman
Langston Hughes
Chester Kallman
Arthur Laurents
Cole Porter
Stephen Sondheim
Gertrude Stein
Virgil Thomson

Dancers and Choreographers

Robert Alton
Josephine Baker
Michael Bennett
Merce Cunningham
Isadora Duncan
Ron Field
Loie Fuller
Robert Joffrey
Ted Shawn
Clifton Webb

Designers

Maude Adams
Elsie de Wolfe
Loie Fuller
Robert Edmond Jones
Charles Ludlam
Livingston Platt
Jean Rosenthal
Hassard Short

Directors and Musical Directors

Robert Alton
Michael Bennett
George Birimisa
Maurice Browne
Al Carmines
Joseph Cino
Cheryl Crawford
Rachel Crothers
George Cukor
Owen Dodson
Lehman Engel

Ron Field
Clyde Fitch
Paul Guilfoyle
Avery Hopwood
Robert Joffrey
Robert Edmond Jones
George Kelly
Eva Le Gallienne
Charles Laughton
Arthur Laurents
Charles Ludlam
Alfred Lunt
Guthrie McClintic
Sanford Meisner
Agnes Morgan
Robert Moore
Robert Patrick
Hassard Short
Megan Terry
John Van Druten
Margaret Webster
Monty Woolley

Performers

Maude Adams
Chris Alexander
Judith Anderson
Jean Arthur
Josephine Baker
Tallulah Bankhead
Gladys Bentley
George Birimisa
Rae Bourbon
Maurice Browne
John Cage
Al Carmines
Lynne Carter
Mady Christians
Joe Cino
Montgomery Clift
Katharine Cornell
Charlotte Cushman

James Dean
Stormé DeLarverié
Elsie de Wolfe
Marlene Dietrich
Julian Eltinge
Lynn Fontanne
Edwin Forrest
Farley Granger
Paul Guilfoyle
Nancy Hamilton
Robert Heide
Annie Hindle
Josephine Hutchinson
Elsie Janis
Danny Kaye
H. M. Koutoukas
Charles Laughton
Eva Le Gallienne
Charles Ludlam
Alfred Lunt
Sanford Meisner
Adah Isaacs Menken
Robert Moore
Agnes Moorehead
Kathleen Mulqueen
Ona Munson
Alla Nazimova
Nance O'Neil
Robert Patrick
Charles Pierce
Gertrude "Ma" Rainey
Bert Savoy
Bessie Smith
Clifton Webb
Margaret Webster
Ella Wesner
Alexander Woollcott
Monty Woolley

Playwrights and Critics

Edward Albee
W. H. Auden

Djuna Barnes
Eric Bentley
George Birimisa
Jane and Paul Bowles
Truman Capote
Rachel Crothers
Mart Crowley
Mercedes de Acosta
Martin Duberman
Clyde Fitch
Robert Heide
William M. Hoffman
Avery Hopwood
Langston Hughes
William Inge
Christopher Isherwood
George Kelly
H. M. Koutoukas
Larry Kramer
Charles Laughton
Arthur Laurents
Charles Ludlam
Carson McCullers
Terrence McNally
Agnes Morgan
John Patrick
Robert Patrick
Cole Porter

Stephen Sondheim
Gertrude Stein
Megan Terry
Virgil Thomson
John Van Druten
John-Claude van Itallie
Gore Vidal
Thornton Wilder
Tennessee Williams
Lanford Wilson
Alexander Woollcott

Producers, Managers, and Agents

Helen Arthur
Maurice Browne
Al Carmines
Joe Cino
Katharine Cornell
Cheryl Crawford
Mart Crowley
Charles Laughton
Eva Le Gallienne
Charles Ludlam
Elisabeth Marbury
Guthrie McClintic
Agnes Morgan
Margaret Webster

Contributors

Billy J. Harbin was Professor Emeritus in the Department of Theatre, Louisiana State University. His essay on actor Monty Woolley appeared in *Passing Performances: Queer Readings of Leading Players in American Theater History* (Ann Arbor, 1998), and on playwright George Kelly in *Staging Desire: Queer Readings of American Theater History* (Ann Arbor, 2002). He coedited with Gresdna A. Doty, *Inside the Royal Court Theatre, 1956–1981: Artists Talk* (Baton Rouge, 1990) and he created and taught the first Ph.D. level seminar at LSU on Queer Theory, out of which his students contributed nineteen biographies to this volume. He was named the 2002 ATHE Outstanding Teacher of Theatre in Higher Education. A member of the National Theatre Conference, he was elected into the College of Fellows of the American Theatre.

Kim Marra is Associate Professor of Theatre Arts and American Studies at the University of Iowa. With Robert A. Schanke, she coedited *Passing Performances: Queer Readings of Leading Players in American Theater History* (Ann Arbor, 1998) and *Staging Desire: Queer Readings of American Theater History* (Ann Arbor, 2002). Her articles and reviews primarily on gender and sexuality in late-nineteenth and early-twentieth century United States theater history appear in *Theatre Survey; Theatre Journal; TDR; Journal of Dramatic Theory and Criticism; Theatre Research International; Theatre Annual; Theatre Topics; New England Theatre Journal; Journal of American History; August Wilson: A Casebook; Staging Difference: Cultural Pluralism in American Theater and Drama;* and *Performing America: Cultural Nationalism in American Theater.* She has served on the editorial boards of *Theatre Survey, Theatre History Studies,* and the Theater in the Americas series of Southern Illinois University Press, and for two terms as a member of the Executive Committee of the American Society for Theatre Research.

Robert A. Schanke is Professor Emeritus of Theatre at Central College, Iowa, where he served as Chair of the faculty research and development committee. His articles on theater history appear in *Theatre Survey, Theatre Topics, Southern Theatre,* and *Central States Speech Journal.* He has contributed to numerous reference books and anthologies, including *Women in American Theatre, Cambridge Guide to American Theatre,* and *Shakespeare Around the Globe* . He is the author of *Ibsen in America: A Century of Change* (Metuchen, NJ, 1988), *Eva Le Gallienne: A Bio-Bibliography* (Westport, 1989), and *Shattered Applause: The Lives of Eva Le Gallienne* (Carbondale, 1992). With Kim Marra, he coedited *Passing Performances: Queer Readings of Leading Players in American Theater History* (Ann Arbor, 1998), and *Staging Desire: Queer Readings of American Theater History* (Ann Arbor, 2002). He was the editor of the journal *Theatre History Studies* and is currently the editor of the Theater in the Americas Series for Southern Illinois University Press. His book *"That Furious Lesbian": The Story of Mercedes de Acosta* (Carbondale, 2003) was named the 2003 Book of the Year by *ForeWord Magazine* in the category of gay/lesbian nonfiction. Both that book and his *Women in Turmoil: Six Plays by Mercedes de Acosta* (Carbondale, 2003) were finalists for 2003 Lambda Literary Foundation awards. He is past Vice-President of the Association for Theatre in Higher Education, a member of the National Theatre Conference, and was elected into the College of Fellows of the American Theatre. In 2004 he received the ATHE award for Sustained Excellence in Editing.

Sam Abel-Palmer has taught at Dartmouth College and the University of Vermont. He is the author of *Opera in the Flesh: Sexuality in Operatic Performance* (New York, 1997), and "Staging Heterosexuality: Alfred Lunt and Lynn Fontanne's Design for Living," *Passing Performances: Queer Readings of Leading Players in American Theater History* (Ann Arbor, 1998). He has also published articles in many professional journals and anthologies. Currently, he is an investigator for the Human Rights Commission in Montpelier, Vermont.

Hamilton Armstrong is a post-doctoral student and instructor at Nihon University in Tokyo, Japan. He is researching kabuki influences in the career of neo-onnagata (contemporary male-to-female cross-dressing performer) Sasai Eisuke. He received the Ph.D. in Theater History and Criticism from Louisiana State University.

Noreen C. Barnes is Director of Graduate Studies in Theatre at Virginia Commonwealth University and heads the MFA in Theatre Pedagogy program. She has served as Editor of SETC/Theatre Symposium, and has contributed articles and essays to various publications and anthologies. Her professional experience includes directing the premiere of Kate Bornstein's "Hidden: A Gender," at Theatre Rhinoceros, dramaturgy for several productions directed by Joseph Chaikin, and direction of Mercilee Jenkins in a solo piece created by Jenkins on bisexuality.

Milly S. Barranger is an Alumni Distinguished Professor at the University of North Carolina at Chapel Hill. She is author of *Margaret Webster: A Life in the Theater* (Ann Arbor, 2004); Margaret *Webster: A Bio-Bibliography* (Westport, 1994); *Theatre: A Way of Seeing* (Belmont, CA, 1980); *Theatre: Past and Present* (Stamford, CT); *Understanding Plays* (New York, 1990); and is coeditor of *Notable Women in the American Theatre: A Biographical Dictionary* (Westport, 1989).

Stephen Berwind is Assistant Professor of Theatre at the University of Toledo. After a nearly twenty-year career as theater manager and freelance director, he earned a Ph.D. from Louisiana State University in 2000, focusing on both the Royal Court and Charles Ludlam.

Martin Blank has been a producer and director of over fifty plays, including several of Thornton Wilder's, in Off-Broadway, regional, and academic theaters throughout the country. In addition, he has published articles on Wilder in *Journal of American Drama and Theater,* and *Theater History Studies,* among others. He is the editor of *Critical Essays on Thornton Wilder* (Boston, 1995) and the coeditor of *Thornton Wilder: New Essays* (West Cornwall, CT, 1999).

Karen C. Blansfield is Assistant Professor in the Department of Dramatic Art at the University of North Carolina at Chapel Hill. She is also a dramaturg and author of essays in several books, journals, and magazines, as well as *Cheap Rooms and Restless Hearts* (Bowling Green, 1988). Her *Michael Frayn: A Research and Production Sourcebook* is forthcoming from Greenwood Press.

Melanie Blood is Associate Professor of Theatre and Assistant Director of the School of Performing Arts at SUNY College at Geneseo. She was also on the faculty at the University of Georgia, Athens, and received her M.A. and Ph.D. from Northwestern University. She has published articles in *Theatre History Studies, Journal of American Theatre and Drama,* and *Modern Drama* and is currently completing a book on the Neighborhood Playhouse. She currently serves as secretary of the Association for Theatre in Higher Education.

Robert Brooks holds a Ph.D. in Theatre from Louisiana State University and is currently an Assistant Professor of Theatre History at Francis Marion University, Florence, SC. His work has appeared in the *American National Biography* and the *Dictionary of Literary Biography.*

Jennifer Jones Cavenaugh is Associate Professor of Theatre at Louisiana State University. She received her doctorate from the University of Washington, and the MFA in Dramaturgy from Brooklyn College. She has published essays in *Modern Drama, American Drama, The New England Theatre Journal,* and *Theatre Notebook.* Her article, "Rebels of Their Sex: Nance O'Neil and Lizzie Borden," appeared in *Passing Performances: Queer Readings of Leading Players in American Theater History* (Ann Arbor, 1998). Her book, *Medea's Daughters: Forming and Performing the Woman Who Kills,* was published by Ohio State University Press in 2003.

Jay Scott Chipman is Associate Professor of Communication and Theater Arts at Nebraska Wesleyan University, where he also serves as Director of Theater. His essay, "A Lifetime in Light: Jean Rosenthal's Careers, Collaborations, and Commitments to Women," appeared in *Staging Desire: Queer Readings of American Theater History* (Ann Arbor, 2002). He has also published in *Theatre Studies,* and *The Gay and Lesbian Literary Heritage* (New York, 1995).

Susan F. Clark is completing a full-length study of *Uncle Tom's Cabin* in popular entertainment entitled *Sold Down the River.* Dr. Clark has taught at Smith College, Emerson College, and the University of Southern Maine. Her articles have appeared in *New Theatre Quarterly, The Journal of Popular Culture,* and *The Drama Review.*

Bud Coleman is Associate Professor in the Department of Theatre and Dance at the University of Colorado at Boulder, where he teaches American Theatre History, acting, and musical theatre. He has a Ph.D. in Theatre History from the University of Texas at Austin.

Amy Cuomo is Assistant Professor in the Department of Mass Communication and Theatre, State University of West Georgia, where she teaches Theatre History, Self Staging, and an interdisciplinary course on feminism, film, and theatre. Her work explores the construction of women on stage and in the media.

Jameson Currier is the author of *Where the Rainbow Ends: A Novel* (New York, 1998), two collections of short stories, *Dancing on the Moon: Short Stories About AIDS* (New York, 1993) and *Desire, Lust, Passion, Sex* (San Francisco, 2004), and a documentary film, *Living Proof: HIV and the Pursuit of Happiness* (1993). In 2003 he was a recipient of a writing fellowship from the New York Foundation for the Arts.

Sherry A. Darling holds a Ph.D. in Drama from Tufts University. She is currently writing a book based on her dissertation "A Critical Introduction to *The Stone Wall: an Autobiography.*" She has taught at Boston College and Suffolk University and is currently working as an historical researcher and archivist.

Mark Fearnow is Professor of Theatre at Hanover College. He is the author of *Clare Booth Luce: A Research and Production Sourcebook* (Westport, 1995) and *The American Stage and the Great Depression: A Cultural History of the Grotesque* (New York, 1997). He is a contributor to *The Cambridge Guide to American Theatre, The Cambridge History of American Theatre,* and the *Oxford Encyclopedia of Theatre and Performance.*

Lesley Ferris is Professor and Chair of the Department of Theatre at The Ohio State University. She has published on issues of gender and performance and is the author of *Acting Women: Images of Women in Theatre* (New York, 1990) and *Crossing the Stage: Controversies on Cross-Dressing* (New York, 1993). Her essay, "Kit and Guth: A Lavender Marriage on Broadway," appeared in *Passing Performances: Queer Readings of Leading Players in American Theater History,* eds. Robert A. Schanke and Kim Marra (Ann Arbor, 1998). A recent essay, "'Cooking Up the Self': Bobby Baker and Blondell Cummings 'Do' the Kitchen," appeared in *Interfaces: Women/Autobiography/Performance/Image,* eds. Sidonie Smith and Julia Watson (Ann Arbor, 2002).

James Fisher, Professor of Theater at Wabash College, has authored five books, including *The Theater of Tony Kushner: Living Past Hope* (New York, 2001). He has published essays and reviews in numerous periodicals, edits *The Puppetry Yearbook,* and is book review editor of the *Journal of Dramatic Theory & Criticism.* Fisher was 1999–2000 McLain-McTurnan-Arnold Research Scholar at Wabash College and was named "Indiana Theatre Person of the Year" in 1997 by the Indiana Theatre Association.

Jon Fraser is Associate Dean and Professor of Theatre, School of Visual & Performing Arts, C.W. Post Campus, Long Island University. He was an Edward Albee Foundation Fellow, and is a playwright living in New York City. He served two terms as treasurer of the Association for Theatre in Higher Education.

Gary Garrison is a Master Teacher and Artistic Director of the Goldberg Department of Dramatic Writing at New York University's Tisch School of the Arts. A published and produced playwright, he is the author of the critically acclaimed book, *The Playwright's Survival Guide: Keeping the Drama In Your Work and Out of Your Life* (Portsmouth, NH, 1999).

Eric Gordon has served as Director of the Workmen's Circle/Arbeter Ring Southern California District since November 1995. In addition to *Mark the Music: The Life and Times of Marc Blitzstein* (New York, 1989), he is coauthor of *Ballad of an American: The Autobiography of Earl Robinson* (Lanham, MD, 1997).

Douglas Gordy is Director of the Media Access Office for Northern California, a program sponsored by the California Governor's Committee for the Employment of Disabled Persons, which helps performers with disabilities find work in the entertainment field.

Lynne Greeley is Assistant Professor at the University of Vermont and has taught theater at the University of Maryland and Johns Hopkins University. She has contributed to journals and books on the subjects of women in theater, feminist criticism, radical theater movements, the pedagogy of theater, and is currently completing a book, *Power Femmes: Performance in Twentieth Century Theatre.*

Lisbeth Herer is a graduate student at Florida State University.

Melissa Hillman is the Artistic Director of Impact Theatre in Berkeley, which specializes in new works by emerging playwrights. She holds a Ph.D. in Dramatic Art from the University of California, Berkeley, and teaches at California State, Hayward, her undergraduate alma mater.

Zoe Coralnik Kaplan, who teaches literature and theater at Marymount Manhattan College and New York University, holds a Ph.D. from the Graduate Center at CUNY in Dramatic Literature, History, and Criticism. She lectures and has published essays on Jane Austen, and she is the author of a biography, *Eleanor of Acquitaine* (Philadelphia, 1987), written for young people.

Joseph Kissane, recently retired, was a professor and administrator at Columbia University. His research interest is the life and career of American playwright George Kelly, out of which came the entry in this volume on Livingston Platt.

Stephen E. Long has taught English and Humanities courses at colleges in Oklahoma and Florida.

William MacDuff received a B.A. in Theater from Columbia University and an M.F.A. in playwriting from UCLA, where he has taught theater history and playwriting for the past seven years.

Christine C. Mather holds a Ph.D. in theater from Louisiana State University and an M.A. from the University of Colorado. She has published articles and reviews and presented papers at numerous conferences, including the IFTR meeting in Canterbury, England.

Krista L. May is Associate Editor of the *World Shakespeare Bibliography*. She earned the Ph.D. in English from the Texas A&M University, after completing her dissertation, *Queering the Modern Subject: Radclyffe Hall, Djuna Barnes, and Modern Discourses of Sexuality*. She is also a freelance writer and has written for *PopMatters* (www.popmatters.com).

Susan McCully teaches playwriting, drama, and gender studies at the University of Maryland, Baltimore County. She researches lesbian and queer theatre, and her one-woman play *Cyber Becomes Electra* has received multiple performances in North America and Europe.

Lee Alan Morrow has a Ph.D. from Northwestern University. He is the author of *The Tony Award Book: Four Decades of Great American Theater* (New York, 1990) and coauthor of *Creating Theater: The Professionals' Approach to New Plays* (New York, 1986). His essay, "Elsie Janis: 'A Comfortable Goofiness,'" appeared in *Passing Performances: Queer Readings of Leading Players in American Theater History* (Ann Arbor, 1998).

Daniel-Raymond Nadon is Associate Professor of Theatre at Kent State University, where he serves on the graduate faculty and teaches Shakespeare, playwriting, acting, directing, and gay and lesbian theater. He was among the first Fulbright scholars to Quebec, where he studied the works of Michael Tremblay.

Jane T. Peterson is an Associate Professor and director of the graduate program at Montclair State University in New Jersey. She is the author of *Women Playwrights of Diversity* (Westport, 1997) and has articles in the *American National Biography, Theatre History Studies, Notable Women in American Theatre,* and the *Encyclopedia of New Jersey.* Her essays on Robert Edmond Jones have appeared in *Staging Desire: Queer Readings of American Theater History* (Ann Arbor, 2002), and *Experiments, Rebels and Disparate Voices* (New York, 2003).

Richele Pitalo holds the M.F.A. in Directing from Louisiana State University.

Jay Plum holds a Ph.D. in theater from the City University of New York. He has published articles on American drama and theater in *Modern Drama, Theatre Survey,* and *African American Review.* His current research explores the relationship among contemporary gay male performance, politics, and history from the experimental productions of Reza Abdoh and Pomo Afro Homos to the musical stages of Broadway.

Paul Sagan directed the original production of George Birimisa's *The Man with Straight Hair*. He lives in San Francisco, where he works as a staff writer for Antenna Audio.

Ray Schultz is Assistant Professor of Theatre at the University of Minnesota, Morris. He holds a B.A. in dramatic literature from New York University and an M.A. in acting and a Ph.D. in theater from Wayne State University in Detroit. He recently published an article on Lanford Wilson's *Burn This* in the *Journal of American Drama and Theatre*.

Judith A. Sebesta teaches courses in theatre history in the School of Theatre Arts at the University of Arizona. She has published essays in *New England Theatre Journal, Theatre Journal, Theatre Annual, OnStage Studies,* and the *Sondheim Review*. Her coedited anthology on women and musical theatre is forthcoming from McFarland Press. She currently is vice president for Conference 2005 of the Association for Theatre in Higher Education.

Jack Sharrar is Director of Academic Affairs for the American Conservatory Theater, where he also teaches in the MFA program and the Young Conservatory. He serves as a Regional Arts Theater Panelist for the National Foundation for the Arts, has taught at Central Michigan University, University of Utah, and Los Angeles County High School for the Arts. He is author of *Avery Hopwood, His Life and Plays* (Jefferson, NC, 1989) contributor to Oxford University Press's *The American National Biography,* and editor of numerous award-winning books of scenes and monologues for young actors published by Smith & Krause. He is a graduate of the University of Michigan and holds a Ph.D. in theater history and dramatic literature from the University of Utah.

Jeffrey Smart, Ph.D., taught at the University of Minnesota-Duluth, Truman State University, the University of South Florida at Sarasota and Virginia Commonwealth University. His research often examined musical theater, and he was a published playwright.

Wendell Stone is an Instructor in the Department of Mass Communication and Theatre at the State University of West Georgia. He is the author of *Caffe Cino: The Birthplace of Off-Off-Broadway* (Carbondale, IL, 2005).

Ginger Strand is a writer and independent scholar. She has contributed essays to *The Believer, Raritan, The New England Review, Theatre Journal, European Romantic Review,* and *American Literary History,* as well as anthologies. Her novel *Flight* will be published in 2005 by Simon and Schuster. She wishes to thank the Council of the Humanities at Princeton University for a Behrman/Perkins fellowship that supported this volume.

David **Vaughan** is the archivist of the Cunningham Dance Foundation and the author of *Merce Cunningham: Fifty Years* (New York, 1997) and of *Frederick Ashton and his Ballets* (New York, 1997). He was a member of the editorial board of the *International Encyclopedia of Dance* (1998). He received the 2000 CORD (Congress on Research in Dance) Award for Outstanding Leadership in Dance Research, and in September 2001, he received a New York Dance and Performance Award ("Bessie") for sustained achievement.

Denise **Walen** is Associate Professor in the Drama Department at Vassar College, where she teaches theater history and dramatic literature. Her reviews and articles have appeared in *Theatre History Studies, Theatre Journal, Theatre Survey, Nineteenth Century Theatre,* and the anthologies, *Women and Playwriting in Nineteenth-Century Britain* and *Passing Performances: Queer Readings of Leading Players in American Theater History.* Her book *Constructing Desire: Homoeroticism in Early Modern Drama* is forthcoming from Palgrave Press.

Lionel **Walsh** is Director of the School of Dramatic Art, University of Windsor, where he teaches acting, improvisation, and character study, and is a certified teacher of the Michael Chekhov Acting Technique. He is a member of Canadian Actors' Equity Association and has worked as a professional actor and director in Canada and the United States. His other publications include an essay on Canadian playwright Brad Fraser in *Censorship: An International Encyclopedia* and a review of Joanna Merlin's *Auditioning—An Actor-Friendly Guide* for *Theatre Topics.* He has been active in the Association for Theatre in Higher Education since 1995, where he has served as focus group representative and pre-conference planner for the Lesbian and Gay Theatre Focus Group, and as a member-at-large on the governing council.

Donald **Whittaker** holds a Ph.D. in Theatre from Louisiana State University. His current research interest is the exploration of the Other in American musical theater.

Eric **Wiley** is Assistant Professor of Theatre at the University of Texas—Pan American. His articles have appeared in the *Drama Review, Theatre InSight,* and *Text and Presentation,* and he has had two original plays produced Off-Off-Broadway.

James **Wilson** is Assistant Professor of English at LaGuardia Community College. He is currently working on a book about lesbian and gay theater and performance in the Harlem Renaissance, *"Bulldykes, Pansies,* *and Chocolate Babies": Performanced, Race, and Sexuality in the Harlem Renaissance.*

Kevin Winkler is Chief Librarian, Circulating Collections, New York Public Library for the Performing Arts. He is the editor of vol. 22 in the Theatre Library Association's monograph series, *Performing Arts Resources,* which focuses on performing arts archives. His articles have appeared in *Theatre History Studies,* and he is a contributor to *Performing Processes: Creating Live Performances* (Intellect Books) and *International Dictionary of Library Histories* (Fitzroy Dearborn).

Mark Zelinsky is Assistant Professor of English at Saint Joseph College in West Hartford, CT. He teaches a wide variety of theater classes and directs the Queenes Companye—an acting troupe with a rich tradition of single gender Shakespearean productions at the Women's College. His articles have appeared in *Tennessee Williams Literary Review* and *Humanities in the South.*

Index

Abatino, Pepito, 40

Abbott, Berenice, 48

Abbott, Cary, 393–94

Abbott, George, 24, 185

Acker, Jeanne, 299

Adams, Annie, 15

Adams, Charles Francis, 143

Adams, John Quincy, 353

Adams, Maude (Ewing Kiskadden), 8, 15–18, 162, 210, 376; and Frohman, 6, 15, 16, 17, 159

Adler, Stella, 176, 279

Agenoux, Soren, 96

Ahrens, Lynn, 276

Akalaitis, Joanne, 71

Albee, Edward, 18–23, 81, 187, 271, 287; and Barr, 20, 116, 359; and Flanagan, 19, 20, 22; and Smith, 20, 339

Albee, Reed and Frances, 18

Alda, Alan, 287

Alexander, Cris (Christopher), 24–25

Allen, Fred, 285

Alton, Robert (Robert Alton Hart), 25–27

Alvarez Quinteros, Serafin and Joaquin, 291

Amaya, Mario, 174

Ames, Winthrop, 105

Anawalt, Sasha, 220

Ancker, Julian, 35

Ander, Kenneth, 134

Anderman, Maureen, 22

Andersen, Hans Christian, 254

Anderson, John, 45

Anderson, Dame Judith (Frances Margaret Anderson-Anderson), 27–29, 71, 109, 247

Anderson, Maxwell, 92, 260

Anderson, Robert, 356

Anderson-Anderson, James, 27

Andress, Ursula, 133

Andrews, Charlton, 201

Angeli, Pier, 133

Anglin, Margaret, 314–16

Anouilh, Jean, 359

Anthony, Mary, 94

Anthony, Susan B., 347, 353

Anton, Robert, 361

Appia, Adolphe, 223, 350

Arbus, Diane, 135

Arden, Eve, 230

Aristophanes, 84

Arlen, Harold, 81

Arlen, Michael, 179, 294

Arliss, George, 179

Armstrong, Louis, 323, 338

Armstrong, Paul, 233

Arnaz, Desi, 185

Arpino, Gerald, 7, 220–21, 222

Artaud, Antonin, 350

Arthur, Helen Jean, 30–32; and Morgan, 7, 30, 32, 290–91, 292

Arthur, Jean (Gladys Georgianna
    Greene), 32–35
Arzner, Dorothy, 297, 299
Ashe, Bruce, 245, 248
Ashley, Elizabeth, 279
Astaire, Fred and Adele, 336
Atkinson, Brooks, 24, 306, 366, 373,
    389; on Bankhead, 44, 45, 46; on
    Capote, 81; on Christians, 91
Auchincloss, Hugh D., Jr., 362
Auden, Constance Rosalie Bicknell,
    36
Auden, George Augustus, 36
Auden, W. H. (Wystan Hugh),
    36–39, 61, 141; and Isherwood,
    36, 37, 38, 212–13; and Kallman,
    38, 227–29
Auer, Sydney and Claire, 70
Austen, Howard, 363
Avian, Bob, 50

Babbitt, Milton, 341
Bacall, Lauren, 157, 289, 311
Bach, Steven, 136, 138
Bachardy, Don, 214
Bacharach, Burt, 288
Bailey, Pearl, 81, 87, 191
Baker, Dorothy, 116
Baker, George Pierce, 290, 314, 325,
    392
Baker, Jean-Claude, 40, 41
Baker, Josephine, 8, 39–42, 87
Balanchine, George, 326
Ball, Thomas, 165
Bancroft, Ann, 23, 250
Banim, John, 164
Bankhead, Tallulah Brockman, 7,
    42–46, 99, 104, 109, 184, 191;
    and Cukor, 119; on de Acosta, 129;
    and female impersonators, 89, 312;
    and Kelly, 44, 236; and Laughton,
    245
Bankhead, William, 43
Banks, Richard, 347
Barber, Samuel, 62, 103
Barclay, James Paul, 283
Barker, Margaret, 109

Barnes, Clive, 117, 312, 333
Barnes, Djuna Chappell, 47–49,
    261, 262
Barnes, Wald and Elizabeth, 47
Barnes, Zadel, 47
Barney, Natalie, 49, 148
Barr, Richard, 20, 116, 289, 359
Barrett, Elizabeth. See Browning,
    Elizabeth Barrett
Barrie, James M., 15, 16, 266
Barry, Gene, 192
Barry, Philip, 307
Barrymore, Ethel, 109, 119, 162, 253
Barrymore, John, 119, 224, 225
Barrymore, Lionel, 224, 301
Barter, Martin, 280
Bates, Blanche, 200
Baudelaire, Charles, 172
Baum, Vicky, 90
Baxley, Barbara, 208, 212, 279
Baylis, Lilian, 370
Beaton, Cecil, 131
Beatty, Warren, 101
Beaumarchais, Pierre Augustin de,
    198
Beckett, Samuel, 20
Behrman, S. N., 390
Belasco, David, 200, 209, 266, 303,
    317
Bell, Arthur, 157
Bell, Robert W., 206
Benchley, Robert, 253
Bender, Milton "Doc," 183
Benet, Stephen Vincent, 246
Bennett, Dorothy, 98
Bennett, Michael, 9, 50–52, 156
Bentley, Eric Russell, 8, 52–56
Bentley, Gladys, 8, 56–58
Beregi, Oscar, 147
Berezin, Tanya, 387
Bergman, Ingmar, 342
Berkelman, Robert George, 139
Berlin, Irving, 86, 329, 366, 391; and
    Short, 335, 336, 337
Berman, Eugene, 297
Berners, Gerald, 347
Bernhardt, Sarah, 29, 253, 376

Bernstein, Leonard (Louis), 24, 59–62, 157, 249; and Copland, 61, 62, 102, 103; and Sondheim, 61, 341
Bickerton, Joseph P., Jr., 317
Bierbower, Jennie Cockrell, 215, 216, 217
Bing, Rudolph, 372
Bingham, Amelia, 162
Binney, Constance, 43
Birabeau, Andre, 99
Bird, Bonnie, 77
Bird, Montgomery, 164
Birimisa, George, 63–66, 96
Bizet, Georges, 337
Blake, Arthur, 311
Blake, Eubie, 39–40
Blast, Bill, 132
Blitzstein, Marc (Marcus Samuel), 7, 66–68, 103, 152, 153, 325
Bloch, Gabrielle (Gab Sorere), 173
Bloodgood, Clara, 162
Bolger, Ray, 182, 185, 191
Bolton, Guy, 268, 320
Bond, Pat, 347
Bone, Robert, 141
Booth, Edwin, 127
Booth, Shirley, 249, 251
Borden, Lizzie, 302
Bordoni, Irene, 201
Borguignon, Serge, 116
Borske, Haal, 96
Bosworth, Patricia, 99, 263
Botticelli, Sandro, 129
Boucicault, Dion, 354
Bouillon, Jo, 41
Boulanger, Nadia, 66, 102, 352
Bourbon, Rae/Ray (Ramon Icarez), 68–69
Bowles, Jane (Sydney Auer), 7, 70–72, 73, 110
Bowles, Paul (Frederick), 7, 70–73
Boyer, Charles, 246, 286
Boynton, Louise, 16
Brackett, Rogers, 134
Braden, John, 198
Bradford, Barbara Taylor, 118

Brady, Diamond Jim, 392
Brando, Marlon, 92, 105, 157, 306, 382; on Clift, 100, 101
Braque, Georges, 346
Brecht, Bertolt, 37, 38, 52, 53, 67, 246
Brennan, Jay, 328, 329
Brenner, Doc, 134
Brewster, Anne, 126
Britt, George, 44
Britten, Benjamin, 38, 62, 103
Broderick, James, 279
Bromberg, J. Edward, 253
Brook, Peter, 81
Brooks, Alfred, 94
Broughton, Henry, 339
Brown, Carolyn, 121, 123
Brown, Danny, 134
Brown, Joe E., 296
Brown, John Mason, 21
Brown, T. Allston, 374
Browne, E. Martin, 86
Browne, Marsie and Frederick Herbert, 73
Browne, Maurice, 73–76, 205
Browning, Elizabeth Barrett, 105, 106, 126, 127
Browning, Robert, 291
Brundred, Jane, 373
Brustein, Robert, 211, 359
Bryant, Charles, 299
Bulgakov, Mikhail, 361
Burke, Kenneth, 48
Burnett, Frances Hodgson, 265–66
Burr, Aaron, 85
Burton, Humphrey, 60, 62
Busch, Charles, 313
Bush, George H. W., 280
Buzzell, Eddie, 297
Byron, Lord (George Gordon Noel), 282, 353

Caan, James, 279
Cage, John, 76–79; and Cunningham, 7, 77, 78, 79, 121, 123
Cahill, Marie, 200
Caldwell, James, 124

Caldwell, Zoe, 28
Callas, Maria, 275
Calthrop, Gladys, 253
Campbell, Mrs. Patrick, 32
Caponi, Gena Dagel, 72
Capote, Joe, 80
Capote, Truman (Truman Streckfus
    Persons), 80–82
Capra, Frank, 33, 34
Carmines, Al (Alvin), 82–86
Carrington, Frank, 292
Carrington, Margaret Huston, 225
Carroll, Pat, 347
Carter, Janice, 306
Carter, Jimmy, 219
Carter, Lynne, 8, 87–89
Carter, Myra, 22
Carville, James, 277–78, 280
Cary, Madeleine, 106
Cassady, Neal, 145
Caulfield, Joan, 34
Causey, Alan, 96
Chaikin, Joseph, 7, 348, 349, 350
Champion, Gower, 158, 191
Chanel, Coco, 50
Channing, Carol, 24, 191, 289
Charlip, Remy, 84, 121
Chatmon, Sam, 324
Chávez, Carlos, 228
Chekhov, Anton, plays of, 244, 254,
    255, 356, 387; Van Itallie's adap-
    tations of, 360, 361
Cherifa (Jane Bowles's lover), 70, 71
Chevalier, Maurice, 184, 217
Childs, Nelisse, 109
Chirikov, Evgeny, 298
Chogyam Trungpa, Rinpoche, 361
Christensen, Peter G., 380
Christians, Mady, 89–93, 371
Christians, Rudolph and Bertha
    Klein, 89–90
Christy, E. P., 170
Ciardi, John, 202
Cino, Joseph, 7, 94–98, 309, 386,
    387; and Heide, 94, 96, 97, 189
Cino, Mary, 94

Claire, Ina, 201, 236
Clarac-Schwarzenbach, Annemarie,
    271–72
Clare, Ada, 283
Clarke, Sarah Jane, 126
Cleveland, W. S., 301
Clift, Bill and Sunny, 98
Clift, Montgomery (Edward Mont-
    gomery), 7, 98–101, 154, 175,
    248; and Lunt, 99, 263
Clifton, Josephine, 164
Clinton, Bill, 280
Clurman, Harold, 22, 109, 187, 212,
    278
Coca, Imogene, 180, 218
Coco, James, 118
Cohan, George M., 150
Cole, J. O., 318
Cole, Jack, 26, 156, 157, 330
Coleman, Emily, 49
Collamore, Jerome, 316
Collison, Wilson, 201
Comden, Betty, 24, 157
Comstock, F. Ray, 224, 267
Connelly, Marc, 260
Conrad, Robert, 164
Cook, Eliza, 125
Coomaraswamy, Ananda K., 77
Cooper, Gary, 245
Cooper, George, 170
Copeau, Jacques, 377
Copland, Aaron, 6, 7, 70, 102–4,
    109, 278; and Bernstein, 61, 62,
    102, 103; and Engel, 152, 153
Corligliano, John, 197, 198–99
Cornell, Katharine ("Kit"), 29,
    104–8, 179, 256; and Hamilton,
    182, 218; and McClintic, 7,
    104–6, 107, 182, 294
Cothran, Tom, 60
Cotsworth, Staats, 208
Coward, Nöel, 24, 230, 239, 294,
    311, 366; and Bankhead, 43, 44,
    45; and the Lunts, 260, 261, 263;
    and Porter, 43, 186, 320, 321; and
    Wilson, 217

Cowell, Henry, 103
Crafton, Allen, 209
Craig, Edith, 370
Craig, Edward Gordon, 147, 223, 350
Craig, John, 314
Craven, Frank, 179
Crawford, Cheryl, 7, 91, 108–11, 254, 371–72
Crawford, Joan, 179, 311, 312, 367
Crawford, Luella Elizabeth (Parker), 108
Crawford, Robert, 108
Cronyn, Hume, 22
Crosby, Bing, 154, 231, 307
Crothers, Rachel, 43, 49, 111–14, 217, 266
Crouse, Russel, 320
Crow, Emma, 127
Crowley, Edward Joseph and Pauline, 114
Crowley, Mart (Edward Martino), 114–18, 287, 288
Cukor, George Dewey, 7, 8, 119–21
Cukor, Victor and Helen (Gross), 119
Cunningham, Merce, 121–24; and Cage, 7, 77, 78, 79, 121, 123
Cushman, Charlotte Saunders, 124–28
Cushman, Edwin Charles (Ned), 127
Cushman, Mary Eliza, 124

Dahdah, Robert, 95
Dakin, Walter, 380, 382
Dale, Alan, 44
Dale, Stormy. *See* **DeLarverié, Stormé**
Dall, John, 175, 248
Dalrymple, Jean, 372
Daly, Augustin, 146
Daly, Tyne, 251
Da Silva, Howard, 253
David, Hal, 288
da Vinci, Leonardo, 241

Davis, Bette, 116; and female impersonators, 88, 89, 311, 312, 313
Davis, Fitzroy, 107
Dawn, Hazel, 201, 293–94, 295, 296
Day, Dorothy, 48
de Acosta, Mercedes, 8, 128–31, 299; and Dietrich, 131, 137; and Duncan, 148, 149; and Le Gallienne, 129, 130, 253; and Munson, 131, 297
Deacy, James, 132, 133
Dean, James Byron, 7, 101, 132–34
Debussy, Claude, 174
DeFoe, Louis Vincent, 200
De Lamar, Alice, 253
DeLarverié, Stormé (Stormy Dale), 88, 134–36
de Legge, Boisey, 324
Del Rio, Delores, 304
DeMille, Agnes, 26
Dennis, Patrick, 25, 192
Dennison, George, 84
Desti, Mary, 148
DeWeerd, James, 133
Dewhurst, Colleen, 21, 22
de Wolfe, Stephen and Georgiana Copeland, 265
de Wolfe Mendl, Elsie (Ella Anderson), 162, 320; and Marbury, 7, 215, 264–68
Diamond, David, 61, 62, 103
Dietrich, Elizabeth Josephine, 136
Dietrich, Marlene, 35, 89, 131, 136–39, 148, 368
Dietz, Howard, 393
Dillingham, Charles, 17
Dillon, Melinda, 21
Dillon, Millicent, 70, 71, 72
Dionne quintuplets, 305
Dodge, Mabel, 48, 224
Dodson, Edith, 142
Dodson, Nathaniel and Sarah, 139
Dodson, Owen, 8, 139–42
Donahue, Jack, 294
Donner, Clive, 310
Douglas, Lord Alfred, 54, 85

Douglas, Kirk, 105
Dowling, Eddie, 294
Dowson, Ernest, 152
Drake, Alfred, 182
Draper, Ruth, 32
Drew, John, 15, 159
Drivas, Robert, 21
Driver, Don, 50
Duberman, Martin Bauml, 8,
    142–46
DuBois, W. E. B., 140, 143
Dudevant, Aurore (George Sand), 283
Duffy, Joseph, Jr., 348
Duffy, Marguerite Cecelia (Henry),
    348
Duffy, Maureen, 113
Duke, Vernon, 393
Dukore, Bernard, 75
Dumas, Alexander *(pere),* 283, 284
Du Maurier, Gerald, 44
Duncan, Elizabeth, 147
Duncan, Isadora (Angela Isadora),
    146–49, 253; and de Acosta, 129,
    148, 149; and Fuller, 147, 148,
    171, 172–73, 174
Duncan, Sandy, 158
Dunne, Dominic, 118
Dunning, Jennifer, 222
Dunphy, Jack, 80–81
Dunsany, Lord, 32, 291
Dürrenmatt, Friedrich, 260, 364
Duryea, Nina Larre Smith, 319
Duse, Eleanora, 149, 254
Duvall, Robert, 279

Eagels, Jeanne, 119
Ebb, Fred, 156, 157, 214, 276
Eckhart, Meister, 77, 78
Edwards, Samuel, 283
Eldridge, Florence, 45
Eliot, T. S., 36, 37, 49, 86, 152
Elizabeth II, queen of England, 29
Elliott, Maxine, 162, 266
Ellis, Havelock, 389
Eltinge, Julian (William Julian Dal-
    ton), 6, 8, 149–52
Emerson, Ken, 169, 170

Emery, John, 44
Engel, Lehman (A. Lehman Engel),
    7, 99, 152–56, 371
Englander, Roger, 198
Enters, Angna, 32
Esbjornsen, David, 23
Esenin, Serge, 147, 148
Euripides, 53, 255
Evans, Maurice, 90, 91, 154, 306;
    and Webster, 370–71, 373
Evensen, Marion, 91
Eyen, Tom, 96, 237

Faber, Roderick, 239
Fagan, J. B., 370
Falk, Peter, 254
Farber, Viola, 121
Farnan, Dorothy, 38
Faulk, Lillie Mae ("Nina"), 80
Fedorova, Alexandra, 221
Ferber, Edna, 109, 119, 120
Ferguson, Elsie, 178–79
Ferrer, José, 109, 371
Fichandler, Zelda, 256
Field, Kate, 126
Field, Ron (Ronald), 50, 156–59
Fielding, Harold, 313
Fielding, Marjory, 25
Fields, Herbert, 183, 184, 393
Fields, Lew, 183
Fierstein, Harvey, 192, 239, 251,
    309, 313
Fine, Sylvia, 229, 230, 232
Finke, William, 325
Finkelstein, Marty, 192
Fisher, Clara, 124
Fisher, Eddie, 286
Fisk, Jim, 374
Fitch, (William) Clyde, 6, 15,
    159–63, 266
Fitzgerald, F. Scott, 278, 346
Flagstad, Kirsten, 227
Flaherty, Stephen, 276
Flanagan, Neil, 95
Flanagan, William, 19, 20, 22
Flanner, Janet, 110
Fleming, Victor, 120

Florence, Lillie, 16
Floyd, John, 201
Foley, Margaret, 126
Fonda, Henry, 180, 218, 247, 364
Fonda, Jane, 89, 100, 252
Fontaine, Joan, 92
Fontanne, Lynn (Lillie Louise), 27; and Lunt, 7, 99, 256, 260–64, 371
Foote, Gene, 157
Foote, Horton, 279, 280
Forbes, Kathryn, 91, 356
Forbes, Malcolm, 56
Ford, Glenn, 306
Ford, John, 33
Ford, Ruth, 118
Foreman, Richard, 347
Fornes, Maria Irene, 84, 348
Forrest, Edwin, 6, 127, 163–67
Forsyth, William, 219
Forsythe, Henderson, 22
Forsythe, John, 306
Fosse, Bob, 51, 156, 158, 279
Foster, Eliza Clayland Tomlinson, 167
Foster, Morrison, 169
Foster, Paul, 96
Foster, Stephen (Collins), 6, 167–71, 198
Foster, William Barclay, 167
Fox, Duane, 157
France, Anatole, 223
Frankau, Pamela, 373
Frederick IX, king of Denmark, 333
Freeman, Florence, 126
Freud, Sigmund, 37, 196
Friedkin, William, 117
Frohman, Charles, 266, 334; and Adams, 6, 15, 16, 17, 159
Frohman, Daniel, 265, 266
Fuller, Loie (Mary Louise Fuller), 7, 171–74; and Duncan, 147, 148, 171, 172–73, 174
Furth, George, 344

Gable, Clark, 120
Gale, Mrs. Lyman, 314

Galileo Galilei, 53, 246
Galsworthy, John, 291
Gandhi, Mahatma, 366
Gantillon, Simon, 32, 291
Garbo, Greta, 106, 129, 131, 137, 148, 213
Garfield, John, 253
Garland, Judy, 120, 157
Garrison, Eula Seeley, 112
Gaskill, William, 86
Gee, Jack, 339–40
Gener, Randy, 237
Genet, Jean, 19
George, Grace, 200
Gershwin, George, 86
Gershwin brothers, 329, 342
Gest, Morris, 224
Gide, André, 53
Gielgud, John, 21, 22, 27–28, 130, 370, 371
Gilder, Jeanette, 266
Gill, Brendan, 319, 320
Gill, Peter, 85
Gilman, John, 190
Gingold, Hermione, 89, 191
Giraudoux, Jean, 260
Gish, Dorothy, 306
Gish, Lillian, 247
Glass, Bonnie, 366
Gleason, Jackie, 307
Glenn, Barbara, 133, 134
Goethe, Johann Wolfgang von, 90, 347
Goetz, Augustus, 53, 132, 133
Goetz, Ruth, 53
Gogol, Nicolai, 53
Gold, Michael, 379
Golden, John, 90
Goldmark, Rubin, 152
Gooch, Betty, 277
Gordon, Ricky Ian, 361
Gordon, Ruth, 378
Gorn, Steve, 361
Gottfried, Martin, 230, 231, 241
Gould, Norma, 330
Goulding, Edmund, 217, 367

Graham, Martha, 32, 152, 221, 330, 332; and Rosenthal, 325, 326, 327, 328

Granger, Farley (Farley Earl Granger II), 7, 175–77, 231; and Laurents, 175, 176, 177, 248

Grant, Cary, 120, 175, 320

Grant, Lee, 280

Granville-Barker, Harley, 223, 291

Gray, David, 201

Greeley, Horace, 150

Green, Adolph, 24, 157

Green, Paul, 109, 153

Green, Silas, 338

Greene, Herbert and Johanna, 32

Greene, Lorne, 279

Greene, Luther, 29

Greenwood, Charlotte, 335

Greet, Ben, 370

Gregory, Paul, 246, 247

Grey, Joel, 279

Griffith, D. W., 301

Grimes, Tammy, 279

Grizzard, George, 21

Grosser, Maurice, 346, 351

Guare, John, 237

Guggenheim, Peggy, 48

Guilbert, Yvette, 291

Guilfoyle, Paul, 177–80, 294, 295–96

Gussow, Mel, 28, 360

Guthrie, Tyrone, 255, 256, 372

Hagen, Uta, 21, 63, 154, 187, 371

Haimsohn, George, 96

Haines, William, 119, 184

Hall, Bernard, 137

Hall, Radclyffe, 130

Halliday, Richard, 110

Hamilton, Alexander, 85

Hamilton, Clayton, 316

Hamilton, Nancy, 107, 180–82, 218

Hamilton, Thomas, 337

Hamlisch, Marvin, 289

Hammarskjöld, Dag, 49

Hammerstein, Oscar, II, 186, 337, 341; and Rodgers, 26, 193, 342, 356

Hammond, Percy, 151

Hampden, Walter, 179

Hampton, Lionel, 323, 338

Hanfstaengl, Putzi, 48

Hanna, Leonard, 318, 321

Han Suyin, 307

Hardwick, Cedric, 93, 246, 286

Harkness, Rebekah, 221

Harlow, Jean, 239

Harris, George, 95

Harrison, Gilbert, 379

Hart, Lorenz ("Larry" Milton), 8, 183–87; and Rodgers, 183–86, 393

Hart, Moss, 99, 107, 229, 366; and Kaufman, 185, 390, 393; and Short, 336, 337

Hart, Robert Alton, Jr., 25

Hartman, Norman "Speedy," 309

Harvey, Louise, 18

Harvey, Sir Martin, 370

Haslund, Fredrik, 141

Hatcher, Tom, 249, 250, 252

Haun, Harry, 289

Hawkes, Howard, 100

Hawkins, Coleman, 338

Hay, Mary, 366

Hayden, Margaret, 92

Hayes, Helen, 109, 256, 391

Hays, Matilda, 126

Hayward, Susan, 306

Hearn, George, 89, 252

Heath, Priscilla, 139

Heckart, Eileen, 251

Heenan, John, 282

Hegamin, Lucille, 323

Heide, Robert, 7, 94, 96, 97, 187–90

Hellman, Lillian, 44–45, 61, 67, 91, 92, 113

Hemingway, Ernest, 346

Henderson, Fletcher, 338

Henderson, Ray, 106

Henri, Robert, 365

Henze, Hanze Werner, 228

Hepburn, Katherine, 50, 180, 249, 311; and Cukor, 119, 120

Herbert, Victor, 392

Herman, Harry and Ruth (Sacks), 190

Herman, Jerry (Gerald), 190–93, 251, 378

Heston, Charlton, 306

Hewitt, William, 67

Hickman, Alfred, 303–4

Hill, Arthur, 21

Hiller, Lejaren, 78

Hiller, Wendy, 373

Hindemith, Paul, 378

Hindle, Annie, 193–95, 374, 376

Hirsch, Foster, 234

Hitchcock, Alfred, 28, 45, 138, 208, 248; and Granger, 175–76, 177; and Wilder, 378

Hoagland, Mrs. Anthony, 113

Hodes, Roberta, 116

Hodgkins, Nan, 17

Hoffman, Morton and Johanna, 196

Hoffman, William M., 96, 196–99, 237, 242

Holland, Anthony, 198

Hollenbeck, Jacob, 365

Hollenbeck, Mabelle, 365, 368–69. See also **Webb, Clifton**

Holliday, Billie, 339

Holm, Celeste, 251

Holm, Hanya, 332

Holman, Libby, 100, 366

Hope, Bob, 218, 285

Hopkins, Arthur, 224, 225, 392

Hopkins, Miriam, 92, 201

Hopwood, Avery (James), 199–203

Hopwood, James and Jule Pendergast, 199

Hosmer, Harriet, 126

Houseman, John, 187, 256, 347, 353, 371; and Rosenthal, 325, 326

Howard, Bart, 68–69

Howard, James, 95

Howard, John Tasker, 169, 170

Howard, Leslie, 105, 179, 294

Howard, Sidney, 234, 376

Howe, Julia Ward, 127

Hughes, James Mercer Langston, 8, 58, 61, 203–5

Hughes, Willie, 161

Hull, Helen Ross, 270

Hull, Howard, 316

Humphrey, Doris, 32, 330

Hurston, Zora Neale, 204

Huston, John, 81, 271

Hutchinson, Josephine, 179, 205–8, 254

Hutton, Betty, 182

Huxley, Aldous, 77

Hyams, J., 133

Hynds, Reed, 210

Ibsen, Henrik, plays of, 112, 141, 179, 377; and Le Gallienne, 253, 254, 255

Inge, Luther Clayton, 208

Inge, Maude Sarah, 208

Inge, William Motter, 19, 208–12

Ionesco, Eugene, 386

Isherwood, Christopher William Bradshaw, 156, 212–15, 356; and Auden, 36, 37, 38, 212–13

Isherwood, Kathleen and Frank, 212

Ives, Charles, 154

Jacker, Corinne, 113

Jackson, Andrew, 306

James, Allan, 96

James, William, 345

Janis, Elsie (Elsie Jane Bierbower), 8, 215–18

Janson, Ellen, 75

Jeffers, Robinson, 28

Jefferson, Thomas, 143

Jewsbury, Geraldine, 127

Joan of Arc, 16, 33, 85, 106, 130

Joffrey, Robert, 7, 9, 218–23; and Arpino, 220–21, 222

Johns, Jasper, 121

Johnson, Andrew, 353

Johnson, James P., 338

Johnson, Lyndon, 191
Johnston, Jill, 123
Jolson, Al, 184
Jones, Fred and Emma Cowell, 223
Jones, James, 307
Jones, Margo, 210–11
Jones, Robert Edmond (Bobby),
   223–27
Jourdan, Louis, 92, 133
Joyce, James, 345, 378

Kahn, Michael, 360
Kahn, Otto H., 253
Kallman, Chester, 38, 227–29
Kander, John, 156, 157, 214, 276
Kanfer, Stefan, 93
Kanin, Garson, 372
Karloff, Boris, 368
Kashevaroff, Xenia Andreyevna, 77
Katz, Leon, 85, 347
Kauffmann, Stanley, 24
Kaufman, George S., 119, 260, 389;
   and Hart, 185, 390, 393
Kaye, Danny (David Daniel Kamin-
   ski), 7, 176, 177, 229–32
Kaye, Nora, 250
Kazan, Elia, 110, 115–16, 133, 273,
   382; and Clift, 99, 100, 101
Kazan, Molly, 273
Keaton, Buster, 33
Keaton, Dianne, 279
Keitel, Harvey, 197
Kellner, Bruce, 201
Kelly, Gene, 26, 175, 182, 185, 307
Kelly, George Edward, 44, 232–37,
   317
Kelly, Grace, 92, 235, 279, 307
Kelly, Patsy, 35
Kelly, Walter, 232
Kemble, Fanny, 127
Kennedy, Laura, 17
Kennedy, Madge, 200
Kennedy, William B., 155
Kenyon, Doris, 201
Kern, Jerome, 86, 150, 268, 342,
   366; and Short, 335, 337

Kerouac, Jack, 145
Kerr, Deborah, 22, 101
Kerr, Jean, 287
Kerr, Walter, 25
Key, Susan, 170
Kierce, Mrs. Kendrick, 269
King, Dennis, 185
Kinsella, Marion, 327
Kirby, Marion, 32
Kirk, Poppy, 131
Kirkwood, James, 45, 118
Kirstein, Lincoln, 326
Kiskadden, James Henry, 15
Kitt, Eartha, 87
Kittredge, George Lyman, 392. *See
   also* **Woolley, Monty**
Kleban, Ed, 155
Kleist, Heinrich von, 53, 54
Klosty, James, 122
Knight, Shirley, 310
Knowles, James Sheridan, 125–26
Knowles, John, 363
Koch administration, 242
Komar, Chris, 121
Kopit, Arthur, 273
Kornfeld, Lawrence, 84
Kostelanetz, Richard, 78
Koussevitzky, Serge, 60
Koutoukas, H. M. (Haralimbus
   Medea), 7, 84, 96, 237–40
Krafft-Ebing, Richard von, 12n. 7,
   389
Kraft, Victor, 102–3
Kramer, Larry, 2, 8, 177, 240–43,
   345
Kramer, Stanley, 101
Krauss, Ruth, 84
Krutch, Joseph Wood, 234, 235
Kushner, Tony, 56, 275

Ladd, Billy, 336–37
Lahr, Bert, 285, 296
Lancaster, Burt, 92, 101
Lanchester, Elsa, 244–45
Langella, Frank, 22
Lansbury, Angela, 192, 250, 252

Lapine, James, 343
Lardner, Ring, 32
Larson, Jack, 353
Larson, Orville, 317
LaRue, Danny, 313
Lasser, Louise, 279
Laughton, Charles, 7, 110, 244–48, 286
Laughton, Robert and Elizabeth, 244
Laurents, Arthur, 8, 61, 248–52, 345; and Granger, 175, 176, 177, 248; and Hatcher, 249, 250, 252
Lawrence, D. H., 240
Lawrence, Gertrude, 156, 366
Lawrence, Pauline, 330
Layard, John, 37
Lee, Canada, 109
Lee, Gypsy Rose, 249
Le Gallienne, Eva, 28, 176, 177, 216, 252–56; and Christians, 90, 91; and de Acosta, 129, 130, 253; and Duncan, 148, 149, 253; and Hutchinson, 207, 208, 254; and Nazimova, 253, 299; and Webster, 7, 110, 254, 371, 372, 373
Lehar, Franz, 336
Lehman, Benjamin Harrison, 29
Le Massena, Bill, 98
Lemon, Courtenay, 48
Le Moyne, Sarah Cowell, 30
LeRoy, Mervin, 207
Lessing, Gotthold Ephraim, 90
Levin, Ira, 289
Levine, James, 199
Levison, Andre, 172
Levy, Jacques, 360
Lewis, Arthur H., 234
Lewis, Edmonia, 126
Lewis, Morgan, 182
Lewis, Robert, 110, 253, 306
Lewisohn, Alice and Irene, 7, 30, 290–91
Lieb, Sandra, 324
Light, James and Susan, 48
Lillie, Beatrice, 181
Lindsay, Howard, 320

Link, Ron, 95
Lion, Jean, 41
Loesser, Frank, 177
Logan, Joshua, 304
Longfellow, Henry Wadsworth, 127
Longwell, Dennis, 279
Loos, Anita, 391
Lori-Parks, Suzan, 348
Lorre, Peter, 305
Lortel, Lucille, 254, 274
Love, Earl, 339
Loy, Myrna, 100
Lubitsch, Ernst, 119, 184, 297
Luders, Gustav, 200
Ludlam, Charles, 9, 239, 257–60
Ludlum, Robert, 307
Lukas, Paul, 91
Lunt, Alfred David, Jr., 49, 316–17, 372; and Clift, 99, 263; and Fontanne, 7, 256, 260–64, 371
Lynde, Paul, 286
Lynn, Diana, 116

MacArthur, Charles, 43, 391
MacDonald, Jeanette, 184
MacDougal, Ronald, 305
MacGowan, Kenneth, 225
Mackaye, Percy, 225
MacLaine, Shirley, 230, 250
Macready, William, 125, 127, 164
Macy, Gertrude, 106–7, 182
Maeder, James, 124
Malin, Jean, 184
Mallarmé, Stéphane, 172
Mamet, David, 279
Mann, Erika, 37
Mann, Theodore, 273
Mann, Thomas, 37, 62, 271
Mann, W. J., 368
Manners, Hartley, 260
Mansfield, Josie, 374
Mantle, Burns, 151, 235
Manulis, Martin, 116
Mao Zedong, 84
Marbury, Elisabeth, 6, 129, 319; and de Wolfe, 7, 215, 264–68

Marbury, Francis and Elizabeth
McCoun, 264–65
March, Frederic, 45, 99
March, Iris, 106
Marcy, Helen, 327
Marie Alexandra Victoria, queen of
Romania, 173
Marlowe, Christopher, 347
Marshall, Glesca, 300
Martin, Arthur, 39
Martin, Mary, 35, 109, 154
Marx, Groucho, 103
Marxism, 37
Mason, Marsha, 118
Mason, Marshall, 95, 197, 198, 386,
387
Mass, Lawrence D., 345
Massey, Raymond, 92, 247
Masteroff, Joe, 214
Mathis, June, 299
Matisse, Henri, 346
Matthews, Carmen, 22
Maugham, Somerset, 311, 334
Maupassant, Guy de, 390
Maurel, Victor, 365
Maxwell, Elsa, 320
May, Elaine, 278
Mayer, Louis B., 367
McCandless, Stanley, 325
McCarthy, Joseph, 111, 251, 372
McClintic, Guthrie ("Guth"),
27–28, 91, 179; and Cornell, 7,
104–6, 107, 182, 294
McCullers, Carson, 21, 110, 269–72
McCullers, Reeves, 270, 272
McDermott, Dana Sue, 226
McDonald, Carrie, 39
McDowell, Jane, 169
McKay, Ellin, 391
McKechnie, Donna, 51
McKenzie, Everett, 328
McKinley, William and Mrs., 215
McNally, Terrence, 8, 20, 21,
273–76
McQueen, Steve, 279
McRae, Bruce, 201

Meisner, Herman and Bertha, 276
Meisner, Jacob, 276
Meisner, Sanford, 8, 176, 276–81;
and Carville, 277–78, 280
Melba, Dame Nellie, 27
Melville, Herman, 241
Mendl, Sir Charles, 268
Menken, Adah Isaacs, 281–84
Menken, Alan, 155
Menken, Alexander Isaac, 281–82
Menken, Josephine, 281
Menotti, Giancarlo, 62, 103
Meredith, Burgess, 253, 256
Merlo, Frank, 110, 382
Merman, Ethel, 190, 273, 320
Merrick, David, 81, 250, 288
Meyer, Peggy, 276–77
Meyerhold, Vsevolod, 350
Meyerowitz, Jan, 205
Michelangelo, 25, 241, 310
Midler, Bette, 158
Mielziner, Jo, 49, 382
Mill, John Stuart, 112
Millay, Edna St. Vincent, 48
Miller, Arthur, 23, 202, 211,
280
Miller, DeWitt, 161, 163
Miller, Gilbert, 245
Miller, Irvin C., 338
Miller, Marilyn, 217, 335, 366
Miller, Willie George, 339
Milligan, Andy, 95
Milne, A. A., 84
Minnelli, Liza, 156
Mitchell, James, 176
Mitchell, Ruth, 149
Mitchum, Robert, 247
Mitropoulos, Dimitri, 60
Molière, Jean Baptiste de, 90, 255
Molnar, Ferenc, 260
Monro, Harold, 73
Monroe, Marilyn, 100
Montague, H. J., 195
Montealegre, Felicia, 60
Mooney, Phoebe, 95
Moore, Robert, 9, 117, 287–90

Moore, Victor, 296
Moorehead, Agnes (Robertson), 35, 246, 284–87
Mordkin, Mikhail, 26
Morgan, Agnes Bangs, 7, 30, 32, 290–92
Morgan, Anne, 267, 320
Morgan, J. P., 267
Morgan, Richard, 338, 339
Morinni, Clare de, 173, 174
Morris, Lloyd, 356
Moss, Arnold, 253
Mostel, Zero, 341
Mueller, Sven von, 90
Mulqueen, Kathleen (Catherine), 179, 292–96; and Dawn, 293–94, 295, 296
Muir, Edwin, 49
Mumaw, Barton, 332–33
Munson, Ona, 131, 296–97
Munt, Maxine, 94
Murdoch, James E., 282
Murray, Brian, 23
Murray, Mae, 366
Myers, Robert, 272

Nabokov, Nicolas, 228
Nabokov, Vladimir, 22
Nall, Adeline, 132
Nash, J. Richard, 132
Nathan, George Jean, 200, 208, 254, 304
Nazimova, Alla (Adelaide Leventon), 49, 253, 296, 297, 298–300; and de Acosta, 129, 299
Neal, Patricia, 305
Negri, Pola, 129
Nemirovich-Danchenko, Vladimir, 297
Nestroy, Johann, 378
Nevelson, Louise, 23
Newell, Robert Henry, 283
Nietzsche, Friedrich, 108
Nix, Malissa Pridgett, 322
Nixon, Richard, 53, 364
Norman, Ruth, 110

Oakes, James, 164–66
Obey, André, 377
O'Brien, Shaun, 24, 25
O'Casey, Sean, 67, 152
Ochs, Adolph, 389
O'Connor, Bob. *See* **Patrick, Robert**
O'Connor, Robert Henderson, 308
Odets, Clifford, 109, 277
O'Horgan, Tom, 95
Oliver, Edith, 71
Oliver, Paul, 323
Olivier, Laurence, 29, 230–31, 247, 289, 368
Olsen, Charles, 78
Omar Khayyam, 146
O'Neil, Nance (Gertrude Lamson), 300–304
O'Neill, Eugene, plays of, 27, 48, 53, 234, 240, 262; and Albee, 20, 23; and Jones, 224, 225
Orlenev, Paul, 298, 299
Orwell, George, 37–38
Osborne, Paul, 133, 307, 387
Overmeyer, Eric, 348

Page, Geraldine, 133, 383
Papp, Joseph, 242
Parish, James, 92
Parker, Dorothy, 43
Parker, H. T., 377
Parkerson, Michelle, 135
Parnell, Peter, 86
Pastor, Tony, 194, 374
Paton, Lee, 187
Patrick, John (Groggan), 304–8
Patrick, Robert (Robert Patrick O'Connor), 7, 197, 308–11; and Cino, 94, 96, 309
Patten, Dorothy, 109
Paxton, Russell, 229
Pearn, Violet, 291
Pears, Peter, 103
Peaslee, Richard, 360
Peck, Gregory, 105, 279, 280
Pelham, Laura Dainty, 75
Pemberton, Brock, 392

Pennington, William, 21
Perkins, Helvetia, 70–71
Peters, Bernadette, 96
Petit, Roland, 221
Peyser, Joan, 62
Pfuel, Ernst von, 54
Philbin, Mary, 33
Picasso, Pablo, 121, 346
Pickford, Mary, 206, 218
Pierce, Charles, 311–14
Piercy, Marge, 202
Pinza, Ezio, 154
Pirandello, Luigi, 53, 90, 377
Plato, 61, 204, 241
Platt, Livingston, 314–18
Plautus, 341
Pleshette, Suzanne, 279
Pollack, Sydney, 279, 280
Pollock, Channing, 200
Poole, Abram, 129
Porcher, Nananne, 327
Porter, Cole, 43, 99, 186, 230,
    318–22, 337; and Thomas,
    319–20, 321, 322; and Webb,
    367; and Woolley, 318, 320, 321,
    392, 393, 394
Porter, Kate (Cole), 318
Porter, Samuel Fenwick, 318
Pound, Ezra, 196
Powell, Dawn, 109
Powell, Dick, 207, 247
Powell, Michael, 197
Powell, William, 201
Power, Tyrone, 105, 247
Prabhavanada, Swami, 213
Preminger, Otto, 248, 289, 367
Prince, Harold, 156, 157, 342,
    343
Proust, Marcel, 241
Pryor, Roger, 92
Pullman, Bill, 23
Purdy, James, 21

Quinn, Peter, 169
Quintero, José, 71, 383
Quinton, Everett, 239–40

Rabb, Ellis, 255
Rabkin, Gerald, 237
Raft, George, 230
Rainey, "Ma" (Gertrude Pridgett), 8,
    322–25, 338, 340
Rainey, William "Pa," 322
Rains, Claude, 33
Rambeau, Marjorie, 200
Rambert, Marie, 221
Rambova, Natacha, 299
Ramon, Florence, 110
Randall, Tony, 24, 279
Rankin, McKee, 300, 301, 302, 303
Rauschenberg, Robert, 78, 121
Reagan, Caroline Dudley, 40
Reagan, Nancy, 222
Reagan, Ronald, 242, 256, 280, 305,
    364
Reagan, Ron (son), 222
Redford, Robert, 250, 252
Redgrave, Lynn, 289
Reed, John, 48, 224
Rehl, Steve, 307
Reich, Wilhelm, 145
Reinhardt, Max, 90, 136, 224, 377
Renwood, Minnie, 172
Reynolds, Debbie, 286
Reynolds, Tim, 84
Rhinock, Joseph L., 43
Rice, Elmer, 91, 93, 204
Rich, Frank, 251
Richards, M. C., 78
Richardson, Ralph, 130
Riggs, T. Lawrason, 319
Rinehart, Mary Roberts, 200, 201
Riva, Maria, 137
Rivera, Chita, 158
Robbins, Jerome, 7, 61, 249; and
    Field, 156, 157, 158
Robbins, Phyllis, 16, 17
Roberts, David, 245
Roberts, Leona, 207
Robeson, Paul, 8, 109, 145, 371, 372
Robinson, Edward G., 33, 92,
    296–97
Robinson, Peter, 300

Rockefeller, John, 366
Rodgers, Richard, 25, 91, 231, 341;
    and Hammerstein, 26, 193, 342,
    356; and Hart, 183–86, 393
Rodin, August, 172
Rodriguez, Pancho, 271
Rogers, Ginger, 91, 368
Romberg, Sigmund, 342
Rome, Harold, 154
Rooney, Mickey, 368
Roosevelt, Eleanor, 106, 182, 268,
    285
Roosevelt, Franklin D., 185, 268
Roosevelt, Theodore, 265
Root, Deane, 169
Rorem, Ned, 62, 345
Rose, Billy, 185
Rosenthal, Jean (Eugenia), 61,
    325–28
Rosner, Paul, 35
Ross, Frank, Jr., 33, 34
Ross, Herbert, 81, 251, 391
Rostand, Edmond, 15, 90
Rostova, Mira, 100, 101
Roth, Philip, 21
Rothenberg, David, 288
Ruehl, Mercedes, 23
Ruggles, Charles, 201
Rummel, Walter Morse, 147
Russell, Bob, 39
Russell, Lillian, 150, 353, 392
Russell, Rosalind, 24
Russo, Vito, 176, 240
Ryan, Annie, 195

Sacco, Nicola, 67
Sachs, Arlene, 133, 134
Sager, Carol Bayer, 289
Saltmarsh, Lessie Margaret, 27
Sand, George (Aurore Dudevant), 283
Sarabhai, Gita, 77
Sardou, Victorien, 266
Sargent, Robert, 84
Saroney, Gilbert, 195
Sarton, May, 253
Sartre, Jean-Paul, 52, 70, 189

Satie, Eric, 351, 352
Sauvage, Henri, 172
Savoir, Alfred, 291
Savoy, Bert, 328–29
Scarborough, Dorothy, 270
Schell, Maximilian, 137, 138
Schiller, Friedrich von, 16, 255
Schmidmann, Joanne, 7, 349–50
Schneider, Alan, 20, 21
Schnitzler, Arthur, 55, 92
Schoenberg, Arnold, 66, 77
Schwartz, Charles, 318, 319, 321,
    392
Scott, Sir Walter, 125
Sedgwick, Edie, 189
Segal, Vivienne, 185, 186
Seldes, Marian, 22
Selznick, David O., 120, 217
Selznick, Lewis J., 298–99
Sergeant, Elizabeth, 226
Sergeant, Winthrop, 327
Seroff, Victor, 147, 148
Setterfield, Valda, 121
Seurat, George, 343
Seward, William Henry, 127
Shakespeare, William, plays of, 90,
    161, 185, 255, 260, 282; Cushman
    in, 125–26; Platt's designs for,
    314–16; Webster's direction of,
    370–71, 372, 373
Shatner, William, 118
Shaw, George Bernard, plays of, 214,
    246, 266, 285, 291, 372; Chris-
    tians in, 90, 93
Shaw, Glen Byam, 247
Shawn, Ted (Edwin Myers Shawn),
    7, 330–34
Shepard, Sam, 237, 309, 360
Sheppard, Jack, 282
Sheridan, Richard Brinsley, 255
Sheriff, R. C., 75
Sherman, Jane, 331
Sherwood, Robert, 99, 260, 263
Shilts, Randy, 242
Shipman, Elaine, 86
Shiras, Charles, 168, 170

Shore, Dinah, 218
Short, Hassard, 303, 334–37
Shubert, J. J., 26, 43
Shubert, Lee, 43, 267, 298
Shubert brothers, 30, 130, 200, 298, 303, 389
Sieber, Marie Elizabeth, 136
Sieber, Rudi, 136
Silverberg, Larry, 280
Simon, John, 242
Simon, Neil, 23, 288, 289
Simpson, Lillian, 340
Sinatra, Frank, 101, 307
Sinclair, Catherine, 164
Sissle, Noble, 39–40
Sledge, Adelaide Eugenia, 43
Slezak, Walter, 91, 185
Smith, Alexis, 320
Smith, Bessie, 8, 20, 323–24, 337–40
Smith, Betty, 202
Smith, Clara, 39, 40
Smith, Clarence, 338
Smith, Hugh, 339
Smith, Jack, 189
Smith, Maggie, 23
Smith, Marguerite Waters, 269
Smith, Michael, 66, 95, 97, 189
Sneider, Vern, 306
Sondheim, Stephen, 50, 61, 193, 340–45; and Hammerstein, 341, 342; and Laurents, 249, 250
Sophocles, 53
Sorere, Gab (Gabrielle Bloch), 173
Stanislavsky, Constantin, 297
Stanley, Charles, 95
Stanwyck, Barbara, 306
Stapleton, Maureen, 105, 279, 289
Starkweather, David, 96
St. Denis, Michael, 377
St. Denis, Ruth, 171, 330–31
Stebbins, Emma, 126, 127
Steenburgen, Mary, 280
Stein, Gertrude, 48, 61, 196, 253, 345–48; and Carmines, 84, 85; and

Hopwood, 201; and Toklas, 85, 345–46, 379
Steinbeck, John, 21, 22, 133
Sternberg, Josef von, 136–37, 297
Sternheim, Carl, 53
Steward, Samuel, 379
Stewart, Ellen, 386
Stewart, James, 175
Stewart, Michael, 378
Still, William Grant, 204
St. John, Christopher (Christabel Marshall), 370
Stokes, Edmond, 374
Stone, John Augustus, 164
Storm, Lesley, 93
Strasberg, Lee, 100, 109, 132, 176, 255; and Meisner, 278, 279
Strauman, Brad, 307
Stravinsky, Igor, 228
Strawbridge, Edwin, 317
Streisand, Barbra, 89, 250
Strindberg, August, 92
Sturges, Howard, 320, 321
Styne, Jule, 341
Sully, Rosalie, 125
Suzuki, D. T., 77
Swanson, Gloria, 109, 311
Swinburne, Algernon, 284
Swindlehurst, Lillie, 165

Talma, Louise, 378
Tamiris, Helen, 32, 332
Tandy, Jessica, 22
Tarkington, Booth, 260
Taubman, Howard, 21
Tavel, Ronald, 96, 258
Taylor, Elizabeth, 100, 101, 118
Taylor, Laurette, 32, 119, 260, 262
Taylor, Mark, 61
Temple, Shirley, 368
Terry, Ellen, 370
Terry, Megan, 7, 8, 348–51, 360
Tharp, Twyla, 219, 222
Thaxter, Phyllis, 263
Thirkfield, Rob, 387
Thomas, Danny, 138

Thomas, Jonathan, 22
Thomas, Linda Lee, 319–20, 321, 322
Thompson, Dorothy, 109
Thompson, Kay, 87, 118, 231
Thomson, Virgil, 7, 8, 103, 153, 351–54; and Bowles, 70, 72; and Stein, 346, 347, 351, 352–53
Thorndike, Sybil, 370
Tipton, Noel, 169
Todd, Michael, 69
Toklas, Alice B., 85, 345–46, 379
Torry, Johnny, 95, 96, 97
Townsend, James, 208
Trimble, James "Jimmy," 362, 363
Trueman, Paula, 32
Tucker, Mary, 269
Tudor, David, 121
Twain, Mark, 15, 184

Uggams, Leslie, 250
Ulrich, Lenore, 201
Upward, Edward, 213

Vaccaro, John, 258
Valentino, Rudolph, 299
Vanderbilt, Anne, 267
Van Druten, John, 91, 92, 93, 156, 354–57; and Isherwood's stories, 213–14, 356
Van Fleet, Jo, 279
Van Gogh, Vincent, 25
van Itallie, Hughes and Marthe (Levy), 357
van Itallie, Jean-Claude, 96, 348, 357–62; and Chaikin, 7, 359, 360, 361
van Itallie, Michael, 358
Van Vechten, Carl, 201, 261
Van Volkenburg, Ellen, 73, 75
Vanzetti, Bartolomeo, 67
Vaughn, David, 86
Verdon, Gwen, 230
Vespucci, Simonetta, 129
Vidal, Gore (Eugene Luther Vidal), 362–64

Vincent, Jack, 329
Vivian, Charles, 195
Voight, Jon, 279
Voskovec, George, 22

Wagner, Robert, 116, 118
Wald, Lillian, 30, 290
Walker, Nancy, 24
Walker, Robert, 175–76
Wallach, Eli, 279, 280
Walters, Charles, 25
Warhol, Andy, 96–97, 189, 190
Waring, James, 84
Warner, Jack, 382
Washington, Booker T., 139
Wasserstein, Wendy, 113
Waters, Ethel, 105, 323
Waters, Lula Carson, 269
Watts, Jonathan, 220
Waugh, Evelyn, 241
Wayne, David, 306
Wayne, John, 100
Weagley, William, 234–35, 236–37
Weaver, Ray, 262
Webb, Clifton (Webb Parmalee Hollenbeck), 7, 24, 365–69, 391
Webster, Benjamin, III, 369
Webster, Daniel, 353
Webster, Margaret, 8, 154, 369–73; and Christians, 90, 91, 92, 93, 371; and Crawford, 109, 110, 254, 371–72; and Le Gallienne, 7, 110, 254, 371, 372, 373
Wedekind, Frank, 53
Weidman, Charles, 32, 330, 332
Weil, Simone, 349
Weill, Kurt, 38, 67, 109, 204, 337; and Engel, 152, 153–54
Weiss, Jeff, 96
Welles, Orson, 33, 105, 152, 325, 371; and Moorehead, 285, 286
Wells, H. G., 258
Werley, Pete, 338
Wertenbaker, Lael, 325, 326, 327
Wesner, Ella, 374–76

West, Mae, 69, 88, 157, 262, 311, 329
West, Morris L., 307
Wharton, Edith, 253, 266
Whitcomb, Ian, 169
White, Christine, 132
White, Edmund, 214
White, Irving, 98
White, Oliver, 110
White, Stanford, 267
Whitman, Walt, 61, 66, 109, 166, 204, 284
Whitney, Anne, 126
Whitty, Mary Louis "May," 369, 370, 372
Wilde, Dolly, 299
Wilde, Oscar, 62, 95, 253, 266; and Douglas, 54, 85; and Fitch, 160–62, 163
Wilder, Amos and Isabella, 376
Wilder, Thornton, 45, 191, 359, 376–80; and Clift, 99–100
Williams, Cornelius Coffin "C. C.," 380, 381
Williams, Edwina Estelle Dakin, 380–81
Williams, Rose, 380, 381
Williams, Tennessee (Thomas Lanier Williams III), 240, 289, 363, 371, 380–85; and Albee, 19, 23; and Bankhead, 45, 46; and Bowles, 70; and Inge, 210, 211, 212; and Isherwood, 213; and McCullers, 271; and Merlo, 110, 382, 383; and Van Druten, 357
Wilson, Doric, 96, 237
Wilson, Gilbert, 217
Wilson, Jack, 320, 321
Wilson, Lanford, 7, 8, 24, 144, 275, 385–88; and Cino, 96, 309, 386, 387; and Hoffman, 197, 198

Wilson, Pete, 280
Wilson, Robert, 347, 360
Winchell, Walter, 41
Windham, Donald, 385
Winter, William, 128
Winters, Shelley, 247
Winwood, Estelle, 43
Wise, Eleanor, 327
Withers, Jane, 304
Wodehouse, P. G., 320
Wolff, Christian, 121
Wood, Audrey, 211, 381
Wood, Cyrus, 294
Wood, Natalie, 116, 118, 289
Wood, Thelma, 48, 49
Woods, Gregory, 205
Woodward, Charles, 116–17
Woodward, Joanne, 279
Woolf, Virginia, 239
Woollcott, Alexander Humphreys, 29, 43, 48, 104, 261, 388–91
Woolley, Monty (Edgar Montillion), 7, 367, 391, 392–95; and Porter, 318, 320, 321, 392, 393
Woolley, William Edgar, 392
Worth, Irene, 21
Wouk, Herman, 247
Wright, Margaret, 86
Wright, Robert, 68
Wynn, Ed, 285, 296

Yacoubi, Ahmed, 72
Yeston, Maury, 155
Young, Wilbur, 56

Zanuck, Darryl, 367
Zaslove, Arne, 85
Zolotow, Maurice, 316
Zorina, Vera, 185